T0336717

Modern Trends Surrounding Information Technology Standards and Standardization within Organizations

Kai Jakobs
RWTH Aachen University, Germany

A volume in the Advances in IT Standards and Standardization Research (AITSSR) Book Series

An Imprint of IGI Global

Managing Director:	Lindsay Johnston
Production Editor:	Christina Henning
Development Editor:	Erin O'Dea
Acquisitions Editor:	Kayla Wolfe
Typesetter:	Kaitlyn Kulp
Cover Design:	Jason Mull

Published in the United States of America by
Information Science Reference (an imprint of IGI Global)
701 E. Chocolate Avenue
Hershey PA, USA 17033
Tel: 717-533-8845
Fax: 717-533-8661
E-mail: cust@igi-global.com
Web site: http://www.igi-global.com

Library of Congress Cataloging-in-Publication Data

Modern trends surrounding information technology standards and standardization within organizations / Kai Jakobs, editor.
    pages cm
 Includes bibliographical references and index.
   ISBN 978-1-4666-6332-9 (hardcover) -- ISBN 978-1-4666-6333-6 (ebook) -- ISBN 978-1-4666-6335-0 (print & perpetual access) 1. Information technology--Standards. 2. Information technology--Management. 3. Standardization. I. Jakobs, Kai, 1957-
  T58.5.M634 2015
  004.068--dc23
                                              2014020099

This book is published in the IGI Global book series Advances in IT Standards and Standardization Research (AITSSR) (ISSN: 1935-3391; eISSN: 1935-3405)

British Cataloguing in Publication Data
A Cataloguing in Publication record for this book is available from the British Library.

All work contributed to this book is new, previously-unpublished material. The views expressed in this book are those of the authors, but not necessarily of the publisher.

For electronic access to this publication, please contact: eresources@igi-global.com.

Advances in IT Standards and Standardization Research (AITSSR) Book Series

Kai Jakobs
RWTH Aachen University, Germany

ISSN: 1935-3391
EISSN: 1935-3405

Mission

IT standards and standardization are a necessary part of effectively delivering IT and IT services to organizations and individuals as well as streamlining IT processes and minimizing organizational cost. In implementing IT standards, it is necessary to take into account not only the technical aspects, but also the characteristics of the specific environment where these standards will have to function.

The **Advances in IT Standards and Standardization Research (AITSSR) Book Series** seeks to advance the available literature on the use and value of IT standards and standardization. This research provides insight into the use of standards for the improvement of organizational processes and development in both private and public sectors.

Coverage

- Standards in the Public Sector
- Economics of Standardization
- Case Studies on Standardization
- Analyses of Standards-Setting Processes, Products, and Organization
- Descriptive Theory of Standardization
- User-Related Issues
- Standards for Information Infrastructures
- Emerging Roles of Formal Standards Organizations and Consortia
- Standards and Technology Transfer
- Multinational and Transnational Perspectives and Impacts

IGI Global is currently accepting manuscripts for publication within this series. To submit a proposal for a volume in this series, please contact our Acquisition Editors at Acquisitions@igi-global.com or visit: http://www.igi-global.com/publish/.

Titles in this Series

For a list of additional titles in this series, please visit: www.igi-global.com

Evolution and Standardization of Mobile Communications Technology
DongBack Seo (University of Groningen, The Netherlands and Hansung University, South Korea)
Information Science Reference • copyright 2013 • 328pp • H/C (ISBN: 9781466640740) • US $195.00 (our price)

Information Technology for Intellectual Property Protection Interdisciplinary Advancements
Hideyasu Sasaki (Ritsumeikan University, Japan)
Information Science Reference • copyright 2012 • 367pp • H/C (ISBN: 9781613501351) • US $195.00 (our price)

Frameworks for ICT Policy Government, Social and Legal Issues
Esharenana E. Adomi (Delta State University, Nigeria)
Information Science Reference • copyright 2011 • 352pp • H/C (ISBN: 9781616920128) • US $180.00 (our price)

Toward Corporate IT Standardization Management Frameworks and Solutions
Robert van Wessel (Tilburg University, Netherlands)
Information Science Reference • copyright 2010 • 307pp • H/C (ISBN: 9781615207596) • US $180.00 (our price)

Data-Exchange Standards and International Organizations Adoption and Diffusion
Josephine Wapakabulo Thomas (Rolls-Royce, UK)
Information Science Reference • copyright 2010 • 337pp • H/C (ISBN: 9781605668321) • US $180.00 (our price)

Information Communication Technology Standardization for E-Business Sectors Integrating Supply and Demand Factors
Kai Jakobs (Aachen University, Germany)
Information Science Reference • copyright 2009 • 315pp • H/C (ISBN: 9781605663203) • US $195.00 (our price)

Standardization and Digital Enclosure The Privatization of Standards, Knowledge, and Policy in the Age of Global Information Technology
Timothy Schoechle (University of Colorado, USA)
Information Science Reference • copyright 2009 • 384pp • H/C (ISBN: 9781605663340) • US $165.00 (our price)

Standardization Research in Information Technology New Perspectives
Kai Jakobs (Aachen University, Germany)
Information Science Reference • copyright 2008 • 300pp • H/C (ISBN: 9781599045610) • US $180.00 (our price)

www.igi-global.com

701 E. Chocolate Ave., Hershey, PA 17033
Order online at www.igi-global.com or call 717-533-8845 x100
To place a standing order for titles released in this series, contact: cust@igi-global.com
Mon-Fri 8:00 am - 5:00 pm (est) or fax 24 hours a day 717-533-8661

Table of Contents

Section 3
Focus on Individual Standards and Sectors

Section 4
Standardisation and Asia

Section 5
About People

Detailed Table of Contents

Section 1
Standardisation and Innovation

Ole Hanseth, University of Oslo, Norway
Petter Nielsen, Telenor Research and Future Studies, Norway

This chapter addresses issues related to how to enable the broadest possible innovative activities by infrastructural technology design. The authors focus on the development of high-level services based on mobile telecommunication technologies that for matters of simplicity are termed the development of a Mobile Internet. The focus of the analysis is how features of the technology itself enable or constrain innovations. The authors do this by looking on a few embryos of the Mobile Internet (primarily the Norwegian CPA platform, but also two pre-CPA platforms in Norway and Japan's i-mode) through the concepts of end-to-end architecture, programmability of terminals, and generativity. This analysis illustrates that the change from closed infrastructures like MobilInfo and SMSinfo to more open ones like CPA and i-mode increased the speed and range of innovation substantially. At the same time, the differences between CPA and i-mode regarding programmability of terminals and the billing service provided by the CPA network enabling the billing of individual transactions also contributed to basically the same speed and range of innovations around CPA as i-mode in spite of the huge differences in investments into the networks made by the owners. However, the analysis also points out important differences between the Internet and the existing Mobile Internet regarding technological constraints on innovations. It points out important ways in which powerful actors' strategies inhibit innovations, and how they embed their strategies into the technology and, accordingly, create technological barriers for innovation.

Chapter 2

This chapter discusses the notion of "responsible innovation" and "value sensitive design". It applies these notions to standardization and more specifically to standard selection. Based on earlier research (Van de Kaa, 2013; Van den Ende, Van de Kaa, Den Uyl, & De Vries, 2012), it is proposed that standards should be flexible to facilitate changes related to ethical and societal values. An acceptable standard can be achieved by involving users in the standard development process. The understanding of standardization and standard selection in particular can be improved by incorporating concepts and theories from the discipline of philosophy. This chapter discusses three conceptualizations of standard selection: market dominance, socio-political acceptance, and acceptability.

Section 2
Looking Inside Standards Setting Organisations

Chapter 3

As the field of ICT standardization has changed from a relatively static, monolithic environment into a very dynamic field in the last two decades, many formal standardization bodies, fora, consortia, and other types of Standards Setting Organizations (SSOs) have emerged. These SSOs have often competed against each other for the same application areas. To a large degree, these changes reflect developments in the field of telecommunications and IT themselves, including liberalization, globalization, rapid changes in technology, and convergence. More than ever before, firms can choose which standard setting body they want to join. Nevertheless, data shows that many firms decide to be members of many relevant bodies at the same time. The aforementioned changes and the multi-SSO memberships of a firm have differently influenced various types of stakeholders, which increases potential tension among members during standardization processes. This chapter intends to study such tension and the effect influenced by the structure and processes of the standard-setting bodies themselves. A framework to analyze tension within given organizational structure and processes based on Giddens' Structuration Theory is proposed. The appealing feature of this theory is that it is neither deterministic at the agent level nor at the structural level, but takes iterative influences between both levels as a starting point. This study shows how an SSO struggles to decrease tension among members and suggests propositions related to the tension that academia and practitioners can apply.

Chapter 4

Industry-led technical standardization is often cited as an example for private governance. And the Digital
Video Broadcasting (DVB) Project is often presented as a particularly successful case of such governance
without government. The successes of the industry-led DVB Project have often been cited as evidence
for the superior governance capacity of private industry. While the commercial and engineering success
of the DVB Project is unequivocal, this chapter raises the question whether it has been equally successful
in governing a complex sector that is confronted by a range of market failures, with direct implications
for important public policy objectives such as media pluralism and diversity.

Chapter 5

The Internet Engineering Task Force (IETF) specification documents corpus spans three decades of
Internet standards production. This chapter summarizes the results of an exploratory study on this corpus
for understanding how this system of standards and its production have evolved in time. This study takes
an alternative perspective, which considers a system like IETF as an organization itself, rather than a
constellation of extra-organizational activities. Thus, how it works and evolves are examined with respect
to its endogenous dynamics rather than by taking it as a system, which responds to requirements coming
from the external environment. The author conducts a longitudinal examination of several features of
these documents, their authorship, their dependency and collaboration network structure, and topics. They
present a review of how the standards corpus evolves into specialized subsystems and a commentary of
findings towards monitoring and managing such standardization processes.

Chapter 6

As part of its "policy project to examine the legal and policy issues surrounding the problem of potential
patent 'hold-up' when patented technologies are included in collaborative standards," the Federal Trade
Commission held an all-day workshop on June 21, 2011. The first panel of the day focused on patent
disclosure rules intended to encourage full knowledge of patents "essential" for a standard and therefore
to prevent patent ambush. When patents are disclosed after a standard is defined, the patent holder may
have enhanced bargaining power that it can exploit to charge excessive royalties (e.g., greater than the
value the patented technology contributes to the product complying with the standard). In this chapter,
the authors present a case study on patent disclosure within the ICT sector. Specifically, they take an
empirical look at the timing of patent disclosures within the European Telecommunications Standards
Institute, the body responsible for some of the world's most prevalent mobile telephony standards. They
find that most members officially disclose their potentially relevant patents after the standard is published,
and sometimes considerably so. On the other hand, the authors also find that the delay in declaring patents
to ETSI standards has been shrinking over time, with disclosures occurring closer to (although for the
most part still after) the standard publication date for more recent standard generations as compared to
earlier ones. This latter finding coincides with ETSI policy changes, suggesting that standards bodies
may be able to improve patent disclosure with more precise rules.

Section 3
Focus on Individual Standards and Sectors

Vladislav V. Fomin, Vytautas Magnus University, Lithuania
Arturas Medeisis, Vilnius Gediminas Technical University, Lithuania

Cognitive radio technology is commonly seen as a promise to form the basis of the next largest breakthrough in the development of ubiquitous wireless broadband services. However, the disruptive nature and complexity of this technology raises a host of associated issues, including the open question on reasons for the slow progression of the innovation. In this chapter, the authors offer a co-evolutionary analysis of the CR innovation context, aiming to reveal a stakeholders' domain, which is best positioned to lead the further CR development. Having analysed the position of CR within technology, market, and regulatory domains, the authors come to conclude that the regulatory domain oversees some of the most crucial enabling factors that may decide the future of CR technology.

Tineke Egyedi, DIRoS, The Netherlands
Sachiko Muto, Delft University of Technology, The Netherlands

This chapter analyzes standardization of mobile phone chargers to explore the role that compatibility standards might play in mitigating the negative impact of ICT on the environment. Building on insights gained from the economics of standards literature, the authors explore how the inherent effects of compatibility standards—such as reducing variety, avoiding lock-in, and building critical mass—can have positive implications for the environment. They argue that current standardization literature and policy have overlooked this important (side) effect of compatibility standards. Excessive diversity and incompatibilities in ICT generate e-waste, discourage re-use, and make recycling economically unviable; the authors, therefore, develop an economic-environmental framework for analyzing sustainability effects of compatibility standards and apply it to the case of mobile phone chargers. They conclude that well-targeted compatibility standardization can be equated to ecodesign at sector level and should be considered as an eco-effective strategy towards greening the IT industry.

Simon den Uijl, Erasmus University Rotterdam, The Netherlands
Henk J. de Vries, Erasmus University Rotterdam, The Netherlands
Deniz Bayramoglu, Technische Universität Darmstadt, Germany

Previous research has shown how various technologies became the market standard. This chapter presents some refined models and applies them to the case of compressed audio formats. The authors analyze the rise of MP3 as the market standard and identify several key factors that contributed to its success. First, a process of formal standardization reduced the number of competing compressed audio formats.

Secondly, enabling technologies, in particular the rise of the Internet, contributed significantly to the success of compressed audio formats. The timing of market entry was important in the sense that when the rise of the Internet took place, MP3 was one of the few fully developed compressed audio formats. MP3 offered technological superiority (high fidelity at low data rate) versus its initial competitors. The technology also benefitted from dedicated sponsors that promoted market adoption. Due to the weak regime of appropriability, audio files in the MP3 format managed to spread quickly over the Internet. Lastly, the availability of complementary assets for MP3 fueled its market adoption and strengthened network externalities on both sides of the platform-mediated network.

Chapter 10

Standards and specifications for public security are missing in many technical aspects as well as the areas of communication protocols and security management. Several technology management research gaps related to this field exist, particularly regarding R&D stage standardisation. This chapter gives insight into the development of a specification (DIN SPEC) for the protection of transportation infrastructure based on civil security research results. Besides providing practical examples for activities related to the popular standardization strategy framework of Sherif, Jakobs, and Egyedi (2007), the chapter suggests its extension. Standardisation challenges and solutions are also unveiled. The chapter finishes by outlining key aspects that may influence the adoption of the specification. Fields of application of the findings include, in particular, fast track standardisation procedures with voluntary implementation of the results, the standardisation of R&D results, and standardisation projects among small groups.

Chapter 11

International e-Customs is going through a standardization process. Driven by the need to increase control in the trade process to address security challenges stemming from threats of terrorists, diseases, and counterfeit products, and to lower the administrative burdens on traders to stay competitive, national customs and regional economic organizations are seeking to establish a standardized solution for digital reporting of customs data. However, standardization has proven hard to achieve in the socio-technical e-Customs solution. In this chapter, the authors identify and describe what has to be harmonized in order for a global company to perceive e-Customs as standardized. In doing so, they contribute an explanation of the challenges associated with using a standardization mechanism for harmonizing socio-technical information systems.

Section 4
Standardisation and Asia

Chapter 12

  Xiaobai Shen, University of Edinburgh, UK
  Ian Graham, University of Edinburgh, UK
  Robin Williams, University of Edinburgh, UK

While users in the rest of the world have been offered 3G mobile phones based on either the CDMA2000 or W-CDMA standards, users in China have the additional option of using phones based on the TD-SCDMA standard. As a technology largely developed by Chinese actors and only implemented in China, TD-SCDMA has been seen as an "indigenous innovation" orchestrated by the Chinese government and supported by Chinese firms. China's support for TD-SCDMA was widely viewed in the West as a ploy to keep the "global" 3G standards, W-CDMA and CDMA2000, out of China, but in 2009, the Chinese government licensed the operation of all three standards. The authors argue that Chinese support for TD-SCDMA, rather than being a defensive move, was a proactive policy to use the TD-SCDMA standard to develop Chinese industrial capacity, which could then be fed back into the global processes developing later generations of telecommunications standards. Rather than being an indigenous Chinese technology, TD-SCDMA's history exemplifies how standards and the intellectual property and technological know-how embedded in them lead to a complex hybridization between the global and national systems of innovation.

Chapter 13

  DongBack Seo, Chungbuk National University, Korea

East Asian countries are booming with both technological and demographic advances. They have traditionally developed their economies by being licensed foreign Information and Communications Technology (ICT) standards and using them to develop their home market and to export products. This chapter proposes that East Asian countries should start to develop a leadership role in global ICT standardizations even though their focuses are currently still primarily on developments in their own nations.

Section 5
About People

Chapter 14

Kai Jakobs, RWTH Aachen University, Germany

This chapter discusses the influence individuals have in the ICT standards development process. The chapter draws upon ideas underlying the theory of the Social Shaping of Technology (SST). Looking through the SST lens, a number of non-technical factors that influence ICT standards development are identified. A literature review on the role of the individual in ICT standards setting and a case study of the IEEE 802.11 Working Group (WG) show that in a standards body's WG, the backgrounds, skills, attitudes, and behaviour of the individual WG members are crucially important factors. Yet, the case study also shows that in most cases employees tend to represent the ideas and goals of their respective employer. The chapter observes that the non-technical factors are ignored all too often in the literature. It argues that a better understanding of the impact and interplay of these factors, specifically including the skills and attitudes of the WG members, will have significant implications both theoretical and managerial.

Chapter 15

Henk J. de Vries, Erasmus University, The Netherlands

This chapter explores how standardization education can be implemented at the national level. Previous studies form the main source for the chapter. This research shows that implementation of standardization in the national education system requires a national policy, a long-term investment in support, and cooperation between industry, standardization bodies, academia, other institutions involved in education, and government. The approach should combine bottom-up and top-down. The chapter is new in combining previous findings to an underpinned recommendation on how to implement standardization education.

Preface

Even today, many still consider Information and Communication Technologies (ICT) standards—and, even more so, standards setting—a necessary evil at best and a downright nuisance at worst. Typically, this is accompanied by the claim that standards represent a barrier to innovation and that they reduce to virtually zero the economic viability of any non-standard yet technically superior solutions. Indeed, the proponents of this view have got a point: standards do reduce variety and may hamper innovation. However, they conveniently ignore the fact that standards also enable innovation. After all, an ICT standard is also a widely agreed platform that provides a level playing field upon which innovations may be built.

Indeed, standards may assume very different roles and be used for equally different tasks. Perhaps most obviously in ICT, they provide for interoperability. This ranges from a simple and mostly technical "plug and matching socket"[1] to the much more complex and still fairly technical interoperability aspects in the field of, say, mobile communication (covering, for example, power levels, frequency bands, communication protocols, encodings, error detection, etc.). Obviously, most ICT would not work without such interoperability standards. Yet, and in some ways much more importantly, standards have a number of non-technical dimensions, too. They:

- **May Create Markets:** Take the GSM[2] standards as an example – without them, digital mobile communication would never have gotten off the ground. The same holds for the TCP/IP standards, the protocols that define the core of the Internet;
- **Are an Important Policy Tool:** Certainly in Europe, where standards have been used extensively to support the creation of a single market. Moreover, standards may be mandated by the European Commission in support of, for example, an industry policy in a certain area;
- **Support Innovation:** While standards are indeed potentially variety-reducing (and thus "innovation-unfriendly"), they also provide a common platform upon which innovations can flourish;
- **May Have Legal Ramifications:** In most countries, this holds primarily for health and safety standards.

This overall economic and policy importance suggests that the money at stake for an individual company may also be substantial, depending on, for instance, whether or not a standard actually materialises and if it has the desired characteristics and features. Obviously, a company can try to influence the process to achieve its goals.

From a firm's perspective, success in standards setting may well have a significant impact on its economic well-being. This impact may materialise through different channels. For example, a proprietary technology may be "ennobled" by becoming a standard. This, in turn, may imply increased revenues due to, for instance, a faster diffusion of the technology. Likewise, a standard enables the emergence of complementing products or services. Alternatively (or additionally), an organisation may capitalise on IPR that has been incorporated into a standard and for which licensing agreements may be made.

The standards working groups in the ICT sector are (almost?) exclusively dominated by the big players – the Ciscos, Intels, Siemens, Ericssons, Huaweis, IBMs (you name them) of this world. Some highly specialised Small and Medium-Sized Enterprises (SMEs) may occasionally also play major roles (oftentimes due to capable and respected representatives). However, things look quite different for "normal" SMEs (i.e. those that mostly just use a technology [as opposed to develop it]). For them, the barriers to standardisation are manifold. For one, the knowledge about the importance of ICT standards is limited. This frequently comes hand in hand with a lack of resources; after all, standards setting is expensive, and without any clearly identified immediate business benefits (as opposed to perhaps less obvious but potentially much more important strategic goals) most SMEs will hesitate to spend serious money on active participation in standards setting.

Standardisation is as much about personalities, diplomacy, negotiation, and in-depth knowledge of the Standards Setting Organisations' (SSOs') policies and bylaws as it is about the technical nuts and bolts. Despite the fact that several SSOs (e.g. ISO, CEN) require their WG members to act in a purely personal capacity (as opposed to, for examples, national or company representative), there is ample evidence that this is not always adhered to. That is, WG members do frequently act in the best interest of their respective employer. To do so effectively requires an adequate level of education and training. This may well be assumed as far as the technical aspects are concerned but not necessarily for the more non-technical abilities. The need for the latter is further reinforced through the increasingly important role China has lately been playing in the international standards arena. In general, dealing with peers from different parts of the world requires a fairly high level of knowledge about, and sensitivity for, cultural aspects. Negotiating with, for example, a delegate from a Chinese company may be very different from negotiations with a representative from the US. Here, great oaks from little acorns may grow and insensitive behaviour may well thwart a promising compromise.

The variety of aspects I have touched upon above (and then some) are also reflected in the chapters of this book. Given this diversity of topics, I found it quite hard to come up with an at least semi-meaningful structure. The book is subdivided into five sections:

1. Standardisation and Innovation.
2. Looking at Standards Setting Organisations.
3. Focus on Individual Standards and Sectors.
4. Standardisation and Asia.
5. About People.

SECTION 1: STANDARDISATION AND INNOVATION

This section comprises two chapters that look at very different aspects of the very interesting—and at times hotly debated—link between standardisation and innovation.

The chapter "Infrastructural Innovation and Generative Information Infrastructures" was written by Ole Hanseth and Petter Nielsen. Here, "generativity" denotes a technology's overall capacity to produce unprompted change driven by large, varied, and uncoordinated audiences. As such, it is a function of a technology's capacity for leverage across a range of tasks, adaptability to a range of different tasks, ease of mastery, and accessibility. By applying this concept, this chapter aims to disclose and to better understand the success and failure of attempts to create the Mobile Internet (as opposed to the "traditional" Internet). It shows that the move from closed (proprietary) mobile infrastructures to more open ones considerably increased the speed and range of innovations. However, it also shows how powerful players' strategies may create barriers to innovation. To overcome such barriers, the chapter concludes that in order to enable more innovations in the realm of the Mobile Internet the programmability of the terminals needs to be improved.

The notion of "responsible innovation" has become increasingly popular. The underlying idea is that innovation should also consider the ethical and social aspects of new technology from the design phase onwards. Standardisation may well be considered part of a technology's design phase. Accordingly, in the second chapter, "Responsible Innovation and Standard Selection," Geerten van de Kaa looks at the process of "standard selection" (i.e. how and why a certain standard eventually reaches dominance). He identifies three dimensions of standard selection: socio-political acceptance, market dominance, and acceptability. In line with the responsible innovation approach, he argues that not just economic aspects ("market dominance") should be considered when studying standard selection. Rather, ethical and consumer values should also be considered, as should functional ones. They will lead to a higher degree of a standard's acceptability.

The two chapters address very different aspects of the link between standards and innovation. However, both highlight the importance of the flexibility of standards for innovations to be built upon them.

SECTION 2: LOOKING INSIDE STANDARDS SETTING ORGANISATIONS

Standards emerge through the cooperation of a group of individuals that together form a working group or a committee under the umbrella of an SSO. It is, therefore, no big surprise that the characteristics of this SSO play a major role in standards setting. These characteristics cover a wide range of aspects – from membership levels to IPR policies to types of deliverables and the speed of their development. The four chapters of this section cover an equally broad ground.

The ICT standardisation environment has become extremely complex and heterogeneous, with dynamic links between SSOs and with each SSO having developed its own governing structures, processes, and policies. These internal characteristics of an SSO contribute to different levels and types of tension among its members. Applying Giddens' Structuration Theory, DongBack Seo's chapter, "Analysis of Various Structures of Standards Setting Organizations (SSOs) that Impact Tension among Members," reviews four influential SSOs (ETSI, IEEE, IETF, OMA). It shows how the different governing structures and systems of these SSOs influence tension among member organisations during the standardisation process. The chapter then offers propositions that can be used to formulate and improve a governing structure in order to decrease these tensions and encourage members to be more positively active in the standardisation process.

Under a government-led technology policy, governments aim to select and possibly enforce technology standards. The chapter "Industry-Led Standardization as Private Governance? A Critical Reassessment of the Digital Video Broadcasting Project's Success Story" by Niclas Meyer analyses under which circumstances governance through industry-led standardisation may represent an alternative to this. The Digital Video Broadcasting (DVB) Project has been a great engineering and commercial success. Yet, this industry-led project could not address many of the governance issues involved in the standardisation of television systems. Industry may not necessarily be willing to engage in a level of standardisation that is necessary to address a range of governance issues involved in, for example, television standardisation, such as the creation of fair competition or media pluralism and diversity. This case study demonstrates that important public interests, such as media pluralism and diversity, cannot and should not be left to industry standard-setters alone.

In the chapter "The Evolution and Specialization of IETF Standards," Mehmet Gencer aims to improve our understanding of how systems of standards are organised, and how they change over time. It presents results of an exploratory, empirical, and longitudinal study on IETF standards and on the underlying collaborative processes. The chapter shows that over time the system of standards changes and assumes a structure comprising increasingly isolated subsystems focusing on relatively independent areas. This effect started in the 1980s. Since then, focus shifted from infrastructural issues to more growth-related problems in the 1990s to security aspects in the 2000s. These findings indicate the increasing complexity of the work on standards specifications and the development of specialisation as the system of Internet standards grows.

How SSOs deal with issues of Intellectual Property Rights (IPR) is one of the most important aspects in ICT standardisation. In the chapter "Assessing IPR Disclosure within Standard Setting: An ICT Case Study," Anne Layne-Farrar analyses IPR disclosure patterns in ETSI. The chapter reveals that most official disclosures at ETSI are made ex post – often many years after the relevant standard components were published. However, the analysis also shows that these delays are shrinking, with a rather more modest improvement from 2G to 3G, but a significant drop from 3G to 4G. Since this drop occurred after ETSI's IPR policy clarification, one may conclude that changes to policy rules can have a significant impact on members' disclosure behaviour.

SECTION 3: FOCUS ON INDIVIDUAL STANDARDS AND SECTORS

The chapters in the previous section looked at various characteristics of SSOs. Regardless of their various differences, these SSOs are in the business of developing technical standards. Accordingly, the five chapters of this section look at a number of individual standards for different fields in the ICT sector.

In fact, the first chapter by Vladislav Fomin and Arturas Medeisis looks at the pre-standardisation phase, which may be placed between R&D and standardisation proper. Their chapter on "Co-Evolutionary Analysis of Cognitive Radio Systems" examines the technology innovation process for Cognitive Radio (CR) from a co-evolutionary perspective. To cover all relevant stakeholders, it does a multi-domain analysis of the CR innovation context covering the three domains: market, technology, and policy. The major conclusion of the chapter is that the policy domain and its stakeholders—primarily the telecommunication regulatory agencies, national/regional governments, and large international standardisation bodies—should assume a more proactive role at the current stage of CR technology development.

ICT is often hailed as a means to achieve sustainability in other sectors, whereas the lack of sustainability of the sector itself is typically neglected. The chapter "Standards for ICT: A Green Strategy in a Grey Sector" by Tineke Egyedi and Sachiko Muto argues that compatibility standardisation has the potential to become a green strategy. They show that all three economic function of standards—information, compatibility, and variety reduction—have effects on sustainability. The case of the standardisation of mobile phone chargers—triggered by an intervention of the European Commission—illustrates how compatibility standards can help reduce energy consumption as well the generation of e-waste in the ICT sector.

The chapter, "The Rise of MP3 as the Market Standard: How Compressed Audio Files Became the Dominant Music Format," by Simon den Uijl, shows how a disruptive technology—the MP3 audio compression technology—can significantly change an industry and offer opportunities to new entrants, but may also cause problems to inattentive incumbents. It gives an account of the events surrounding the development and eventual market success of the MP3 standard and explains why competitors like Apple's AAC and Microsoft's WMA did not succeed in breaking its dominance. The case shows that technological superiority is only important if it is in line with consumer needs, that the first mover advantage is only relevant when it targets the key applications, and that it is next to impossible to identify the killer application of a new technology up-front.

The subsequent chapter also looks at the factors that contribute to the success of a standard, albeit from a completely different angle and for an entirely different technology. Simone Wurster discusses the "Development of a Specification for Data Interchange between Information Systems in Public Hazard Prevention: Dimensions of Success, Related Activities, and Contributions to the Development of Future Standardisation Strategy Frameworks." Deploying six dimensions to describe the success factors of a standardisation project, she describes a standardisation initiative that successfully linked research and standardisation. The project's success was supported by the small size of the working group and by the virtual absence of competition inside the group. Appropriate marketing measures were also important, as was the view towards future developments of the specification.

Perhaps somewhat in contrast to the previous success stories, Stefan Henningsson's chapter on "Achieving Standardization: Learning from Harmonization Efforts in E-Customs" describes an attempt on standardisation that has thus far been only partly successful. The fact that e-customs standardisation needs to address, and accommodate, both social (organisational processes and practices) and technical (network hardware and software) aspects is identified as the main underlying reason. The chapter highlights the importance of moving from research on IT standards to research on IS standards. IT standards compliance is a necessary but not sufficient condition for leveraging the benefits that are typically expected from standardisation.

SECTION 4: STANDARDISATION AND ASIA

Over the past couple of years, the ICT standardisation landscape has changed due to the increasingly important role that Asian countries, most notably China, have assumed. With a clear standardisation strategy, quite a number of large and internationally successful companies and a huge internal market, China clearly has the potential—and the desire—to play a leading role in ICT standardisation.

In the chapter "Standards Development as Hybridization and Capacity Building," Xiaobai Shen, Ian Graham, and Robin Williams provide a socio-technical analysis of the 3G environment in China. They argue that the competition between the "indigenous" TD-SCDMA technology and the globally implemented W-CDMA and CDMA2000 platforms should not be seen as a standards war. Rather, all systems are largely based on the same Intellectual Property (IP). This interrelatedness implies that the global standardisation processes will become more fluid, and that IP and expertise generated during local or national standards development (like TD-SCDMA) will be fed back into the international process.

Looking at the four Asian Tigers (Hong Kong, Singapore, South Korea, and Taiwan) and China, DongBack Seo explains how some Asian countries (most notably Korea and China) have been transforming themselves to ICT standard-setters. In the chapter "Are Asian Countries Ready to Lead a Global ICT Standardization?" she argues that Asia as a whole may well have the clout to lead global ICT standardisation, but that none of the individual nations has all of the necessary characteristics to go it alone. To overcome this limitation, the EU might serve as a role model. Even then, however, it will be necessary to cooperate with the EU and the US rather than try and fight these regions through regionally developed standards.

SECTION 5: ABOUT PEOPLE

At the end of the day, standards are developed by people. Unfortunately, those who actually populate the SSOs' working groups, or may do so in the future, are perhaps the most frequently ignored group of stakeholders.

The chapter on "The Role of the Individual in ICT Standardisation: A Literature Review and Some New Findings," by yours truly, aims to at least slightly improve this situation. Through a brief literature review and a case study, it highlights the fact that these individuals' views, ideas, preferences, hidden agendas, etc. exert a significant impact on the development of a standard. It also argues that these people, whether knowingly or unintentionally, act as "shape agents" during the process – typically on behalf of their respective employer. This is due to the fact that they are influenced by the corporate environment within which they work, including any technical, strategic, and economic goals or preferences as well as corporate values or beliefs.

To do their job properly, these people need an adequate level of education and training. To this end, the final chapter, by Henk de Vries, discusses "How to Implement Standardization Education in a Country." It identifies three barriers for the implementation of standardisation education: the lack of the topic's appeal to students, the limited willingness of teachers to include the topic in their courses, and the lack of awareness of the importance of standardisation education for industry and government representatives. Experiences from the APEC countries (who are leaders in standardisation education) shows that the national standards bodies play an important role in overcoming these barriers.

Kai Jakobs
RWTH Aachen University, Germany

ENDNOTES

[1]   Well, perhaps not that simple and technical. It took the (European) mobile phone industry about two years to agree to the introduction of a standardised charger based on the micro-USB plug.
[2]   Global System for Mobile Communications, originally Groupe Spécial Mobile, a set of standards for second generation mobile communication. It succeeded a number of standards for analogue mobile communication that never became popular to any extent worth mentioning.

Section 1
Standardisation and Innovation

Chapter 1
Infrastructural Innovation and Generative Information Infrastructures

Ole Hanseth
University of Oslo, Norway

Petter Nielsen
Telenor Research and Future Studies, Norway

ABSTRACT

This chapter addresses issues related to how to enable the broadest possible innovative activities by infrastructural technology design. The authors focus on the development of high-level services based on mobile telecommunication technologies that for matters of simplicity are termed the development of a Mobile Internet. The focus of the analysis is how features of the technology itself enable or constrain innovations. The authors do this by looking on a few embryos of the Mobile Internet (primarily the Norwegian CPA platform, but also two pre-CPA platforms in Norway and Japan's i-mode) through the concepts of end-to-end architecture, programmability of terminals, and generativity. This analysis illustrates that the change from closed infrastructures like MobilInfo and SMSinfo to more open ones like CPA and i-mode increased the speed and range of innovation substantially. At the same time, the differences between CPA and i-mode regarding programmability of terminals and the billing service provided by the CPA network enabling the billing of individual transactions also contributed to basically the same speed and range of innovations around CPA as i-mode in spite of the huge differences in investments into the networks made by the owners. However, the analysis also points out important differences between the Internet and the existing Mobile Internet regarding technological constraints on innovations. It points out important ways in which powerful actors' strategies inhibit innovations, and how they embed their strategies into the technology and, accordingly, create technological barriers for innovation.

DOI: 10.4018/978-1-4666-6332-9.ch001

1. INTRODUCTION

The Internet as we know it is a standard and infrastructure spurring innovation and fuelling entrepreneurship in an unprecedented fashion. Its counterpart for mobile phones – the Mobile Internet – has however only modestly, at its best, become such an arena for entrepreneurship. The success of the Internet has been explained in different ways, but a central factor has been the flexibility and openness of its design. With an outset in the concept of loose coupling from software engineering and the argument for locating intelligence in the fringes (the so called end-to-end argument) in network architecture design, Jonathan Zittrain (2006) have ventured more deeply into these matters and coined the key success factor of Internet as its *generative* capacity. More particularly, Zittrain define generativity as a technology's capacity for leverage across a range of tasks, adaptability to a range of different tasks, ease of mastery, and accessibility. This conceptual framework illuminate that the essential flexibility of Internet as an infrastructure is not limited to its modularity and decentralized network architecture, but also the way in which it enable and leverage innovation performed by third-party contributors.

In this article, we discuss two early 'instances' of the Mobile Internet, namely the Japanese i-mode and the Norwegian CPA platform. By applying the concept of generativity, our aim is to disclose and to better understand the success and failure of attempts to create the Mobile Internet. By comparing with the Internet, we discern what generative capacities the i-mode and CPA platforms offer, how the capacities have developed and the motivations behind their development. Our contribution thus lies in a deeper insight in the successfulness of different approaches to the Mobile Internet in the way in which they support innovation.

Standardization is, of course, a critical issue in the development of all kinds of information infrastructures, and so also the Mobile Internet. Our primary focus is not explicitly on standards, but rather on issues and concepts, like architecture and the concept of generativity, that have huge influence on actors' strategies for developing infrastructures, including strategies for developing standards and what kind of standards that are needed. Accordingly, we also contribute to the literature on standardisation with an extended perspective on flexibility, namely generativity.

The rest of this paper is designed like this. In section 2, we frame the concept of standardisation in the broader literature on standards and flexibility. In section 3, we describe our research methodology and approach. In section 4, we introduce the CPA and i-mode in brief, before we in section 5 compare and discuss their generative capacities. In the last section 6, we draw implications related to the further developments of the Mobile Internet as well as reflect on the applicability of the concept of generativity.

2. A CHANGING 'WORLD OF STANDARDS' AND THE NEW NEEDS FOR FLEXIBILITY

The research presented in this paper is part of a growing interest in research on infrastructure standardisation in general and on the tension between standardisation and flexibility within ICT in particular. This increasing interest is a result the transformation of the 'world of standards' (Brunsson & Jacobsson, 2002). This transformation is a result of the growth in the number and importance of standards due to the so-called convergence of telecommunications and information technologies. This convergence leads to the development of a whole range of new standards, and new kinds of standards, in particular domain specific ones like standards for Electronic Patient Records (see for instance Hanseth et al., 2006).

The necessity of flexibility, as well as the contradiction between standards and flexibility has been a central topic in the literature on standardisation. In this section, we describe how changes in information and telecommunication technologies

(ICTs) have brought new requirements for flexibility. From a perspective on flexibility as the seamlessly fit of objects into larger systems as well as the standards adaptability to contextual changes, the very nature of today's ICTs also require them to be flexible in the sense of enabling and promoting innovation, and in particular innovation by third party contributors. Namely, they must be *generative* to endure and grow.

Technological changes within telecommunications and ICT have brought many new actors into this field. Telecommunication standardisation used to be taken care of by (a limited number of) service providers and equipment manufacturers. With the digitalisation of telecom, computer manufacturers and software companies also got involved. This technological change opened up possibilities for a broad range of new services. The development of such services involved even more actors – even users (big and small companies, professionals like medical doctors, etc.) (Jakobs, 2000). These services also implied a need for new kinds of standards which raised new challenges. Some of these new and hard challenges were related to the fact that the standards for high level services needed to satisfy much more complex user practices (in particular compared to the simple ones supported by traditional telecommunications which just enabled users to dial a number, talk, and hang up.) (Bowker & Star, 1999; Foray, 1994; Hanseth & Monteiro 1997; Jakobs 2000). The ongoing 'convergence' of the ICT and the media sectors further increases the current technological and institutional complexity and variety as well as increases the speed of change. These changes partly triggered, and were partly taking place in parallel, with the deregulation of the telecommunication sector. The deregulation increased competition, which again brought more actors into the picture at the same time as it changed the relations between the actors involved.

Standardised systems such as large scale ICT solutions and infrastructures tend to become accumulatively change resistant as they grow and diffuse (Egyedi, 2002; Hanseth et al., 1996). Thus, to endure, these systems have to be prepared for change to avoid becoming obsolete (Tassey, 2000). Standards must allow for growth and change through various means of flexibility to avoid this. Flexibility of standards and infrastructures has become increasingly important as the "world of standards" has changed as described above. The fundamental principle for making technological systems flexible is modularization, allowing some components to be kept stable while others are changed without implications for the rest of the system. This also applies to standards and infrastructures (Hanseth et al., 1996).

2.1. Flexibility and Generativity

The success of the Internet has triggered many discussions about lessons to be learned for how to develop infrastructures, and in particular large scale ones. In the later years, the 'essence' of the Internet has been much in focus among some 'cyberlaw' scholars discussing regulation of cyberspace. An issue of interest for some of these has been how to regulate cyberspace or the Internet so that unwanted use (for instance distribution of child pornography and music, and film and software piracy) is constrained at the same time as the qualities of the Internet that have made it so successful are maintained. The qualities of the Internet that these scholars have identified as important to maintain is the speed and scope of innovations that the Internet has allowed and triggered – regarding both the Internet itself and its use. We will here introduce three "cyberlaw" scholars and the aspects of the Internet they have highlighted and discussed.

Lawrence Lessig (2001) has stressed the importance of location of functions close to the application that uses the function, the so-called end-to-end architecture, originally proposed by Saltzer et al. (1984). This is a central principle to provide flexibility by systems design. The point this principle is making is that functionality in communication networks only can be appropriately implemented if based on knowledge that only exists close to the applications standing at the endpoints of a communication system. Thus, the network should not control how it grows, the applications should. Both Lessig (2001) and David (2005) exemplify this argument by illustrating the Internet as a network where intelligence is in the fringes. Since the network is not optimised for any application but open for and inviting the unexpected and surprising, innovations can flourish without changes in standards or the network itself. The important role of the end-to-end architecture in the success of the Internet is also underscored by historian Janet Abbate (1994, 1999) in her analysis of the history of the Internet. The relationship between the end-to-end architecture and innovation is brilliantly analysed by Barbara von Schewick (2010). Abbate (1994) also demonstrates the substantial difference this end-to-end architecture represented in relation to traditional telecommunication (where all functionality is in the network and not in the ends (i.e. the telephones)) and argues convincingly that this was an important explanation why the Internet won the 'war' against the ISO/OSI standards (Abbate 1994).[1] The discussion about the importance of the Internet's end-to-end architecture has more recently turned into a broader one also focusing on the importance of platform based architectures and the evolution of platform centric ecologies, typical examples being the iPhone and Android platforms and their respective ecologies (Gawer, 2009; Tiwana et al., 2010),

Yochai Benkler (2006) develops this end-to-end argument one step further by underscoring the mutual dependence of the end-to-end architecture of the network and (easily) programmable terminals in terms of general purpose computers. Benkler base his argument on contrasting programmable computers and appliances. An appliance is a device with a limited and well defined set of functions which (normally) cannot be modified after the users have bought it. Typical examples include washing machines, radios and telephones (traditional ones, at least). By large, such devices have computers inside, but their software cannot (normally at least) be modified by its users. Benkler is worried that several proposals for increasing security and stop harmful use of the Internet, i.e. cyberspace regulation, will constrain the Internet users ability to program their computers, i.e. turn them into appliances. An example of this is found in the proposed 'trusted computing' technology and how this may be implemented and ways in which it might be enforced by law.[2]

Jonathan Zittrain (2006) develops this argument yet another step by means of the concept of *generative technology*. He argues that the success of the Internet is closely linked to its generativity, and that regulation of cyberspace must carefully avoid doing harm to this. Generativity is "the essential quality animating the trajectory of information technology innovation." (ibid., p. 1980). It "denotes a technology's overall capacity to produce unprompted change driven by large, varied, and uncoordinated audiences" (ibid.). Zittrain argues that the grid of PCs connected by the Internet has developed in such a way that it is exceptionally generative. Zittrain defines generativity more detailed as a function of a technology's capacity for leverage across a range of tasks, adaptability to a range of different tasks, ease of mastery, and accessibility. This also makes it clear that generativity includes but also extends the matters of flexibility to include more than modularity and end-to-end architecture. *Leverage* describes the extent to which these objects enable valuable accomplishments that otherwise would be either impossible or not worth the effort to achieve. *Adaptability* refers to the breath of a technology's use without change and the readiness with which it might be modified to broaden its range of uses. A technology's *ease of mastery* reflects how easy it is for broad audiences to adopt and adapt it: how much skill is necessary to make use of its leverage for tasks they care about, regardless of whether the technology was designed with those tasks in mind. *Accessibility* – the more readily people can come to use and control a technology, along with what information might be required to master it, the more accessible the technology is.

In the remainder of this paper we will discuss two examples of Mobile Internet infrastructures and discuss the importance of generativity in relation to such infrastructures and how generativity can be promoted.

3. RESEARCH METHODOLOGY

Standards are widely accepted as being of strategic value, thus standards develop through a process where multiple actors pursue their strategies and agendas. Our research approach is based on an understanding of the processes of standard making as being open and situated as well as being understood differently by the various actors involved. Our empirical data is based on an empirical case study of the CPA, as well secondary data such as books and papers related to i-mode. Inspired by Star (1999), our 'reading' of how CPA emerged revealed a highly complex process that was not primarily network operator driven. Further insights were gained into local contingencies, the properties of the standard and the achievements of those engaged in developing the standard.

The research presented here started in 2002 and continued until late 2004. Since CPA appeared as inseparable from its context, a case study approach was adopted (Yin, 1994), following an interpretative perspective (Klein & Myers, 1999; Orlikowski & Baroudi, 1991; Walsham, 1993, 1995). We found our role as researchers to involve describing, interpreting, analysing and understanding the social world of the involved actors (Klein & Myers, 1999; Orlikowski & Baroudi, 1991).

Starting out by interviewing the manager of the CPA within one of the network operator, our attention was directed towards how close the standard was interrelated with other (internal) technical platforms as well as actors within the

business sector. We also found the appearance of the relationship between the various actors and their coordination interesting, which further guided us also to study how CPA was initially conceived and implemented. Thus, to understand the standard, the study reached both back in time towards the predecessors of CPA, out into the business sector as well as out into the more 'global' setting by studying internationalisation attempts.

A total of 39 formal interviews were conducted with managers, heads of sales and system developers in a total of 23 different organisations, official of government agencies and forums (listed in Table 1), including the two Norwegian network operators. The interviews lasted typically 45 minutes to an hour; they were all recorded, transcribed and notes were taken. The interviews did not follow a strict interview guide, but focused on discussing the very nature of CPA, its development and operation. As the interviews progressed, certain issues were also identified and focused on. In addition to the interviews, data was also collected from studying standard documents and specifications, websites and the trade press.

While giving a broad understanding of the standard as well as its context, this approach came with certain challenges. Since we did not operate within the borders of one or a few organisations, we had to negotiate access and justify the participation of the interviewees in a variety of different organisations, ranging from 5-men businesses to

Table 1. Interviews

Type Organisation	No. Interviews
Network operator	18
Aggregator	6
Small content provider	5
Integrator	2
Forum/consortia	2
Government	4
Content producers	2
Total	39

network operators with 20,000 employees. While this required different approaches to gain access, maintaining access to all these organisations was not feasible. Another challenge was to identify the important actors related to CPA, both historically and related to the business sector. To access these 'hard-to-reach' populations, a snowball strategy (Vogt, 1999) was used.

The data analysis was interpretive and based on our capacity to conceptualise the essential topics in our data. In our analysis, we broadly focused on the industry's market structure, the nature of the services and the standard to include a broad context of influential factors as the actors' aims, institutions and organisations and their strategies. During the transcription of the interviews, the key themes were identified. The themes subsequently acted as input to discussions and guided the further analysis of the transcripts as well as the topic for new interviews. In parallel with this, the research has been guided by presentations and discussions at several seminars, workshops and conferences.

4. THE CPA AND I-MODE AS INSTANCES OF THE MOBILE INTERNET

In this section we describe the Norwegian CPA and the Japanese i-mode infrastructure as instances of the Mobile Internet. Since our empirical research is limited to the CPA infrastructure, we use considerable more space to introduce this infrastructure than i-mode. I-mode is also a better known case, and we limit our focus to its core, its idiosyncrasies and where it differs from the CPA.

Our focus is on the development, diffusion and use of CPA and i-mode in Norway and Japan respectively. However, it is worth keeping in mind that CPA has been successfully transferred to countries like Malaysia, Hungary and Ukraine (Hanseth et al., 2012), while many huge and costly efforts aimed at transferring i-mode to Europe has failed (Tee & Gawer, 2009). Tee and Gawer

(ibid.) explains this with the fact that i-mode's architecture reflects the structure of the mobile telephone industry in Japan but not the one found in Europe.

4.1. The Predecessors of CPA: MobilInfo and SMSinfo

In 1997, both Norwegian mobile phone network operators introduced platforms for mobile content services, respectively MobilInfo and SMSinfo. Inspired by information services on wired phones, the operators started to use SMS as a channel for information services. The technical platform of MobilInfo and SMSinfo were built more or less ad-hoc and largely independent from the existing internal systems of the network operators. Even if introduced at the same time, these platforms were outcomes of independent initiatives and launched for the purpose of differentiation. As "walled garden" approaches, it was the network operators that proactively took imitative and invited different information providers to "mobilise" their content. The network operators took the advantage of existing information feeds from providers such as newspapers, traffic information centres and the meteorological institute, and turned them into mobile information services. In addition, the network operators also offered a few non-utility services, such as jokes and bible citations. All in all, it was the network operators that identified potential services, developed the necessary interfaces, took responsibility for the marketing, and controlled the whole value chain of these services.

Even if MobilInfo and SMSinfo certainly influenced their successor (CPA), they did not create much of a success. First, the network operators had very limited resources to invest in service innovation and development, not to say marketing activities. Since they were the only one in this game, little was done to develop and promote the services. Second, providing non-utility services was seen as a risk of jeopardizing the brands of the operators. Therefore, few new services were introduced. Third, the services could not be premium charged (i.e. SMS messages charged to the user at a rate higher than a standard SMS), rendering any business model impossible. Thus, the stake of the operators as well as the content providers in the platforms never became revenue. As a result, the service offerings did not develop beyond simple information services and fairly prudent entertainment under the control of the network operators.

4.2. The Case of the Norwegian CPA

The CPA is an infrastructure for value added content services for mobile phones in Norway. The CPA infrastructure basically supports three tasks; the production, preparation and marketing of mobile content services; transportation (requests and deliveries) of services between producers and consumers; and handling the involved billing transactions. As described above, this service sector was in Norway up until 1999 based on the network operators providing separate infrastructures and network operators controlled the whole value chain. The introduction of CPA broke up this vertical integration into functional domains, enabling and requiring a range of new roles and actors. The provision of services will in the case of CPA usually involve:

- Content producers (producing ringtones, jokes, news, music, weather information, etc.);
- Content providers (preparing content for mobile phones and developing new service concepts);
- Aggregators collecting a rich variety of content and possibly integrating these in larger service concepts;
- Media windows (i.e. newspapers, magazines, TV-broadcasters, etc.) providing space for marketing;

- Software companies; and
- Network operators providing transportation and billing services.

Linked to the core of its business idea, CPA is a joint undertaking by both the two Norwegian mobile network operators. On the one hand, they provide the same set of functions and a common service level (i.e. functionality, level of capacity, etc.), but not a single technical interface towards content providers. On the other, they provide a common user interface for content service consumers. Thus, CPA enables the consumers to acquire content services through some simple and standardised steps.

A key element of the CPA is that service usage is billed over the regular mobile phone bill. Since the consumer is already registered with one of the network operators, there is no need for cumbersome registration and confirmation of personal data, credit card number etc. Services are requested with an SMS sent to a short number (four digit number such as 2004), and when the network operator to which the consumer subscribe receives the SMS at its SMSC (message centre), the message is recognized as a service request and the CPA platform forwards it to the appropriate content provider over a TCP/IP connection (as illustrated in Figure 1).

When the content provider receives the request, they produce and return the requested content back to the network operator. In addition, the content provider also specifies the rating class of the service, i.e. the cost which the consumer is to be charged. The network operator requests their billing system with a CDR (Call Data Record) to handle the request according to the rating class before returning the content to the customer. Finally, when the subscriber pays his mobile phone bill, the revenue is split based on a standardised split model between the network operator and the content provider. The content of these transactions are not monitored by the network

Figure 1. Content services transactions on the CPA

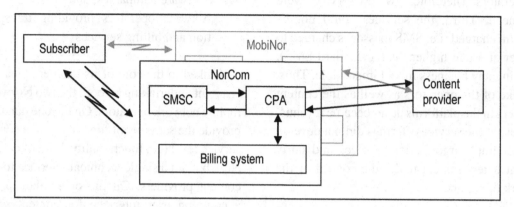

operators. However, it is to their discretion to react to complaints and close down services they find violating Norwegian law and consumer rights.

One prominent aspect with the CPA is that it is based on 'premium Mobile Terminated (MT) billing'. This means that the return message originating from the content provider is premium rated, i.e. charges the receiver for more than the cost of a regular SMS. Giving the content providers the possibility to charge several times for one request, this further enables subscription or push services as well as services that are requested from other sources than an SMS, in particular the Internet. Such subscription services have been growing in popularity and include services informing you about goals scored in matches your favourite football team is playing, "powder alarms," i.e. alarms informing you when a certain amount of powder snow has fallen in a certain skiing destination, etc.

Of course, as owners of the underlying mobile telecommunication Infrastructures, including the billing systems, the network operators were central actors in the establishment of the CPA infrastructure. But their recent efforts have been modest and catered primarily to increasing traffic. At the same time, several application houses are active in building add-ons to the underlying infrastructure to enable new services and service concepts. Examples include software to collect votes, and produce and visually present numbers

and statistics on ballots in relation to TV-shows, as well as software which presents on-screen comments and questions posted by SMS to discussions/talk-shows.

To summarise, the key components of the CPA are:

- **Business Model and Revenue Sharing Model:** Network operators provide a *standardised business model* for premium rated content services to the content providers. Operators allow any content provider to distribute their content to all subscribers, offering public market access as well as economies of scale in billing. In addition, they offer a *standardized revenue sharing model* (i.e. it is non-negotiable). The maximum charge is 60 NOK (approx Euro 7.50) and the predefined revenue split favours the network operator from 54 to 29 percent.

- **Equivalent Functionality, Architecture, and Service Level:** The content providers are offered basically the same functionally and service level, even if the interfaces to the network operators' implementation of CPA platforms differs. The services are provided by means of an infrastructure based on a common architecture. This infrastructure is, however, implemented differently by the different network operators.

Both interfaces are based on content providers initiating a TCP/IP connection to the respective CPA platforms. At the same time, aggregators provide interfaces which hide the differences between the operators' implementations of CPA for the majority of the content providers. This reduces time-to-market for content providers and lowers the barrier of up-front investments to connect to the CPA. Further, it also lessens the administrative burden of network operators as smaller content providers find it more convenient to connect through the aggregators.

- **Administration and Use of Rating Classes and Short Numbers:** Based on their public market approach, network operators have also *standardised their administration and use of short numbers and rating classes*. This adds to the transparency of the market by being the basis for a standardised way of marketing the services.

- **Guidelines for Consumer Protection:** Further, in order to reduce the risk of 'offensive' services being provided and marketed or marketed fallaciously, the network operators have *standardised guidelines* describing which services cannot be provided over CPA as well as how to market the services in a consumer friendly manner.

- **Interface for Service Acquisition:** By providing a *standardised interface for service acquisition* – the user interface, every mobile phone user in Norway has easy and transparent access to content services. Independent of which operator they subscribe to as well as the type of subscription and calling plan, subscribers can access the same services, from the same short number and for the same price. This also makes the marketing of services simpler as instructions for service requests become easier to read for the consumers.

This also illustrates that the development of standards was a key element in the development of the CPA infrastructure. However, it is worth noting that there was a great variety of kinds of standards defined, not just "traditional" technical standards. At the same time, the standards were not specified in detail, only at a more general level. We find both issues to be key elements in the CPA infrastructure's success.[3]

So, why did the network operators choose this particular approach in Norway? In short, the developers and the promoters of CPA had the experiences with MobilInfo and SMSinfo and were operating with scarce resources and did not have a strong and convincing business case. Thus, they had to work without the costs of the usual grand marketing campaigns, they had to circumvent the need to change the billing system (as it would have been too cumbersome and time consuming, if possible at all) and they managed to postpone technical systematisation and documentation. Therefore, CPA was developed in a bottom-up fashion where only a few enthusiasts, working for the operators and a couple content providers, set up a pilot version of the infrastructure and a few pilot services using it. The successful demonstration of these attracted more content providers and other actors. As the use of the infrastructure expanded, it was polished and extended and the standard defining it worked out. Rather than a traditional telecommunication standardization model, i.e. a formal top-down process focusing on formal and detailed technical specifications, the standardization model was more driven by 'rough consensus and running code' – i.e. in line with the slogan describing the Internet standardization approach.

While the network operators implemented technical CPA platforms, content providers were similarly important in their persistent belief and pursuit for its realisation. In this process, aggregators found their role in providing support for smaller content providers where the standard did not suffice. In addition, and perhaps more important, they developed and introduced add-ons and extensions to the platform, enabling new services and service concepts. At least partially resulting from these circumstances, the cost of implementing and operating CPA platforms became marginal for the network operators. The costs and further the risks involved primarily rested with the content providers.

4.3. The Case of the Japanese i-Mode

Japan enjoys the highest diffusion rate of the Mobile Internet, and the major network operator NTT DoCoMo with its i-mode standard offers a range of services of which the most popular are travelling information, SMS equivalent e-mail services, weather and news, music, games and entertainment (Ishii, 2004). NTT provides the content providers a business model where they can charge for monthly subscriptions or for packet transmission. The users' acceptance of NTT Do-CoMo's i-mode has been found remarkably high, and i-mode have been identified as a unique success case incomparable to other mobile content services (presented by e.g.(MacDonald, 2003)).

While CPA has had little strategic value for the operators, i-mode is based on NTT exploiting content services for strategic purposes. Where CPA is public and transparent across mobile networks, i-mode is used by NTT for differentiation purposes to attract and retain customers. Because of its strategic importance, NTT has spent significantly more resources on, but also limit the range of services offered to their own users with a 'walled garden' approach. Where the providers of the CPA delegates the responsibility and the related costs of designing, introducing and administering services to other actors in the market, NTT not only take editorial responsibility, but has also introduced a large bureaucratic organization to administer their service portfolio. Changes and extensions to the i-mode is the responsibility of

the network operator, and where innovation is pursued by content providers it is under NTT's central scrutiny. Thus, only if a new service fit the service portfolio and is perceived to have the potential to create revenue, it is accepted. In the case of CPA, anyone can add new components and services on the fly without prior evaluations and approval. Thus, where a 'walled garden' approach leaves the network operators with considerable risk, CPA redistributes most of the risk among a large number of other actors.

When it comes to penetration rate and the number of users, the i-mode story is quite different compared to the CPA. In Japan, the Mobile Internet are in general (including the competing Mobile Internet standards Sky web and EZ-web) available for 36 percent of the total population (Ishii, 2004). In the case of CPA, the penetration of CPA is following the mobile phone penetration, which is more or less saturated. While 82 percent of the mobile phone users subscribed to mobile internet services in Japan, only 53 percent of the mobile phone users actually use the services. i-mode users also have to register for the service and have a certain i-mode phone.

5. DISCUSSION: I-MODE, CPA AND GENERATIVITY

We will now discuss how infrastructures supporting distribution of information to mobile devices (phones) may enable or constrain innovation and development of new information distribution services. We will do so by exploring how the various features of the Internet that has been proposed as explanations of its success (in terms of rapid diffusion and development of new services and capabilities). Based on this understanding, our aim is to shed light on how infrastructure design enable and constrain innovative development of new mobile content services. We will first discuss the role of end-to-end architectures, and then the programmability terminals, and finally generativity.

Our discussion draws upon the network architecture and concepts illustrated in Figure 2. We split the collection of computing and communication technology involved in the requesting and delivering content into network and terminals. The terminals will normally be of two kinds: computers (run by content providers) and (subscribers') handsets. We denote the total collection of technology an infrastructure.

5.1. Mobile Internet and Innovations

Early platforms for distributions of content to mobile phones (like MobilInfo and SMSinfo) represented substantial innovations. However, the actual services were not new. From a service perspective it was all about copying just a few very simple services from the Internet domain into the mobile domain. And the success in terms of number of users and usage was modest. With the emergence of CPA and i-mode the speed of innovations, in terms establishing successful services in the mobile domain, increased dramatically. But most services established were still basically copied from the Internet domain. Genuinely new services are still only modestly present.

We see the speed and degree of innovations related to CPA and i-mode as basically on the same level and so also their usage. However, we see the range of services based on CPA as a bit beyond that of i-mode and so also usage compared to the size of the populations and markets in Norway and Japan. But there is a huge difference we would like to point at: the success of the CPA was achieved without any significant investments from the operators' sides, while DoCoMo made huge investments in i-mode.

When comparing innovations related to CPA and i-mode to the Internet there is also a huge difference in terms of speed and rate of innovations and the innovations of brand new services (like file sharing networks and services, community services like you-tube and Facebook, blogging technologies and services, etc.).

5.2. End-to-End Architecture

We will now look at the architecture of the various networks and how they relate to the end-to-end principle.

5.2.1 MobilInfo and SMSinfo

The architecture of MobilInfo and SMSinfo are definitively *not* end-to-end. The operators asked

Figure 2. Basic architectural and conceptual framework

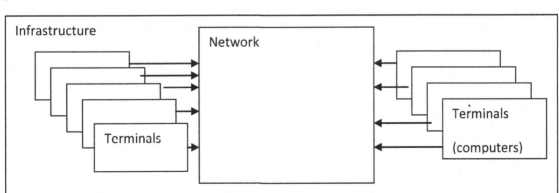

potential content providers for relevant content. When agreement was reached, the operators received the actual information in one form or another and prepared it for distribution to their subscribers and made it available on their own in-house servers. Content providers were not linked to the platform as such at all, even though real time information like stock exchange rates was received through a computer communication link. So in this case, all information and the technology used to transfer it to users were located in the network and full controlled by the network operators.

5.2.2 The CPA

The CPA platform represented a significant change in architecture compared to the previous proprietary platforms - basically towards an end-to-end architecture where more of the overall functionality was located in the fringes. In this case, what was 'taken out' of the network, was primarily moved to the content providers' computers. But more functionality was also put into the subscribers' handsets.

The CPA network included two main functions. First, it transported SMS messages between content providers' computers and subscribers' handsets. Second, the network included the billing systems so that the transactions could be billed. This network enabled any content provider to establish any kind of service that could be supported by the SMS transport services and that could be billed by the billing system. That means that the content providers could develop any software that on the bases of received SMS messages generated SMS messages. The content sent to subscribers' handsets may also include WAP-push messages and Java software to run in the handsets that have such a capability.

However, the CPA infrastructure is still not fully based on a pure end-to-end architecture. Substantial – and important – 'intelligence' still

remains located in the network. This includes first of all the billing systems. Their complexity, and accordingly their 'resistance' to change, implies that they constrain innovation. For instance, subscription services cannot be implemented if the billing system is based on so-called MO billing[4]. The billing systems are controlled by the telecom operators. This gives them opportunities to block innovations by others if they want to do so for strategic or other purposes[5]. But also the billing function may be extended by adding functionality in the terminals and without modifying the (billing system running in the) network. This happened on one occasion when it was discovered that the operators' billing system did not have the capacity to bill all transactions. One of the first Idol competitions on television where the viewers could vote by sending SMS resulted in a very high number of messages sent to the TV channel over the CPA platform within a short period of time. These messages generated more billing transactions than what the billing systems were able to process. Accordingly, the overall billing system had to be changed. In this case, the modifications required to bill all transactions was actually done to the software running in the "end," i.e. on the TV channel's computers. The modified version of the software of the TV channels stored the information required to bill the transactions and transferred them to the operators in chunks of a size and at a frequency adapted to the billing systems' processing capacity.

5.2.3 i-Mode's Architecture

i-mode's architecture is close to identical to that of the CPA platform. It includes the same two basic functions – transfer of requests for content and content plus billing. However, both transfer and billing functionality are different. Requests for content and content transfer are based on the HTTP protocol (requests for the content identified by a url and transferring content as C-HTML). Billing of subscribers is based on monthly subscription rates, not individual transactions. But information about individual transactions is stored in order to calculate the 'sales' and income of each content provider.

5.2.4. Mobile Platforms vs. Internet

The CPA and i-mode infrastructures' architecture is rather similar. The Internet does not include billing system and the data transfer protocols (TCP/IP) provide a bit more general data transfer service the CPA and i-mode. In addition the Internet is more symmetrical that the terminals connected are of the same kind (general computers) while CPA and i-mode aim at enabling communication between mobile phones and computers. Even though (more recent models) mobile phones run TCP/IP and may be connected to the Internet, so far neither CPA nor i-mode facilitates arbitrary TCP/IP based communication between mobile phones.

5.2.5 Summary

This discussion shows that there are substantial differences regarding the various mobile content infrastructures' architecture. The architectures of CPA and i-mode are close to the same (related to end-to-end). Their architectures are close to end-to-end. MobilInfo and SMSinfo, however, are almost as far from end-to-end as you may get. And we find strong evidence support the assumption that these differences in architectures also explain a significant part of the differences when it comes to speed and range of innovations. But the architectures of CPA and i-mode do not conform as closely to the end-to-end principle as the Internet. And we do see this difference as part of the explanation of the differences that still exists between the mobile and the Internet domains when it comes to range and speed of innovations.

5.3. Programmability of Terminals

The ultimate programmable device is the modern computer. We will first discuss briefly the features making the computer a powerful programmable device, then the programmability of mobile phone technologies and finally the CPA and i-mode platforms respectively. Early proprietary platforms like MobilInfo and SMSinfo did not offer any possibilities for programming of terminals at all.

5.3.1 Defining Programmability

What first of all makes a device programmable is the possibility of controlling it by means of software. But it is still easier to write software for some devices than others. This depends on the power of the available programming language and the environment supporting the software development activity (i.e. tools supporting the writing, debugging and testing the software). Second, the programmability of a device depends on its basic functionality – usually made available through an operating system. This may include functions like file system, multitasking, support for real time applications, network and communication capabilities, etc. Third, programmability depends on the device's capacity in terms of screen size and quality, keyboard and other input devices available, and the capacity of the processor, storage, and networking technologies. Programmability may also be indirectly affected by other issues like degree of standardization.

As already mentioned, computers are in general the ultimate programmable device. Over the years its programmability has increased as the computers capacity and to some extent also its functionality has increased. For instance, the availability of the Internet has increased the possibilities of developing distributed systems of all kinds. However, recent suggestions for how to solve various security problems (hacking, distribution of viruses, illegal file sharing, etc.), in particular the ideas of 'trusted computing', have made some worried that PC's programmability will be seriously reduced and that they may be turned into mere appliances (Benkler, 2006; Zittrain, 2006).

5.3.2 Programmability of Mobile Phones

Originally mobile phones were appliances with no capabilities for being (re-)programmed after they had left the manufacturers. Over the years, however, they have evolved rapidly towards generalized computers. And the most advanced (3G) phones seem to have all capabilities of modern computers – except screen size and keyboard. But the toolkits – like powerful DBMS systems and libraries for writing various kind of software – seem to be limited in number and maturity in comparison. But the most significant difference seems to be the number of ways in which both handset manufacturers and telecom operators in various ways block possibilities for changing programs that are initially put into the handsets and in that way reduced the handsets' programmability for third parties (see for instance (Benkler, 2006)). So, even though the programmability of mobile phones over the years has increased, there is still an enormous gap between mobile phones and PC's in this regard.

5.3.3 CPA vs. i-Mode

The basic computational model of i-mode is a transaction model, or more precisely send requests for web-pages and then receiving those pages. And i-mode is linked to the specific i-mode phone which cannot be programmed. So i-mode only allows programming of the terminals by the content providers. And these terminals can most easily be programmed by formatting content in C-HTML or more generally by writing software that by receiving HTTP requests as input produces C-HTML pages.

The computational model of the CPA infrastructure is basically the same as for i-mode: it allows phone users sending SMS messages to request some content service and when receiving an SMS a content provider may produce and return any kind of information that the requesting user's phone is capable of receiving (SMS, ring tones, music, java programs, etc., depending on the model). And the programmability of content providers' terminals is, then, beyond that of i-mode. The CPA platform works for all mobile phones. That means that the power of the programming language of the users' terminals varies. This point is of less importance in the western world where powerful smartphones have gained a dominant position. However, in the developing world (of which some countries have adopted the CPA platform) where the mobile dominates over the fixed line Internet, cheaper and simpler phones are crucial.

5.3.4 Summary Programmability

There is a substantial and significant difference regarding programmability between closed and proprietary infrastructures like MobilInfo and SMSinfo on the one hand and i-mode and CPA on the other. But the programmability of the CPA infrastructure's terminals also goes significant beyond that of i-mode. But at the same time, there are also significant and substantial differences between CPA and i-mode on the one hand and the Internet on the other. And these differences are crucial parts of the explanation of differences in range and speed of innovations.

5.4. Generativity

We will now turn to the concept of generativity. We will discuss the generativity of the various platforms (PC & Internet, CPA and i-mode) by discussing how they relate to each of the five aspects of generativity included in Zittrain's definition.

5.4.1 Allowing Unprompted Change by a Large, Varied, and Uncoordinated Audience

The extent unprompted change by a large, varied, and uncoordinated audience is allowed is to a large extent determined by an infrastructure's architecture (how close it is to end-to-end) and the programmability of the terminals. Proprietary and closed networks like MobilInfo and SMSinfo, because of their lack of both end-to-end architecture and programmability of terminals, do not allow or enable any change by anybody except by the network operators themselves. But this issue goes beyond these two technological features. For instance, network operators' policies and the conditions they set for using their network also have impact on to what extent "unprompted change by a large, varied, and uncoordinated audience" is allowed or possible.

CPA clearly appears as an infrastructure where those who control the network do not involve themselves in the innovative activities. New services are developed and added on the fly, without any evaluation or notification of the network operators. As long as new services do not violate Norwegian laws and a few formal guidelines, anything goes. At the same time, aggregators and other facilitators have taken the role of coordinating the relationship with and technical interfaces to the different operators. They do neither control new services.

NTT DoCoMo has a very different approach to control and coordination. Even if their strategy have changed over the years, the business model and payment system only apply for the official content. Official content is content that have been considered and evaluated as suitable by the content specialists of DoCoMo. As a result, innovation is not only a time consuming and bureaucratic process, but also risky since it is the employees of DoCoMo and not the users to decide its ap-

propriateness. At the same time, DoCoMo argue that this process is highly appreciated by their customers as they can be sure that the content is of high quality.

5.4.2. Capacity of Leverage across a Range of Tasks

Capacity of leverage are largely determined by the terminals programmability, i.e. what kind of useful services that can be developed based on the programming tools available in the terminals. But it also derives from the services offered by the network. And the CPA and i-mode offer one service of particular relevance: billing. The availability of this kind of service enable business models required for the successful development of certain services. And in this respect these two networks contains one form of capacity for leverage not available on the Internet.

Both the CPA and i-mode are infrastructures that enable the transportation and billing of mobile content services. Both infrastructures provide third-party contributors an attractive business model, business models that make it worthwhile producing and offering content. At the same time, direct invoicing of users or using alternatives such as credit cards is not justified because of the relatively small transactions involved. While CPA billing is on a per transaction basis (also enabling subscription services), i-mode only offers monthly subscriptions. The i-mode approach is therefore less attractive when it comes to offer services which trigger immediate consumption as it requires signing up for a subscription first.

Offering billing services to the content providers, the network operators offers their capability of billing and the content providers can leverage on the operators existing customer relationships. The cost of adding the billing of content services to existing phone bills is marginal compared to the cost of content providers formalising new billing relationships and perform billing of small transactions.

While the business models are attractive, the CPA has been criticized for favouring the network operators. Beyond the economic argument, the content providers are concerned that the cost of using the infrastructure only allows for low-cost services. Providing services which are more costly in terms of investments in technology and production is thus rendered impossible.

While CPA is less attractive revenue share wise, it is more so market wise. While i-mode only is accessible for NTT DoCoMo customers and i-mode users, CPA is available for any Norwegian mobile phone user. While the size of NTT's customer base still make providing content worthwhile, the limited Norwegian market renders provision of services to only a section of the market much less attractive.

The capacity of leverage represented by the billing systems points to another interesting and important conclusion: the limits of the end-to-end architecture. Its existence breaks with the end-to-end principle at the same time as it enables the provision of certain services that would otherwise be almost impossible to develop.

5.4.3 Adaptability to a Range of Different Tasks

Adaptability is also closely linked to programmability. In fact, we have problems in seen that adaptability goes beyond the issue of programmability, at least in relation to the technologies considered in this article.

5.4.4 Ease of Mastery

Both CPA and i-mode appear as relatively simple infrastructures for content providers. In the case of the CPA, only a minimal set of functionality is available, meaning that it easy to understand and

to use or implement, and it is cheap and easy to provide new services based on it. It is also easy to *change* when new requirements are revealed. Actors such as aggregators and integrators and the services and interfaces they provide also add to the simplicity. Further, the completeness in the sense of a mixture of marketing, use of short numbers, rating classes, etc. also make CPA easier to master. In the case of i-mode, basic knowledge in C-HTML is the primary requirement to provide services.

Network operators are challenged by the complexity and inflexibility of billing systems. Both in the case of the CPA and i-mode, there is no need for the content providers to be involved in and be knowledgeable in the underlying billing systems.

On a general level, the nature of programming language appears as a contradiction between ease of mastery and programmability as a more task specific (and what is often called a more high level) programming language is easier to learn while a more general and abstract one has wider applicability.

Ease of mastery is also influenced by non-technical issues like availability of text books, degree of standardization, number of knowledgeable persons around, etc. For instance, the huge number of text books available around the Internet (from "Internet for dummies" like books to books on narrow and specialized issues) and the widely distributed knowledge of the Internet make the Internet easier to master for both users and developers than CPA and i-mode.

5.4.5 Accessibility

I-mode appears with limited accessibility both for end-users and for content providers. On the one side, services are only accessible for i-mode customers, on the other, the content for the official sites are filtered by NTT. In this sense, i-mode is not a network that anyone can join – a strategic choice by NTT to make its network more attractive than other networks. In comparison to this 'walled garden' approach, CPA appears more like an "open garden" where services are accessible for any user, and any service can be provided.

Where the threshold for providing i-mode services primarily lies in the filtering process of NTT, the substantial costs of connecting to the CPA infrastructures and the revenue share model may hamper content providers launching new services using the CPA.

5.4.6 Summary

The concept of generativity can to a large extent be seen as the sum of end-to-end and program-mability of terminals. Accordingly, the analysis of the various infrastructures' generativity brings us to basically the same conclusion as the discussion of their architectures and programmability. However, the analysis adds a few important results. First of all, we see the concept of generativity to be broader in the sense that it also includes aspects going beyond the purely technological. An example of this is the role of the operators' (and other actors') strategies and policies regarding issues like openness. Generativity is also a more holistic than the sum of end-to-end and program-mability. This is illustrated by the billing system example. The fact that this service is provided by the network, contradictory to the end-to-end principle, increases the programmability of the terminals in certain ways. Services provided by the network also matters – not only that everything should be in the end-points.

5.5. "3ʳᵈ Generation" Mobile Internet

Technologies and services related to what we in this article call the Mobile Internet have changed dramatically over the years. We can say that SMSinfo and MobilInfo represented the 1ˢᵗ generation of such technologies, CPA and i-mode the 2ⁿᵈ, while today's' smartphones like iPhone and Android phones represent the 3ʳᵈ. Of

these the last "generation" looks very much like the traditional PC based Internet. However, this generation of Mobile Internet still shares many of its predecessors' roots in traditional telecom. Smartphone manufacturers and telecom operators still have significant control over this market and put various constraints on the Mobile Internet's generativity compared to the traditional one. This is exemplified with the fact that "apps" for an iPhone only can be downloaded from Apple's iTunes service, that you need a certificate issued by Apple to run the "app," and that Apple put lots of restrictions on what kind of apps that they allow on the iPhone (Tilson et al., 2012). In addition, the CPA platform is still relevant. It is the platform that gives content providers access to the operators' billing systems, and is, accordingly, required if content providers want their customers to pay for the their content.

5.6. Future Research: Beyond Generative Technology

The concept of generativity is gaining increased attentions and popularity related to innovation in general and related to digital technologies in particular. The concept is used to address more than how aspects of the technology play a role in innovation processes. This gives us clear indications that more research on the infrastructural innovation and generative information infrastructures will be fruitful. We will here briefly other aspects of the concepts of generativity which we strongly believe will be useful to explore in further research.

Framed within organizational thinking, David A. Lane (2011) presents a theory of innovation built around complexity and the cognitive processes in innovation. This theory consists of two main concepts: exaptive bootstrapping and generative relationships. The concept of exaptive bootstrapping describes how technologies emerge and evolve. Lane describes these processes as a 5-step algorithm driven by positive feedback (ibid.,

p. 69): 1) new artefacts are designed to achieve some particular attribution of functionality; 2) organizational transformations are constructed to proliferate the use of tokens of the new type; 3) novel patterns of human interaction emerge around these artefacts in use; 4) new attributions of functionality are generated – by participants or observers – to describe what the participants in these interactions are obtaining or might obtain from them; and 5) new artefacts are conceived to instantiate the new attributed functionality.

Lane (ibid p. 71) claims that "the most important cognitive process in innovation is the generation of new attributions" and that "the most important communication process involve the aligning of attributions among agents." Accordingly, Lane understands innovation as a collective and social activity. Under situations of uncertainty and change, identities and attributions change, and agents need to track these changes carefully in their attributions of identity of the significant agents and artefacts in their world. The process of monitoring and interpreting identities requires discourses with other agents. These discourses are channeled through the agents' informational and interpretive social networks. And from these networks, generative relationships emerge. This perspective on generativity will be central in this paper.

New attributions arise in the context of a particular kind of relationship among agents which Lane call generative. And the generative potential of relationships among agents and their modes of interaction depend on five characteristics: aligned directedness, heterogeneity, mutual directedness, appropriate permissions, and action opportunities. Generative relationships may link actors from the same firm, groups of actors from more than one organization engaged in joint projects, or agents working together under the auspices of a market system. The important point is that in generative relationships, agents have *aligned directedness* which means that their interactions are focused on achieving similar transformations. In addi-

tion, generative relationships are characterized by *heterogeneity*. Even if having the same overall aim to support a stable system, innovative agents have to seek out and build strong relationships with others agents that differ substantially terms of e.g. competence, social positions and access to resources. Another aspect of generative relationships is *mutual directedness*. This implies that a group of heterogeneous actors, which have different experiences and perceive the world differently, engage with each other in a way where they see each other's worldview and experiences as a resource rather than assuming the world views different from one's own to be wrong – which often happens. The generative potential of relationships also depends upon what the individual actors are allowed to do, i.e. what Lane calls *permissions structures*. And, finally, the generative potential depends upon whether the actors have appropriate *action opportunities*, i.e. the possibility to engage with one another in interactions that result in transformations not just in their own attribution, but in the structure of agent-artefact space.

The concept of generative relationships is highly relevant in organizational settings where structures are fixed and the innovative potential limited. It points to alternative, and indeed more *ad hoc* and uncertain, processes in which new ideas and innovations emerge from such relationships within and outside organizations. Generative relationships are not centrally controlled or planned, but can be released and let to emerge by management in situation where the future landscape is uncertain. Through generative relationships, a better understanding of what is happening inside and outside the organization, emerging shifts and the possibility of future action can develop based on multiple and differing perspectives.

In some ways similar to the generative relationships concept, van Osch and Avital (2010) have suggested the term "generative collectives" and analyzed how the structures of different types of collectives produces different generative capacity. This perspective is at the same time primarily focused on a collective understanding of the future, shared interests and mutual engagement, and gives little if any attention to (the potential in) heterogeneity. Further, it does not clearly link collectives and their thinking and action to organizational structures.

The concepts of generative technologies and generative relationships are both focused on innovation. And they both concern how innovation is emergent and the outcome of human actors exploring new ideas and opportunities. They address the challenge of understanding how innovation happens in complex settings and how different technological and social environments in different ways enable innovation.

At the same time, the generative technologies perspective focuses on attributes of technologies as the enabler for innovation, where the generative relationships perspective focuses on the attributes of the organizational setting of human actors involved in innovation and the relationships between them. In this way, they are complementary. While different technologies have different capacities to facilitate innovation, innovation cannot be seen as independent of human activity. And human activity will be influenced by other humans as well as the properties of the technology they are working with. This complementarity has also been picked up by Avital and Te'eni (2009) when they argue that the extent to which innovation will take place depends on an appropriate combination of a generative technology and a generative collective of users and developers. When these elements are matched in a successful way there is a generative fit between the two.

6. CONCLUSION

We will now conclude our analysis of how to enable or constrain infrastructural innovations in the Mobile Internet domain by means of the concepts of end-to-end architecture, programmability of terminals and generativity.

This analysis illustrates that the change from closed infrastructures like MobilInfo and SMSinfo to more open ones like CPA and i-mode increased the speed and range of innovations substantially. At the same time the differences between CPA and i-mode regarding programmability of terminals, and the billing service provided by the CPA enabling the billing of individual transactions, also contributed to, at least, basically the same speed and range of innovations around CPA as i-mode in spite of the huge differences in investments into the networks made by the owners. But the analysis also points out important differences between the Internet and the existing Mobile Internet regarding in particular technological constrains on innovations. It also points out important ways in which powerful actors' strategies inhibit innovations and how they embed their strategies into the technology and, accordingly, creates technological barriers for innovation. These issues are first of all linked to the programmability of terminals. So we will conclude that the by far most important issue regarding the enabling of more innovations related to the Mobile Internet is to improve the terminals programmability. In this, the concept of generativity with its focus on the grid – that is the mobile phone network and terminals, has shown as fruitful.

REFERENCES

Abbate, J. (1994). The Internet Challenge: Conflict and Compromise in Computer Networking. In J. Summerton (Ed.), *Changing large technical systems* (pp. 193–210). Boulder, CO: Westview Press.

Abbate, J. (1999). *Inventing the Internet*. Cambridge, MA: MIT Press.

Avital, M., & Te'eni, D. (2009). From Generative Fit to Generative Capacity: Exploring an Emerging Dimension of Information Systems Design and Task Performance. *Information Systems Journal*, *19*(4), 345–367. doi:10.1111/j.1365-2575.2007.00291.x

Benkler, Y. (2006). *The Wealth of Networks. How Social Production Transforms Markets and Freedom.* New Haven, CT: Yale University Press.

Bowker, G. C., & Star, S. L. (1999). *Sorting things out: Classification and Its Consequences.* Cambridge, Massachusetts: The MIT Press.

Brunsson, N., & Jacobsson, B. (2002). The Contemporary Expansion of Standardization. In N. Brunsson, & B. Jacobsson (Eds.), *Associates. A World of Standards.* New York: Oxford University Press. doi:10.1093/acprof:oso/9780199256952.003.0001

Clark, D. D., Sollins, K., Wroclawski, J., & Faber, T. (2003). Addressing Reality: An Architectural Response to Real-World Demands on the Evolving Internet. In *Proceedings of ACM SIGCOMM.* ACM. doi:10.1145/944760.944761

Clark, D. D., Wroclawski, J., Sollins, K. R., & Braden, R. (2002). Tussle in Cyberspace: Defining Tomorrow's Internet. In *Proceedings of SIGCOMM'02.* Pittsburgh, PA: ACM. doi:10.1145/633057.633059

David, P. A. (2005). *The beginnings and prospective ending of "end-to-end": An evolutionary perspective on the internet's architecture.* SIEPR Discussion Paper No. 01-04. Retrieved from http://siepr.stanford.edu/publicationsprofile/567

Egyedi, T. M. (2002). Standards enhance system flexibility? Mapping compatibility strategies onto flexibility objectives. In *Proceedings from EASST 2002 Conference.* University of York.

Foray, D. (1994). Users, Standards and the Economics of Coalitions and Committees. *Information Economics and Policy*, *6*(3-4), 269–293. doi:10.1016/0167-6245(94)90005-1

Gawer, A. (2009). *Platforms, Markets and Innovation.* Cheltenham, UK: Edvard Elgar. doi:10.4337/9781849803311

Hanseth, O., & Monteiro, E. (1997). *Understanding Information Infrastructures.* Unpublished Manuscript. Retrieved from http://heim.ifi.uio.no/~oleha/Publications/bok.pdf

Hanseth, O., Monteiro, E., & Hatling, M. (1996). Developing information infrastructure: The tension between standardisation and flexibility. *Science, Technology & Human Values*, *21*(4), 407–426. doi:10.1177/016224399602100402

Hanseth, O., Nielsen, P., & Alhponse, J. (2012). *Fluid Standards: The Case of Mobile Content Serices.* Unpublished manuscript. Retrieved from http://heim.ifi.uio.no/~oleha/Publications/FluidStandardsNielsenHanseth.pdf

Jakobs, K. (2000). *User Participation in Standardization Processes - Impact, Problems and Benefits.* Berlin: Vieweg Publishers.

Klein, H. K., & Myers, M. D. (1999). A set of principles for conducting and evaluating interpretive field studies in information systems. *Management Information Systems Quarterly*, *23*(1), 67–94. doi:10.2307/249410

Lane, D. A. (2011). Complexity and innovation dynamics. In C. Antonelli (Ed.), *Handbook on the Economic Complexity of Technological Change.* Cheltenham, UK: Edward Elgar Publishing. doi:10.4337/9780857930378.00008

Lemley, M. A., & Lessig, L. (2000). The End of End-to-End: Preserving the Architecture of the Internet in the Broadband Era. *UCLA Law Review, 48*(925). doi:10.2139/ssrn.247737

Lessig, L. (2001). *The future of ideas: the fate of the commons in a connected world.* New York: Random House.

Orlikowski, W. J., & Baroudi, J. J. (1991). Studying information technology in organizations: research approaches and assumptions. *Information Systems Research, 2*(1), 1–28. doi:10.1287/isre.2.1.1

Saltzer, J. H., Reed, D. P., & Clark, D. D. (1984). End-to-End Arguments in Systems Design. *ACM Transactions on Computer Systems, 2*(4), 277–288. doi:10.1145/357401.357402

Star, S. L. (1999). The Ethnography of Infrastructure. *The American Behavioral Scientist, 43*(3), 377–391. doi:10.1177/00027649921955326

Tassey, G. (2000). Standardization in technology-based markets. *Research Policy, 29*(4-5), 587–602. doi:10.1016/S0048-7333(99)00091-8

Tee, R., & Gawer, A. (2009). Industry Architecture as a Determinant of Successful Platform Strategies: A Case Study of the I-Mode Mobile Internet Service. *European Management Review, 6*(4), 217–232. doi:10.1057/emr.2009.22

Tilson, D., Sørensen, C., & Lyytinen, K. (2012). Change and Control Paradoxes in Mobile Infrastructure Innovation: The Android and iOS Mobile Operating Systems Cases. In *Proceedings of the 45th Hawaii International Conference on System Science (HICSS 45).* IEEE. doi:10.1109/HICSS.2012.149

Tiwana, A., Konsynski, B., & Bush, A. A. (2010). Platform Evolution: Coevolution of Platform Architecture, Governance, and Environmental Dynamics. *Information Systems Research, 21*(4), 675–687. doi:10.1287/isre.1100.0323

Trimintzios, P., Hall, C., Clayton, R., Anderson, R., & Ouzounis, E. (2011). *Resilience of the Internet Interconnection Ecosystem.* European Network and Information Security Agency. Retrieved from https://www.enisa.europa.eu/activities/Resilience-and-CIIP/critical-infrastructure-and-services/inter-x/interx/report

van Osch, W., & Avital, M. (2010). Generative Collectives. In *Proceedings of ICIS 2010.* ICIS.

van Schewick, B. (2010). *Internet Architecture and Innovation.* Cambridge, MA: The MIT Press.

Vogt, W. P. (1999). *Dictionary of Statistics and Methodology.* Thousand Oaks, CA: SAGE Publications.

Walsham, G. (1993). *Interpreting information systems in organizations.* Chichester, UK: Wiley.

Walsham, G. (1995). Interpretive Case Studies in IS Research: Nature and Method. *European Journal of Information Systems, 4*(2), 74–81. doi:10.1057/ejis.1995.9

Wu, T. (2010). *The Master Switch: The Rise and Fall of Information Empires*. New York: Knopf Publishing Group.

Yin, R. K. (1994). *Case study research: designs and methods*. Thousand Oaks, CA: Sage Publications Inc..

Zittrain, J. (2006). The Generative Internet. *Harvard Law Review, 119*, 1974–2040.

KEY TERMS AND DEFINITIONS

Flexibility: The ability of a system to respond to potential internal or external changes affecting its value delivery, in a timely and cost-effective manner.

Generative Relationships: May link actors engaged in joint projects or working together under the auspices of a market system. These actors' interactions are focused on achieving similar transformations.

Generative Technology: A technology that is never fully complete, that has many uses yet to be conceived of which the public can be trusted to invent and share.

Generativity: A technology's overall capacity to produce unprompted change driven by large, varied, and uncoordinated audiences.

Information: Knowledge or facts about someone or something.

Infrastructure: A shared, evolving, open, standardized, and heterogeneous installed base.

Innovation: The development and implementation of new ideas by people who over time engage in transactions with others within an institutional context.

Mobile Content Services: Services delivered to or used with mobile phones via public telecommunications networks.

ENDNOTES

[1] Even though the Internet's end-to-end architecture has contributed significantly to the Net's successful evolution, its future is uncertain. The Internet's growth has generated new demands. For instance, issues such as security, illegal distribution of spam, music, and child pornography have become major concerns. Many actors are arguing that these issues demand technological mechanisms (filters and security technologies, like trusted computing) to be put into the Net. Network providers also argue that they have to implement quality of service mechanisms to guarantee better services for those willing to pay for them, in order to afford further expansion of their bandwidth capacities. Scholars like Benkler (2006), David (2005), Lemley and Lessig (2000), Wu (2010) and Zittrain (2006) are worried that the proposals for addressing these issues will destroy the end-to-end architecture and turn the Internet into an appliance, as well as dramatically reduce the rate of innovations related to the Internet in the future. Other researchers argue that the Internet's architecture has to change to *allow* further growth (Clark et al., 2002, 2003; Faratin et al., 2008). This relates to "tussles in cyberspace" emerging out of the growth in number and variety of Internet Service Providers. This makes their relationships complex, and the conditions for sustainable and coordinated growth of the Internet are eroding. A new architecture is also considered necessary to maintain, or preferably enhance, the Internet's resilience (Trimintzios et al., 2011).

[2] This argument is spelled out in detail by Benkler (2006), se in particular pages 409 – 10.

3   The standardization approach of the CPA effort is more extensively discussed by Hanseth et al. (2012), labeling the standards "fluid."

4   Mo billing means that billing is "mobile originated," i.e. the billing takes place when the mobile phone sends an SMS. The alternative billing strategy is MT, i.e. "mobile terminated" billing which means that billing takes place when the mobile phone receives the message. See also section 4.2.

5   Examples include content of pornographic or racist nature and services that violate consumer rights.

Chapter 2
Responsible Innovation and Standard Selection

Geerten van de Kaa
Delft University of Technology, The Netherlands

ABSTRACT

This chapter discusses the notion of "responsible innovation" and "value sensitive design". It applies these notions to standardization and more specifically to standard selection. Based on earlier research (Van de Kaa, 2013; Van den Ende, Van de Kaa, Den Uyl, & De Vries, 2012), it is proposed that standards should be flexible to facilitate changes related to ethical and societal values. An acceptable standard can be achieved by involving users in the standard development process. The understanding of standardization and standard selection in particular can be improved by incorporating concepts and theories from the discipline of philosophy. This chapter discusses three conceptualizations of standard selection: market dominance, socio-political acceptance, and acceptability.

1. INTRODUCTION

The standardization process can be broadly distinguished in three stages: standard development, standard selection, and standard implementation (Hesser, Feilzer, & de Vries, 2007). To date, researchers from multiple disciplines have studied these three stages using a multitude of methods and theoretical approaches. When studying the second stage, standard selection, researchers have focused on the process in which standards achieve dominance in the market. This involves both theory building studies (using mostly case studies) and theory testing studies (using e.g., surveys). In attempting to explain standard dominance, these scholars have applied different perspectives including evolutionary economics (Anderson & Tushman, 1990; Tushman & Anderson, 1986; Utterback & Abernathy, 1975), network economics (Farrell & Saloner, 1985; Katz & Shapiro, 1985), and innovation management (Schilling, 1998; Suarez, 2004). In these studies, the emphasis is on standard selection in terms of market share. Scholars offer different strategies that can be applied to positively influence the installed base (market share) given the existence of network effects. Standard selection can also be reached when standards are institutionalized (e.g.,

DOI: 10.4018/978-1-4666-6332-9.ch002

enforced by regulators) leading to socio-political acceptance[1] of standards. Essentially, there are two conceptualizations of standards selection: standard dominance in the market and socio political acceptance / institutionalization of standards.

This chapter applies a novel discipline to standardization: 'philosophy' or more specifically 'ethics of technology'. Standard selection can also be studied in terms of notions such as 'value sensitive design' and 'responsible research and innovation'. By incorporating these concepts, our understanding of standardization in general and standard selection in particular can be improved.

Recently, there has been increased attention for responsible research and innovation, as evident by Horizon 2020 (*European Union Framework Programme for Research and Innovation*). Researchers have also begun to focus on responsible research and innovation (Owen, Macnaghten, & Stilgoe, 2012; Stilgoe, Owen, & Macnaghten, 2013). Recently, a paper published in the International Journal of IT Standard and Standardization Research referred to the concepts of responsible innovation and value sensitive design in relation to standardization (Van de Kaa, 2013). This chapter is an extension of that paper. The paper refers to the Kaleidoscope conference in 2013 and the role of standards: "sustainable communities will combine human-oriented technologies and human values [...] for this to occur, standards are indispensable" (Van de Kaa, 2013). As argued before (Van de Kaa, 2013) this might be reached by applying concepts and methods from the area of responsible research and innovation. According to Van de Kaa (2013): "standards should be developed according to the principles of value sensitive design [...] during its development and after its realization, a standard should be flexible to facilitate changes related to ethical and societal values surrounding the technology (such as privacy, security, and reliability)."(Von Schomberg, 2011).

2. THEORY

Responsible research and innovation can be defined as "a transparent, interactive process by which societal actors and innovators become mutually responsive to each other with a view on the (ethical) acceptability, sustainability and societal desirability of the innovation process and its marketable products (in order to allow a proper embedding of scientific and technological advances in our society)" (von Schomberg 2011b as cited by Owen et al., 2012). Two points from this definition are especially interesting: (1) the notion that next to innovators, such as firms, societal actors, such as consumers, should be involved in the innovation process and (2) in the innovation process, aspects such as 'acceptability' and 'sustainability' should be taken into account. At a workshop during the Kaleidoscope conference 2013, Professor van den Hoven discussed the concept of responsible innovation. In his summary of this workshop, Van de Kaa (2013) reports:

Van den Hoven talked about the topic of responsible innovation which is a form of ethics and technology development. Van den hoven referred to the Lund declaration which emphasizes that 'European research must focus on the grand challenges of our time'. He stressed that the grand challenges (e.g. climate change and sustainable energy) are mentioned in the UN millennium goals and are potential focus areas of horizon2020 (the European Union framework for research and innovation). Van den Hoven argued that innovations should be geared to these grand challenges and argues that if we do not do so the innovations will not be successful and we will fail to benefit from the innovations. For example, in the Netherlands, the establishment and introduction of the electronic patient record system and the smart metering system failed because of the fact that security and privacy considerations (ethical aspects) were not sufficiently taken into account. Sometimes, it is difficult for technologies to satisfy different values simultaneously and trade-offs should be made. For example, in the case of Closed Circuit TV systems, the example used in the presentation of Van den Hoven, cameras that provide sharp images (and thus provide full security) will decrease consumer's privacy considerably. He argues that the challenge is to come up with a technology that is both secure and that enables privacy. In fact, the challenge is to implement different values such as privacy and security in the technological artefacts that we develop (such as standards).

According to Van den Hoven, innovations will not be successful if they do not occur in a responsible manner. It can be argued that the same holds for standards. The standard development process should be conducted in a responsible way in order to achieve success (in terms of standard selection).

Responsible innovation may be incorporated if innovations are developed according to the principles of value sensitive design. During his workshop, Professor van de Poel presented the ideas behind value sensitive design. In his summary of the workshop, Van de Kaa (2013) reports:

One way to make sure that values are incorporated in the innovations that we develop is to apply the notion of value sensitive design [...] Value sensitive design is: "A systematic attempt to include values of ethical importance in design". In this respect it is important to identify the stakeholders involved and their values, understand what these values entail, and how these values can be embodied in the design (Friedman, Kahn, & Borning, 1996) [..] this may be accomplished by translating the values into specific design requirements for technological artefacts such as standards (in fact, many standards are inspired by considerations of safety, compatibility or security). Van de Poel explained the notion of a values hierarchy in which values (such as safety) are translated to norms (such as

reduction of risks) which are subsequently translated to design requirements (concrete goals). Using this notion it is possible to translate values to norms and design requirements but it can also be used to reconstruct the values and norms that underlie specific design choices so as to possibly arrive at additional design requirements that were not taken into account prior.

If the notion of value sensitive design were to be applied to standardization, the first step would be to conduct a stakeholder analysis using e.g., De Vries et al. (2003). Subsequently, the values that these stakeholders deem important should be mapped. Ultimately, they can be translated to design requirements for standards, which could then be taken into account during the standardization process.

Ample research has been conducted on standards selection in the market. Scholars have identified various factors for standard selection (Schilling, 1998; Suarez, 2004; Van de Kaa, Van den Ende, De Vries, & Van Heck, 2011). These researchers mostly offer economic and strategic factors that explain standard dominance. Other researchers focus on the institutionalization of standards (Backhouse, Hsu, & Leiser, 2006). Little research has been conducted on standard acceptability while this may be an important aspect that contributes to standard dominance. In essence, it can be argued that when a standard is more acceptable to end users, these end users will be more encouraged to adopt that standard increasing its installed base. Van de Kaa (2013) uses the example of the standards battle for wireless home network communication which illustrates the significance of applying value sensitive design to standards in order to increase standard acceptability:

... in the 1990s two standards, WiFi and HomeRF, were competing. At the end of the 1990s significantly more companies adopted HomeRF as compared to WiFi. Using the extant literature on standard selection one might expect that HomeRF would

have achieved market dominance because of its large installed base. However, WiFi achieved market dominance [...] the WiFi standard was more flexible which partly contributed to its dominance. For example, in 2004, changes were incorporated in the standard to resolve security issues which led to an increase in WiFi's stakeholder network size. One could view this as an example of a situation of responsible innovation whereby values (privacy) are translated to design requirements (the security protocol) and subsequently incorporated in technological artefacts (standards) so as to increase the acceptability and market uptake of the standard. (Van de Kaa, 2013).

3. PROPOSITIONS AND DISCUSSION

In the workshop organized at the Kaleidoscope conference 2014 and in the paper subsequently published in the International Journal of IT Standards and Standardization Research, three propositions (relating responsible innovation to standardization) were raised:

- "During its development and after its realization, a standard should be flexible to facilitate changes related to ethical and societal values surrounding the technology (such as privacy, security, and reliability).
- Standards should always be developed according to the principles of responsible innovation and value sensitive design in order for them to achieve social acceptance (and thus market dominance).
- To facilitate value sensitive standard design, consumer organizations or individual consumers should always be present during standard development." (Van de Kaa, 2013).

These propositions argue for value sensitive standardization. By involving consumers, though e.g., consumer organizations in the standardiza-

tion process, important ethical and social values may be learned. Subsequently, these can be incorporated in the standard, leading to increased standard acceptability and acceptance among end users. However, during the technology development process consumers may not always be aware of the social and ethical values that surround a technology. For example, in the case of Wireless communications, the standards were developed at the start of the digital era and at that time, consumers may not have been aware of the ethical aspects surrounding the new technology that are now very important such as privacy with respect to personal data. These ethical values gradually become apparent as consumers apply the products in which the standards are implemented. In the case of WiFi, the products are the routers. The need for a security protocol for WiFi arose when people attempted to hack routers. When this occurred, the standard had already been introduced in the market. This shows the importance of standard flexibility, also in the selection stage. A problem with a flexible standard in the selection stage is that once the installed base increases, people may become locked into the standard. When the standard is then changed, the compatibility that the standard enables may be compromised. Standards should be flexible until widespread adoption occurs. They can be flexible in the first three stages of the Suarez model (Suarez, 2004) and should become more fixed in stage 4: after a 'clear early front-runner' has appeared in the market and before one of the standards has achieved dominance (Suarez, 2004). Then, in stage 5, standards can be more fixed and compatibility can be guaranteed. One way to accomplish this is to leave certain parts of the standards intentionally open ('blank spots') (Van de Kaa, 2013). These 'blank spots' may be filled when the need arises (or when it becomes apparent that a certain value becomes important). A problem with involving consumers in formal standardization organizations is that the negotiations that take place within these organizations can become technically complex at times, often making it difficult for consumers to grasp the contents of the discussions. To solve this issue, Van de Kaa (2013) suggests including "persons that translate the difficult technical information to laymen terms so that the knowledge is known to the consumer audience." Another possible solution could be to ask the technical experts involved during the negotiations to put themselves in the consumer's shoes. Consumers could be offered prototypes of products in which the envisioned standard is implemented (possibly in an experimental setting) and consumers could be questioned about possible ethical problems that may arise during their use. These ethical problems can be inventorized and categorized under values, which may subsequently be taken into account during the standard development process.

4. CONCLUSION

The current paper argues that to fully understand standard selection, a broader approach is needed than just focusing on a firm in its economic environment (Table 1, second level). Functional and ethical consumer values also need to be considered (Table 1, first level) and may lead to increased technology acceptability and thus to technology selection (Van de Kaa, 2013; Van den Ende et al., 2012). The institutional level (Table 1, third level)[2] also plays an important role. Many (regulatory) institutions exist that may impact the socio-political acceptance of standards and, in this sense, the black box of government needs to be opened (Van de Kaa, Greeven, & van Puijenbroek, 2013). *To fully understand standards battles, each of these three levels need to be considered and the actors in these levels should be aligned*, for example, by means of network governance (Van de Kaa et al., 2013; Van den Ende et al., 2012). Ideally, to achieve technology success, networks of actors and technology co-evolve (Van den Ende et al., 2012). This is illustrated in Table 1.

Three conceptualizations of standard selection (on three different levels of analysis) can be distinguished: socio-political acceptance, market dominance, and acceptability. Most research on standards battles focuses on the grey area in Table 1 and is starting to broaden to the white areas. In the literature on standard selection, a comparable shift in focus can be observed. Researchers have started to approach the problem of standard selection as a multi-level problem and have gradually broaden their focus to the first and third level (Afuah, 2013; Miller & Tucker, 2009).

There are ample directions for further research. According to Narayanan et al. (2012), there is a need for more integrative research with respect to standards, which incorporates multiple views. Future research can contribute to this integrative

Table 1. Research perspectives on standard selection

	Main Actors	Independent Variables (Selection)	Dependent Variable	Example Papers
3rd level: multi-actor system	(Regulatory) institutions	Smart governance Policy	Socio-political acceptance of standards (institutionalization)	(Backhouse et al., 2006; Nickerson & Zur Muhlen, 2006; Van de Kaa et al., 2013)
2nd level: firms in an economic environment	(networked) Firms	Complementary assets Economic mechanisms	Market acceptance of standards (market dominance)	(Schilling, 1998, 2002; Suarez, 2004; Van de Kaa, Rezaei, Kamp, & De Winter, 2014; Van de Kaa et al., 2011; Van de Kaa, Van Heck, De Vries, Van den Ende, & Rezaei, 2014)
1st level: consumer values	Consumers	Responsible innovation Value sensitive design	Consumer acceptability of standards (acceptability)	(Van de Kaa, 2013)

research by approaching the issue of standard development and selection as a multi-level problem. In the second proposition raised in Section 3, it is assumed that standard acceptability is related to (or even positively influences) standard dominance. However, the relationship between the two concepts, dominance and acceptability, have not been studied before nor has it been tested. In fact, the relationship between the three concepts (standard dominance, socio-political acceptance, and acceptability) has not been researched and this could be an interesting area for further research. Then, the first step is to attempt to clearly define and to distinguish between the three conceptualizations of standard selection as mentioned in Table 1. It would be interesting to examine how these concepts are interrelated. This will also contribute to more integrative research.

ACKNOWLEDGMENT

We thank the NWO research program 'maatschappelijk verantwoord innoveren' for funding part of the research leading to this chapter.

REFERENCES

Afuah, A. (2013). Are network effects really all about size? The role of structure and conduct. *Strategic Management Journal*, *34*(3), 257–273. doi:10.1002/smj.2013

Anderson, P., & Tushman, M. L. (1990). Technological discontinuities and dominant designs: A cyclical model of technological change. *Administrative Science Quarterly*, *35*(4), 604–633. doi:10.2307/2393511

Backhouse, J., Hsu, C., & Leiser, S. (2006). Circuits of power in creating de jure standards: Shaping an international information systems security standard. *Management Information Systems Quarterly*, *30*(Special Issue), 413–438.

De Vries, H. J., Verheul, H., & Willemse, H. (2003). *Stakeholder identification in IT standardization processes.* Paper presented at the Workshop on Standard Making: A Critical Research Frontier for Information Systems. Seattle, WA.

Farrell, J., & Saloner, G. (1985). Standardization, compatibility, and innovation. *The Rand Journal of Economics*, *16*(1), 70–83. doi:10.2307/2555589

Friedman, B., Kahn, P. H., & Borning, A. (1996). Value Sensitive design and information systems. In P. Zhang, & D. Galletta (Eds.), *Human-computer Interactions and Management Information Systems: Foundations* (Vol. 6, pp. 348–372). Armonk, NY: M.E. Sharp.

Hesser, W., Feilzer, A. J., & de Vries, H. J. (2007). *Standardisation in Companies and Markets*. Hamburg: Helmut Schmidt University.

Katz, M. L., & Shapiro, C. (1985). Network externalities, competition, and compatibility. *The American Economic Review*, *75*(3), 424–440.

Miller, A. R., & Tucker, C. (2009). Privacy Protection and Technology Diffusion: The Case of Electronic Medical Records. *Management Science*, *55*(7), 1077–1093. doi:10.1287/mnsc.1090.1014

Narayanan, V., & Chen, T. (2012). Research on technology standards: Accomplishment and challenges. *Research Policy*, *41*(8), 1375–1406. doi:10.1016/j.respol.2012.02.006

Nickerson, J. V., & Zur Muhlen, M. (2006). The Ecology of Standards Process: Insights from Internet Standard Making. *Management Information Systems Quarterly*, *30*(Special issue), 467–488.

Owen, R., Macnaghten, P., & Stilgoe, J. (2012). Responsible research and innovation: From science in society to science for society, with society. *Science & Public Policy*, *39*(6), 751–760. doi:10.1093/scipol/scs093

Schilling, M. A. (1998). Technological lockout: An integrative model of the economic and strategic factors driving technology success and failure. *Academy of Management Review, 23*(2), 267–284.

Schilling, M. A. (2002). Technology success and failure in winner-take-all markets: The impact of learning orientation, timing, and network externalities. *Academy of Management Journal, 45*(2), 387–398. doi:10.2307/3069353

Stilgoe, J., Owen, R., & Macnaghten, P. (2013). Developing a framework for responsible innovation. *Research Policy, 42*(9), 1568–1580. doi:10.1016/j.respol.2013.05.008

Suarez, F. F. (2004). Battles for technological dominance: An integrative framework. *Research Policy, 33*(2), 271–286. doi:10.1016/j.respol.2003.07.001

Tushman, M., & Anderson, P. (1986). Technological discontinuities and organizational environments. *Administrative Science Quarterly, 31*(3), 439–465. doi:10.2307/2392832

Utterback, J. M., & Abernathy, W. J. (1975). A dynamic model of process and product innovation. *Omega, 3*(6), 639–656. doi:10.1016/0305-0483(75)90068-7

van de Kaa, G. (2013). Responsible innovation and standardization: A new research approach? *International Journal of IT Standards and Standardization Research, 11*(2), 61–65. doi:10.4018/jitsr.2013070105

van de Kaa, G., Greeven, M., & van Puijenbroek, G. (2013). Standards battles in China: Opening up the black-box of the Chinese government. *Technology Analysis and Strategic Management, 25*(5), 567–581. doi:10.1080/09537325.2013.785511

van de Kaa, G., Rezaei, J., Kamp, L., & De Winter, A. (2014). Photovoltaic Technology Selection: A Fuzzy MCDM Approach. *Renewable & Sustainable Energy Reviews, 32*, 662–670. doi:10.1016/j.rser.2014.01.044

van de Kaa, G., Van den Ende, J., De Vries, H. J., & Van Heck, E. (2011). Factors for winning interface format battles: A review and synthesis of the literature. *Technological Forecasting and Social Change, 78*(8), 1397–1411. doi:10.1016/j.techfore.2011.03.011

van de Kaa, G., Van Heck, H. W. G. M., De Vries, H. J., Van den Ende, J. C. M., & Rezaei, J. (2014). Supporting Decision-Making in Technology Standards Battles Based on a Fuzzy Analytic Hierarchy Process. *IEEE Transactions on Engineering Management, 61*(2), 336–348. doi:10.1109/TEM.2013.2292579

van den Ende, J., van de Kaa, G., den Uijl, S., & de Vries, H. J. (2012). The paradox of standard flexibility: The effects of co-evolution between standard and interorganizational network. *Organization Studies, 33*(5-6), 705–736. doi:10.1177/0170840612443625

Von Schomberg, R. (2011). Prospects for technology assessment in a framework of responsible research and innovation. In Technikfolgen abschatzen lehren: Bildungspotenziale transdisziplinarer Methoden (pp. 39–61). Springer

Wüstenhagen, R., Wolsink, M., & Bürer, M. J. (2007). Social acceptance of renewable energy innovation: An introduction to the concept. *Energy Policy, 35*(5), 2683–2691. doi:10.1016/j.enpol.2006.12.001

KEY TERMS AND DEFINITIONS

Acceptable: "Agreed or approved of by most people in a society" (Hornby 2000).

Flexibility: "The extent to which the format can be changed to suit new conditions or situations" (Van de Kaa 2014, Hornby 2000).

Market Dominance: "A design is dominant in a certain product category when more than 50% of new installations use the technology for a significant amount of time" (Van de Kaa 2011).

Responsible Research and Innovation: "A transparent, interactive process by which societal actors and innovators become mutually responsive to each other with a view on the (ethical) acceptability, sustainability and societal desirability of the innovation process and its marketable products (in order to allow a proper embedding of scientific and technological advances in our society)" (von Schomberg 2011b as cited by Owen, Macnaghten et al. 2012).

Socio-Political Acceptance: Socio-political acceptance is defined as "social acceptance on the broadest, most general level" (Wurstenhagen et al. 2007).

Standard Selection: The stage in the standardization process from initial launch of a standard to selection of that standard.

Standard: "Approached specification of a limited set of solutions to actual or potential matching problems, prepared for the benefits of the party or parties involved, balancing their needs, and intended and expected to be used repeatedly or continuously, during a certain period, by a substantial number of the parties for whom they are meant" (De Vries 1999).

Value-Sensitive Design: "An approach to the design of technology that accounts for human values in a principled and comprehensive manner throughout the design process" (Friedman 1999).

ENDNOTES

[1]   See Wurstenhagen et al. (2007) for an explanation of the phenomenon of socio-political acceptance.

[2]   Though recently, more and more researchers are focusing on this level.

Section 2
Looking Inside Standards Setting Organisations

Chapter 3
Analysis of Various Structures of Standards Setting Organizations (SSOs) That Impact Tension among Members

DongBack Seo
Chungbuk National University, Korea

ABSTRACT

As the field of ICT standardization has changed from a relatively static, monolithic environment into a very dynamic field in the last two decades, many formal standardization bodies, fora, consortia, and other types of Standards Setting Organizations (SSOs) have emerged. These SSOs have often competed against each other for the same application areas. To a large degree, these changes reflect developments in the field of telecommunications and IT themselves, including liberalization, globalization, rapid changes in technology, and convergence. More than ever before, firms can choose which standard setting body they want to join. Nevertheless, data shows that many firms decide to be members of many relevant bodies at the same time. The aforementioned changes and the multi-SSO memberships of a firm have differently influenced various types of stakeholders, which increases potential tension among members during standardization processes. This chapter intends to study such tension and the effect influenced by the structure and processes of the standard-setting bodies themselves. A framework to analyze tension within given organizational structure and processes based on Giddens' Structuration Theory is proposed. The appealing feature of this theory is that it is neither deterministic at the agent level nor at the structural level, but takes iterative influences between both levels as a starting point. This study shows how an SSO struggles to decrease tension among members and suggests propositions related to the tension that academia and practitioners can apply.

DOI: 10.4018/978-1-4666-6332-9.ch003

INTRODUCTION

For a long time, standardization has been a relatively static process. Within a certain field (e.g. telecommunications industry), it was evident how standard-setting institutions had developed and maintained standards. Within this kind of field, demand was relatively homogeneous, so the requirements and job boundaries for a Standard Setting Organization (SSO) were clear.

Due to environmental and technological changes such as liberalization, globalization, fast technological (r)evolution, and network convergence, the demand for standardization processes within the field of Information and Communications Technologies (ICT) has changed and become more and more heterogeneous. Consequently, companies create new standardization consortia or forums when they consider that the existing SSOs can not satisfy their needs, because the governing structures and processes of those SSOs become too political with lots of tension among members (Bekkers and Seo, 2008). For example, ITU could not efficiently manage the NGN activities, because each member country would like to provide a chairman.

The growing number of standard-setting bodies and their dynamic relationships pose challenges for not only companies who need to participate in those bodies but also SSOs themselves who compete against each other in standardizing a technology including incumbent SSOs. Each SSO develops different levels and types of tension among its members, because it has its own governing structures and processes. Consequently, it challenges companies to deal with a different governing structure and process by SSO. To be competitive, SSOs need to ease the level and type of tension among its members. For this reason, it is necessary to understand the heterogeneous levels and types of tension as well as how structures of SSOs impact the creation, increase and decrease of tension.

Thus, it is important to analyze SSOs' governing structures in standardizing a technology, because these structures greatly influence tension among members within a SSO according to Giddens' Structuration theory. The Structuration theory, which will be explained in the section of Theoretical Background, acknowledges the significances of social structure and members of a society. A given social structure directs members to behave in a certain way. On the other hand, interactions among members influence the evolution of the social structure. In this sense, the social structure can affect the creation, increase, and decrease tension among members. In a SSO context, this idea can be amplified considering that a SSO has distinct governing structure and members join in the SSO with specific purposes. Based on Structuration theory, this paper will reveal 1) how different governing structures and systems of various SSOs influence tension among member organizations in standardizing technology and 2) suggest propositions that can be used to formulate and improve a governing structure and systems so that it can decrease tension among members and encourage them to be more positively active in standardization processes. This paper will particularly review four influential SSOs to understand and identify different levels and types of tensions as exploratory research instead of exhaustingly examining all SSOs. Data collection was done through reviewing academic and non-academic papers that discussed with experts the functionalities and structures of the various SSOs. In addition, six semi-structured interviews were held with representatives of various companies who are members of many SSOs including the European Telecommunications Standards Institute (ETSI).

For academia, this paper contributes in identifying the heterogeneity of SSOs in different levels and types of tension based on the governing structures and processes of SSOs. SSOs may use this proposed analysis to improve their governing structures and standardization processes to attract more members and maximize the effectiveness and efficiency of technology standardizations. Practitioners including companies as well as policymakers involved in SSOs can also apply the findings of this study to improve their standards strategies and policies through understanding and analyzing various governing structures and processes of different SSOs.

THEORETICAL BACKGROUND

There is little doubt that Information and Communication Technologies (ICT) have been a backbone of the ubiquitous society. The ubiquitous society means that wherever and whenever people can connect to Internet regardless access points (e.g., mobile phone, desktop computer, and tablet computer) and media (wireless network, satellite, and fiber optic cable). Due to the complexity of technologies and systems, many organizations from different industries including consumer electronics, telecommunications, and information technology networks, as well as governments, must work together to standardize components, technologies, and systems. In this way, they can provide seamless products and services as a whole in a ubiquitous society. Seamless products and services allow users to access to Internet through their devices (e.g., mobile phone, desktop computer, and tablet computer) and use general services without any barriers (e.g., re-configuring). To fulfill this demand for technology standardization, the number of SSOs increases and these SSOs have formulated their own governing structures that impact greatly standardization processes. To analyze how different governing structures of various SSOs influence tension among members during standardization processes, Giddens' Structuration theory is adopted.

Anthony Giddens (1984) introduced the Structuration theory that bridges two lopsided theories of social systems, for example, agency- versus structure-centered theories. This theory recognizes the significance of both individual actors and societal structure. It means that all actors behave in certain ways influenced by the context of the existing social structure. At the same, their thoughts and behavior contribute the formation and evolution of the social structure. Thus, there is mutual relationship between a social structure and members who live and form the social structure instead of one side overwhelming the other side.

The reason to select Structuration theory is related to the research question – how the governing structure of a SSO influences the tension among members in standardizing technologies. Researchers have applied Actor-Network Theory (ANT) and Game theory to analyze technology standardization processes (Seo, 2013). These theories are useful to analyze dynamic relationships and inter-activities among members within a given governing structure that has the sets of rules and policies. However, the interest of this study is how various governing structures of SSOs differently influence dynamic relationships and inter-activities among members without assuming or taking any given structure. To answer this research question, Giddens' Structuration theory is applied. In this paper, the term of structure is narrower than the original structure used by Giddens. Strucutre in this research implies administrative rules and governance structures within a SSO, while Giddens' social structure refers to governance rules, policies, and social practices within a society.

Below explains how the proposed conceptual model (Figure 1) works. A number of organizations (actors) formed a SSO with a certain governing structure such as rules and policies. For example, the *European Telecommunications Standards Institute* (ETSI) is rooted on the GSM group. *European Conference of Postal and Telecommunications Administrations* (CEPT), whose acronym came from its French name (*Conférence Européenne des administrations des Postes et des Telecommunications*), founded this GSM group.

Figure 1. Conceptual structuration model for standardization within a SSO

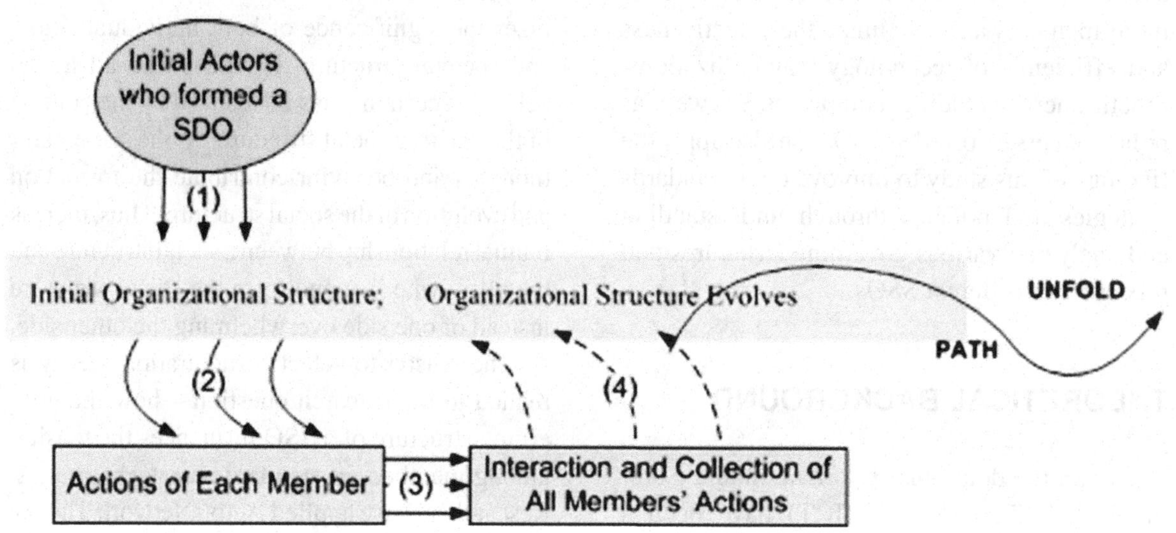

In 1959, 19 members established CEPT. The original 19 members were monopoly-holding national *Post, Telegraphy and Telephony* (PTT) bureaus. (1) Therefore, the initial governing structure was formed by these 19 members. (2) This initial governing structure influenced the activities of members. For instance, one of membership policies was allowing only European PTT to be a member. (3) However, as environment changes such as market needs, liberalization in the telecommunications industry, and changes in member organizations, the existing organizational structure provided constraints rather than enablers to members' activities. Also, CEPT itself grew with 7 new members during its first ten years. (4) Therefore, the technology development, the change of market competition, and the entrance of new members stimulate the dynamic of interactions among members. These accumulated dynamics feed back to the organizational structure to evolve. This recursive and mutual relationship between the governing structure of CEPT and members has continued. This phenomenon is exactly what Giddens tries to explain and analyze through Structuration theory in the social context.

To apply this concept more concretely, we need to understand how the *structure* of a SSO forces members to behave in certain *systematic* ways and creates *modes* that reinforce the given structure. Below explains these three concepts that support the Structuration Theory.

According to Giddens' book (1984) about the constitution of society, *structure* refers to "rules and resources, or sets of transformation relations, organized as properties of social systems," *system* is defined as "reproduced relations between actors or collectivities, organized as regular social practices," and *structuration* is identified as "conditions governing the continuity or transmutation of structures, and therefore the reproduction of social system" (p. 25). Due to the fact that these definitions are for studying the constitution of society, they are rephrased and redefined to research governing structures and processes of SSOs as follow: *structure* as recursively and objectively formulated sets of rules and policies members should follow as long as the sets are valid, *system* as legitimately reproduced activities and interactions conducted by members, and *structuration* as modes that encourage members to act and interact in certain ways to reinforce the given structure (see Table 1).

Based on the conceptual model (Figure 1) and rephrased definitions of three concepts for

Table 1. Definitions of three concepts

	Structure	System	Structuration
Giddens (1984: p. 25) In social context	Rules and resources, or sets of transformation relations, organized as properties of social systems.	Reproduced relations between actors or collectivities, organized as regular social practices.	Conditions governing the continuity or transmutation of structures, and therefore the reproduction of social system.
In the context of standardization	Recursively and objectively formulated sets of rules and policies members should follow as long as the sets are valid.	Legitimately reproduced activities and interactions conducted by members.	Modes that encourage members to act and interact in certain ways to reinforce the given structure.

the context of technology standard (Table 1), the structures of four influential SSOs are analyzed and compared to understand and identify different levels and types of tensions among members.

DATA AND METHODOLOGY

Data for this study was collected, by means of desk research, focusing on academic and non-academic papers discussing the functionalities and structures of the various SSOs. Six semi-structured interviews were also conducted with representatives of companies that were typically involved in many SSOs including the following SSOs. Four SSOs were selected – 1) European Telecommunications Standards Institute (ETSI), 2) Internet Engineering Task Force (IETF), 3) Open Mobile Alliance (OMA), and 4) Institute of Electrical and Electronics Engineers (IEEE) – on the basis of preparatory talks with SSOs' members. Interviewees were asked to talk frankly, not

as representatives of their firms, in order to get a genuine view on how SSOs work and what kind of tension exists. Based on the literature review (e.g., Brenner et al., 2005; IEEE, 2013; IEEE, 2014a,, 2004b; OMA, 2014) and interviews, numbers of issues are identified. These issues are well matched with the definitions of three concepts from Structuration theory that were rephrased for the context of technology standardization (see Table 2).

There are seven identified issues: 1) membership (admission and joining decision by actors), 2) decision-making structure, 3) Intellectual Property Rights (IPR) policies, 4) initiating new work, 5) third-party specifications, 6) local vs. global focus, and 7) performance (see *Related issues* in the Table 2). The first three items (membership, decision-making structure, and IPR policies) are fundamental rules and policies of a SSO that form its structure. Following these rules and policies, all members systematically conduct their activities including items 4) and 5) (initiating new work and third-party specifications). These are the most

Table 2. Related to issues by three concepts

	Structure	System	Structuration
In the context of standardization	Recursively and objectively formulated sets of rules and policies members should follow as long as the sets are valid.	Legitimately reproduced activities and interactions conducted by members.	Modes that encourage members to act and interact certain ways to reinforce the given structure.
Related issues	• Membership (Admission and joining decision by actors). • Decision-making structure. • IPR policies.	• Initiating new work. • Third-party specifications.	• Local vs. global focus. • Performance.

important activities chosen by interviewees and by the review of the documents and reports of the four SSOs. It is notable that specifying standards is not selected. It is because all the fundamental and important decisions are made during the initiating new work and these decisions are just operationalized when specifying standards. Then, the interaction and collection of all members generate certain modes (structuration) that encourage to maintain the existing structure and system. However, these modes can positively or negatively influence the focus and performance of a SSO. Therefore, the structuration of a SSO will be evaluated by analyzing its focus and performance (items 6 and 7).

This study is an exploratory research. Given the number of interviews, it cannot be claimed that the study is complete or representative. Still, having chosen stakeholders from different actor groups (equipment manufacturers, network operators, public bodies) and including firms with a different background of technological preferences (from telecom and computer industries) as interviewees, the most relevant perspectives are included without giving preferential treatment to one perspective at the expense of the others – except, possibly, for smaller firms. It is also useful to note that there was a surprising degree of consensus about many of the issues discussed in this research, despite differences in perspective.

Being an exploratory study, this research heavily relies on a limited set of interviews. Thus, it is not aimed to present a fully representative or authoritative view, but it is aimed to provide interesting and valuable views on how various governing structures of different SSOs influence tensions among members in the field of ICT.

STRUCTURE

Literature and interviewees identify three items (membership, decision-making rules, and IPR policies) that are fundamental pillars supporting the structure of a SSO. These items are critical guidelines for members to develop standards strategies and behave in standardizing technologies within the SSO. Below illustrates how each item is a part of the structure and related to tension among members.

Membership Structure

Membership policy is the most fundamental component for SSOs' structures (Jakobs et al., 2010; Jakobs, 2011). SSOs exist by the grace of its stakeholders, usually (but not always) by its members. For this reason, membership levels, distribution (balance between various industrial categories), and admission rules are significant for the structure of a SSO (Lemstra et al., 2010). ETSI and OMA offer membership to organizations (either for profit or not for profit), while IEEE is primarily based on individual based membership, even though it introduced an additional company membership lately. IETF, in contrast, does not have the concept of members at all.

Individual membership, as used by IEEE, certainly has its benefits. It caters nuanced discussions, not necessarily following the delineations of companies' interest and strategies. Individual members can feel strong incentives (e.g. peer recognition and personal satisfaction) to give their best. However, these advantages come at a price. In IEEE, the large majority of members indeed represent a firm, visible or not (Jakobs, et al., 2010; Jakobs, 2011; Luna, 2007). As a result, firms seek ways to represent their interests by sending as many individuals as possible to the meetings in order to influence the decision-making process. This leads to considerable tension, because other individuals or (smaller) firms perceive that their legitimate inputs or views are suppressed by the large and organized corporate manipulations exerted by parties with vested interests (Jakobs, et al., 2010; Jakobs, 2011). A very visible and well-documented event where this happened was the initial development of IEEE 802.20 standard for mobile telecommunications (Bekkers and Seo, 2008; Luna, 2007). Some leading firms in this area reportedly sent many experts to the meetings so that they could buy votes to enforce their own interests. For example, Qualcomm (and Kyocera) were accused to play this game for their Wimax-competing proposal (for more details, see Luna, 2007). When this caused a public uproar, IEEE found out that the companies in question had violated the IEEE rules. Thus, the entire standards activity was revamped and re-started. Consequently, this incident illustrated one drawback in the individual-based membership that can increase tensions among members to monitor each other.

Respondents (all working in established telecommunication firms) were also critical towards the non-member structure of IETF, particularly when it comes to the (perceived) fairness of the decision-making process (see below).

Concerning membership balance (i.e. the degree to which the various stakeholder categories are sufficiently represented), SSOs that consist of heterogeneous groups of members based on their industries (e.g., telecom and computer) have more tension than SSOs with homogeneous members. For example, as one interviewee points out, in IETF, participants from telecommunications firms have the feeling that their interests are not taken duly into account, and they have to fight against the concurrence of views from members based on computer industry (Bekkers and Seo, 2008; Dickerson, 2004). Based on the analysis of interviews and the literature review, four propositions related to membership structure are developed. These propositions provide a hint to decrease tension among members.

Proposition 1a: Organization-based membership is negatively related to tension among members.

Proposition 1b: Individual-based membership is positively related to tension among members.

Proposition 1c: Non-membership structure is positively related to tension among members.

Proposition 1d: The heterogeneity of member groups based on the industrial category is positively related to tension among members.

Positively related to tension refers to increasing tension. For example, individual-based membership is likely to increase tension among members.

Decision-Making Structure

Although virtually all bodies would claim that 'consensus' is the leading principle, their decision-making structures have been implemented in different ways. As membership structure does, this structure influences the tension among members. Depending on a structure, members perceive whether their opinions are fairly reflected in the decision-making process or ignored by other members who try to manipulate the process.

For example, due to the fact that IETF has no membership structure (see above), it cannot have a balloting/voting system either. Instead, the so-called Working Group chairs and Area directors have powerful autonomy to take decisions. During meetings and e-mail discussions, individual members should strive for 'rough consensus' (implying that unanimity is not strictly necessary). Nevertheless, the chairs and directors can make decisions at their own discretion if necessary. Every member in IETF has the right to get involved, but as the most interviewees pointed out, some members perceive that only privileged small groups of insiders have actual influence in the decision-making process (Bekkers and Seo, 2008). Although there are public meetings with high attendance, participants hardly have a chance to bring issues to the table unless they are considered to be an 'authority' by the insiders in the specific technical area. One interviewee comments: 'you can compare it with voting by humming: who hums hardest will determine the outcome.' Considering this situation, it is not surprising that there is considerable tension among members.

The SSOs that do have membership and voting structures need to make a key choice on voting rules. One of the most interesting issues for them is the choice between weighted voting on the one hand and one-member-one-vote on the other. Whereas the weighted voting is unusual for individual membership models (e.g. IEEE), it has been regularly used in organization-based membership models (e.g. ETSI), even though some newly formed SSOs with organization-based membership adopted un-weighted voting structure (e.g. The 3rd Generation Partnership Project [3GPP]). Interviewees state that there is increasing support for the one-member-one-vote policy, because this structure seems fair and tends to reduce entry barrier for new members. Another concern in decision-making structure to which we need to pay attention is possibly discriminating voting rules based on member types (e.g. members industrial categories or geographical origins). For example, governments may be categorized as non-voting observers. Another example is a voting right discrimination against members' geographical origins that is still used in ETSI. However, it is increasingly debated whether this rule should be maintained. This is one of the evidences for the recursive part in the proposed model. Many members perceive more constraints than benefits from this rule, so they interact with each other and collectively try to change this existing structure. With these analyses, three propositions are developed as below.

Proposition 2a: No voting structure is more positively related to tension among members than a voting structure.

Proposition 2b: Weighted voting structure is more positively related to tension among members than one-member-one-vote structure.

Proposition 2c: Voting structure that discriminates members based on their industrial category or regional origin is positively related to tension among members.

IPR Policies

As shared by many people, IPR policies are most contentious factor in SSOs' structures. IP-owning companies vigorously participate in standards processes in order to ensure that the final specification includes technologies covered by their patents. Especially with the advent of technology-only firms, the interests of the various members become even more diverse. Technology-only firms refer to companies that have a business model fully or largely based on licensing income, not from producing standard-compliant goods. As a result, it is more difficult for all members to agree on a technology specification.

There are a number of contrasting different aspects among members that increase the tension. For example, there are 1) IPR holding versus non-IPR holding companies, 2) vertical integrated versus IP-only companies, 3) status quo versus new members, and 4) companies with large IPR portfolio versus with small IPR portfolio. There are also other debatable issues such the value of IPR (essential or non-essential) and market share.

IPR rules are also a very important consideration for firms whether or not to join SSOs. In a recent small-scale survey of large firms that are active in various SSOs, all respondents indicate that they carefully study the IPR policy before joining any SSO, even though some of them have been members of more than 150 SSOs. Some will also reconsider their memberships if significant changes in the IPR policy are made (Updegrove, 2003).

As shown in Table 3, most SSOs request all IPR holders to declare their IPR and be prepared to license its essential IPR at Fair, Reasonable and

Table 3. IPR policies of four SSOs and World Wide Web consortium (W3C)

SSO	Main Character of IPR Policy
IEEE	Voluntary ex-ante disclosure of licensing terms since early 2008, including a RAND option.
IETF	• Preference for IPR-free standards. • Otherwise RAND, though decisions may be made to divert from this. • Implementation requirement is believed to relieve IPR problems. • Declarations from parties other than the IPR holder itself are allowed (and encouraged).
OMA	"Standard" RAND policy
ETSI	"Standard" RAND policy, now also 'passively' allowing voluntary ex-ante disclosure of licensing terms.
W3C (not under study here)	Royalty-free (RC) obligation

Non-Discriminatory (RAND) conditions. RAND policies, when used in the current patent-intensive strategies of members, show several shortcomings. For example 1) it is not feasible to calculate and analyze the cost and benefit of certain technologies that are potential to be a part of standard; 2) RAND terms are inherently vague; and 3) there are possible problems for companies to over-claim and under-claim. (See Bekkers and Seo, 2008 for a more discussion of these and more shortcomings of RAND).

At this point, there is no single SSO that does successfully address all (or even most) of these issues in its structure as IPR policies. For instance, excessive licensing fees by non-members cannot be effectively addressed in an SSO policy. However, the perceived problems with RAND have led to many heated discussions in the last few years. Consequently, some of SSOs, for example, ETSI studied whether it should revise its IPR policy, even though it did not change much, while IEEE introduced a brand new IPR policy (Department of Justice, 2007). This is another example of the recursive part in the conceptual model (see Figure 1) – *the interaction and collection of all members' actions, the structural changes*. SSOs have tried to restructure their IPR policies based on the demands from their members.

Without doubt, one of the most interesting recent developments is the adoption of a voluntary ex-ante licensing policy in IEEE (Bekkers and Seo, 2008; Luna, 2007). In such a policy, an IP owner can choose to disclose its licensing rates before the technology is made a part of a standard (instead of disclosing these rates only once the standard is ready). Interviewees regard it as a very interesting move, and their view is best described as moderately positive. Voluntary ex-ante licensing schemes can reduce uncertainty that has been one of the central problems. It can be used to facilitate a sensible cost/benefit analysis in order to decide on the inclusion of a certain technology in standard, so members can choose among several technologies (if available). IPR-holders may compete to offer the most attractive combination of technology and licensing terms. Some interviewees, however, feel that they would not opt to declare licensing conditions beforehand. One of interviewees say, "*It is like asking a chess-player, at the start of the match, to denounce what his 20th move will be.*" However, as long as the scheme is *voluntary*, they have the right not to do so. With these analyses, two propositions related to IPR policies are developed.

Proposition 3a: The heterogeneity of member groups regards to IPR ownership and strategies is positively related to tension among members.

Proposition 3b: Voluntary ex-ante licensing schemes are negatively related to tension among members.

SYSTEM

As mentioned, system is about legitimately reproducing activities and interactions among members. In this section, two items (initiating new work and third-party specifications) are identified as most important activities for SSOs. When all members of a SSO conduct these activities, they have formed certain behavior patterns over a period under the given SSO's structure. The following illustrates how each activity is systematically formulated and related to tension among members.

Initiating New Work

Long-term success for an SSO depends on its capabilities to identify and initiate relevant new work on a continuous basis. In this matter, some SSOs cover a broad scope of subjects (e.g. ISO), so they are able to attract new subjects. However, SSOs that started as a one-issue club might have problems to maintain their positions once they standardize all necessary technologies in the given issue. Many SSOs are somewhere in between these two extremes. In fact, they often compete against each other for new works in competitive environment. This is not always appreciated by firms that are members of multiple SSOs (as many firms are), who argue that competing works between SSOs lead to duplication of their efforts and uncertainty about potential standards. As a result of difficulties in finding new work, some SSOs feel that their pipelines are drying up (Bekkers and Seo, 2008). For example, all the interviewees expressed their concerns that ETSI has fewer and fewer new works.

There are several issues in identifying new works. First, an SSO should develop criteria, rules, and procedures to identify an acceptable new work item. Second, it has to be decided who has principle responsibility for initiating a new work item (member, SSO management team, board, or specialized task force). Third, an SSO needs to be sure that participants are willing to allocate resources to standardize the new work item, because the members are who develop standards, not the SSO itself.

One challenge here is that the status quo members might resist new work items that are found to be attractive by other members. They might do so for a variety of reasons, including the threat of new innovative works that could take over their existing products or services in the market, so they might prefer to have these works done in another SSO. With this observation, one proposition is constructed.

Proposition 4: A dominant role for established status quo members is positively related to tension in initiating new work.

Third-Party Specifications

It is quite usual that a SSO develops a technology specification from scratch to implementable status. However, there is also a (renewed) demand for the SSO to approve already developed technology specifications by others as standards. For example, it is possible to submit ready-made specifications through the Publicly Available Specifications (PAS) procedure in ETSI (Bekkers and Seo, 2008). In the case of IEEE, third party specifications are allowed as input (Luna, 2007). Organizations may be interested to feed their technology specifications into well-known SSOs, because the standards these SSOs produce (a) may be more favorable from the legal point of view (in case of formal SSOs); (b) are likely to be well disseminated and accessible to other interested parties; (c) are conceived as a 'quality stamp'; (d) signal stable specifications to provide a solid basis for product development; (e) allow eventual ambiguities, omissions and errors to be found and corrected; (f) tend to be maintained well.

There are quite a few successful examples of such a working mode: IETF works completely on the basis of external specifications, European Computer Manufacturers Association (ECMA –

now known as European association for standardizing information and communication systems) received the Compact Disc (CD) as an external specification among many others. In addition, ETSI accepted various broadcasting standards, including the Digital Video Broadcast (DVB) as a standard that is widely used for digital television services.

However, it becomes contentious when there are competing technologies developed by internal task forces as well as submitted as external specifications. While all the interviewees were in strong favor of promoting the use of external specifications, in many cases, SSOs have struggled when they try to apply this system, because external specifications can compete against another potential technology candidate that a SSO has been developing. This is particularly true for SSOs that are vertically integrated. A vertically integrated SSO means a standard-making body that develops a technology standard from scratch. This problem is observed more often in IEEE and ETSI than in IETF, ITU, ISO and ECMA. Meanwhile the issue of third-party specifications is ongoing, vertically integrated SSOs tend to run into a situation that there are competing technologies developed by internal task forces and by submitted as external specifications, which potentially create tensions among members who are involved in these two technologies. Based on these analyses, one proposition is suggested.

Proposition 5: In the matter of third-party specifications, vertically integrated SSOs are more positively related to tension among members than none vertically integrated SSOs.

STRUCTURATION

Structuration refers to the emerged conditions governing the continuity of transmutation of structures, so it encourages members to reproduce systematical activities. Thus, structuration is not given and nor static, but formulated and evolved depending on the changes of structure and systematic patterns that members have formed to conduct certain activities shown in the previous section (System). For these reasons, analyzing the structuration of a SSO implies what kind of modes the SSO provides for its members to conduct activities in standardizing technologies. If the SSO provides positive modes, it will create virtuous cycle to make its structuration more constructive. As a result, it will eventually decrease tension among members and attract more new members. Otherwise, the structuration falls in vicious cycle that creates more tension unless the SSO changes its structure to stimulate the changes of members' behavioral patterns. This section illustrates two items (local versus global focus and performance) that evaluate SSOs' structuration related to tension among members.

Local vs. Global Focus

Traditionally, different SSOs have focused on issues in standardizing technologies based on local demands. While some SSOs such as ITU, ISO, and IEC really started as a global SSO without any formal or actual focus on any single region in particular, others have local concentration. Although most of these formally local SSOs have increasingly begun to address issues for the global market, they still inherit local features in their laws and procedures such as membership balance, power distribution, and technical focus. For example, ETSI was founded as a local SSO in Europe. Supported by European Union, ETSI has statutes, rules, and procedures that distinguish between members from Europe and other regions. Members from the European region can become 'Full Members', while others from non-European regions can only become 'Associate Members' that have fewer rights. Only Europe-based members can be candidates for board membership, which is a valuable way to influence standardization processes. Although SSOs like ETSI seem open to change such discrimination, there are many legislative obstacles to overcome including resistance from the status quo members. Consequently, ETSI still has a local focus while considering a global market.

Proposition 6: Expanding the market without changing the existing structure and system of a SSO is positively related to creating negative modes that increase tension among members.

Performance

There are many dimensions to evaluate the performance of a SSO. Two of most important dimensions by the interviewees are 1) the relevance of technologies that SSOs try to standardize and 2) the speed of standardization process. Members compare what kinds of technologies various SSOs work on and evaluate how relevant these technologies are to their interests.

Overall, interviewees stress the current high relevance of IEEE and OMA, because these SSOs are standardizing technologies that are highly important in the next few years. However, IETF is graded low in the relevance, even though IETF standardized TCP/IP protocol that has been one of the most widely implemented standards, because there is not many new and important works related to technology standardizations. It is because many incumbent players – especially, companies in the telecom industry – feel uncomfortable with this SSO, therefore, they bring their activities elsewhere. ETSI has been criticized as well in this perspective. According to some interviewees, ETSI is not regarded as important as it used to be. They perceive that ETSI's current or potential works are not important to the market. The relevance issue is significantly related to the item, "(4) initiating new work" in the System section. Members formulate behavior patterns under the structure and system in initiating new works. At the same time, they evaluate how these works are

relevant to their businesses. If they are frustrated with initiating new works or evaluate the technologies in progress with lower relevance, they can go to another SSO to standardize the technologies that they want. The frustration means increasing tension among members, because some of them are unhappy with the existing works while others do not recognize the need of new works. Thus, the given structure and system of a SSO that have the high tension (especially, for the issue of initiating new work) tend to have the low relevance of technologies.

Proposition 7a: The structure and system of a SSO that are positively related to tension among members are negatively related to the relevance of technologies in standardization.

Another dimension of performance is the speed of standardization process. Formal SSOs are known as slow in process. This is often said to be the reason why firms go to another type of SSOs such as forum or consortium. However, this claim is not always true. For example, when IETF standardized Session Initiation Protocol (SIP), it took longer than many comparable standards in formal SSOs. The problem was that it was "[...] claimed to suffer from low speed when either (1) the number of volunteers is too low and (2) when there are too many volunteers, with too many different opinions" (one of interviewees). He explained, "Consortia allow you to make speed, which is very important: the timing of the SSOs output is key to the business success. However, this does not mean that consortia are always made of like-minded organizations. Also in consortia, you have many different types of actors, representing different interests. However, the risk is considerably lower that there are participants who deliberately try to delay or block the standardization effort. There is really less gaming (instead, groups already divide before and join different consortia)." As the interviewee mentioned, the structure and system of a SSO can provide a room for some members to play a game that delays the speed of standardization process such as too much heterogeneous membership base and the absence of voting structure. Therefore, the given structure and system are related to the performance in the speed of standardization process.

Proposition 7b: The structure and system of a SSO that are positively related to tension among members are negatively related to the speed of standardization process.

CONCLUSION AND DISCUSSION

The structuration of a SSO provides conditions governing the continuity of the existing structure, so members can reproduce the system through their activities and interactions. Thus, the structuration is closely co-dependent with the structure and system. If the structuration is static, which means that the structure and system are static as well, it will increase the tension among members as suggested in Proposition 6.

Proposition 6 illustrates the need for organizations to change their structure and system if they want to expand or alter target market so that they maintain the consistency between their regional focus and target market. Otherwise, the inconsistency increase the tension among members and consequently, it will impact their performance.

Reversely thinking, it means that we can fathom the tension among members through analyzing the performance of a SSO (Proposition 7a and 7b), because of the difficulty in measuring the tension. It is not surprising that the tension is negatively related to the SSO's focus and performance. This is why organizations must decrease the tension to increase their focus and performance. Perhaps, organizations should also focus on decreasing the tension, not just increasing the performance.

From these analyses, recommendations are 1) self-evaluating tensions among members by applying the propositions; 2) being flexible to change the structuation of a SSO instead of insisting on a static structuation; and 3) paying attention to decrease tensions among members, because it is related to the performance of a SSO.

In this research, how the structure and system of an organization are related to the tension (Proposition 1a through Proposition 5) is explained. Table 4 summarizes these Propositions and their relations to the tension ('+' for a positive relation, '-' for a negative relation).

Although this research is exploratory, applying these propositions to four SSOs (ETSI, IEEE,

Table 4. Summary of Proposition 1a through Proposition 5

Concepts	Propositions
Structure	Proposition 1a: Organization based membership (-) Proposition 1b: Individual based membership (+) Proposition 1c: Non-membership structure (+) Proposition 1d: The heterogeneity of member groups based on the industrial categories (+)
	Proposition 2a: Absence of voting structure (+) Proposition 2b: Weighted voting structure (in contrast with one-member-one-vote) (+) Proposition 2c: Voting structures that discriminate members based on industrial categories or regional origins (+)
	Proposition 3a: The heterogeneity of member groups regards to IPR ownership and strategies (+) Proposition 3b: Voluntary ex-ante licensing schemes (-)
System	Proposition 4: Dominant role for status quo members (+)
	Proposition 5: In the matter of third-party specifications, vertically integrated SSOs (+)

OMA, and IETF) demonstrates the feasibility of the proposed framework to analyze tension among member (See Table 5).

ETSI that have generally high tension provides negative modes in the geographic focus and low performance in the relevance of technologies, while IEEE and OMA that have medium or low tension overall offer positive modes in the geographic focus and high performance in the relevance of technologies. Although IETF has low performance in the relevance of technologies, it provides medium modes in the geographic focus because of the medium tension in initiating new work.

The contributions of this paper are: 1) providing the framework to analyze and fathom the tension among members within an organization; 2) suggesting a way to identify problematic issues in the structure or system that create or increase the tension; and 3) proposing an approach to evaluate overall tensions and performances between organizations (as shown Table 5). For academia, this research offers new avenue to analyze the tension among members and the performances of SSOs related to the tension. For practitioners, the proposed framework can be used in tension management. SSOs can apply this study to create or modify their structures and systems to decrease the tension while increasing the performance. Companies who are parts of members in many SSOs can use the framework to analyze and compare various SSOs so that they can select SSOs to maximize their resources in standardizing technologies.

Some of limitations are the selected issues (items) are based on the number of interviewees, so it does not have full external validity. These items can be improved further. Due to the fact that this research focuses on SSOs, researchers should consider other issues to study the tension in other types of organizations. However, the conceptual framework (Figure 1 and Table 1) is still applicable to analyze other types of organizations. Another limitation is that the framework should be validated more with richer empirical data, because this research is exploratory.

Table 5. Result (Evaluation) of applying of propositions to four SSOs

	ETSI	IEEE	OMA	IETF
P1: Membership	Low	High/medium	Low	High
P2: Decision-making structure	High/medium	Low	Low	High
P3: IPR policies	High	Medium	Medium	Medium
P4: Initiating new work	High	Medium	Medium	Medium
P5: Third party specifications	High	Low	Medium	Low
P6: Geographic focus	Generally, High – Negative modes (Inconsistence)	Generally, Medium/low – Positive modes	Generally, Medium/low – Positive modes	Generally, High/medium – Medium modes
P7: Performance	Generally, High – Low performance	Generally, Medium/low – High performance	Generally, Medium/low – High performance	Generally, High/medium – Low performance

REFERENCES

Bekkers, R., & Seo, D. (2008). *Quick Scan for best practices in ICT standardisation: What ETSI could learn from other standards bodies. Commissioned by the Directorate of Energy and Telecommunications, Dutch Ministry of Economic Affairs*. Utrecht: Dialogic.

Brenner, M., Grech, M., Torabi, M., & Unmehopa, M. (2005). The open mobile alliance and trends in supporting the mobile services industry. *Bell Labs Technical Journal*, *10*(1), 59–75. doi:10.1002/bltj.20079

Department of Justice. (2007). Response to Institute of Electrical and Electronics Engineers, Inc.'s Request for Business Review Letter. Washington, DC: DoJ.

Dickerson, K. (2004). Operator strategies for maximising the benefits of standardisation. Academic Press.

Giddens, A. (1984). *The Constitution of Society*. Berkeley, CA: University of California Press.

IEEE. (2013). *IEEE Standards Association Operations Manual*. New York: Authors.

IEEE. (2014a). *IEEE Constitution and Bylaws*. New York: Authors.

IEEE. (2014b). *IEEE Policies*. New York: Authors.

Jakobs, K. (2011). How People and Stakeholders Shape Standards - The Case of IEEE 802.11. In J. Filipe, & J. Cordeiro (Eds.), *Web Information Systems and Technologies 2010, LNBIP*. Springer. doi:10.1007/978-3-642-22810-0_1

Jakobs, K., Lemstra, W., Hayes, V., Tuch, B., & Links, C. (2010). Creating a Wireless LAN Standard: IEEE 802.11. In J. Groenewegen, & V. Hayes (Eds.), *The Innovation Journey of WiFi*. Cambridge University Press. doi:10.1017/CBO9780511666995.006

Lemstra, W., Groenewegen, J., & Hayes, V. (2010). *The Innovation Journey of WiFi*. Cambridge University Press. doi:10.1017/CBO9780511666995

Luna, L. (2007, January). Reality game. *Mobile Radio Technology*.

OMA. (2014). *Open Mobile Alliance: Policies and Terms of Use*. Retrieved from http://openmobilealliance.org/about-oma/policies-and-terms-of-use

Seo, D. (2013). *Evolution and Standardization of Mobile Communications Technology*. Hershey, PA: IGI Global. doi:10.4018/978-1-4666-4074-0

Updegrove, A. (2003). Darwin, Standards and Survival. In The standards edge: Dynamic tension. Ann Arbor, MI: Bolin Communications.

KEY TERMS AND DEFINITIONS

ETSI: European Telecommunications Standards Institute.

IEEE: Institute of Electrical and Electronics Engineers.

IETF: Internet Engineering Task Force.

OMA: Open Mobile Alliance.

SSO: Standard Setting Organization.

Structuration Theory: it was introduced by Anthony Giddens and it bridges two lopsided theories of social systems, for example, agency-versus structure-centered theories.

Structure: Recursively and objectively formulated sets of rules and policies members should follow as long as the sets are valid.

Tension: A strained state among members with a standard setting organization.

Chapter 4
Industry–Led Standardization as Private Governance?
A Critical Reassessment of the Digital Video Broadcasting Project's Success Story

Niclas Meyer
Fraunhofer Institute for Systems and Innovations Research ISI, Germany

ABSTRACT

Industry-led technical standardization is often cited as an example for private governance. And the Digital Video Broadcasting (DVB) Project is often presented as a particularly successful case of such governance without government. The successes of the industry-led DVB Project have often been cited as evidence for the superior governance capacity of private industry. While the commercial and engineering success of the DVB Project is unequivocal, this chapter raises the question whether it has been equally successful in governing a complex sector that is confronted by a range of market failures, with direct implications for important public policy objectives such as media pluralism and diversity.

INTRODUCTION

At the example of the DVB, Project, this chapter examines whether and, if so, under what circumstances governance through industry-led standardization processes, may provide a solution to the challenges posed to conventional government-led technology policy, in which governments try to select and enforce technology standards. These challenges of government-led standardization policy are well illustrated by the history of government involvement in interna-

tional and European high-definition television (HDTV) standardization. First, the case of HDTV standardization demonstrated the difficulties of global governance where governments need to collaborate and agree to common measures. When HDTV standardization was first brought onto the agenda of the CCIR (Consultative Committee for International Radio) by the government of Japan the international community failed to overcome its divergent interests and to find agreement on a common standard. As each government sought to install its domestic technology as the international

DOI: 10.4018/978-1-4666-6332-9.ch004

standard, the negotiations quickly erupted into an international standards war, which could not have been any more passionate, as demonstrated by the following statement by an executive of the French company Thomson:

High-definition television was to be the [Japanese'] ultimate weapon—an instrument with which to squeeze their European competitors out of their own domestic market and blitzkrieg the wide-open American market. In short, move in for the kill [...] This was to be the new Verdun. (Interview with an unnamed Thomson executive in The Economist (The world at war, 1990)

Secondly, the story of HDTV standardization also demonstrated the information problems faced by governmental actors that seek to influence standardization processes in high tech industries. Upon the initiative of the French government and the European Commission close to €1 billion in public subsidies were sunk into the development of an HDTV standard, which was never deployed (Cawson, 1995; Peterson & Sharp, 1998). Many commentators began to refer to this failure to support their arguments that governmental actors should stay out of technical standardization processes (Cave, 1997; Cawson, 1995; Galprin, 2002; Levy, 1997).

The subsequent success of the industry-led Digital Video Broadcasting (DVB) Project was then celebrated by the critics of government interventionism as evidence for the superior governance capacity of industry-led technical standardization processes. DVB standardization was a great engineering and commercial success (de Bruin & Smits, 1999; Cave, 1997; Reimers, 2006). Its standards are today used in nearly one billion devices all over the world (DVB Project, 2013, p. 2). This led many commentators to the conclusion that industry knew best what technical standards were needed and how to develop these

and that government should stay out of industry standardization processes (de Bruin & Smits, 1999; Dai, 2008; Watson, 2005).

This article challenges this conclusion. From an engineering and from a commercial perspective the success of the DVB Project cannot be disputed. Governance, however, is concerned with the solution of all sorts of interaction problems that occur in the economy and society at large. In the case of digital television, governance is concerned with the creation and regulation of the market as a level playing field on which companies compete for the benefit of the consumer. Governance is also concerned with a range of other public policy objectives, such as media pluralism and diversity. As argued below, standardization has a critical impact on all of these governance issues. Therefore, this chapter will raise the question whether and, if so, to what extent, the DVB Project was able to address these governance issues.

The following Section provides a brief introduction to and definition of the concept of governance, which is applied in this chapter. This is followed by a detailed empirical investigation of the DVB case.

GOVERNING THROUGH STANDARDS

This chapter starts from the institutionalist premises that economic exchange cannot take place or create value without the presence of institutions, such as property rights, antitrust rules, contract law, enforcement mechanisms, payment systems etc. (see North, 1990; Fligstein, 1996). The process of creating and maintaining these institutions is described as governance. It is the institutionalized social coordination that is necessary to produce and implement collectively binding rules or to provide collective goods (Mayntz, 2004). As market competition depends on institutions to function properly or to take place at all, markets cannot provide governance, i.e. the institutions that constitute and govern them themselves. Governance, by definition, is thus a coordinative, non-competitive process.[1]

Traditionally, governance was provided by government. Faced with an accelerating pace of technical change and economic internationalization, however, governmental actors increasingly find themselves unable to provide the public goods and the coordination that they used to be able to provide. Technical change challenges the governance capacity of governmental actors. They often lack the technical expertise and market information that is necessary to keep pace with—not to mention influencing the direction of—these developments. Given their size and ability to adopt and enforce legally binding decisions, public actors are considered influential. But for their lack of information they are unable to use this influence in a purposeful way. This was also demonstrated by the above-mentioned case of European HDTV standardization, where large amounts of public subsidies were sunk in an outdated technology that was never deployed. And even where public entrepreneurs had this information and expertise, Auriol and Benaim (2000) and David (1990) suggest, they would only have a 'narrow time window' to intervene before markets were locked in and before their technical knowledge became obsolete.

Economic internationalization, in turn, tends to undermine the governance capacity of governmental actors for it requires governance across and beyond jurisdictional barriers. Since there is no world government which could provide governance on a global level, international governance requires national governments to cooperate. Such intergovernmental cooperation, however, is often difficult. Given heterogeneous national interests, it tends to be quite slow and prone to run into bargaining gridlocks. These cooperation problems are exacerbated by the fact that intergovernmental decision-making is usually based on the principle

of consensus, which opens the door for hold outs and other bargaining strategies that further complicate and prolong the consensus-building process.

In this context governance without government, that is governance by and through private, i.e. non-state actors, is gaining more and more attention (Hall & Biersteker, 2002; Peters & Pierre, 1998; Porter, 2005). As governments are still commonly expected to provide the same functions of governance that they used to be able to provide, they often actively encourage the inclusion of non-governmental actors (Braithwaite, 2002, 2005; Eberlein & Grande, 2005, p. 151; Knill & Lehmkuhl, 2002, p. 42).

The advantage of governance through non-governmental actors, such as private industry, appears to be that non-governmental actors' operations tend to be less constrained by jurisdictional boundaries and tend to possess superior market information and technical expertise. Technical standardization through the various international standards setting organization represents a good example for such governance without government. Both formal standards-organizations (such as the ISO, IEC etc.) as well as informal standardization consortia fulfill a wide range of governance functions. At one end of the spectrum, they develop reference and quality standards signal consumers that a specific product or service is "fit for purpose" (ISO, 2005, p. 10), complying with a set of health, safety, or environmental quality levels etc. By resolving information asymmetries regarding the quality of products between buyers and sellers (Akerlof, 1970), technical standards can significantly increase the efficiency of economic transactions. Compatibility and interface standards, in turn, govern the technological and transactional interconnectivity between different goods and services (David & Greenstein, 1990; David & Steinmueller, 1994, p. 218). This paper shall focus on the latter. Whereas private standardization consortia may be less active in the case of quality standards, they play an increasingly central role in the provision of compatibility standards. As both formal organizations and private consortia can, in principle, fulfill similar governance functions, this paper does not distinguish between the two and refers to both as industry-led organizations as opposed to government-led regulatory processes, in which industry is not officially involved.

Governance through industry-led standardization appears to have two advantages over governance through governmental regulation. It is considered to be based on superior information and it is expected to allow for more flexible and timely governance than could be provided by public rule-makers (Abbott & Snidal, 2001, p. 345). The private participants of the standardization organizations always have a market incentive to update their information and to monitor market trends and technological developments continuously (Abbott & Snidal, 2001, p. 365; David, 1985, 1990).

An increasing number of policy-makers around the world—especially, though not exclusively, the European Commission—are building on governance through industry-led standardization (European Commission, 2004a, p. 2; 2004b, 2008). Günter Verheugen, the previous vice-president of the European Union (EU) Commission, for instance, suggested that:

This [industry standardization] is an excellent example of better regulation [...] We thus avoid that legislation becomes overloaded with excessive technical details, we guarantee flexibility because European Standards can be easily adapted and reviewed [...]. Günter Verheugen (CEN, 2005)

In the EU, quasi-regulatory tasks are therefore often delegated to industry standard-setters, namely CEN, CENELC and ETSI. The removal of technical barriers to trade by legislative processes, as set out in the 1969 General Programme on the Removal of Technical Obstacles to Trade, had turned out to be too cumbersome and time-consuming (Egan, 2001, pp. 78-81). The legislative process was often held up by the politicization

of minor technical issues of legislation. For this reason the *New Approach* to technical harmonization and standardization was introduced in 1985 (European Council, 1985). It was meant to circumvent the decision-making problems of the European policy-making process, which Scharpf (1988) named the 'joint-decision trap,' by privatizing market regulation. Under the *New Approach* the task of removing the remaining 'technical' barriers to market integration was delegated to the European standard setting organizations.[2] At the same time new standard setting organizations, such as the DVB Project, have started to emerge, which provide governance through standardization in a wide variety of fields. Given their wide prevalence and the central role that technical standards play in the governance of advanced market economies, governance through standardization could be interpreted as evidence for the superior governance capacity of private compared to public governance.

DIGITAL VIDEO BROADCASTING STANDARDIZATION

This Section examines the success of the DVB Project as a form of private governance. The DVB Project, was and still is the main driver behind digital television standardization. Its creation and institutional design was a direct response to the debacle of European HDTV standardization mentioned above. This is also reflected in the four principles upon which it was build. First, it was decided that the development and standardization of digital television should--from operators, content producers down to TV-set manufacturers--include the entire value chain (DVB Project, 1993, Article2(1)).[3] In its first year, the DVB grew from 83 to 147 firms (de Bruin & Smits, 1999, p. 14). Today, it includes 200 firms (DVB Project, 2013).

Secondly, the DVB Project broke with the tradition of consensual decision-making and introduced the possibility of majority voting to prevent the body's broad membership from delaying joint decision-making and to reduce the risk that individual members would be able to pursue hold out strategies.[4]

Thirdly, the DVB Project was meant to seek independence from governmental influence. "We decided at an early stage that we had to keep it [the DVB] away from any regulatory influence," Peter Kahl, the first president of the DVB project, was argued (Homer, 1994).[5]

Finally, the standardization process was meant to be 'market driven.' For that purpose, the DVB Project was divided into separate Technical and Commercial Modules. While latter were meant to formulate commercial requirements, such as functionality, cost targets and deadlines, the role of the former were deliberately limited to the transposition of these commercial requirements into technical specifications. This 'market driven' approach was meant to ensure that standards were specified in accordance with companies' business demands and that they would only be developed if and when they can be translated to products with "direct commercial value" (DVB Project, 2010). According to an early participant in the DVB Project this approach was the result of the:

[...] the burned fingers (or perhaps burnt-out cheque books) in the age of MAC and HD-MAC. [...] The engineers now realized that, before designing a new broadcast system, it was necessary to decide what the system should do for the public and how much it should cost to be successful on the European domestic market. (Wood, 1995)

This approach is considered to have contributed greatly to the success of DVB standards (Reimers, 1997, p. 28; Dai, 2008, p. 1; DVB Project, 2010). It allowed the DVB Project to respond to the commercial opportunities in a more timely fashion than other standard setting organizations.

Given these four principles, the institutional design of the DVB Project can be considered as rather progressive. A priori it can be expected to be more likely to develop common standards and thus to provide governance without government than less progressive organizations. To assess whether and to what extent this was the case, the following two Sections provide an in-depth analysis of the development of two of the technological cornerstones of digital television: Digital transmission and conditional access.

Digital Transmission Standardization

As a result of its innovative organizational structure, the DVB Project could celebrate its first success soon after its foundation in 1993. By 1994, the DVB Group quickly agreed to a common set of standards for satellite (DVB-S), cable (DVB-C) and, shortly thereafter, terrestrial (DVB-T) transmission via a common compression technology (MPEG-2).[6] Due to cooperation agreements with ETSI and CENELEC, the DVB Group could feed these technical specifications into the latter's standardization processes. ETSI and CENELEC simply rubber-stamped the DVB Project's specifications and transformed them into formal European standards (Grimme, 2001).

As a result of this first success the literature, without exception, has been quite positive about the European digital television standardization project (de Bruin & Smits, 1999; Cave, 1997). Dai (2008) even goes as far as to present the case of digital television standardization—in comparison to European HDTV standardization—as evidence for the superior governance capacity of private industry and as an argument for non-intervention:

The spectacular failure and the unexpected success of DVB have certainly dealt EU policy-makers, including the European Commission, the Coun-

cil of Ministers, and the French Government, a powerful blow. The EU finally accepted in 1995 that the outcome of technological standardization should be determined by market forces, rather than policy makers. (Dai, 2008, p. 61)

Not without *schadenfreude*, Dai (2008, p. 60) argued that, "[i]t is rather ironic that television viewers in France," a country which the author associates with interventionist industrial policies, "today are beginning to experience digital TV from the non-official DVB project, rather than the officially favored HD-MAC technology!" According to Dai this stands in stark contrast to the United Kingdom (UK), which he considers to be a rather non-interventionist country, where digital television is striving.

From an engineering perspective, the development of this technology clearly was a great success. The DVB overcame tremendous technological challenges and pushed the technological frontier into the digital age.[7] This stood in sharp contrast to the above-mentioned European HDTV technology, which, despite large government subsidies, was already outdated before its development was completed. This appears to confirm the expected informational advantage of industry compared to government.

From a governance perspective, however, the DVB's compression and transmission standardization process was not as successful. The problem was that instead of developing a single common standard—or at least multiple interoperable standards—distinctly incompatible standards were adopted for satellite, cable and terrestrial broadcasting.[8] To make things worse, different countries adopted subtly different versions of the three transmission standards. Even different generations of the same technology, such as DVB-C and DVB-C2, were made incompatible. Philip Laven, the DVB Project's current director, later stated that:

There are now more than 1500 digital satellite TV services using DVB standards in Europe [...] Regrettably, to receive all 1500 satellite services, you would need many different digital TV set-top boxes. The reality is that there is a serious problem with inter-operability. (Laven, 2002, p. 3)

From a governance perspective, however, a single common standard or at least multiple interoperable standards would have been preferable for two reasons: First, a single intermodal standard could have significantly accelerated the market take-up of digital television by maximizing economies of scale and scope and creating the basis for a competitive market for set-top boxes, which would have brought down the retail price of digital TV equipment. The lack of a single transmission standard, however, undermined scale economies and is hence considered to have "cost real money".[9] It is held, at least partially, responsible for the relatively slow market penetration of digital television (Brown & Picard, 2004, p. 2; Cawley, 1997, p. 2). The high retail prices of set-top boxes were one of the main reasons why the consumer switch-over to digital television has been slower than expected.

Secondly, a single common standard or intermodal interoperability would have increased competition on the service provision side of the market. Competition across the three modes would have (1.) resolved significant antitrust problems within the individual markets—especially the have brought competition into the naturally monopolistic infrastructure side of the cable market—(2.) brought down the price of television services, and (3.) it could have accelerated the switchover from analog to digital television. Incompatible standards, by contrast, decreased intermodal competition by raising the switching costs for consumers. Modal incompatibility meant that if consumers wanted to switch from one mode to another they had no choice but to purchase new transmission equipment, stacking up towers of set-top boxes in their living rooms (Brown & Picard, 2004, p. 2). Given high initial equipment prices, however, consumers were unlikely to do so and would thus stay with their old provider. This is not to suggest that a maximum level of variety reduction is always necessary. In the case of digital television, however, it clearly was. From the governance perspective, it can thus be argued that DVB transmission standardization was not a success.

Even if it would not have been possible to use the same technology for all three modes the Japanese example demonstrates that it would have been technically feasible to develop an interoperable system that functions across modes and minimizes switching costs for consumers. However, cable, satellite and terrestrial operators deliberately chose to develop incompatible systems for each mode. In the face of technical convergence and market liberalization, the incumbent operators saw incompatible standards as an opportunity to minimize competition between the different modes of broadcasting—i.e. satellite, cable and terrestrial.

The reason why the DVB developed incompatible standards nonetheless was that governance concerns did not play a role in the standardization process. The standard-setters deliberately chose incompatible standards to minimize competition among each other and across modes.[10] The problem hence was not that standard setters were unable to adopt the necessary standards because of decision-making problems. The problem was that they were unwilling to do so. They were more concerned with their current market shares than the opportunity to maximize the size of the future market. The standard-setters cooperation thus appears to have been closer to competition-reducing collusion than market-making governance.

Although the DVB's transmission and compression standardization may have been a great commercial and engineering success, it clearly illustrates the limits of industry-led standardization as a form of governance without government. It shows that even where companies would be able to agree to the required standard—there neither appear to have been technological nor proprietary problems—industry standard-setters are unable to provide the necessary governance. Interestingly, this view was also shared by Philip Laven, the DVB Project's current director:

[I]n the strange world of digital TV, many operators have deliberately chosen standards that are unique to their services. This suggests that self-regulation will not be successful in this area. (Laven, 2002, p. 6, emphasis added)

Although this case study does not directly lend itself to an empirical investigation of this issue, theoretically it is rather straightforward to conceive of ways in which governmental interventions might have lead to superior outcomes. To achieve the optimal level of variety reduction governmental actors might have forced the DVB by law or regulation to adopt a single common standard for all three modes of television transmission. This could have been done in a technologically neutral way, thus avoiding the infamous information problems of public actor interventions. The bigger problem would have been that national laws or regulations can only have a limited success in a market which is as international as the consumer electronics market. An EU level intervention, however, might have sufficed. If manufacturers and broadcasters were forced to apply a multi-modal standard in the European market, they may not have altered their products and services for non-European markets.

Conditional Access Standardization

This Section investigates the governance capacity of industry-led standardization processes at the example of the DVB's attempts to standardize conditional access systems. Conditional access constitutes the technological basis of pay TV and its standardization succeeded the above-described development of transmission standards. While pay TV used to be a small niche market in most European countries, it was expected to play a central role in the governance of the newly created digital television market because of two reasons (see Ypsilanti, & Sarrocco, 2009, p. 196).

First, conditional access was crucial for the commercial viability, sustainability and size of the digital television market. Because advertising revenues were not going to rise proportionally with the larger number of channels that digitalization allowed broadcasters to submit they had to look for new revenue streams (see Lyle, 2008, p. 125). Conditional access systems allowed broadcasters to scramble their television systems and to restrict the consumption of their program to paying customers.[11] This was expected to open the market to a larger number of broadcasters and content providers, not only increasing competition among companies but also increasing the size of the market overall. In order to achieve this, however, it was necessary that all market participants—both incumbents and potential insurgents—gained access to the revenue streams of pay TV. An open conditional access standard was necessary.

In the absence of such a standard, access to the revenue streams of pay TV was going to remain limited to a small number of firms, impairing the overall growth of digital television markets as well as the competition upon them. The problem is rooted in a first-mover advantage resulting from two factors (Nolan, 1997, p. 601). First, companies managing to obtain a critical mass of subscribers before their competitors would be able to exploit economies of scale and reduce retail prices of the set-top boxes containing their conditional access systems thus setting off a bandwagon effect of accumulative sales. Secondly, consumers were discouraged to switch from one pay TV provider to another as long as set-top box prices were non-negligible. Once having purchased one conditional access decoder—which, in the early days, could cost up to €1,000—consumers were unlikely to acquire another one only to access services from another pay TV provider. As a result only one

firm would gain access to the revenue streams of pay TV. To prevent a monopolization of pay TV markets and to cease the technological opportunities provided by digitalization an open standard for conditional access was necessary.

The first mover advantage and the dominant position that can result from it is well illustrated by the emergence of satellite-based pay TV in the UK. Sky TV, which was owned by Rupert Murdoch's News International Corporation, began transmission two years before BSB, its main competitor. With the help of an aggressive penetration pricing strategy—leasing receivers to new subscribers at minimal cost and charging low introductory rates—Sky TV quickly build up an installed base of 1.5 million consumers before BSB entered the market. This initial lead turned out to be irrevocable. Only 7 month after going on air, BSB collapsed and had no choice but to merge with Sky TV—forming BSkyB (British Sky Broadcasting) (Hart, 2004, p. 36). Within one year, BSkyB managed to break even and has held a dominant position in the British satellite broadcasting market since (see Grindle, 2002, pp. 6-7). Many third party providers complained about the terms which BSkyB obliged them to accept to gain access to its conditional access system called Videocrypt. To prevent that this bottle neck would be carried over into the digital era, it was necessary to develop a common non-proprietary standard for digital conditional access that could provide a large number of companies with equal access to a the revenue streams of pay TV.

Secondly, a common standard was also necessary to maintain and promote media pluralism and diversity. In markets characterized by a high degree of market concentration, Hotelling (1929) demonstrated, companies tend to target the same middle ground of consumers by providing a relatively homogeneous range of products (i.e. programs) to maximize sales (i.e. viewing time and thus advertising revenues). This 'Hotelling effect' was recently confirmed by a study of the British Department for Culture, Media, and Sport

(2001, Paragraph 1.5). It suggested that companies with a significant market presence tend to 'super-serve' a median audience of young adults rather than to address the full range of cultural, ethnic and religious niche markets. Only where new companies were able to enter the market and competition intensified would companies employ product differentiation strategies and start to offer a more heterogeneous range of programs catering to niche markets and minority interest (Biggam, 2000). This, however, could only be achieved through a common open standard. In its absence, the opportunity to increase media pluralism and diversity via a diversification of the television market would be sacrificed. It was feared that television programs would "[..] be dominated by the TV culture of quiz shows featuring stripping housewives, squeezing out educational and public interest programmes," as suggested by Arlene McCarthy, Member of the European Parliament (EP, 2001).

To maximize the size and competitiveness of the digital market and to optimize its contribution to media-pluralism and diversity, it was necessary to create a common and open standard. The remainder of this section will examine whether and to what extent the DVB Project was able to develop such a standard.

As a potential solution, Public and free TV operators proposed a system called Multicrypt, which could be described as a form of maximum standardization. Multicrypt was based on the Common Interface, a standardized socket integrated in the set-top boxes that would allow consumers to access any pay TV operator's programs by inserting the given operator's credit-card-sized decoder card into an open and non-proprietary set-top box. Proponents of Multicrypt argued that it would mean lower risk and lower cost for consumers, which would no longer be forced to buy a whole new decoder to watch another pay TV operators' programs. Consumers merely need to acquire the given provider's decoder card. This also reduced their risk of being stranded with a set top box that

has lost the 'standards war' to another set-top box. In the medium to long run, its proponents argued, Multicrypt would lead to deeper levels of market penetration of digital television and increase competition between conditional access services and create a common European market for conditional access decoders and content. Both could be produced at a larger scale and thus be sold at a lower price. Multicrypt had the advantage that no rules or regulations were required to guarantee third party access to digital television markets.

The incumbent pay TV operators, however, opposed the Multicrypt solution. They each sought to use the installed base of consumers acquired in analogue pay TV markets to launch proprietary systems, which would give them a dominant position in the market (Verse, 2008, p. 226). Therefore, they sponsored the Simulcrypt system, which, in turn, could be described as a form of minimum standardization. It was intended to allow third parties to transmit streams of encrypted information simultaneously through the incumbents' proprietary broadcasting system—hence the name 'Simulcrypt' (Levy, 1997, p. 668)—without standardizing conditional access as a whole. While this opened their conditional access systems to third parties, it also meant that the incumbent pay TV broadcasters would have been able to control and dictate the conditions of third party access themselves. Public and free TV broadcasters and manufacturers therefore vehemently opposed the Simulcrypt option, claiming that it gave pay TV operators too much market power.

Given this divergence of interests between the incumbent pay TV broadcasters—BSkyB, Canal+ and Nethold—on the one side; and public service and free TV broadcasters, on the other, the DVB Project soon found itself in a stalemate. "Those who drive the market at the beginning want to protect their market and they want Simulcrypt. Those who don't want to be debarred, favour Multicrypt," the gridlock was summarized by Robin Crossley, of SES Astra (in M. Brown, 1995). At a closer look, this stalemate could be described with the classic hold-out problem. While public service and private broadcasters as well as potential market insurgents depended on the standardization of conditional access to create—and gain access to—the digital pay TV market, incumbent pay TV operators did not depend on such a standard. This allowed them to hold out agreement and force their negotiation partners to make costly concessions.

These concessions were eventually spelled out in the DVB Project's conditional access compromise, which comprised both Simulcrypt and Multicrypt.[12] And in order to appease regulators and competition authorities, the legal departments of BSkyB and Filmnet drafted a voluntary and nonbinding code of conduct on fair reasonable and non-discriminatory conditions (FRAND) for third party access to digital decoders (Levy, 1997, p. 668). The incumbent pay TV operators celebrated the compromise as a good example of successful self-regulation: "This underscored the recognition [...] that commercial actors were well placed to find a solution for a perceived market distortion," it was argued (Eltzroth, 2007).

At a closer look, however, this compromise rather demonstrates the problems of industry-led standardization as a form of private governance. While the conditional access technologies—particularly the common scrambling mechanism—developed by the DVB Project may also have been a great engineering success and while the compromise may have been a great commercial success to some companies, the DVB Project failed to adopt a standard that would have maximize the size and competitiveness of digital television markets and wasted an opportunity to increase media pluralism and diversity.

The first problem of the compromise was that although it formally included Multicrypt, it meant that Simulcrypt—and thus minimum-standardization—would prevail. It allowed the incumbent pay TV operators to use their installed base of consumers to promote their proprietary Simulcrypt and to consolidate their dominant position. While market insurgents were free to use Multicrypt, they had no means of compensating their second-mover disadvantage.[13] The incumbents' proprietary control over Simulcrypt allowed them to fend off market insurgents. Second movers never stood a chance. This was demonstrated, for instance, by the bankruptcies of the British ITV Digital in April 2002 and the Spanish Quiero TV soon after (Iosifidis, Steemers, & Wheeler, 2005, pp. 112-114; Iosifidis, 2007). The companies that were not immediately driven into bankruptcy, such as TPS in France or OnDigital in the UK, could never develop into serious competitors of the incumbent pay TV operators (see Levy, 1999, pp. 65-67; Rediske, 1996). Given their second-mover disadvantage market insurgents were often forced to employ costly penetration pricing strategies and invest in premium content such as football or blockbuster movies to obtain enough consumers to break even. In the UK, for instance, this resulted in ITV Digital's overbidding on Premier League football rights had pushed the consortium into insolvency (Iosifidis et al., 2005, pp. 112-114). In Spain, Quiero TV failed because it could not afford to give their set-top-boxes away for free as its competitors Canal Satellite Digital and Via Digital were able to do. Instead Quiero TV had to sell its decoders for around €400 to €500 (Iosifidis et al., 2005, pp. 112-114; Iosifidis, 2007). The European pay TV markets continue to be dominated by the incumbent operators. This was a direct consequence of the failure to adopt a common and open conditional access standard.

Given the vagueness and lack of a commonly accepted definition of FRAND, the pay TV operators obligation to grant access under such conditions also turned out to be insufficient to guarantee third party access and thus to create a more competitive market. In other industries this often led to lengthy and costly litigations, acting as an additional deterrent to market entry. The fact that these litigations almost always eventually lead to an agreement does not mean that FRAND has made much of a contribution to the resolution of the underlying hold-out problems mentioned above. In a hold-out situation the party holding out will always settle, albeit not without negotiation significant concessions from their negotiation partners. That is the objective of any hold out strategy. Furthermore, the fact that there have not been such litigations in the case of conditional access should not be interpreted as evidence that FRAND was working either. This rather demonstrates the significance of the lack of a common standard as an entry deterrent. Pay TV markets continue to be dominated by a limited number of incumbent operators.

Some commentators, such as EU Commissioner Liikanen, however, argued that the conditional access compromise "[...] led to the creation of strong vertical pay TV markets" (Liikanen, 2001). In contrast to horizontal markets, which would be based on open and universal standards, vertical markets are based on competing, proprietary standards, in which service providers control every aspect of the value chain, such as set-top boxes, conditional access systems, and interactivity (A. W. Brown, 2005). In many industries vertical markets might suffice. In the specific case of television and broadcasting, however, vertical markets were clearly suboptimal. In order to exploit the Hotelling effect and thus to increase media pluralism and diversity, horizontal markets are necessary. That is because vertical markets, by definition, can only sustain a much smaller number of firms than would be necessary to make use of the 'Hotelling effect.' Given the high sunk costs involved in entering the market and building up an installed base of consumers, the market size only allows a limited number of firms to break even.

As a result, Europe remained stuck with a limited number of broadcasters that 'super-served' a median audience with a lowest common denominator of content. This is not to say the structure and concentration of digital television markets is more

worrying than the structure of the old analogue television markets. However, a good opportunity was sacrificed to create a more competitive and dynamic digital television market that might have increase media pluralism.[14]

Just as the DVB Project's failure to agree to a single multi-modal transmission standard the episode of conditional access standardization thus, too, illustrates the limits of governance without government in the form of private industry standardization. It shows that where companies have heterogeneous technological or proprietary preferences or where their strategic interests are at stake, they are unlikely to agree to a single common standard. Industry may reach a compromise involving multiple and incompatible standards, as in the case of the DVB Project's conditional access compromise. But where variety reduction is necessary to achieve optimal outcomes—as in the case of transmission and conditional access standardization—such a compromise is insufficient.

Different to the case of transmission standardization, however, the problem was not that standard-setters were unwilling to adopt a common standard. In the case of conditional access standardization they were unable to find a consensus. Despite the fact that the DVB Project had adopted the principle of majority voting, the Pay TV providers were able to hold-out agreement. This suggests that industry standard-setters are faced with the same decision-making problems as governmental actors meeting in intergovernmental organizations such as the EU or the United Nations. To the public policy literature, which often conflate industry into a unitary actor which has one interest only and that is to thwart governmental interferences with their business, this is a relatively new finding. This chapter, however, demonstrates that non-governmental actors' preferences may be just as heterogeneous as governmental actors' preferences. For this reason, the delegation of governance functions to non-governmental actors should not be expected to solve the decision-making problems common to intergovernmental bargaining arrangements. Intergovernmental decision-making problems merely seem to be replaced by private decision-making problems.

CONCLUSION

Although the DVB Project has been a great engineering and commercial success, this chapter showed that the industry-led DVB project could not address many of the governance issues involved in the standardization of television systems. Governance through industry-led standardization, as in the case of DVB, may be based on better market information and technological expertise than governance through governmental regulation. This case study demonstrated, however, that industry may not necessarily be willing to engage in a level of standardization that is necessary to address a range of governance issues involved in television standardization, such as the creation of fair competition or media pluralism and diversity. The short term interests of the standard-setters involved in the DVB Project prevented them from adopting a multi-modal standard which could have maximized the size of the market in the long run. Instead, they focused on weakening their competitors and strengthening their own market position.

Secondly, the governance capacity of industry standard-setters is limited, for they face the same decision-making problems that often tend to constrain intergovernmental decision-making. In the case of conditional access standardization the participants of the DVB Project failed to agree to a single common standard. Instead the status quo prevailed and multiple technologies were introduced. This turned out to have had devastating consequences for the market introduction of digital television as well as media pluralism and diversity.

Because most standardization organizations merely seek to solve specific engineering or business problems and do not see themselves as providers of governance, it may be unreasonable to measure their success by their contribution to governance. However, the agreements that standards setters adopt, or fail to adopt, as so many economic transactions, can create significant externalities. And if standards setters fail to internalize these externalities themselves, different ways need to be found to do so. Ways may need to be found for governmental actors to protect the public interest and to intervene where industry standardization fails, however difficult this may be. This case study demonstrated that important public interests, such as media pluralism and diversity, cannot and should not be left to industry standard-setters alone.

ACKNOWLEDGMENT

For their comments and suggestions the author is indebted to four anonymous reviewers as well as the organizers and participants of the 16th Annual conference of the European Academy for Standardization (EURAS) in Kaunas, where a first draft of this chapter was presented. Furthermore, the author would like to express his gratitude to 13 interviewees, which granted invaluable insights into the world of DVB standardization.

REFERENCES

Abbott, K., & Snidal, D. (2001). International 'standards' and international governance. *Journal of European Public Policy*, 8(3), 345–370. doi:10.1080/13501760110056013

Akerlof, G. (1970). The Market for 'Lemons': Quality Uncertainty and the Market Mechanism. *The Quarterly Journal of Economics*, 84(3), 488–500. doi:10.2307/1879431

Auriol, E., & Benaim, M. (2000). Standardization in decentralized economies. *The American Economic Review*, *90*(3), 550–570. doi:10.1257/aer.90.3.550

Biggam, R. (2000). Public service broadcasting: The view from the commercial sector. *Intermedia*, *28*(5), 21–23.

Braithwaite, J. (2000). The New Regulatory State and the Transofrmation of Criminology. *The British Journal of Criminology*, *40*(2), 222–238. doi:10.1093/bjc/40.2.222

Braithwaite, J. (2005). Neo-liberalism or regulated capitalism. *RegNet Occasional Paper, 5*.

Brown, A., & Picard, R. (2004). The long, hard road to digital television in europe. In *Proceedings of 6th World Media Economics Conference*, (pp. 12–15). Retrieved Apr. 14, 2010, from http://www.cem.ulaval.ca/pdf/brown_picard.pdf

Brown, A. W. (2005, Jan.). Interoperability, standards and sustainable receiver markets in the European Union. *EBU Technical Review*, 1–16.

Brown, M. (1995, Apr. 11). Who will rule the airwaves?; Those outside the BSkyB camp fear Murdoch is poised to 'do it again'. *The Independent* (London), p. 22.

Cave, M. (1997). Regulating digital television in a convergent world. *Telecommunications Policy*, *21*(7), 575–596. doi:10.1016/S0308-5961(97)00031-1

Cawley, R. A. (1997). European aspects of the regulation of pay television. *Telecommunications Policy*, *21*(7), 677–691. doi:10.1016/S0308-5961(97)00036-0

Cawson, A. (1995). High-Definition Television in Europe. *The Political Quarterly*, *66*(2), 157–173. doi:10.1111/j.1467-923X.1995.tb00460.x

CEN. (2005). *Standards are a concrete contribution for the relaunch of the Lisbon strategy for growth and employment in the European Union*. Retrieved from http://www. cen.eu/CENORM/news/pressreleases/interviewverheugen.asp

Dai, X. (2008). Guiding the Digital Revolution: Is European Technology Policy Misguided? In J. Hayward (Ed.), *Leaderless Europe* (pp. 47–65). Oxford, UK: Oxford University Press. doi:10.1093/acprof:oso/9780199535026.003.0004

David, P. A. (1985). Clio and the Economics of QWERTY. *American Economic Review*, *75*(2), 332–336.

David, P. A. (1990). Narrow windows, blind giants and angry orphans: the dynamics of systems rivalries and the dilemmas of technology policy. In F. Arcangeli (Ed.), *Innovation diffusion* (Vol. 3). New York: Oxford University Press.

David, P. A., & Greenstein, S. (1990). The economics of compatibility standards: An introduction to recent research. *Economics of Innovation and New Technology*, *1*(1-2), 3–41. doi:10.1080/10438599000000002

David, P. A., & Steinmueller, W. E. (1994). Economics of compatibility standards and competition in telecommunication networks. *Information Economics and Policy*, *6*(3-4), 217–241. doi:10.1016/0167-6245(94)90003-5

de Bruin, R., & Smits, J. (1999). *Digital Video Broadcasting: Technology, Standards, and Regulations*. Boston, London: Artech House.

Department for Culture, Media, and Sport. (2001). *Consultation on media ownership rules*. Retrieved Sept. 6, 2010, from www.culture.gov.uk/PDF/media_ownership_2001. pdf

DVB Project. (1993, Sept. 10). *Memorandum of understanding*. Retrieved May 25, 2010 http://www.immagic.com/eLibrary/ARCHIVES/GENERAL/DVB_CH/D001213M.pdf

DVB Project. (1994a, Sept. 27). *DVB Agrees conditional access Package. Press Release.* Retrieved May 25, 2010, from http://www.DVB.org/documents/press releases/pr005_DVB%20agrees%20conditional%20access%20package.940927. pdf

DVB Project. (1994b). *DVB GA 2 (94) 9 rev. 1, Appendix 1: Code of Conduct -Access to Digital Decoders*. Author.

DVB Project. (2010). *History of the DVB Project.* Retrieved May 25, 2010, from http: //www.DVB. org/about_DVB/history/

DVB Project. (2013, May.). *DVB Fact Sheet.* Retrieved January 25, 2013, from http://www.dvb.org/resources/public/factsheets/DVB-Project_Factsheet.pdf

Eberlein, B., & Grande, E. (2005). Reconstituting Politcal Authority in Europe: Transnational Regulatory Networks and the Informalization of Governance in the European Union. In E. Grande, & L. Pauly (Eds.), *Complex sovereignty: reconstructing political authority in the twenty-first century* (pp. 146–167). Toronto, Canada: University of Toronto Press.

Egan, M. (2001). *Constructing a European market: standards, regulation, and governance*. Oxford, UK: OUP. doi:10.1093/0199244057.001.0001

Eltzroth, C. (2007, Dec. 31). *IPR Policy of the DVB Project: Commentary on Article 14 MoU DVB*. Retrieved July 9, 2010, from http://www.DVB.org/membership/ipr_policy/IPR_commentary0712.pdf

Ely, S. (1995, Winter). MPEG video coding. A simple introduction. *EBU Technical Review*, 12–23. Retrieved July 6, 2010, from http://www.ebu.ch/en/technical/trev/trev_frameset-index.html

European Commission. (1993, Nov. 17). *Digital Video Broadcasting: A Framework for Community Policy*. COM(93) 557 final. Retrieved Aug. 26, 2010, from aei.pitt.edu/3116/

European Commission. (2004a). *The role of European standardisation in the framework of European policies and legislation*. Communication from the Commission to the European Parliament and the Council. Retrieved from http://ec.europa.eu/enterprise/standards_policy/role_of_standardisation/doc/context_en.pdf

European Commission. (2004b). *Commission staff working document: The challenges for European standardisation*. Retrieved from http://ec.europa.eu/enterprise/standards_policy/role_of_standardisation/doc/staff_working_document_en.pdf

European Commission. (2008). Communication from the Commission to the Council, the European Parliament and the European Economic and Social Committee. *Towards an increased contribution from standardisation to innovation in Europe*. COM(2008) 133 final. Retrieved from http://ec.europa.eu/enterprise/standards_policy/standardisation_innovation/doc/com_2008_133_en.pdf

European Council. (1985). *Council Resolution on a new approach to technical harmonisation and standards*. Retrieved Sept. 1, 2013, from http://eur-lex.europa.eu/legal-content/EN/TXT/PDF/?uri=CELEX:31985Y0604(01)&from=EN

European Parliament (EP). (2001, Dec. 10). *Debate on electronic communications networks and services*. Retrieved Sept. 1, 2010, from http://www.europarl.europa.eu/sides/getDoc.do?type=CRE&reference=20011210&secondRef=ITEM-005&format=XML&language=EN

Fligstein, N. (1996). Markets as politics: A political-cultural approach to market institutions. *American Sociological Review*, *61*(4), 656–673. doi:10.2307/2096398

Galperin, H. (2002). Can the US transition to digital TV be fixed? Some lessons from two European Union cases. *Telecommunications Policy, 26*(1-2), 3–15. doi:10.1016/S0308-5961(01)00050-7

Grimme, K. (2001). *Digital television standardization and strategies.* Boston: Artech House Publishers.

Grindle, P. (2002). *Standards, Strategy, and Policy. Cases and Stories.* Oxford, UK: Oxford University Press.

Hall, R., & Biersteker, T. (Eds.). (2002). *The emergence of private authority in global governance.* Cambridge, UK: Cambridge Univiversity Press. doi:10.1017/CBO9780511491238

Hart, J. A. (2004). *Technology, Television, and Competition - The Politics of digital TV.* Cambridge, UK: Cambridge University Press. doi:10.1017/CBO9780511490941

Homer, S. (1994, May 16). Science: The day of digital TV is dawning; Steve Homer charts the progress of technology that is going to give us clearer television pictures. *The Independent* (London), 21.

Hotelling, H. (1929). Stability in competition. *The Economic Journal, 39*(153), 41–57. doi:10.2307/2224214

Iosifidis, P. (2007). Digital TV, digital switchover and public service broadcasting in Europe. *Javnost-The Public, 14*(1), 5.

Iosifidis, P., Steemers, J., & Wheeler, M. (2005). *European television industries.* London: British Film Institute.

ISO. (2005). *FAQ.* Retrieved from http://www.iso.org/iso/en/faqs/faq-standards.html

Knill, C., & Lehmkuhl, D. (2002). Private actors and the state: Internationalization and changing patterns of governance. *Governance: An International Journal of Policy, Administration and Institutions, 15*(1), 41–63. doi:10.1111/1468-0491.00179

Laven, P. (2002). Workshop OBS/IViR/EMR 2002: Co-regulation of the Media in Europe. In Proceedings of Co-regulation of the Media in Europe: Co-regulation of the Media in Europe. Florence: European University Institute.

Levy, D. A. L. (1997). The regulation of digital conditional access systems. A case study in European policy making. *Telecommunications Policy, 21*(7), 661–676. doi:10.1016/S0308-5961(97)00035-9

Levy, D. A. L. (1999). *Europe's Digital Revolution: Broadcasting regulation, the EU and the nation State.* London: Routledge. doi:10.4324/9780203278284

Liikanen, E. (2001, Mar. 27). *EBU Conference, Public service broadcasting in eEurope.* Brussels: RAPID 01/143.

Lyle, D. (2008). The Digital Revolution -What Does it Mean for Advertising? In G. Terzis (Ed.), *European Media Governance: The Brussels Dimension* (pp. 121–128). Bristol: Intellect Ltd.

Mayntz, R. (2004). Governance im modernen Staat. In A. Benz (Ed.), *Governance – Regieren in Komplexen Regelsystemen: Eine Einführung* (pp. 65–76). Wiesbaden: Verlag für Sozialwissenschaften. doi:10.1007/978-3-531-90171-8_4

Nolan, D. (1997). Bottlenecks in pay television: Impact on market development in Europe. *Telecommunications Policy, 21*(7), 597–610. doi:10.1016/S0308-5961(97)00037-2

North, D. C. (1990). *Institutions, institutional change and economic performance. Political economy of institutions and decisions.* Cambridge: Cambridge University Press. doi:10.1017/CBO9780511808678

Peters, B., & Pierre, J. (1998). Governance without government? Rethinking public administration. *Journal of Public Administration: Research and Theory, 8*(2), 223–243. doi:10.1093/oxfordjournals.jpart.a024379

Peterson, J., & Sharp, M. (1998). Technology Policy in the European Union. In N. Nugent, W. E. Paterson, & V. Wright (Eds.), *The European Union Series.* London: Macmillan Press.

Porter, T. (2005). The Private Production of Public Goods: Private and Public Norms in Global Governance. In E. Grande, & L. Pauly (Eds.), *Complex sovereignty: reconstituting political authority in the twenty-first century* (pp. 217–237). Toronto, Canada: University of Toronto Press.

Rediske, M. (1996, May 11). Die Telekom als Kontrolleur. *TAZ,* 7.

Reimers, U. (1997, February). DVB-T: the COFDM-based system for terrestrial television. *Electronics & Communication Engineering Journal,* 28.

Reimers, U. (2006, January). DVB: The Family of International Standards for Digital Video Broadcasting. *Proceedings of the IEEE, 94*(1), 173–182. doi:10.1109/JPROC.2005.861004

Scharpf, F. W. (1988). The Joint-Decision Trap. Lessons From German Federalism an European Integration. *Public Administration, 66*(3), 239–278. doi:10.1111/j.1467-9299.1988.tb00694.x

Verse, A. (2008). Conditional access für das Digitale Fernsehen. In U. Reimers (Ed.), DVB-Digital Fernsehtechnik: Datenkompression und Übertragung (3rd ed., pp. 221–228). New York: Springer-Verlag.

Watson, A. B. (2005, January). Interoperability standards and sustainable receiver markets in the European Union. *EBU Technical Review,* 1-16. Retrieved May 3, 2014, from https://tech.ebu.ch/docs/techreview/trev_301-eu.pdf

Wood, D. (1995, Winter). Satellites, science and success: The DVB story. *EBU Technical Review,* 4–11. Retrieved May 25, 2010, from http://www.ebu.ch/en/technical/ trev/trev_266-wood.pdf

World at War. (1990, August 4). *The Economist, UK Edition,* 65.

Ypsilanti, D., & Sarrocco, C. (2009). *OECD Communications Outlook 2009.* Retrieved May 3, 2014, from http://www.oecd.org/sti/broadband/oecdcommunicationsoutlook2009.htm

KEY TERMS AND DEFINITIONS

Conditional Access: Technological basis of pay TV that limits access to programs to fees paying users.

Digital Television: Digital technology succeeding analogue television.

Governance: Social coordination that is necessary to overcome coordination problems, to implement collectively binding rules or to provide collective goods. Not limited to government. Also non-governmental actors can provide governance functions.

Hotelling Effect: An effect of monopolistic competition where companies tend to target the same middle ground of consumers by providing a relatively homogeneous range of products to maximize sales.

Interoperability: Ability to operate different systems or technologies together.

Public Policy: Government policy in the pursuit of the public good.

Regulation: Hierarchical intervention in market competition. Not limited to government. Also non-governmental actors can regulate markets.

Standardization: The process whereby technical standards are developed.

ENDNOTES

[1] Therefore, this chapter is not concerned with competitive standardization processes leading to the installation of *de facto* standards.

[2] These included CEN (European Committee for Standardization), CENELEC (European Committee for Electrotechnical Standardization) and ETSI (European Telecommunications Standards Institute).

[3] It was also decided that participation should not be limited to European firms and actively sought the participation of Japanese and Korean players (Interview 3 with a member of the DVB Group, 2010).

[4] According to the DVB's memorandum of understanding (MoU), "[a]ll reasonable efforts shall be taken to ensure decisions of the Board are taken on the basis of consensus. However, when a consensus on an issue cannot be achieved ...a call for an indicative vote may be made...If the indicative vote indicates a favorable outcome but a consensus is nonetheless not achieved, a call for a deciding vote may be made [...]" (DVB Project, 1993, Article 6(4)).

[5] The Commission recognized this arguing that "the group is an independent body and

draws its strength from this. It will not be appropriate therefore that the Commission [...] becomes a member of the group" (European Commission (EC), 1993, p. 24).

[6] MPEG-2 was just undergoing standardization in the International Standardization Organization (ISO) and International Electrotechnical Commission (IEC) (Ely, 1995, p. 12).

[7] By reducing bandwidth requirements, for instance, digital compression technology allowed satellite broadcasters to deliver between 6–12 digital channels at the cost of one analogue channel (Wood, 1995).

[8] Each is based on different technologies, namely QPSK modulation, QAM and Coded OFDM respectively (Reimers, 2006, pp. 175-176).

[9] Interview 11 with a representative of the broadcasting industry (2010).

[10] The incumbent telecoms operators, for instance, that controlled cable television in most European countries were keen to minimize competition from satellite television, which was rapidly gaining more and more market shares during the early 1990s. Similarly, terrestrial television providers—public and private—sought to shield themselves from the growing competition from both cable and satellite pay TV operators.

[11] The first conditional access system, Videocrypt, was developed by Rupert Murdoch's Sky TV in 1990. Conditional access allowed Murdoch to make his investments in alleged 'premium content'—such as Premier League football and Hollywood blockbusters—profitable (Levy, 1997, p. 668).

[12] The compromise also included the DVB Project's Common Scrambling Mechanism and the recognition of (DVB Project, 1994a, 1994b).

[13] The incumbent Pay TV providers had no incentive to include Common Interfaces in their set-top boxes. And although they

were not allowed to prevent manufacturers from including them they had no incentive to do so because they would not be paid for it. This meant the failure of Multicrypt. If third parties wanted to enter the pay TV market, they had to negotiate access to the proprietary and unstandardized Simulcrypt systems of the incumbent providers.

14   Moreover, it is interesting to note that in many European countries, such as Germany, pay TV never seems to have gained a permanent foothold. The lack of common standards seems to have undermined the growth of the pay TV market overall. More content diversity and the availability of larger variety of niche programming might have attracted more consumers.

Chapter 5
The Evolution and Specialization of IETF Standards

Mehmet Gencer
Istanbul Bilgi University, Turkey

ABSTRACT

The Internet Engineering Task Force (IETF) specification documents corpus spans three decades of Internet standards production. This chapter summarizes the results of an exploratory study on this corpus for understanding how this system of standards and its production have evolved in time. This study takes an alternative perspective, which considers a system like IETF as an organization itself, rather than a constellation of extra-organizational activities. Thus, how it works and evolves are examined with respect to its endogenous dynamics rather than by taking it as a system, which responds to requirements coming from the external environment. The author conducts a longitudinal examination of several features of these documents, their authorship, their dependency and collaboration network structure, and topics. They present a review of how the standards corpus evolves into specialized subsystems and a commentary of findings towards monitoring and managing such standardization processes.

1. INTRODUCTION

Information and Communication Technology (ICT) industry is strongly dependent on standards and this dependency is increasing. Despite the wider debate on whether standardization is an obstacle to, or catalyst of, innovation, most actors in the Software and Internet technology industry seem to embrace standardization, and, in particular, open standards (Capek et al., 2005). Increasing numbers of industry consortia in the ICT industry are being formed in order to deliver the standards needed, and play a major role in

the standardization process (Blind et al., 2010). While dominant firms' attempts to impose their own technologies occasionally create conflicts in the standardization process, there is a general tendency in the ICT industry to embrace collaborative processes of standards creation in the public domain (Garcia, 1992; Bonaccorsi et al., 2006; Simcoe, 2006).

Driven by either industry consortia or formal bodies, participation in the standardization process seems to be becoming more widespread in the ICT and other similar industries. This is particularly true for Internet technologies, where mobility of

DOI: 10.4018/978-1-4666-6332-9.ch005

digital information over the globe across a variety of hardware and software platforms demands a high level of compatibility and durable standards. Certain levels of this technology stack favor formal or semi-formal standardization bodies like the Internet Engineering Task Force (IETF), Institute of Electrical and Electronics Engineers (IEEE), or ISO. Despite extensive collaboration within these bodies, or perhaps because of it, the creation of standards is often delayed or even fails completely (Besen & Farrell, 1991); both outcomes are costly for the industries that rely on these standards.

Recently research on standardization is concerned with a variety of issues including motivations for standardization, its impact on, and diffusion into industry, legal issues, and business strategies related to standardization. On the other hand, empirical studies concerning how standards are produced are rather rare. An understanding of how production takes place in standardization bodies, how systems of standards are organized, and how all these change over time, can contribute to our understanding of failures and delays in standardization.

This revised report (Gencer, 2012) is an attempt to contribute in this direction. We present results of an exploratory empirical study building upon our previous work (Gençer et al., 2006) concerning Internet standards published by the IETF and the collaborative processes involved in their production. We follow these processes through several decades of IETF's existence to explore how its features and internal dynamics effect development of a systems of standards. In addition to conventional exploratory statistics, we borrow concepts, methods, and tools from social network analysis to examine production related features and referential relations of standards in relation with the ways in which a system of standards change over time and assumes a structure consisting of subsystems specialized on relatively independent areas. Our study (1) highlights long term trends in the volume, composition, and collaborative features of IETF output, (2) examines longitudinal changes and compartmentalization in the interdependency structures of IETF driven standards using social network analysis methods, (3) analyses topics of structural specialization, and (4) explores and discusses changes in the subject focus of the standardization community and consequences of certain structural changes for the future of standardization work.

The next section summarizes the background literature and describes the research methodology adopted in the study. Then we present the IETF case and the data set used in this research, along with the analysis methods employed. In the following sections we first present findings regarding changes in the features of standards and the extent of collaboration in their production. Then we summarize findings about changes in interdependency structures through the decades, and explore how the system of standards evolves into relatively independent subsystems specialized on particular problematics. Finally we discuss consequences of the findings for the standardization process, followed by a summary of our conclusions.

2. BACKGROUND AND METHODOLOGY

Existing research on standardization tends to focus on subjects such as the way in which standards diffuse into industries and affect innovation and their relation to the competitive strategy and performance of firms (Choi et al., 2011). While there are several studies which concern systems of standards as a whole and the processes within them (e.g. Egyedi 2003), the majority of research take the firm/organization level as the unit of analysis. Similarly, a good portion of MIS research concerns standards to some degree, but its focus is on the business organization or intra-organization level, and the role attributed to standards is not explicit or clear (West, 2003). At the opposite end, research on technological systems (Allen & Sriram, 2000) focuses on the relation between standards and whole societies or industries. As a consequence our understanding of how the systems of related standards are produced at the intersection of organizations, and how such systems change over time, is limited, fragmented, and assumes that a system of standards is shaped by external environment which imposes requirements on it, thus ignoring its internal dynamics entirely.

Among the few exceptions is a study by Nickerson and Muehlen (2006) which uses institutional theory to study evolution of the bodies that form Internet standards. They note that "economic self-interest alone cannot explain all aspects of the Internet standard-making process... An approach that describes an ecology (a set of relations between different standards institutions, ideas, and participants) provides needed explanations"(Nickerson & Muehlen, 2006, pp17). Using relational examination, Gamber et al. (2008) analyze the referential relations between clusters of standards in an industry, and identify spillover effects in standards clusters similar to the case of patents. Although yet limited in terms of scope and practical implications, these lines of research indicate the value of relational analysis for understanding internal dynamics of systems of standards, separate from the market dynamics surrounding these systems.

Concepts and methods developed in the field of social networks research provide a powerful basis for such relational analysis. Empirical methods developed in this field are based on the mathematical concept of graph which is used to represent relations between people in a variety of social phenomena from relations between school children, to corporate board interlocks (Scott, 2000). A rich variety of graph based metrics have been proposed to assess features of individuals, groups, or whole networks in relation to knowledge processes, power, and trust in social systems (see Wasserman & Faust 1994 for a review). One finds numerous different social network metrics for assessing different aspects of same structural feature (Scott, 2000), such as the 'information centrality'

which considers collaborative relations, versus 'structural hole' which considers competition and opportunity. Often these structural measures are subjected to different frames of interpretation depending on the social phenomena of interest.

With the recent growth in the popularity of the term "social networks" in reference to Internet based virtual communities, the field has experienced a boom in the availability of network visualization and analysis tools. In addition, these new fields of application have stimulated research interest in study of social groups and cliques. Beyond the well known concept of 'small worlds' (Watts, 1999) which refers to the highly clustered nature of relations in social and natural phenomena, social networks researchers have started to further develop techniques and concepts to understand clustering and its dynamics in social systems.

2.1. Social Networks Analysis Methods

Generality of structural assessment methods and tools, and the rich variety of frames of interpretation makes social networks analysis a useful resource for understanding the endogenous dynamics of systems of standards and the processes within these systems. Network structural metrics, together with a repertoire of their interpretations in various applications provide a suitable tool set for investigation of systems of artifacts such as groups of standards. Parts of the empirical study presented here borrow centrality measures and visualization tools from social network analysis to explore essentially non-social referential relations within a corpus of Internet standards. While social network analysis is rather weak in terms of longitudinal analysis methods, we use the relevant metrics and visualizations to compare non-overlapping time frames in order to understand how the IETF corpus evolves over the several decades of its history.

Although this is mainly an empirical study of the referential relations between standards, we have applied certain network metrics to co-authorship relations as well, in order to assess possible similarities between the relational structure of artifacts (standards) and of their producers (standards authors).

An essential network metric used in this study is *in-degree centrality*, which is simply a count of references made to a standard from other standards documents. This is a direct measure of 'local' importance of a standard within the system. We also refer to measures such as *betweenness centrality* (Wasserman & Faust, 1994) which assesses the 'global' role of an element in integrating the system.

Measures such as in-degree or betweenness centrality are used to assess the features of individual elements in a system of relations. However, one is often interested in the emergent sub-systems within the larger system. Such sub-systems are groups of elements which are relatively highly interconnected with each other. If the system at hand represents friendship relations, for example, a group of friends can be identified by looking at the fact that they come together more often with people within the group, in comparison with people outside the group. Since such sub-systems/communities are emergent features of a system, several methods have been proposed for their identification. Some of these methods allow one to assess 'how much' a system is compartmentalized into sub-systems, by considering the number of sub-systems and how isolated these systems are. For this purpose we have used commonly implemented metrics of *clustering coefficient* (Watts & Strogatz, 1998) and *modularity* (Blondel et al., 2008) as a measure of how much a system is compartmentalized, specifically to measure how the structure of IETF standards becomes specialized as the system grows over time.

2.2. Topic Analysis Methods

A document corpus such as IETF RFCs contain a great deal of information in document contents in addition to relational information. Topic analysis is a content analysis method which is applied to a document corpus to quantitatively discover the key concepts around which a document corpus is organized.

Topic analysis is essentially a clustering method in which one tries to cluster documents with respect to their feature measures. In its common form the feature set consists of term/word occurrence counts for each document. Since the number of features is very high the problem does not lend itself easily to more conventional clustering methods. Nonetheless, fueled with the emergent needs of Internet era for classifying large amounts of text documents for search and browsing, research has produced several topic clustering methods in recent years (Aggarwal & Zhai, 2012). Majority of these methods start off with a document-term matrix of features, then apply probabilistic (Blei, 2012), matrix based (Seung & Lee, 2001), or dimension reduction based (Hofmann, 1999) methods for clustering. A side product of clustering is measures that indicate which words best represent a topic.

In this study we have chosen the non-negative matrix factorization (NMF) method (Seung & Lee, 2001; Aggarwal & Zhai, 2012) for topic analysis, due to its computational efficiency (since the IETF data set is relatively large) and its competitive performance in terms of clustering quality (Aggarwal & Zhai, 2012). If we denote the $n \times d$ document-term matrix for a corpus of n documents by A, NMF tries to minimize

$$\left\| A^T - UV^T \right\|$$

Here U is an $n \times k$ matrix, where k is the number of clusters of our choosing. Therefore the method tries to approximate the feature matrix with document-cluster associations in U, and cluster-word associations in V. At the end of the process the V matrix indicates how much each word in the corpus vocabulary represents each cluster. One can use top randking words for each cluster to examine a topic. As with most clustering methods there is no best way to determine the number of topics. In this study we have tried a range of values for k, and examined an established measure for clustering quality (Hoyer, 2004) to decide on this value.

3. THE IETF STANDARDS

Internet standards date back to the beginning of the conception and engineering of the Internet within ARPA (Advanced Research Projects Agency) in 1969. As Internet technology emerged from its defense project cocoon, IETF was established in 1986 as a civil organization, which remains intimately connected to Internet and one of the important platforms that drives the processes for production of Internet standards (Alvestrand, 2004). Most, if not all, standards produced before 1986 were later cataloged by IETF.

IETF organizes three open meetings in a year. As Alvestrand notes in his insider review of IETF processes, decision making is not based on voting, but on "rough consensus and running code" (2004, p1372). The formal output of IETF processes is published as part of the "Request for Comments" (RFC) document series, which contains "each distinct version of an Internet standards-related specification" (Bradner, 1996, p5).

Although all RFCs are standards related specifications, only some are Internet standards. Among other types of RFCs is, for example, those called BCP (Best Current Practice) which "standardize the results of community deliberations about statements of principle or conclusions about what is the best way to perform some operations or IETF process function" (Bradner, 1996, p6). Only some RFCs contain specifications which are intended to become standards (so called standards track). Other than these, IETF publishes RFCs which are categorized by labels such as 'experimental' or 'informational', whose circulation is seen beneficial to the Internet standards community. Table 1 presents a list of standards and non-standards track RFC types, along with their common abbreviations. The order of these listings indicates an increasing 'level' of RFC types. For example a specification enters the standards track as a proposed standard, and over time, and depending on community feedback, may escalate to draft standard, then to standard level.

IETF has established rules and procedures for the format and content of different types of documents, how they circulate and progress in their relevant tracks, etc. Not all standards-track specifications progress towards becoming a standard and their status depends on community feedback from their application. Since its establishment, IETF has maintained good support from, and representation of, the industry. The authorship of RFC documents demonstrates this support, as most authors are company representatives, although many academics are also involved in the process.

Table 1. Types of RFC documents published by IETF

STANDARDS TRACK (In Order of Maturity)
PS: Proposed Standard
DS: Draft Standard
S: Standard
NON-STANDARDS TRACK
BCP: Best Current Practice
E: Experimental
I: Informational
H: Historic

The number of RFCs published by IETF each year indicates a growing trend as shown in Figure 1. Alvestrand's (2004) report covering numbers of participation to meetings up to 2003 indicates a boom which subsided in the year 2000. However, there seems to have been a new wave of activity in recent years. Figure 1 exhibits an ongoing increasing trend in IETF's RFC publication counts, overlaid with peaks, as shown.

4. DATA-SET AND ANALYSIS METHODS

IETF makes available both meta-data and complete texts for each of its RFC documents, some of which date prior to IETF's establishment in 1986. We have used custom software to retrieve both meta-data and texts to produce the necessary data sets. Among the meta-data about each

Figure 1. Number of RFCs published by IETF each year, with peaks of activity marked

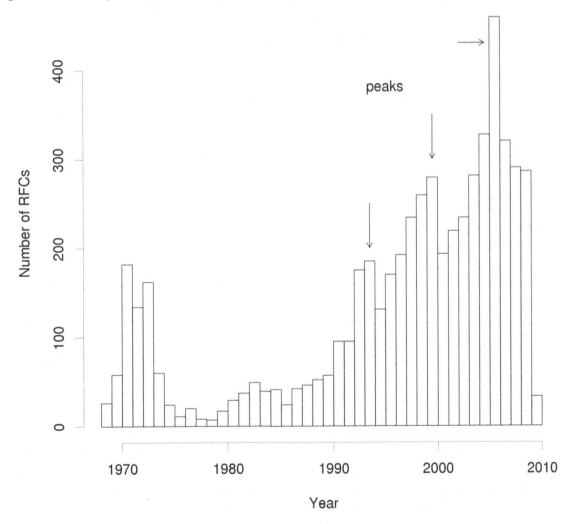

RFC are the year of publication, list of authors, and RFC type. In cases where specification in an RFC obsoletes an existing one, this information is also included in its meta-data, thus providing information about both the life-times of and relations between RFCs. Although some of these meta-data were not collected in earlier RFCs and were retrospectively attached by IETF, the meta-data is generally reliable. We have further analyzed RFC texts with custom software to extract referential relations between documents. The data used for this study included 5781 RFC documents.

These pieces of information are used to generate the following set of data for each RFC in the IETF corpus:

1. *Year* of publication.
2. List of document authors, whose length we denote as *number of authors*.
3. Current *type* of document, where possible types are listed in Table 1.
4. Whether the RFC is replaced by publication of another one, and if so the identification of replacement. For such RFCs we have also added the *lifetime* information of RFC by checking the difference between the year of publication of the RFC and the one which replaces it. The lifetime data is available only for 882 such documents.
5. The referential relations between RFCs are generally not available other than the references implied by one making another obsolete (although the meta-data scheme appears to reflect intentions to include such referential information). For this reason we have resorted to scanning document texts using a custom computer program. As a result of this process, we have found which other RFCs are mentioned in an RFC body, and how often (i.e. the strength of reference). The *number of dependencies* in each RFC is appended to a per RFC data set which denotes the number of those RFCs which an RFC has references to. The reference strengths are used for visualization and analysis of the interdependency network.
6. Titles of RFCs are used for topic analysis.

The referential relations between RFCs form the basis of a directed network of dependency relations. Figure 2 demonstrates how such a network is formed. If an RFC document mentions another one, a directed edge from the former to the latter is added to the network, and edge weight is set to the number of times the latter RFC is mentioned in the text.

The data set is analyzed using descriptive tools from the R statistics package (R Development Core Team, 2009). In addition to this data set, the strengths of references are used to lay out the interdependency network of the RFC corpus, which is, in turn, analyzed and visualized using the ORA software toolkit for social network analysis (Carley et al., 2009) and Gephi (Bastian et al., 2009). The interdependency network is represented as a directed and weighted graph (Scott, 2000) in which the vertices are RFC documents, edge direction corresponds to referencing direction, and the weight of an edge is found by counting the number of occurrences of the referenced RFC in the referencing RFC document's text.

In order to conduct topic analysis we have first produced a document-term matrix containing counts of each word in each RFC document title. We have adopted the common approach of stemming each word and further processing of the matrix to use more informative tf-idf measure instead of simple word counts (Jones, 1972). We have used Python Natural Language ToolKit (Bird et al., 2009) and SciKit (Pedregosa et al., 2011) software packages for this purpose. NMF analysis was done using SciKit and SciPy software (Oliphant, 2007).

The additional analysis on RFC document titles using topic analysis allowed us to triangulate the results of social network analysis concern-

Figure 2. An example of referencing relations between RFC documents. In this example RFC-2 is mentioned twice in the text of RFC-1, thus the relation strength is two. In the other relations the relation strength is one.

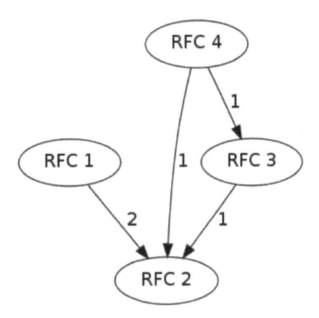

ing specialization of the IETF standards system. The analysis not only confirmed the number of specialized subsystems in each case, but also provided the words representing topical content of each subsystem.

5. CHANGES IN IETF STANDARDIZATION OUTPUT AND PROCESS

The volume and composition of the IETF documents published each year reveal certain aspects of the evolution of IETF standards and their production. The total number of IETF RFCs published each year is shown in Figure 1. This output volume is composed of different types of documents. The composition of publication volume across different types of documents is shown in figures 3(a) and 3(b), separately for standards track, and non-standards track RFCs . When interpreting this data one must remember that the IETF was established in 1986, although some RFCs were released prior to that and included in the IETF data set. Therefore fluctuations prior to this year, during what we may call the infancy period of Internet related institutions, are disregarded here. The composition has shown that a large portion of documents in this period are labeled as 'unknown', which justifies the decision to disregard this early period in the context of this study.

These data for RFC publication volume exhibit two distinct features: (i) there is a consistent increase trend in volume continuing to the present day, and (ii) there are peaks of output volume overlaid with this increase trend, approximately every six years. These peaks are marked in Figure 1, and seems to be common in standards and non-standards track volumes in Figures 3(a) and 3(b).

The first of these features is rather expected, since IETF has retained its role uninterruptedly since its formation, and the spread of Internet use increased demand for the production of an increasing volume of standards. The plot of document

Figure 3. Changes in the volume and composition of standards and non-standards track RFCs over the years.

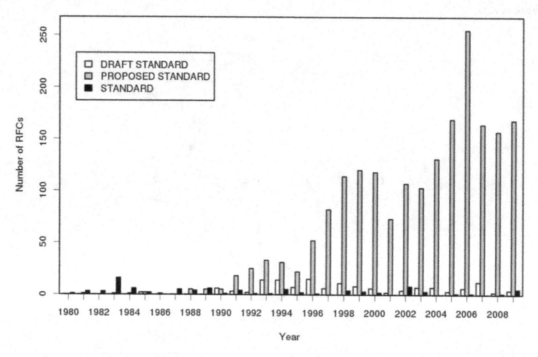

(a) Standards track RFCs over the years

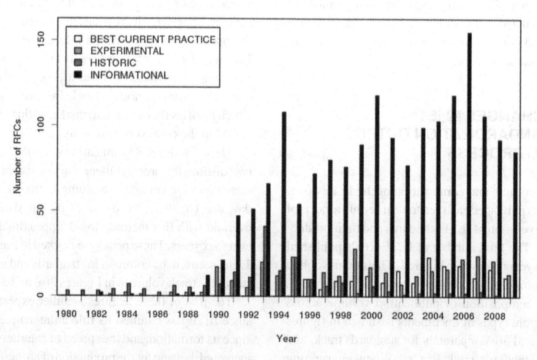

(b) Non-standards track RFCs over the years

production volume composition with respect to the type attributes of documents, shown in figures 3(a) and 3(b), also reveals some changes over time. The majority of recent output is composed of PS (proposed standard) and I (informational) type documents, which are at the less mature levels of their respective tracks. Although BCP and E type documents display a steady volume for the same period, volume is low. On the other hand, more mature specifications, i.e. those of DS (draft standard), S (standard), or BCP (Best Current Practice) type, have a low and more or less stable volume. This data therefore suggests that over time it takes increasingly more refinement stages and more extended collaboration to produce mature standards and specifications. Recent updates by IETF to its processes seems to acknowledge a slowdown and reflect the need to make these processes both more inclusive (of independent contributors) and faster (by adopting parallel approval processes)[1] . This seems to be similar to the task of modifying complex artifacts such as software (Ghezzi et al., 2002) which becomes more complex and time consuming as the product grows. More interestingly, the result also shows that IETF specifications production increasingly relies on two document types (I and PS types). This, in turn, prompts a further question concerning whether use of too many types makes coordination for standards production more difficult, and whether this is the reason for the community converging on a small subset of document types.

Changes in RFC document volume composition hint at the changes in how standards production progresses. Dependency relations between standards and the extent of their authorship can provide further explanations about such changes. Figures 4(a) and 4(b) show the changes in two related features through years in box-plot form: number of dependencies (references) and number of authors. Both measures exhibit a clearly increasing trend after 1986. This data shows that

it takes more people and wider consideration of, and integration with, existing standards to produce a new one. This resonates with the above finding that it takes more stages and requires more corrections for proposed standards to mature into standard status.

The second feature of RFC production volume, that it has an episodic nature, worths more attention. Systems science can provide a probable interpretation for these episodes. As Simon (Simon, 1962) describes, while a system grows, relatively distinct subsystems emerge within the larger system as the need arises. Such an evolutionary pattern over time may well be expected from the system consisting of the IETF specifications corpus. If that is the case, the IETF community's attention should be shifting between these subsystems depending on the immediate and common expectations within the community. It seems reasonable to expect that a contemporary challenge will invite efforts to create a set of interrelated specifications, with these efforts becoming a major attractor of the attention of IETF community. Indeed, the special attention of the community to security and virtual private network related technologies, which was noted by Alvestrand (2004) in reference to the state of IETF affairs in year 2003, shows itself in the emergence of a relatively independent subsystem of specifications which we shall discuss in the following sections. However, creation and stabilization of such a subsystem of standards or non-standards track specifications will probably start with a low volume of output, and only after reaching a consensus on key issues will it then exhibit a higher output volume. Definitive ascertainment of the causes of this episodic volume requires further qualitative and quantitative work on both the RFC corpus and the IETF community.

Exploration of document lifetimes in this study was limited to a small portion of the RFC document corpus and we did not observe any apparent temporal pattern; hence no results are reported here.

Figure 4. Distributions of number of dependencies and number of authors of RFCs published each year. The solid boxes mark the first and third quartiles of the distributions with the mean value shown as a bold line, whereas the bubbles beyond the dotted whiskers show individual extreme values in data.

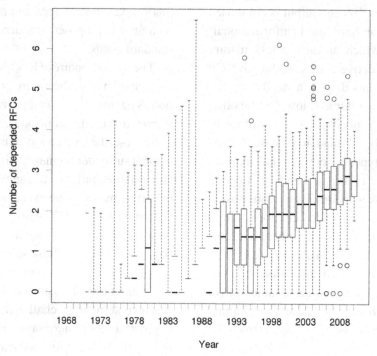

(a) Number of dependencies of RFCs published each year.

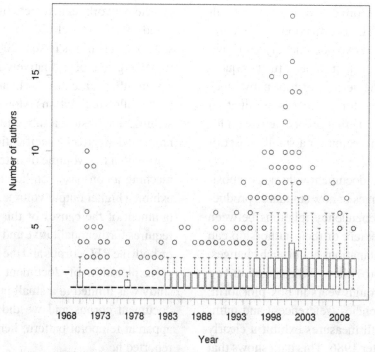

(b) Numbers of authors of RFCs each year.

6. RFC CORPUS STRUCTURE: CHANGE AND SPECIALIZATION

It is only in rare cases that one has extensive records of a community's work and the interactions involved in conducting a collective work. On the other hand the outcomes of such work, often reveal essential features of their production. This is the case for IETF community, since it is possible to determine interdependencies between RFC documents produced by the community, which to some extent reflects the collaborative structures underlying their production.

The features of the RFC interdependency network structure explored in this section are presented below, first for the whole RFC corpus, then for the three decades between 1980 and 2010. A visualization of the network structure for the whole RFC corpus is shown in Figure 5 which was created with the network analysis tool Gephi (Bastian et al., 2009). In this visualization, each vertex corresponds to an RFC and each edge corresponds to a referencing relation. The graph contains only the core subset of RFCs, however, since full visualizations of such large networks usually convey little information (Bender-Demoll & Mcfarland, 2006). Thus the visualization in this figure shows, not all, but only most important nodes, selected on the basis of the *in-degree* measure that is often used in social network analysis as an essential measure of positional importance (Wasserman & Faust, 1994; Scott, 2000; Nooteboom, 2008). Graph vertices (RFCs) are shown in sizes proportional to their in-degrees.

6.1. The Whole RFC Corpus

Figure 5 demonstrates the historical build up of referential relations between IETF RFCs. A variety of RFCs from different years depend on

Figure 5. The dependency network structure of the whole IETF RFC corpus, with only the most central nodes (90 out of about 6.000) included in the visualization. The sizes of vertices representing RFCs are proportional to their in-degrees, while the lengths of the arrowed edges representing referential relations are proportional to reference strength/count.

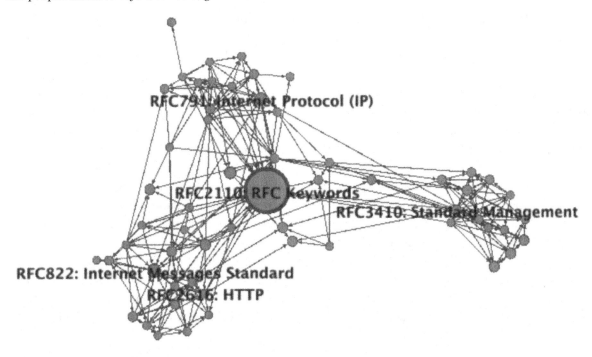

one another, thus the corpus is not a collection of isolated islands of documents but an interconnected group whose connections do not follow any initial plan. Nevertheless, as is common in most real networks the RFC corpus network exhibits a "small worlds" structure (Watts, 1999). One can observe several subgroups which are tightly connected to one another, more so than they are connected to documents in other subgroups. The visualization only shows labels of the most central RFCs in their respective subgroups, for readability reasons.

The distinctive subgroups in Figure 5 are: (i) the subgroup of user level application protocols such as HTTP (the standard protocol for the transfer of web pages) and MIME (standard for file attachments in e-mail and web pages), at the bottom left of the figure, (ii) the subgroup of network management related protocols, at the right of the figure, and (iii) the subgroup of basic data transfer protocols such as the Internet Protocol (IP). Since the latter subgroup is essential to the operation of the Internet and depended on by others, it has a relatively higher proportion of links to other subgroups compared to within-group links. At the center of Fig. 5 is an RFC which defines numerous keywords that are frequently referenced from other RFCs. It is an example of similar RFCs which bind the system of RFCs, and which typically define standards for the specification of standards.

The measure of betweenness centrality (which assesses the integrative role of an element in a graph) points to different elements in the system from those indicated by the direct measure of in-degree centrality. The highest betweenness centrality in this graph belongs to RFC2279 which specifies a standard for universal character encoding to support multiple content languages in a variety of situations. The second rank in terms of betweenness centrality is RFC2049 which specifies improvements to support a variety of content types on the Internet. This finding highlights the pressures on Internet standardization efforts stemming from both globalization and increasing content variety. It is worth noting here the utility of ostensibly irrelevant social network analysis methods and metrics in exposing systemic features of the structure of a network which is itself not social.

6.2. Changes in the Structure of Standards and Collaboration

We next look at the structures for the three decades of the 1980s, 1990s, and 2000s separately. The network for RFCs published between 1980-1990 is shown in Figure 6(a), one for the period 1990-2000 is shown in Figure 6(b), and one for the 2000s is shown in Figure 6(c).

Changes in the network structure, seem to indicate an ongoing compartmentalization of the RFC corpus. This prompts us to question whether the same may be true for the structures of collaborative work behind standards production. Findings in social studies (Kogut, 2000; Langlois & Robertson, 1992) suggest that such an evolutionary path towards progressive specialization may well be the case for systems of standards and the work behind their production.

While the tools of social network studies do not provide well developed longitudinal methods to assess such changes in the structure, a comparison over the decades is possible. For such a comparison we have used some measures to assess the level of compartmentalization separately for the network of each decade. As described in the social network analysis methods section above, there are metrics proposed in the literature which assess compartmentalization of a network by looking at how it is partitioned into sub-systems and how isolated these sub-systems are from one another. For this purpose we have applied two commonly used metrics of *clustering coefficient* and *modularity* available in the two corresponding software tools of Gephi (Blondel et al., 2008; Bastian et al., 2009) and ORA (Watts & Strogatz, 1998; Carley et al.,

Figure 6. Dependency network structure of RFCs produced in different decades, with limited numbers of most central nodes included in each. The sizes of vertices representing RFCs are proportional to their in-degrees, while the lengths of arrowed edges representing referential relations are proportional to reference strength/count.

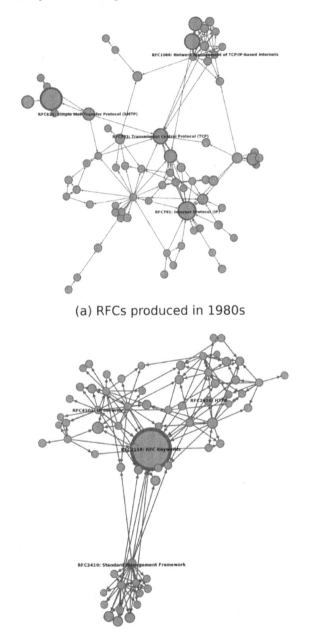

(a) RFCs produced in 1980s

(b) RFCs produced in 1990s

(c) RFCs produced in 2000s

2009), respectively. These metrics were applied to the RFC networks of the three decades separately, to make sure that relative changes in the two metrics are in check with one another. One of the metrics is also applied to the co-authorship networks of the corresponding decades to check whether the compartmentalization of the system of standards is, as we expected, in parallel with that of the collaboration behind its production. The results are shown in Table 2.

These results show an increase in compartmentalization from 80s to 90s, followed by stability from the 90s to the 2000s. This is in general agreement with the system science insight that a growing system gets more compartmentalized in time, and the stability achieved during the last decade is parallel to that of activity. In addition,

the results provide preliminary support for our expectation that compartmentalization of the organization of production (co-authorship network) parallels that of the products, while determining the particular characteristics of the parallelism between the two requires further study.

The results of analysis of topics in the RFC documents is presented in Table 3. Number of topics/clusters which best explain the corpus content parallels the results of structural analysis, as the number of clusters has increased from 2 to 4. The results also indicate the number of RFC documents in each cluster/topic.

We will now look at each decade to interpret the analysis results as a whole, in the context of standardization problematic of each decade.

Table 2. Changes in compartmentalization of RFC corpus and co-authorship network for three decades, using two measures: (#1) modularity (Blondel et al., 2008), and (#2) clustering coefficient (Watts & Strogatz, 1998).

Network/Measure	1980s	1990s	2000s
RFC, #1	0.453	0.581	0.563
RFC, #2	0.133	0.164	0.171
Co-authorship, #1	0.785	0.851	0.803

Table 3. Results of topic clustering applied to RFC titles for three separate decades

Decade	# Topics	Topic Keywords
1980s	355	protocol, Internet, official, specification, network, standard, transfer, ARPA, message, mail
	21	number, assigned, Internet, location, terminal, option, subnet, telnet, broadcast, ethic
1990s	232	Internet, standard, official, protocol, message, IAB(Internet Architecture Board), mail, architecture, process, encoding
	180	management, object, definition, SMIV2(Structure of Management Information), base, information, interface, network
	414	protocol, version, PPP, network, control, specification, SNMPv2, access, point
	770	service, extension, IP, SMTP, MIB, network, address, security, directory
2000s	171	access, directory, lightweight, LDAP, protocol, control, operation, schema, attribute, specification
	271	session, initiation, SIP (Session Initiation Protocol), protocol, event, description, SDP (Session Description Protocol), header, package, requirement
	1125	manage, network, IPv6, information, mobile, base, IP, switch, object, label
	1327	Internet, extension, security, protocol, message, authentication, version, key, service, transport

1980s

This decade's structure seems to reveal the beginnings of the emergence of specialized sub-groups within the system. At the center of the graph are standards labeled TCP and IP, which are abbreviations of protocol names that are the most essential standards for transfer of digital data packets over the Internet between computers. Two peripheral subgroups seem to be emerging in the 80s: (i) the application level standards which specify the content structure of data carried in the Internet for specialized uses such as e-mail (top of the figure), and (ii) network management related standards (bottom of the figure). This structure indicates that the focus of work in the 1980s decade is making the Internet communication infrastructure work, with the newly emerging interest in network scaling and use of Internet communication for services like e-mail.

Topic analysis results in Table 3 also show the presence of two groups. Relatively small size of management related documents group indicate that once the problem of making devices communicate reliably is more or less settled, issues related to management of the Internet has emerged as a new problematic. This is highlighted in the topic keywords of cluster two of this decade, which relates to assignment of IP addresses and subnets. An interesting keyword in this topic is "ethics". A closer look at the corpus (e.g. RFC1087) indicates that the Internet designers and authorities has been facing certain dilemmas to keep the growing Internet accessible to all, while maintaining its reliability, thus discussing the trade-off in ethical terms.

1990s

In this decade the network management group continues to be distinguishable (top right of the figure). The application level specifications subgroup also continues to exist (bottom of the figure), but the activity is now concentrated on the HTTP protocol which is at the center of web technologies that started to become popular after 1991. At the center of the network are groups of specifications which attempt to clarify both the standards for RFC authoring (e.g. RFC keywords) and matters such as assigned numbers which become an important issue for the growing Internet. These are numbers which globally standardize the computer port addresses web page services must use, etc. The problematic of work in the 90s decade seems to be two fold: (i) to sustain compatibility between the increasing variety of technologies, and (ii) to impose structure and discipline on the community's work under an increasing production load.

Topic analysis for this decade has indicated that 2 or 4 topics are appropriate, where the latter is presented in Table 3. Topics 2, 3, and 4 appears to be related to technical aspects of compatibility in relatively independent technical domains, while topic 1 is related to terms and organization of standards making process.

2000s

The network for the 2000s exhibits a different structure with some subsystems of standards becoming relatively more isolated from the network core. Specifically, the network management subgroup (bottom of the figure 6(c)) is relatively more isolated than it was previously. A newly emerging subgroup at the top left contains RFCs related to Internet protocol security. The emergence of this subgroup reflects the increasing concern with Internet security and its use in electronic commerce in the new millennium with the spreading of web usage. The third subgroup, at the top right, is once again related to application level specifications, and HTTP remains the most important standard in this subgroup. The keyword definitions RFC remain the most central document.

Topic analysis results show the Internet security problematic as a distinct cluster (topic 4), which is also the largest group of the decade. However, the rest of topics goes somewhat orthogonal to what structural grouping shows, e.g. showing session management as a distinct topic. This difference only indicates that analysis of content and structure in such a standard corpus promises a richer interpretation of the standardization process, but requires further work.

7. DISCUSSION OF FINDINGS

The findings reported here reveal several features of the IETF's RFC specifications corpus and the way it has changed over time. An obvious feature of the IETF corpus is that it is a growing system. The findings here demonstrate some important properties of this system. First of all, the production output level suggests that this system acts or reacts as a whole. The output volume of RFCs published by the IETF exhibit fluctuations, or episodes, marked with seemingly regular peaks. The changes in the system's output suggest that IETF is an organization in the traditional sense and that it reacts to environmental demands as a whole. However, empirical investigations focusing on the motivations and behavior of standardization process participants (e.g. commercial firms) are mostly blind to such system level features. In other words, our results underline the need to consider a system of standardization such as IETF as an organization with its own identity, organizational culture, dynamics, goals, etc.

Some reports on the IETF in the literature seem to support this interpretation. Bradner (Bradner, 1999) describes how IETF work is structured to improve efficiency and work focus, and how certain practices are employed to increase output quality. Alvestrand's account of the IETF (Alvestrand, 2004) speaks of a strong work culture, how participants associate certain elements of organizational identity with the IETF, and in addition indicates that this organization as a whole directs its attention to certain contemporary challenges. A contrary view that a system such as the IETF is

simply a constellation of the extra-organizational activities of contributors from different organizations would neither concur with these accounts, nor explain the non-random, episodic output volume of the IETF standardization process reported here. Even when one considers the possibly conflicting agendas of IETF contributors, such aspects are well suited to be investigated within organizational research frameworks.

Presence of episodes in organizational output is not a widely known phenomenon and our research methods are not suitable to offer a full explanation. However, looking at Alvestrand's account in conjunction with our findings, we suggest that since organizational attention is possibly focused on a certain few contemporary challenges, the episodes reflect how these challenges are tackled, then a basic consensus on their solution is reached, and eventually reflected in IETF specifications. If one subscribes to the view that IETF is an organization with shared goals and relatively unified focus, it makes sense to assume that RFC production within the IETF proceeds through such phases of organizational problem solving. A full explanation of this episodic output, however, will require a qualitative and retrospective study.

The second property of the IETF system, which is somewhat contrary to the first, is that, as the system grows, it becomes divided into specialized subsystems. This is evident in the structural changes in the RFC interdependency networks. While such compartmentalization is at first contrary to the view of the IETF as a unified system, it is a common evolutionary path in organizational growth (Aldrich, 1999). Our findings also reveal that the level of compartmentalization has stopped increasing during the last decade, and in parallel the production volume of RFCs has started to decline. Since the demand for Internet related standards appear to be growing, this indicates that IETF's position in Internet standardization is shrinking, possibly in parallel with other standards organizations taking over certain sub-fields. In addition, we have found that it takes more authors, deeper consideration of existing specifications, and more revisions to develop specifications into mature standards. In considering these findings together, it should be asked whether it is inevitable that the work of standards production in a growing system of standards become more complex or inefficient. More precisely, it is worth considering whether such inefficiency could be addressed by introducing changes in administrative or organizational practices. A failure to address growth, and the structural changes it brings about, may eventually lead to further inefficiency and shrinking of IETF's role in Internet standardization.

8. CONCLUSION

This study explored features of production and relational structure of Internet standards related specifications produced by the IETF, as it has grown through several decades. By combining social network analysis approaches, we have investigated changes in standards production in relation to the network structure. The findings reported here indicate the increasing complexity of the work on standards specifications, and development of specialization as the system of Internet standards grows. Certain longitudinal features of IETF production call for a view of this 'task force' as an organization with relatively unified goals and focus, rather than merely a collection of contributions from different organizations.

REFERENCES

Aggarwal, C. C., & Zhai, C. (2012). A survey of text clustering algorithms. In *Mining text data* (pp. 77–128). Springer. doi:10.1007/978-1-4614-3223-4_4

Aldrich, H. (1999). Organizations evolving. *Sage (Atlanta, Ga.)*.

Allen, R. H., & Sriram, R. D. (2000). The role of standards in innovation. *Technological Forecasting and Social Change, 64*(2-3), 171–181. doi:10.1016/S0040-1625(99)00104-3

Alvestrand, H. (2004, September). The role of the standards process in shaping the internet. *Proceedings of the IEEE, 92*(9), 1371–1374. doi:10.1109/JPROC.2004.832973

Bastian, M., Heymann, S., & Jacomy, M. (2009). Gephi: An open source software for exploring and manipulating networks. In Proceedings of International AAAI Conference on Weblogs and Social Media. AAAI.

Bender-Demoll, S., & Mcfarland, D. A. (2006). The art and science of dynamic network visualization. *Journal of Social Structure, 7*(2), 1–38.

Besen, S. M., & Farrell, J. (1991). The role of the ITU in standardization. *Telecommunications Policy, 15*(4), 311–321. doi:10.1016/0308-5961(91)90053-E

Bird, S., Klein, E., & Loper, E. (2009). *Natural language processing with python*. O'reilly.

Blei, D. M. (2012, April). Probabilistic topic models. *Communications of the ACM, 55*(4), 77–84. doi:10.1145/2133806.2133826

Blind, K., Gauch, S., & Hawkins, R. (2010). How stakeholders view the impacts of international ict standards. *Telecommunications Policy, 34*(3), 162–174. doi:10.1016/j.telpol.2009.11.016

Blondel, V. D., Guillaume, J.-L., Lambiotte, R., & Lefebvre, E. (2008, October). Fast unfolding of communities in large networks. *Journal of Statistical Mechanics, 2008*(10), P10008. doi:10.1088/1742-5468/2008/10/P10008

Bonaccorsi, A., Giannangeli, S., & Rossi, C. (2006). Entry strategies under competing standards: Hybris business models in the open source software industry. *Management Science, 52*(7), 1085–1098. doi:10.1287/mnsc.1060.0547

Bradner, S. (1996, October). *The internet standards process – Revision 3* (No. 2026). RFC 2026 (Best Current Practice). IETF. (Updated by RFCs 3667, 3668, 3932, 3979, 3978, 5378, 5657, 5742)

Bradner, S. (1999, February 22). Open sources: Voices from the open source revolution (o'reilly open source). In *The Internet Engineering task Force*. O'Reilly.

Capek, P. G., Frank, S. P., Gerdt, S., & Shields, D. (2005). A history of ibm's open-source involvement and strategy. *IBM Systems Journal, 44*(2), 249–257. doi:10.1147/sj.442.0249

Carley, K., Reminga, J., Storrick, J., & DeReno, M. (2009). *Ora users guide (Tech. Rep.)*. Carnegie Mellon University, School of Computer Science, Institute for Software Research.

Choi, D. G., Lee, H., & Sung, T. (2011). Research profiling for standardization and innovation. *Scientometrics, 88*(1), 259–278. doi:10.1007/s11192-011-0344-7

Egyedi, T. M. (2003). Consortium problem redefined: Negotiating democracy in the actor network on standardization. *International Journal of IT Standards and Standardization Research, 1*(2), 22–38. doi:10.4018/jitsr.2003070102

Gamber, T., Friedrich-Nishio, M., & Grupp, H. (2008, January 21). Science and technology in standardization: A statistical analysis of merging knowledge structures. *Scientometrics, 74*(1), 89–108. doi:10.1007/s11192-008-0105-4

Garcia, D. L. (1992). Standard setting in the united states: Public and private sector roles. *Journal of the American Sociaety for Information Science, 43*(8), 531–537. doi:10.1002/(SICI)1097-4571(199209)43:8<531::AID-ASI3>3.0.CO;2-Q

Gencer, M. (2012). The evolution of ietf standards and their production. *International Journal of IT Standards and Standardization Research, 10*(1), 17–33. doi:10.4018/jitsr.2012010102

Gençer, M., Oba, B., Özel, B., & Tunaloğlu, V. S. (2006). Open source systems, ifip working group 2.13 foundation on open source software 2006. In E. Damiani, B. Fitzgerald, W. Scacchi, & M. Scotto (Eds.), Organization of Internet Standards. Springer.

Ghezzi, C., Jazayeri, M., & Mandrioli, D. (2002). *Fundamentals of software engineering*. Upper Saddle River, NJ, USA: Prentice Hall PTR.

Hofmann, T. (1999). Probabilistic latent semantic indexing. In *Proceedings of the 22nd annual international acm sigir conference on research and development in information retrieval* (pp. 50–57).

Hoyer, P. O. (2004). Non-negative matrix factorization with sparseness constraints. *Journal of Machine Learning Research, 5*, 1457–1469.

Jones, K. S. (1972). A statistical interpretation of term specificity and its application in retrieval. *The Journal of Documentation, 28*(1), 11–21. doi:10.1108/eb026526

Kogut, B. (2000). The network as knowledge: Generative rules and the emergence of structure. *Strategic Management Journal, 21*(3), 405–425. doi:10.1002/(SICI)1097-0266(200003)21:3<405::AID-SMJ103>3.0.CO;2-5

Langlois, R. N., & Robertson, P. L. (1992). Networks and innovation in a modular system: Lessons from the microcomputer and stereo component industries. *Research Policy, 21*(4), 297–313. doi:10.1016/0048-7333(92)90030-8

Nickerson, J. V., & Muehlen, M. Z. (2006). Standard making, legitimacy, organizational ecology, institutionalism, internet standards, web services choreography. *MIS Quarterly, 30*(SI), 467–488.

Nooteboom, B. (2008). In S. Cropper, M. Ebers, C. Huxham, & P. S. Ring (Eds.), *The oxford handbook of inter-organizational relations* (pp. 607–634). Oxford University Press.

Oliphant, T. E. (2007). Python for scientific computing. *Computing in Science & Engineering*, *9*(3), 10–20. doi:10.1109/MCSE.2007.58

Pedregosa, F., Varoquaux, G., Gramfort, A., Michel, V., Thirion, B., & Grisel, O. et al. (2011). Scikit-learn: Machine learning in Python. *Journal of Machine Learning Research*, *12*, 2825–2830.

R Development Core Team. (2009). R: A language and environment for statistical computing. Vienna, Austria: Author.

Scott, J. (2000). Social network analysis. *Sage (Atlanta, Ga.)*.

Seung, D., & Lee, L. (2001). Algorithms for non-negative matrix factorization. *Advances in Neural Information Processing Systems*, *13*, 556–562.

Simcoe, T. S. (2006). Open innovation: Reaching a new paradigm. In H. Chesbrough, W. Vanhverbeke, & J. West (Eds.), Open standards and intellectual property rights. Oxford University Press.

Simon, H. A. (1962). The architecture of complexity. *Proceedings of the American Philosophical Society*, *106*(6), 467–482.

Wasserman, S., & Faust, K. (1994). *Social network analysis*. Cambridge. doi:10.1017/CBO9780511815478

Watts, D. J. (1999). Networks, dynamics, and the Small-World phenomenon. *American Journal of Sociology*, *105*(2), 493–527. doi:10.1086/210318

Watts, D. J., & Strogatz, S. H. (1998, June 04). Collective dynamics of 'small-world' networks. *Nature*, *393*(6684), 440–442. doi:10.1038/30918 PMID:9623998

West, J. (2003). *Proceedings of the workshop on standard making: A critical research frontier for information systems*. Academic Press.

KEY TERMS AND DEFINITIONS

Collaboration: Co-authorship in standardization process.

Ethics: Moral discussions regarding Internet standards.

IETF: The Internet Engineering Task Force, which steers standardization process for the Internet.

Open Standards: Publicly available standards.

Social Network Analysis: Relational analysis of social systems, such as standards co-authorship.

Standards Evolution: Changes in the structure of a standards corpus.

Standards Specialization: Specialization of a system of standards into specialized sub-systems.

Systems Thinking: An approach in understanding parts of a system in relation to the whole, rather than in isolation.

Topic Analysis: Techniques for clustering of documents based on their textual content.

ENDNOTES

[1]   An IETF memo summarizes policy changes to make standardization process more inclusive of independent contributors (http://tools.ietf.org/id/draft-klensin-rfc-independent-02.txt, retrieved Nov. 10, 2011). However, the statistics of RFC editor still indicate a relatively longer processing time for independent contributions (http://www.rfc-editor.org/overview.html, retrieved Nov. 10, 2011).

Chapter 6
Assessing IPR Disclosure within Standard Setting:
An ICT Case Study

Anne Layne-Farrar
Charles River Associates, USA

ABSTRACT

As part of its "policy project to examine the legal and policy issues surrounding the problem of potential patent 'hold-up' when patented technologies are included in collaborative standards," the Federal Trade Commission held an all-day workshop on June 21, 2011. The first panel of the day focused on patent disclosure rules intended to encourage full knowledge of patents "essential" for a standard and therefore to prevent patent ambush. When patents are disclosed after a standard is defined, the patent holder may have enhanced bargaining power that it can exploit to charge excessive royalties (e.g., greater than the value the patented technology contributes to the product complying with the standard). In this chapter, the authors present a case study on patent disclosure within the ICT sector. Specifically, they take an empirical look at the timing of patent disclosures within the European Telecommunications Standards Institute, the body responsible for some of the world's most prevalent mobile telephony standards. They find that most members officially disclose their potentially relevant patents after the standard is published, and sometimes considerably so. On the other hand, the authors also find that the delay in declaring patents to ETSI standards has been shrinking over time, with disclosures occurring closer to (although for the most part still after) the standard publication date for more recent standard generations as compared to earlier ones. This latter finding coincides with ETSI policy changes, suggesting that standards bodies may be able to improve patent disclosure with more precise rules. [1]

1. INTRODUCTION

The Federal Trade Commission (FTC) has been interested in the timeliness of patent disclosure within standard setting organizations (SSOs) – and the lack thereof leading to patent ambush – for many years now. It brought its first-failure-to-disclose case in the mid 1990s, against Dell[2]. At the time, Dell was participating in the standard consortium VESA, on the development of a computer bus standard, but Dell failed to disclose that at least one of Dell's patents would read on the

DOI: 10.4018/978-1-4666-6332-9.ch006

standard. The FTC found that Dell's failure to disclose its relevant IPRs violated US antitrust law, at which point Dell agreed not to assert its patent against companies implementing the VESA bus standard. The next case of this ilk came in 2002, when the FTC began its long running Rambus case[3]. Rambus was accused of failing to disclose relevant patents and patent applications, along with other deceptive conduct. The European Commission took up the cause a few years later, in 2007, when it sent Rambus a Statement of Objections that argued Rambus has violated Article 102 of the Treaty for the Functioning of the EU by abusing a dominant position[4].

Commentators on the various competition agency cases have largely been in agreement that failing to adequately disclose intellectual property rights (IPR) that might be essential to implement a standard early on in the standard development process is conduct that, at a minimum, should be discouraged and that in the extreme may constitute an antitrust violation (Besen & Levinson, 2009)[5].

Some argue that a failure to disclose patents coupled with deceptive behavior aimed at keeping the IPR from coming to light amounts to anticompetitive conduct – hence the Rambus investigation and the many related private lawsuit claims[6]. Others argue that non-disclosure of IPRs in standards is more appropriately deemed a breach of contract with the standards body, but nonetheless agree that deceptive failure to disclose should be stopped (Kobayashi & Wright, 2009)[7].

The economic theory underlying the concern over a failure to timely disclose IPR is one of exploitation. If licensors, especially those that are upstream specialists (like Rambus), are seen as withholding relevant patent disclosures while standard discussions are underway within an SSO, disclosing their patents only after the standard had been defined and member firms may be "locked into" the chosen technology, then those licensors can charge "excessive" licensing fees. In particular, licensors following this kind of opportunistic strategy can not only charge licensing

fees based on the value their IPR contributes to products conforming to the standard but also can appropriate some portion of licensees' upfront and irreversible investments to implement the standard in the downstream market – the definition of patent hold up.

As may be evident from the description above, two key conditions (perhaps among others) underlie the ability to practice patent ambush. The first is SSO members' lack of knowledge of the undisclosed patents, or an element of surprise. If potential licensees were unaware of a licensor's IPR on technologies important for a standard during its development, then the licensor would be able to use the element of surprise after these firms were irrevocably committed to the standard – that is, after they had made unrecoverable investments – to hold up licensees by charging "excessive" royalty rates that exploited the cost of switching to any alternative technologies. In contrast, had member firms known of the licensor's IPR in advance of defining and implementing the standard, especially at a time when the licensors' technology may have faced competition from other technologies viable for use in the standard, then such exploitation would not be possible. With ex ante knowledge of the IPR, the SSO members could either have voted an alternative technology into the standard, excluding a given licensor's patented technology altogether, or else they could have negotiated fair and reasonable royalties (RAND) with a particular licensor ex ante, under the credible threat of switching to one of the alternative technologies.

A second key condition required for profitable patent ambush is the presence of viable alternative technologies ex ante. If the licensor's patents faced reasonable substitutes before the standard was voted on and the licensor attempted to charge more for a license than its technology was perceived to be worth, then potential licensees could simply turn to the next best substitute; the licensor has little to no bargaining power in this case. If instead the patented technology is unique and irreplaceable – at least at a reasonable cost for the standard components at issue – then even if the SSO members had known about the licensor's IPR in advance of defining the standard they would nonetheless not have been able to credibly threaten to exclude the technology from the standard. In this latter case, the licensor has bargaining power even ex ante and without resort to any exploitation of switching costs derived from a lack of disclosure.

With unique patented technology, with no meaningful or viable substitutes, the question is whether the licensor can still exploit licensees' ex post irreversible investments to implement the standard. If the technology truly is essential for the standard under development, then the only credible alternative to taking a license, either ex ante or ex post, is to abstain altogether from producing products implementing the standard. Of course, ex post a licensee may already have made its irreversible investments, which will likely affect its willingness to walk away, but clearly the degree to which ex post IPR disclosure can play a role is considerably weakened in this scenario as compared to the case where viable alternatives are available ex ante. In fact, under certain circumstances it can make financial sense for SSO members to pay somewhat more than a patent's "incremental value" over the next best alternative, even before any irreversible investments are made, if the profits available to licensees through implementing the standard with the patented technology are higher than the profits available without it[8] (Layne-Farrar, Llobet, & Padilla, 2014).

Given the two conditions necessary for patent ambush to be successful, it is interesting to examine whether SSO participants do indeed disclose their relevant patents ex ante, during standard development. This question is the focus of the remainder of this paper. In particular, I present quantitative analysis of IPR disclosures within one important ICT SSO, the European Telecommunications

Standards Institute (ETSI), to provide a case study of patent disclosure behavior. While ETSI is the standards body responsible for important European mobile telephony standards (namely GSM, UMTS/WCDMA, LTE) these standards are important in the US and many other parts of the world as well. The global importance of the ETSI standards is reflected in its membership, which includes over 700 firms from over 60 countries, including the US, Canada, China, Taiwan, Japan, Australia, Israel, Russia, etc.

The remainder of the paper is organized as follows. The following section (Section 2) lays out the empirical approach taken, describes the data used to conduct the analysis, and presents the results. Section 3 then concludes. In an ideal world, the analysis would cover disclosure patterns at numerous SSOs to control for any institutional or cultural differences. Unfortunately, the data do not exist to allow for such a cross SSO comparison. Instead, the analysis here is based on IPR disclosures made to ETSI because it offers a look at important standards with relatively detailed data in comparison to the very limited public records at other SSOs.

The analysis reveals two key findings. First, most official IPR disclosures at ETSI are made ex post – often many years after the relevant standard components were published. While it is impossible to precisely define the demarcation line between "ex ante" and "ex post" (as explained below), analysis using a reasonable definition for that dividing line indicates that the majority of the official IPR disclosures at ETSI have been made "ex post".

A second key finding from the analysis is that the timeliness of IPR disclosures at ETSI has been improving over time. This is evident when we consider disclosure delays over the years and when we compare the delay in disclosing patents between the older generation mobile telecom standard (2G standard) with newer generations of that standard (3G and 4G). The average disclosure delay for the 2G wireless standard is 2 years; that figure falls slightly to 1.91 years for 3G, but drops considerably to 0.75 years for 4G[9]. During the analysis period, ETSI altered its IPR disclosure rules. The findings thus suggest that SSO policy changes to clarify IPR rules can have an impact by improving member disclosure behavior.

2. QUANTIFYING PATENT DISCLOSURES

As explained above, the analysis here focuses on the timing of patent disclosures to ETSI as compared to the contemporaneous status of the standards under development at the SSO. Ideally, this study would consider numerous standards bodies to understand general disclosure norms and any variation amongst organizations or across industries. Unfortunately, most SSOs do not make public the data required for that assessment. ETSI is notable in this regard because it maintains an extensive database that, among other things, contains information on members' patent disclosures. These disclosures represent the official written notices that member firms make to ETSI, although it is important to note that other informal (verbal) notices could have come earlier[10]. To keep the analysis manageable, I restrict my focus to ETSI projects related to the development of the mobile telecommunication standards, which are among the most popular in terms of implementation[11].

Formal IPR disclosure rules are spelled out clearly in ETSI's Guide on IPR[12]. As a result, all members are informed on where to look for the list of potentially essential IPR declared for any standard, project, or technical specification in which they are active. Moreover, it is my understanding that working group meetings (where the nitty gritty details of the standard specifications

are determined) typically begin with the group's chair reminding attendees that potentially essential IPR should be disclosed as soon as practicable.

2.1 The Data

The key element of any empirical analysis of IPR disclosure timing is obviously the definition of what constitutes "ex post" versus "ex ante". While a precise identification of this point is quite difficult given that standards tend to evolve over time (meaning there are really numerous "ex ante / ex post" demarcations), for the purposes of this analysis we can rely on an objective proxy. Specifically, "ex post" can be discerned by comparing the disclosure date for a patent named as essential for the implementation of a particular standard component to the publication date for that standard component's technical specifications. Under this approach, when disclosure dates precede the relevant publication dates, they can be considered "ex ante", named before the component was voted upon; when they follow publication dates, they can be considered "ex post".

In order to assess the timing of patent disclosures made to ETSI, I collected all mobile telecom-related patent declarations made to ETSI by member firms as of December 23, 2010[13]. I include both granted patents and patent applications in the analysis. A typical disclosure posted on ETSI is presented in Table 1.

Each IPR declaration is supposed to indicate the standard project that the patent reads on (such as GSM, UMTS, or LTE), the specific work item, deliverable or technical specification (TS) relevant for the patent, and the version number for the TS (reflecting the evolution of the standard's specification details over time). As the example in Table 1 illustrates, a given patent declared to ETSI can identify more than one deliverable. In other words, the same patent may be relevant for

Table 1. Representative ETSI IPR disclosure entry

Company Name	Nokia Corporation
Project	UMTS
Patent title	Communication of pictorial data by encoded primitive component pictures
Country of registration	UNITED STATES
Application No.	
Patent No.	6137836
Countries applicable to App./Patent	
Work Item or ETSI Deliverable No. with Section and Version	3GPP TS 26.140 Section:4.8 Version:5.2.0; ETSI TS 126.140 Section:4.8 Version:5.2.0; 3GPP TS 26.234 Section:2 Version:5.4.0; ETSI TS 126 234 Section:2 Version:5.4.0
Declaration date to ETSI	7/6/2005
Notes	The SIGNATORY and/or its AFFILIATES hereby declare that they are prepared to grant irrevocable licenses under the IPRs on terms and conditions which are in accordance with Clause 6.1 of the ETSI IPR Policy, in respect of the STANDARD, to the extent that the IPRs remain ESSENTIAL.
Other Patents/Applications in same family with countries	
Status	Active

multiple components of a particular standard and may even be relevant for multiple generations of a standard[15]. The TS and version number define the precise component of the standard for which the patent holder believes the disclosed patent may be essential.

Within the analysis here, a "declaration" is defined as each patent declared to ETSI regardless of the number of technical specifications that the declaration reads on. An "entry", on the other hand, is defined as each combination of a technical specification and a version made within a declaration. Some declarations therefore have multiple entries.

For each unique entry I collected the TS version publication date. This date is the proxy "standardization" date that determines a disclosure entry's ex ante or ex post status. While it is clear that standards tend to evolve over a long period of time, and a particular version is just one iteration of that evolution, publication marks an official consensus among the working group members

that the specification in the published version is the one to be adhered to (at least until replaced by a subsequent published version). Therefore, a TS may continue to evolve after publication, but if so it will have a higher version number associated with it. These publication dates therefore offer reasonable points in time to separate ex ante from ex post, in relation to components of the overall standard. Comparing an entry's disclosure date (the date of the official IPR declaration letter posted to ETSI) to the TS version publication date listed in the patent's declaration therefore defines the timing of the disclosure for the analysis presented here.

Because this study is centered on disclosure timing, certain fields were critical to the analysis. Any declaration that did not provide a declaration date or a specific deliverable was deleted from the dataset. In addition, I deleted declarations that were subsequently withdrawn (presumably because the IPR holder determined they were not essential)[16].

Many of the declarations made to ETSI have patents filed with and/or granted by the US Patent and Trademark Office (USPTO), the European Patent Office (EPO), the Japanese Patent Office (JPO), plus many other smaller jurisdictions, such as individual European nations. All patent jurisdictions in the declarations were included in the data. The final dataset contains 14,127 declarations made up of 34,571 entries[17].

Even though there are over 34,000 entries in the overall dataset, only a third of those entries are complete in that they contain all the necessary data for the analysis (version number and deliverables). Table 2 summarizes the completeness of the data. The companies that report a version number but have no deliverable information are excluded from the analysis because timing cannot be determined for these declarations. This leaves 14,102 declarations, 34,546 entries.

Table 3 below shows the jurisdictional distribution of the declarations and entries. The US is the most common jurisdiction. Roughly 27% of the complete entries and declarations (first panel) have the US as country of registration. Of the partial declarations/entries (second panel), roughly 37% list the US as the country of registration.

As a final description of the data, Table 4 presents the top ten assignees by declarations made. In total, 47 different entities account for 4,915 complete declarations (first panel). Only 10 ETSI members have made more than 100 complete declarations: Nokia, Motorola, Qualcomm, InterDigital Technology, Nokia Siemens, Ericsson, Samsung, NTT Docomo, Siemens, and Philips Electronics. These ten firms account for 87% of all complete entries.

2.2. Disclosure Timing in the Aggregate

Consider first the complete records: those declarations that provide all information necessary for calculating the difference between the date of disclosure and the date the standard component was finalized. Figure 1 below presents the difference, in quarter increments, between the date of the official IPR disclosure and the date of the declared TS version publication date. A negative one indicates that the patent was declared one year prior to the listed TS version publication (e.g., ex ante) while a positive one indicates that the patent was declared one year after the listed TS version publication date (e.g., ex post).

As the figure clearly shows, the overwhelming majority of the complete entries were made after the publication of the technical specification named as relevant by the patent holder. Only 710 (11.3%)[18] of the complete entries were made ex ante. While most entries were declared ex post, the distribution is highly skewed with a mean of 1.5 years delay between publication date and declaration, a mode of 4 months, and a median of 6 months. In other words, many official declarations were made shortly after the relevant publication

Table 2. Breakdown of declarations and entries

	Number of Declarations	Number of Entries
Number in Initial Sample	14,127	34,571
No Deliverables (excluded)	25	25
With Deliverables but no Version	9,187	22,689
With Deliverables and Version	4,915	11,857
Final Numbers	14,102	34,546

Note: The number of declarations includes all declarations that have at least one complete entry (i.e., deliverable and version information are included).

Table 3. Breakdown of declarations and entries by jurisdiction

Country of Registration	Number of Declarations	Number of Entries
Final Dataset with Version		
United States	1,314	3,182
European Patent Office	474	1,007
Patent Cooperation Treaty	429	919
Japan	297	704
Germany	294	685
Korea (Republic of)	275	597
China, Taiwan & Hong Kong	261	721
United Kingdom	142	253
France	122	242
Other	1,307	3,547
Total	4,915	11,857
Final Dataset with Deliverables, No Versions		
United States	3,361	8,318
China, Taiwan & Hong Kong	1,183	2,105
European Patent Office	525	1,214
Patent Cooperation Treaty	496	716
Japan	482	1,208
Korea (Republic of)	278	744
Canada	258	839
Finland	214	483
Other	2,390	7,062
Total	9,187	22,689

Note: The number of declarations includes all declarations that have at least one complete entry (i.e., deliverable and version information are included).

date. The distribution has a very long tail, however, indicating that 1,792 (28.54%) declarations were made two or more years after the relevant version was published.

As shown in Figure 2, the same pattern emerges when we consider the average delay for the broader group of those declarations that have at least one complete entry. These initial calculations suggest that ex post declarations are quite common within ETSI.

Another way to consider the data is by ETSI project. Figure 3 breaks the disclosure data down for the four largest standard projects at ETSI dur-

ing the timeframe analyzed[19]. The oldest project included is GSM, the 2G mobile standard, which had its first component vote in 1990[20].

The modal declaration for this project is 4 months after the relevant publication date; the median delay is 7.5 months. GPRS is the next project, representing an evolution of 2G (often referred to as 2.5G), with its first publication date in 1997. The modal delay is again 4 months after publication, but this project has a lower median of 4.5 months. The third group analyzed is the 3G standard, which had its first publication in 1999[21]. While the mode is far lower at less than one month,

Table 4. Breakdown of entries and declarations by company

Company	Number of Declarations	Number of Entries
Final Dataset with Deliverables, With Versions		
Nokia Corporation	962	1,595
Motorola Inc	773	1,551
Qualcomm Incorporated	581	3,728
InterDigital Technology Corp.	502	1,205
Nokia Siemens Networks	296	373
Ericsson AB	284	376
Samsung Electronics Co., Ltd	283	345
NTT Docomo, Inc.	240	513
Siemens AG	188	402
Philips Electronics N.V.	146	146
Other	660	1,623
Total	4,915	11,875
Final Dataset with Deliverables, No Version		
Nokia Corporation	1,465	2,446
Qualcomm Incorporated	1,313	4,127
InterDigital Technology Corp.	1,135	3,680
Motorola Inc	830	5,389
InterDigital Patent Holdings Inc	644	1,437
Huawei Technologies Co., Ltd	628	743
Samsung Electronics Co., Ltd	544	703
LG Electronics Inc.	413	540
Philips Electronics N.V.	383	432
ZTE Corporation	232	312
Other	1,600	2,880
Total	9,187	22,689

Note: The number of declarations includes all declarations that have at least one complete entry (i.e., deliverable and version information are included).

the median delay is 11 months, higher than the GSM median and considerably higher than the GPRS median. The 4G standard, which had its first publication in 2002, thus far has a 4 month median delay and a modal delay of 11 months[22].

Considering the proportion of declarations made no more than one year after the relevant standard publication date presents another picture of ETSI's IPR disclosure conduct. Only 47.2% of the GSM declarations were made within one year of the relevant publication, whereas 87.4% meet this criterion for GPRS, 34.2% met it for 3G, and 82.1% met it for 4G. GPRS therefore has the tightest period of declarations, although the more recent 4G is close behind.

Table 5 considers the data in terms of a simple before and after calculation, by standard generation. While the statistics above indicate that disclosure delays have been falling over time, the table above makes it clear that the majority of IPR

Figure 1. Patent disclosure timing (Complete entries)

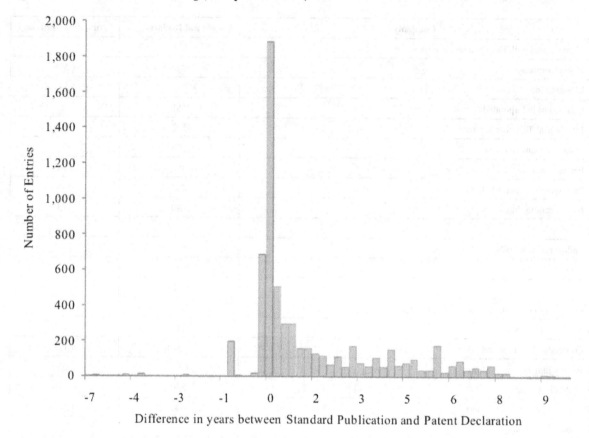

disclosures at ETSI are still ex post, even for the most recent mobile telecom generation.

Based on the statistics and charts above, the project level analysis suggests that average disclosure times have generally tightened over the years, but not in any consistent or smooth fashion[23]. Despite the general improvement, however, the majority of declarations continue to be made ex post and the disclosure timing distribution continues to have a long right tail.

2.3. Firm Level Analysis

Differences in timing are further explored by considering company level data. First consider the simple average and the median delay for the more active ETSI members in terms of the number of

declarations and entries. Table 6 below looks at the top 10 ETSI members with 100 or more entries.

While many of the average delays are small (falling under a year), Table 6 makes clear that late IPR declarations are a broad practice for ETSI's mobile telecom standards. Entries are declared to ETSI on average about 1.5 years after the relevant technical specification is adopted.

The average delay in declaration across firms ranges from 0.49 years (Ericsson) to 3.66 years (Philips)[24]. Of the 43 firms that have at least one complete entry, only 2 have an average difference between declaration and publication date that indicates ex ante disclosures (i.e., a negative average). However both of these firms, Dilithium Networks and LG Electronics, are relatively minor contributors, having only 6 complete entries in total[25].

Figure 2. Average patent disclosure timing (Declarations with at least one complete entry)

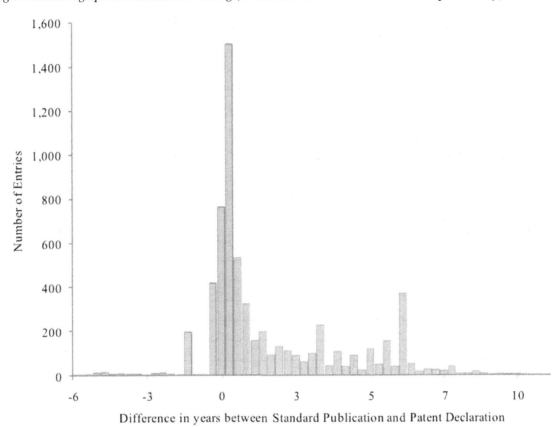

Figure 3. Average patent disclosure timing (Declarations with at least one complete entry)

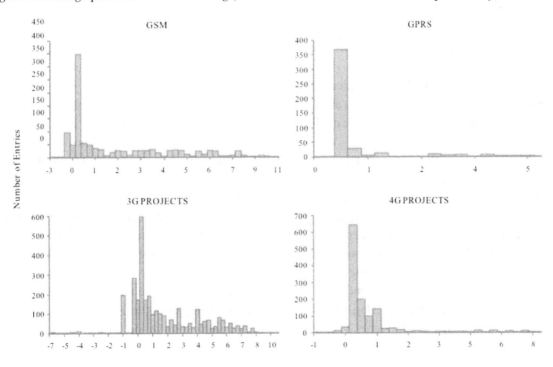

Table 5. Declarations and entries made by ex ante and ex post by standard

Project	Number of Entries	Ex Ante	% Ex Ante	Ex Post	% Ex Post
2G	1,159	100	8.6%	1,059	91.4%
2.5G	461	1	0.2%	460	99.8%
3G	3,314	562	17.0%	2,752	83.0%
4G	1,346	47	3.5%	1,299	96.5%

Table 6. Average entry disclosure timing by company

Company	Number of Entries	Average Delay in Years	Median Delay in Years
Nokia Corporation	1,331	0.61	0.40
Qualcomm Incorporated	1,130	0.64	0.37
InterDigital Technology Corp.	1,126	3.45	4.19
NTT Docomo, Inc.	476	2.29	0.92
Ericsson AB	344	0.49	0.16
Siemens AG	324	1.71	1.14
Nokia Siemens Networks	304	2.21	0.92
Samsung Electronics Co., Ltd	257	1.20	0.46
Coding Technologies	149	0.50	0.57
Philips Electronics N.V.	136	3.66	2.93
Other	703	1.65	1.05
Total	6,280	1.58	0.50

Note: The number of entries includes all entries that have version number and publication information.

Median delays tell a very similar story. Ericsson has the lowest median delay at around two months, while InterDitigal Technology has the highest at 4.19 years. And again, of the 43 firms with at least one complete entry, Dilithium Networks and LG Electronics are the only firms with ex ante median declaration dates.

Next consider an analysis of complete entries that examines the different telecom projects to which the firms assigned their declarations, presented in Table 7[26]. Disclosure lag appears to have tightened considerably between 2G and 2.5G technology, but increased again somewhat from 2.5G to 3G. 4G lags are inconsistent across firms, with some showing improvement from 3G and others increasing the disclosure lag. On average, 2.5G entries are declared roughly 8 months earlier than 2G entries; 3G entries are declared roughly 6 months earlier than 2G entries; and 4G entries are declared somewhat more than 1 year earlier than 2G.

It is important to note that firms tend to make many IPR declarations at once. In other words, official disclosure is "lumpy" and does not occur smoothly over time. The table below shows the highest count and proportion of complete entries and declarations by firm.

As the table indicates, a single declaration date tends to cover double digit percentages of a given firm's total disclosed IPR. In fact, two firms posted all of their relevant IPR on a single date. The fact that declarations come in bursts is not surprising given the time and cost involved in identifying patents to declare as potentially read-

Table 7. Mean and median differences in entry disclosure timing by company and project—2G through 4G

Company	2G Mean	2G Med.	2.5G Mean	2.5G Med.	3G Mean	3G Med.	4G Mean	4G Med.	Overall Mean	Overall Med.
Nokia Corporation	1.50	0.89			0.31	0.39	0.33	0.25	0.61	0.40
Qualcomm Incorporated	0.36	0.36	0.36	0.36	1.08	0.37			0.64	0.37
InterDigital Technology	3.69	4.37			3.19	3.69	4.27	4.52	3.45	4.19
NTT Docomo, Inc.					4.64	5.39	0.61	0.46	2.29	0.92
Ericsson AB	5.99	6.65	1.67	1.67	3.75	4.65	0.23	0.16	0.49	0.16
Siemens AG	2.05	1.51	2.00	1.49	1.63	1.02	0.44	0.43	1.71	1.14
Nokia Siemens Networks	3.99	3.12			3.13	3.03	0.52	0.46	2.21	0.92
Samsung	1.05	0.93			1.71	0.97	0.30	0.15	1.20	0.46
Coding Technologies					0.50	0.57			0.50	0.57
Philips Electronics					3.66	2.93			3.66	2.93
Other	2.82	3.32	1.05	0.52	1.78	1.29	0.48	0.30	1.65	1.05
Total	2.00	0.62	0.67	0.37	1.91	0.93	0.75	0.25	1.58	0.50

Note: The number of entries includes all entries that have version and publication information.

Table 8. Counts of entries and declarations with the same declaration date

Company	Date with Most Declarations Entries	Date with Most Declarations Declarations[24]	Top 2 Most Declaration Dates Entries	Top 2 Most Declaration Dates Declarations
Nokia Corporation	187 (14%)	187 (22%)	256 (19%)	235 (27%)
Qualcomm Incorporated	1,029 (91%)	513 (88%)	1,124 (99%)	576 (99%)
InterDigital Technology	326 (29%)	326 (66%)	989 (88%)	463 (93%)
NTT Docomo, Inc.	129 (27%)	68 (31%)	211 (44%)	132 (60%)
Ericsson AB	74 (22%)	57 (21%)	144 (42%)	106 (40%)
Siemens AG	69 (21%)	33 (20%)	107 (33%)	58 (35%)
Nokia Siemens Networks	79 (26%)	60 (25%)	122 (40%)	103 (43%)
Samsung	76 (30%)	74 (33%)	140 (54%)	122 (54%)
Coding Technologies	149 (100%)	29 (100%)	149 (100%)	29 (100%)
Philips Electronics	136 (100%)	136 (100%)	136 (100%)	136 (100%)
Other[25]	508 (81%)	298 (79%)	613 (90%)	377 (91%)

Note: The number of entries includes all entries that have version and publication information.

ing on a standard currently under development. In light of the effort involved, firms appear to make such determinations infrequently, on an as-needed basis. For this reason, while ETSI members may make blanket oral statements in working group meetings without naming particular patents (which would put other members present at the meeting on notice that some IPR is forthcoming), it is likely that many provide patent-specific details only with official written notifications. In this case, the official notices would take on additional importance in that they provide specificity, allowing potential licensees to move beyond the mere existence of IPR and into an evaluation of the particular patents.

Figure 4 corroborates the finding that official disclosures come in waves. As the chart below illustrates, declarations peaked in 2004, with 2005 and 2009 showing spikes as well.

Figure 4. Entries by publication year

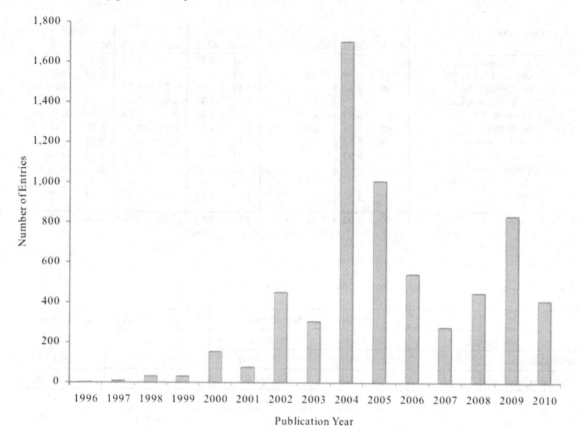

2.4. Are Delays Shrinking?

As was shown in the prior section, even though there is variation in the average delay, almost all ETSI members, and certainly all the major industry players, typically declare their patents to ETSI after the relevant standard component (TS) has been published. As also noted, however, overall the average delay for later projects (3G and 4G) is lower than for earlier projects (2G). In this section, the pattern over time is further explored by conducting a variety of statistical analyses. If members are shortening their disclosure lags, it could be the case that ETSI is taking a more active stance on late disclosure of intellectual property, or that members are fully aware that competition agencies like the EC and the FTC are cracking down on such behavior, or simply that members

are generally more aware of regulatory concern about patent ambush and are therefore making a greater effort to disclose their relevant patents in a more timely fashion.

In fact, ETSI records indicate that a policy change may be responsible for at least some portion of the improved timeliness of IPR disclosures. In November 2005, at its 46th General Assembly, ETSI adopted a modification to its IPR Policy. Specifically, the wording of clause 4.1 of the Policy changed from "Each MEMBER shall use its reasonable endeavors, in particular to timely inform ETSI of ESSENTIAL IPRs..." to "...each MEMBER shall use its reasonable endeavors, in particular during the development of a STANDARD or TECHNICAL SPECIFICATION where it participates, to inform ETSI of ESSENTIAL IPRS in a timely fashion..."[27]. Thus, after 2005, what "timely" meant became considerably more precise and was defined in relation to the development of standards and technical specifications.

Table 9 shows the number of entries by TS publication year along with the average and standard deviation in disclosure delay. There is a clear downward pattern beginning in the late 1990s; the average delay is markedly lower for the later years, dropping from 3.66 in 1996 to 0.25 by 2010. A similar pattern can be seen for the median delay over time. The trend is clear: ETSI members are declaring their intellectual property more quickly after publication of the relevant standard component[28]. That being said, even as late as 2010 the disclosure norm at ETSI remains ex post and improvements in timeliness have yet to translate into substantial ex ante disclosure.

Regression analysis is presented next. I run a regression of the difference in years between declaration and publication on year-specific fixed effects. Table 10 shows the results. The baseline is the average delay in the beginning year (1996), represented by the constant; the coefficients on the years indicate the presence and extent of any delay (negative numbers indicate shorter delays as compared to 1996). There is a decline in the first couple of years, followed by an increase in the length of the average delay, which peaks around 2001. Most of the early coefficients, however, are not statistically significant, meaning they are not likely any different from the base year 1996 (although this result may be partially driven by the fact that in the early years we have considerably fewer entries than in the later ones). A structural break appears to occur in 2004, when the length of the average delay collapses from 3.66 years to about 1.03 years (3.66-2.63), a change that is highly statistically significant. The timing of this break suggests that debate in anticipation of the ETSI General Assembly rule change may be responsible. From 2004 on all the differences relative to the baseline are statistically significant. Interestingly,

Table 9. Summary statistics of complete entries by year of publication of the relevant technical specification

Year	Number of Entries	Mean Delay in Years	Median Delay in Years	Standard Deviation
1996	2	3.66	3.66	1.01
1997	8	2.43	2.46	1.25
1998	32	3.06	2.56	1.66
1999	31	4.00	3.32	1.86
2000	155	4.04	4.18	2.66
2001	78	5.13	4.48	2.46
2002	452	4.52	5.63	2.69
2003	305	4.59	6.16	2.42
2004	1,702	1.03	0.36	1.75
2005	1,007	1.32	0.86	2.15
2006	541	1.93	2.56	1.81
2007	276	1.26	1.40	1.37
2008	448	0.67	0.88	1.19
2009	833	0.43	0.25	0.42
2010	410	0.25	0.18	0.29
Total	6,280	1.58	0.50	2.24

Note: The number of entries includes all entries that have version and publication date information.

disclosure delay increases from 2005 to 2006 (the year after the ETSI policy rule went into effect), but from 2007 on there is a consistent decline in disclosure delay[29].

When considered in tandem, these results confirm the results from the previous sections, suggesting that overall ETSI members are declaring their intellectual property more quickly after publication of the relevant component specification, albeit still ex post. The figure below summarizes the findings, noting the start dates for each standard generation, as well as the date of ETSI's policy change.

When viewed in the aggregate, the results presented in this section point to two distinct findings. First, declarations occur most often ex post, after the relevant technical specification for the patents being declared has been published. This is true even after ETSI revised its IPR Policy to more explicitly define that "timely" disclosure means during the development of the standard. Second, there is strong evidence that while declarations remain ex post on average, ETSI members are becoming quicker to declare relevant patents after publication of a standard and that trend has been continuing for many years now.

3. CONCLUSION

Over the past 15 years, the majority of IPR disclosures relevant for mobile telecom standards developed at ETSI have been made ex post, coming after the publication of the component the patent is declared as relevant for. While the modal delay in disclosure has fallen steadily over time,

Table 10. Regression analysis: Dependent variable is the difference in years between declaration and publication date

Year	Coefficient	Robust Standard Error	P>|t|	
1997	-1.231	0.653	0.059	
1998	-0.601	0.583	0.303	
1999	0.340	0.604	0.573	
2000	0.383	0.549	0.486	
2001	1.474	0.577	0.011	*
2002	0.864	0.522	0.098	
2003	0.935	0.525	0.075	
2004	-2.629	0.508	0.000	**
2005	-2.336	0.511	0.000	**
2006	-1.729	0.512	0.001	**
2007	-2.397	0.513	0.000	**
2008	-2.992	0.509	0.000	**
2009	-3.226	0.506	0.000	**
2010	-3.410	0.506	0.000	**
Constant	3.657	0.506	0.000	**
N	6,280			
R-sq	0.373			

Notes: $*p<0.05$, $**p<0.01$

Figure 5. Entry disclosure delays by year of publication of relevant technical specification

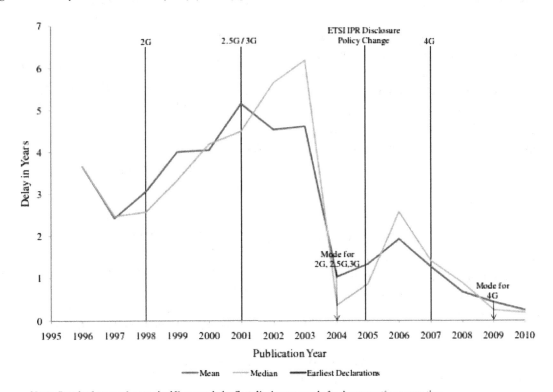

Note: Standard generation vertical lines mark the first disclosures made for the respective generation.

from a peak of 7.39 in 2002 down to -0.92 (i.e., ex ante) in 2005 and then back up again to 0.29 in 2010, most IPR disclosures at ETSI continue to be made ex post.

The good news is that disclosure delays are falling. Indeed, the marked shift in disclosure delay is seen at the time ETSI was debating the IPR policy clarification that was eventually adopted at General Assembly, indicating that the rules do matter. If the trend toward more timely disclosures continues, we would expect the transition from ex post to ex ante disclosure to occur eventually. However, the lumpy nature of IPR disclosures, as companies review their IPR holdings only periodically and then make disclosures in broad tranches, suggests that at least some patents will always be declared ex post, just as a practical matter.

To the extent that it takes time after a standard has been published for ETSI members to make irreversible investments in implementing the standard, modest delays in IPR disclosure of a few months may not be problematic from a licensing perspective. If standard implementers still have enough time to negotiate licenses without any investment lock-in, then patent hold up cannot be practiced[30]. Indeed, if implementation investments take over a year to complete, then the "ex post" clock may not start ticking until that point, regardless of when technology votes occur. This logic would imply that the ex ante/ex post demarcation is firm specific, triggered by an individual member's irreversible investments, and is not universal to the standard overall. This is an interesting avenue for future research.

ACKNOWLEDGMENT

The author thanks Roger Brooks, Damien Geradin, Daniel Garcia-Swartz, A. Jorge Padilla, and Richard Taffet for helpful comments and suggestions and Charmaine Alcain, Dhiren Patki, and Sokol Vako for invaluable research support. Financial support for early rounds of the research underlying this paper was provided by Qualcomm.

REFERENCES

Besen, S., & Levinson, R. (2009). Standards, intellectual property disclosure, and patent royalties after Rambus. *North Carolina Law Review*, *10*(233). Retrieved from http://jolt.unc.edu/sites/default/files/Besen_Levinson_v10i2_233_282_0.pdf

Kobayashi, B., & Wright, J. (2009). Substantive preemption, and limits on antitrust: An application to patent holdup. *Journal of Competition Law & Economics*, *5*(469).

Layne-Farrar, A., Llobet, G., & Padilla, J. (2014). Payments and participation: The incentives to join cooperative standard setting efforts. *Working Paper*. Retrieved from http://papers.ssrn.com/sol3/papers.cfm?abstract_id=1904959

ADDITIONAL READING

European Commission. (2009). *Antitrust: Commission accepts commitments from Rambus lowering memory chip royalty rates* (Press Release). Retrieved from http://europa.eu/rapid/press-release_IP-09-1897_en.htm?locale=en

European Telecommunications Standard Institute. (2014). *ETSI Intellectual Property Rights Policy*. Retrieved from http://www.etsi.org/images/files/IPR/etsi-ipr-policy.pdf

European Telecommunications Standard Institute. (2014). *ETSI IPR Online Database*. Retrieved from http://ipr.etsi.org/

Leopold. G. (2007, February 12). Rambus ruling to fuel reforms. *InformationWeek*. Retrieved from http://www.informationweek.com/rambus-ruling-to-fuel-reforms/d/d-id/1051803?

Patterson, M. (2002). Inventions, industry standards, and intellectual property. *Berkeley Technology Law Journal*, *17*(1043).

United States Federal Trade Commission. (1996). *Decision in the matter of Dell Computer Corporation, Docket No. C-3658 Consent Order, etc., In regard to alleged violation of section 5 of the Federal Trade Commission Act* (Commissioner Azcuenaga dissenting). Washington, DC. Retrieved from http://www.mwe.com/info/pubs/ftc_volume_decision_121_(January_-_June_1996) pages_561-655.pdf

United States Federal Trade Commission. (2002). *In the matter of Rambus Incorporated Docket No. 9302* (Complaint). Washington, DC. Retrieved from http://www.ftc.gov/enforcement/cases-proceedings/011-0017/rambus-inc-matter

KEY TERMS AND DEFINITIONS

Bargaining Power: The leverage that one party has over another during licensing negotiations.

Case Study: An empirical inquiry that investigates a contemporary phenomenon within its real-life context; when the boundaries between phenomenon and context are not clearly evident; and in which multiple sources of evidence are used.

Essentiality: Patents whose covered technology is necessarily infringed by compliance with a standard.

FRAND: Fair, Reasonable, and Non-Discriminatory licensing commitments.

IPR: Intellectual Property Rights.

Patent Ambush: The practice of hiding patents on technology incorporated into a standard, so as to take advantage of lock-in after the standard is codified.

ENDNOTES

[1]   The ideas and opinions in this paper are exclusively the author's, as are any errors. Comments should be sent to alayne-farrar@crai.com.

[2]   Fed. Trade Comm'n Decisions, in the Matter of Dell Computer Corporation, Docket No. C-3658 Consent Order, etc., in Regard to Alleged Violation of Sec. 5 of the Federal Trade Commission Act, May 20, 1996 (Commissioner Azcuenaga dissenting).

[3]   Fed. Trade Comm'n, in the Matter of Rambus Incorporated Docket No. 9302, Complaint, June 18, 2002, ¶ 119 at 31.

[4]   See http://europa.eu/rapid/pressReleasesAction.do?reference=IP/09/1897&format=HTML&aged=1&language=EN&guiLanguage=en

[5]   The debate surrounding the Rambus case is illustrative. While many aspects of that case have been the subject of much debate and controversy, the general notion that IPR holders should disclose ex ante was not in dispute. See e.g., Stanely M. Besen & Robert J. Levinson, Standards, Intellectual Property Disclosure, and Patent Royalties After Rambus, 10 NC J. L. & TECH 233 (2009) available at http://jolt.unc.edu/sites/default/files/Besen_Levinson_v10i2_233_282_0.pdf; Mark R. Patterson, Inventions, Industry Standards, and Intellectual Property, 17 Berkley Tech. L. J. 1043 (2002); George Leopold, Rambus Ruling to Fuel Reforms, INFORMATIONWEEK, Feb 12, 2007.

[6]   "The foregoing conduct by Rambus, during and after its involvement in JEDEC's JC-42.3 Subcommittee, has materially caused or threatened to cause substantial harm to competition and will, in the future, materially cause or threaten to cause further substantial injury to competition and consumers…" See Fed. Trade Comm'n, in the Matter of Rambus Incorporated Docket No. 9302, Complaint, June 18, 2002, ¶ 119 at 31; see also Rambus Inc. v. Infineon Techs. Ag, 318 F.3d 1081 (Fed. Cir. 2003).

[7]   See e.g., Bruce H. Kobayashi & Joshua D. Wright, Federalism, Substantive Preemption, and Limits on Antitrust: An Application to Patent Holdup, 5 J. COMPETITION L. & ECON 469 (2009).

[8]   See Anne Layne-Farrar, Gerard Llobet, and Jorge Padilla, Payments and Participation: The Incentives to Join Cooperative Standard Setting Efforts Journal of Economics & Management Strategy, Volume 23, Number 1, Spring 2014, 24–49.

[9]   The mean difference is statistically significant at the 1% level. The medians for the two generations are, however, not statistically different from one another, at 0.63 and 0.93 for 2G and 3G, respectively

[10]   The official letters submitted to ETSI therefore provide a "lower bound" on IPR disclosure. Some IPR may have been announced earlier, during working group meetings but we cannot know who was in the room at the time nor who heard the announcement. Thus, the letters are the first disclosure that has universal access and which provides documentation

[11]   Standard projects included are: 3GPP, 3GPP/AMR-WB, 3GPP/AMR-WB+, 3GPP/EMS, AMR, GERAN, GPRS, GSM, GSM/AMR-NB, GSM/TDMA, LCS, LCS-128 Pos, LTE, Lawful Interception, Smart Card, UICC,

UMTS, UMTS FDD, UMTS/CDMA and WCDMA

[12]   ETSI Guide on IPR; Note that 3GPP is an umbrella organization of which ETSI is a part. According to the 3GPP website, "Individual Members shall be bound by the IPR Policy of their respective Organizational Partner [ETSI in this case]. Individual Members should declare at the earliest opportunity, any IPRs which they believe to be essential, or potentially essential, to any work ongoing within 3GPP. Declarations should be made by Individual Members to their respective Organizational Partners."

[13]   These data are available online. I collected declarations to the following mobile telecom related ETSI projects: 3GPP, 3GPP/AMR-WB, 3GPP/AMR-WB+, 3GPP/EMS, AMR, GERAN, GPRS, GSM, GSM/AMR-NB, GSM/TDMA, LCS, LCS-128 Pos, LTE, Lawful Interception, Smart Card, UICC, UMTS, UMTS FDD, UMTS/CDMA and WCDMA.

[14]   Id.

[15]   For example, a patent may be originally disclosed for the 2G mobile telecom standard, GSM, but reiterated for 2.5G (GPRS) or 3G (UMTS).

[16]   Only the standard projects listed in supra note 11 were included in the analysis.

[17]   ETSI reports a total of 25,827 declarations made to mobile telecom projects as of December 23, 2010. I made sure that patent numbers were of an appropriate format (i.e. patent number was not given as N/A, cancelled, pending, fallen, removed, to be completed, or to be provided) and that it did not contain any alpha/numeric characters that designate year of submission or document type submitted (character placement and document code description vary across jurisdictions). I then extracted the multiple entries of each declaration and made each combination of a declaration and an entry as one observation resulting to 38,335 observations. Of these I deleted 478 withdrawn declarations, 1,287 blanket patents (e.g. application number and patent number = missing, n/a, pending, PCT, unpublished, to be provided, unknown, cancelled, Fallen, Removed) and 1,999 non- relevant projects (e.g. declarations where project not in 2G, 2.5G, 3G or 4G). I then removed complete duplicates that matched across the following fields: company name, project, patent title, declaration date, deliverables, country of registration, status countries applicable application/publication). Duplicate entries were then removed from the dataset (i.e. all other fields being equal including version numbers, ETSI TS 125 101 and 3GPP TS 25.101 is considered as just one declaration). To match the ETSI declarations with the correct Version Publication Dates, I also ensured that the technical specifications as well as the version numbers were consistent in format with the variables in the Version Publication dataset. Where version number is not complete (i.e., Version:5.X.Y, Version: Release 8, Release 6) the version number released right after the declaration date was used. If no other declarations with the same release number were made after the declaration date, the publication date of the same version family right before the declaration date was used. I then visually inspected the data for any mismatch in the grouping that could have caused to exclude relevant declarations or include irrelevant observations. After these processes, the dataset contained 14,127 declarations and 34,571 entries.

[18]   Note that even though 11,857 entries included a version number I was only able to find the publication dates for 6,280 entries due to incomplete information in the ETSI website or ambiguities in the entry itself.

[19]   No other project reached significant numbers of declarations to warrant separate analysis.

[20]   GSM includes the following: GSM, GSM/AMR-NB GSM/TDMA, LCS, LCS-128 Pos, Lawful Interception and UICC.

[21]   3G Projects include 3GPP, 3GPP/AMR-WB, 3GPP/AMR-WB+, 3GPP/EMS, UMTS, UMTS FDD, UMTS/CDMA, WCDMA, AMR, and Smart Card.

[22]   4G Projects include LTE.

[23]   Statistical tests comparing the mean differences in entry disclosure timing by project confirm that the observed differences are statistically significant. In particular, Bonferroni multiple mean comparison tests were run. Results on file with the author.

[24]   I treat the 33 firms with the lowest number of entries as a single entity for this analysis. I confirmed the results of Table 6 by conducting multiple mean comparison tests. The tests indicate that all but two firms make their declarations late (i.e. each firm's average is statistically significantly higher than zero).

[25]   Both of these firms are included in "Other" in Table 5.

[26]   The ETSI projects have been classified as follows: 2G—GSM, GSM/AMR-NB, GSM/TDMA, GERAN, LCS, LCS-128 Pos, Lawful Interception, and UICC; 2.5G—GPRS; 3G—3GPP, 3GPP/AMR-WB, 3GPP/AMR-WB+, 3GPP/EMS, UMTS, UMTS FDD, UMTS/CDMA, WCDMA, Smart Card, AMR; 4G—LTE.

[27]   See ETSI Guide on Intellectual Property Rights (IPRs), Version adopted by Board #70 on 27 November 2008, 4.6.1 History of Changes, p. 61.

[28]   Regressing the average delay on the publication year produces a negative and statistically significant coefficient, as seen in Table 9. This suggests that censoring of the data toward the late years does not drive the regression result.

[29]   If the General Assembly and the rule change that resulted from it increased awareness of the importance of IPR disclosure within telecom standards development, this spike could reflect firm representatives returning from the General Assembly and instructing their staff to review their portfolios anew, in order to make more comprehensive disclosures in the wake of the IPR policy change.

[30]   The time and expense of shifting the standard specification to an alternative technology, should one exist, would still remain though.

Section 3
Focus on Individual Standards and Sectors

Chapter 7
Co–Evolutionary Analysis of Cognitive Radio Systems

Vladislav V. Fomin
Vytautas Magnus University, Lithuania

Arturas Medeisis
Vilnius Gediminas Technical University, Lithuania

ABSTRACT

Cognitive radio technology is commonly seen as a promise to form the basis of the next largest break-through in the development of ubiquitous wireless broadband services. However, the disruptive nature and complexity of this technology raises a host of associated issues, including the open question on reasons for the slow progression of the innovation. In this chapter, the authors offer a co-evolutionary analysis of the CR innovation context, aiming to reveal a stakeholders' domain, which is best positioned to lead the further CR development. Having analysed the position of CR within technology, market, and regulatory domains, the authors come to conclude that the regulatory domain oversees some of the most crucial enabling factors that may decide the future of CR technology.

1. INTRODUCTION

The concept of Software Defined Radio (SDR) – a radio system in which RF emissions and operational parameters could be defined and re-configured by software – has been discussed since mid 80-ties with the first commercial products arriving to the market in the early 90-ties (Kloch et al., 2009). In 1999 Mitola and Maguire (1999) introduced the concept of Cognitive Radio (CR) – a kind of an application built on top of the SDR technological base to enable "intelligent" on-the-

fly self-reconfiguration of the radio system to adapt to the instantaneous state of the spectrum-space environment as well as to real-time user requirements.

As a technology innovation, CR was conceived as a promise to overcome the limitations of the existing international governance system for radio spectrum allocation, under which the key resource of wireless communications systems – the radio spectrum – is rigidly divided into chunks (bands), and the bands are strictly associated with specific applications. The "intelligent" re-configuration

DOI: 10.4018/978-1-4666-6332-9.ch007

feature of CR might allow dissociating specific bands from specific technologies/applications, thus boosting overall efficiency of spectrum use. More specifically, the possibility to dynamically access the underutilized chunks of spectrum, known as "white spaces", would allow accessing opportunistically the bands that would be otherwise considered closed for access by new spectrum users. This paradigm is referred to as "Opportunistic Spectrum Access" or "Dynamic Spectrum Access" (DSA).

More than a decade down the road since the concepts of CR and DSA were proposed, the SDR-based radio systems remain mostly restricted to the narrow niches of heavy-duty high-end infrastructure devices such as tactically agile military equipment and complex (multi-standard) base stations of cellular telephony systems that utilize re-configurability in order to become more easily adapted to evolving radio interface specifications by simple software upgrades. Meanwhile, the true CR still remains the subject of the R&D efforts and only few commercially oriented pilots have been deployed on a very limited geographical scale.

The pattern of CR development does not fit easily into popular theoretical frameworks on technology innovation – the niche technology so far hasn't found its way to the broader market.

As of today, it seems that nascent CR industry is disoriented by apparent failure of initial DSA vision to make quick progress to market and as a result it is increasingly unclear where the impetus for the CR innovation and commercialization advancement should come from. To find out which domain or stakeholder is better positioned to take the lead in formulating the vision, requirements and coordinating standardization work, we conduct a co-evolutionary analysis of the heterogeneous context in which the CR develops.

2. ONE PHENOMENON, MANY PERSPECTIVES: CR THROUGH THE PRISM OF TECHNOLOGY INNOVATION

2.1 The Phenomenon of CR

The term 'cognitive' in CR refers to the distinctive – intelligent – features of the radio system, namely its ability to derive real-time information about its local radio environment, analyse this within the context of its own technical capabilities, applicable regulatory policy rules as well as user communications requirements and based on that analysis make autonomous decisions on the best possible way to configure itself for carrying out the communications task at hand (Doyle, 2009). It is postulated that by carrying out this autonomous and environmentally conscious adaptive operation, the CR would be able to make the most optimal use of available radio frequency resources and installed network infrastructure and thus ensure highly reliable anywhere-anytime communications (Haykin, 2005).

CR was meant to start off a new disruptive development cycle in wireless telecommunications industry – a global behemoth in economic and technological terms. Contemporary developments in that industry find their roots in the policy, technology, and market developments of the 1980s. It may be therefore worth to take a short digress to review some of the lessons learned over those years.

Since the 1984 European Council's (EC) Recommendation 84/549/EC, which aimed to "stop the fragmentation of the European market, to help users to have cheap prices, and to help the European industry to have a wide market", as well as 1987 and 1990 EC's Green Papers outlining a common approach in the field of tele- and satellite communications, a European ICT market has been oriented towards common standards and user services (Fomin, 2001; Paetsch, 1993).

The case of GSM is likely to be the most often quoted success story of the European standards development. The harmonized common market regulation may confidently be called one of success factors for GSM, as the then developed policy forced EU countries to allow GSM handsets to freely roam across the entire European region.

Ever since the dawn of deregulation of the European telecommunications market, politicians argue for more competition and better telecommunication services for the public (Tardy & Grøndalen, 2010). Users seek lower prices of and wider accessibility to broadband access, and operators seek to satisfy the growing demand for mobile broadband while striving to overcome capacity limitations due to lack of the radio spectrum (Tardy & Grøndalen, 2010).

The success of GSM standard, also referred to as Second Generation (2G) technology, built the ever-growing market base for standards evolution towards third (3G, such as UMTS) and fourth generation (4G, such as LTE or WiMAX) technologies. The 3G and 4G had then to balance the strong demand for broadband services with certain technological uncertainties posed by ever competitive deregulated market in which regulators had been gradually shying away from championing particular technologies. As a result, the technological evolution took very careful progression in the market whereas new radio technologies were being introduced as add-on rather than replacement of older generations. It is this multi-standard operational environment, which spawned the way to commercialization of professional SDR solutions, such as re-configurable base stations. The evaporating availability of radio frequencies for mobile network operation due to radio spectrum being overcrowded by different technologies cre-

ated a need for autonomously reconfigurable CR solutions, especially on the side of user handsets to address the re-configurability and shortage of frequencies in the most elegant way.

Clearly, the radio spectrum, to this date, is a cornerstone of the global wireless industry. Each wireless system has an assigned (often exclusively) frequency band, and each wireless device "must have one RF module (and related antennas) for each wireless communication system being supported like GSM/UMTS, RFID, GPS, DVB-H or FM-radios" (Kloch et al., 2009).

Such reliance of the wireless industry on having access to suitable radio spectrum is both an enabler and a bottleneck of innovation process at the same time. The strict frequency assignment along with the associated lengthy and rigid international process of administrative frequency allocation often results in inefficient use of this critical resource that is equally important to service provisioning of existing systems and the appearance of innovative designs and applications (Federal Communications Commission, 2010b). While satisfying the demands of policy and market stakeholders would require finding ever "more frequencies" for provision of spectrum-hungry services, such as e.g., broadband wireless Internet access, measurements have repeatedly shown that at any location at any time a large portion of the spectrum is actually not used (Tardy & Grøndalen, 2010). It is in this context that the advent of CR, and more specifically – its promise of DSA paradigm of opportunistic spectrum access, can be seen as bringing a disruptive transformation to the extant relationships between the industry stakeholders. Other than DSA, the CR technology promises improved management and optimization of the radio networks through load balancing, easier deployment and adaptability (the "Self-Organized Network" - SON concept), as well as radio resource usage optimization, among other (Mueck et al., 2010), which also means freeing service providers from the strict association of specific bands to specific radio access technologies (RATs) (Tardy & Grøndalen, 2010). All such improvements on network organization and operation side represent important, albeit non-disruptive technological developments that are actively pursued by cellular industry and is well featured in newest editions of 3GPP standards.

However, while the latter technology of reconfigurable networks had been slowly finding its way to the professional market, in keeping up with the need to address the new generations of multi-RAT network provisioning, at the same time the fully-fledged CR operation of the DSA kind, especially for non-infrastructure based autonomous user terminal devices remains an elusive target. It may be seen that after 15 years since its inception, the CR operation of the DSA variety is still lingering in the very first phase of technological development, which could be described as "R&D race" (Suarez, 2004). Until the first milestone – a commercial prototype – had been reached, the prospects of CR will be marred by the uncertainties of nascent R&D competition. The situation with CR development is further complicated by the fact that so far there does not appear any strong leading firm, a champion of the CR technology that would drive the development and prototyping, including the sponsorship of technological standard. However, the research shows that it is the absence of clearly defined business case that prevents the appearance of firm-champions and more active development of CR technologies (Fomin & Medeisis, 2012).

2.2 The Many Perspectives on Innovation

Theories on evolution of technology characterize the development of infrastructural/disruptive technology as punctuated equilibrium (Levinthal, 1998), in which technological advancement is seen as a linear process of change, where technology evolves through several stages (see Figure 1). First market introduction takes place in niche markets, in which technologies gradually improve through competition and reach maturation, ready to evolve out of the niche as soon as there are changes in wider environment which create a fit between the general market needs and the evolving niche technology, or when the changes render the old technology inadequate (Schot & Geels, 2007). Here, different stages imply different sets and "orientations" of factors affecting the innovation process – if at the "R&D" stage technological viability is the key, then at the "Innovation/market introduction" stage the development must be supported by sound economic model, and, later, the advancement through "Broader diffusion" stage depends on institutional and cultural context (Schot & Geels, 2007). Given that for the moment the CR development seems to be stuck in the very first phase, one may apply this theoretical lens to deduce explanation that pending market introduction and thus slow market uptake of CR is the result of absence or deficiency of CR business models and their associated technology use scenarios.

The critics of evolutionary technology model argue that entrepreneurial actions in bringing

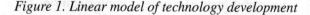

Figure 1. Linear model of technology development

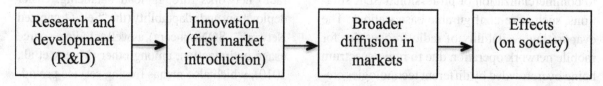

R&D output to the market in complex technology systems' context are too "heavy" to be leveraged by individual firms (Van de Ven, 2005). Studies of large technical systems (LTS, see Hughes, 1993) refute the linear logic of technology development activities and instead highlight the messiness, heterogeneity, and complexity of technological development (Schot & Geels, 2007), where multiple system builders are dealing with intricately intertwined economic, political, and technology factors in their attempt to create and stabilize a network of key stakeholders, technology, and its use scenarios (Fomin & Lyytinen, 2000; Schot & Geels, 2007). If stabilized, such network becomes a cradle for successful innovation and diffusion to the broader market. Applying this theoretical lens to deduce explanation for slow market uptake of CR would require a scholar to seek the "missing threads" in the socio-techno-institutional web holding together the activities and the actants of the CR innovation.

Attempting to reconcile the linearity with the heterogeneity, the "innovation journey" approach to innovation (Van de Ven et al., 1999) postulates that evolutionary stages must be supported by a process infrastructure, which includes, among other, basic scientific knowledge, financing mechanisms, consumer markets, R&D, manufacturing, institutional arrangements, etc. (Van de Ven et al., 1999). The institutional arrangements here are needed to legitimize and *standardize* a new technology (Schot & Geels, 2007). Strategic niche management (SNM) approach (Schot & Geels, 2007; Schot et al., 1994) further posits that *stable technology* is the precondition for the innovation journey to proceed with market introduction and diffusion (Schot & Geels, 2007). For the technology to become stable (i.e., to be standardized), the innovation process must be facilitated by the creation of technological niches, i.e. "protected spaces" where actors could experiment with new technologies in real-life situations. Pilot projects and demonstration projects should allow firms, policy makers, users and other stakeholders to

interact and facilitate mutual learning processes (Schot & Geels, 2007). Applying this theoretical lens to deduce explanation for slow market uptake of CR would require a scholar to reveal the obstacles preventing technology to stabilize or protected niche to form, or both.

The aforementioned perspectives adopting the network (web) view on technology innovation process can be complemented by the studies, which specifically focused on the role of standards. The role of *technology standards* as enabling or crucial factors in building and stabilizing the heterogeneous innovation network has been addressed in a number of innovation studies that specifically focused on the development of complex wireless technologies and services (Fomin & Lyytinen, 2000; K. Lyytinen & King, 2002; Yoo et al., 2005). Lyytinen and King (2002) argued that standards are the only means by which complex technology innovation can see a broad market adoption. Yoo et al. (2005) argued that (1) technology standards become the binding elements in creating networks of diverse players pursuing the development of the same technology, (2) standards offer ways to integrate and generate technical knowledge that is critical for the successful implementation of the infrastructure; and (3) standards help regulate and create markets. On the other hand, it was argued that overly strict standardization policies or rapid standardization processes are likely to lead to lock-ins to obsolete or inferior (technological) solutions (Fomin et al., 2008; Yoo et al., 2005).

The role of standards in innovation process, where neither the standard-based product(s) nor the market(s) have been developed yet can only be discussed within the context of *anticipatory standardization. Anticipatory standards* define future capabilities of technology or services *ex ante* in contrast to *ex post* standardizing existing practices or capabilities through *de facto* standardization in the market. In doing so, they embed significant technological or process innovations into the technical specification which are "intended to guide the emergence of new technologies and consequently indicate far ahead in advance the market's ability to signal the features of products that users will demand" (David, 1995, p.29). *Anticipatory standardization* in the context of CR, then, can be seen as "a network of events that create and coordinate institutionally-bound and contextualized technological repertoires (capabilities) to be adopted among a set of heterogeneous actors" (K. J. Lyytinen et al., 2008, p.2).

To summarize, the popular theoretical frameworks to technology innovation seem to agree on two issues: (1) there are different innovation contexts which must be considered – technological, economic, institutional; and (2) developing a stable network of heterogeneous actors (around a technology standard, regulatory decree, market practice, or else) is a prerequisite for successful innovation.

In this context, the current state of CR development can be regarded as an *anticipatory technology standardization process* (K. J. Lyytinen et al., 2008), as no dominant technology design(s) has emerged, and no broad market deployment(s) has taken place. This leaves open the question *what kind of stabilizing element is needed* for the CR innovation process to succeed. Given the complexity of the process and heterogeneity of actors-network to be created and stabilized, it is unclear whether the sought-for stabilization would materialize in a form of a technology standard, established market niche, regulatory regime, or some mix of the above (or something else yet). Yet, it is argued that the nascent technological proposition could receive the sufficient push into the marketplace only when (self-perceived) interests of the different actors are well aligned (Anker, 2010). It is then even less certain as to whether the necessary alignment of interests of different actors-stakeholders could emerge as the ultimate catalyst of change.

To yield a better understanding as to which domain of the CR innovation process has a greater potential to contribute to the network stabilization process, in the following section we show

an attempt at a multi-domain analysis of the contextual environment in which CR innovation is taking place.

3. CO-EVOLUTIONARY ANALYSIS OF THE CR INNOVATION PROCESS

Given the complexity of CR innovation process and heterogeneity of current and potential key stakeholders who may take a lead in developing CR-related standards, in makes sense to examine technology innovation process from a co-evolutionary perspective. Co-evolutionary analysis rests on a presumption that for each group of stakeholders there are factors, which being largely under the discretion of that particular group of stakeholders, interact with factors that are in part or fully external, but which may be influenced by a different group of stakeholders (Bauer et al., 2007; Chena et al., 2007). Previous studies on telecommunications standards development, which focused on the co-evolutionary dynamics of the market, distinguished three main stakeholder groups (or market domains): technology/innovation, policy/regulation, and economics/market (see Figure 2).

Two or more units in such a co-evolutionary system are said to co-evolve, if they each have a significant impact on each other. Events in one area affect (but do not fully determine) developments in related ones in anticipated and unexpected ways (Bauer et al., 2007). Thus, existing technology standards can constrain or foster the ability of service providers to deploy new features and services. Business decisions affect or are affected by policy choices and the technology standards. The evolution and overall performance of the whole industry is thus subject to interaction of and coordination between stakeholders representing the co-evolving domains.

Previous authors (K. Lyytinen & King, 2002) refer to the co-evolutionary process as "a large systemic innovation, which demands coordination of multiple independent and heterogeneous actors

Figure 2. Relationships between the innovation system, market place and the regulatory regime (K. Lyytinen & King, 2002). See also Figure 1 "Co-evolutionary dynamics" in Bauer et al., (2007).

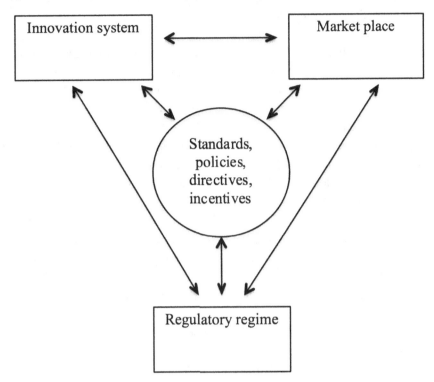

to ensure compatibility and interoperability across different systems." Adopting the lens of systemic innovation, analysis of the development, standardization and commercialization of CR would require examining the stakes those "heterogeneous actors", or stakeholders, bring to the table.

3.1 The Market Domain

In the context of this paper we are looking at the market domain through the prism of the service providers' business proposition to the end user - the consumer. This means that we are excluding from the analysis different market players that the service provision segment could be made of. Such simplification is warranted because the future structure and revenue sharing models of the service provisioning in the field of CR is not yet clear and may take various complex forms, as e.g. discussed in (Delaere & Ballon, 2008).

It is intuitive to assume that critical value proposition of CR to the consumer should be low(er) price and low(er) complexity, including billing complexity1, as compared to the current paradigm's services. According to a survey of telecommunication market consumers (European Commission, 2009a), the biggest thing that keeps people from using mobile broadband services is the high pricing (42%), followed by technology implementation problems (31%). However, supply diversity (Delaere & Ballon, 2008) should be retained to preserve competition.

The lessons of "cost control" strategy of 3G operators in Europe entering the market under strong competition from 2G operators/services seem to be feasible for the introduction of CR services, too. For example, when launching 3G services in highly saturated 2G UK's market, Hutchinson's '3' UMTS service was drawing customers purely on the basis of a voice package that effectively gave complete control of costs by offering a high number of inclusive minutes (Stewart et al., 2003). Also, when introducing 3G, mobile operators were interested in providing cost-effective mobile data services and thus capitalize on solution of the digital divide problem. Mobile data services and their cost reduction options were taking an important part in UMTS business planning for operators in different European countries.

The cost control factor aspect is tightly related to extant operator's strong position as "holders" of sophisticated billing systems. Telcos and MNOs have installed on their networks billing systems which permit the service providers to bill per second of voice or video call, per message or per kilobyte of data, or for any other transaction. Associated with billing are the security and authentication systems that make it secure and trustworthy (Stewart et al., 2003). "Rather than having just one way of billing, this sophisticated billing system allows operators to package 'service products' to bill for any unit – a piece of information, a photograph, a phone call, irrespective of any actual costs to deliver, or relative the cost of another service product" (Stewart et al., 2003).

Combination of SIM identification with the power of billing systems potentially allow use of many different wireless access systems into one bill for the end user (Stewart et al., 2003), thus rendering the complexity of supplied services simple in the eyes of consumer. Should new CR-enabled services lack the billing and access simplicity of the current paradigm, adoption of services is likely to see retardation.

"The next big thing" after 3G in the wireless broadband may become the rubric of "Future Wireless Home Networks", which was seen as one of important demand drivers for CR systems. The DSA-based spectrum access would give the home networking a solid basis for flexible unlicensed development beyond the current confines of ISM bands (most notably the 2.4 GHz band which had long become a key case of overcrowded commons). Not burdened by spectrum licenses,

home wireless networking based on IEEE 802.11 technology (Wi-Fi) has in the last decade become a truly pervasive technology (Nekovee, 2009). Already today a large majority of Europeans who have an Internet connection to home and own a computer are using Wi-Fi routers at home. In the future, the wireless traffic in home environment will grow exponentially, as the Future Wireless Home Networks will embrace not only Internet connection for computers, but also media servers (High Definition TV, video and audio), wireless cameras and game consoles wirelessly connected to the Internet and one another (Nekovee, 2009). Moreover, the concept of Unlicensed Mobile Access (UMA) and Multi-path TCP (MPTCP) technologies as part of "Future Wireless Home Networks" also covers novel seamless voice and data communication possibilities, with enabling multi-mode handsets to roam between 2G/3G/4G and home Wi-Fi networks without disrupting active voice calls or data sessions. While the growth in home networking traffic would depend on having a wired high-speed Internet connection to home, predominantly meaning Fibre to the Home (FTTH), nevertheless the ultimate home connectivity would be realized wirelessly due to growing proliferation of laptop PCs and smart-phones/tablets as the prime devices for using Internet services on their own or as a complement to fixed devices (the point in case being the concept of "second screen" as the key enabler of interactive TV, whereas a smartphone/tablet PC is used as an interactive console to complement a such stalwart fixed device as TV set). This is well evidenced by the fact that today the FTTH providers employ wireless routers as the terminating device (a Home Gate-Way – HGW) at customer premises. Another important driver for wireless home networking is the "femto-cell" concept driven by the cellular operators. Femto-cells could indeed provide a win/win situation for both the operator (reducing risk of traffic overload of their wide-area network) and the customer (having a multi-functional wireless access solution of a home cell that could provide both voice and broadband data to mobile/portable terminals while enjoying favorable pricing on the provided services).2

CR is also expected to be widely deployed by Wireless Internet Service Providers (WISPs) to offer metro-area broadband coverage systems for business enterprises, as long as these services can protect incumbent licensed users as well as be commercially viable (Borth et al., 2008). For a long time this was one of key applications driving the R&D activities aiming to offer DSA operations in TV bands (TV White Spaces – TVWS concept). Possibility of using TVWS would give access to large (8 MHz in Europe) channels suitable for high-speed broadband transmissions (Borth et al., 2008). Besides, there are better propagation characteristics in the VHF and UHF TV bands compared to that in other higher frequency unlicensed bands (e.g. 2.4 GHz or especially the 5 GHz bands used for Wi-Fi). The technical features of TV bands influence commercial viability of the CR systems utilizing - lower total cost of ownership than competing systems (Borth et al., 2008).

To summarize, for the consumers, the introduction of CR-based technologies might offer improved access to a plethora of existing and future innovative RATs and operations in different frequency bands. The CR standards would enable the mobile user "roam freely between different spectrums and choose preferable radio bearer according to cost and QoS", thus resulting in "Always Best Connected" paradigm (Damljanovic & Sippola, 2010). However, the attractiveness and utility of services in the mobile environment is not a static concept and thus its adequacy must be examined thoroughly "as a function of place, time, and social setting (e.g. commuting, shopping, or in need of medical assistance)" (J. I. Mitola, 2009).

3.2 The Technology Domain

For the manufacturers (equipment vendors) the shift to CR standards-based technologies would help shift innovation from hardware (HW) to software (SW) paradigm. This would also bear direct implications for other players in the technological domain: service providers (network operators) and application providers. Both of the latter could benefit from the SW-based technology paradigm: the service providers would see quickening of their network technology updating cycles while the application providers would further capitalize on the opportunities the SW-centered technological environment would provide them.

When device and service features can be altered by software, competition implies faster sequences of updates and improvement of operating behavior of technology. SDR and CR could improve the economic benefits for industry (and the consumers) by reducing the equipment implementation costs (European Commission, 2009b). Indeed, mobile telephony service providers have had one of their feet in this paradigm for at least since the introduction of the GSM networks. Annual or semi-annual firmware/software upgrades to network equipment helps mobile operators keep up with the growing demand for spectrum-hungry services through introduction of new GSM/UMTS standards and techniques into the communication network.

CR should lower the production costs for the manufacturers due to the shift from hardware-based rigid design to flexible "software-can-do-all" architecture (Collins, 2010; McHale, 2010). The volume of terminal and infrastructure equipment will be a driver for additional cost reduction opportunities (European Commission, 2009b). While telecommunications equipment manufacturers have since long been producing firmware upgradeable network and consumer devices, to date, CR remains an uncertainty, which means that manufacturers don't have solid incentives to invest into developing the technology. Besides, the cognitive features are likely to create higher entry barriers for manufacturing CR compared to conventional radio- and telephony- equipment, as the new technology is more complex (McHale, 2010). This can lead to a chicken and egg dilemma

- technology vendors will wait for large operators to announce the support for the technology to realize that there is a sufficient volume potential (Tardy & Grøndalen, 2010), while the operators, on the other hand, wouldn't support the technology, unless it is standardized and embraced by the manufacturers (European Commission, 2009b).

The inherent feature of CR technology to provide seamless multi-band access bode well for price savings on the network level. Motorola (Motorola Inc., 2007) points to operating frequency band costs as having the greatest cost implications. Motorola's prediction was that potential saving from deploying 3G/UMTS across various bands (in particular 900 MHz band) could reduce deployment/expansion costs up to 60%. This is already happening today with the deployment of LTE technologies in the 900 MHz band (790-862 MHz), known as "Digital Dividend" band, as it was freed from use for TV broadcasting thanks to its conversion from analogue to more efficient digital technologies. However this expansion of mobile LTE technologies into a new 900 MHz band did take place without relying on the CR paradigm, which further reduced the incentives for developing CR technologies and standards as pre-requisite of further developments.

So nowadays the only remaining attraction of CR to mobile industry is if it were to offer possibility of DSA to some new bands that would be otherwise inaccessible due to their allocation to other primary services. This is called the "traffic offloading" concept and it makes sense as the real time ad hoc interim access to otherwise unavailable spectrum might be still helpful for releasing at least some of the traffic from metro-area cellular networks during times of peak traffic load (busy hour). Thus the TVWS still remain of potential interest (Borth et al., 2008; Nekovee, 2009), even though their attractiveness had been of recently diminished due to reduction of TV bands (i.e. after extracting the "Digital Dividend" part) and the resulting densification of TV transmitters. Nevertheless, the so called White Space Devices (WSD)

are likely to become the first ubiquitous CR-type of devices on the market, whose introduction is driven by the possibility of having opportunistic access to the unused patches of radio spectrum in prime-value TV UHF bands.

The FP7's End-to-End Efficiency (E3) project (FP7, 2011), which aimed at integrating CR wireless systems in the Beyond 3G (B3G) world, carried out a research among operators and vendors, resulting in a list of expected value propositions and bottlenecks. From operators' position, perspective value propositions would be:

1. Operations in multi-radio access technologies environment (user terminal selecting the preferred network in data broadcasting services, working across national and international current and legacy networks);
2. Spectrum usage improvement and spectrum efficiency (secondary use of spectrum, dynamic spectrum allocation, flexible spectrum management);
3. Improvement of network operations (CapEx and OpEx reductions, RAN self-management);
4. Network scalability, upgradable equipment;
5. Stability of operations, good network performance.

Of these five propositions, only the 1st and 3-5th had been developing, whereas the 2nd one, the DSA, had been handicapped by the stalling development of CR technologies.

To summarize, there may be seen two major incentives for equipment vendors and operators in supporting CR standards development. The first would be the fact that CR helps shifting operation-defining features of technology from hardware to software, which implies faster sequences of updates and improvement of operating behavior of the equipment (and the application services it supports), as well as reduces the equipment implementation costs (European Commission, 2009b). The second would be linked to technological enabling of mechanisms for opportunistic access to radio spectrum for new wireless networks and applications (see next sub-section for more on that).

3.3 The Policy Domain

For the regulators, the promised CR paradigm may ease the growing pressure of spectrum allocation problem (due to fast growing demand for wireless data communications, for example) as well as endless dilemma of administratively choosing the most appropriate (worthy) recipient of any "new" spectrum. Therefore, centralized policy based management and control in the radio communications domain must be changed to accommodate self-organization of spectrum management operations (European Commission, 2009a).

With the world being increasingly challenged by natural disasters and emergency situations, one of the greatest beneficiaries of DSA might be the so called Public Protection & Disaster Relief applications, often associated with military, police and other governmental services (Damljanovic & Sippola, 2010). In situations where particular spectrum is overcrowded due to e.g., disaster-provoked escalation in the number of calling parties, mobile devices operating in one frequency band could change the RAT and have access to other parts of spectrum. A new CR based DSA standard could bring end to the currently existing fragmentation in emergency communications in Europe, where some countries adopted TETRA, while other – did not. By flipping the coin, however, it could be observed that if appropriate regulatory policies were set in place, the opportunistic spectrum access paradigm enabled through CR would allow civil users "borrowing" parts of the governmental (in particular - military) spectrum, not of which might be used in the normal circumstances of peace.

The concepts of CR imply certain architectural functionalities, two of which are that of flexible spectrum access and re-configurability of devices and networks. Self-organization and decentral-

ized control could necessitate the introduction of (different type of) central controlling entities (Damljanovic & Sippola, 2010; E2R II, 2007), which would be charged with defining the rules for interacting with competitors, acquiring spectrum, getting access to users, ensure that the transaction or administrative costs for spectrum users are as low as possible, prevent users withholding spectrum from trading for speculative reasons or other strategic motives, and ensuring that sufficient radio spectrum is available for emergency services, distress calls, military users and other institutions that serve the public interest, among other (E2R II, 2007). In the TVWS concept this central controlling entity took form of the "Geolocation Database" as the master manager of the WSDs deployed in its service area.

If the aforementioned requirements can be fulfilled, mobile communications customers would be granted always-best connectivity for optimally serving equipment and users, in terms of QoS and cost, and seamless mobility for rendering the users agnostic of the heterogeneity of the underlying infrastructure, while ensuring the consistency of application provision in the overall service area (European Commission, 2009b; Mueck et al., 2010). These "mobility and heterogeneity" features imply, among other, moving away from the traditional individual rights of use of spectrum where a license per operator is required to the so-called general authorization scheme with license-exempt or light-licensing regimes (Tardy & Grøndalen, 2010).

If no license is required, the equipment will solely have to comply with a pre-defined set of regulatory conditions. In the case of light licensing regime, the users of spectrum are to identify themselves and comply with the set of regulatory conditions (Tardy & Grøndalen, 2010) . While these changes may be beneficial to new entrant service providers and equipment manufacturers, the drawback with the license-exempt usage for regulators and incumbent service providers is that the more users, the more interference (Tardy &

Grøndalen, 2010). Therefore it is of paramount importance to construct the regulatory conditions for unlicensed use of CR so that they provide convincing insurances to regulators and incumbent service providers that the feared explosion of interference would not happen.

In the CR paradigm, it can be very difficult to monitor spectrum for interference, because sharing of spectrum by CR transceivers would make it difficult, if not impossible, to detect excessive sources of interference (Damljanovic & Sippola, 2010). This, in turn, may prevent the service provider from ensuring previously agreed QoS (Tardy & Grøndalen, 2010).

On the other hand, doing nothing and prohibiting CR is also not a viable regulatory option since regulators anyway always have to balance with new appearing sources and risks of interference (Damljanovic & Sippola, 2010). In that regard it could be noted that the current European Union's "New Approach" to regulation, such as the existing R&TTE Directive relevant to the field of telecommunications, is primarily based on self-declaration of product conformity with a set of essential minimum requirements and neither includes type approval nor registration of the equipment nor equipment identifier (Mueck et al., 2010) for certain conditions and certain classes of equipment. This means that the regulators have previously opened up the opportunities for industry self-regulation and therefore it would be now hard to change that trend.

In Europe, the regulatory support for CR can be said to have started from 2007, when the European Commission issued to CEPT in 2007 a Mandate on the "Technical considerations regarding harmonisation options for the Digital Dividend" (Medeišis 2014). The resulting CEPT Report 24 (2008) provided a high level policy framework for all further European developments in this field (Medeišis 2014). In the following years, with the involvement of national regulatory bodies a number of CR-oriented technical reports were produced3.

Standardisation became another important element of the European regulatory support for CR technologies. European Telecommunications Standardisation Institute (ETSI) has taken a leading position in this with dedicating a number of Technical Committees (TCs) to CR and related wireless technologies (Medeišis 2014). The key ETSI group of relevance to CR is the TC Reconfigurable Radio Systems (TC RRS). However, given the complexity and fuzzy outlook of the full scale CR technology, the key focus of ETSI work today is directed at a better defined areas of developing the standards for WSD operation (ETSI, 2014) as well as re-configurable radio systems, as implied by the very name of TC RRS.

Given the ambiguity surrounding the nature of future CR services, and potentially big stakes involved in developing CR-based markets, one may assume standardization and regulatory efforts will be more and more directed towards interface standardisation (Fomin, Sukarevičienė, and Lee 2014) – CR systems standardisation "is really about interface standardisation", and not about CR-as-a-system (Mueck and Bekkers 2013).

However, standardisation focused (solely) on interfaces is not likely to give sufficient impetus to the CR innovation. Not only novel tools are needed for the paradigm-changing CR services. Orchestration of regulatory action (Anker 2010, Medeišis 2014) and business model development (Sukarevičienė 2014) are needed in creating totally new communications solutions and services.

To summarize, it could be concluded that for regulators (and policymakers in the broader sense) the CR could offer a promising new operational paradigm for substituting (in some bands) or complementing (in general) previous rigid administrative practices of spectrum assignment by new mechanisms of flexible market/industry self-regulation. It should be however noted, that this premise of broader market self-regulation may sometimes appear being against the regulators' instinctive bureaucratic self-interests in that it would be eroding their very own *raison d'être*.

Therefore regulators need an incentive for moving in that direction, e.g. as the one provided by co-evolutionary forces from market and technological segments, as well as from the higher levels of socio-economic development policies.

In that respect it could be also noted that regulatory steps alone, and especially if they are not brought to the necessary level of detail, will not bring about the expected change in technological regime or market development break-through. The point in case is an example TVWS policy developments in the United States. The FCC formally announced its intention to open TVWS for unlicensed use already in 2002. Then for decade the FCC hasn't approved a single radio device to use the TV bands, so complicated was the regulatory task of determining how TV stations and domestic TV receivers can share spectrum with WSDs (Hazlett, 2010). The resolution of that stalemate was only made possible thanks to subsequent, more detailed FCC ruling on the subject (Federal Communications Commission, 2010a), which was echoed by similar developments in Europe, most notably in the UK (Ofcom, 2008). Interestingly, these latest policy-making initiatives are being made in the context of significant lobbying by the various technological and market stakeholders, including industrial champions like Google. This again demonstrates the virtues of co-evolutionary development discussed in this chapter.

3.4 Summary on Co-Evolutionary Analysis

Multi-domain analysis of the CR innovation context suggests that those *service providers* and wireless equipment manufacturers who do not have sufficiently large stake in existing networks and technologies are the two groups that should be most interested in "disruptive" opportunities offered by CR. For these two groups the cognitive technology and associated (anticipated) regulatory flexibility should act as both the catalyst for technological and business development as well as door-opener to access the spectrum markets which were traditionally characterized as having stringent entry barriers for new players.

It may be also noted that *the policy domain* is especially well positioned to influence the overall developments in the related domains. This is because in technology and market domains we see many forces and factors that are of intuitive or general nature, whereas in policy domain the factors and forces appear to be of well manageable nature.

This leads us to suggest that the major conclusion of the co-evolutionary analysis is that the policy domain and its stakeholders – primarily the independent national regulatory agencies for telecommunications, but also the national governments at large and international (standardization) bodies (ITU, EU, etc.) should assume more proactive role at the current stage of technology development – i.e., they are better positioned to succeed in establishing an actor-network and leading it by creating windows of opportunities for new technological paradigms. Thus the policymakers could develop and promote the vision for technology and business development and coordinate activities of CR innovation processes.

4. CONCLUSION

The CR technology clearly represents the major potential force that could form the basis of the next largest breakthrough in the development of ubiquitous wireless broadband services. However, after more than a decade of R&D development the technology did not deliver on its promise of bringing disruptive change to the telecommunications markets.

In this work we reviewed different streams of literature on technology evolution to gain a better understanding on concept and status of CR innovation process. The development of CR today can be best conceptualized as anticipatory multi-thread standardizing process (K. J. Lyytinen et al., 2008) aimed at creating a platform for future technologies. The role of standardization in bringing CR to the market is essential (Kwak et al., 2011; Stewart et al., 2011), as non-standardized technologies can not be expected to bring a disruptive change on a global scale. For CR to become a "next big thing" in the world of telecommunications, global economies of scale must be created.

At the backdrop of an absent obvious leader in CR development, we conducted a co-evolutionary analysis to reveal a stakeholders' domain, which is favorably positioned to take a lead in CR development process. Based on the analysis, we conclude that the regulatory domain and regulatory stakeholders represent some of the most crucial enabling factors that may decide the future of CR technology.

ACKNOWLEDGMENT

This work was supported in part by COST Action IC0905 TERRA "Techno-Economic Regulatory framework for Radio spectrum Access for Cognitive Radio/Software Defined Radio" (www.cost-terra.org).

REFERENCES

Anker, P. (2010) Cognitive radio, the market and the regulator. *Proc. IEEE Symposium on New Frontiers in Dynamic Spectrum Access Networks*. doi:10.1109/DYSPAN.2010.5457912

Bauer, J. M., Ha, I. S., & Saugstrup, D. (2007). Mobile television: Challenges of advanced service design. *Communications of the Association for Information Systems, 20*, 621–631.

Borth, D., Ekl, R., Oberlies, B., & Overby, S. (2008). Considerations for successful cognitive radio systems in us tv white space. In *Proceedings of DySpan*. DySpan. doi:10.1109/DYSPAN.2008.61

CEPT. (2008). *CEPT Report 24: A Preliminary Assessment of the Feasibility of Fitting New/future Applica-Tions/services into Non-Harmonised Spectrum of the Digital Dividend (namely the so-Called 'White Spaces' between Allotments)*. Retrieved from http://www.erodocdb.dk/

Chen, C., Watanabe, C., & Griffy-Brown, C. (2007). The co-evolution process of technological innovation—an empirical study of mobile phone vendors and telecommunication service operators in japan. *Technology in Society, 29*(1), 1–22. doi:10.1016/j.techsoc.2006.10.008

Collins, L. (2010). *'Whisky and soda' solution to software-defined radio architecture*. IET Collective Inspiration.

COST. (2009). *Cost action ic0905 "Techno-economic regulatory framework for radio spectrum access for cognitive radio / software defined radio (terra)"*. Retrieved from http://www.cost-terra.org

Damljanovic, Z., & Sippola, U. (2010). *Towards digital innovation theory: Cognitive radio report*. Academic Press.

David, P. A. (1995). Standardization policies for network technologies: The flux between freedom and order revisited. In R. W. Hawkins, R. Mansell, & J. Skea (Eds.), *Standards, innovation and competitiveness: The politics and economics of standards in natural and technical environments* (pp. 15–35). Aldershot, UK: Edward Elgar.

Delaere, S., & Ballon, P. (2007). *Model implications of a cognitive pilot channel as enabler of flexible spectrum management. In Proceedings of 20th Bled eConference eMergence: Merging and Emerging Technologies.* Bled, Slovenia: Processes, and Institutions.

Delaere, S., & Ballon, P. (2008). Multi-level standardization and business models for cognitive radio: The case of the cognitive pilot channel. In *Proceedings of the 3rd IEEE Symposium on New Frontiers in Dynamic Spectrum Access Networks (DySPAN'08).* Chicago, IL: IEEE.

Doyle, L. (2009). *Essentials of cognitive radio. Cambridge wireless essential series.* Cambridge, UK: Cambridge University Press. doi:10.1017/CBO9780511576577

E2R II. (2007). *The e2r ii flexible spectrum management (fsm) - Technical, business & regulatory perspectives.* Author.

ETSI (2014). *Final Draft Standard EN 301 598: White Space Devices (WSD); Wireless Access Systems operating in the 470 MHz to 790 MHz TV Broadcats band; Harmonised EN covering the essential requirements of Article 3.2 of the R&TTE Directive. ETSI, February 2014.* Author.

European Commission. (2009a). *Future networks. The way ahead!* Brussels: Information Society and Media Directorate General.

European Commission. (2009b). *Radio spectrum policy group report on "Cognitive technologies". Final draft.* Brussels: Information Society and Media Directorate-General.

FP7. (2011). *Fp7 project ""End-to-end efficiency (e3)".* Retrieved from https://ict-e3.eu

Federal Communications Commission. (2010a). *Second memorandum opinion and order 10-074 in the matter of unlicensed operations in the tv broadcast bands* (Technical paper). Federal Communications Commission (FCC).

Federal Communications Commission. (2010b). *Spectrum analysis: Options for broadcast spectrum (Technical paper): Federal Communications Commission.* FCC.

Fomin, V. V. (2001). *Innovation, standardization, and sustainable development of cellular mobile communications on three continents.* Paper presented at the The 6th EURAS Workshop on Standards, Compatibility and Infrastructure Development. Delft, The Netherlands.

Fomin, V. V., & Lyytinen, K. (2000). How to distribute a cake before cutting it into pieces: Alice in wonderland or radio engineers' gang in the nordic countries? In K. Jakobs (Ed.), *Information technology standards and standardization: A global perspective* (pp. 222–239). Hershey, PA: Idea Group Publishing. doi:10.4018/978-1-878289-70-4.ch014

Fomin, V. V., & Medeisis, A. (2012). In search of sustainable business models for cognitive radio evolution. *Technological and Economic Development of Economy.*

Fomin, V. V., Pedersen, M. K., & de Vries, H. J. (2008). Open standards and government policy: Results of a delphi survey. *Communications of the Association for Information Systems, 22*(April), 459–484.

Fomin, V. V., Sukarevičienė, G., & Lee, H. (2014). State-of-the-Art in Policy and Regulation of Radio Spectrum. In *Cognitive Radio Policy and Regulation Techno-Economic Studies to Facilitate Development of Cognitive Radio.* Springer.

Haug, T. (2002). A commentary on standardization practices: Lessons from the nmt and gsm mobile telephone standards histories. *Telecommunications Policy, 26*(3-4), 101–107. doi:10.1016/S0308-5961(02)00003-4

Haykin, S. (2005). Cognitive radio: Brain-empowered wireless communications. *IEEE Journ. on Sel. Areas in Communicatons, 23*(2), 201–220. doi:10.1109/JSAC.2004.839380

Hazlett, T. (2010). Putting economics above ideology. *Barron's Editorial Commentary*. Retrieved from http://online.barrons.com/

Hughes, T. P. (1993). The evolution of large technological systems. In W. E. Bijker, T. P. Hughes, & T. J. Pinch (Eds.), *The social construction of technological systems: New directions in the sociology and history of technology* (pp. 51–82). Cambridge, MA: MIT Press.

Kloch, C., Bilstrup, B., Vesterholt, C. K., & Pedersen, T. P. (2009). *Roadmap for software defined radio - a technology, market and regulation perspective*. Danish Technological Institute.

Kwak, J., Lee, H., & Fomin, V. V. (2011). The governmental coordination of conflicting interests in standardisation: Case studies of indigenous ict standards in china and south korea. *Technology Analysis and Strategic Management, 23*(7), 789–806. doi:10.1080/09537325.2011.592285

Levinthal, D. A. (1998). The slow pace of rapid technological change: Gradualism and punctuation in technological change. *Industrial and Corporate Change, 7*(2), 217–247. doi:10.1093/icc/7.2.217

Lyytinen, K., & King, J. L. (2002). Around the cradle of the wireless revolution: The emergece and evolution of cellular telephony. *Telecommunications Policy, 26*(3-4), 97–100. doi:10.1016/S0308-5961(02)00002-2

Lyytinen, K. J., Keil, T., & Fomin, V. V. (2008). A framework to build process theories of anticipatory information and communication technology (ict) standardizing. [JITSR]. *International Journal of IT Standards and Standardization Research, 6*(1), 1–38. doi:10.4018/jitsr.2008010101

McHale, J. (2010). *Software-defined radio technology is enhancing communications in military and commercial applications worldwide*. Military & Aerospace Electronics.

Medeišis, A. (2014). European Regulatory Developments Related to CR. In Cognitive Radio Policy and Regulation Techno-Economic Studies to Facilitate Development of Cognitive Radio. Academic Press.

Mitola, J., & Maguire, G. (1999). Cognitive radio: Making software radios more personal. *IEEE Personal Communications, 6*(4), 13–18. doi:10.1109/98.788210

Mitola, J. I. (2009). Cognitive radio architecture evolution. *Proceedings of the IEEE, 97*(4), 626–641. doi:10.1109/JPROC.2009.2013012

Motorola Inc. (2007). *Minimizing the cost of umts/hsxpa networks*. Motorola, Inc.

Mueck, M., Piipponen, A., Kalliojarvi, K., Dimitrakopoulos, G., Tsagkaris, K., & Demestichas, P. et al. (2010). Etsi reconfigurable radio systems – status and future directions on software defined radio and cognitive radio standards. *IEEE Communications Magazine, 48*(9), 78–86. doi:10.1109/MCOM.2010.5560591

Nekovee, M. (2009). A survey of cognitive radio access to tv white spaces. *International Journal of Digital Multimedia Broadcasting*.

Ofcom. (2008). Ofcom awards spectrum licence to qualcomm uk spectrum ltd (news release). *Office of Communications* Retrieved May 23rd 2008, from http://www.ofcom.org.uk/media/news/2008/05/nr_20080516b

Paetsch, M. (1993). *The evolution of mobile communications in the u.S. And europe: Regulation, technology, and markets*. London: Artech House.

Schot, J., & Geels, F. (2007). Niches in evolutionary theories of technical change. *Journal of Evolutionary Economics*, *17*(5), 605–622. doi:10.1007/s00191-007-0057-5

Schot, J., Hoogma, R., & Elzen, B. (1994). Strategies for shifting technological systems. *Futures*, *26*(10), 1060–1076. doi:10.1016/0016-3287(94)90073-6

Stewart, J., Dorfer, W., Pitt, L., Eskedal, T., Gaarder, K., & Winskel, M. et al. (2003). *Cost and benefit of use scenarios. The selection environment for mimo-enabled multi-standard wireless devices including cost benefit analysis of various convergence technologies*. Edinburgh, UK: University of Edinburgh.

Stewart, J., Shen, X., Wang, C., & Graham, I. (2011). From 3g to 4g: Standards and the development of mobile broadband in china. *Technology Analysis and Strategic Management*, *23*(7), 773–788. doi:10.1080/09537325.2011.592284

Suarez, F. F. (2004). Battles for technological dominance: An integrative framework. *Research Policy*, *33*(2), 271–286. doi:10.1016/j.respol.2003.07.001

Sukarevičienė, G. (2014). Business Scenarios and Models for Use of Geo-Location Database in TV White Spaces. In Cognitive Radio Policy and Regulation Techno-Economic Studies to Facilitate Development of Cognitive Radio. Academic Press.

Tardy, I., & Grøndalen, O. (2010). Which regulation for cognitive radio? An operator's perspective. *Telektronikk*, *1*, 105–120.

Van de Ven, A. H. (2005). Running in packs to develop knowledge-intensive technologies. *Management Information Systems Quarterly*, *29*(2), 368–378.

Van de Ven, A. H., Polley, D., Garud, R., & Venkataraman, S. (1999). *The innovation journey*. New York: Oxford University Press.

Yoo, Y., Lyytinen, K., & Yang, H. (2005). The role of standards in innovation and diffusion of broadband mobile services: The case of south korea. *The Journal of Strategic Information Systems*, *14*(3), 323–353. doi:10.1016/j.jsis.2005.07.007

KEY TERMS AND DEFINITIONS

Anticipatory Standardization: A process of developing anticipatory standards, i.e., standards, which define future capabilities of technology or services ex ante in contrast to ex post standardizing existing practices or capabilities through de facto standardization in the market.

Co-Evolutionary Analysis: Analysis of a system, in which two or more units are said to co-evolve, i.e., they each have a significant impact on each other.

Co-Evolutionary Process: A large systemic innovation, which demands coordination of multiple independent and heterogeneous actors to ensure compatibility and interoperability across different systems.

Cognitive Radio (CR): A kind of an application built on top of the SDR technological base to enable "intelligent" on-the-fly self-reconfiguration of the radio system to adapt to the instantaneous state of the spectrum-space environment as well as to real-time user requirements.

Software Defined Radio (SDR): A radio system in which radio frequency (RF) emissions and operational parameters could be defined and re-configured by software.

ENDNOTES

[1]   Billing complexity is considered to exist if the end user is forced to enter into a billing relationship with more than one actor, which complicates an essentially transparent

service to the user and decreases user value (Delaere & Ballon, 2007).

[2] The point here is that when user deploys femto-cell at home, it collects the traffic from the domestic mobile devices and routes it to the network over the DSL or fiber by which the femto-cell is connected. This means that this traffic is off-loaded from over-the-air radio access channels of the operator. For the operator this means lower overall loading of base stations, hence fewer number of them needed in a city assuming eventual broader proliferation of femto-cells. Lower number of base stations is a substantial saving for the operator. These savings (or part of them) the operators are likely to pass over to the user in a form of reduced or payment-free tariffs in the "home-cell" to compensate for the subscribers' willingness to install a micro-base station at home.

[3] See e.g., ECC Reports 159, 185, 186.

Chapter 8
Standards for ICT:
A Green Strategy in a Grey Sector

Tineke Egyedi
DIRoS, The Netherlands

Sachiko Muto
Delft University of Technology, The Netherlands

ABSTRACT

This chapter analyzes standardization of mobile phone chargers to explore the role that compatibility standards might play in mitigating the negative impact of ICT on the environment. Building on insights gained from the economics of standards literature, the authors explore how the inherent effects of compatibility standards—such as reducing variety, avoiding lock-in, and building critical mass—can have positive implications for the environment. They argue that current standardization literature and policy have overlooked this important (side) effect of compatibility standards. Excessive diversity and incompatibilities in ICT generate e-waste, discourage re-use, and make recycling economically unviable; the authors, therefore, develop an economic-environmental framework for analyzing sustainability effects of compatibility standards and apply it to the case of mobile phone chargers. They conclude that well-targeted compatibility standardization can be equated to ecodesign at sector level and should be considered as an eco-effective strategy towards greening the IT industry.

INTRODUCTION

Following a much-publicized intervention by the European Commission, the mobile phone industry finally agreed in 2009 – after dragging its feet for two years – to introduce a standardized charger based on the micro-USB plug. In the Commission's communication surrounding the process, it was explicitly announced that by introducing compatibility there would be a reduction in the generation of e-waste and a significant benefit for the environment. The phone charger case illustrates that compatibility standards can contribute fundamentally towards improving the sustainability of the information and communication technology (ICT) sector.

In the remainder of the chapter we first consider the need to limit the direct impact of the ICT sector on the environment – which is negative and growing rapidly – by reviewing figures on energy consumption, use of scarce resources and e-waste. We briefly introduce the variety of sustainability-

DOI: 10.4018/978-1-4666-6332-9.ch008

targeted standardization activities already being undertaken by actors worldwide, before looking more closely at the sustainable impact of compatibility standards as such. Based on their effects on the market, we extend our economics of standards framework to include implications for the environment. These effects are illustrated by the mobile phone chargers case. Finally we discuss the potential use of compatibility standardization to achieve sustainability policy goals.

ICT AS A SOLUTION OR PART OF THE PROBLEM?

Implicit in many recent policy reports about the contribution of ICT as an enabler for sustainability in other sectors (Climate group, 2008; Capgemini 2009) is the assumption that ICT itself is a clean a sector. The negative externalities1 generated by the sector are often disregarded. For example, the influential *Climate Group* study (2008) notes that fifteen percent of the CO_2 emissions in 2020 can be saved by applying smart ICT in other sectors. However, the direct environmental and rebound effects, that is, the unintended side effects that negate the intended environmental benefits, are ignored or covered up (e.g. Climate Group, 2008, p.50). The parallels between current promises of ICT towards making an environmental contribution and the hopes held in the 1990s entail a warning. The rebound effects of the paperless office (direct, primary environmental effect) and teleworking (indirect, secondary environmental effect) have become classic examples (Egyedi & Peet, 2003; Van Lieshout & Huygen, 2010). While teleworking was hailed as a means to reduce mileage to work, studies show that it increased other transport (e.g. Travel during leisure time); and while ICT was expected to reduce paper use (i.e., 'de-materialization'), in reality – and primarily because of computers – between 1988 and 1998 it increased by a quarter (O'Meara 2000, p.129).

Indeed, in stark contrast with the immaterial notion conveyed by concepts such as 'virtual', 'web' and 'the cloud', the impact of ICTs on the environment is highly concrete. It relates to the energy and materials used in manufacturing products; the packaging and logistics of distribution; the energy and material consumption during use; and disposal at end-of-life. At each of these stages, standards can play a sustainability-enhancing role. Here, we focus on the two key problems of energy use and e-waste.

Energy Use

ICT is responsible for a growing proportion of the global energy consumption and greenhouse gas emissions. In a high profile report titled 'The Internet Begins with Coal' Mills (1999) already cautioned about the large amount of energy required for Internet use. He calculated that half a kilogram of coal was needed to send a file of 2MB. The energy consumption of the Internet, which was at the time eight percent of the total energy consumption of the United States, was estimated to rise within twenty years to 30 - 50 percent. Although Mills was accused of exaggerating (Koomey et al. 1999), he was justified in highlighting the rapid growth of the Internet and the enormous amount power which ICT requires (OECD, 2009, p.15). A major culprit is the energy necessary to cool the heat released by ICT equipment. In fact half the electricity in server rooms is spent on air conditioning (Clevers & Verweij 2007, p.22). Given the rising number of ICT users worldwide, number of ICT devices per person, capacity of processors, need for data storage and the trend toward always-on (ITU, 2008, p.4), it is to be expected that the current energy consumption of the ICT sector will increase further.

In 2006, the electricity consumption of ICT in the Netherlands amounted to 8.4 terawatt hours per year (Clevers & Verweij, 2007). This is equivalent to a capacity of 960 megawatt per hour. To indicate the extent of the problem: two nuclear power plants with the capacity of the one in Borssele, the Netherlands, would not be sufficient to generate this amount of energy. In this figure of 8.4 terawatt hours the energy required for the mining of raw materials, the production of ICT and the recycling of electronic devices are excluded. The Dutch ICT industry association ICT~Office estimates that the electricity consumption of ICT in the Netherlands is about eight percent of the total Dutch energy consumption (ICT ~ Milieu, 2009). In Europe, ICT products and services already consume 7.8 percent of the electricity and this proportion is projected to grow to 10.5 percent by 2020 (Forge, Blackman, Bohlin, & Cave, 2009).

Scarcity of Raw Materials

Scarce and expensive metals are used to make ICT products, such as cobalt in batteries, indium for LCD screens, gold for connections between components, and platinum in hard disks (Van Huijstee & De Haan, 2009). Annually 3 percent of the mined gold and silver, 13 percent of palladium and 15 percent of the cobalt are used for PCs and mobile phones (UNEP, 2010). The high prices of these scarce resources on the world market contribute to making these mines into stakes of regional wars (UNEP, 2010, p.48). For example, the profits from extracting cobalt and tin in the Democratic Republic of Congo play such a politically destabilizing role (SOMO, 2008).

The short lifespan of many IT and consumer electronic products in industrial countries intensifies the problem of scarce resources. Computers are often replaced after two or three years and cell phones often after less than two years (Wilde & De Haan, 2009; Van Huijstee, de Haan, Poyonen, Heydenreich, & Riddselius, 2009). Service providers may offer free cell phones (with charger) for an extended service subscription (Van Huijstee et al 2009, p.7). In these industrial countries, many sub-markets are already saturated and growth in the ICT industry increasingly depends on the demand for replacement.

Substitution is encouraged by improving equipment (faster and more memory), but also by new software releases that require increased computing capacity (Hilty, 2008; Ohanjanyan & Haven, 2000). While the new release arrives on the market, the next one is already on the roll. Such planned obsolescence (Overeem, 2009, p.56) has a major impact on the environment particularly because software and hardware markets are strongly intertwined. It discourages re-use of equipment and leads to more electronic waste.

E-Waste

The short lifespan of electronics also exacerbates the problem of their disposal at end-of-life. Currently, global e-waste generation is growing by about 40 million tons a year (UNEP, 2009b) and is an increasing health hazard in the developing world (Williams, Kahhat, Allenby, Kavazanjian, Kim, & Xu, 2008). Discarded ICT products are only partially repaired and reused. While the bulk of used metals can be recovered from the remainder of the waste (Van Huijstee & De Haan 2009, p.8), other raw materials undergo changes during the manufacturing process. Chemical reactions with other substances make their recovery impossible.

Because recycling is labor intensive, there is an economic imperative to ship waste to countries where labor is cheaper. Toxic waste is therefore being exported overseas to countries like the Philippines, India and China where the precious metals make informal handling of ICT waste a lucrative business. This is a problem for two reasons. From the perspective of recovering raw material, informal recycling is much less effective. For example, in Europe more than 95 percent of the gold can be recovered, compared with 25 percent when recovered in China and India (Van Huijstee & De Haan, 2009). Also from an ethical and societal point of view, informal recycling is a major problem. In an environment with "open air burning, acid baths and toxic dumping" children and adult workers run serious health risks (BAN / SVTC, 2002, p.1). Toxic bromide flame retardants used in fire-resistant coatings are released and affect the development of fetuses and their nervous system. The lead that enters the blood-stream of children affects their IQ and damages the nervous system (CREM, 2008, p.29). So far, the most ambitious attempt to address the e-waste problem has come from two EU directives. The European Directive on the restriction of the use of certain hazardous substances in electrical and electronic equipment (2002/95/EC) is designed to address the use of toxic substances in ICT equipment. The Guidelines on Waste Electrical and Electronic Equipment (2002/96/EC), WEEE in short, aims specifically at reducing ICT waste (Huygen & Van Lieshout, 2010). The WEEE is of interest because it makes ICT producers to a certain extent responsible for recycling their products, i.e., it aims at internalizing the environmental costs of the ICT industry.

ECONOMICS OF STANDARDS

Scholarly interest in standardization has grown during the last two decades particularly from economists (Swann, 2010), which reflects Borraz'

statement that, "there is practically no economic activity nowadays that is not framed, whether partly or totally, by standards" (Borraz, 2007, p.57). Unless indicated otherwise, in this chapter the term 'standard' refers to committee standards2. A committee standard3 is a documented specification "established by consensus (…), that provides, for common and repeated use, rules, guidelines or characteristics for activities or their results, aimed at the achievement of the optimum degree of order in a given context" (adapted from ISO/IEC, 2004, p. 8).4 This definition includes standards developed by formal standards bodies (e.g. International Organization for Standardization, ISO), standards consortia (e.g. World Wide Web Consortium, W3C) and professional organizations (e.g. Institute of Electrical and Electronics Engineers, IEEE).

From an economic perspective, committee standards represent three key functions (first column of Table 1; extracted from Swann, 2000). First, they have an informative function. They make life easier because we can refer to them and thus reduce informational transaction costs (Kindleberger, 1983). Such costs may entail, for example, the time and resources required to

Table 1. Economic-environmental framework: Market and sustainability effects

Function of Standards	Effects on the Market	Effects on Sustainability
Information	Increase market transparency. Reduce transaction costs. Correct adverse selection. Facilitate trade.	Ease consumer choice for green products and services.
Compatibility	Create network externalities. Increase competition. Decrease vendor lock-in.	Counteract planned obsolescence and forced upgrades. Extend useful life of products and their complements. Facilitate growth of re-use markets and viability of green products.
Variety reduction	Allow economies of scale. Build critical mass.	Reduce use of resources and waste. Create favourable condition for investing in green innovations. Ease automated disassembly and improve conditions for recycling. Can increase environmental efficiency gains in process design.

establish a common understanding. Standards reduce the costs of negotiations because "both parties to a deal mutually recognize what is being dealt in" (Kindleberger, 1983, p. 395). They reduce transaction costs between producers and costumers by improving recognition of technical characteristics and avoidance of buyer dissatisfaction (Reddy, 1990). They reduce the search costs of customers because there is less need to spend time and money evaluating products (Jones & Hudson, 1996). Because the information provided by standards increases market transparency, standards help to correct the occurrence of 'adverse selection'. Adverse selection takes place if the supplier of an inferior product gains market share through price competition because the supplier of a high quality product has no means to signal this information to potential consumers. Standards that contain information about quality will help suppliers to signal this information and minimize the likelihood that consumer selection is based on wrong assumptions. Moreover, because of increased market transparency, standards facilitate trade particularly in anonymous international markets, where parties to the transaction do not know each other.

Second, the committee standards we focus on also have a compatibility function. Compatibility can be of two types (David & Bunn, 1988, pp. 172):

- Complementary when subsystems A and C can be used together, e.g. plug and socket; and
- Substitutive when subsystems A and B can each be used with a third component C to form a productive system, e.g. the USB interface of a digital camera (A) and of an external hard disk (B) vis a vis the USB interface of a laptop (C).

Technical compatibility is achieved by using gateway technologies, that is, "a means (a device or convention) for effectuating whatever technical connections between distinct production sub-systems are required in order for them to be utilised in conjunction, within a larger integrated production system." (David & Bunn, 1988, p. 170). Notably, compatibility standards fall within this category. They interconnect and integrate subsystems in a way that allows subsystems from different suppliers to work together and replace each other. That is, standardized gateways loosen technical interdependencies between complementary and substitutive subsystems (Egyedi & Verwater-Lukszo, 2005), which is tantamount to increasing system flexibility (Egyedi & Spirco, 2011, p. 3), and reduce market interdependencies. They create a more open and competitive market. Because interfaces are standardized, consumers can more easily switch between providers and products, and are less easily locked-in (Farrell & Saloner, 1985), enhancing the market's overall economic efficiency. Standards also create a more innovative market environment as they facilitate the emergence of standards-based clusters of new economic activity. Example are the cluster of paper processing equipment and office products (e.g. printers, copiers, fax machines, binders) that has developed around the A-series of paper formats (ISO 216); and the cluster of Internet services based on TCP/IP.

The third main economic function of committee standards is that of variety reduction. It is heavily intertwined with the informative and compatibility functions discussed above. While the current formal definition of committee standard speaks more generally of "achieving an optimum degree of order in a given context" (ISO/IEC, 2004), an earlier definition of the Dutch standards body more explicitly mentions "(…) [creating] order or unity in areas where diversity is needless or undesirable" (Van den Beld, 1991). The principle aim of committee standards is to reduce needless and unhelpful variety by agreeing on a specification that can serve as a shared point of reference. Reduced variety facilitates economies of scale (i.e., cheaper units) and helps build the critical mass required for markets to take off.

By reducing needless and unhelpful variety, the market becomes more transparent (information function of standards) and runs more efficiently (compatibility function). The first two columns of Table 1 summarize the main functions and market effects of compatibility standards. As we will illustrate below, the functions information, compatability and variety reduction, offer a lens for identifying potential sustainability-enhancing effects of compatability standards.

STANDARDS FOR SUSTAINABILITY

Standards and sustainability are related in two distinct ways: some standards specifically aim to contribute towards a better environment while others have a different aim (e.g. creating compatibility) and inadvertently make a positive contribution. We start below with a brief overview of environment-oriented standards activities, These differ from the compatability standards discussed in the subsequent section because they explicitly target sustainability issues. In the case of the compatability standards, increased sustainability is as it were a side effect – albeit a potentially significant one, as we will argue.

Environmental Standards

A wide range of sustainability-oriented standards policies and initiatives exists. Some are general and thus also relevant to ICT. The 2010-2013 Action Plan for European Standardisation of the European Commission, for example, lists a number of proposed actions and mandated activities including the development of standards for energy efficiency (e.g. Smart Grids) and sustainability (e.g. air quality). Examples of generic standards initiatives are the management standards of the ISO 14000 and ISO 26000 series, and the standards for collecting data on, for example, climate change. ISO 14001 lays down basic requirements for the environmental management of an organization. Its

model for continuous improvement is applicable to any organization interested in establishing and maintaining an environmental management system, including those in the domain of consumer electronics (Singhal, 2006). Examples of more specific standards in the 14000 series include ISO 14044 on the requirements and guidelines for a product life cycle assessment and ISO 14062 on integrating environmental aspects into product design. Likewise, ISO 26000 is a management system standard that provides organizations guidance on social responsibility. Its scope includes guidelines for corporate responsible behavior towards the environment, covering issues such as sustainable use of resources, climate change mitigation and sustainable consumption.

Moreover, to evaluate and compare environmental policy options agreed methods are needed for data collection as well as standard indicators and statistics. In this regard, the standards developed by ISO, IEEE, the Organization for Economic Co-operation and Development (OECD) and the World Meteorological Organization (WMO) play a fundamental role (e.g. ISO/NP 14067-2 on quantifying and communicating the carbon footprint of products).

Meeting the challenge of a sustainable ICT sector has also become an important focus for many standards organizations. The ISO/IEC Software and Systems engineering Sub-Committee (JTC1/SC27) has worked on life cycle assessments and developed a standard on the corporate governance of information technology (ISO/IEC 38500:2008). Recognizing that ICT is responsible for a growing proportion of the global energy consumption and greenhouse gas emissions, a large majority of standards initiatives focuses on the energy efficiency of ICTs during use. The Alliance for Telecommunications Industry Solutions (ATIS), the European Committee for Electrotechnical Standardisation (CENELEC), Energy Star, the European Telecommunications Standards Institute (ETSI), the International Electrotechnical Commission (IEC), ISO, and the International

Telecommunication Union (ITU) have all developed standards aimed at improving the energy efficiency of electronic equipment. A number of recent initiatives are targeting the energy efficiency of networks and data centers (OECD, 2009b; ITU, 2009a).

Sustainability Effects of Compatibility Standards

Most initiatives discussed above focus on the use of standards as a means to improve eco-efficiency. However, the ICT sector also needs to become more eco-effective (Appelman, Osseyran, & Warnier, 2013). Few people realize that eco-effectiveness can also be a side-effect of compatibility standards, as we argue. We use the economic framework introduced earlier, that is, the main functions and market effects of compatibility standards, to explore this argument and induce in a systematic way the effects of compatibility standards as they relate to the environment. This approach allows us to formulate propositions that can usefully extend the framework to include environmental effects and serve as a starting point for further research. Table 1 column 3 summarizes the environmental effects mentioned in the propositions according to the most relevant – but in most cases closely interrelated - functions of compatibility standards at stake, i.e.: information, compatibility and variety reduction.

- **Standards Extend the Useful Life of Products, Peripherals and Accessories, Thereby Counteracting Planned Obsolescence:** By reducing variety and creating compatible complements and substitutes within and between (sub)systems, standards facilitate the replacement of some parts and the reuse of others. They facilitate refurbishing and replacement of spare parts and peripherals. For example, the carbon footprint of upgrading a PC

with a new RAM module is significantly smaller than manufacturing a new PC. Compatible interfaces increase the possibility for such upgrades and therefore increase product longevity. The same reasoning applies to interfaces between products and their peripherals. Standardizing these interfaces extends the longevity of peripherals and accessories.

- **Standards Reduce the Use of Scarce Resources and E-Waste:** Because product parts and complementary peripherals are less likely to become obsolete when a system is changed or upgraded, fewer will be replaced (less use of resources) and discarded (less waste).

- **Standards Counteract the Environmental Burden of Forced Upgrades:** A side effect of compatibility standards is that standards loosen interdependencies between (sub)systems and their providers. They reduce the likelihood of supplier lock-in and prevent situations in which consumers must keep abreast with forced ICT upgrades (e.g. because support for older software versions is withdrawn). Standards thus counteract the environmental burden of lock-in and forced upgrades.

- **Compatibility Standards Facilitate the Growth of Re-Use Markets:** Because standards facilitate refurbishing, replacement and reuse, the value of second-hand ICTs increases. Without standardized interfaces, well-functioning printers, game consoles, etc. might not be in demand for reuse market because consumers cannot be certain that they will find compatible complements and substitutes (e.g. cartridges and games). In the past, re-use and re-manufacturing have not been considered important economic activities. They tend to be neglected in economic analyses (Williams et al., 2008). However, the rising scarcity of resources makes it probable that these economic activities – along with recycling – will become increasingly significant.

- **A Level Playing Field Increases the Viability of Producing Green ICT:** Committee standards create a level playing field and increase competition among suppliers. Therefore, where there is demand for 'green' products, companies will have an incentive to compete on sustainable product features. Consumer independence from vendors is a prerequisite to achieve such a market.

- **Standardization Can Help Build a Critical Mass for Products and Thereby Creates a More Favourable Condition for Investing in Green Innovations:** The uncertain outcome of wars between rival technologies can lead to a hold-up of investments (Williamson, 1979): producers will postpone investments for fear of investing in a 'losing' system and having to write off sunk costs (i.e., costs that are specific and irreversible and which therefore cannot be retrieved). The same hesitations exist on the consumer-side. Consumers will postpone their purchases and the market will stagnate. An agreed standard is needed for the market to take off. This also applies to the market for 'green innovations' such as the need for a standardized charger for electric vehicles. The European Commission has issued an industry-endorsed (ACEA, June 24 2010) mandate to the European standards organizations for a common European charger on the grounds that incompatibilities would fragment the market and impede commercial success (European Commission, 2010, June 29).

- **A Transparent Market Makes It Easier for Consumers to Choose Green ICT:** Increased market transparency and reduced complexity due to information and variety reduction, and increased competition due to compatibility will make the ICT industry more susceptible to 'green' consumer demands (e.g. energy efficient production and use of ICT, demands for repair and replacement of parts). A transparent market allows producers to charge more for sustainable products. Consumers who are aware of the negative environmental externalities of ICT, will be better positioned to recognize and select 'green' and upgradable products and services, and thus to avoid adverse selection.

- **Standardized Interfaces Ease Automated Disassembly of Products and Thereby Improve Conditions for Recycling:** Ecological design is critical to green ICT because the energy and environmental costs of the product's lifecycle are determined in the design phase (EU, 2009, Article 7). Currently the emphasis has been on designing energy efficient ICT, which is also the main focus of *European Directive 2009/125/EC of 21 October 2009 establishing a framework for the setting of ecodesign requirements for energy-using products ecodesign.* However, ecodesign can also extend to product design that has the end-of-life of products in mind – for example the design of ICT products with standard clips and fasteners to more easily disassemble and efficiently recycle them (Van Huijstee and De Haan, 2009, p.16). Standardized interfaces between complementary subsystems can facilitate the automated disassembly of products. Increased automation of such processes would make recycling less labor-intense and heighten its economic viability.

- **Standards Facilitate Economies of Scale Which Could, Theoretically, Lead to Environmental Efficiency Gains:** Compatibility standards ease larger-scale production. This could lead to environmental benefits if production processes are then organized in a way that is more efficient in terms of energy use and the raw material required. Similarly, efficiency gains in transport could also reduce energy consumption. However, facilitating economies of scale could equally lead to more production and associated rebound effects. This proposition should therefore be treated with caution.

The positive environmental side effects of compatibility standards are summarized in Table 1 column 3. They concern product design (e.g. replaceability of parts and recyclability of raw material) as well as process design (e.g. material and energy efficiency). The main side-effects coincide with three design principles of the cradle-to-cradle approach (McDonough & Braungart, 2002): elimination of the concept of waste; the output of a system should provide nutrients for the biosphere or the technosphere; and no downgrading of material should occur; or, in terms of the Life Principles in biomimicry (Benyus, 2002; Biomimicry 3.8), compatibility standards foremost contribute to the principle 'be resource (material and energy) efficient'.

If correct – and elaborate research would be needed to further test, specify and quantify these effects – the combined propositions would be a plea for considering compatibility standardization as specific form of eco-design at sector level. While such research falls outside the scope of this chapter, in the following we explore the initial tenability of our propositions in a preliminary case study.

EXAMPLE: A STANDARDIZED CHARGER FOR MOBILE PHONES

In 2009 there were an estimated four billion mobile phones globally and about 500 million in Europe (Forge et al., 2009). In 2008 roughly 1.2 billion mobile phones were sold with as many chargers.

At least half of the sales was to replace 'old' phones. 51,000 tons of chargers were discarded that year (GSMA, 2009).75

European Commission's Initiative to Standardize

In February 2009, the European Commissioner for Enterprise and Industry, Günter Verheugen, made headlines, saying he was tired of waiting for industry to standardize the connector for mobile phone chargers, and threatened mobile phone manufacturers with regulation. He was concerned about the amount of electronic waste produced by consumers throwing away incompatible but still functioning chargers when switching phones. Given that chargers can weigh twice as much as the handsets themselves, the effects of fewer of them being produced, distributed and disposed would be substantial. It was not the first time the issue was raised. Already in December 2006 the Chinese government had announced that China would switch to the micro-USB connector ("China Spells out National Standard for Cell Phone Chargers", 2006). The industry, represented by the Open Mobile Terminal Platform, responded to the Chinese call by announcing standardization on the micro-USB connector in September 2007. But for a long time nothing happened (ANEC, 2009).

Faced with Verheugen's ultimatum, the industry signed a Memorandum of Understanding (MoU) with the Commission6 in June 2009 to develop a micro-USB standard. The European Standards Organisations (ESOs) were to facilitate implementation of the agreement. The standard was to lead to less hassle for consumers and have a positive environmental impact. In the words of the Commission: "The environmental benefits of harmonising chargers are expected to be very important: reducing the number of chargers unnecessarily sold will reduce the associated generated electronic waste, which currently amounts to thousands of tons." (European Commission, 2009) While the MoU only covered EU territory, the market for mobile phones is essentially global. Therefore, the MoU was also expected to have an impact elsewhere, which was particularly relevant given the rapid growth of mobile phone ownership also in the developing world (UNEP, 2010). In October 2009 also the International Telecommunication Union (ITU) announced that micro-USB would be its point of departure for work on the Universal Charger Solution. This 'energy-efficient one-charger-fits-all new mobile phone solution' would result in a fifty percent reduction in standby energy consumption and be up to three times more energy-efficient than an unrated charger (ITU, 2009c).

Although consumers were disappointed that the European Commission did not simultaneously address the connectors of other electronic devices (ANEC, 2009), Verheugen's proposal was widely welcomed - also by industry (UNEP, 2009). It helped industry to meet the requirements of the European WEEE Directive.7

Environmental Effects of a Standard for Mobile Chargers

The arguments the European Commission used to standardize mobile phone chargers illustrate many of the key environmental effects of compatibility standards discussed above. That is, a common standard will extend the useful life of chargers. It will facilitate their reuse. Fewer will be replaced, reducing the amount of e-waste generated. One (shared) charger will suffice for multiple phones. The storage of different types of plugs will be avoided – thus reducing the required amount of raw materials needed to produce additional plugs and reducing the amount of waste that would need to be managed. By standardizing plug and socket, a main cause of vendor lock-in and planned obsolescence in the mobile phone market is addressed.

Our extended economic framework points to additional environmental effects as well, i.e., that such standards are also likely to

- Facilitate the growth of re-use markets for chargers and mobile phones. Arguably, a second hand mobile phone would have more value if one could be certain to find a charger for it;
- Provide an incentive to compete on and invest in sustainable product features by creating a level playing field (including design for automated disassembly and energy efficiency). Standardization is an important step in unbundling the compatible complements of phone and charger; and
- Make it easier for consumers to influence the market (i.e. demand and select e.g. 'green' chargers).

CONCLUSION: COMPATIBILITY STANDARDS: A GREEN STRATEGY

ICT is sometimes hailed too uncritically as a means to achieve sustainability in other sectors. The lack of sustainability of the sector itself is neglected. Predictions about the increasing use of ICT worldwide and the Internet, in particular, signal a growing, serious environmental problem. While there are major national and European directives on hazardous substances, electronic waste and ecodesign, the perspective that compatibility standardization can have inherent positive environmental effects, as we argue in this chapter, has not been included so far as an – at times significant – policy angle in its own right. While usually initiated for economic purposes, compatibility standardization has, as we argue, the potential to become a green strategy, contributing towards addressing the growing problem of energy use and scarcity of precious resources in the ICT sector. We recommend that this vantage point is investigated further.

Research is needed that examines whether compatibility standardization can, indeed, be regarded as a form of ecodesign at sector level.

This requires, first, case studies that determine whether the environmental effects we identify are correct, complete, and/or have unforeseen rebound effects. They will help to further elaborate the economic-environmental framework developed in this chapter. Second, complementary quantitative data is needed about the environmental impact of compatibility. Third, although all parties, industry included, say they benefit from standardization, the example of the mobile phone chargers emphasizes that self-coordination by industry is not self-evident. We recommend a systematic analysis of the circumstances under which instances of market failure can take place in the light of our economic-environmental framework.

ACKNOWLEDGMENT

This chapter was originally based on a translation of a Dutch chapter 'Interoperabiliteitstandaarden voor ICT: Een groene strategie in een grijze sector', in: Valerie Frissen & Mijke Slot (Eds.), *Jaarboek ICT en Samenleving 2010, 7de editie: De duurzame informatiesamenleving,* Gorredijk: Media Update, pp. 221-239. It was strongly revised in response to comments from three anonymous reviewers of the SIIT conference (Berlin, September 2011), whom we dearly thank for their feedback and subsequently published as an article in *International Journal of IT Standards & Standardization Research, 10/1*, pp.35-48. In this chapter we have again introduced a few improvements.

REFERENCES

ACEA. (2010, June 24). *Auto manufacturers agree on specifications to connect electrically chargeable vehicles to the electricity grid.* European Automobile Manufacturers' Association. Retrieved from http://www.acea.be/index.php/news/news_detail/auto_manufacturers_agree_on_specifications_to_connect_electrically_chargeab

ANEC. (2009). *ANEC Newsletter, No.102–December 2009.* Retrieved from http://www.anec.org/anec.asp?rd=453&ref=02-01.01-01&lang=en&ID=251

Appelman, J. H., Osseyran, A., & Warnier, M. (Eds.). (2013). Standardization as ecodesign at sector level. In Green ICT & energy: From smart to wise strategies. London: CRC Press.

BAN/SVTC. (2002). *Exporting Harm: The High-Tech Trashing of Asia.* Seattle, WA: BAN/SVTC.

Beld, J.W. van den (1991). Technical standards not always commercially desirable. *Elektrotechniek- Elektronica, 2,* 22-24. (in Dutch)

Benyus, J. M. (2002). *Biomimicry: innovation inspired by nature.* New York: Perennial.

Borraz, O. (2007, January). Governing standards: The rise of standardization processes in France and in the EU. *Governance: An International Journal of Policy, Administration and Institutions, 20*(1), 57–84. doi:10.1111/j.1468-0491.2007.00344.x

Capgemini (2009). *Trends in mobility.* Utrecht: Cap Gemini/Transumo. (in Dutch)

China Spells out National Standard for Cell Phone Chargers. (2006, December 19). *People's Daily.* Retrieved from http://english.peopledaily.com.cn/200612/19/eng20061219_334047.html

Clevers, S. H., & Verweij, R. (2007). *ICT in flow. Inventory of electricity use by the ICT sector & ICT-equipment.* The Hague: Ministry of Economic Affairs. (in Dutch)

Climate Group. (2008). *Smart 2020: Enabling the low carbon economy in the information age.* Retrieved from http://www.theclimategroup.org/publications/2008/6/19/smart2020-enabling-the-low-carbon-economy-in-the-information-age/

CREM. (2008). *An analysis of the flows of electronic waste in The Netherlands.* Amsterdam: Greenpeace. Retrieved from http://www.greenpeace.org/usa/en/

David, P. A., & Bunn, J. A. (1998). The Economics of gateway Technologies and Network evolution: Lessons from Electricity Supply History. *Information Economics and Policy, 1988*(3), 165–202.

Egyedi, T., & Muto, S. (2010). Interoperability standards for ICT: A green strategy in a grey sector. In Yearbook ICT and Society 2010 (7th ed.). Gorredijk: Media Update. (in Dutch)

Egyedi, T., & Spirco, J. (2011). Standards in transitions: Catalyzing infrastructure change. *Futures, 43*(9), 947–960. doi:10.1016/j.futures.2011.06.004

Egyedi, T., & Verwater-Lukszo, Z. (2005). Which standards' characteristics increase system flexibility? Comparing ICT and batch processing infrastructures. *Technology in Society, 27*(3), 347–362. doi:10.1016/j.techsoc.2005.04.007

Egyedi, T. M., & Peet, D.-J. (2003). *Informatics & sustainable development.* Nijmegen: UCM/KU. (in Dutch)

European Commission. (2009, June 29). *Harmonisation of a charging capability of common charger for mobile phones – Frequently Asked Questions* [Press Release]. Retrieved from http://europa.eu/rapid/pressReleasesAction.do?reference=MEMO/09/301

European Commission. (2010, June 29). *Towards a European common charger for electric vehicles* [Press Release]. Retrieved from http://europa.eu/rapid/pressReleasesAction.do?reference=IP/10/857&format=HTML&aged=0&language=EN&guiLanguage=en

Farrell, J., & Saloner, G. (1985). Standardization, compatibility, and innovation. *The Rand Journal of Economics, 16*(1), 70–83. doi:10.2307/2555589

Forge, S., Blackman, C., Bohlin, E., & Cave, M. (2009). A green knowledge society: An ICT policy agenda to 2015 for Europe's future knowledge society. A Report for the Ministry of Enterprise, Energy and Communications, Government Offices of Sweden. Chiltern Close, UK: SCF_Associates.

GSMA. (2009, February 17). *GSM World agreement on Mobile phone Standard Charger* [Press Release]. Retrieved from http://www.gsmworld.com/newsroom/press-releases/2009/2548.htm

Hilty, L. M. (2008). *Information Technology and Sustainability. Essays on the Relationship between ICT and Sustainable Development.* Books on Demand GmbH, Norderstedt.

ICT~Milieu (2009). *ICT environmental monitor.* Woerden: ICT~Office/ICT~Milieu. (in Dutch)

ITU. (2008). *ITU and Climate Change.* Geneve: ITU.

ITU. (2009a). ITU-T Focus Group on CT and Climate Change. In *Deliverable 1: Definitions.* Geneva: ITU. Retrieved from http://www.itu.int/dms_pub/itut/oth/33/07/T33070000030001M-SWE.doc

ITU. (2009b). *ITU-T Focus Group on CT and Climate Change. Deliverable 2: Gap Analysis.* Geneva: ITU.

ITU. (2009c, October 22). *Universal phone charger standard approved—One-size-fits-all solution will dramatically cut waste and GHG emissions* [Press Release]. Retrieved from http://www.itu.int/newsroom/press_releases/2009/49.html

Jones, P., & Hudson, J. (1996). Standardization and the cost of assessing quality. *European Journal of Political Economy, 12*(2), 355–361. doi:10.1016/0176-2680(95)00021-6

Kindleberger, C. P. (1983). Standards as public, collective and private goods. *Kyklos, 36*(3), 377–396. doi:10.1111/j.1467-6435.1983.tb02705.x

Koomey, J., Kawamoto, K., Nordman, B., Piette, M. A., & Brown, R. E. (1999). *Initial comments on "The Internet begins with coal"*. Memorandum (LBNL-44698). Berkeley: Berkeley Lab. Retrieved from http://www.zdnet.com/news/networking/2007/09/20/micro-usb-to-be-phone-charger-standard-39289524/

Krechmer, K. (2006). Open Standards Requirements. *The International Journal of IT Standards and Standardization Research, 4* (1).

Lipsey, R. G., & Steiner, P. O. (1979). *Economics: An Introductory Analysis*. New York: Addison Wesley.

McDonough, W., & Braungart, M. (2002). *Cradle to Cradle: Remaking the Way We Make Things*. New York: North Point Press.

Mills, M. P. (1999). *The Internet begins with coal: A preliminary exploration of the impact of the Internet on electricity consumption*. Arlington, VA: The Greening Earth Society.

O'Meara, M. (2000). Harnessing Information Technologies for the Environment. In *State of the World 2000* (pp. 121–141). Washington, US: The Worldwatch Institute.

OECD. (2009a). *OECD communications outlook 2009*. Paris: OECD.

OECD. (2009b). *Towards Green ICT Strategies: Assessing Policies and Programmes on ICT and the Environment*. Paris: OECD. Retrieved from www.oecd.org/dataoecd/47/12/42825130.pdf

Ohanjanyan, O. & Haven, A. (2000). *From Microchip to Megamarket*. Internal document. (in Dutch)

Overeem, P. (2009). *Reset: Corporate social responsibility in the global electronics supply chain*. Amsterdam: GoodElectronics & MVO Platform.

Reddy, N. M. (1990). Product of self-regulation: A paradox of technology policy. *Technological Forecasting and Social Change, 38*(1), 49–63. doi:10.1016/0040-1625(90)90017-P

Singhal, P. (2006). *Integrated Product Policy Pilot on Mobile Phones, Stage III Final Report: Evaluation of Options to Improve the Life-Cycle Environmental Performance of Mobile Phones*. Espoo, Finland: Nokia Corporation.

SOMO (2008), *Mobile Connections: Supply Chain Responsibility of Five Mobile Phone Companies*. Amsterdam: SOMO.

Swann, G. M. P. (2000). *The Economics of Standardization*. London: Department of Trade and Industry, Standards and Technical Regulations Directorate. Retrieved from https://www.gov.uk/government/uploads/system/uploads/attachment_data/file/16506/The_Economics_of_Standardization_-_in_English.pdf

Swann, G. M. P. (2010). *The Economics of Standardization: An Update*. Report for the UK Department of Business, Innovation and Skills. Retrieved from http://www.bis.gov.uk/assets/biscore/innovation/docs/e/10-1135-economics-of-standardization-update.pdf

UNEP. (2009b) *Recycling – From E-Waste to Resources*. Nairobi: United Nations Environment Programme. Retrieved from www.unep.org/pdf/Recycling_From_e-waste_to_resources.pdf

UNEP. (2009a). *Guideline on the Awareness Raising-design considerations: Mobile Phone Partnership Initiative – Project 4.1*. Basel: United Nations Environment Programme. Retrieved from http://www.basel.int/industry/mppi/MPPI%20Guidance%20Document.pdf

UNEP. (2010). *UNEP yearbook 2010: New science and developments in our changing environment*. Nairobi: United Nations Environment Programme. Retrieved from http://www.unep.org/yearbook/2010

van Huijstee, M., & de Haan, E. (2009). *E-Waste*. Amsterdam: SOMO. Retrieved from http://somo.nl/publications-nl/Publication_3289-nl/at_download/fullfile

van Huijstee, M., de Haan, E., Poyhonen, P., Heydenreich, C., & Riddselius, C. (2009). *Fair Phones: It's Your Call: How European mobile network operators can improve responsibility for their supply chain*. Amsterdam: SOMO.

van Lieshout, M., & Huygen, A. (2010). ICT and the environment – Could it be a byte more? In Yearbook ICT and Society 2010 (7th ed.). Gorredijk: Media Update. (in Dutch)

Wilde, J., & de Haan, E. (2006). *The High Cost of Calling: Critical Issues in the Mobile Phone Industry*. Amsterdam: SOMO.

Williams, E., Kahhat, R., Allenby, B., Kavazanjian, E., Kim, J., & Xu, M. (2008). Environmental, Social, and Economic Implications of Global Reuse and Recycling of Personal Computers. *Environmental Science & Technology, 42*(17), 6446–6454. doi:10.1021/es702255z PMID:18800513

Williamson, O. (1979). Transactions-Cost Economics: The Governance of Contractual Relations. *The Journal of Law & Economics, 22*(2), 233–262. doi:10.1086/466942

KEY TERMS AND DEFINITIONS

Compatibility Standards: (Also called interface or interoperability standards). A technical agreement that allows two elements or subsystems to work together and/or function as a whole.

Eco-Design: The design of a product or process in a manner that addresses ecological concerns and improves their environmental performance.

Economic-Environmental Framework: A conceptual framework that identifies potential economic and environment impacts of compatibility standards.

Energy Use: The amount of energy required for IT services and by electronic equipment.

E-Waste: Waste from electronic equipment.

Mobile Phone Chargers: Equipment needed to charge mobile phones.

Scarcity of Raw Material: The lack of basic material for producing IT equipment.

Sustainability: Improving the quality of human life while living within the carrying capacity of supporting eco-systems (United Nations Environment Programme).

ENDNOTES

[1]   Externalities are the costs or benefits of a transaction incurred or received by members of society but not taken into account by the parties to the transaction. Externalities disappear when they are included in the cost estimate and become internalized. Externalities can be negative, e.g. polluting industry can drive down the value of houses in the area, or positive, e.g. a well-maintained park increases the value of houses in the neighborhood. (Lipsey & Steiner, 1979) The environment-related negative externalities of ICT production and use are often not in included in the calculated transaction costs.

[2]   The second sense in which the term 'standard' is often used, is that of *de facto standards,* that is, specifications that underlie products and services with a significant market share. An example is the PDF specification of Acrobat Reader. Initially this specification was not

meant to become a shared standard, that is, to be referred and built to by third parties; but its wide use has turned it into one.

3   The term 'open standard' is avoided because the debate it raises could distract the reader from the point we are trying to make. For the interested reader we point to Krechmer (2006).

4   We omitted "and approved by a recognized body" from the original definition in order to avoid – a mostly theoretical - discussion about which standards body is 'recognized' and which one is not, and to widen the term's applicability to widely used, non-formal committee standards as well.

5   This is based on the estimation that 1.2 billion mobile phones were sold in 2008. Given that between 50 and 80 percent of these were replacement handsets, this would amount to 51,000 - 82,000 tons of replacement chargers every year. (GSMA, 2009; based on data from UNEP, Gartner, European Commission Integrated Product Policy Pilot on Mobile Phones, University of Southern Queensland).

6   The fourteen companies who signed the MoU were Apple, Emblaze Mobile, Huawei Technologies, LGE, Motorola, NEC, Nokia, Qualcomm, Research in Motion, Samsung, Sony Ericsson, TCT Mobiles, Texas Instruments and Atmel.

7   For possible answers to why market coordination did not happen before see Egyedi & Muto (2010).

Chapter 9
The Rise of MP3 as the Market Standard:
How Compressed Audio Files Became the Dominant Music Format

Simon den Uijl
Erasmus University Rotterdam, The Netherlands

Henk J. de Vries
Erasmus University Rotterdam, The Netherlands

Deniz Bayramoglu
Technische Universität Darmstadt, Germany

ABSTRACT

Previous research has shown how various technologies became the market standard. This chapter presents some refined models and applies them to the case of compressed audio formats. The authors analyze the rise of MP3 as the market standard and identify several key factors that contributed to its success. First, a process of formal standardization reduced the number of competing compressed audio formats. Secondly, enabling technologies, in particular the rise of the Internet, contributed significantly to the success of compressed audio formats. The timing of market entry was important in the sense that when the rise of the Internet took place, MP3 was one of the few fully developed compressed audio formats. MP3 offered technological superiority (high fidelity at low data rate) versus its initial competitors. The technology also benefitted from dedicated sponsors that promoted market adoption. Due to the weak regime of appropriability, audio files in the MP3 format managed to spread quickly over the Internet. Lastly, the availability of complementary assets for MP3 fueled its market adoption and strengthened network externalities on both sides of the platform-mediated network.

DOI: 10.4018/978-1-4666-6332-9.ch009

1. INTRODUCTION

The recent downfall of the iconic photography company Kodak, caused by the paradigm shift from analog to digital photography, is a clear example of an innovative market leader that was among the first to identify a radical innovation but chose to bypass the opportunity because it cannibalized its existing market. Clayton Christensen first described this 'innovator's dilemma' in his bestselling book (Christensen, 1997). He showed that an excessive customer focus may prevent firms from creating new markets and finding new customers for the products of the future. As they unwittingly bypass opportunities, such firms clear the way for entrepreneurial companies to catch the next wave of industry growth.

In the last two decades, we have witnessed how audio codecs, in particular the MP3 audio compression format (also known as the MPEG-1 Layer 3 standard), changed the music industry. In 1995, when a representative of one of the organizations behind MP3 presented the idea of compressed audio distribution using the Internet and copy protection to the music industry, they replied "It all sounds very interesting, but what does this have to do with us?". Not only did the music industry fail to embrace the opportunity for music distribution over the Internet, but so did the market leaders in consumer audio equipment which were involved in audio compression.

This paper examines the rise of the MP3 audio compression technology, from its inception to when it became the dominant music format. It shows how a disruptive technology can change an industry and offer opportunities to new entrants. In the following sections, we will summarize previous research on platforms and platform competitions,

and describe our research methodology. This is followed by a detailed case description, case analysis and our conclusions.

2. THEORETICAL OVERVIEW

The body of literature on management of technology and innovation, labels compressed audio formats as platform technologies. Platforms are products, technologies or services consisting of core components which remain stable, and interfaces which allow the core components to operate with complements as one system (Baldwin & Woodard, 2009). Interfaces are often codified into standards. Platforms may occur on multiple levels of a product's architecture: a personal computer is a platform, and its operating system as well. Platforms may enable 'platform-mediated networks', facilitating the interaction between two groups of users, the supply network (which provides complementary products) and the demand network (Eisenmann et al., 2006). For example, in the case of the Compact Disc platform, the record labels constitute the supply network and the consumers constitute the demand network. Other well-known examples where content providers and consumers interact through platforms can be found in the video (e.g. VHS and DVD) and videogame industry (e.g. PlayStation). The platform's value to a user depends on the size of the network on the other side, and the two networks attract each other (Rysman, 2009). This phenomenon whereby the functionality for a user increases, i.e. complementary goods become more plentiful and lower in price, if more users join is known as cross-side or indirect network externalities (Arthur, 1994; Arthur, 1996; Eisenmann et al., 2006; Liebowitz

& Margolis, 1994). Platforms can also experience same-side or direct network externalities, whereby an increase in the number of users on one side of the network makes the platform either more or less valuable to users in that network. Since platform mediated networks are prone to externalities, industries governed by platform technologies often have a single platform that has a dominant market share, or in other words, can be regarded as the market standard.

The field of innovation management includes a significant collection of academic papers and books on platforms competing to become the market standard, including VHS versus Betamax (Cusumano et al., 1992; Rosenbloom & Cusumano, 1987), Blu-ray versus HD-DVD (Gallagher, 2012), color television versus black and white television (Willard & Cooper, 1985), and various generations of video game consoles (Gallagher & Park, 2002; Schilling, 2003; Shankar & Bayus, 2003). Organizations that obtain technological market dominance can potentially earn near-monopoly rents (Schilling, 2005), whereas those that are unsuccessful forfeit most of the investment in their technology. These 'winner-take-all' markets demonstrate very different competitive dynamics than markets where competitors coexist relatively peacefully, as they often have a single tipping point which shifts the balance to one side.

Eisenmann (2008) has shown that there are roughly four different models for organizing platforms: proprietary, licensing, joint venture and shared. As Figure 1 shows, these models differ by the number of platform sponsors (parties that control the technology and participation rights) and platform providers (parties mediating interactions between users in two-sided networks). The platform sponsors of competing platforms often choose different models. The specific situation dictates which model works best. During a platform competition, a model may evolve towards a hybrid form by implementing aspects of another model.

Previous research by Suarez (2004) provides a framework which links eight factors (technological superiority, complementary assets and credibility, installed base, strategic maneuvering, regulation, network effects and switching cost, regime of appropriability, and characteristics of the technological field) to a five-phase division of a platform competition: R&D build-up, technical feasibility, creating the market, decisive battle, and post dominance. Suarez posits that a platform competition can be described in terms of a few key milestones, and each marks the start of a new phase in the competition. The start of the R&D build up can be traced back to the moment when a pioneer firm or research group starts applied R&D aimed at the technological innovation.

Figure 1. Models for organizing platforms (adapted from Eisenmann, 2008)

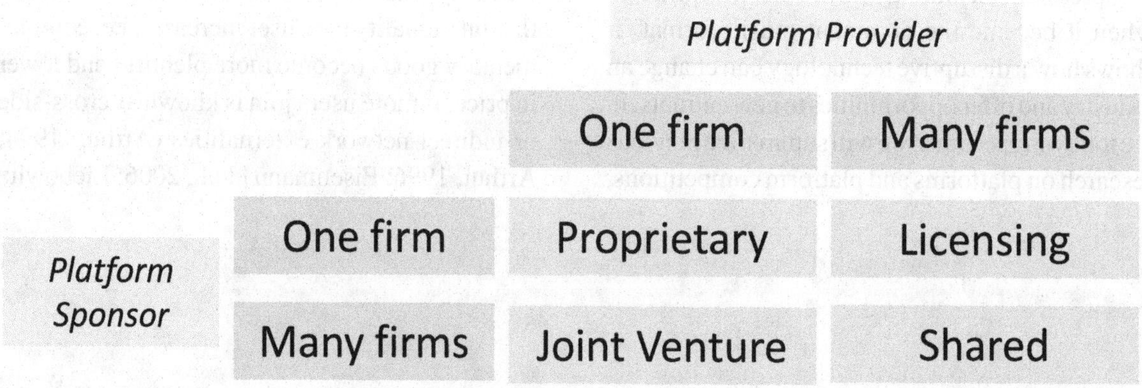

		Platform Provider	
		One firm	Many firms
Platform Sponsor	One firm	Proprietary	Licensing
	Many firms	Joint Venture	Shared

The second milestone is the appearance of a first working prototype based on the technological innovation. This marks the start of the 'technical feasibility' phase during which platform sponsors start to prepare for market entry. The phase of creating the market is triggered by the market introduction of a first commercial product of the new technology. After the platform competition has commenced, a particular design can become a front-runner. The presence of this front-runner is the fourth milestone and marks the start of the decisive battle. The front-runner has the best chance of winning the competition, as its larger installed base tends to create a bias towards the technology with the largest market share. Finally, a specific technological design achieves dominance and the competition moves into the last phase: post dominance.

3. RESEARCH METHODOLOGY

In order to study the rise of MP3 as the market standard, we have refined Suarez's phase division of a platform competition, and combined these with factors known to influence the decision of users in two-sided networks to adopt a particular technology.

In the emergence of a market standard, a new technology needs to compete against alternatives, displace the existing de-facto standard, and be cautious not to be leapfrogged by a substitute. While studying platform competitions, we found that a platform first becomes dominant in a specific market niche, and then competes for dominance in a product category. An example of this is the video industry where Blu-ray first competed against HD-DVD and became the dominant platform for high-definition video storage and distribution, but is currently competing with DVD for dominance in the product category. We modified Suarez's model accordingly by adding the phase 'Winning the mass market' and renaming some of the other phases to better fit our ideas. An overview of the phases is shown by Figure 2.

To determine which factors influence the adoption of a particular technology by users in two-sided networks, we examined 40 papers in academic journals on the emergence of market standards, and identified and consolidated the factors which influence users to adopt a particular technology. The resulting overview provided 46 factors (Den Uijl & De Vries, 2008). By combining these factors with the six phases in a data matrix, we created a framework for identifying which factors influenced the rise of MP3. The

Figure 2. Six phases of platform competition (adapted from Suarez, 2004)

factors in the data matrix function as a checklist in each phase of the platform competition. We used the same list of factors to determine the number of factors found in previous case studies (Christensen, 1993; Cusumano et al., 1992; David, 1985; David & Bunn, 1988; Gallagher & Park, 2002; Garud & Kumaraswamy, 1993; Garud et al., 2002; Khazam & Mowery, 1994; Rosenbloom & Cusumano, 1987; Shankar & Bayus, 2003; Smit & Pistorius, 1998; Tripsas, 1997; Wade, 1995; Willard & Cooper, 1985) and identified up to 22 factors per case.

To analyze the MP3 case, we first collected data and made a chronological case description. Then we defined the phases of the platform competition by determining when the milestones occurred. Subsequently we identified which factors influenced the platform competition at each phase. Data was collected from several sources. Written documents such as academic papers (Denegri-Knott & Tadajewski, 2010) and market intelligence reports from independent market research firms, and public announcements were used to gain a general insight. Based on the initial desk research, a preliminary case study analysis was performed. To complement and triangulate the data from the literature and gain an in-depth understanding of the platform competition, we conducted ten focused interviews with key people from parties involved in the platform competition (e.g. Fraunhofer, Philips, AT&T, Thomson). These interviews were conducted during 2011-2012. Each interview lasted between hand an hour and three hours. To ensure consistency and reliability, interview guidelines were used. We compared the findings from archival sources to the findings of the interviews, and the results were communicated to the interviewees for verification. The data were complemented by documents which were sent by the interviewees, or studied at their offices. In the subsequent sections, the case will be described using the results in the data matrix.

4. THE EVOLUTION OF AUDIO FORMATS AND THE ORIGINS OF MP3

The first time sound was mechanically reproduced, was in 1877 when Thomas Edison invented the phonograph. The device used a tinfoil wrapped cylinder or wax-coated cardboard cylinder on which the music was stored. This invention created a market for prerecorded music. The wax phonograph cylinder dominated the recorded sound market during the early 20th century. During the 1910s phonographs using flat double-sided records became the dominant audio technology and 78 revolutions per minute became the standardized speed in 1925. As technology improved, consumers became interested in better recording quality. This led to the market introduction of the 33-rpm and 45-rpm records in 1932 and 1949 (Langlois & Robertson, 1992). Sales of the 45-rpm format took off with the emergence of rock and roll music (Spanias et al., 2007), and the 33-rpm and 45-rpm records became the dominant format for albums and singles respectively. In 1963, the compact cassette tape format was introduced and became an instant success with accessories for home, portable, and car use (Musmann, 2006). Nevertheless, it took twenty years to replace the 33-rpm and 45-rpm records as the dominant format (as shown by Figure 3). In 1982 the introduction of the Compact Disc Digital Audio (CD), marked the transfer of analog to digital audio storage. The CD took over the dominant position in 1991, thereby becoming one of the fastest technologies to obtain market dominance.

Shortly after the compact cassette tape format had been introduced and the 33-rpm and 45-rpm records dominated the market of recorded music, some academic and corporate (e.g. Bell Labs) visionaries recognized that audio and video transmission over telephone lines could result in new products and services. However, this required

Figure 3. Volume of recorded music products sold in the United States by format[1]

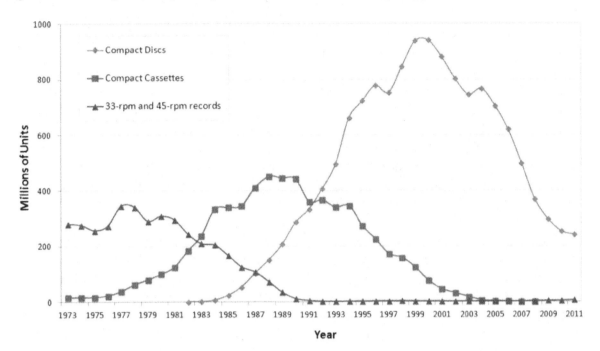

digitalized data and high data rate transmission. One of these visionaries was Professor Musmann of the University of Hannover (Germany), who focused on data reduction by encoding the amplitudes. In 1977, he managed to reduce the bit rate of moving images by a factor of three thousand to 64 kbit/s, which brought transmission via telephone lines and satellites within reach. In the early 1970s, another visionary, Professor Seitzer of the University of Erlangen (Germany), had the idea to compress and transmit audio data in high quality over telephone lines. As improvements were made to telecommunications infrastructure, he shifted his focus to transmitting music. This shift in focus was necessary to justify his research on data reduction. The industry was losing its interest in data reduction, due to the advances in optical transmission using optical fibers. Seitzer wondered what could be promoted as a step forward when using a digital phone line of 64 kbit/s, so he came with the idea of transmitting music

over the telephone network from a central music database. He applied for a patent in 1977, which was granted in December 1982. The patent was subsequently offered to the industry (e.g. Bosch, Telefunken, Grundig, Philips and Siemens), however no-one believed that there would be a need for the invention and it was discontinued in 1988. In 1979, Prof. Seitzer's team developed the first digital signal processor capable of audio compression, creating the basis for developing audio compression schemes.

5. THE RISE OF MP3 AS THE MARKET STANDARD

The following sections describe the subsequent phases in the rise of MP3, and identify the relevant factors and tactics that influenced the platform competition.

5.1 R&D Build-Up (1982-1986)

The first steps towards MP3 started with the development of ATC (Adaptive Transform Coding), which started in 1982 when a young German Engineer named Karlheinz Brandenburg was hired as a PhD student by Professor Seitzer at the University of Erlangen. He set out to work on digital audio coding for music transfer over a phone line, and to show the practical feasibility of Professor Seitzer's patented idea. To devise a functional algorithm for digital audio encoding, Brandenburg required a cross-disciplinary approach, combining knowledge from various fields such as psychoacoustics and quantization. The University of Erlangen had a broad knowledge base, and by consulting many of his colleagues, Brandenburg managed to learn about these disciplines. The difficulty was in combining these into a working algorithm.

In 1986, Brandenburg achieved a major breakthrough when he read an article in a scientific journal, which proposed to combine several concepts in a different sequence. Brandenburg had also experimented with these concepts, and decided to develop a new algorithm based on the different sequence, and aimed at speech encoding. The tests of the new algorithm showed that the idea worked properly, compressing speech much more than before without a noticeable decline in quality. The result was a 'proof of concept' of the algorithm and something new compared to what other people were working on. In the folloing year, he further revised and improved the algorithm in iterative steps. During this period he needed computer capacity to perform the tests, which was provided by Deutsche Thomson. The result was the ATC algorithm for speech encoding. After Brandenburg reached his breakthrough, he presented his findings at international conferences and learnt about other parties (e.g. Institut fur Rundfunktechnik and Bell Labs) that were working on a solution to the same problem.

5.2 Preparing for Market Entry: Reducing the Level of Competition (1987-1992)

In 1987, the European Union funded EUREKA project for Digital Audio Broadcasting (DAB) started. The aim was to deliver near-CD quality audio programmes in digital form to domestic receivers. A powerful algorithm was required that would allow audio compression so that it could be transferred via the Integrated Services Digital Network (ISDN). The project embraced research institutes and industries from 29 European countries including electronic equipment manufacturers (e.g. Philips and Thomson), public and private broadcasters (e.g. IRT, CCETT and France Telecom), and regulatory bodies. The Fraunhofer Institute for Integrated Circuits (set up in 1985 as a department of the Fraunhofer Gesellschaft[2]) and the University of Erlangen participated with the ATC algorithm and a large team (including Brandenburg). Although ATC was suitable for speech encoding, encoding music was more difficult. So the team worked on overcoming the problems of encoding music signals with ATC. They named the resulting algorithm Optimum Coding in the Frequency domain (OCF). Fraunhofer compiled this on signal processors, made dedicated hardware, and managed to build the first real-time OCF encoding/decoding device in the same year they started. Before this development, it would take several hours to encode or decode seconds of music.

At the International Conference on Acoustics, Speech, and Signal Processing in 1987, Brandenburg attended a presentation of an Australian university. Brandenburg managed to reproduce their ideas and use this to make significant progress in the encoding efficiency and audio quality of OCF. At the same conference Fraunhofer and AT&T Bell Labs presented their work on music encoding and discovered they had independently developed a similar algorithm. Just like the University of Erlangen, AT&T Bell Labs had the required core competences: the underlying technologies for audio compression were conceived at AT&T in the 1920s and 1930s (Spanias et al., 2007; Sterne, 2012). Since the two approaches were similar, this offered a good basis to collaborate on developing the algorithm. So after Brandenburg finished his PhD in 1989, he went to AT&T Bell Labs to perform Postdoctoral research till 1991. In return, the collaboration gave AT&T access to Fraunhofer's hardware expertise, which they were lacking. However, AT&T was not focused on music, but on speech encoding, and consequently research on music encoding was not really valued An interviewee mentioned AT&T's attitude was "we're not going to make any money on this". As a result, AT&T gave Fraunhofer co-ownership of e.g. the intellectual property rights and code during their collaboration.

In 1988, the Japanese telecommunications company NTT took a leading role in establishing a standard for digital video and audio encoding. The head of NTT's research laboratory, Hiroshi Yasuda, realized that market adoption of encoding required a worldwide standard. His approach was to make a standard for computer networks, whereby the data would be stored in the computer. At that time, the CD was the only means to play and store video and audio real time, and its short access time made it suitable for interactive communications. So it was important to include the CD in the standard as storage medium. To facilitate the standard development process, Yasuda approached a prominent standard development organization, the International Organization for Standardization (ISO). As a result of Yasuda's efforts, the ISO established the Motion Picture Expert Group (MPEG) in 1988 to develop a digital coding standard for video and audio signals. Two experts were appointed to lead the efforts (audio and video) in the MPEG: Didier LeGall (AT&T Bell Labs) for video and Prof. Musmann (University of Hannover) for audio. Since the CD

had a bit rate of 1.5Mbit/s, Yasuda, Musmann and LeGall decided to split up the available data rate: 1.24 Mbit/s for video, and the rest (256 kbit/s) for audio while keeping the sound quality intact. The parties issued a document describing the goals for the technical specifications. In the same year ISO posted a call, inviting interested parties to join the MPEG. NTT, AT&T Bell Labs, University of Hannover, and Deutsche Thomson were the first parties that joined. Subsequently, the first working group meeting was planned, and an invitation – open to all interested parties – was widely distributed.

At the same time, the EUREKA project struggeled to select an audio encoding format. During a EUREKA project meeting, the Chair proposed that the parties would work towards a single solution in the MPEG-1 audio working group, and the result would be adopted for DAB. The members agreed and submitted their DAB proposals to the MPEG-1 working group.

The first meeting of the MPEG-1 audio working group was organized by Deutsche Thomson in Hannover (Germany) in December 1988 and was attended by approximately 20 company representatives. They appointed Professor Musmann as chair of the audio working group. They also defined the system requirements and selected applications (CD-ROM for audio and video, Digital Audio Tape Recorder, and Digital Audio Broadcasting). As part of the standardization process, task forces were formed to set commercial and technical requirements (aspects on which the compression algorithms would be tested and their measure of importance), and define objective test criteria.

After the first meeting, Professor Musmann issued a call for proposals. He received fourteen proposals before the deadline of June 1989. Professor Musmann subsequently had to conceive a process that would lead to a single solution supported by all participants. From June to October 1989, he studied the proposals, and found they could be divided in four groups (see Figure 4).

Figure 4. Coding concepts and members of the four groups (adapted from Mussman, 2006)

Company	Country	Coding Concept
CCETT	France	**MUSICAM** Subband coding with more than 8 subbands
IRT	Germany	
Matsushita	Japan	
Philips	Netherlands	
AT&T	USA	**ASPEC** Transform coding with overlapping blocks
France Telecom	France	
Fraunhofer Gesellschaft	Germany	
Deutsche Thomson-Brandt	Germany	
Fujitsu	Japan	**ATAC** Transform coding with non-overlapping blocks
JVC	Japan	
NEC	Japan	
Sony	Japan	
BTRL	Great Britain	**SB/ADPCM** Subband coding with less than 8 subbands
NTT	Japan	

His suggestion to work towards a solution in four groups was accepted by all parties. As a result, Fraunhofer, AT&T, Thomson and France Telecom started to work together and each made their contribution: Fraunhofer's OCF filterbank, AT&T's PXFM perceptual model, Thomson's window and block switching, and France Telecom's entropy coding. The four clusters set up research groups which had six months to develop hardware that combined the ideas of the members in the group. Since most of the companies in the MUSICAM and ASPEC clusters had already worked together in the DAB project, they had an important advantage over the other two clusters.

In July 1990, during the 4th meeting of the working group, the progress of the clusters was tested. It became apparent that the ATAC and SB/ADPCM cluster could not get their hardware for real time processing functioning properly (at that time the hardware for the real time processing was difficult to develop, and the required signal processors were developed not long before). As a result, it was not possible to complete the full range of tests, and much additional work was required to reach the level of the other two proposals. Since the MPEG audio standard had a strict deadline to be completed by the end of 1991, there was no time for the two clusters to catch up, so Professor

Musmann suggested that the companies in ATAC and SB/ADPCM to join the MUSICAM and ASPEC clusters. Only few companies actually did, and the others remained involved in the working group as neutral parties.

During the next meeting in September, the tests results were discussed. These showed MUSICAM had achieved the best overall results. The outcome was based on an agreed formula that took into account audio quality, complexity (which translates into cost of the integrated circuit for the decoder and encoder), delay and some other parameters. Although ASPEC and MUSICAM scored similarly on most tests, the difference in complexity was 10:1. However, ASPEC showed better audio quality at low bit rates, and several parties (including AT&T and two parties involved in testing the codecs: BBC and Swedish Radio) were dissatisfied with the idea that a codec with better results on the low bit rate would not be included in the standard. As a result, the MPEG-1 audio working group feared that the national standards bodies would vote down the outcome (especially the US standards body, ANSI, due to the influential role of AT&T). Since MUSICAM inherently consisted of two layers (Layer 1 was aimed at the Digital Compact Cassette application, and Layer 2 was aimed at the DAB application), the working group managed to reach consensus by agreeing to add a third layer for lower data rate applications that would be backwards compatible to Layer 1 and 2. Layer 1 had a data rate of 192kbit/s, Layer 2 had a data rate of 128kbit/s, and Layer 3 was set at 64kbit/s (reducing the original sound data from a CD by a factor of 12). The latter was selected to enable data transfer over ISDN. Brandenburg became responsible for writing the Layer 3 specification, under the review of two people from MUSICAM. While writing the Layer 3 specification, Brandenburg had to mix the different technologies in order to maintain the good performance of ASPEC at low data rate, while maintaining compability with Layer 1 and 2.

During an intermediate test event in Paris in June 1991, the results showed that Layer 1 and 2 were nearly completed. But the working group found there were problems in meeting the requirements for Layer 3. After this test, one of Professor Musmann's PhD students discovered a mistake had been made while combining ASPEC and MUSICAM. He came up with a solution on how to reduce the efficiency impairment of the combined technologies and improve the sound quality. But due to the lack of interest from the University of Hannover, this idea was patented by Fraunhofer. The day before the Layer 3 team had to deliver their equipment for the final test, the Fraunhofer team managed to solve a software bug which greatly increased the audio quality and resulted in meeting the quality requirements.

The last test before completing the specification was conducted in October 1991 in Hannover. The group concluded that most of the problems that had been found at the intermediate meeting in June were solved. Since the deviations from CD sound quality were minor and there was little time before the deadline, they agreed to include Layer 3 in the MPEG-1 audio standard. MPEG-1 audio was finalized in November 1991. The complete MPEG-1 standard, which comprised both audio and video, was approved as ISO/IEC IS 11172 in November 1992. The standard was published several months later.

The MPEG-1 standardization process and the willingness of its participants to collaborate greatly reduced the amount of competition among compressed audio formats. Nevertheless, next to Layer 2 (which became the audio compression format for DAB), there were several other audio compression formats that competed for market adoption. Sony renamed the ATAC technology to ATRAC and implemented this in their products such the portable music player MiniDisc which was launched in 1992. Dolby was very active with a proprietary format, AC-1, which they introduced in 1987 at the beginning of the High Definition

Television (HDTV) standardization process (Todd et al., 1994). In 1989, they introduced AC-2 which had better audio quality and a reduced bit-rate. Finally, in 1991 AC-3 (also known as Dolby Digital) was introduced, which was implemented in a commercial cinema product and later also in HDTV and DVD.

5.3 Initiating Market Adoption: Finding the First Applications (1993-1996)

After the MPEG-1 audio standard was published, it became clear that this was no guarantee for Layer 3 to be utilized in an application. Unlike the MU-SICAM supporters, the ASPEC supporters were not strongly positioned to implement the MPEG-1 audio standard. Fraunhofer focused on applied science, AT&T and France Telecom offered telecom services whereby music compression was out of scope, so this left Thomson (which was active in the consumer electronics field) as the only ASPEC supporter able to implement Layer 3 in products. To overcome this problem, the Fraunhofer team took it upon themselves to find applications for Layer 3. They made an effort to promote the application of Layer 3 by attending many conferences, giving demonstrations, and by creating a website to inform interested parties about the technology. They also searched for applications they could service themselves. Due to the relatively high complexity of Layer 3, the implementation required a market which was not sensitive to the price of the integrated circuit. This led them to the radio broadcasting market. Between 1989 and 1992, Fraunhofer had sold a small series of equipment that was able to encode music (first using OCF and later ASPEC) and could be distributed via low-cost ISDN telephone lines, and in 1993 these were converted to MPEG-1 Layer 3. These systems were used by, for example the Christian Science Publishing Society and the U.S. Army Research Laboratory. They also did contract research for professional ISDN broadcasting systems

and speech announcements for buses to customers such as Philips Kommunikations Industrie (PKI), Dialog4, NSM Löwen and Meister Electronic. These parties were interested to use high quality low bitrate audio coding because this allowed them to save cost by using fewer cables or less data storage. These were small initial markets for the technology and showed its advantages. In that same year, Telos Systems (at that time a small US based firm) was the first to buy a MPEG-1 Layer 3 license and the equipment to encode and distribute MPEG-1 Layer 3 for newscasting of sport matches. Telos was successful with the system, and afterwards purchased additional equipment. This increased the visibility of MPEG-1 Layer 3 in the industry. In addition, Telos introduced Fraunhofer to other companies. One of these was one of the first internet service providers, and the respective contact person later switched to Microsoft. The resulting relationship with Microsoft later became important to the market adoption of Layer 3.

In 1993, Fraunhofer established a partnership with Thomson for their essential patents on Layer 3. Since Thomson was experienced in licensing negotiations, they agreed that Thomson would focus on the consumer market and provide licenses on the combined patent portfolio (approximately 18 patent families) while Fraunhofer would service the professional market with equipment. Although Thomson actively licensed the combined patent portfolio to all commercial enterprises interested in using Layer 3, a license from them alone was not sufficient since it did not include the MUSI-CAM patents. In order to obtain access to these, companies had to negotiate a license with the Italian company SISVEL, which Philips, IRT and CCETT appointed as the licensing agent for their combined MPEG-1 patent portfolio in 1996.

After the ISO MPEG audio standard was finalized, several companies started developing chipsets for Layer 2, a prerequisite for implementing the technology in mass-produced devices. To enable this for Layer 3, the Fraunhofer team entered into discussion with the German company

Intermetall. The two companies got acquainted during the EUREKA project. Intermetall had just developed a new chip, and were looking for a complex task to showcase its capabilities. Layer 3 was ideal for this due to its complexity. Intermetall was also interested to provide receiver chips for the DAB digital radio. Although DAB was based on Layer 2, Intermetall was hoping that DAB would eventually move toward Layer 3. This led to the development of the Layer 3 decoder chip prototype, which became available in 1994. The Fraunhofer team used this chip to develop a prototype of a portable Layer 3 player. The device was battery powered, used an EEPROM decoder chip to store and play music, and had 1MB memory. At that time, memory was expensive. A portable player with sufficient memory to store one hour of music would have cost several thousands of US Dollars. Using Moore's law (Moore, 1965) which states that the number of transistors per semiconductor (and thereby the amount of bits that can be stored on a chip) doubles roughly every two years, they calculated that solid state memory would become attractively priced for the mass market around 2000. The prototype was shown publicly for the first time at an academic conference in fall 1994. Even though the idea of storing music on solid state memory was not new, it attracted substantial academic interest.

In the same year, the Fraunhofer team held an internal meeting about the commercialization strategy. They identified a rapid increase in the adoption of the World Wide Web and the interest of its users to share music through this new means of communication as an important opportunity, and realized there was a limited window of opportunity to establish Layer 3 as dominant audio distribution format in this niche. Fraunhofer was aware of the development of the World Wide Web because Brandenburg had used Usenet (a hybrid between e-mail and web discussion forums) during

his postdoc at AT&T to exchange research results with the University of Erlangen. The interest to share music via the Internet became apparent in 1993, when the Internet Underground Music Archive (IUMA) started sharing music of independent artists over File Transfer Protocol (FTP) and Gopher sites in Layer 3 format. The IUMA was founded by a group of Californian engineers that had attended the MPEG-1 audio working group meetings. Their intention was to develop a new distribution method for music of independent bands, eliminating the need for record companies. At that time, it was commonly known that a CD-ROM drive (which was introduced in the personal computer market in 1985) could be used to "rip" the music (which was stored using Pulse Code Modulation which digitally represented sampled analog signals, and this signal had no copy protection mechanism) from an audio CD. The IUMA used a software program to grab songs as WAV files and an encoder (based on the source code which was published in part 4 of the MPEG-1 audio standard) to convert and compress the files to Layer 3 format for storage, computer playback and Internet distribution. The IUMA showed that the Internet was a suitable means to exchange music. The Layer 3 format was used because it had several important advantages compared to its alternatives. It was one of the few formats that was fully developed, it required a low data rate (while maintaining good quality) which matched well with the requirements for music transfer over the Internet (the vast majority of Internet users accessed it through a 56 kilobit per second dial-up modem), and it had shown to provide high quality audio at low bitrates in the radio station market. The interest for music distribution over the Internet was enabled by the developments in personal computers, which became capable of playing good quality audio due to the implementation of sound cards. In order to capitalize on the limited window of opportunity and facilitate the use of Layer 3 on the Internet, in July 1994 Fraunhofer released the first software MP3 encoder called L3enc on their web site for US$250. These developments enabled Layer 3 to cross over from the professional market to the consumer market.

In July 1995, the Fraunhofer team renamed MPEG Layer 3 to MP3 because it was shorter and easier to utilize, and changed the file extension to .mp3. They released a media player named WinPlay3 later that year. WinPlay3 was the first real-time MP3 audio player for PCs running Microsoft's Windows, and could be downloaded from the Internet. Previous to the release of the application, audio compressed with MP3 technology had to be manually decompressed by the users prior to listening.

In the same year, Fraunhofer started selling and licensing encoder hardware boards for the PC domain. In addition, the software company Macromedia obtained a license on MP3 and integrated the encoder and decoder in their Shockwave media (audio and video) player. Soon thereafter Xing Technology and RealNetworks introduced their streaming media players: Streamwork and RealAudio. The RealAudio media player could play MP3 but also used a propietary format called RealAudio which was based on Dolby's AC3. According to statistics from International Webcasting Association in September 1997, the web broadcasting (e.g. radio stations transmissions) market share of RealAudio almost reached 90%. Although the RealAudio player was popular during the early years of the Internet, it was surpassed in market share by Microsoft's media player in 2000.

The years 1995 and 1996 saw the emergence of what came to be known as the 'MP3 scene' (Spilker and Höier, 2013) With easy access to MP3 encoders, Internet users started to rip their own MP3 files from CDs and make them available on the Internet. So-called 'warez groups' competed to release music first and offer the widest assort-

ment. MP3 files began to circulate on university servers, enthusiast home pages, IRC chat channels, free webspace services, and FTP servers (Burkart and McCourt, 2006).

In 1996, another competitor, Liquid Audio, entered the stage. The company had developed a website where customers could purchase, download and play music using its own software player, encoded in a proprietary, secure format. In order to create the compression format, the company had worked with Dolby. By 1999, Liquid Audio had enlisted over 200 partners and affiliates that agreed to sell or distribute music in the Liquid format (Hause, 2000). Major labels EMI and BMG and several hundreds of small labels were using the Liquid format and another major label, Warner Music, was utilizing Liquid's server software. However, the format was hindered by its PC-only playback capabilities, since there was little support from integrated circuit vendors and therefore could not be implemented in portable compressed audio players.

MP3's lack of copy protection spurred its popularity for illegal music distribution, but this feature was unintentional. Fraunhofer was able to offer copy protection, but they also wanted to agree upon a standard with the record labels. However, at that time the record labels did not recognize the increasing popularity of the Internet and the potential impact on their business model. In 1995, the Fraunhofer team participated in a European project: Music on Demand. Only the small record labels participated in the project. Fraunhofer held a presentation about digital rights management, however the record labels failed to recognize the urgent need to discuss the topic. Fraunhofer also contacted the project leader of a European project on real time audio encoding on PCs. This project included participants from the computer and music industry, and it was the first time Fraunhofer established contact with the major record labels in the music industry. During a meeting at BMG

Ariola in Munchen, the major record labels said "it all sounds very interesting, but what does this have to do with us?".

5.4 Gaining Critical Mass in the Internet Music Distribution Market: The Rise of Complementary Assets (1997-1999)

Several years after the Internet music distribution market started, several compressed audio formats were competing for market adoption and MP3 was in the lead. In 1997, AAC, a technologically superior audio compression format joined the competition. The initial idea to start with the development of AAC can be traced back to the end of 1992. At that time, the MPEG-1 audio working group finalized the first MPEG audio standard, and MPEG continued with the development of the next standard by starting the MPEG-2 audio working group. This working group focused on developing an audio compression format that could be used for low data rates, enable multi-channel sound, and would be compatible with the MPEG-1 audio standard. However, during this development there were concerns that the backwards compatibility requirement put too many restrictions on the capabilities of the new format. In 1993, the MPEG-2 audio working group decided to compare the new format to two codecs that were not compatible with MPEG-1: Dolby's AC-3 and AT&T's new Perceptual Audio Coder (PAC). In January 1994, the test results became available, showing that AC-3 and PAC were better than the newly developed backwards compatible codecs. Subsequenty, the MPEG-2 audio working group started a new work item on 'non backwards compatible coding'. Several parties submitted proposals. After testing these, the working group decided to move forward by combining the proposals of Fraunhofer, AT&T, Dolby and Sony. Their respective proposals showed good results and were technically similar. The parties together created the AAC codec, which was final-

ized in April 1997. After the AAC standard was finalized, industry insiders expected the market would switch to the new format. An interviewee reported: "From a technical perspective MP3 had lost its right to exist after AAC became available". However, market adoption was hindered due to two reasons. First, after the AAC codec became available, the standard developers wanted to put different licensing constraints on AAC, making it difficult to obtain a license on the 'standard-essential' patents. This issue was solved when the parties agreed on a collaborative patent licensing program in 1998. As result, the first implementations of AAC entered the market in 1999. By this time, MP3 had an extensive installed base and a large number of complementary products. Secondly, Dolby was appointed by the patent holders to act as the licensing agent (in 2003 this role was appointed to VIA Licensing, a Dolby subsidiary), while the company was simultaneously marketing its proprietary AC-3 codec, causing a conflict of interest.

In 1997, two important events boosted the market adoption of MP3. Firstly, the MP3 decoder software was hacked by an Australian student and published on-line as freeware. Due to the lack of a regime of appropriability, this could not be counteracted and Fraunhofer and Thomson decided to support the distribution of unrestricted MP3 media players. Secondly, Microsoft obtained a license from Thomson (Handelsblatt, 2000), and included MP3 in their Windows Media Player (WMP) 6.1. This media player was the multimedia platform that came with Windows 98 as the default front end for playing audio and video files, and since Windows was the dominant personal computer operating system, many consumers had access to WMP. Microsoft included MP3 rather than AAC in WMP 6.1 mainly because it was already a popular codec with much available audio content, but also because AAC was not finalized in time to be included in WMP 6.1.

In the same year, the type of complementary assets for MP3 broadened with the launch of the world's first commercially available portable players that could store and play MP3 files and websites for MP3 file sharing. The portable MP3 player was introduced by Audio Highway and contained software for uploading MP3 audio content to a personal computer and then downloading it onto the portable MP3 player. The device had no moving parts, therefore (unlike the compact disc) the music did not skip when consumers were exercising or driving. The portable MP3 player used Intermetall's first commercial Layer 3 decoder chipset which had become available the previous year. About half a year later, the South Korean company SaeHan introduced the MPMan, which was the first mass produced portable MP3 player. The first dedicated website for sharing MP3 files was MP3.com. It quickly became one of the most popular websites on the Internet that offered the possibility to stream, play and store MP3 encoded music.

A media player called Winamp, introduced in 1997 as MP3 playback engine, was distributed as shareware and quickly became a success (Paxton, 2000) due to the expanding penetration of multimedia computers and high-speed Internet connections. Within months of its first release, Winamp was consistently topping the download list at shareware sites, and was downloaded over 3 million times within the first years of its release (Alderman, 2001). New media players were entering the market, and the user base quickly expanded. At the same time, new websites started offering MP3 songs for free download, and other sites allowed people to upload music, creating a virtual market for free music. In addition, most people did not notice or care that this trading of music was illegal.

In 1998, the Recording Industry Association of America (RIAA) began to take notice and started to actively shut down these websites. However, the number of sites that were started significantly outnumbered those that were shut down. Since people could only listen to the music on their computer, the problem for the recording

industry was limited. Later that year, Diamond Multimedia, a large company with retail distribution capabilities, entered the market with its own portable MP3 player: the Rio PMP300 (Paxton, 2000). This became the first commercially successful portable MP3 player. With the prospect of MP3 moving off the PC and into the mainstream, the RIAA filed a lawsuit against Diamond for encouraging illegal music copying. This lawsuit attracted much press coverage, ironically bringing MP3 under the attention of the mainstream, creating mass-market awareness and increasing demand for portable MP3 players and MP3 files.

In October 1998, Diamond Multimedia, Good-Noise, MP3.com, MusicMatch, and Xing Technology founded the MP3 Association to promote MP3 technology as the standard for downloadable music, thereby increasing both the visibility and use of the technology. In addition, the organization pooled together legal resources to strengthen its lobbying efforts, while attempting to improve the relationship with the recording industry.

In June 1999, the user-friendly peer-to-peer music sharing site Napster was launched. Although there were already websites which facilitated file sharing (e.g. IRC and Hotline), Napster specialized exclusively in MP3 files and presented an interface that made it easy to find the audio file of interest. The result was a system whose popularity generated an enormous selection of downloadable MP3 files. By the end of the first week, Napster had 15,000 users, and this number had grown to over 25 million by 2001. Due to Napster's popularity, the RIAA filed a lawsuit against the website end of 1999, based on the Digital Millennium Copyright Act (DMCA). The DMCA had been passed in the United States at the end of 1998, and criminalized services that controlled access to copyrighted works. This legislation gave the RIAA a strong legal basis to strike against the rising popularity of websites that facilitated sharing MP3 files.

Although Microsoft had a license on the MP3 technology, in 1999 they introduced a proprietary format named Windows Media Audio (WMA) with copy protection. This new format became a serious competitor to MP3. Microsoft, as a strong market player, aggressively pushed WMA as the market standard. They bundled WMA with the release of the fourth version of Windows Media Player in 1999, and licensed their codec to other software providers so users would not be tied to WMP. They embedded support for WMA in other products using Windows, such as set-top boxes, and used marketing slogans to manage industry expectations. At the CES conference in 2000, Microsoft requested its licensees to mention that WMA was 'twice as good as MP3' on their booths. However, the technological superiority of WMA over MP3 was not evident. There were tests that showed both codecs gave similar results. Microsoft had two reasons to introduce WMA. First, they wanted to be free of license payments, and secondly they believed an alternative audio

compression format with adequate copy protection could win the support of the music industry and gain significant market traction.

By the time WMA entered the market, MP3 had gathered significant momentum and held a large advantage over other compressed audio formats due to its significant installed base, availability of songs in the MP3 format, and complementary assets (software and hardware players). Strong direct and indirect network externalities helped to increase this momentum. By 1999, MP3 was regarded as the market standard for Internet distribution of music, and the Internet had become a fast growing medium for information, communication and entertainment exchange (see Figure 5), reaching 35% penetration among U.S. households, at a 49% consumer PC penetration (Fraunhofer IIS, 2012).

Figure 5. Percentage of American adults using the Internet 2000-2010 (source: Pew Research Center, 2012)

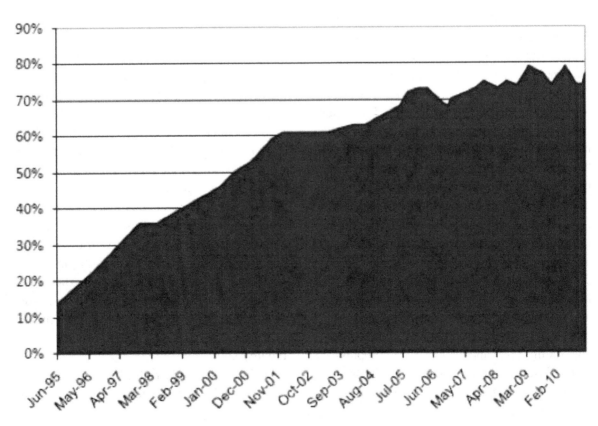

5.6 Winning the Mass Market: The Power of Network Effects (2000-2009)

Although by 2000, MP3 was regarded as the market standard for music distribution over the Internet, it still needed to replace the Compact Disc as the dominant format for music storage and distribution. Simultaneously there were several physical formats (of which MiniDisc was the most prominent) on the market that aimed to replace the CD. MPEG-1 Layer 2, one of MP3's first competitors, was no longer an important contender. DAB did not achieve the commercial success that was expected and the format resided in several very successful applications for video distribution (Video CD and Digital Video Broadcasting).

In 2000, several major consumer electronics players (e.g. Philips, Sony, Sanyo, Sharp, Samsung and LG) entered the market for portable MP3 players. The major consumer electronics company Panasonic and the personal computer company Apple (with its first generation iPod) joined the competition in 2001, and in the same year MP3 file sharing websites KaZaa and Bittorrent were launched. In 2004, KaZaa's popularity peaked, and the same happened for Bittorrent in 2006. The combination of an increase in availability of portable MP3 players and websites providing MP3 files created strong network effects and reinforced the market adoption of MP3. Between 2000 and 2007, the market adoption of portable MP3 players grew rapidly (see Figure 6). The first boost (between 2000 and 2002) resulted from the large number of companies entering the portable MP3 player market, especially the major consumer electronics players. The second boost (between 2003 and 2006) was caused by the network effects and the market tipping towards the MP3 format. This was also driven by the popularity of Apple's portable compressed audio player, the iPod, which turned out to be the ´killer application´ of the compressed audio players. iPod sales were a significant part of the MP3 player sales (see Figure 6).

In 2000, the major record labels BMG, Sony, EMI and Warner (which had been working with Liquid Audio and RealNetworks) decided to use Microsoft's WMA format for online music downloads because of its copy protection and its tie-in to Windows Media Player (Geek.com, 2000). This significant increase in content support boosted WMA's market traction and made it the major up-and-coming competitor in the audio codec domain. However, the additional support from the music industry hardly resulted in compressed audio players supporting the format, limiting the use of WMA to the computer. When the market adoption for portable MP3 players accelerated, and Apple's iPod (which supported several audio codecs, amongst which MP3, but not WMA) became successful, the window of opportunity for WMA in the portable compressed audio market closed. In an attempt to boost compressed audio player support, Microsoft launched the Zune in 2006. However, this did not become successful.

Up to 2001, MiniDisc players, which could be used to record and play music in Sony's proprietary ATRAC codec, had the highest market adoption in the compressed audio player segment. MiniDisc was launched by Sony in 1992, taking a proprietary approach and focusing on the portable music player market after the ATAC audio compression format was removed from the MPEG-1 audio standardization process. MiniDisc players quickly became popular in Japan, accounting for most of the worldwide sales. Although Sony was the major sponsor behind MiniDisc, they also licensed it to others (in 2001 Sony's player shipments constituted 25% of the MiniDisc market). Despite MiniDisc's early entry in the portable compressed audio player market, the format failed to gain critical mass outside Japan. After 2001, sales of portable MP3 players exceeded those of MiniDisc players. Sales of MiniDisc players peaked in 2001 and then decreased sharply (see Figure 7).

In February 2001, the US Ninth Circuit Court of Appeal ruled that Napster should stop allowing

Figure 6. Sales of portable compressed music players from 1998-2008 (Sources: Ethier, 2008; Abel, 2008; Apple Inc., n.d.; Nihon Keizai Shimbun, 2000)

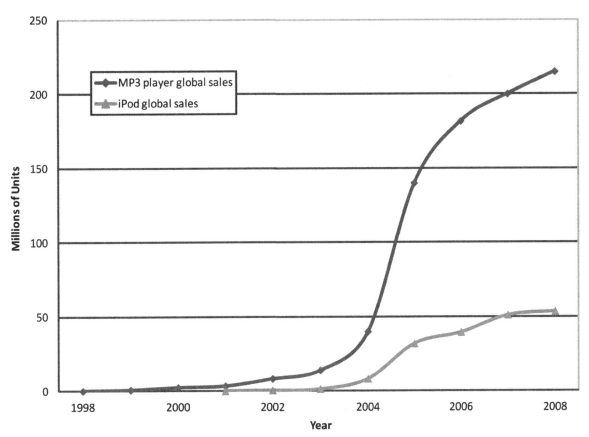

music fans to share copyrighted material (Smith & Wingfield, 2003). However, not all attempts of the RIAA were successful. In April 2003, the court ruled that Grokster and Streamcast Networks could continue to distribute Internet file-sharing software, forcing the music industry to intensify the legal pursuit of individuals who distributed copyrighted works online. By July 2003, the RIAA had issued hundreds of federal subpoenas demanding Internet service providers and some universities to turn over names of users suspected of illegally sharing music. Several months later, the RIAA filed 261 lawsuits against individuals who allegedly illegally used file-sharing software to distribute copyrighted music online.

Amidst all this turmoil, in 2003 Apple launched iTunes 4.0 (version 1.0 was introduced in January 2001 as an MP3 media player for Apple's Mac operating system) which contained a new feature: the iTunes Store. The iTunes Store was a proprietary software-based online digital media store where consumers could purchase music files in the AAC format including Apple's Fairplay data rights management. The use of a strong data rights management system was a prerequisite from the record labels to make their music catalogues available for iTunes (Jobs, 2007). The AAC codec was very suitable to Apple's needs, because it provided high audio quality at low bitrates and its design allowed an extension with a DRM implementation.

Figure 7. Volume of MiniDiscs sold from 1994-2011[3]

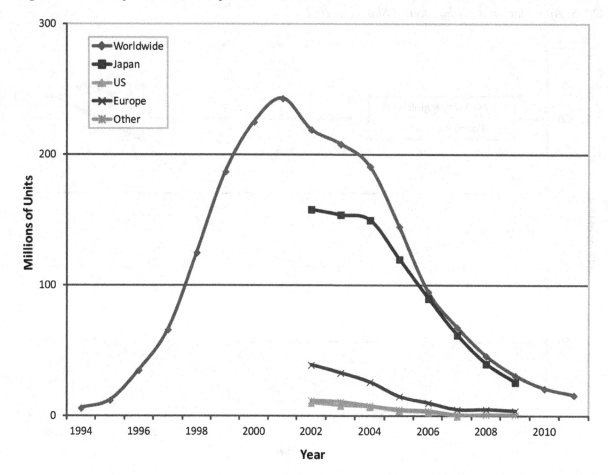

Apple's Fairplay software restricted purchased song playback to Apple products. When the iTunes Store was launched, it had content support from the five major record labels (EMI, Universal, Warner, Sony Music Entertainment, and BMG). During this time, the iPod was becoming increasingly popular, and the iTunes Store allowed iPod users easy access to a broad selection of music and to download songs legally. Consumers were thrilled, and the iTunes Store quickly became a success. The store sold about 275,000 tracks in its first 18 hours in business and more than one million in its first 5 days. In August 2004, Apple announced that the iTunes Store was the world's number one online music service. It had over one million songs available for download in the US, more than 100 million songs had been downloaded and the store had more than 70 percent market share of legal downloads for singles and albums (Apple Inc., 2004). The success of the iPod and the iTunes Store proved to be a potent combination and reinforced the market adoption of both products.

With the introduction of portable MP3 players, compressed audio formats competed more directly with CDs. This initiated the decline of CD sales. In 2004, the share of physical CDs and digital music acquired by US customers was almost equal

(Josephson, 2005). The market started to reach a tipping point, whereby MP3 was taking over the dominant position from the CD (see Table 1).

MP3's market share in the music industry is difficult to measure since its use is largely based on unpaid music acquisition. Based on CD sales data and paid downloads (see Figure 8) and the market share of the different ways of music acquisition (see Table 1), we calculated the volume of unpaid music acquisition between 2006 and 2009 (see Figure 8). The volume of unpaid music acquisition surpassed the CD sales in 2006. While much of the unpaid music acquisition was based on the MP3 format, alternate formats were also. In addition, some paid downloads used MP3 files (for example, from the Amazon MP3 store). With the drop in CD sales, and the rise of compressed audio formats, MP3 became the dominant audio format. However, in order to pinpoint when this actually occurred, we need an indication of the

Table 1. Market share of music acquisition by US consumers[5]

	2004	2005	2006	2007	2008	2009
Physical CDs	51%	n.a.	41%	32%	27%	22%
Digital	49%	n.a.	59%	68%	73%	78%
Paid downloads			7%	10%	13%	15%
iTunes				69%	68%	69%
Amazon MP3					5%	8%
Rhapsody				2%	3%	4%
Zune				1%	2%	3%
Napster				4%	2%	2%
Other				24%	20%	14%
Un-paid music acquisition			52%	58%	61%	63%
P2P			27%	33%	n/a	29%
Burned from others			40%	33%	n/a	17%
Ripped from others			33%	33%	n/a	19%
Music transferred from external hard drive						29%
Music downloaded from digital storage locker						5%
Market share per compressed audio format						
MP3	72%			64.3%[6]	62.5%	60.9%
WMA	19.6%			17.5%	17%	16.6%
iTunes (AAC)	4.3%			10.1%	11.6%	13.3%
Other	3.9%			8%	8.9%	9.3%
Market share of music formats						
MP3				43.7%	46.2%	48.7%
WMA				11.9%	12.4%	12.9%
AAC				6.9%	8.5%	10.4%
CD				32%	27%	22%
Other				5.5%	5.9%	6%

Figure 8. Volume of music products sold in US from 2000-2011[4]

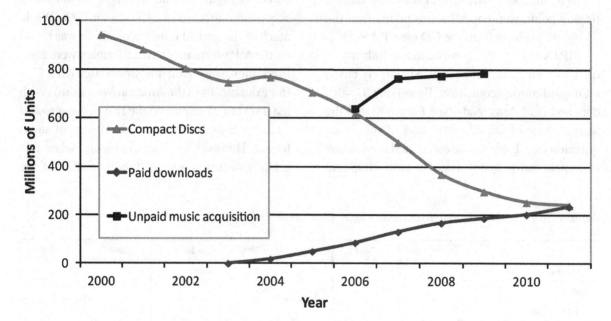

market share of the audio compression formats that were used for music distribution. The last available research on this was conducted in 2004 by the NPD Group, and provided the following results: 72% market share for MP3, 19.6% for WMA, 4.3% for AAC, and 3.9% for other formats (CNET, 2004). When we cross reference these figures with the actual market development of paid and unpaid music acquisition, and extrapolate the figures for MP3, we find that by 2009 the MP3 format had nearly obtained 50% market share of of music acquisition by US customers.

However, the extrapolation does not account for the positive effect that the rapid market adoption of portable MP3 players had on the market share of MP3. This suggests it likely exceeded 50% by 2009 (perhaps already in 2008) and can therefore be regarded as the dominant music format in the US.

5.7 Post Dominance (2010-Ongoing)

As we have seen from Figure 8 and Table 1, the market share of paid downloads is increasing fast.

This is largely driven by Apple's iTunes store which uses the AAC format. As Table 1 shows, the market share of AAC in terms of the overall music formats has grown relatively fast, but its absolute growth is similar to that of MP3. With the introduction of the iPhone in 2007 and the iPad in 2010, Apple leveraged its iTunes store to cellphones and tablet computers. The rapid market adoption of the iPhone and iPad boosted the adoption of AAC. As the MP3 standard was finalized in 1993, most essential patents will be expired by 2013, lowering the cost for a MP3 license and making the format more commercially attractive. Both MP3 and AAC will benefit from the steady decrease of the CD, and although AAC could take over the dominant position from MP3 at some time, this is not likely to happen any time soon.

6. CASE ANALYSIS

It took MP3 17 years from the start of its development to become the market standard for music on the Internet (see Figure 9). At that time, it was still far from becoming the dominant music format. While competing against the CD as incumbent dominant format, the adoption of MP3 experienced a period of rapid growth and within nine years it had become the overall dominant music format. By modeling an S-curve (Foster, 1986) on the market adoption of MP3, we can see the importance of the phases from a market adoption perspective. It was useful to add the phase of 'winning the mass market' to our scope of analysis, because during this period MP3's market adoption increased the most (see Figure 9). At present, MP3 is in a phase where the market is mature and saturated. This is often the time when a new platform emerges to compete for the position of dominant platform (Anderson & Tushman, 1990; Clark, 1985; Dosi, 1982; Foster, 1986). As noted in the previous section, the market share of paid downloads (which

is mainly driven by the AAC codec) is steadily increasing and could challenge MP3 for market dominance.

Over the lifetime of MP3, there were several audio compression formats that competed for market dominance. The first major competitor for MP3 was MPEG-1 Layer 2. Initially, this technology had more market adoption. However, contrary to expectations, DAB failed to become a market success. With the rise of the Internet, the adoption of MP3 quickly surpassed that of MPEG-1 Layer 2. The parties behind Layer 2 did not foresee the market of music distribution over the Internet, and the Internet had initially specific technological characteristics that gave MP3 a distinct advantage over Layer 2. However, while the Internet started to boom, the competing format AAC became available and various parties expected the market

Figure 9. Phases, respective timeframes and milestones in the rise of MP3 as the market standard

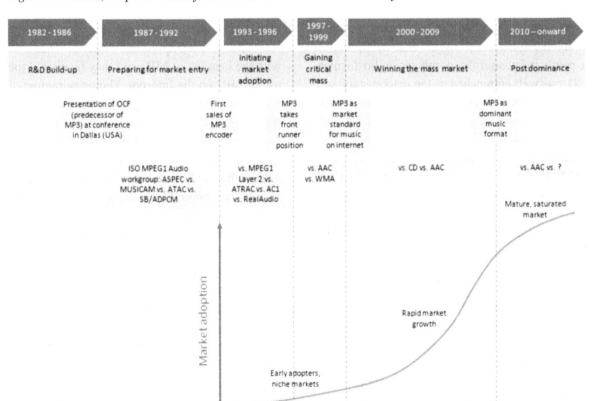

to switch to the new format. However, the market adoption of MP3 accelerated while the adoption of AAC progressed slowly. On the one hand, this was due to certain developments that benefitted the adoption of MP3 (the license to Microsoft and the hacked decoder), but on the other hand, it was also caused by certain errors by the AAC supporters (e.g. assigning the patent licensing and format promotion to a party that had a conflict of interest). When Microsoft launched its WMA on the market in 1999, MP3 had already become the dominant music distribution format on the Internet, and the first popular portable players had been launched on the market. However, during 2000 and 2001, WMA quickly gained market share. The rise of WMA was countered by rapid market adoption of portable compressed audio players supporting MP3, especially the iPod. WMA's market entry was too late and it missed the boost in market adoption caused by portable compressed audio players. The combined growth of portable players supporting MP3 and their positive reinforcement on the popularity of MP3 files sharing websites enabled the market to tip towards MP3, and as a result it became the dominant audio format. CD was well entrenched as the market standard, and much time (approximately 16 years after it entered the market) and momentum was required for MP3 to take over its position. Sony's MiniDisc technology could have been a significant threat to MP3. If it had replaced the CD between 1992 and 2000, the outcome of the competition against MP3 would have been unclear.

We identified 27 factors that influenced the platform competition. Following the detailed description in the previous sections, we determined nine key factors that enabled MP3 to become the dominant format (see Figure 10 for an overview). As can be seen from Figure 10, the focal point of the key factors is the phase of 'Initiating market adoption'. The combination of factors reflects the efforts to harness available chances and accelerate the initial momentum. In the period when mass market applications for compressed

music formats emerged, the level of competition was reduced by the MPEG-1 audio standardization process (stimulating parties to collaborate and develop a single standard). The rise of MP3 was enabled by four technologies: the rise of the Internet, the CD which digitized music without content protection, personal computers with sufficient processing power and sound cards, and low cost integrated circuits able to perform real time encoding/decoding (leading to the introduction of portable MP3 players). The timing of MP3's market entry was another key factor. When the rise of the Internet took place, MP3 was one of the few fully developed audio compression formats, and it offered the highest compression ratio while maintaining near CD audio quality. The high compression ratio made it technologically superior to other formats. MP3 had very dedicated sponsors, Fraunhofer and Thomson, that actively promoted its use and had the endurance to explore various market niches. Before the Internet gained rapid market adoption, Fraunhofer managed to identify music distribution over the Internet as a 'killer application' that matched well with the benefits of MP3 and they facilitated the use of MP3 on the Internet. The weak regime of appropriability, caused by MP3's lack of content protection and the difficulty to enforce rights on the Internet, allowed MP3 files to be shared easily, made it difficult for the RIAA to take action against this, and made Fraunhofer and Thomson release their control over the use of MP3 decoders after the software was published as freeware by an Australian student. The popularity of MP3 was not only due to its technological benefits, but also caused by the availability of complementary assets: the large number of websites offering MP3 files and MP3 (software and hardware) players. Lastly, direct and indirect network effects created self-reinforcing mechanisms that tipped the market towards MP3.

As noted in the theoretical overview, MP3 is a platform technology that enables 'platform-mediated networks'. In general, platforms face the

Figure 10. Nine key factors that influenced the platform competition through the six phases of platform competition

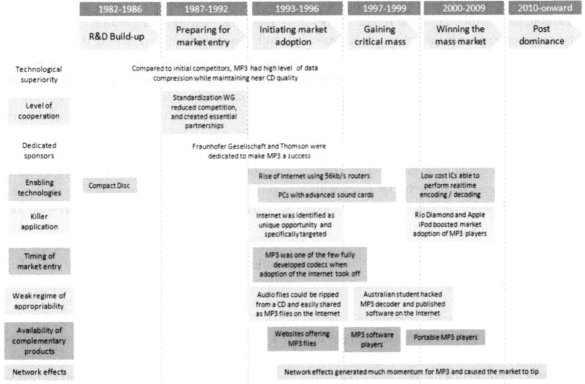

difficulty that they first require support from the supply network (e.g. content providers such as record labels or film studios) before they can attract users from the demand network. A key differentiator of MP3 was that the demand network and supply network were one and the same. Consumers could copy music from a CD and transform this into an MP3 file for sharing on the Internet, whereas its predecessors and competitors were dependent on the support of record labels. Although platform mediated networks have strong (often indirect) network externalities, we have seen that when the demand and supply network become the same, the direct and indirect network externalities overlap and reinforce each other. This results in unparalled network effects which transforms an industry by undermining the position of the incumbent supply network. The turnover of the global music industry plummeted from roughly $36.9 billion in 2000 to $15.9 billion in 2010 (IFPI, 2001; IFPI, 2011), and whereas the music industry was dominated by six major record labels in 1998, mergers reduced this to four major labels by 2005.

The success of MP3 was also influenced by the evolution of its organizational design. Of the four modalities suggested by Eisenmann (2008), MP3 was initially organized as a shared platform. As shared platforms require governance arrangements, platform sponsors must decide whether to organize under the auspices of an informal alliance, a new industry association, or an established Standard Development Organization (SDO). During the phase of 'preparing for market entry', several parties decided to collaborate in an SDO's standardization process. This provided a level playing field for the various participants, reduced the amount of competition and created alliances that sponsored the resulting standard. Subsequently the main platform sponsors, Fraunhofer and Thomson, had to find the initial market niches where market adoption would take root and grow. The organizational design evolved by including elements from a licensing mode. Fraunhofer and Thomson entered into a joint licensing agreement and actively licensed their patents. This enabled many platform providers to enter the market and target various applications. The result was a significant amount of momentum which could not be counteracted by powerful sponsors with a proprietary platform approach, or industry associations enforcing legislation.

7. CONCLUSION

The paradigm shift towards compressed audio in the music industry is a textbook example of Christensen's Innovators Dilemma. The incumbent parties were among the first that were able to benefit but passed the opportunity on to others since they failed to recognize that the technology would be successful in the market. Whereas Christensen's lessons are derived from the hard disc drive industry, the MP3 case shows that similar events occur with platform technologies. Not only did the market leaders in consumer audio equipment fail to embrace the opportunity, but so did the content providers. This latter point is where the MP3 case adds to Christensen's lessons.

Our study adds to the field of platform competitions, by showing that platform mediated networks can have a demand and supply network which are one and the same. When the demand and supply network are one and the same, the direct and indirect network externalities overlap and reinforce each other. This enables fast market adoption and undermines the position of the incumbent supply network.

We add to the work of Eisenmann (2008) by illustrating how a platform's organizational mode may evolve over time, and how these changes affect the platform competition. We subscribe to Eisenmann's claim regarding the importance of selecting the right organizational mode, but the case shows that the success of a particular organizational mode heavily depends on various other factors, such as the timing of market entry and the availability of complementary goods. A platform's organizational mode has an influence on these factors, but with multiple platforms competing in the market the influence is vice-versa.

The case of the MP3 audio compression format shows that the road to becoming the market standard is complex, involves many factors that influence the process, and takes many years. The case confirms known success factors, but also adds nuances;

- Technological superiority is a multifaceted concept whereby customer requirements are leading. Before audio compression formats, the history of music formats shows that a format had to have superior audio quality to become the market standard. While MP3 did not provide superior audio quality, it managed to outcompete the CD because the technology provided superior performance on other customer requirements;

- First mover advantage is only relevant when targeting the key applications. Several studies (e.g. Cusumano et al., 1992; Suarez, 2004) have shown that being first to enter a market provides an advantage in building up an installed base. As the case shows, technologies often have several applications and competing in the right market is more important than being first;

- The killer application follows from product proliferation. It is difficult to identify up-front which application will drive a technology's market adoption to the extent that it becomes the market standard. When implementing the technology in various products and addressing different applications, the chance to find the killer application increases.

We conclude that adding a sixth phase to Suarez's model was an important modification which enhanced our understanding of how technologies become the dominant platform. If we had taken Suarez's approach, the 'decisive battle' would have resulted in MP3 becoming the dominant format for music on the Internet, and the 'post-dominance' phase would have constituted the period when MP3 competed with the CD. As we see in this case, MP3 first became dominant in the niche of music distribution over the Internet, and subsequently competed with CD for the overall dominant music format. This distinction is essential for our understanding of how MP3 became the dominant format and underpins our assumption that a platform technology first becomes dominant in a niche market before competing for dominance in the product category.

REFERENCES

Abel, I. (2008). From technology imitation to market dominance: The case of iPod. *Journal of Global Competitiveness*, *18*(3), 257–274. doi:10.1108/10595420810906028

Alderman, J. (2001). *Sonic boom: Napster, MP3, and the new pioneers of music*. Cambridge, UK: Perseus Publishing.

Anderson, P., & Tushman, M. L. (1990). Technological Discontinuities and Dominant Designs: A Cyclical Model of Technological Change. *Administrative Science Quarterly*, *35*(4), 604–633. doi:10.2307/2393511

Apple Inc. (2004, August 10). *iTunes music store catalog tops one million songs*. Retrieved April 29, 2012, from http://www.apple.com/pr/library/2004/08/10iTunes-Music-Store-Catalog-Tops-One-Million-Songs.html

Apple Inc. (n.d.). *Form 10-Q (quarterly report)*. Retrieved from http://investor.apple.com/sec.cfm?ndq_keyword=&DocType=Quarterly

Arthur, W.B. (1994). Positive feedbacks in the economy. *The McKinsey Quarterly, 1*, 81-95.

Arthur, W. B. (1996, July-August). Increasing Returns and the New World of Business. *Harvard Business Review*, 100–109. PMID:10158472

Baldwin, C. Y., & Woodard, C. J. (2009). The architecture of platforms: A unified view. In *Platforms, Markets and Innovation*. Cheltenham, UK: Edward Elgar Publishing Limited. doi:10.4337/9781849803311.00008

Burkart, P., & McCourt, T. (2006). *Digital music wars: Ownership and control over the celestial jukebox*. Lanham, MD: Rowman and Littlefield.

Christensen, C. M. (1993). The rigid disk drive industry: A history of commercial and technological turbulence. *Business History Review*, *67*(4), 531–588. doi:10.2307/3116804

Christensen, C. M. (1997). *The Innovator's Dilemma: When New Technologies Cause Great Firms to Fail*. Boston, USA: Harvard Business School Press.

Clark, K. B. (1985). The interaction of design hierarchies and market concepts in technological evolution. *Research Policy*, *14*(5), 235–251. doi:10.1016/0048-7333(85)90007-1

CNET. (2004, October 15). *MP3 losing steam?* Retrieved on April 29, 2012, from http://news.cnet.com/MP3-losing-steam/2100-1027_3-5409604.html

Cusumano, M. A., Mylonadis, Y., & Rosenbloom, R. S. (1992). Strategic maneuvering and mass-market dynamics: The triumph of VHS over Beta. *Business History Review*, *66*(1), 51–94. doi:10.2307/3117053

David, P. A. (1985). Clio and the Economics of QWERTY. *The American Economic Review*, *75*(2), 332–337.

David, P. A., & Bunn, J. A. (1988). The economics of gateway technologies and network evolution: Lessons from the electricity supply history. *Information Economics and Policy*, *3*(2), 165–202. doi:10.1016/0167-6245(88)90024-8

Den Uijl, S., & De Vries, H. J. (2008). Setting a technological standard: Which factors can organizations influence to achieve dominance?. In *Proceedings 13th EURAS Workshop on Standardisation. Aachener Beiträge zur Informatik, Band 40*. Aachen: Wissenschaftsverlag Mainz in Aachen.

Denegri-Knott, J., & Tadajewski, M. (2010). The emergence of MP3 technology. *Journal of Historical Research in Marketing*, *2*(4), 397–425. doi:10.1108/17557501011092466

Dosi, G. (1982). Technological paradigms and technological trajectories. *Research Policy*, *11*(3), 147–162. doi:10.1016/0048-7333(82)90016-6

Eisenmann, T. (2008, Summer). Managing Proprietary and Shared Platforms. *California Management Review*, *50*(4), 31–53. doi:10.2307/41166455

Eisenmann, T., Parker, G., & Van Alstyne, M. W. (2006, October). Strategies for two-sided markets. *Harvard Business Review*, *84*(10), 92–101. PMID:16649701

Ethier, S. (2008). *The Worldwide PMP/MP3 Player Market: Shipment Growth to Slow Considerably*. In-Stat report.

Foster, R. (1986). *Innovation; The Attacker's Advantage*. New York: Summit Books.

Frainhofer, I. I. S. (2012, March 22). *Die MP3 Geschichte*. Retrieved March 22, 2012, from http://www.iis.fraunhofer.de/en/bf/amm/diemp-3geschichte/zeitleiste/

Gallagher, S., & Park, S. H. (2002). Innovation and Competition in Standard-Based Industries: A Historical Analysis of the U.S. Home Video Game Market. *IEEE Transactions on Engineering Management*, *49*(1), 67–82. doi:10.1109/17.985749

Gallagher, S. R. (2012). The battle of the blue laser DVDs: The significance of corporate strategy in standards battles. *Technovation*, *32*(2), 90–98. doi:10.1016/j.technovation.2011.10.004

Garud, R., Jain, S., & Kumaraswamy, A. (2002). Institutional entrepreneurship in the sponsorship of common technological standards: The case of Sun Microsystems and JAVA. *Academy of Management Journal*, *45*(1), 196–214. doi:10.2307/3069292

Garud, R., & Kumaraswamy, A. (1993). A., Changing Competitive Dynamics in Network Industries: An Exploration of Sun Microsystems' Open Systems Strategy. *Strategic Management Journal*, *14*(5), 351–369. doi:10.1002/smj.4250140504

Geek.com. (2000, November 1). *Warner Music likes Windows Media*. Retrieved on April 29, 2012, from http://www.geek.com/articles/news/warner-music-likes-windows-media-2000111

Group, N. P. D. (2006). *Annual digital music study survey of U.S. consumers 2006*. Author.

Group, N. P. D. (2007). *Annual digital music study survey of U.S. consumers 2007*. Author.

Group, N. P. D. (2009). *Annual digital music study survey of U.S. consumers, 2009*. Author.

Group, N. P. D. (2012, March 6). *Maintaining customers has been the key to a reinvigorated music market, according to NPDs annual music study*. Retrieved on April 29, 2012, from www.npd.com/wps/portal/npd/us/news/pressreleases/pr_120306

Handelsblatt. (2000, September 6). *Interview: Die Musikindustrie schläft weiter.* Retrieved on March 22, 2012, from http://www.handelsblatt.com/archiv/interview-mit-den-mp3-erfindern-interview-die-musikindustrie-schlaeft-weiter/2003290.html

Hause, K. (2000). *The future of the music industry: MP3, DVD audio and more.* IDC report.

International Federation of the Phonographic Industry (IFPI). (2001, April). *2000 recording industry world sales.* IFPI.

International Federation of the Phonographic Industry (IFPI). (2011, March). *The recording industry in numbers: The recorded music market in 2010.* IFPI.

Jobs, S. (2007). *Thoughts on Music.* Apple Inc. Press Release. Retrieved from http://www.apple.com/fr/hotnews/thoughtsonmusic/

Josephson, I. (2005, April 4). Presentation for NARM. *NPD Music Year.*

Khazam, J., & Mowery, D. (1994). The commercialization of RISC: Strategies for the creation of dominant designs. *Research Policy, 23*(1), 89–102. doi:10.1016/0048-7333(94)90028-0

Langlois, R. N., & Robertson, P. L. (1992). Networks and innovation in a modular system: Lessons from the microcomputer and stereo component industries. *Research Policy, 21*(4), 297–313. doi:10.1016/0048-7333(92)90030-8

Liebowitz, S. J., & Margolis, S. E. (1994). Network Externality: An Uncommon Tragedy. *The Journal of Economic Perspectives, 8*(2), 133–150. doi:10.1257/jep.8.2.133

Moore, G. E. (1965). Cramming more components onto integrated circuits. *Electronics, 38* (8).

Musmann, H. G. (2006, August). Genesis of the MP3 audio coding standard. *IEEE Transactions on Consumer Electronics, 52*(3), 1043–1049. doi:10.1109/TCE.2006.1706505

Nihon Keizai Shimbun. (2000, August 9). *Minidisc player/recorder shipments rise.* Retrieved on April 29, 2012, from http://www.telecompaper.com/news/minidisc-playerrecorder-shipments-rise

Paxton, M. (2000). *Portable Digital Music Players Ride the MP3 Wave.* Cahners In-Stat Group Report.

Pew Research Center. (2012, March 22). *Internet use over time.* Retrieved on March 22, 2012, from http://www.pewinternet.org/data-trend/internet-use/internet-use-over-time/

Rosenbloom, R. S., & Cusumano, M. A. (1987). Technological Pioneering and Competitive Advantage: The Birth of the VCR Industry. *California Management Review, 29*(4), 51–76. doi:10.2307/41162131

Rysman, M. (2009). The economics of two-sided markets. *The Journal of Economic Perspectives, 23*(3), 125–143. doi:10.1257/jep.23.3.125

Schilling, M. A. (2003). Technological Leapfrogging: Lessons from the U.S. Video Game Console Industry. *California Management Review, 45*(3), 6–32. doi:10.2307/41166174

Schilling, M. A. (2005). *Strategic Management of Technological Innovation.* New York: McGraw-Hill.

Shankar, V., & Bayus, B. L. (2003). Network effects and competition: An empirical analysis of the home video game industry. *Strategic Management Journal, 24*(4), 375–384. doi:10.1002/smj.296

Smit, F. C., & Pistorius, C. W. I. (1998). Implications of the Dominant Design in Electronic Initiation Systems in the South African Mining Industry. *Technological Forecasting and Social Change, 59*(3), 255–274. doi:10.1016/S0040-1625(98)00006-7

Smith, E., & Wingfield, N. (2003, September 9). The high cost of sharing. *The Wall Street Journal,* pp. B1, B8.

Spanias, A., Painter, T., & Venkatraman, A. (2007). *Audio signal processing and coding*. Hoboken, NJ: John Wiley & Sons, Inc. doi:10.1002/0470041978

Spilker, H. S., & Höier, S. (2013). Technologies of Piracy? Exploring the Interplay Between Commercialism and Idealism in the Development of MP3 and DivX. *International Journal of Communication*, 7, 2067–2086.

Sterne, J. (2012). *The meaning of a format*. Durham, NC: Duke University Press. doi:10.1215/9780822395522

Suarez, F. F. (2004). Battles for technological dominance: An integrative framework. *Research Policy*, *33*(2), 271–286. doi:10.1016/j.respol.2003.07.001

Todd, C. C., Davidson, G. A., Davis, M. F., Fielder, L. D., Link, B. D., & Vernon, S. (1994). *AC-3: Flexible Perceptual Coding for Audio Transmission and Storage*. Paper presented at the 96th Convention of the Audio Engineering Society. New York, NY.

Tripsas, M. (1997). Unraveling the Process of Creative Destruction: Complementary Assets and Incumbent Survival in the Typesetter Industry. *Strategic Management Journal*, *18*(S1), 119–142. doi:10.1002/(SICI)1097-0266(199707)18:1+<119::AID-SMJ921>3.3.CO;2-S

Wade, J. (1995). Dynamics of Organizational Communities and Technological Bandwagons: An Empirical Investigation of Community Evolution in the Microprocessor Market. *Strategic Management Journal*, *16*(S1), 111–133. doi:10.1002/smj.4250160920

Willard, G. E., & Cooper, A. C. (1985). Survivors of Industry Shake-Outs: The Case of the U.S. Color Television Set Industry. *Strategic Management Journal*, *6*(4), 299–318. doi:10.1002/smj.4250060402

KEY TERMS AND DEFINITIONS

Case Study: An intensive study of a single unit for the purpose of understanding a larger class of (similar) units.

Compressed Audio Format: Audio compression is a form of data compression designed to reduce the size of audio files. Audio compression algorithms are typically implemented in computer software as audio codecs.

De-Facto Standard: A standard that has emerged through market forces.

MP3: An audio compression format (also known as the MPEG-1 Layer 3 standard).

Paradigm Shift: A change in the basic assumptions, or paradigms, within the ruling theory of science.

Platform Technology: A technology from which various products can emerge without the expense of a new process/technology introduction.

Standardization: The formulation, publication, and implementation of guidelines, rules, and specifications for common and repeated use, aimed at achieving optimum degree of order or uniformity in a given context, discipline, or field.

Standards Battle: The fight for dominance in the market between two functionally equivalent standards.

ENDNOTES

[1] Data provided by the Recording Industry Association of America. Data is compiled by accounting firm PricewaterhouseCoopers on behalf of the Recording Industry Association of America. It is the RIAA's estimate of the size of the U.S. recorded music industry based on data collected directly from the major music companies (which create and/or distribute about 85% of the music sold in the U.S.).

2   The Fraunhofer Gesellschaft is a German research organization with a focus on applied science.

3   Based on various press releases, statistical data, and reports of the Japan Recording-Media Industries Association (JRIA).

4   Based on various sources: Data provided by the Recording Industry Association of America (RIAA); NPD, 2006, 2007, 2009. In order to match RIAA data with figures from NPD and compare music acquisition across formats, we utilized the NPD Group methodology and used an equivalent of 10 standalone digital tracks for each CD album (NPD, 2012).

5   Based on various market research reports of the NPD Group on how music was acquired from 2004-2009.

6   Figures in grey marked zones are based on market share data from 2004, extrapolated based on actual data from 2007-2009.

Chapter 10

Development of a Specification for Data Interchange between Information Systems in Public Hazard Prevention:
Dimensions of Success, Related Activities, and Contributions to the Development of Future Standardisation Strategy Frameworks

Simone Wurster
Berlin University of Technology, Germany

ABSTRACT

Standards and specifications for public security are missing in many technical aspects as well as the areas of communication protocols and security management. Several technology management research gaps related to this field exist, particularly regarding R&D stage standardisation. This chapter gives insight into the development of a specification (DIN SPEC) for the protection of transportation infrastructure based on civil security research results. Besides providing practical examples for activities related to the popular standardization strategy framework of Sherif, Jakobs, and Egyedi (2007), the chapter suggests its extension. Standardisation challenges and solutions are also unveiled. The chapter finishes by outlining key aspects that may influence the adoption of the specification. Fields of application of the findings include, in particular, fast track standardisation procedures with voluntary implementation of the results, the standardisation of R&D results, and standardisation projects among small groups.

DOI: 10.4018/978-1-4666-6332-9.ch010

1. INTRODUCTION

1.1 Public Security, Standards, and Standardisation Needs

The global intensity and frequency of terrorist attacks since the turn of the century show the vulnerability of modern societies and the need for protecting so-called critical infrastructures (see European Commission, 2004). Several recent studies highlight the need for security-related standards, e.g. ECORYS (2009), ESRIF (2009), the European Commission (2008, 2011a) and the European Council (2010). Standards and specifications for public security are missing in many technical aspects, as well as the areas of communication protocols and security management.

Sinay (2011) defines security as 'a system of measures, including their embodiments and their interactions, designed to ward off intentionally destructive activity resulting in injury or material damage'. The current global market size for security technologies and services is estimated at 100 billion Euros (approximately 143 billion US dollars), and the annual growth rate is predicted at a minimum of approximately 5% for the next few years (see ECORYS, 2009).

Standardisation is 'the activity of establishing and recording a limited set of solutions to actual or potential matching problems directed at benefits for the party or parties involved balancing their needs and intending and expecting that these solutions will be repeatedly or continuously used during a certain period by a substantial number of the parties for whom they are meant' (de Vries, 1999, p. 13). Blind (2004), as well as Swann (2000, 2010), offer an extended overview of the many advantages standardisation provides for the parties involved. To stimulate lead markets for security-related technologies and services, standards and specifications may provide a knowledge and technology transfer, connect relevant stakeholders, foster innovative demand, provide innovation-enhancing regulatory frameworks, intensify competition and increase exportability (see Blind, 2008a). Although some scientists are closely involved in standardisation processes, many researchers not only in the security field do not use the special opportunities that standardisation can offer to them (see Blind & Gauch, 2007).

The present study was part of the German project InfraNorm (2010-2013). Its goal was to initiate the development of standards and specifications for the protection of transportation infrastructure based on R&D stage standardisation and to provide a standardisation manual for the participants of the German Framework Program 'Research for Civil Security'.

1.2 Standardisation Instruments for Researchers

Standardisation is an important catalyst for innovation and modern societies need to include new knowledge from the research field in standards to promote innovation and competitiveness (see Blind, 2009; EXPRESS, 2010; CEN-CENELEC STAIR, 2011). But there are obstacles. The project INTEREST examined the barriers that prevent researchers from getting involved in standardisation. Three categories of barriers were identified: a lack of resources, the standardisation process itself and the lack of awareness and visibility of standards and standardisation processes. The third category illustrates in particular that researchers are not aware of the potential benefits of active participation in standard-setting (Blind & Gauch, 2007; INTEREST, 2006). Emphasising these issues, the report on the future of European (EU) standardisation stresses the need to improve mutual awareness and cooperation between standardizers, innovators, and the research communities (see EXPRESS, 2010). As a solution, the CEN-CENELEC Working Group STAIR (STAndardisation Innovation and Research) published the Integrated Approach for Standardization, Innovation and Research which links the specific stages of research, development and innovation (R&D&I) and standardisation, see Figure 1.

In March 2011 STAIR published a paper on the operationalisation of the integrated approach in the future common strategic framework for EU research and innovation (CEN-CENELEC STAIR, 2011). A month later the European Commission formulated a 'Strategic Vision for Standards' (European Commission, 2011b) which highlights the role of standards for innovative products and processes and explains a number of issues concerning the improvement of the standardisation process. The European Parliament has adopted the regulation on European Standardisation in first reading in September 2012. According to the document, standardisation process should be accelerated, simplified and modernised (see Scapolo, Churchill & Viaud, 2013).

Standardisation organizations have developed different types of processes and products to address the need to save time and to foster the diffusion of innovation via standardisation. In addition, a CEN-CENELEC Research Helpdesk is being established (see CEN-CENELEC, 2014). A suitable instrument on both a European and an international level is the 'Workshop Agreement' which is offered by the European standardisation organisation CEN and the international standardisation organisation ISO. The specific documents are called CEN Workshop Agreement (CWA) and International Workshop Agreement (IWA). Workshop Agreements are consensus documents. They represent the output of a workshop, which is open to all stakeholders (see Hatto, 2013; CEN, 2014a; ISO, 2014). Developed in 10 to 12 months, they are quickly available to address specific market requirements. Their main fields of application are areas which are not the subject of more formal standardisation and they can ultimately become a European Norm or international standard (EN or IS). According to Hatto (2013), they 'are ideal as

Figure 1. The Integrated Approach for Standardization, Innovation and Research (Source: CEN CEN-ELEC STAIR, 2011)

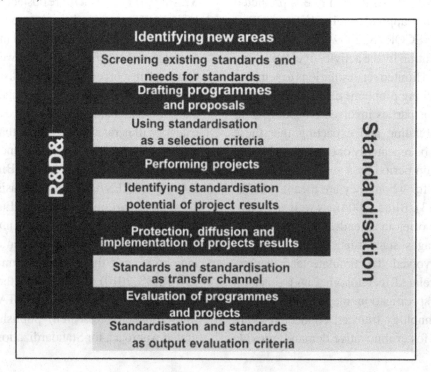

fast deliverables for emerging areas' and 'might be the ideal route for delivering a standard based on results from a research project'. Workshop Agreements usually have a limited lifespan of three years. After this period, or earlier if appropriate, they can be transformed into another type of standard. Withdrawing them is also possible.

There are two additional possible deliverables in ISO and one in CEN which offer interesting conditions for researchers (see Hatto, 2013). They are most suitable for topics that are still under development or which have not reached a sufficient state of maturity for more formal standardisation. These are international Technical Specifications (TS) and their equivalent CEN TS as well as international Publicly Available Specifications (PAS) (see ISO, 2014 and CEN, 2014b). Like IS and EN, TS typically contain requirements that must be satisfied in order to demonstrate compliance. In contrast to EN, there is no compulsion on members of CEN to implement CEN TS or to abolish conflicting national standards. PAS are similar to TS but they focus on an earlier stage of the technological development. They are usually developed in less than 12 months. According to Hatto (2013), they act as an early stage deliverable to encourage a move towards more formal standardization.

1.3 DIN Specifications (DIN SPECs)

Funded by the European Union, the project IN-TEREST examined the barriers that prevent researchers from getting involved in standardisation. Three categories of barriers were discovered: lack of resources, the standardisation process itself and the lack of awareness and visibility of standards and standardisation processes, which includes the lack of awareness of the potential benefits of active participation in standard-setting (see Blind & Gauch, 2007; INTEREST, 2006).

Standardisation organizations have developed different types of processes and products to address the need to save time. Examples on the European

and international level were described in section 1.2. On national level, the DIN German Institute for Standardisation, for example, created the new instrument 'DIN Specification' (DIN SPEC). Several kinds of DIN SPECs were created. This article focuses on DIN SPECs based on procedures to develop public available specifications, DIN SPEC (PAS) – DIN SPEC as the abbreviation.

While German DIN standards (DIN Norms) are developed based on full consensus decisions of all stakeholders, the development of a DIN SPEC does not require the involvement of all stakeholders. Therefore, the work leads to a quicker result. In contrast to the development of a DIN Norm which may take up several years, a DIN SPEC will be released several months after its submission to the DIN (see Figure 2). Its development takes place in existing standards committees or in project-related committees.

The development of a DIN SPEC is characterized by four phases: proposal stage, development, publication and review. The standardisation process begins with a standardisation proposal to the DIN. After receiving approval, the initiator creates the business plan. The document is published on the website of the DIN for four weeks and has to include the statement that the standardisation process is open to every interested party. To participate in the project notification must be given within a specified period. After the expiration of the publication deadline, the working group is established. A DIN secretary supports the process.

The development of the specification contains four elements: a kick-off meeting, manuscript preparation, draft publication (optional) and incorporation of comments (optional).

The kick-off meeting includes the adoption of the business plan by considering any comments received in the publication phase. Normally, a chairman or a chairwoman is appointed at the beginning of the meeting.

The preparation of the manuscript is the main activity of the standardisation process. The phase ends when the working group reaches consensus on

Figure 2. Comparison between DIN Standards and DIN SPECs. Source: DIN e.V. (in German).

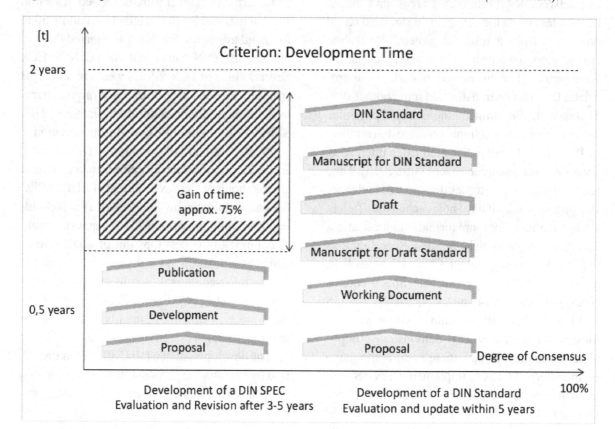

the contents of the relevant DIN SPEC. Optionally, the manuscript can be published online for public comment for four weeks, followed by a discussion of the comments by the working group regarding a possible incorporation into the manuscript. The next step is the adoption of the specification by the working group by majority decision.

The subsequent publication must be approved by the Director of the DIN. Then, the DIN secretary submits the document to the DIN department of quality control. Normally, the specification is then published and also made available via internet.

After three years a review is carried out by the DIN. Comments received during the validity period of the DIN SPEC are discussed. The review leads to four conclusions: revision of the

DIN SPEC, withdrawal and revision, as well as the withdrawal of a DIN Norm. The preparation of a European or international document is also possible.

2. LITERATURE REVIEW AND RESEARCH GAP

Based on their economic function, four types of standards can be distinguished: (1) semantic standards; measurement and testing standards (2); quality and variety reducing standards (3) and interface and compatibility standards (4) (see Blind, 2004). With regard to the position in the product cycle, Sherif (2001) identified three types of standards. According to his classification, standards can be anticipatory, participatory, or responsive.

Anticipatory standards are standards 'that must be created before widespread acceptance of devices or services'. Participatory standards 'proceed in lock-step with implementations that test the specifications before adopting them' and responsive standards 'occur to codify a product or service that has been sold with some success' (Sherif, 2001, p. 2).

R&D stage standardisation is a specific kind of participatory standardisation used in practice (see e.g. DIN, 2012). It is a proactive approach to questions of standardisation very early on in the overall innovation process, which can then benefit from the timely formulation of recommendations on structural aspects of the product/system that is to be developed.

In many fields, investigating factors of success and performance indicators is of great scientific interest (see e.g. Cooper & Kleinschmidt, 1987, 1990, 1995; de Brentani, 1991; Ernst, 2002; Liu & Arnett, 2000).

Efficiency and effectiveness are important goals for projects (see e.g. Kisielnicki & Sroka, 2005). Specific performance indicators research in this field is for example, done by Boehlje and Schiek (1998), Clarke (1999) and Janecek and Hynek (2010). While Clarke (1999) defines success as the effectiveness of a project, Boehlje and Schiek (1998) and Janecek and Hynek (2010) investigate factors that lead to efficiency in organizations. Therefore, we define factors of success for the purpose of this study as a number of characteristics that have an impact on both the efficiency and effectiveness of a project or organization.

Sherif et al. (2007) offer a framework to investigate project management issues leading to successful standardisation projects. According to Sherif et al. (2007), 'successful standards have to respond adequately and timely to societal needs in terms of user requirements, regulatory constraints and unstated assumptions, whether collective or individual.' In this context, the authors describe 'the need to define a way to evaluate and measure the quality of standards'. They identified six dimensions which are important or, quoting the introduction of the first dimension, even 'essential for the success of a project' (p. 8). The list includes the dimensions scope management, time management, quality management, cost management, resource management and documentation management. Regarding time management Egyedi (2006) adds: If a standard '(…) includes too many details at an early stage of the life cycle [of the technology], the wrong aspects may be included. If standardisation takes place late in the life cycle but does not respond to specific end-user demands, it may be irrelevant.'

To ensure interoperability, which is one important outcome of appropriate quality management, Egyedi (2006) offers a comprehensive list of recommendations related to the drafting of standards, the pre-implementation and the post-implementation.

In addition to the extended work of Sherif et al. (2007), Loewer (2006) and Pfetsch (2008) investigate negotiation strategies and Riefler (2008) shows, that higher homogeneity of interests facilitates a standardisation process, whereas higher heterogeneity of organization types in a standardisation project raises the acceptance of a standard. The author also shows that the size of a standardisation group is important. Small groups facilitate decision making while more effort may be needed to influence the target group to adopt the results.

Pfetsch (2008) focuses specifically on workshops, conflicts and negotiations as a communicative mode of problem solving. Based on a description of specific styles of negotiations, he explains success strategies of confrontational or integrative conflict management. He also emphasizes the importance of hard and soft factors in the negotiation process, depending on the different stages of negotiations and of the conflict cycle.

Additionally, Pfetsch (2008) identifies seven rules for successful negotiations in standard setting.

Regarding the stages that follow the standardisation process Blind (2008b) investigates factors influencing the lifetime of telecommunication and information technology standards. Success factors in particular are not investigated.

Pioneering research concerning formal security-related standards and standardisation was done by Blind (2008a). Yet, there is little empirical insight into the field available so far.

- Little is known about the establishment of security standards, particularly in the field of R&D stage standardisation.
- Although Sherif (2001) identified three standard types with regard to different positions of standards in the technology cycle, there has not been much research done about R&D stage standardisation and related anticipatory and participatory standards.
- Little is known about the standardisation of common results of joint research projects.
- The development of DIN SPECs and its success factors have not yet been investigated.

Based on a survey and a case study, this chapter aims at providing new scientific insight into that field.

3. RESEARCH OBJECTIVES

Based on the research gap described before, key research activities in the project InfraNorm were intended to offer answers to the following central question: How can security researchers establish standards and specifications successfully? Three sub-questions were derived:

1. Which activities characterized the successful development of the standard or specification?

2. Which challenges occurred?
3. Which solutions were found?

With regard to question 1, definitions of success dimensions and related indicators are needed. While a key foundation was given by Sherif et al. (2007), InfraNorm aimed at addressing specific problems that researchers in the German security research program asserted were related to security-specific standardisation. In order to consider their needs appropriately, a preliminary analysis of such problems was needed. Therefore, a survey was conducted. The questionnaire used consisted of 14 questions in eight topic areas and was sent to approximately 300 German researchers in the field of civil security. The completion of the questionnaires took place between May and July 2011. 48 persons participated in the survey.

In order to offer additional insight into the barriers that prevent researchers from getting involved in standardisation investigated by INTEREST (2006) the German security researchers were asked for their opinion on what barriers prevent participation in the security-related standards. They were asked to rate the importance of eleven barriers in total. The three most significant barriers include the use of other forms of exploitation of R&D results, the time required and the necessary costs. All findings support the results of INTEREST (2006).

The aim of revealing perceived risks in security-related standardisation had particularly high priority. Therefore, the participants were asked to give a risk assessment. Specific risks related to security-standards were identified, for example ethical risks including privacy-related risks and the risk of misusing the security-standards information for criminal purposes.

Another question dealt with addressed the risks of conflict in the standardisation process. Six central aspects were identified: the identification of mutual benefits, consensus-building,

Intellectual Property Rights (IPR), administrative problems and delays, specific aspects in an international context, as well as the users' resistance and problems of acceptance.

A following question focused on the risks of conflict within the different stages in the standardisation process. Typical stages of the standardisation process include the initiation of the project (Phase 1), the development (Phase 2), the release of a standard (Phase 3), its utilization (Phase 4), as well as the revision (Phase 5). On the basis of those, the participants were asked to develop a ranking of the phases according to the perceived conflict potential in each of these stages. Phase 2 was ranked first, hence viewed to bear the biggest potential for conflict, followed by Phase 1, Phase 5 and Phase 4. The stage 'release' (Phase 3) is allocated the least conflict potential.

Based on the survey, seven issues were selected for investigating success factors to overcome potential problems: resources and time required (related to Phase 1), consensus-building, IPR, specific problems related to security-related standards (related to Phase 2); acceptance of a specification (related to Phase 4); as well as the further development of the standard as an issue of Phase 5.

A comparison between these aspects and the success dimensions offered by Sherif et al. (2007) lead to the following results:

- Appropriate scope management lays the foundation for the future acceptance of a specification. This dimension also covers the avoidance of specific conflicts (which may for example lead to frustrated participants leaving a working group) and addresses problems of specific delays.
- Problems related to resources are well addressed by Sherif et al's (2007) dimension 'resource management'.

- This dimension also covers the avoidance of remaining problems related to consensus-building and conflicts within a working group.
- Concerns regarding the time required are reflected by Sherif et al's (2007) dimension 'time management'.
- Solutions for problems related to security-standards are a specific issue. They were included in the quality management dimension. In contrast to the other topics of this dimension, ensuring the avoidance of misuse of a specification for example is mandatory for security-related standardisation. This aspect requires special attention.
- Usability of a specification can also be addressed by this dimension.
- Besides appropriate scope management, quality management is similarly essential to ensure the future acceptance of a specification.
- Appropriate document management may also help to ensure usability. Furthermore, it addresses problems related to language issues reflecting general problems in the international standardisation projects mentioned in the InfraNorm survey.
- IPR, which are not explicitly covered by Sherif et al. (2007), are regarded as an issue of 'scope management' (search for relevant IPR), resource management (management of potential conflicts) as well as quality management (use of alternative options).
- The further development of the specification is a specific problem but has certain similarities with aspects related to the quality management category. Therefore, it will be analysed in the context of this category.

In summary, Sherif et al's (2007) framework offers a foundation to address the specific problems perceived by the participants in the German security research program. Particular attention was paid to the integration of specific security-related issues into the framework. However, the identified solution is not regarded as optimal. Since ensuring appropriate solutions for these issues is mandatory for security standardisation, the absence of a specific dimension related to them in the framework bears the risks of 'forgetting' the implementation of necessary measures. Therefore, an alternative approach will be described in section 9.

As mentioned before, three research questions were formulated. Based on Sherif et al's (2007) work, an extension of the first question was derived: Which activities characterize the successful development of the standard or specification? How are a) scope management, b) time management, c) quality management, d) cost management, e) resource management and f) documentation management executed? In this context, Sherif et al's (2007) work also draws attention to additional problems not mentioned by the participants of the survey described before.

As shown in section 2, Sherif et al. (2007) offer a list of indicators showing that the scope is not well managed. Therefore, the following questions were derived: Does the scope match the intended use? Were there changes that led to delays? Have there been inappropriate compromises? Did frustrated participants leave the working group due to change in scope?

Regarding time management it was shown before, that the development of a DIN SPEC is theoretically possible within six months. The realization in individual cases depends on the relevant project, its content, the project group as well as the project management skills of the chairman. Regarding the starting point of the project, specific conditions are given by the time frame of the project InfraNorm. Therefore, we identify successful time management of a working group in the InfraNorm context by comparing the time required for the development of the relevant DIN SPEC with the 'optimal' time span of six months.

Results of appropriate quality management include the conformity of the specification to its scope and the technical requirements of the target group as well as the avoidance of incompatible implementations. Therefore, two key questions were derived: Is there conformity to the scope and the technical requirements? And: Are there incompatible implementations? An additional question is: Are specific security-related issues addressed appropriately?

Questions related to cost management are: Did the project team pay attention to backward compatibility? And are there reference implementations? R&D stage standardisation projects may build on R&D projects, which include a technical pre-version of the standard. Therefore, specific sources of success regarding cost management are usable.

Resource management is mainly linked to the management of human resources. Therefore, relevant questions are: Have there been rivalries? And: Did conflicts occur?

Two occurring questions are related to document management: Is supplemental material offered? And, with specific regard to international working groups, how are language issues managed in drafting the documents?

The main goal of investigating activities related to the six dimensions of success in the case study of the following sections is showing aspects leading to the realization of desired outcomes or to the absence of important problems.

Additionally, it would be very interesting to offer information about the success of the specification itself by referring to the number of users, the number of implementations etc. This is not possible yet but a short estimation will be given at the end of this article.

4. RESEARCH DESIGN

According to Yin (2011), qualitative research has become a popular form of research in many academic and professional fields. A case study is a qualitative research strategy 'which focuses on understanding the dynamics present within single settings' (Eisenhardt, 1989, p. 534). An advantage of qualitative research is that it facilitates insight into new fields, e.g. based on case studies. According to Yin (2008), case studies are particularly suitable if 'how' or 'why' (p. 8) questions are to be answered. Publications in the field of standardisation based on case study research include for example Bekkers (2001), Blind (2003), Blind and Iversen (2004), de Vries, de Vries, and Oshri (2008), Iversen (2004), Iversen, Bekkers, and Blind (2006) and van de Kaa (2009). Nevertheless there is a huge research gap in the area of public security research.

As mentioned before, the six categories of standardisation quality identified by Sherif et al. (2007) were chosen as the foundation of the in-depth analysis of the project described in section 5. They were extended by specific issues regarding security-related standards and the further development of R&D-based standards. The case study methodology was chosen to give a deep insight how security-related DIN SPECs based on R&D results are developed.

The preparation of the InfraNorm standardisation manual includes the task of providing in-depth information about standardisation processes to develop DIN SPECs based on the specific standardisation activities within the project. This task was easily combinable with the research methodology 'participant observation.' Participant observation is a field research method and offers a specific methodology for case study research. It simultaneously combines 'document analysis, interviews ..., direct participation and observation as well as introspection' (Flick, 2002, p. 139). Researchers go directly to the social system under investigation and collect data there (see DeWalt & DeWalt, 2002). For the execution of the case studies an action plan was completed which included a case study plan and a monitoring scheme for the attendance at meetings of the working groups and discussions

with participants, the preparation of field notes, the analyses of project documents and protocols as well as the completion of case study reports.

During the project minutes of the meetings were kept; relevant information was extracted and categorized. The focus was on activities related to the specific categories defined previously. Additionally, there was a feedback round during the final meeting of the project. The minutes of the meeting were used in the same way.

Possible challenges like the definition of system boundaries and the diffusion of the DIN SPEC were identified early on and documented by the working group. The identification of additional challenges was based on coding of the author's field notes and protocols. Subsequently, the documents were scanned to identify possible solutions and to include them into the relevant categories.

5. DESCRIPTION OF THE STANDARDISATION PROJECT

5.1 Introduction

The exchange of information between various IT systems in civil hazard prevention often requires the implementation of complex, proprietary data interfaces. Recurring implementation efforts and maintenance overhead, however, may be reduced by a communication standard. Therefore, the objective of developing the DIN SPEC was to lay the foundation for interoperability between respective information systems.

The developed DIN SPEC describes a data exchange format for information systems in public security. It includes syntactic and semantic requirements for the exchange of data. Its aim is to lay the foundation for basic interoperability between information systems. The core topic is the definition of a message exchange format between information systems of different organizations whose communication is already established. This allows the respective developers of these systems, hereafter to develop a data interface. Via this interface, a unique semantic data exchange is carried out. Since the exchanged content can be diverse, the document considers this on a relatively high level of abstraction. The document specifies generalized categories of information, which can reflect a large part of the information exchange.

The standardisation project was built on the results of three former projects within the German Framework Program - Research for Civil Security. One project had a leading function. Standardisation was intended right from the beginning of the project. Therefore, resources to develop the DIN SPEC were well-organized.

The working group included two university employees, four company representatives, a secretary of the DIN German Institute for Standardisation as well as the author of this article who was a permanent guest of the working group, but was not involved in the development of the specification. Therefore, the risk of being biased regarding the research activities should be limited.

The university employees realized the importance of offering a specification for data exchange to exploit other R&D results. Additional plans to use the specification will be explained later in more detail. Mainly they included a demonstrator and reference implementations. Besides writing publications, the researchers identified the development of a specification as a means to exploit R&D results with a lasting impact.

The companies are vendors of security solutions. They also realized the need for standardised interconnections. Furthermore, they wanted to give their customers the opportunity to use a modern standard without being dependent on a proprietary solution. One company member of the working group described his interest in the standardisation project as follows:

A primary goal related to the committee work was using contacts with other companies in the same subject area as [we] are. Through working on such a project with common goals, we

obtained an insight into the thinking and working methods of other companies in an industry that is an important partner for our customers ... in everyday business. Of course we also wanted to give impulses in the standardisation process, to include important topics based on our experience with our customers.

The decision to develop a DIN SPEC had several reasons:

- According to section 1, its development is faster than the development of a DIN Norm.
- Its development was also regarded as faster and easier than the development of a European or international specification or standard without losing this option.
- Based on the three German projects it was easy to find partners.
- Without the need to coordinate dates among partners from different countries and by avoiding extensive travelling cost and language problems, a fast and efficient process was expected.

Nevertheless the working group regards the option of further internationalization activities as very interesting. As mentioned before, a DIN SPEC is normally used for three years. After this period decisions regarding further steps will be made. Later it will be described how the working group will evaluate the specification after one year to decide on further steps, including the development of a European or international standardisation project based on the DIN SPEC.

To understand the needs of the target group and their requirements for the specification workshops, round tables for interviews were done within the research project before standardisation effort itself started. The project team worked closely together with different stakeholders like the Red Cross, fire fighters, the Federal Agency for Technical Relief (THW), the Federal Police and the State Police.

5.2 Initiation of the Project and Kick-Off Meeting

The standardisation project formally started in spring 2011 with the development of the business plan and a subsequent kick-off meeting in July 2011. Table 1 gives an overview of the key characteristics of the project.

For developing the DIN SPEC, the participants agreed on arranging three meetings in three consecutive months in an attempt to approve the DIN SPEC by the end of the fourth quarter of 2011. The initiator, an engineer of the participating university, was elected as chairman.

In Germany, data exchange in civil hazard prevention is embedded in federal structures. Therefore, the aim of the project was to address specific preconditions of data interchange in the context of federalism. An analysis of existing standards showed that no solutions for such issues existed. The aim of the DIN SPEC is to enable communication while maintaining different methods for doing so. Thus, the present effort sets itself apart by focusing on flexibility and semi-structuring.

One of the first identified tasks was to establish a common understanding of the target audience of the DIN SPEC, which has subsequently been specified to include dispatchers at control centres, software producers and developers.

Instead of using IT systems, paper-based records were common in many application fields at control centres at the time of initiating the project. Thus, the development of the DIN SPEC has been a proactive effort.

The working group attached importance to generating a benefit for all participants. Therefore, the chairman called for a transparent display of each member's viewpoint and everyone's contribution to the process. Throughout the initiation phase interactions with external stakeholders were important as well. Out of five prospective partners two could not be convinced to become project participants. Reasons given included that the initiative would entail giving up several advantages that proprietary solutions bring along. Another company indicated interest in the initiative, but lacked resources needed for contributing to the standardisation process.

The most important result of the initiation phase concerns the definition of the scope of the DIN SPEC. Additional technical requirements that have been defined include, in particular, accuracy, completeness, avoiding redundancy, avoiding any extra effort for operators, as well as offering the opportunity to plan the implementation effort appropriately.

5.3 1. Workshop (August 2011)

One core theme of the workshop was the issue of scope with regard to content and the technical principles of the data transfer. Furthermore, the structure and contents of the first draft version of the DIN SPEC were discussed in detail.

As shown before, the project's environment is characterized by federalism. For example, the names of firemen's' ranks vary throughout the country. Similarly, there are many different categories of emergency vehicles and various types of dispatch centres. Therefore, the DIN SPEC focuses on flexibility and semi-structuring.

Several participants favoured an application of the DIN SPEC in a state of its emergency, while other participants preferred usability for data exchange in both exceptional and regular situa-

Table 1. Key characteristics of the project

Type of Standard	DIN SPEC on data exchange format
Initiator	university (coordinator of several projects within the security research program)
Foundation	three projects of the German security research program
Participants	2 university employees, 4 company representatives
Duration	6 months
Realization	kick-off meeting, 3 workshops, final meeting, conference calls

tions. In the case that only exceptional situations are covered, another SPEC for regular situations would be necessary. However, both specifications might be incompatible with each other. Consequently, at a following meeting it was decided that the DIN SPEC may enable data exchange in both exceptional and regular situations. Moreover, it was important for the working group to formulate no restrictive requirements. They deliberately avoided demanding use of specific GIS software.

5.4 2. Workshop (September 2011) and 3. Workshop (Beginning of November 2011)

The workshops were prepared in an iterative way by not only sending out multiple revised versions of the DIN SPEC, but also by incorporating comments sent by the working group via e-mail. The second workshop yielded several resolutions. All participants were satisfied with the accomplishment realized so far.

The agenda of the third workshop included the clarification of remaining issues as well as the inclusion of additional change requests within open discussion rounds. A proposal to allow the implementation of parts of the DIN SPEC to promote its dissemination, inasmuch as the actors involved agree on the types of the exchanged information, was discarded. This would have created problems, if a new player entered into this type of communication relationship.

Specific activities were done to ensure appropriate certification activities would be related to the specification in the future. Moreover, the participants reflected on possible further steps after the publication, including deliberations on developing a Norm or a European specification.

5.5 Final Meeting (End of November 2011)

In preparation of the workshop, another version of the DIN SPEC was issued by the chairman, sent

out and commented on by the working group via e-mail. Above all, the agenda included the finalization of the draft version and issuing measures.

To evaluate the project results thus far, specific screening criteria were defined and applied, including 'internationalization potential' and 'expandability'. Internationalization potential was assessed and ensured by a possible coverage of the DIN SPEC's contents by the encoding format UTF-81, an English XML-nomenclature, an internationally applicable XML-framework and broad semantic definitions which enable the application of the specification in additional countries.

The foundation of the criteria 'expandability' is particularly concerned with the aspect that in case of future updates or extensions, users using version 1 may still be enabled to communicate, i.e. previous elements need to be compatible with newer versions.

5.6 Conference Call (End of December 2011) and Publication

The key goal of the conference call was the approval of the DIN SPEC. The conference call was carried out using Microsoft Office LiveMeeting, so that the current document was visible for all participants. Changes discussed could thus be incorporated into the document immediately. Again, the concern was raised that no one who buys and implements a first version of the specification can be forced to update his or her system to the next version. Respective measures have been taken. The adapted version was subsequently released for publication. Reflecting on the results, one member of the working group described the benefits of the specification as follows:

An important benefit for [our company] is related to the simplification of our own development of interfaces and software solutions. We regard a collaborative development of such interfaces, not only across companies but also across industries, as a great value added (...). In relations with our customers, [our company] can play the role of a pioneer and offer innovative solutions and further developments. ... Finally, we hope that the work in this standardisation process is positive marketing, and that it increases our awareness, especially in industries in which we do not operate yet.

5.7 Further Measures

In order to ensure an appropriate diffusion of the DIN SPEC, marketing measures have been planned. Public relations activities are being carried out by every related organization. Several implementations by all partners were planned as reference systems. The intention was to have synergies with other research projects. A member of a university planned on providing a specific open source implementation, along with articles in specialized journals and conference contributions. The first activities were undertaken and several articles were published.

In terms of the content, rather than promoting the DIN SPEC itself, it appeared to be more effective to promote the standardised exchange or the application, respectively. The business representatives also highlighted the topic on their website.

After one year, considerations for further development of the DIN SPEC on the participant's level are envisaged. For guaranteeing further development of the DIN SPEC even in the case of a change of employer by group members, strategic measures were introduced as a precaution.

6. SUCCESS FACTORS OF THE STANDARDISATION PROJECT

According to Sherif et al's (2007) activities leading to successful standardisation projects can be described by using the six dimensions scope management, time management, resource management, quality management, cost management and documentation management. As shown in

section 3, they were extended by specific aspects of security-related R&D-stage standardisation.

The occurrence of the six success dimensions in this case study is described below. The case study also unveiled a need for a further extension of Sherif et al's (2007) framework, e.g. regarding the further development of a specification and its lifecycle management. These issues were, for example, included in the dimension 'document management'. Table 2 summarizes the results.

The InfraNorm survey, which was mentioned previously, showed that most German security researchers do not have any experience in standardisation. However, the chairman's prior experience in standardisation issues, as well as his possession of the rare combination of experience in security research and standardisation, benefited the process. It influenced many dimensions positively.

Regarding scope management the foundations of the project were laid by the identification of a need for standardisation that has not yet been covered. Uniqueness compared to other standards was carefully ensured. No other standardisation committee had addressed the relevant data exchange based on the specific requirements of federalism.

Reflecting recommendations from ETSI (2012), requirements of the heterogeneous target group were analysed in detail through workshops, interviews, etc. and could be used as a key foundation of the standardisation project. The added value of the DIN SPEC was clearly defined.

Based on the aim of serving a broad target audience, standardisation alternatives focusing on one scenario or type of dispatch centres only, were ruled out. For any decision, emphasis was put on the later acceptance of the DIN SPEC, mainly by purposefully investigating and accounting for requirements of the target audience.

While changes in scope may have different reasons, Sherif et al. (2007) stress the importance of an appropriate management of the relevant situations. A change in the project was related to the usability of the DIN SPEC for data exchange in

Table 2. Success factors of the standardisation project and their effects based on Sherif et al. (2007)

Dimension of Success	Activities in the Project	Related Effects
Scope Management	• Well-defined added value based on interviews, workshops, etc. within a research project. • Investigation of existing standards and clear definition of unique content. • Focus on a broad target audience.	• Scope matches intended use. • No delays due to changes. • No situations with 'frustrated participants leaving the working group' due to change in scope. • No committee with similar activities.
Time Management	• Appropriate link between R&D and standardisation combined with appropriate resource planning. • Effective time management.	DIN SPEC could be finished after a few months.
Quality Management*	• Projection of reference implementations. • Specific decision not to allow the implementation of parts of the DIN SPEC only. • Appropriate strategies to avoid use of the DIN SPEC other than for its intended purposes. • Projection of certification activities. • Monitoring responses to the DIN SPEC for about one year in order to decide on further actions.	• Linkage with the scope and the technical requirements. • Avoidance of misuse.
Cost Management	• Sensibility for backward compatibility, in case of pre-defined additional options in the future backward compatibility ensured. • Use of identified synergies with R&D projects regarding reference implementations. • Usability of the DIN SPEC for data exchange in both exceptional and regular situations. • Avoidance of additional DIN SPECs and risk of incompatibilities. • Assurance of internationalization and further migration.	• No lock-ins in out-dated versions in the future. • Avoidance of wrong implementations. • Avoidance of investment in additional interfaces.
Resource Management	• Appropriate composition of the working group. • Transparency of goals and the contributions of partners.	• No rivalries. • No powerful actor who took the agenda and changed the scope.
Document Management	• Additional publication of an XML scheme for data interchange between information systems in civil hazard prevention. • Implementation of measures to guarantee continuity in the working group's work despite changes in staff.	• Usability of the specification. • Ensuring availability of up-dates.
* including management of specific security issues		

both exceptional and regular situations. Through an appropriate re-definition of the application fields of the DIN SPEC, not only the need for an additional SPEC, but also the risk of incompatibilities has been avoided.

The project clearly benefited from this change. It also showed the interrelation between scope management and cost management, another dimension of success identified by Sherif et al. (2007).

Time management was organized well. Being able to build on the results of the requirement analyses, the working group could work efficiently as a small group without competition. They also examined what could be realized within the constrained time frame given for developing the DIN SPEC. Thus, time targets and the realization of certain elements were balanced. Hereby, the working group showed the willingness to eliminate some of the possible elements of the specification.

The project was able to be finished quickly. The publication took place early in the technology lifecycle. Therefore, the problem of being too late was avoided, but there are not very many systems that can use the specification so far. Therefore, the diffusion of the specification will need time.

Regarding quality management, conformity to the different requirements was ensured. Specific considerations were related to appropriate data protection. Therefore, the project team also ensured that misuse of the specification could be avoided. Regarding the risk of incompatible implementations the working group found out that residual risk cannot be avoided.

As an aspect of cost management it was important to ensure backward compatibility and thereby secure investment. Another aspect of good cost management was the proactive avoidance of an additional specification for data exchange in regular situations.

The possibilities of internationalization and of further developing the DIN SPEC are assured by multiple measures. Internationalization is possible through, for example, use of English XML-nomenclature, of an internationally applicable XML-framework and of broad semantic definitions. First internationalization activities started.

Regarding functionality, future versions of the DIN SPEC may particularly consist of more categories to describe security risks and incidents. Nevertheless, communication between systems using the current and following versions of the DIN SPEC is made possible regarding the exchange of information related to the core categories of information.

Various measures to support the adoption of the specification were planned.

As mentioned in section 3, resource constraints are often a barrier hindering standardisation activities. In this case, standardisation was planned by the time that funding for an R&D project had been applied for and was included in resource planning. Activities to prepare for the standardisation project were integrated into the project and

helped save time later. As described earlier, the working group could work efficiently as a small group without competition, allowing them to work without conflict. Resource management was well organized. Goals and planned contributions of the members were openly presented. No specific conflict occurred. As mentioned before, the working group attached importance to generating a benefit for all participants. Right from the beginning the group adopted the principle from the Harvard negotiation project: 'All parties should benefit from the options chosen and should receive mutual gains' (see Pfetsch, 2008, p.58).

The specification was written in the native language of the working group members. Therefore several problems related to document management could be avoided but they may occur later. The publication of an XML scheme of specific aspects of the specification helps the target group to use the specification in the right way.

So far, no specific success factors related to Intellectual Property Rights occurred. One prospective partner could not be convinced to become a project participant because the initiative would entail giving up unique selling propositions that proprietary solutions bring along. The issue is discussed in the next section.

The supporters of the DIN SPEC aim at triggering strong demand for systems, which can communicate based on the DIN SPEC in security-related public procurement. The realization may function as a key factor to make the DIN SPEC successful.

7. CHALLENGES AND A SOLUTION-ORIENTED APPROACH

The working group faced challenges. One challenge the group faced right at the beginning of the project. As described in chapter 1 and chapter 6, was not possible to involve two potential partners and experts in the standardisation effort as desired. In one case this was caused by the resource restrictions of an SME, while the other potential partner preferred to promote his own proprietary solutions. Fortunately, the working group could compensate the potential knowledge gap by the expertise of its members.

The definition of system boundaries was regarded as another challenge. Different requirements regarding data interchange in civil hazard prevention exist. Yet, this challenge was anticipated by a broad focus of the DIN SPEC. Risks of over- or under-specification, as well as appropriate solutions, were identified.

A meaningful influencing factor for the future diffusion of the DIN SPEC is to what extent currently existing systems can operate on the basis of the DIN SPEC and to what degree these can be updated or changed.

A detailed discussion about the diffusion of the DIN SPEC will follow in the next section. A further diffusion of the specification on a European or international level needs additional standardisation effort and will also depend on the kind of security communication within the different countries.

8. PREVIEW ON THE DIFFUSION OF THE SPECIFICATION FROM THE VIEWPOINT OF STANDARDISATION THEORY AND FIRST RESULTS

The adoption of the specification depends on the behaviour of different groups of stakeholders, which, in particular, include users of information systems, vendors who offer solutions based on the new specification, as well as vendors of other proprietary solutions. In order to counteract any diffusion-averting effects, various measures have been defined.

Using the specification for data interchange requires the involvement of several actors who participate in the interchange relationships. One

issue will be how the supporters of the specification will be able to stimulate network effects within the target group (see e.g. Katz & Shapiro, 1985, 1994).

Related success factors are mainly discussed in research on the establishment of de facto standards. They include:

- The perceived added value of the new solution (see e.g. Blind, 2004),
- The target group's expectations regarding the success of the new specification (see e.g. Farrell & Saloner, 1987; Shapiro & Varian, 1999a,b),
- Their current investment in other solutions (see e.g. Arthur, 1989; Shapiro & Varian, 1999a,b),
- Their perceived switching costs (see e.g. Arthur, 1989; Shapiro & Varian, 1999a,b),
- The target group's willingness to switch (see e.g. Farrell & Saloner, 1987).

Comments within the standardisation community showed that those factors identified as influencing the establishment of de facto standards may be relevant for formal standards as well. The further development of the DIN SPEC will show to what extent they will be important for its success. In this context, the supporters of the new specification also face the challenge of convincing stakeholders who prefer manual work instead of using technology for the activities the specification addresses. The utilization of the DIN SPEC thereby demands the willingness to accept changes in the process of current tasks. An important aspect therefore is to obtain promoters within the respective organizations who introduce the new solutions to their employees in an appropriate way.

In addition to the advantages of being based on an open specification, it will also be important that the relevant technical solutions can compete with the current solutions regarding additional characteristics (see e.g. Blind, 2004), for example usability, reliability, robustness, customer service, updates, complementary products, etc.

Shapiro and Varian (1999a) stress the significance of gathering allies in support of a new standard, of managing expectations by assembling these allies and by making claims about a standard's current or future popularity. Their findings highlight the importance of similar activities related to the DIN SPEC of this study.

The specification offers a variety of opportunities to address different needs of the target group and allows for use in many different contexts. Its developers are aware of a certain risk that these positive characteristics might lead to fragmentation to some extent and to barriers in the data interchange between specific users groups. To avoid this, a recommendation for the implementation of the specification is given but a certain risk cannot be eliminated.

As mentioned before, the success of the specification may also depend on the reactions of current vendors of proprietary solutions. Fortunately, innovation history also includes many examples of promotors of previous solutions who reacted too late to replace a specific new solution (see e.g. Christensen, 1997).

9. SUMMARY AND FINAL REMARKS

Sherif et al. (2007) identified six dimensions to describe success factors of a standardisation project. Broadly, their concept proved to be applicable for relevant standardisation questions in the German Framework Program - Research for Civil Security. To show the practical realization of these success factors, a case study was done.

The investigated project gave an example of linking research and standardisation appropriately. The intended use of the specification in future

R&D projects and the intended exploitation of synergies to promote the future success of the investigated DIN SPEC display specific interrelations between R&D and standardisation.

The working group could work efficiently as small group without competition, allowing for work without conflict. Therefore, assumptions about the size of the standardisation group and its efficiency given by Loewer (2006) were confirmed. To avoid problems regarding the acceptance of a new standard or specification mentioned by Loewer (2006) in-depth analyses of the target group's requirements were conducted.

The ability of the new specification to enable appropriate emergency-related and regular applications simultaneously, as well as the avoidance of several incompatible specifications, can be regarded as key success factors related to the specific security-related aspects of the project.

The findings also show the importance and nature of appropriate marketing measures to promote further steps in the lifecycle of the specification. Furthermore, they stress the importance of facilitating the further migration of a specification. A particular influencing factor regarding the diffusion of such a specification in the field of civil hazard prevention is related to public procurement.

Challenges within the standardisation process and a solution-oriented approach were also unveiled in this case study. The solution-oriented approach includes several measures that still need to be tested in practice. The working group is aware of certain risks such as that the measures might not be implemented appropriately or lead to the desired results.

Several results of the case study seem to be quite specific and therefore difficult to generalize but there are also results of general interest, e.g.:

- The need to plan R&D stage standardisation together with the relevant project to ensure availability of resources.

- The added value of linking activities to prepare for standardisation with other tasks of relevant R&D projects to save time in the standardisation process.
- The added value of identifying synergies between activities intended at the exploitation of relevant R&D results and activities to promote the diffusion of a new specification.
- The added value of identifying synergies between activities to promote the diffusion of a new specification and future R&D projects regarding the utilization of the specification.
- The need to pay attention to the further development of a specification.

Even the composition of the working group helps to derive aspects of general interest. Since the working partners already knew each other from common R&D projects, this helped avoid conflicts and helped to fulfil quality criteria related to (human) resource management defined by Sherif et al. (2007).

Additionally, regarding security research projects, the following advice was derived:

- Establish appropriate relationships to public procurers.
- Ensure usability of standards and specifications in both exceptional and regular situations, if possible.
- Implement appropriate strategies to avoid the use of a security-related specification or standard for other than its intended purposes.

In contrast to DIN Norms or EN standards, the implementation of DIN SPEC's, as well as the implementation of Workshop Agreements or Technical Specifications from the European standardisation committees CEN and CENELEC, for example, is voluntarily. This reduces additional risks of conflict.

The findings also show potential for an extension of Sherif et al's (2007) work based on different stages in the standardisation process, the standard lifecycle and different types of standards:

- **Specifying Preconditions:** The first aspect is related to preconditions of the projects. The chairman in the case study was experienced in standardisation, which is unusual for R&D stage standardisation. This aspect is regarded as a key influence on the six dimensions, e.g. regarding scope and quality as well as time and resource management.
- **IPR Management:** IPR aspects are not covered explicitly. Although it is possible to integrate this topic into other dimensions, a separate dimension would be helpful.
- **Lifecycle Management:** A third recommendation concerns the further development of the standard, the development of new versions etc. This leads to a call for a dimension 'lifecycle management' or 'versions management'.
- **Management of Industry-Specific Issues:** Sherif et al's (2007) article focuses on ICT standards. The importance of particular aspects may be different in other industries. For example a working group, which writes a quality standard for steel normally does not have to look at interoperability. The development of standards for civil security bears specific risks, for example in the fields of ethics and privacy. A specific dimension to analyze these issues might have been helpful. Similar problems may occur in other industry contexts, too. Therefore, it might be valuable to use industry-specific aspects as a separate area of investigation.
- **Management of Specific Issues Related to the Relevant Type of Standard:** Sherif et al's (2007) main focus is on interoperability standards. Therefore, several as-

pects in their article are related to interoperability and compatibility. Other kinds of standards, such as quality or terminology standards may have different requirements, which need to be considered appropriately.

Blind (2004) as well as Swann (2000, 2010) offer an extended overview of the many advantages standardisation provides for the parties involved but the project INTEREST showed that many researchers do not know them and that they need to be motivated appropriately. One of InfraNorm's goals was to contribute to the realization of that aim in the field of civil security by demonstrating the advantages of standardisation for the parties involved and by showing how risks can be avoided.

ACKNOWLEDGMENT

The author would like to thank the Federal Ministry of Education and Research (BMBF) for the financial support.

REFERENCES

Arthur, W. B. (1989). Competing Technologies, Increasing Returns, and Lock-in by Historical Events. *The Economic Journal*, *99*(394), 116–131. doi:10.2307/2234208

Bekkers, R. (2001). *The development of European mobile telecommunications standards: An assessment of the success of GSM, TETRA, ERMES and UMTS*. Eindhoven: Eindhoven University of Technology.

Blind, K. (2003). Patent Pools - A Solution to Patent Conflicts in Standardisation and an Instrument of Technology Transfer: The MP3 Case. In *Proceedings of the 3rd IEEE Conference on Standardisation and Innovation in Information Technology (SIIT 2003)*, (pp. 27-35) Delft: TUD-TBM. doi:10.1109/SIIT.2003.1251192

Blind, K. (2004). *The Economics of Standards: Theory, Evidence, Policy*. Cheltenham: Edward Elgar Publishing.

Blind, K. (2008a). Standardisation and Standards in Security Research and Emerging Security Markets. In *Proceedings of the Fraunhofer Symposium 'Future Security', 3rd Security Research Conference*, (pp. 63-72). Stuttgart: Fraunhofer IRB Verlag.

Blind, K. (2008b). Factors Influencing the Lifetime of Telecommunication and Information Technology Standards. In T. M. Egyedi, & K. Blind (Eds.), *The Dynamics of Standards* (pp. 155–180). Cheltenham: Edward Elgar Publishing. doi:10.4018/978-1-59904-949-6.ch024

Blind, K. (2009). *Standardisation: A catalyst for innovation*. Retrieved from http://publishing. eur. nl/ir/repub/asset/17558/EIA-2009-039-LIS.pdf

Blind, K., & Gauch, S. (2007). Standardisation benefits researchers – Standards ought to be developed in parallel to the research processes. *Wissenschaftsmanagement*, Special 2/2007 (English Version), 16-17.

Blind, K., & Iversen, E. (2004). *The Interrelationship between IPR and Standardisation: Patterns and Policies*. Retrieved from http://eprints.utas. edu.au/1282/1/Blind_Iversen2004Euras.pdf

Boehlje, M., & Schiek, W. (1998). Critical success factors in a competitive dairy market. *Journal of Dairy Science*, *81*(6), 1753–1761. doi:10.3168/ jds.S0022-0302(98)75744-3

Brentani, U. (1991). Success Factors in Developing New Business Services. *European Journal of Marketing*, *25*(2), 33–59. doi:10.1108/03090569110138202

CEN. (2014a). *CEN Workshop Agreements (CWAs)*. Retrieved from http://www.cen.eu/pages/ default.aspx

CEN. (2014b). *Technical Specifications (TS)*. Retrieved from http://www.cen.eu/pages/default. aspx

CEN-CENELEC. (2014). *CEN-CENELEC Research Helpdesk*. Retrieved from http://www.cen. eu/cen/Services/Innovation/Pages/default.aspx

CEN-CENELEC STAIR. (2011). *The Operationalisation of the Integrated Approach: Submission of STAIR to the Consultation of the Green Paper "From Challenges to Opportunities: Towards a Common Strategic Framework for EU Research and Innovation funding"*. Retrieved from http://www.cencenelec.eu/research/pages/default.aspx

Christensen, C. M. (1997). *The Innovator's Dilemma: When New Technologies Cause Great Firms to Fail*. Boston, MA: Harvard Business Review Press.

Clarke, A. (1999). A practical use of key success factors to improve the effectiveness of project management. *International Journal of Project Management, 17*(3), 139–145. doi:10.1016/S0263-7863(98)00031-3

Cooper, R. G., & Kleinschmidt, E. J. (1987). Success Factors in Product Innovation. *Industrial Marketing Management, 16*(3), 215–223. doi:10.1016/0019-8501(87)90029-0

Cooper, R. G., & Kleinschmidt, E. J. (1990). New Product Success Factors – A Comparison of Kills versus Successes and Failures. *R & D Management, 20*(1), 47–63. doi:10.1111/j.1467-9310.1990.tb00672.x

Cooper, R. G., & Kleinschmidt, E. J. (1995). Benchmarking the Firm's Critical Success Factors in New Product Development. *Journal of Product Innovation Management, 12*(5), 374–391. doi:10.1016/0737-6782(95)00059-3

de Vries, H., de Vries, H., & Oshri, I. (2008). *Standards-Battles in Open Source Software. The Case of Firefox*. London: Palgrave Macmillan. doi:10.1057/9780230595095

de Vries, H. J. (1999). *Standardization: A Business Approach to the Role of National Standardization Organizations*. Boston: Kluwer Academic Publishers.

DeWalt, K. M., & DeWalt, B. R. (2002). *Participant observation: a guide for fieldworkers*. Walnut Creek, CA: AltaMira Press.

DIN. (2012). *Research & Development Phase Standardisation*. Retrieved from http://www.ebn.din.de/cmd?level=tpl-home&languageid=en

ECORYS. (2009). *Study on Competitiveness of the EU Security Industry*. Retrieved from http://ec.europa.eu/enterprise/policies/security/files/study_on_the_competitiveness_of_the_eu_security_industry_en.pdf

Egyedi, T. M. (2006). Experts on causes of incompatibility between standard-compliant products. In Enterprise Interoperability, (pp. 553-563). Berlin: Springer.

Eisenhardt, K. M. (1989). Building Theories from Case Study Research. *Academy of Management Review, 14*(4), 532–550.

Ernst, H. (2002). Success factors of new product development: A review of the empirical literature. *International Journal of Management Reviews, 4*(1), 1–40. doi:10.1111/1468-2370.00075

ESRIF. (2009). *ESRIF Final Report*. Retrieved from http://ec.europa.eu/enterprise/policies/security/ files/esrif_final_report_en.pdf

ETSI. (2012). *Making better standards: Practical ways to success*. Retrieved from http://portal.etsi.org/mbs

European Commission. (2004). *Critical Infrastructure Protection in the fight against terrorism (COM/2004/0702)*. Retrieved from http://eur-lex. europa.eu/LexUriServ/LexUriServ.do?uri=COM :2004:0702:FIN:EN:PDF

European Commission. (2008). *Towards an increased contribution from standardisation to innovation in Europe*. Retrieved from http:// eur-lex.europa.eu/LexUriServ/ LexUriServ.do? uri=COM:2008:0133:FIN:en:PDF

European Commission. (2011a). *Programming Mandate Addressed to CEN, CENELEC and ETSI to Establish Security Standards*. Retrieved from ftp://ftp.cencenelec.eu/CENELEC/ EuropeanMandates/M_487.pdf

European Commission. (2011b). *Communication from the Commission to the European Parliament, the Council and the European Economic and Social Committee: A strategic vision for European standards: Moving forward to enhance and accelerate the sustainable growth of the European economy by 2020, COM(2011) 311 final*. Retrieved from http://eur-lex.europa.eu/LexUriServ/Lex-UriServ.do?uri=COM:2011:0311:FIN:EN:PDF

European Council. (2010). *The Stockholm Programme - An Open and Secure Europe Serving and Protecting Citizens*. Retrieved from http:// eur-lex.europa.eu/LexUriServ/LexUriServ. do?uri=OJ:C:2010

EXPRESS [Expert Panel for the Review of the European Standardisation System]. (2010). *Standardization for a competitive and innovative Europe: a vision for 2020. Report delivered to the European Commission in February 2010*. Retrieved from http://ec.europa.eu/enterprise/policies/european-standards/files/express/ exp_384_express_report_final_distrib_en.pdf

Farrell, J., & Saloner, G. (1987). Competition, Compatibility and Standards: The Economics of Horses, Penguins, and Lemmings. In H. L. Gabel (Ed.), *Product Standardisation as a Competitive Strategy* (pp. 1–21). Amsterdam: Elsevier Science.

Flick, U. (2002). An introduction to qualitative research (2nd ed.). London: SAGE Publications.

Hatto, P. (2013). *Standards and Standardisation. A practical guide for researchers*. Retrieved from http://ec.europa.eu/research/industrial_technologies/pdf/practical-standardisation-guide-for-researchers_en.pdf

INTEREST. (2006). *INTEREST: Integrating Research and Standardisation: A Guide to Standardisation for R&D Organisations and Researchers*. Retrieved from http://www-i4.informatik.rwth-aachen.de/Interest/ Manual_R%26D.pdf

ISO. (2014). *ISO deliverables*. Retrieved from http://www.iso.org/iso/home/standards_development/deliverables-all.htm?type=pas

Iversen, E. (2004). Case Study: TETRA. In *Study on the Interaction between Standardisation and Intellectual Property Rights* (pp. 167–174). Retrieved from http://ftp.jrc.es/EURdoc/eur21074en. pdf

Iversen, E., Bekkers, R., & Blind, K. (2006). Emerging coordination mechanisms for multiparty IPR holders: Linking research with standardisation. *Industrial and Corporate Change, 21*(4), 901–931.

Janecek, V., & Hynek, J. (2010). Incentive System as a Factor of Firms' Efficiency Improvement. *E & M Ekonomia Management, 13*(1), 76-90.

Katz, M., & Shapiro, C. (1994). Systems Competition and Network Effects. *The Journal of Economic Perspectives, 8*(2), 93–115. doi:10.1257/jep.8.2.93

Katz, M. L., & Shapiro, C. (1985). Network Externalities, Competition, and Compatibility. *The American Economic Review*, *75*(3), 424–440.

Kisielnicki, J., & Sroka, S. (2005). Efficiency and Effectiveness of Management in Project Oriented Organizations: The Role of Information Technology in the Organizations. In *Proceedings of the 2005 Information Resources Management Association International Conference: Managing Modern Organizations Through Information Technology*, (pp. 83-87). Hershey, PA: IGI Global.

Liu, C., & Arnett, K. P. (2000). Exploring the factors associated with Web site success in the context of electronic commerce. *Information & Management*, *38*(1), 23–33. doi:10.1016/S0378-7206(00)00049-5

Loewer, U. M. (2006). *Interorganisational standards*. Heidelberg: Physica.

Pfetsch, F. (2008). Bargaining and Arguing as Communicative Modes of Strategic, Social, Economic, Political Interaction. In J. Schueler, & A. Hommels (Eds.), *Bargaining Norms. Arguing Standards* (pp. 52–65). The Hague: STT Netherlands Study Centre for Technology Trends.

Riefler, B. (2008). *The Composition of Working Groups in Industry-Specific Standardisation Organizations*. Retrieved from http://www.ivr.uni-stuttgart.de/mikro/RePEc/stt/ download_dpaper/composition_of_ working_groups.pdf

Scapolo, F., Churchill, P., & Viaud, V. (2013). *A possible future for the standardization system through the lens of additive manufacturing*. Paper presented at the Kick-Off meeting of the STAIR AM platform. Brussels, Belgium.

Shapiro, C., & Varian, H. R. (1999a). Art of Standard Wars. *California Management Review*, *41*(2), 8–32. doi:10.2307/41165984

Shapiro, C., & Varian, H. R. (1999b). *Information Rules: A Strategic Guide to the Network Economy*. Cambridge: Harvard Business Review Press.

Sherif, M. H. (2001). *Contribution Towards A Theory Of Standardisation In Telecommunications*. Retrieved from www-i4.informatik.rwth-aachen.de/~jakobs/siit99/proceedings/Sherif.doc

Sherif, M. H., Jakobs, K., & Egyedi, T. M. (2007). Standards of quality and quality of standards for Telecommunications and Information Technologies. In M. Hoerlesberger, Elnawawi, & M., Khalil, T. (Eds.), Challenges in the Management of New Technologies (pp. 427-447). Singapore: World Scientific.

Sinay, J. (2011). Security Research and Safety Aspects in Slovakia. In K. Thoma (Ed.), *European Perspectives on Security Research* (pp. 81–89). Berlin: Springer. doi:10.1007/978-3-642-18219-8_7

Swann, P. (2000). *The Economics of standardization: Final Report for Standards and Technical Regulations Directorate Department of Trade and Industry*. Retrieved from http://www.dti.gov.uk/files/file11312.pdf

Swann, P. (2010). *The economics of standardisation: an update*. Report for the UK Department of Business, Innovation and Skills (BIS). Complete Draft. Version 2.2, 27 May 2010. Retrieved from https://www.gov.uk/government/uploads/system/uploads/attachment_data/file/16509/The_Economics_of_Standardization_-_an_update_.pdf

van de Kaa, G. (2009). *Standards Battles for Complex Systems. Empirical Research on the Home Network*. Rotterdam: Erasmus Research Institute of Management.

Yin, R. K. (2008). *Case study research, design and methods* (3rd ed.). Newbury Park: Sage Publications.

Yin, R. K. (2011). *Qualitative Research. From Start to Finish*. New York: Guilford Pubn.

KEY TERMS AND DEFINITIONS

Anticipatory Standards: Standards 'that must be created before widespread acceptance of devices or services' (Sherif, 2001).

Data Interchange: Process of sending and receiving data in such a manner that the information content or meaning assigned to the data is not altered during the transmission (EN 14968:2006-08).

DIN SPEC (PAS): Public available specifications developed at the German standardisation organisation DIN.

Integrated Approach: Integrated Approach for Standardization, Innovation and Research which links the specific stages of research, development, innovation and standardization (CEN-CENELEC STAIR, 2011).

Participatory Standards: Standards that proceed in lock-step with implementations that test the specifications before adopting them' (Sherif, 2001).

Public Security: Protection against threats by terrorism and severe and organized crime (European Commission, 2011).

Publicly Available Specification (PAS): Normative document representing the consensus within a working group (ISO, 2014).

Security: System of measures, including their embodiments and their interactions, designed to ward off intentionally destructive activity resulting in injury or material damage (Siney, 2011).

Specification: Document stating requirements (ISO 15378:2011-11).

Standardisation: 'Activity of establishing and recording a limited set of solutions to actual or potential matching problems directed at benefits for the party or parties involved balancing their needs and intending and expecting that these solutions will be repeatedly or continuously used during a certain period by a substantial number of the parties for whom they are meant' (de Vries, 1999).

Workshop Agreements: Consensus documents, represent the output of a workshop, which is open to all stakeholders.

ENDNOTES

[1] UTF-8 (8-bit UCS Transformation Format) is the dominant character encoding for Unicode-characters. UCS hereby refers to Universal Character Set.

Chapter 11
Achieving Standardization:
Learning from Harmonization Efforts in E-Customs

Stefan Henningsson
Copenhagen Business School, Denmark

ABSTRACT

International e-Customs is going through a standardization process. Driven by the need to increase control in the trade process to address security challenges stemming from threats of terrorists, diseases, and counterfeit products, and to lower the administrative burdens on traders to stay competitive, national customs and regional economic organizations are seeking to establish a standardized solution for digital reporting of customs data. However, standardization has proven hard to achieve in the socio-technical e-Customs solution. In this chapter, the authors identify and describe what has to be harmonized in order for a global company to perceive e-Customs as standardized. In doing so, they contribute an explanation of the challenges associated with using a standardization mechanism for harmonizing socio-technical information systems.

1. INTRODUCTION

The line of trucks waiting to cross the Finish-Russian border is sometimes up to 20 kilometres long. The connection is not obvious at a first glance, but this is actually partly a standardization problem. In this paper we give the foundation to explain how lack of working standards is related to the 20 kilometres queue.

In an increasingly globalized and interconnected world organization of processes across national and organizational borders becomes increasingly important. The subject of how organizations organize processes between organizations is largely unexplored ground, and one of the most topical subject to organizational researchers (Ahrne et al. 2007; Brunsson and Jacobsson 2000; Brunsson et al. 2012). In the globalized world organizational processes span across national borders and the traditional domains of behaviour regulating bodies (Elenurm 2007; Lorentz 2008; Ahrne 2011).

In settings where hierarchical structures are not available for enforcing behaviour, standards is a frequently attempted managerial technique

DOI: 10.4018/978-1-4666-6332-9.ch011

to regulate activities and to achieve harmonization in behaviour (Brunsson and Jacobsson 2000, Brunsson et al. 2012). Several organizations, including the UN, the World Customs Organization (WCO) and the European Commission (EC), are currently engaged in activities to standardize digital information flows in relation to customs processes. As the world steadily is becoming more globalized, companies are active in several parts of the world, which leads to a steady increase of both regional and inter-regional trade. The administrative burden for global companies has become a painful cost item on the balance sheet.

At the same time as international trade increases there is also an increasing need for more extensive customs controls due to diseases such as bird flu, and mad cow-disease as well as increased threat from terrorists and increasing tax-fraud. The move towards what is called e-Customs (here defined as "digital transfer of information needed for customs processes") is supposed to solve the seemingly impossible equation of increasing security, traceability and control of export and import while simultaneously decreasing the administrative burden for companies and customs authorities.

To leverage the benefits of digitalization of customs processes, the task of standardizing e-Customs through focusing on customs-related information systems (IS) has turned out to be a critical challenge (Rukanova et al., 2010, Klein et al. 2012). Organizations such as the United Nations (UN), European Union (EU), Association of Southeast Asian Nations (ASEAN), and other regional economic organizations are all active players in the process of standardizing all the world's e-Customs initiatives (Klievink & Lucassen 2013).

However, standardizing e-Customs is especially complex since it means standardization of IS that contains both social (organizational processes and practices) and technical (hardware and software in the computerized network) components (Hanseth and Braa 2001, Hanseth 2014).

The technical sides of such systems cannot be approached ignoring the social use situation, and vice versa the use and functionality cannot be approach without recognizing technical limitations and boundaries (Kolltveit et al. 2007, Henfridsson & Bygstad 2013). The limited research that exists on standards tend to address either only social (e.g., Brunsson and Jacobsson 2000; Schwartz and Tilling 2009) or technical (e.g., Sherif 2007) application areas.

Despite much effort put into the standardization activity, there are signs that this standardization this far has only partly been successful in its attempt to harmonize behaviour and lower total costs. Or, as described by Henningsson and Zinner Henriksen (2011, p. 368) some of the traders are longing for the "good old paper-days". Taking departure in this dilemma, the objective of the paper is to identify and describe what has to be harmonized in order to that a global company should perceive e-Customs as standardized. This entails the identification of sources why e-Customs solutions, seen as IS, can deviate from each other. Given the limited collective understanding of management through socio-technical standards (Lyytinen and King 2006), a fundamental view of what is to be standardized is a prerequisite for further studies on the political and social processes forming parts of the socio-technical standard.

In the next section we will present previous literature on standardization in international trade, and develop a conceptualization of IS standards implementation deviation, necessary to understand how use of socio-technical standards may deviate from the intentional use. Thereafter we present the case of standardization of the European e-Customs. Based on existing literature and our empirical investigations, we suggest a taxonomy for sources of divergence in e-Customs implementation. Given the taxonomy we discuss and make tentative suggestions on how these problems can be met. Finally we provide conclusions for practice and academia.

2. THE INFORMATION INFRASTRUCTURE OF INTERNATIONAL TRADE

International trade is continuously growing in volumes and in number of shipments worldwide. Trade is generally considered an important driver for economic development and is encourage by most governments (Bjørn-Andersen and Henningsson 2009). However, trade is also considered something that needs to be controlled and monitored. Concerns over terrorists using international shipments in their attacks, the spread of contagious diseases, and increased tax fraud has caused consumers and governmental agencies to demand enhanced control and traceability of products from producer to end consumer.

The need for control over international trade has fueled the development of technology-based solutions that are related to the control and supervision of goods moving in the trade system. Supervision and control is normally the concern of national customs authorities. Customs deals with the administrative procedures related to import and export. It registers what goes where to who, making sure that tax and excise is paid in the right amount to the right authorities. The actually burden of providing the information is commonly delegated to traders, who are stuck at the border unless they can provide the required data for clearing their goods.

2.1 Standardization

International trade has turned into a veritable showcase for different kinds of standards and standardizing bodies. Since the birth of national states, governments have used regulation to protect the national interests and territory. However, the attempts to harmonize and coordinate national regulation are almost equally old as national regulation itself. In 1923 the League of Nations established the Convention on the simplification of Customs formalities and in 1947 the General

Agreement on Tariffs and Trade (GATT) was concluded. Today international organizations such as the UN and the World Customs Organization (WCO) are active players that try to increase order in international trade through standardization. The international and national initiatives are complemented by regional initiatives. EU, ASEAN, and the East-African Community (EAC) are example of regional organizations that provide trade-related standards.

In the absence of hierarchical or market structures to enforce behaviour, management through standards is a possible way to achieve coordination among independent actors (Brunsson & Jacobsson, 2000). Standardizing through the creation of structures is also one of the most effective managerial toolboxes as suggested in the classic framework for exertion of power (Markus & Bjørn-Andersen, 1987) as standards are often perceived as less obtrusive than other regulations. But standardizing IS pose a particular set of challenges on the standardizing body due to its socio-technical nature (Hanseth et al., 2006). Introducing the European e-Customs standard as defined by Regulation (EC) No 648/2005 has the outspoken managerial objective to harmonize European customs processes by an IS standard, in order to provide a common interface to companies active in several European countries. However, as we shall demonstrate with our analysis, standardising IS is not as easy as one might expect in spite of the obvious advantages if all actors standardized their corresponding IS.

The topic of IS standardization represents a long term issue that has remained unresolved for decades. It has been argued that "standardization forms a key feature of modernization" (Hanseth, Jacucci, Grisot, & Aanestad 2006). E-Customs is by the EU seen as a modernization project and standardization should accordingly be addressed. Although it is recognized that standards and standard-setting agencies are prerequisites for successful implementation of e-Customs, agreeing on international standards and achieving interoperability between different standard-based systems across the EU member states and at an international level remains still a great challenge (Henriksen et a., 2008). The standardization challenge is among other factors driven by socio-political traits, which influence the collaboration across organizations (Broks & Geradin, 2011; Damsgaard & Lyytinen, 1998; Damsgaard & Lyytinen, 2001).

2.2 Deviation in Standards Implementation

In this chapter, standards implementation deviation refers to the intentional or unintentional variance in the implementation of a standard. Variance in the implementation of a standards means that the standard might not do its job of harmonizing organizational behaviour. In the case study reported on later on in this chapter the standard investigated is the European e-Customs standard as defined by Regulation (EC) No 648/2005. Standards implementation deviation then in this particular case refers to the variance in the IS that the standard is supposed to cover: the national e-Customs solutions. Consequently, to understand standards implementation deviation in socio-technical IS standards, one must understand the sources for variation in implementation that exist.

Stories of intentional and unintentional standards implementation deviation are frequent in the business press. Microsoft's use of Sun's Java standard (Blundon, 1997) is one classical example of an intentional standards extension. Organizations may also choose to only adopt parts of an existing standard - intentional partial standards adoption. The reasons for intentional deviation from the standard might be both strategic and technical (Egyedi & Dahanayake, 2003). The focus of this chapter, however, is unintentional standards implementation deviation which is a less explored phenomenon (Egyedi & Dahanayake, 2003).

While information technology (IT) software and hardware can be duplicated and sold as complying to a particular standard, IS are specific to the organizational or inter-organizational context in which they are implemented (Iivari, 2003). As standards gets implemented, they become dynamic and might present a variance in their implementation. Jakobs (2008) describes how an organization implementing a WLAN decides to stick to one vendor even though there is other equipment that claim to conform to the same standard. The reason is that as the standard gets implemented, small deviations occur that makes interoperability problematic. Folmer et al. (2009) describes how strategies for international domain standards get 'localized' when attached to meanings in a local context.

IS can be defined on three different levels: technical, infological, and organizational (Iivari, 2003). Consequently, deviation sources can be found on each of these three levels.

Egyedi and Dahanayake (2003) addressed deviation sources on a technical level. They found that these deviations stemmed from pure errors, ambiguities, and specification to parallel options, and functional deviation. Jakobs (2008) found that technical level deviations could be the result of both implementation and installation of standards. Inter-organizational standards are based on a data model, describing which data should be transferred through the system are intended to eliminate such differences. If ambiguities, inconsistencies, or options exist in the data model, deviation in the implemented IS is possible.

The infological level of IS exists in a language context (Iivari, 2003). This means that the objective of an information system is to supply its user with information to support its activities. The interpretation and meaning of transferred data is another potential source of IS deviation (Gustafsson et al., 1982). A parallel can be made to how international domain names are localized into national contexts, as explained by Folmer et al. (2011). In the case of e-Customs, deviations can occur because data fields such as "means of transport", "description of goods", and "exporter" are interpreted differently in each e-Customs implementation. An exporter might be the company that produced the goods and who is now sending it to the customer, but it might also be the logistics service provider that actually transports the goods across the border. In some cases it is even the receiving part who actually acts as exporter. The same problems exist for almost all data that is shipped: shall weight of goods be specified with or without wrapping? How does one write an appropriate description? Is the receiving part represented by its name or organizational number, and if so the organizational number in which country? Data transferred in the IS should have similar meanings to its users. Data meaning is another potential source of implementation deviation.

The organizational level of IS refers to a process view of how data is transformed through the systems to its users. IS can be seen as work systems that as one constituent part contains a work process (Alter, 2003). To complete transfer the user has to manipulate the system by a logic that is partly built into the system and partly defined by the implementation context. The process view addresses when to send which data and to whom. It is possible that national customs offices wants some part of the data model to be submitted to VAT-controlling authorities, some data to health authorities, and some data to the authority responsible for controls of dangerous goods. When and where data is transmitted is defined by the IS' work process, which is a third source of standards implementation deviation.

Figure 1 summarizes the above discussion on sources of variance forming the origin of socio-technical standards implementation deviation. Although the three levels of deviations described above are important sources for variations in implementation of standard, they are to the best of our knowledge not explicitly combined in the literature as a framework for sources of deviation. In the absence of previous works the deduction of a tentative framework based on closely related research is a possible way forward. Examples by Egyedi and Dahanayake (2003), Jakobs (2008),

Figure 1. Conceptualization of socio-technical standards implementation deviation

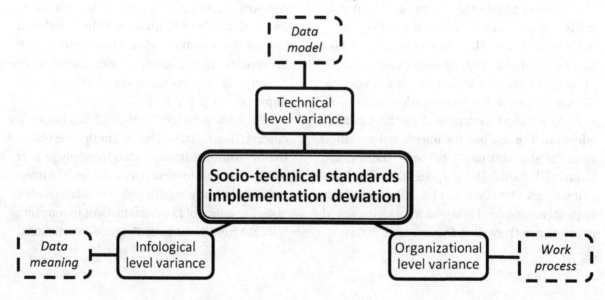

Folmer et al., (2009) indicates that the levels may play important roles in why standard implementations deviates.

3. RESEARCH APPROACH

This chapter presents a case study of e-Customs standardization from the perspective of Arla. The case study presented is a structured case study mainly inspired by Carroll and Swatman (2000). The goal of our study is to induct concepts and theories from empirical observations (Eisenhardt, 1989; Carroll & Swatman, 2000). The structured case study approach suggested by Carroll and Swatman (2000) and applied by, for instance, Grimsley and Meehan (2007), includes guidelines for the process of developing knowledge and theory based on empirical data. It does not prescribe specific data collection techniques or ways of analyzing the data, but outlines a framework for how to develop knowledge and theory. The main steps are in their approach to develop an initial conceptual framework, to collect and analyze empirical evidence, and to reflect on the result in order to induce knowledge. In that regard it is similar to the approach suggest by Eisenhardt's (1989) approach to develop theories from case studies. However, there are several differences between the approaches suggested by Carroll and Swatman (2000) and Eisenhardt (1989). The first is that Carroll and Swatman approach has a strong interpretative legacy whereas Eisenhardt belongs to a more positivistic tradition. Another difference is the view on theory building. Eisenhardt (1989) describes this as a fairly straight forward linear process with iterations (i.e. follow the eight steps and theory will emerge at the end), whereas Carroll and Swatman view the process of theory building as process based on iterations between conceptual framework, data collection and analysis, and reflection where new theories, data, conceptual framework may be introduced

until saturation is reached. In the reminder of the section we will describe how we have adopted the structured case approach.

The research presented in this chapter was part of a large EU-funded research programme. The programme investigated problems and opportunities associated with customs in several businesses and industries from the perspectives of governments, traders, shippers, and IT providers. The programme was a joint research and development project with representatives from government, business and academia.

3.1 The Case Company

Arla Foods (Arla), a company of about 20,000 employees, is the largest producer of dairy products in Scandinavia and the second largest producer of dairy products in Europe. Arla's stated mission is: "To offer modern consumers milk-based food products that create inspiration, confidence and well-being". Arla covers the entire spectrum of dairy products sold in markets across the world. Arla produces 7% of the total milk processed in Europe. Measured by litres of processed milk it is the largest dairy company in Europe. Arla was born after a merger between a Swedish and a Danish dairy company. The merger was a part of a general consolidation trend in Europe; the actors in the food industry is steadily becoming fewer but larger. Arla has production plants in Denmark, Sweden, Poland, UK, Saudi Arabia, Argentina, Brazil, USA and Canada.

3.2 Data Collection and Analysis

The data used in this chapter has been collected via different means including company visits, nine workshops involving all partners of the project, five general project meetings, four specific meetings on food trade with stakeholders involved in the business, email exchange after meetings, study of minutes and other written documentation provided by the food producer and the national customs authorities. Minutes of meetings taken by researches have been distributed to all participants for approval and commenting. During the project extensive written reporting in the form of deliverables has been produced due to the character of the project, which is EU-funded. These sources of data provide a robust material for documenting data which in nature is unstructured and qualitative.

The data collected in the project covered many different theoretical perspectives and areas of interest as the project objective is to find a solution to a real world problem. The idea of approaching e-Customs standardization from a traders perspective originates from workshops with Arla and Danish Customs. Following the idea four interviews were made with Arla to understand how the e-Customs standardization affected the organization. Interviews were recorded and documented by notes. The interviews were guided by the initial findings and theoretical concepts accounted for in Section 2 of this chapter.

4. E-CUSTOMS STANDARDS AND INTEROPERABILITY

In the 1980's, a company that was an active exporter or importer on the European market had to deal with a set of more than 200 different forms to cover different customs procedures, in different countries and for different modes of transport. As a response to the call for a reduction of the administrative burden for economic operators in an all the time more and more globalized arena for businesses the single administrative document (SAD) and related legislation was introduced in the EU. SAD, specified by the EC in Regulation No 1875/2006 and No 648/2005, presented a general form for all types of customs declarations that was applicable to 18 European countries.

The original SAD was introduced January 1st, 1988. Originally 18 countries did employ the document as standard for their customs declaration.

In 1993 the SAD disappeared from trade within the EU as a result of the creation of a common internal market. Ten years later, in 2003, the SAD was reintroduced. The plan was to adapt to the evolution that had occurred since its first creation. The required data to submit was reduced by about a quarter, but perhaps more important was the further diffusion of the SAD as a standard for customs declarations. When the reformed SAD and attached legislation was taken into practice by 2007, the format was adopted by more than 30 countries, including for example Russia.

The SAD was originally a set of 8 copies of the same document printed on carbon paper which was handed out to the different authorities during the journey of the goods. All copies had a specific purpose. The first copy was for the country were export formalities where carried out, the second was used for statistics in the export country, the third copy was returned to the exporter, and so on. Some fields where mandatory to collect for all countries, while some fields were optional to collect. The SAD standardized data was submitted to national customs and with one and the same operation a company could do export clearance, issue the transport document (customs), and prepare the clearance in the country of destination.

Since a few years, Arla submits data needed for customs procedures when exporting from Denmark electronically through the Danish "e-Export system" which has been massively diffused among Danish exporters (Bjørn-Andersen et al., 2007). Customs messages can still be sent through a paper-based equivalent that is possible to use for companies who by some reason do not want to or is not able to submit export data electronically. The paper-equivalent is still based on the SAD.

The data model in the e-Export system is fundamentally a field by field translation of the SAD-fields that the Danish customs were using prior to the computerization. These are the mandatory fields to submit. Since it's the same data that is submitted now, as before, the meaning of that data has settled among European customs organizations. In the development of SAD, a substantial amount of work was devoted to establishing joint understanding of how data items should be understood.

The e-Export system can be reached through either UN/EDIFACT (United Nations/Electronic Data Interchange For Administration, Commerce and Transport) messages or XML (Extensible Markup Language) messages. At present there are no international standards for electronic customs declaration messages through XML. Regarding UN/EDIFACT directory D96.B is used. The sent messages are based on a range of UN/EDIFACT documents.

Besides the mandatory fields the SAD presents a number of optional fields that national customs can demand if they want to. In reality, this have in led to that different XML schemas are used for the data transfer related to export declarations. Although not investigated, it is very unlikely that any two European countries would have implemented exactly the same XML schema without purposely collaborating on the matter. Consequently, although not deviating from the stipulated data model the transferred data differs from country to country. Besides the differences in data model, e-Customs also differs in the mode of transfer between company and customs, as well as in timing of implementation. New regulation is implemented at different dates in each country.

For the work process, the EU has searched to outline generic process models for how export declarations are made. On a high level, these processes are followed in both Denmark and Sweden. However, on a level with higher granularity there are difference when data is submitted, inspections are made and how inspections are made. Processes such as risk analysis are still implemented differently depending on the local risks.

The implications for European exporters are grave. Arla investigated the cost of developing a module for interfacing to Swedish customs and were given the offer of about 100,000 Euro. Bearing in mind that it has to be considered normal

that factual development cost is most often up to twice of calculated costs and that maintenance costs throughout the lifetime of a system is normally much higher than the development cost, implementing electronic export declarations to Swedish customs would be a fairly costly development. Therefore, Arla has chosen not to implement electronic transactions with Swedish Customs.

5. A TAXONOMY OF E-CUSTOMS STANDARDS IMPLEMENTATION DEVIATION

Although Danish and Swedish customs both have adopted the European e-Customs standard launched by the European Commission, to report the customs data electronically Arla has to implement and maintain two separate interfaces to the two e-Customs implementations. Even though Arla is one of the largest dairy companies in Europe and must be regarded as one of the more frequent exporters in Europe, the cost of implementing and maintaining the new system extensions has been estimated to exceed the benefits in efficiency by e-Customs. When complying with the standard does not mean that the objective of harmonization is met it is a relevant question to ask why. We refer to these reasons as the deviation sources of e-Customs.

This section analysis why Arla perceives the e-Customs solutions implemented as different, and the sources of variance that leads to the difference. The analysis takes its starting point in the three sources of standards implementation deviation as outlined in Figure 1.

It should be said that the European e-Customs initiative is far from finalized, but directives regarding export declaration is already being implemented in the two investigated countries. Therefore differences in how these regulations were interpreted, adapted to the national context and implemented can already be seen. Our objective was to describe sources of standard divergence, and as viewpoint to identify divergence we used Arla that has to deal with both Danish and Swedish customs. To assess the usefulness of our initial framework, the question is whether it can explain the differences between the two e-Export systems? Or, in other words, if harmonization in the three stipulated dimensions would imply that Arla is able to deal with the two customs organizations using the same IS? The answer is no. As will be explained in the following, the frame has to be extended with at least three empirically derived sources of deviation. But let us start with recapturing how the first three sources of standards implementation deviation played out in the European e-Customs case.

The *data model* was not completely standardized. Although both Denmark and Sweden based their data models on the SAD, the standard for data model allowed for optional data fields. In consequence, Arla had to submit different data sets to the Danish and Swedish customs.

The *data meaning*, was standardized in the work with the SAD. Although a few optional data fields are not standardized in terms of meaning, these are the national fields that are not used pan-European. All data that is exchanged European-wide seems to be interpreted similarly by the European customs authorities.

For *work processes*, some standardization was achieved by high level process descriptions. However, this was on a high level. There was still a difference in when data was submitted, and to whom, as some of the detailed processes where depending on local context. For example the risk analysis that should take into account local risk factors.

As far as the authors of this chapter has been able to identify, a fourth, fifth and sixth source of deviation are largely ignored in the current regulations and directives. Even if the same data, with the same meaning is transferred there can be deviations in the way data is transferred. We refer to this as the *mode of transfer*. Comparing the e-Export systems we found that the mode of transfer dif-

fered in encryption required for submission and in requirement of digital signature. Currently neither Danish nor Swedish customs employs encryption, but considering the data submitted this is a must for future developments. In Sweden, legislation demands identification of the person who submits data, therefore Swedish customs employs digital signature since long. Danish customs does not. As will be further elaborated later, this source of deviation may be very difficult to deal with due to the roots in national legislation.

Timing is an almost ignored aspect of implementation deviation. On a very general level the EU has set deadline for the phases of e-Customs, but on a practical level national customs are free to implement regulation and updates during a time span. As updates, modification and alternations are frequent during systems development processes and as the systems development process of European e-Customs is likely to be ongoing for a long time, timing of implementation creates at the same time different systems in all European countries.

Finally, the example of need for digital signature is only one example where national and regional legislation differs when it comes to customs processes. The EU has recently introduced the concept of Authorized Economic Operator (AEO), which is a certification that gives certified companies trade facilitations. A similar certification does not exist in for example China. So, how should Chinese customs react to the certification? Currently it is ignored, which erases all facilitations the AEO receives in the EU when trading with China since all paper based certificates and forms has to be produced to Chinese customs. Somehow, for Arla to be able to benefit fully from the e-Customs implementation, the *underpinning legislation* has to be standardized in the markets where Arla is active.

Recapitulating both theoretically and empirically derived sources of deviation we found six distinct sources of deviation: a) declaration process, b) data model, c) data meaning, d) mode of transfer, e) timing in implementation, f) underpinning legislation. The six sources are summarized in Table 1 as *A taxonomy of deviation sources in e-Customs implementations*.

It is noteworthy that all six sources of deviations are so crucial that only the slightest deviation severely damages the harmonization idea. A new step in the work processes, slightly different data models, incompatible meaning of data fields, different encryption techniques, or different implementation dates would from the perspective of Arla force different versions of e-Customs connections. Although development cost for each deviation might be limited seen in isolation, the complexity of having to maintain 27 e-Customs solutions for the pan-European trader is a substantial overhead cost, which is reducing the competitiveness of EU companies. And it is problematic, since it can be avoided, if government agencies across the EU collaborated to a higher degree on standards. In the next we will discuss possible ways of dealing with deviations in the implementation of standards.

6. DISCUSSION AND CONCLUSION

Through the current harmonization-efforts European export declaration processes has becoming more similar. But, as shown above, close is not close enough if the ambition is to substantially lower cost for pan-European business. In order to leverage true benefits all of the six areas of standardization have to be harmonized. Since

international trade is exactly international, some of these issues cannot be solved nationally or regionally, but has to be addressed globally. This section discuss two approaches for dealing with socio-technical standards implementation deviation in international trade: the first one is to increase harmonization through international collaboration, the second one is the potential of creating technical solutions to live with deviating standards implementations.

6.1 Overcoming Deviation: International Collaboration

Although the technical aspects of an e-Customs solution are complex problems to solve, our understanding of the problems put forward in this chapter is that the real challenge lies in establishing the collaborative momentum that enables change in the human and organizational dimensions of the e-Customs solution. In line with what, for example, Bjørn-Andersen (1980) and Monteiro and Hanseth (1996) write, we have seen that you cannot understand the technical aspects of the e-Customs solution without understanding the human and organizational context into which the technical infrastructure is embedded. Despite all actors possibly seeing the point of a well-functioning solution, the interested parts are likely to have rival objectives that have to be consolidated.

In the case of the European trade, pan-European traders wish for one single way to deal with national customs organizations, regardless from

Table 1. A taxonomy of deviation sources in e-Customs

	Deviation Source	Description
A	Work process	Logic by which the IS is manipulated to fulfil its use.
B	Data model	Data processed by the IS.
C	Data meaning	The meaning of processed data for IS' users.
D	Mode of transfer	How data is transferred through the IS.
E	Time of implementation	When the IS and changes to the IS are implemented.
F	Underpinning legislation	Legislation that set the frame for customs processes.

which country they export, but the desirable way differs, depending on the nature (time sensitivity, product type, etc.) of the trader's business. Similarly, the 27 member states' customs organizations of the EU have different interests in the infrastructure, depending on the importance of trade to the country, previous customs systems, existing integration with other national systems and embedding into legislation. The multiple layers of business, national governmental authorities, and international bodies are creating a complex alignment situation (Rukanova et al., 2009). Our experience is also that quite often the actors that share a mutual interest in an intra-organizational solution such as the e-Customs solution are not even aware of this common interest.

What we can learn from viewing international trade from a standardization perspective is the necessity of a common platform where all actors with an interest the e-Customs solution can meet on neutral ground. This role of creating neutral ground can be played by actors such as the UN and the WCO, who are picking up this task in some areas, but the key point is that it does not happen by itself. Someone who does not have an apparent interest in a specific solution must catalyse the process.

6.2 Overcoming Deviation: Interoperability and Interfaces

Although there are international organisations dedicated to developing standards for e-Customs, a widespread adoption of these standards in the short run will not be realistic. This is partly due to the fact that national actors are responsible for different parts of the e-Customs infrastructure. National solutions are developed and implemented with regard to a number of national contingencies, including political will, economic capacity and technical sophistication. This means that countries will adopt new solutions for e-Customs and international trade, subject to different priorities regarding fraud security and trade facilitation.

In addition, many standards have only recently been developed or are still on the drawing table. Therefore existing solutions and those that will be developed in the near future will not conform to these standards. It will take time before governmental agencies and traders are ready to make new investments and shift to international standards. In consequence, for a long time ahead the actors of international trade will have to live with some degree of deviation in the implementation of e-Customs.

However, even though diversity of standards and solutions will exist, it does not mean that efforts in the area of e-Customs cannot proceed. To enable co-existence of different standards and solutions, interoperability tools are essential. Related to e-Customs and international trade, Ulankiewicz et al., (2010) outlines interoperability challenges on three levels for international trade: data and message level, platform level, and process level. Basically, these three levels conform to the three levels of standards implementation deviation discussed earlier in this chapter: technical, infological, and organizational levels.

Essentially, an interoperability approach implies the construction of interfaces that make co-existence of standards implementations with variance in the implementation possible. Overcoming deviation will thus mean not to erase any difference, but simply learning to live with differences. There are, however, limitations to this approach as we see it. Interoperability through interfaces cannot make fundamentally different solutions co-exist. For example, if one country's legislation demands that some data is reported, and this data is not part of the collected data set, then no interoperability tools can convert nothing to data. Another problem might be areas where two mutually excluding alternatives are required. For example, where one country holds the individual who makes a custom declaration responsible for the declaration, and the other country holds the organization for which the individual work as responsible. Creating standardization and harmonization through collaboration will still be the fundamental approach to address the hurdles of standardization deviation. Interoperability tools can overcome minor frictions, but never erase fundamental logical inconsistencies.

6.3 Conclusion

The relevance of seeking to explain the reasons for standards compliance not fulfilling the managerial objective should not be limited to the context of customs. Research on IS and standards is limited despite the increasing importance in managing and using IS (Lyytinen & King, 2006). In addition, the existing research has mostly investigated content of new anticipatory standards rather than processes and factors that explains why and how standards emerge, are used and with which consequences (Lyytinen & King, 2006). Among the explanatory works, standards development is almost exclusively the focus leaving the subject of standards implementation almost unexplored (Egyedi, 2007; Egyedi & Dahanayake, 2003; Söderström, 2004). The exceptions include a few writings on institutional factors of standardizing organizations that eventually leads to implementation problems (e.g. Egyedi, 2007; Damsgaard & Lyytinen, 2001b; King et al., 1994). Not at least the past stream of EDI research has highlighted the need for synchronization between standards on IS and organizational level (e.g. Brousseau, 1994; Ko et al., 2009; Legner & Schemm, 2008), but not specifically addressed the different levels as sources of deviations.

With this chapter we contribute towards an improved understanding of the challenges associated with using standardization mechanism for socio-technical information systems. The harmonization of behavior through standardization has proven difficult (e.g. Aanestad & Jensen, 2011; Broks & Geradin, 2011). Socio-technical standardization is particularly difficult since it means standardization that contains both social

(organizational processes and practices) and technical (hardware and software in the computerized network) components (Hanseth and Braa 2001).

In this chapter we identify and describe what has to be harmonized in order to that a global company should perceive e-Customs as standardized. In our investigation we found that differences in the implementation of e-Customs systems potentially could originate from six distinct sources. In addition to the previously known deviation stemming from a) work processes, b) data model, and c) data meaning, we found three new potential deviation sources in d) mode of transfer, e) timing of implementation, and f) underpinning legislation. All these sources seems to be of the nature that even the slightest deviation in any of the areas leads to the standard failing to meet its objective of increased efficiency.

The idea behind the above mentioned regulations of total electronic data transmission is that it will lead to security increase, higher transparency and less fraud, while not adding to increasing the administrative burden on pan-European actors. So far the results have been that:

- Security, traceability and control have increased.
- The cost of reaching the new level of security, traceability and control without electronic submission of data seem to be higher in most cases.
- The additional burden on pan-European companies has not yet been lowered but rather increased as a result of the new export declaration processes.

We believe that to a large extent this is due to the current deviations in the implementations of export declaration processes, which are in a clear conflict with the idea of creating one common, inner European market place. With the current situation, if a company is active on one member country and would like to expand business with another production and export facility, everything else being equal, the cost is higher if placing that facility in another country than the country that the company is already exporting from due to the need of creating new export processes and developing a new electronic channel to the national customs.

We believe that this research highlights the importance of taking the step from research on IT standards to research on IS standards. As heavily emphasized in the IS literature, IT has no organizational value in its own right, but only as an enabler for information sharing. What we show in this research is that IT standards compliance is a prerequisite but not sufficient requirement for leveraging the benefits that is expected by standardization. More research is needed to understand the potential and problems with regulating behaviour by IS standardization.

ACKNOWLEDGMENT

This research is part of the integrated project ITAIDE (Nr.027829), funded by the 6th Framework IST Programme of the European Commission (see www.itaide.org). The ideas and opinions expressed by the authors do not necessarily reflect the views/insights/interests of all ITAIDE partners.

An outline of this chapter was presented at the 'Common ICT Standards or Divided Markets: the EU and China'-workshop in conjunction with I-ESA conference (Interoperability for Enterprise Software and Applications). Feedback on this presentation from workshop participants was implemented in this version of the chapter.

REFERENCES

Aanestad, M., & Jensen, T. B. (2011). Building nation-wide information infrastructures in healthcare through modular implementation strategies. *The Journal of Strategic Information Systems*, 20(2), 161–176. doi:10.1016/j.jsis.2011.03.006

Ahrne, G., & Brunsson, N. (2011). Organization outside organizations: The significance of partial organization. *Organization*, 18(1), 83–104. doi:10.1177/1350508410376256

Alter, S. (2003). Sorting Out Issues About the Core, Scope, and Identity of the IS Field. *Communications of the AIS, 12*(41).

Bjørn-Andersen, N., Razmerita, L., & Zinner-Henriksen, H. (2007). The streamlining of Cross-Border Taxation Using IT: The Danish eExport Solution. In G. O. J. Macolm (Ed.), *E-Taxation: State & Perspectives - E-Government in the field of Taxation: Scientific Basis, Implementation Strategies, Good Practice Examples* (pp. 195–206). Linz: Trauner Verlag.

Blundon, W. (1997). How Microsoft is broadening Java's scope. *Java World*. Retrieved from http://www.javaworld.com/article/2077608/learn-java/how-microsoft-is-broadening-java-s-scope.html

Brooks, R. G., & Geradin, D. (2010). *Interpreting and enforcing the voluntary FRAND commitment*. Available at http://papers.ssrn.com/sol3/papers.cfm?abstract_id=1645878

Brousseau, E. (1994). EDI and inter-firm relationships: Toward a standardization of coordination processes? *Information Economics and Policy*, 6(3-4), 319–347. doi:10.1016/0167-6245(94)90007-8

Brunsson, N., & Jacobsson, B. (2000). *A world of standards*. Oxford, UK: Oxford University Press.

Brunsson, N., Rasche, A., & Seidl, D. (2012). The dynamics of standardization: Three perspectives on standards in organization studies. *Organization Studies*, 33(5-6), 613–632. doi:10.1177/0170840612450120

Carroll, J. M., & Swatman, P. A. (2000). Structured-case: A methodological framework for building theory in information systems research. *European Journal of Information Systems*, 9(4), 235–242. doi:10.1057/palgrave.ejis.3000374

Damsgaard, J., & Lyytinen, K. (2001). The role of intermediating institutions in the diffusion of electronic data interchange (EDI): How industry associations intervened in Denmark, Finland, and Hong Kong. *The Information Society*, *17*(3), 195–210. doi:10.1080/01972240152493056

Damsgaard, J., & Trading, E. (1998). International trade at the speed of light: Building an electronic trading infrastructure in Denmark, Finland, and Hong Kong. In *Proceedings of the IFIP 8.2 and 8.6 Joint Working Conference on Information Systems: Current Issues and Future Changes*. IFIP.

Damsgaard, J., & Truex, D. (2000). Binary trading relations and the limits of EDI standards: The Procrustean bed of standards. *European Journal of Information Systems*, *9*(3), 173–188. doi:10.1057/palgrave.ejis.3000368

Egyedi, T. M. (2007). Standard-compliant, but incompatible?! *Computer Standards & Interfaces*, *29*(6), 605–613. doi:10.1016/j.csi.2007.04.001

Egyedi, T. M., & Dahanayake, A. (2003). Difficulties implementing standards. In *Proceedings of Standardization and Innovation in Information Technology*. Academic Press.

Eisenhardt. (1989). Building Theories from Case study Research. *Academy of Management Review*, *14*(4), 532-550.

Folmer, E., Bekkum, M., & Verhoosel, J. (2009). Strategies for using international domain standards within a national context: The case of the Dutch temporary staffing industry. In *Proceedings of Innovations for Digital Inclusions, 2009. K-IDI 2009. ITU-T Kaleidoscope*. IEEE.

Gal, U., Lyytinen, K., & Yoo, Y. (2008). The Dynamics of IT Boundary Objects, Information Infrastructures, and Organisational Identities: The Introduction of 3D Modelling Technologies into the Architecture, Engineering, and Construction Industry. *European Journal of Information Systems*, *17*(3), 290–304. doi:10.1057/ejis.2008.13

Grimsley, M., & Meehan, A. (2007). e-Government information systems: Evaluation-led design for public value and client trust. *European Journal of Information Systems*, *16*(2), 134–148. doi:10.1057/palgrave.ejis.3000674

Gustafsson, M. R., Karlsson, T., & Bubenko, J. J. (1982). A declarative approach to conceptual information modelling. In T. W. Olle, H. G. Sol, & A. A. Verrijn-Stuart (Eds.), *Information Systems Design Methodologies: A Comparative Review* (pp. 93–142). Amsterdam: North-Holland.

Hanseth, O. (2000). The economics of standards.. In C. U. Ciborra (Ed.), *From control to drift: The dynamics of corporate information infrastructures* (pp. 56–70). Oxford, UK: Oxford University Press.

Hanseth, O. (2014). *Developing Pan-European e-Government Solutions: From Interoperability to Installed Base Cultivation The Circulation of Agency in E-Justice* (pp. 33–52). Netherlands: Springer.

Hanseth, O., & Braa, K. (2001). Hunting for the treasure at the end of the rainbow. Standardizing corporate IT infrastructure. *Computer Supported Cooperative Work*, *10*(3-4), 261–292. doi:10.1023/A:1012637309336

Hanseth, O., Jacucci, E., Grisot, M., & Aanestad, M. (2006). Reflexive Standardization: Side Effects and Complexity in Standard Making. *Management Information Systems Quarterly*, *30*, 563–581.

Henfridsson, O., & Bygstad, B. (2013). The generative mechanisms of digital infrastructure evolution. *Management Information Systems Quarterly*, *37*(3).

Henningsson, S., & Bjørn-Andersen, N. (2009). *When standards is not enough to secure interoperability and competitiveness for European exporters*. Paper presented at the 17th European Conference on Information Systems. Verona, Italy.

Henningsson, S., Bjorn-Andersen, N., Schmidt, A., Fluegge, B., & Zinner Henriksen, H. (2011). Food Living Lab – Complexity of Export Trade. In Y.-H. Tan, N. Bjørn-Andersen, S. Klein, & B. Rukanova (Eds.), *Accelerating Global Supply Chains with IT-Innovation* (pp. 3–29). Berlin: Springer. doi:10.1007/978-3-642-15669-4_5

Henningsson, S., Budel, R., Gal, U., & Bjorn-Andersen, N. (2010). ITAIDE Information Infrastructure (I3) Framework. In Y.-H. Tan, N. Bjørn-Andersen, S. Klein, & B. Rukanova (Eds.), *Accelerating Global Supply Chains with IT-Innovation*. Berlin: Springer.

Henningsson, S., & Zinner Henriksen, H. (2011). *Inscription of Behaviour and Flexible Interpretation in Information Infrastructures: The case of European e-Customs. Journal of Strategic Information Systems.*

Iivari, J. (2003). Towards Information Systems as a Science of Meta-Artifacts. *Communication of the AIS, 12*, 568–581.

Jakobs, K. (2008). *The IEEE 802.11 WLAN Installation at RWTH Aachen University: A Case of Voluntary Vendor Lock-In The dynamics of standards.* London: Edward Elgar.

King, J. L., Gurbaxani, V., Kraemer, K. L., McFarlan, F. W., Raman, K. S., & Yap, C. S. (1994). Institutional factors in information technology innovation. *Information Systems Research, 5*(2), 139–169. doi:10.1287/isre.5.2.139

Klein, S., Reimers, K., Johnston, R. B., Barrett, M., Modol, J. R., Tan, Y.-H., & Henningsson, S. (2012). Inter-organizational information systems: from strategic systems to information infrastructures. In *Proceedings of the 25th Bled eConference*, (pp. 302-319). Academic Press.

Klievink, B., & Lucassen, I. (2013). Facilitating Adoption of International Information Infrastructures: A Living Labs Approach. In M. A. Wimmer, M. Janssen, & H. J. Scholl (Eds.), *Electronic Government* (pp. 250–261). Berlin: Springer. doi:10.1007/978-3-642-40358-3_21

Kolltveit, B. J., Hennestad, B., & Grønhaug, K. (2007). IS projects and implementation. *Baltic Journal of Management, 2*(3), 235–250. doi:10.1108/17465260710817465

Lyytinen, K., & King, J. L. (2006). Standards making: A critical research frontier for information systems research. *Management Information Systems Quarterly, 30*(5), 205–411.

Markus, M. L., & Bjørn-Andersen, N. (1987). Power Over Users: Its Exercise By System Professionals. *Communications of the ACM, 30*(6), 498–504. doi:10.1145/214762.214764

Rukanova, B., Bjorn-Andersen, N., van Ipenburg, F., Klein, S., Smit, G., & Tan, Y. H. (2010). Introduction. In Y.-H. Tan, N. Bjørn-Andersen, S. Klein, & B. Rukanova (Eds.), *Accelerating Global Supply Chains with IT-Innovation* (pp. 3–29). Berlin: Springer.

Sherif, M. H. (2007). *Standardization of business-to-business electronic exchanges.* Paper presented at the Standardization and Innovation in Information Technology. New York, NY. doi:10.1109/SIIT.2007.4629329

Söderström, E. (2004). *B2B Standards implementations: issues and solutions.* (Ph D Doctoral Dissertation). Stockholm.

Ulankiewicz, S., Henningsson, S., Bjorn-Andersen, N., & Fluegge, B. (2010). Interoperability Tools. In Y.-H. Tan, N. Bjørn-Andersen, S. Klein, & B. Rukanova (Eds.), *Accelerating Global Supply Chains with IT-Innovation*. Berlin: Springer.

KEY TERMS AND DEFINITIONS

Case Study: A method of inquiry that centres on in-depth exploration of an empirical case.

E-Customs: Digital transfer of information needed for customs processes.

Information Infrastructure: A heterogeneous IT-based solution for information exchange.

International Trade: Trade that spans national and regional borders.

Socio-Technical Standard: A standard that combines social and technical protocols.

Standard: A social and/or technical protocol aimed at achieving conformity.

Standardization: The mechanism of achieving conformity through introducing a standard.

Standards Deviation: Voluntary or involuntary deviance from the intended use of a standard.

Section 4
Standardisation and Asia

Chapter 12
Standards Development as Hybridization and Capacity Building

Xiaobai Shen
University of Edinburgh, UK

Ian Graham
University of Edinburgh, UK

Robin Williams
University of Edinburgh, UK

ABSTRACT

While users in the rest of the world have been offered 3G mobile phones based on either the CDMA2000 or W-CDMA standards, users in China have the additional option of using phones based on the TD-SCDMA standard. As a technology largely developed by Chinese actors and only implemented in China, TD-SCDMA has been seen as an "indigenous innovation" orchestrated by the Chinese government and supported by Chinese firms. China's support for TD-SCDMA was widely viewed in the West as a ploy to keep the "global" 3G standards, W-CDMA and CDMA2000, out of China, but in 2009, the Chinese government licensed the operation of all three standards. The authors argue that Chinese support for TD-SCDMA, rather than being a defensive move, was a proactive policy to use the TD-SCDMA standard to develop Chinese industrial capacity, which could then be fed back into the global processes developing later generations of telecommunications standards. Rather than being an indigenous Chinese technology, TD-SCDMA's history exemplifies how standards and the intellectual property and technological know-how embedded in them lead to a complex hybridization between the global and national systems of innovation.

DOI: 10.4018/978-1-4666-6332-9.ch012

INTRODUCTION

In January 2009 the Chinese government licensed three network operators to operate third generation(3G) mobile phone networks on three incompatible air interface standards: W-CDMA, CDMA2000 and TD-SCDMA (Time Division Synchronous Code Division Multiple Access). While W-CDMA and CDMA2000 had been implemented by operators around the world, China Mobile's use of TD-SCDMA was the platform's first large-scale implementation. TD-SCDMA has been described as "China's own 3G standard" (Fan, 2006), the "Chinese self-developed standard" (Yan, 2007), "China's... TD-SCDMA" (Kshetri, Palvia, & Dai, 2011), "China's TD-SCDMA standard" (Low & Johnston, 2010), "home-grown technology" (Wu, 2009), "China's homegrown telecommunications standard" (Hsueh, 2011) and "China's... locally developed standard" (Kwak, Lee, & Chung, 2012). This chapter provides a socio-technical analysis of this highly complex IT technology and argues that rather than see the competition amongst the three platforms as a standards war between an indigenous Chinese technology and two global competitors, TD-SCDMA should be seen as a hybrid technology that has emerged through an on-going process of greater engagement by China in global standards development, and that the knowledge generated in China during the development of TD-SCDMA technologies feeds back into global standards development. Detailed descriptions of the development of TD-SCDMA have been produced by Chinese writers, in particular Gao et al. (2012) and Hong et al. (2012), but their focus on the roles of Chinese actors reinforces the perception that TD-SCDMA is an indigenous Chinese technology. In contrast, we shall describe how TD-SCDMA developed through the growing engagement of China with global standards development and, rather than view the process as a clash between two immutable innovation systems, we argue that the history of TD-SCDMA is best understood as a process of hybridization between the global and Chinese systems of telecommunications innovation.

Our analysis is based on a case study of the development of TD-SCDMA conducted within the China EU Information Technology Standards Research Partnership, supported by EU FP7.[1] The case used a combination of primary and secondary data. The former included interviews with actors involved in the development of TD-SCDMA from its beginnings as a collaboration between Chinese actors and Siemens, the European telecommunications equipment supplier, through to the launch of TD-SCDMA in 2010 as a commercial service in China. The interview data was supplemented by discussions in four workshops in China and Europe with industrial experts and policy-makers. Secondary data consisted of academic literature, general and specialised media reports and the official documents of governments and corporations. In this investigation the motivations of key actors were sometimes opaque and claims by actors, in particular the Chinese government agencies, treated with scepticism by many respondents[2]. However, through triangulation, it was possible to reconstruct an STS account of the social processes which have shaped TD-SCDMA.

1. DYNAMICS IN THE MOBILE TELECOMMUNICATIONS INDUSTRY

Telecommunications and telecommunications equipment was identified as a strategically important 'pillar' industry in the Chinese 10th and 11th five year plans. The economic reforms had successfully transformed the Chinese telecommunications industry from being an impediment to economic development in the early 1980s to become its most vibrant sector by the mid-90s. Since 1986, China's five-year plans have emphasised the importance of high technology R&D and innovation (Ure,

2007). Chinese government policy required China to open up its market to foreign players and to build up indigenous technological capability by nurturing domestic players (Shen, 1999).

The development of telecommunications equipment supply in China is well documented (Cai & Tylecote, 2008; P. Gao & Lyytinen, 2000; Harwit, 2008; Shen, 1999; Wu, 2009): the old system of state controlled supply was broken up and a new controlled competitive environment created. The most significant institutional change was a reorganisation of the government ministries in 1998, with the Ministry of Information Industry replacing the Ministry of Post and Telecommunications and Ministry of Electronic Industry. This was followed by a "pseudo-liberalisation" (Pearson, 2005) reorganisation of state-owned companies to create controlled competition between players, but keeping the competing companies in state ownership. In 1999 the state telecommunications agency, China Telecom, was split into three parts (fixed-line, mobile and satellite), establishing China Mobile and China Satcom to take over the mobile and satellite sectors, leaving China Telecom to remain in the fixed-line services. In 2002, China Telecom was further split geographically into North and South, creating China Netcom to operate in the North (Harwit, 2008). The state monopoly was replaced by oligopoly between several state-owned companies. Such an industrial structure in the telecommunications sector allows continual political 'interference' by the state (Pearson, 2005). A key stage in forcing this process was the negotiation of China's accession to the World Trade Organization (WTO) in 2001, leading to the opening up of Chinese markets to foreign firms, to the allowing of foreign investment, the creation of regulated markets, the enforcement of anti-monopoly law (G. Li, 2008), intellectual property law, the introduction of consumer protection, and the development of greater transparency in the relationship between government and industry. The negotiation between China and the United States of China's WTO ac-

cession was long, arduous and often acrimonious (Nakatsuji, 2001), with the US keen to ensure entry to the large and growing Chinese market in genral, but for their telecommunications suppliers in particular. Following these negotiations the Chinese telecommunications operator Unicom were instructed by the Chinese government to negotiate with Qualcomm, the US corporation with ownership of a large part of CDMAone intellectual property, to establish a national Chinese CDMAone 2G network (Mock, 2005), taking over the small-scale network operated by Great Wall, even though GSM was also being rolled out across China. US negotiators also feared that China would use the licensing of TD-SCDMA, which was a recognised international standard, as a means of keeping the other two 3G mobile systems out of China, and so put China under pressure to commit to being open to all international 3G platform standards. In April 2004 at the US-China Joint Commission on Commerce and Trade (JCCT) it was announced that the Chinese government would support technology neutrality with regard to the adoption of 3G telecommunications standards and that telecommunications service providers in China would be allowed to choose which standard to adopt, depending on their individual needs. This position was reiterated in a 2006 JCCT meeting, when the government further agreed to issue licences for all technologies employing 3G standards in a technologically neutral manner that did not privilege one standard over others.

Mobile telecommunications in China experienced rapid growth during the second half of the 1990s. In 2003 China became the largest world market when the total number of China's mobile subscriptions overtook that of the US, making the telecommunication sector China's fastest growing industry. Since WTO entry, the industry had become more open to foreign multinationals. The world's leading telecommunications equipment suppliers had all established presences in China and become major players in the Chinese telecommunications equipment market, although all but

Motorola had to do this by setting up joint ventures with Chinese firms. Chinese investment in early 2G infrastructure benefited the foreign multinationals more than the Chinese firms because most of the advanced technologies were developed by foreign multinationals. China became a "global factory" (Ernst, 2007), at the same time, using the global market to access technologies (Zhan & Tan, 2010), but the more foreign technology China used, the more royalty fees they had to pay.

Although Chinese companies were developing their own products with support from the State Commission of Science and Technology, these products were less sophisticated and less attractive to the Chinese market than products developed by Western multinationals. In 2004 an official in the high technology department of MII commented that "developing technology is less attractive than buying technology".[3] Service operators preferred network equipment developed by foreign multi-nationals and consumers also favoured foreign branded handsets. As a result, foreign brands dominated large cities and affluent areas, leaving Chinese handsets to find their buyers in rural, less developed regions. Chinese companies ZTE and Huawei sought growth through exports to developing countries, but formulated longer-term strategies to combine acquiring foreign advanced technologies with developing their own ones, allowing them to develop their resources and expertise gradually.

2. THE THIRD 3G WAY: TD-SCDMA

The genesis of TD-SCDMA is complex, resulting from the intersection of two trajectories. One started from the efforts of a group of Chinese IT professionals working in the US, and the other from a consortium of European companies. These two paths collided in the ITU's specification of three standards for the air interfaces of third generation

(3G) mobile telephony in 2000. Dr. Guanhan Xu had drafted a blueprint for Synchronous Code Division Multiple Access (or SCDMA) as an interface for wireless devices to connect to networks. Xu had completed his PhD in 1991 at the Stanford University Information Systems Lab under Professor Thomas Kailath specialising in smart antenna technology. Smart antenna technology was being developed in the US for military radar and telecommunications systems, and the Information Systems Lab at Stanford University was the world's leading laboratory in this area. After one year of post-doctoral research, Xu took a position as an assistant professor at the University of Texas in Austin and established his own laboratory researching the use of smart antennas in civil wireless telecommunications. He developed the joint detection system for smart antennas to enhance the coverage and eliminate interference of radio signal transmission. [4]

Together with two Chinese colleagues, Wei Chen and Sanqi Li, Xu believed that their knowledge could be used in China in developing its own technological capabilities (J. Li, 2007). Before returning to China, they contacted the Chinese Academy of Telecommunications Technology, where Sanqi Li worked before he went to the US in 1989, and received a positive response (J. Li, 2007). They registered a private company, Cwill Telecommunications Inc, in Texas in 1994 and planned to grow their business in China (Bloomberg, 2013; China Youth Daily, 2009). In 1995, with the approval of the Ministry of Posts Telecommunications, CATT and Cwill established a joint venture, Xinwei Telecommunications Inc., to develop smart antennas and SCDMA (Synchronous CDMA).

Meanwhile, on the other side of the World in Europe, Siemens, in alliance with Nortel, Alcatel, Motorola, Italtel, Bosch and Sony Europe, was working on TD- CDMA (Time Division CDMA) as an air interface standard for linking mobile devices to base-stations in the next generation of mobile telecommunications. In opposition to Siemen's TD-CDMA consortium, Ericsson, Nokia and NTT DoCoMo were collaborating to develop a competing frequency-division (FD) interface. TD uses a single frequency with uplink and downlink segments synchronised into a single band, where FD uses separate frequencies. Network operators favoured FD because it was a simpler technology and more highly developed, so represented less technical risk and promised earlier implementation. At an ETSI meeting in Paris on 29th January 1998 Europe's vendors and operators chose the FD-based W-CDMA standard air interface for the European 3G mobile system, with the prospect that the standard would also be adopted in Asia where Japanese NTT DoCoMo was working with Nokia and Ericsson on W-CDMA with 16 Asian operators in 11 countries (Scott-Joynt, 1998). For European mobile network operators W-CDMA offered a clear transition from their GMTS networks. Similarly, US operators supported CDMA2000, the FD system sponsored by Qualcomm, which had a clear transition path from their current 2G CDMA networks.

A Chinese telecommunication delegation, sponsored and organised by the Ministry of Science and Technology, visited Siemens and Siemens saw collaboration with CATT as a way to develop a rival 3G standard combining their TD- CDMA expertise with the Chinese development of SCDMA. An emigre Chinese IT professional, Dr Wanlin Li, working for Siemens at its German Headquarters after completing his study in Karlsruhe Institute of Technology, Germany (Business Weekly, 2005), helped with the collaboration between the Chinese delegation and the Siemens senior managerial team. The outcome was a memorandum of understanding to develop the merged system, TD-SCDMA, being signed between the two sides in July 1998 (Zhan & Tan, 2010). A TD-SCDMA blueprint proposal was drafted and sent to the Chinese MPT for approval.

The MPT eventually made the decision and gave a green light only a week before the ITU's deadline for submission on 31 June 1998.

TD-SCDMA technology had some distinctive features compared to other two 3G standards, W-CDMA and CDMA2000. TD (time division) uses a single radio frequency to carry traffic both ways, unlike FD (frequency division) which needs two simultaneous channels, making the uplink/downlink transmission more efficient and reducing interference. TD-SCDMA allows full network coverage over macro cells, micro cells, and pico cells and is well-suited for internet data transmission, where the volumes of data in the two directions are unbalanced (Three-G.net, 2011). China's proposal for TD-SCDMA was accepted by ITU as one of the three 3G standards in IMT-2000 in May 2000 and was then also recognised by the 3GPP consortium[5] in March 2001. In IMT-2000 the ITU agreed on a single underlying standard for 3G mobile network infrastructure, but with five radio interfaces based on three different access technologies (FDMA, TDMA and CDMA), with both W-CDMA and CDMA-2000 using CDMA, and TD-SCDMA using TDMA.

A market intermediary, the TD-SCDMA Forum, was formed in December 2000, bringing together the main Chinese operators and equipment suppliers and involving also some international firms (Datang, 2010). Datang Telecommunications Technology is a state owned enterprise that grew out of the Chinese Academy of Post and Telecommunications Technology (CAPTT), under the then Ministry of Post and Telecommunications (former body of Ministry of Information Industry before the separation of Telecommunications from the Post industry). It had been one of the parent companies of Xinwei, the joint-venture with the US-registered Cwill. A representative of Datang sat as the Chairman of the Xinwei board, while Cwill personnel took the posts of CEO and CET (J. Li, 2007). In 2002, Datang Mobile was established, dedicated to TD-SCDMA related business.

3. APPLICATION OF TD-SCDMA: BUILDING THE ENTIRE SUPPLY CHAIN

The Chinese government mobilised actors across industry by forming the TD-SCDMA Industry Alliance (TD-SCDMAIA) involving Datang Mobile, Soutec, Holley, Huawei, Lenovo, ZTE, CEC and Potevio. The first "TD-SCDMAIA Summit Meeting" was held in early 2003 to deal with "practical" problems such as the sharing of IPR, investment and the potential market. The TD-SCDMA Industrial Alliance has since become an important body in the development of TD-SCDMA. Datang saw its IPR transferred to this body, which then had responsibility for licensing it. It has also acted as the vehicle for drawing on government funding for TD-SCDMA's development and commercialisation.

In 2002 155 MHz of radio spectrum in a band previously controlled by the military was allocated to TD-SCDMA by the Ministry of Information Industry (Liu, 2010). This was seen as an important signal that the government was determined to support the project and companies swiftly assembled around the standard. The attitude of the Chinese press towards TD-SCDMA also changed, and the atmosphere became more supportive of TD-SCDMA, which was recognised as complementary to the 'western' standards and part of building a "mixed" network. As a result of the more established status of TD-SCDMA, an increasing number of enterprises joined the Industry Alliance between 2003 and 2008, with expertise ranging from core network, RAN (radio access network), terminal, chips, testing instrument, antenna to direct amplifier station.

According Zhan and Tan (2010), the development and industrialisation of TD-SCDMA received very substantial Chinese government financial support from 1989 onwards. Coordinated by the National Development and Reform Commission, with the Ministry of Information Industry and Ministry of Science and Technol-ogy, the government provided the R&D subsidy of RMB 708 million to support the TD-SCDMA development and commercialisation (Xu, 2005). In the early stages, funds were from the "national 863 programme", and the "national 973 programme" which are administered by the Ministry of Science and Technology. For the Ministry of Science and Technology (MOST), IT has always been a field of a high priority. Many IT development projects fall into the responsibility of its Department of High and New Technology Development and Industrialization. Some other funding supporting TD-SCDMA came from the National Foundation of Nature Science of China, which funds university research. CATT had also received regular research funding from MII. During the industrialisation stage, TD-SCDMA had also obtained financial support directly from the National Development and Reform Commission (Zhan & Tan, 2010).

On 9th February 2006 the "National Guideline on Medium-and Long-Term Program for Science and Technology Development (2006-2020)", in alignment with the "Hu-Wen New Deal", promulgated a policy specifying the crucial role of technology standards in national S&T advancement and industrial development. The 11th Chinese 5-Year plan of 2006 moved away from the previous strategy of "trading technology for market" to a much stronger focus on "endogenous innovation". Ure (2007) quotes Premier Wen: "We need to promptly develop core technologies and improve systems integration in some important industries and create technologies, products and standards for which we own intellectual property rights".

Given the new political momentum, TD-SCDMA gained full support from the highest level of the government. Many saw TD-SCDMA as representing an opportunity for the Chinese government to implement its policy of promoting indigenous technology. At this point the government leaders increasingly became confident in backing the TD-SCDMA mobile telecommunications standard as a national strategic technology development. In January 2006, MII formally announced TD-

SCDMA to be a "Telecommunication Industry Standard" in China, even though China Mobile was by then trialling WCDMA. Small scale testing in three cities in 2006 proved that TD-SCDMA was technically viable. The policy of licensing three standards instead of one was not changed, though it was unclear how this would happen. AFX News Limited reported in November 2006 that Jiang Yaoping, vice minister of Information Industry Ministry, had said at a conference when asked if the government would subsidize companies deploying TD-SCDMA, 'we keep neutral on the selection progress for 3G standards, and support all the 3G standards including W-CDMA, CDMA2000 and the home-developed TD-SCDMA.'

The challenges facing China in launching a national TD-SCDMA network were significant. A strong operator was needed, which would be able to test, plan and launch the 3G services. A network would need a variety of handsets compatible for the TD-SCDMA standard to be available. China Mobile, the largest and state-owned operator, was the obvious choice for the task. Chinese companies, including big players like Huawei and ZTE, were increasingly seeing each other as competitors, so collaboration across the different sectors amongst service providers, equipment and component suppliers would have been unlikely without the coordination of the government. In the middle of June 2008, Minister of MIIT, Li Yizhong, met with TD-SCDMA technical experts, and asserted that there would be "no failure but success" in TD-SCDMA, and organised a meeting on June 25, 2008 to discuss the further advance of TD-SCDMA's implementation. In the following day, the president of China Mobile declared that they would "make every effort" to ensure a TD-SCDMA service during and after the Beijing 2008 Olympic games. On July 2 2008, MIIT, working with other related departments, established a cross-ministry coordinating group, and allocated 34 special work packages to respective offices. On 12 July 2008, China Mobile formally joined the TD-SCDMAIA. In August 2008 the first licences for TD-SCDMA handset production were issued by the MIIT, and the subsequent steps towards full commercialisation announced. China Mobile committed 20 billion Yuan (about 2 billion Euro) of investment to build up 10 core networks in 8 cities (Beijing and Shanghai had 2 core networks each) and to carry out commercial-scale testing.

Even after the formation of the TD-SCDMA Industrial Alliance, firms in China were still waiting for the government to give clear signals on which of the 3G platform standards would be launched and how large a market each would become. In 2002 Huawei was the leading player in producing WCDMA network equipment while ZTE was the leader in CDMA2000 (Gao & Liu, 2012). Firms would not re-allocate their resources to TD-SCDMA without a clear and strong signal from the market and the government. The long-waited strong signal did not arrive until China Mobile was officially instructed by the government to deploy TD-SCDMA in the beginning of 2009, leaving China Unicom and China Telecom to operate W-CDMA and CDMA2000 networks respectively.

Standards development is dynamic. With the specification of the three competing 3G systems complete, operators and equipment suppliers globally moved on to the development of the next generation of mobile technology, 4G. The ITU's aim in co-ordinating 4G standards development as LTE (Long Term Evolution) was again to avoid the emergence of incompatible standards, but again allowing the emergence of FD and TD versions of LTE. China has taken a lead role in TD-LTE standards development, the TD version of LTE, but unlike with TD-SCDMA, the development of TD-LTE has been supported by global firms to develop dual use TD/FD LTE devices and TD-LTE has been chosen over FD-LTE by operators outside China, notably Softbank in Japan and Bhatia in India.

4. ACADEMIC INTERPRETATIONS OF THE TD-SCDMA SAGA

The case of TD-SCDMA has been widely analysed. In reading accounts of TD-SCDMA is important to recognise the subtle differences between the technical definition of TD-SCDMA as the distinctive air interface, standardised relatively early in the story, and TD-SCDMA as the name for the whole implementable system using that standard, which came much later.

Viale et al (2012) analyse TD-SCDMA development and implementation as "a path dependent process of competition between standards", drawing on the well-established literature on the economics of market standardisation (Stango, 2004). However, the control of the three network operators by the Chinese government means that it is difficult to identify the market shaping the relative success of the three platforms, unlike in classic standards wars, for example ODF versus OOXML in document standards (Blind, 2011) or in competing modem standards (Augereau, Greenstein, & Rysman, 2006). The pivotal role of the Chinese government, inconsistent signals about the government's commitment to TD-SCDMA (Gao & Liu, 2012), conflicts between government ministries and a suspicion that the commitment to implement all three systems was a deception, all generated academic interest in the analysis of the government's policy towards 3G telecommunications. This policy analysis splits into two distinct phases. Prior to the decision to license the three competing platforms Western analysis interpreted the Chinese policy to develop TD-SCDMA as strategy to keep non-Chinese technologies out of the Chinese market and avoid payment of licensing fees (Kennedy, 2006; Kennedy, Suttmeier, & Su, 2008; Suttmeier & Xiangkui, 2004). TD-SCDMA was viewed through the lens of recent experience of the development of a Chinese wireless local radio network standard, WAPI, seen as an attempt to keep Wifi out of the Chinese market

(Gao, 2007; Lee & Oh, 2006; Lee & Oh, 2008; van de Kaa, Greeven, & van Puijenbroek, 2013). Following the licencing of the three platforms, the focus of the academic discourse moved from the US to China, where Chinese academics with access to key participants have focused on the role of TD-SCDMA development in building up Chinese capability in mobile technology (Gao & Liu, 2012; Hong et al., 2012; Kwak et al., 2012).

We argue that all three of these interpretations of TD-SCDMA development gain strength by underplaying the significance of non-Chinese knowledge in the early stages of the development of the interface, as provided by Siemens, and by overlooking the extent to which the implementable system uses intellectual property generic across all three 3G platforms. Whether arguing from outside China that TD-SCDMA was an attempt to close off the Chinese market or later arguing from inside China that TD-SCDMA represents China leapfrogging Western competitors, writers needed to emphasise the indigeneity of TD-SCDMA.

5. STANDARDS DEVELOPMENT AS HYBRIDIZATION

We have shown that the development of TD-SCDMA is a complex entangling of the national and the global; with the technology's implementation depending upon Chinese actors developing a viable system, the Chinese government mandating its use by China Mobile, but with the involvement of multinational companies, foreign intellectual property and TD-SCDMA's early recognition as a global standard. Drawing on cultural studies, Pieterse (1994) and Kraidy (2005; 2002) argue that globalization is not a homogenising force, leading to global convergence on a Western institutional model, but rather is leading to hybridization, where the resulting institutions mix elements of the local and the foreign. Standardisation processes, whether in global bodies such as the ITU or national processes, are as much cultural institutions as the systems of education or popular culture that hybridization theory has most frequently been applied to. The hybridization thesis predicts that instead of the globalised process emulating the processes of a hegemonic country (generally assumed to be the United States) and then overwhelming distinctive national processes, the global process is a hybridization between cultures and when the global institutions collide with national institutions, local hybrids emerge. Zachary (2000) argues that cultural complexity and the resulting hybridity are keys to successful innovation, as large numbers of novel mongrel practices emerge, many of which fail but some become established. Ostry and Nelson (1995) argue that national innovation systems are moving from *techno-nationalism*, with a focus on developing indigenous innovations and avoiding hybridization, towards *techno-globalism*, where innovation processes span national boundaries, implicitly triggering innovation through hybridization. In resisting this trend, the development of national standards is one route to implement a policy of techno-nationalism, and Kennedy et al (2008) identified twelve areas where distinctive Chinese IT standards had been promulgated. Suttmeier and Xiangkui (2004) however interpreted these Chinese innovations as *neo-techno-nationalist* (Yamada, 2000), combining state commitment to the development of a national standard with the involvement of foreign firms and the use of foreign intellectual property, hybridizing between the local and the global. Reimers and Li (2007) quote a Chinese source that estimated that in 2005 Nokia, Siemens, Qualcomm, Motorola and Alcatel-Lucent held 66% of the IPR in the TD-SCDMA air interface, while Steen (2011) quotes another Chinese source as claiming that in 2008 Datang, Huawei and ZTE only held 30% of the IPR. Steen notes that a fully operational system based on the TD-SCDMA interface would therefore almost certainly have much less than 30% Chinese-owned IPR.

As TD-SCDMA was developed, Chinese firms, foreign multinational enterprises and the Chinese government have all been monitoring each other, following the development of the technology and watching market demand. The Chinese government also had various agenda on the table supported by different departments and industries. Our interview in 2007 with a high ranking MII official indicates that all these issues were concerns of the government at different stages. As far as the MII was concerned then, the industry had been benefiting enormously from FDI and technologies of foreign multinationals. For the long term in such an environment with rapid technological changes, they recognise that it is important for industry to keep the door open to advanced technologies, whoever develops them. The implication of this strategy is that the Chinese government had recognised that the strategy should be to draw on non-Chinese technology, build on it, generate innovations and feed this knowledge back into international technology development. The officials interviewed in 2004 referred to the past experience of a self-sufficiency policy and considered this approach would not help domestic companies to become competitive, and ascertained that promoting Chinese technology only would run a high risk of China being locked into one technology which might become obsolete. At the time of WTO accession it was assumed in the West that Chinese technology policy was essentially techno-nationalist, so arm-twisting an agreement to open the Chinese market to non-Chinese technologies was seen as a victory, but in retrospect the agreement has strengthened Chinese industry by broadening their experience in global technology development.

In 1999 Shen (1999) noted that China leap-frogged generations of telecommunications switching technology technology to move from being passive adopter of Western technology to become a significant global innovator. Similarly, the development of TD-SCDMA became a sand-pit in which Chinese actors developed their knowledge of the complexities of assembling a sophisticated IT infrastructure from disparate standards and components, refined their knowledge in areas of telecommunications technology that are of increasing global strategic significance and, not insignificantly, engaged with the political complexities of global standards development. Kipnis (2012) argues that the emergence of distinctively different internet and educational standards in China is a process of nation-building that reinforces national identity, but is not a process divorced from international institutions. Similarly, the development of TD-SCDMA was a process of community-building across Chinese industry, government and academia. Implementing an infrastructural technology became an obligatory point of passage for the disparate actors in the Chinese national system of telecommunications innovation technology, and through this it was a stepping-stone on China's progression from being a consumer of foreign technologies and standards into a major player in the development of future telecommunications standards.

6. CONCLUSION

It is unhelpful to see TD-SCDMA technology as a Chinese "indigenous" technology standard engaged in, and losing, a standards war with competing global standards as this obscures the complex interactions involved between China and the rest of the World. From the viewpoint of STS studies, we have established that the key players involved in TD-SCDMA development and deployment were diverse and dispersed across the US, Europe and Asia, and that this included technical specialists, business firms and government organisations. The TD-SCDMA system implemented in China is largely built on intellectual property and standards shared with the competing systems, and

the intellectual property and expertise generated within the development of TD-SCDMA were fed forward into Chinese engagement in global 4G standards development.

The TD-SCDMA case has generated a wide literature, but analysis has frequently focused on using the case to uncover the innovation policy machinations of the Chinese government, treating TD-SCDMA as a Chinese platform technology in competition with European and American rivals. Prior to 1999 China was a user of telecommunications system standards developed elsewhere. The rejection of TDD by Western operators created an opportunity for the Chinese state and Chinese companies to co-opt a TD version of 3G telephony as a Chinese technology. The evolution of TD-SCDMA was slow and fraught, leading to a system that was clearly Chinese, in the sense that it has only been implemented in China, but not a truly "indigenous technology" as it is built from global standards. The process of turning the original air interface specification and the common components of IMT-2000 into an implementable system provided a valuable opportunity for China to develop its innovative capacity and to gain knowledge of the processes and politics of global standards development.

Fomin (2012), developing the concept of "liquid modernity" (Bauman, 2000), argues that the development and use of standards is becoming increasingly hybridised, with standards becoming malleable and adapting to accommodate tensions between their loci of development and use. The TD-SCDMA case demonstrates that as technologies become more complex and future iterations are built upon accumulated intellectual property, it becomes almost impossible to imagine a truly indigenous technology, as any new standards will be hybridising with existing knowledge elsewhere, and even if you could imagine this pure untainted national technology, its very existence would impact on standards development in other countries and globally. Historically, international standards development has been dominated by actors from North America, Europe and Japan, but as the processes become more diverse due to increasing engagement by actors from emerging economies, hybridization theory suggests that the global processes and standards will become more fluid to accommodate this diversity and allow the emergence of local variations, which will generate knowledge which will then be fed back into the global community.

REFERENCES

Augereau, A., Greenstein, S., & Rysman, M. (2006). Coordination versus differentiation in a standards war: 56K modems. *The Rand Journal of Economics*, *37*(4), 887–909. doi:10.1111/j.1756-2171.2006.tb00062.x

Bauman, Z. (2000). *Liquid modernity*. Cambridge: Polity Press.

Blind, K. (2011). An economic analysis of standards competition: The example of the ISO ODF and OOXML standards. *Telecommunications Policy*, *35*(4), 373–381. doi:10.1016/j.telpol.2011.02.007

Bloomberg. (2013). *Company Overview of Cwill Telecommunications, Inc*. Retrieved from http://investing.businessweek.com/research/stocks/private/snapshot.asp?privcapId=27274

Business Weekly. (2005). *Li Wanlin: 3G- the China's dream*. Retrieved from http://tech.sina.com.cn/t/2005-12-08/1632786691.shtml

Cai, J., & Tylecote, A. (2008). Corporate governance and technological dynamism of Chinese firms in mobile telecommunications: A quantitative study. *Research Policy*, *37*(10), 1790–1811. doi:10.1016/j.respol.2008.07.004

China Youth Daily. (2009). *Guanghan Xu: the first one who helped China spawned into Chinese own 3G standard*. China Youth Daily.

Datang. (2010). *Datang history*. Retrieved from http://www.datanggroup.cn/templates/T_Contents/index.aspx?nodeid=16

Ernst, D. (2007). Beyond the 'Global Factory' model: Innovative capabilities for upgrading China's IT industry. *International Journal of Technology and Globalisation*, *3*(4), 437–459. doi:10.1504/IJTG.2007.015459

Fan, P. (2006). Catching up through developing innovation capability: Evidence from China's telecom-equipment industry. *Technovation*, *26*(3), 359–368. doi:10.1016/j.technovation.2004.10.004

Fomin, V. V. (2012). Standards as Hybrids. *International Journal of IT Standards and Standardization Research*, *10*(2), 59–68. doi:10.4018/jitsr.2012070105

Gao, P. (2007). Counter-networks in standardization: A perspective of developing countries. *Information Systems Journal*, *17*(4), 391–420. doi:10.1111/j.1365-2575.2007.00262.x

Gao, P., & Lyytinen, K. (2000). Transformation of China's telecommunications sector: A macro perspective. *Telecommunications Policy*, *24*(8-9), 719–730. doi:10.1016/S0308-5961(00)00059-8

Gao, X. D., & Liu, J. X. (2012). Catching up through the development of technology standard: The case of TD-SCDMA in China. *Telecommunications Policy*, *36*(7), 531–545. doi:10.1016/j.telpol.2012.01.006

Harwit, E. (2008). *China's telecommunications revolution*. Oxford: Oxford University Press. doi:10.1093/acprof:oso/9780199233748.001.0001

Hong, Y., Bar, F., & An, Z. (2012). Chinese telecommunications on the threshold of convergence: Contexts, possibilities, and limitations of forging a domestic demand-based growth model. *Telecommunications Policy, 36*(10-11), 914–928. doi:10.1016/j.telpol.2012.07.013

Hsueh, R. (2011). *China's regulatory state: a new strategy for globalization.* Ithaca: Cornell University Press.

Kennedy, S. (2006). The Political Economy of Standards Coalitions: Explaining China's Involvement in High-Tech Standards Wars. *Asia Policy,* (2), 41-62.

Kennedy, S., Suttmeier, R. P., & Su, J. (2008). *Standards, Stakeholders, and Innovation: China's Evolving Role in the Global Knowledge Economy.* Academic Press.

Kipnis, A. B. (2012). Constructing Commonality: Standardization and Modernization in Chinese Nation-Building. *The Journal of Asian Studies, 71*(3), 731–755. doi:10.1017/S0021911812000666

Kraidy, M. (2005). Hybridity, or the cultural logic of globalization. Philadelphia, PA: Temple University Press.

Kraidy, M. M. (2002). Hybridity in cultural globalization. *Communication Theory, 12*(3), 316–339. doi:10.1111/j.1468-2885.2002.tb00272.x

Kshetri, N., Palvia, P., & Dai, H. (2011). Chinese institutions and standardization: The case of government support to domestic third generation cellular standard. *Telecommunications Policy, 35*(5), 399–412. doi:10.1016/j.telpol.2011.03.005

Kwak, J., Lee, H., & Chung, D. B. (2012). The evolution of alliance structure in China's mobile telecommunication industry and implications for international standardization. *Telecommunications Policy, 36*(10-11), 966–976. doi:10.1016/j.telpol.2012.07.017

Lee, H., & Oh, S. (2006). A standards war waged by a developing country: Understanding international standard setting from the actor-network perspective. *The Journal of Strategic Information Systems, 15*(3), 177–195. doi:10.1016/j.jsis.2005.10.002

Lee, H. J., & Oh, S. J. (2008). The political economy of standards setting by newcomers: China's WAPI and South Korea's WIPI. *Telecommunications Policy, 32*(9-10), 662–671. doi:10.1016/j.telpol.2008.07.008

Li, G. (2008). Moving towards unsustainability: A study of the Chinese telecommunications regulation. *International Journal of Private Law, 1*(1/2), 47–68. doi:10.1504/IJPL.2008.019432

Li, J. (2007, September 10). Behind the Curtain of 3G Standard. *Commercial Weekly.*

Liu, X. (2010). China's catch-up and innovation model in IT industry. *International Journal of Technology Management, 51*(2/3/4), 194 - 216.

Low, B., & Johnston, W. J. (2010). Organizational network legitimacy and its impact on knowledge networks: The case of China's TD-SCDMA mobility technology. *Journal of Business and Industrial Marketing, 25*(6), 468–477. doi:10.1108/08858621011066053

Mock, D. (2005). *The Qualcomm Equation: How a Fledgling Telecom Company Forged a New Path to Big Profits and Market.* New York: AMACOM.

Nakatsuji, K. (2001). Essence of Trade Negotiation: A Study on China's Entry for WTO. *Ritsumeikan Annual Review of International Studies, 14*(1), 15–34.

Ostry, S., & Nelson, R. R. (1995). *Techno-nationalism and techno-globalism: conflict and cooperation.* Washington, D.C.: Brookings Institution.

Pearson, M. (2005). China's WTO Implementation in Comparative Perspective. In R. Keith (Ed.), *China as a Rising World Power and its Response to Globalization*. London: Routledge.

Pieterse, J. N. (1994). Globalization as hybridization. *International Sociology*, *9*(2), 161–184. doi:10.1177/026858094009002003

Reimers, K., & Li, M. (2007). Effectiveness of the international 3G standardisation process and implications for China's 3G policy. *International Journal of Public Policy*, *2*(1/2), 124–139. doi:10.1504/IJPP.2007.012279

Scott-Joynt, J. (1998). *ETSI Pulls Off 3G Deal And Wins Asian Support*. Retrieved from http://www.totaltele.com/view.aspx?ID=425641

Shen, X. (1999).. . *The Chinese Road to High Technology.*, *256*. doi:10.1057/9781403905505

Stango, V. (2004). The Economics of Standards Wars. *Review of Network Economics*, *3*(1), 1. doi:10.2202/1446-9022.1040

Steen, H. U. (2011). Indicators of development or dependency in disguise? Assessing domestic inventive capacity in South Korean and Chinese infrastructural ICT standards. *Telecommunications Policy*, *35*(7), 663–680. doi:10.1016/j.telpol.2011.06.004

Suttmeier, R. P., & Xiangkui, Y. (2004). China's Post-WTO Technology Policy: Standards, Software, and the Changing Nature of Techno-Nationalism. *NBR Special Report, 7*.

Three-G.net. (2011). *3G Standards*. Retrieved from http://three-g.net/3g_standards.html

Ure, J. (2007). *China Standards and IPRs*. Hong Kong: Working Paper for the EU-China Trade Project.

van de Kaa, G., Greeven, M., & van Puijenbroek, G. (2013). Standards battles in China: Opening up the black box of the Chinese government. *Technology Analysis and Strategic Management*, *25*(5), 567–581. doi:10.1080/09537325.2013.785511

Vialle, P., Song, J. J., & Zhang, J. (2012). Competing with dominant global standards in a catching-up context. The case of mobile standards in China. *Telecommunications Policy*, *36*(10-11), 832–846. doi:10.1016/j.telpol.2012.09.003

Wu, I. S. (2009). *From iron fist to invisible hand: the uneven path of telecommunications reform in China*. London: Eurospan.

Xu, X. Y. (2005). *TD-SCDMA Testing*. Retrieved from http://www.tdscdma-forum.org/en/pdf-word/200561413101910889.doc

Yamada, A. (2000). *Neo-Techno-Nationalism: How and Why It Grows*. Columbia International Affairs Online.

Yan, H. (2007). *The 3G Standard Setting Strategy and Indigenous Innovation Policy in China: Is T-SCDMA a Flagship?* (DRUID Working Paper No. 07-01). Academic Press.

Zachary, G. P. (2000). *The global me: new cosmopolitans and the competitive edge: picking globalism's winners and losers*. London: Nicholas Brealey Pub.

Zhan, A. L., & Tan, Z. X. (2010). Standardisation and innovation in China: TD-SCDMA standard as a case. *International Journal of Technology Management*, *51*(2-4), 453–468.

KEY TERMS AND DEFINITIONS

3G: The third generation of mobile telecommunications technology (i.e. the successor to GSM).

Case Study: An intensive study of a single unit for the purpose of understanding a larger class of (similar) units.

CDMA2000: Another 3G air interface standard, developed by Qualcomm.

Hybridization: Here: development of a standard as a cross between global and local/national interests and technologies.

Indigenous Technology: Technology developed by players from one country or region.

Mobile Telecommunications: The exchange of data via mobile devices and a wireless network.

TD-SCDMA: Time Division Synchronous Code Division Multiple Access; an air interface standard considered by some as an indigenous Chinese technology.

W-CDMA: Wideband Code Division Multiple Access; the major UMTS (Universal Mobile Telecommunications System) air interface standard and a competitor of TD-SCDMA.

ENDNOTES

[1]   The China EU Information Technology Standards Research Partnership was part funded under the European Union under Grant agreement no. 217457. The TD-SCDMA case-study was developed by a research team also involving Dr James Stewart, Dr Ian Graham and Prof Robin Williams, project coordinator, with assistance from Mr Chengwei Wang. This chapter draws, inter-alia on material from Project Deliverable 11: *Final report on Standards dynamics in domain of Mobile Telephony: mobile broadband from 3G to 4G* available on-line at the project website http://www.china-eu-standards.org. Some of this work has been published as Stewart et al. 2011.

[2]   It had been the stated policy of the Chinese government to license three standards of 3G mobile telephony, but up to the point that the licensing took place many respondents, in China and outside China, assumed that this was a smokescreen and that the result would either be the licensing of the "Chinese" standard, TD-SCDMA, keeping foreign technologies out, or a licensing of the "foreign" technologies".

[3]   A personal interview with two officials in MII on 23/04/2004 by our team member, X. Shen for a different research project.

[4]   Interview with a design engineer working on wireless telecommunication environment at a lab of Nortel, on August 2010.

[5]   The 3rd Generation Partnership Project (3GPP) is a collaboration between various regional consortia to develop third-generation (3G) mobile phone system specifications and standards which will then be put forwards within the ITU framework. It is also involved in development of a world-wide 4th Generation (4G) standardization process under the title Long Term Evolution (LTE).

Chapter 13

Are Asian Countries Ready to Lead a Global ICT Standardization?

DongBack Seo
Chungbuk National University, Korea

ABSTRACT

East Asian countries are booming with both technological and demographic advances. They have traditionally developed their economies by being licensed foreign Information and Communications Technology (ICT) standards and using them to develop their home market and to export products. This chapter proposes that East Asian countries should start to develop a leadership role in global ICT standardizations even though their focuses are currently still primarily on developments in their own nations.

1. INTRODUCTION

Traditionally, U.S.A and Europe have led Information and Communications Technology (ICT) standardizations (Seo, 2013). However, along with the economic and technological globalization, some Asian countries have grown rapidly over the past two decades (Lee & Oh, 2008). Although they started their industrial developments by adopting or adapting ICT standards from U.S.A and Europe to manufacture products, they have recently gained more capabilities to develop innovative technologies for global standards themselves (Seo, 2013).

In the early 1990s, Japan was the only developed country in the Asian region that had tried to make its second-generation wireless telecommunications system, Personal Digital Cellular (PDC), an international standard, but it was not successful (Seo, 2010). Since then, the ICT standardization environment has changed drastically. The globalization of economies, the liberalization of industries, the fast development of ICT, the revolution of Internet, and the emergence of Asia countries as major ICT producers and consumers all contribute to this environmental change.

As globalization grows and ICT is further developed, more and more Asian countries are interested in becoming involved with ICT standardization. It was impossible for Japan to make its technology an international standard almost two decades ago. Now, can it be possible for Asian countries to develop and globally standardize their

DOI: 10.4018/978-1-4666-6332-9.ch013

technologies as European countries did? Do they have the global leadership qualities necessary to lead ICT standardizations? These are the main questions I will try to answer through this paper.

National prosperity does not simply grow out of a nation's labor pool and its currency's value, but it depends on the capacity of its industry to innovate and upgrade (Porter, 1990). Based on Porter's *the competitive advantage of nations*, this research explains how some Asian countries have been transforming themselves to ICT standard-setters.

This paper is organized as follow: first, the brief historical background of ICT standardization by region is presented. Second, the current status of ICT capabilities by region is explained. Third, roles in East Asia are evaluated. Finally, a conclusion is addressed.

2. HISTORICAL BACKGROUND OF ICT STANDARDIZATION BY REGION

The historical background of ICT standardization by region provides a basic understanding of nations' approaches to ICT standards and standardization. With the collapse of the Soviet Union, the breakup of AT&T in U.S.A., the privatization of the postal, telegraph, and telephone (PTT) unit in Western Europe, and the ICT developments in the U.S.A and Western Europe in the 1980s, the environment was favorable for companies and authorities in these two regions – the U.S.A and European Union - to standardize ICTs internationally (Bekkers & Smits, 1998). This was especially true for the telecommunications industry, which required large investments in networks and infrastructures before commercializing products or services. These regions could lead ICT standardizations because they had ICT innovation, production, and consumption powers, while the rest of world was under-developed. A notable exception was Japan. Some electronic companies from Japan such as Sony and JVC were able to internationally standardize their electronic products (e.g. Video Home System as a videotape format) through market competitions that can produce *de facto* standards. However, the EU and U.S.A. led most ICT standardizations, particularly in the cases of *de jure* standards (for the explanations of *de facto* and *de jure*, please see De Vries [2006]).

During the late 1980s and early 1990s, four Asian countries, the so called four Asian Tigers (Hong Kong, Singapore, South Korea, and Taiwan) emerged as fast developing countries, while China and India have received increasing attention since the late 1990s and 2000s. Therefore, it is important to overview the historical backgrounds of ICT standardizations in these regions as well as those in the EU, U.S.A. and Japan.

2.1. Europe

The primary aim of the European Union (EU) regulation is to create a large 'home market' with harmonized, homogeneous, and liberalized EU-wide competition. Harmonization can only be achieved through standards. Therefore, standards have played a central role in European plans for unification and industrial development (Lathia, 1995).

The increasing demand for harmonization had led to the introduction of the 'New Approach' in 1985, which was a detailed plan to achieve a common market by 1992. The new approach was essentially aimed at creating a single European market by reducing trade barriers among member states. The approach was successful in unifying standard activities through three European standardizing organizations: European Committee for Standardization (CEN), European Committee for Electrotechnical Standardization (CENELEC), and European Telecommunications Standards Institute (ETSI). "The European system is much more centralized. Traditionally, it did not follow a sector-based approach; rather, the three ESOs mirror the structure of the international standarisation system (ISO [International Organization for Standardization] → CEN; IEC [International Electrotechnical Commission] → CENELEC; ITU-T [International Telecommunication Union - Telecommunication] → ETSI)" (Jakobs, 2009: p. 2, [these parts] are inserted by the authors).

Having a unified ICT standard among EU members provides an opportunity to make it a global ICT standard. A global ICT standard in this paper refers to an international ICT standard that has been adopted around the world as one of the dominant technologies whether it is accepted as a de-jure or de-facto. First, the commitment of EU members presents enough market size as an installed base. Second, many organizations involved in a standardization start to share the same goal of expanding the market for their standard – *let's make a pie bigger before fighting for a piece.* Third, the successful operation of the ICT standard among EU members proves the compatibility and interoperability of the technology.

One of the most famous examples is European second generation wireless telecommunications system, Global System for Mobile (GSM) (originally named as *Groupe Spécial Mobile*), which became one of the most successful global standards, even though it was not initially intended that way. Although European nations focused on standardizing an ICT within Europe at the beginning, they realized a great opportunity to make their technology a global standard.

More recently, the EU has become aware of the danger of excessive government involvement, especially with the rise of consortia in ICT standards setting: '…consortia and fora are playing an increasing role in the development of standards, … the European Standards Organisations have to recognize these facts and re-design policies, processes and organizational structures, in close collaboration with stakeholders and in particular the industry…' (European Commission, 2004).

However it is still known that the European Commission (EC) plays a central role in encour-

aging European standard-setting organizations to develop harmonized European standards (Jakobs, 2009).

Despite fully recognizing its role as a global leader in standardizing ICTs, unfortunately, the EU's approach is still very much focused on the geographical boundaries of Europe. While its recent undertakings have opened the gates for more international participants, the EU is still very much the center of focus, with others are being 'allowed' to jump on the EU bandwagon (Bekkers & Seo, 2008).

2.2. U.S.A.

According to the Office of Technology Assessment (OTA), direct government intervention to coordinate private standard-setting efforts, promotion of a single private Standards Setting Organization (SSO), or provision of direct financial subsidies to selected private SSOs are inappropriate (US Office of Technology Assessment, 1992). The US government favors the market regulation over government's interference in ICT standardizations.

Although American National Standards Institute (ANSI) is a national standards body in the U.S.A., it has relatively little influence on standards setting. However, ANSI-approved standard-setting organizations such as Institute of Electrical and Electronics Engineers (IEEE), Telecommunications Industry Association (TIA), and Alliance for Telecommunications Industry Solutions (ATIS) are involved in many international standardization activities (Jakobs, 2009). The interests of these organizations are presented through ANSI in international SSOs (e.g. International Electrotechnical Commission [IEC] and International Organization for Standardization [ISO]).

In addition, community-based SSOs, such as the Internet Engineering Task Force (IETF) and the World Wide Web Consortium, and private consortia are playing a central role in standardizing ICT in the U.S. market and have become very influential in the global market. It is known that the expansion of the consortia's influence is based on their faster processes and higher subject specializations than those of traditional SSOs on ICT standardizations possess (Winn, 2005), even though these reasons are not always applicable.

2.3. Asia

2.3.1 Japan

Japan has been presented as the most developed country in Asia, often seen as equivalent to other developed countries on European and American continents. The Japanese government has been strongly involved in ICT developments and standardizations and used ICT standardizations as a way to lead its industries to grow further. Government involvement has brought mixed results, especially, for ICT standardizations. Domestically, the involvement has stimulated ICT development and economic and market growth, but these impacts could not reach beyond its territory. For example, the Japanese government developed its own standard, Personal Digital Cellular (PDC) with the aspiration to make it an international standard, especially for developing countries in Asia, so that Japanese companies could benefit from this technology standard (Komiya, 1993; Seo, 2010). Although it brought fast development in the domestic wireless communications market, it failed as an international standard. The PDC standard made the Japanese market technologically isolated from the rest of world. This isolated standard has limited the abilities of Japanese companies (e.g. wireless system and handset manufacturers) to export their products to the world market (Seo, 2010).

Therefore, the Japanese government realized that it could not internationally standardize a technology by itself. For this reason, the Japanese government and companies actively invited,

and cooperated with the European companies to develop and internationally standardize one of the third generation wireless telecommunication technologies, Wide-band Code Division Multiple Access (WCDMA). Consequently, Japanese companies were able to escape from the technological isolation and this provided them with more opportunities to export their products to the world market than the 2G wireless telecommunication standard period allowed for.

Given the way in which Japan managed its standardization, the exclusively dominant role of Japan in Asia has been diminishing as other Asian countries have started to develop their own economies, including the four Asian Tigers (Hong Kong, Singapore, South Korea, and Taiwan) in the late 1980s and early 1990s, followed by China and India in the late 1990s and 2000s.

2.3.2 Four Asian Tigers

The Asian Tigers have developed strong economies over past decades and have become significant users of new technologies. However, until recently, these countries have mainly been adopters of new technologies from other nations.

While Singapore and Hong Kong (now, as a part of China) have focused on development within the financial field, South Korean and Taiwan have concentrated on the development in the information, communications, and electronic industries. Many small and medium enterprises (SMEs) have been the backbone of the Taiwanese economy, while several large conglomerates have led the South Korean economy. Due to their developments in concentrated areas, South Korea and Taiwan are much keener to invest in ICT developments than Singapore and Hong Kong. In particular, the South Korean government and companies have become much more ambitious to develop and standardize new technologies, because national resources and capabilities can be concentrated on those several conglomerates. While in Taiwan, the national resources and capabilities are distributed over many SMEs.

One example is South Korea's choice of Code Division Multiple Access (CDMA) as its 2G wireless telecommunications standard. The South Korean government decided to adapt the CDMA technology from an American company, Qualcomm, despite knowing that GSM was available and would be the standard in Europe. It was a risky decision, because it required a great amount of investment, considering that the CDMA technology was not approved commercially (Seo, 2010). It was possible for the South Korean government to drive the country in this direction, because it could ask those several conglomerates to cooperate by investing their resources and capabilities. This kind of decision would not have been possible for the Taiwanese government to pursue, because of its industrial and economic structure. To make similar decisions, the Taiwanese government would have to persuade many SMEs to participate. Another problem is whether these SMEs have similar desires and enough resources to participate in this kind of a risky project.

The risky decision of South Korea paid off. South Korea was able to build and improve its resources and capabilities in developing and producing mobile telecommunications systems. Consequently, South Korea realized the significances of innovating and standardizing ICT earlier than any of the other Asian Tigers. Among the four tiger countries, South Korea appeared to be the country that can best leverage its strategies in the international standardization arena.

Although South Korea benefited from the commercial success of CDMA by gaining manufacturing capabilities and exporting wireless telecommunication related products, the Korean companies also had to pay a large amount of royalty fees to foreign companies (e.g. Qualcomm) for manufacturing products that used core technologies from the CDMA standard. However, South Korea would otherwise have most likely been locked into foreign companies in implementing and operating the 2G wireless telecommunications system if it had chosen the already commercialized GSM or PDC (Seo, 2013). Developing and standardizing a home-ground technology became a national interest of South Korea, but South Korea was also well aware of the Japanese case of the technological isolation. Thus, the South Korean government and companies started to create sophisticated standards strategies that provided more compatible, acceptable, and flexible technologies to persuade foreign organizations. One example is how the Korean government reconciled with the U.S. government and companies in standardizing its national mobile Internet platform – Wireless Internet Platform for Interoperability (WIPI). A detailed description of the case can be found in the paper of Lee and Oh (2008).

2.3.3 China

Recent political and economic developments have made China a force to be reckoned with. However, the rise of China is often exaggerated. While there are over a billion people in China, only a fraction of those people currently have reliable and significant access to Internet and other ICT infrastructures needed for technology development (see Figure 1). In addition, only selected people are able to receive proper education to be effective knowledge workers (see Figure 2). One thing not to underestimate is that even a small fraction of a population of this size can still be larger than the national population of a small country like The Netherlands. It is worthwhile to provide more historical background information for the case of China as it is the largest country by population in the world, is under communist rule, and is developing rapidly.

Although there is hype about China, it is also true that firms have taken an interest in China and China has taken a more open approach to foreign investors. As one of the fastest growing countries, China has tried to gain power with

Figure 1. Amount of fixed broadband connections per 100 inhabitants (ITU, 2013). Note: individual nations within EU are different, but the data from all members in 2013 is aggregated and averaged.

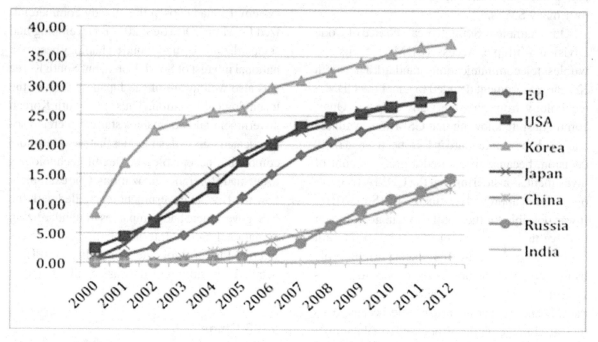

Figure 2. Tertiary education gross enrollment ratio (UNESCO, 2013). Number of pupils or students enrolled in a given level of education, regardless of age, expressed as a percentage of the official school-age population corresponding to the same level of education. For the tertiary level, the population used is the 5-year age group starting from the official secondary school graduation age.

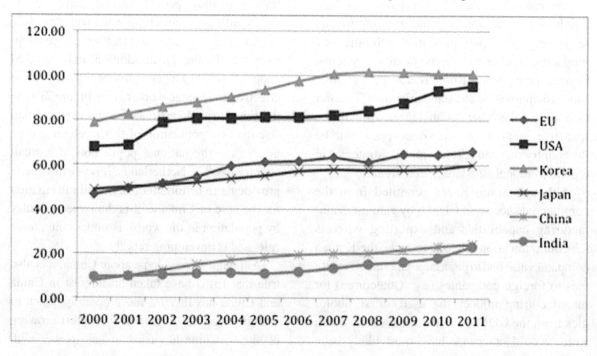

international organizations as well. In the field of ICT standards, the Chinese government established Standardization Administration of the People's Republic of China (SAC) in April 2001 and participated in many international standards setting organizations such as the International Organization for Standardization (ISO) and the International Electrotechnical Commission (IEC) through SAC. Although more Chinese companies (e.g. Huawei and ZTE) and organizations (e.g. China Communications Standards Association [CCSA] and China Electronics Standardization Institute [CESI]) have participated in ICT standardizations, it is known that the State Council has a great power over ICT standardizations and other domestic matters (Steen, 2011; Suttmeier & Yao, 2004).

Chinese technology policy leaders have increased their interest in developing and standardizing China's own technologies (Ping, 2013). Although Suttmeier and Yao (2004) perceived the Chinese efforts in standardizing ICTs under 'neo-techno-nationalism' and Lee, Chan, and Oh (2009) believed that China tried to align different strategies from 'techno-nationalism' to 'techno-globalism' on a case-by-case basis, it is believed that the ambition of the Chinese government is strongly based on 'techno-nationalism' (Seo, 2013). To support this claim, two examples are provided below. Techno-nationalism refers a technology policy that reflects national interests prior to others. It tends to have a closed market to protect national companies and technologies (Lee, Chan, & Oh, 2009; Suttmeier & Yao, 2004). Techno-globalism on the other hand focuses on global interests based on market competition. It tends to have more liberal and open policies to make a market for fair competition (Lee, Chan, & Oh, 2009; Suttmeier & Yao, 2004). Neo-techno-nationalism lies between Techno-nationalism and Techno-globalism, including policies such as adopting open competition with national interests

(for a detailed discussion of these three concepts, see Lee, Chan, and Oh [2009] and Suttmeier and Yao [2004]).

For example, China tried to standardize Wireless LAN Authentication and Privacy Infrastructure (WAPI) that was not compatible with Wi-Fi chips for its domestic market in 2003 (Lee & Oh, 2008). The Chinese government distributed the technical details of the encryption algorithm to only 24 Chinese companies and required both imported and domestically produced equipment (e.g. any wireless devices) to have WAPI. It meant that all foreign companies needed to cooperate with one of these Chinese companies to produce wireless devices in China or export them to China, even though they could be the competitors of the Chinese company. This is an example of 'techno-nationalism' (Lee, Chan, & Oh, 2009). Lee, Chan, and Oh (2009) illustrated the case of Time Division Synchronous Code Division Multiple Access (TD-SCDMA) as an example of 'techno-globalism,' because China invited Siemens to develop TD-SCDMA as its 3G wireless technology standard and opened its market for all three 3G standard (WCDMA, CDMA2000, and TD-SCDMA). However, it seemed that the Chinese government did not have any choice but to choose techno-globalism for the TD-SCDMA case because of the following reasons. First, China did not have the technological capabilities to develop a 3G technology by itself (Seo, 2013). Therefore, it needed help from a foreign company that was at least capable of developing a 3G technology and willing to transfer its knowledge to China (Stewart, Shen, Wang & Graham, 2011). Siemens' proposal for a 3G standard in Europe was not well accepted even though a few elements (e.g., the case of Time Division Duplexing (TDD) in unpaired spectrum) were included in the final version (Seo, 2013). As such, Siemens was likely to be excluded from standardization activities in Europe. Therefore, Siemens was the most appropriate partner for China that could commit to developing its 3G standard (Seo, 2013). Second, the existing 2G systems in China were based on GSM and CDMA. CDMA2000 was a natural migration path for the CDMA system and WCDMA was considered as the next generation of the GSM system. The CDMA2000 and WCDMA had been commercialized since 2000 and 2001 respectively in other nations when China finally released 3G licenses to its wireless service providers in January 2009 (Seo, 2013). Therefore, there had been a lot of pressure on the Chinese government to release 3G licenses for CDMA2000 and WCDMA when the slow development of TD-SCDMA had delayed the Chinese wireless market moving toward 3G for many years (Stewart, Shen, Wang, & Graham, 2011).

For these reasons, it is too early to say that the Chinese policies are moving from 'techno-nationalism' to 'neo-techno-nationalism' or 'techno-globalism.' It is more reasonable to say that the Chinese policies are still based on 'techno-nationalism,' but it adopts 'neo-techno-nationalism' or 'techno-globalism' when it does not have a choice.

One thing we should bear in mind without overestimating or underestimating the Chinese situation is that China is transforming to an innovator of ICT from an adopter of ICT standards, as will be explained in the section "3. Current Status of ICT Capabilities," even though there are areas to be improved. According to Figure 1 and Figure 2, the Chinese social and technological environments are behind those of more advanced Asian countries, but China has tried to play a key role in ICT standardization based on its specific governing structure and the large domestic market. For example, the Chinese government has encouraged ICT standard-related organizations and companies to participate in international standards setting organizations (Fomin, Su, &

Gao, 2011). In fact, some Chinese companies have provided chairpersons to various study groups in the ITU-T. However, despite this fact, we cannot say that China as a country plays a leading role in internationally standardizing ICT yet.

2.3.4 Other Asian Countries

Although many other Asian countries have developed their economies (e.g. India and Vietnam), they largely lack activities as developers in standardizing ICTs. They are mainly playing an adopter role that is also important in an ICT standard value chain. However, this paper explores a potentially leading role for Asia in a global ICT standardization. Thus, I will focus on South Korea, Japan and China, countries that tend to play an important role in standardizing ICT.

3. CURRENT STATUS OF ICT CAPABILITIES

Given the historical background in ICT standardization by region, I move to assess the current status of ICT capabilities by region to answer the research questions: is it possible for Asian countries to develop and globally standardize their technologies as European countries did? Do they have the global leadership skills necessary to lead ICT standardizations?

Based on Porter (1990), nations can achieve competitive advantage through the innovation activities of its national organizations and companies. It means that nations that have innovation capabilities can lead the developments of technologies, industries, and markets. There is a close relationship between ICT innovation and standardization. ICT standardizing comes after innovation activities. However, not all innovative technologies become standards (Ernst, 2013).

For an ICT to become a standard, it requires not only technological innovation but also political maneuver (Steen, 2011).

Thus, as a necessary requirement to become a standard-setter, it is important to assess whether a region has ICT innovative capabilities or not (Ernst, 2013). Many Asian countries used to be simple consumers of ICT products. It means their ICT markets were fully locked-into a few foreign suppliers. Among these countries, some of them (e.g. Japan, South Korea, China) were able to move their positions to ICT producers, because many companies in the U.S. and Europe outsourced products under their brand names. Then, these countries had encouraged their national companies to develop their own brands and technologies to decrease the high royalty fees for foreign intellectual property (e.g., patents) (Fomin, Su, & Gao, 2011). Although the Asian region has become the largest producer of ICT, a great portion of their revenue traces back to the ICT innovators in the U.S. and Europe.

To move from importers (consumers) of ICT products, to producers of ICT products, to ICT innovators and finally to ICT standard-setters, different levels and types of capabilities are required for each stage. To standardize an ICT, an organization needs enough market size to build an installed base as well as the technological capability and capacity to provide necessary technologies (David & Steinmueller, 1994; Farrell & Saloner, 1986). In addition, it must develop sophisticated strategies and policies to persuade other nations to adopt the technology. Therefore, I first review the current statuses of ICT capabilities of South Korea, Japan, and China, comparing them to those of the EU and U.S.A.

3.1 ICT Development

ICT development in Asia has really taken off in the last two decades. The development of infrastructure and the availability of a skilled workforce are key requirements for ICT development and diffusion throughout the region. One of the most significant indicators in measuring the development of infrastructure is the amount of fixed broadband connections per 100 inhabitants as shown Figure 1.

According to the ITU ICT statistics database (Figure 1), South Korea has had the largest amount of broadband connections per inhabitant since 2000, followed by U.S.A., Japan, and EU. However, Russia, China, and India have had much lower amounts. Even for mobile broadband connections in 2010, South Korea had 27,783,865 connections (about 57% of the national population); Japan had 22,047,060 connections (about 17.3% of the national population); and China had only 4,824,000 connections (about 0.4% of the national population) (Mobile Broadband, 2010). This means that the infrastructure developments of South Korea and Japan were comparable to those of the EU and U.S.A., while those of China and India were far behind. Thus, we should not overestimate the Chinese market, even though this small portion can be a great size. From another perspective, the Chinese market has still a lot of room to grow.

Figure 2 shows the gross enrollment ratio of people entering into tertiary education (education beyond high school level) by country. This is one way to measure the availability of a skilled workforce. The gross enrollment ratio of people entering into tertiary education in South Korea has been more than 90% since 2004. The ratios in the US are lower, and even lower in the EU and Japan than the ratio in South Korea, but all have been above 50%, which indicates that these countries have secured a relatively skilled workforce.

However, the figure of China is much lower than the figures of South Korea and Japan. The Chinese government also shared its concern regarding the lack of skilled workforce (Suttmeier & Yao, 2004). To make the situation worse, many highly educated people in China prefer to continue their studies abroad and often decide to stay there after finishing their studies. Therefore, it is fair to say that China is rather behind than other standard-setting countries in securing knowledge workers.

3.2 ICT Consumption and Production

Asia has provided the largest production and consumption of ICT related products and services. However, Asian countries have been relying on innovative technologies from the EU and U.S.A. This is especially true for newly developing countries like China and India.

South Korea and Japan used to pursue a license agreement from innovating companies, mainly in the U.S.A. and Europe, to manufacture ICT products. This kind of the license agreement gave South Korea and Japan an opportunity to improve their resources and capabilities in manufacturing and developing ICTs. These resources and capabilities are now becoming a base for them to develop their own technologies.

Since patenting in the ICT field has become a significant indicator to measure technology innovation (Blind & Jungmittag, 2008), I can use patent-related statistic data to analyze how a country is moving from an ICT producer to innovator. The term, "innovator" in this paper is used broadly, meaning a country that has a lot of innovative activities, which are measured by the number of granted patents and the percentage of patent applications approved and granted. Since the ICT global market has evolved based on many technologies from the EU and U.S.A., I consider the EU and U.S.A., and a country that has equivalent patenting activities to the EU and U.S.A. as an innovator. Figure 3 shows the number of granted patents by country/region since 2000. The figure clearly illustrates the rapid increase of the number of granted patents in South Korea, Japan, and China.

As indicated in the previous version of this paper (Seo & Koek, 2012), Japan has had the largest number of granted patents even in 1995, which

Figure 3. Number of granted patents by country/region (WIPO, 2013). Note: the EU values are based on its 2013 member base.

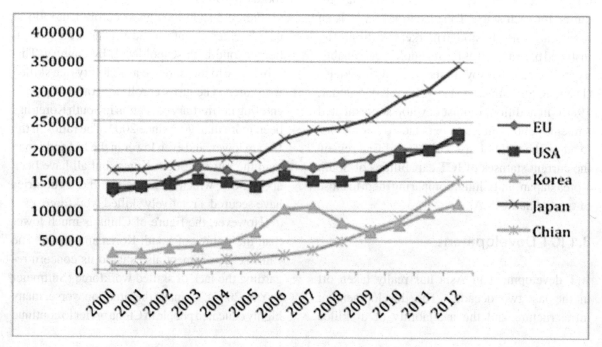

means that it has been a comparable innovator to the EU and U.S.A. since the 1990s. Especially, the number of granted patents by Japan has grown much larger than those by EU and U.S.A. In 2012, the number of granted patents by U.S.A. exceeded that by EU. Meanwhile, South Korea moved quickly to be an innovator, but fell back in 2008, and then the number of granted patents by South Korea has grown steadily. The interesting phenomenon and different from the previous version of this paper (Seo & Koek, 2012) is about China's fast growth in gaining the large number of granted patents, which started to exceeded South Korea since 2009. The growth rates for the numbers of granted patents by Japan and China are much more steeper than those of EU, U.S.A. and Korea.

While many parts of the world experienced a declining number of patent filings by 10 percent in 2009 because of the global financial and economic crisis, South Korea, Japan, and China had 2.1 percent, 3.7 percent, and 29.7 percent growth on filing patents, respectively (IPR-Helpdesk, 2010). Figure 4 shows the percentage of patent applications that were actually approved and granted

by nation/region from 2000 to 2012. Although this Figure does not reflect the complexity and significance of a patent, it provides the indication of a general capability to gain patents, because innovators competed for similar technologies at the time. Figure 4 reveals interesting facts. First, South Korea and Japan are more able to file patent applications that are likely to be approved and granted than EU and U.S.A. In fact, South Korea and Japan have gradually increasing the relevant capabilities for their applied patent applications to be approved and granted, while those capabilities in the EU and U.S.A have fluctuated. Second, different from the astonishing growth of the number of granted patents by China (Figure 3), China has struggled to improve the approval rate of patent applications for a decade, which is 21% lower than EU in 2012 (Figure 4).

According to the number of granted patents (Figure 3) and the percentage of patent applications approved (Figure 4), the Japanese capabilities in ICT innovation have been much more competitive compared to those of the EU and U.S.A. South Korea is successfully transforming to an ICT in-

Figure 4. Percentage of patent applications approved and granted by country/region (WIPO, 2013). Note: the EU values are based on its 2013 member base.

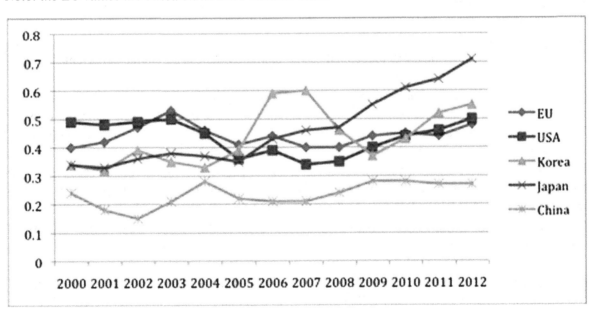

novator from a follower and adopter, especially in improving the approval rate of patent applications. Meanwhile, China is also rapidly transforming to an ICT innovator in term of gaining the number of granted patents, but it needs to improve related capabilities for its applied patent applications to be approved and granted.

4. ROLES OF EAST ASIA (SOUTH KOREA, JAPAN, AND CHINA)

Asia has already played a significant role in ICT productions and is likely to play a critical role in ICT standardizations soon. As Asian economies grow larger and become more important in the world, it is expected that Asian countries may take a central role in developing policies for internationally regulated ICT standardizations.

The currently prevalent approach in global ICT standardizations is through consortia in many areas (e.g., Blu-ray Disc Association and Open Mobile Alliance). While formal SSOs are struggling to globally standardize ICTs because of the conflicting interests among their members, consortia benefit from this and take over the roles of SSOs, creating a globally unregulated ICT standards field (Bekkers & Seo, 2008). Although there is a conflict among members in a consortium, members tend to actively reconcile over a conflict. If some members cannot find a way to reconcile, they will create another consortium to standardize the technology they pursue. For example, some members (Hitachi, Panasonic, Philips, Pioneer, Sony, and Thomson) created a competing consortium to standardize the technology of Blu-ray Disc, when they could not find a way to reconcile the conflict over selecting a technology. For formal SSOs, it is almost impossible for members to create another competing formal SSO when a similar situation happens.

The EU uses a different model from other regions and private consortia, where three overarching SSOs (CEN, CENELC and ETSI) aim to develop harmonized standards for its member nations. The approach is much more regulated than private consortia and ensures compatibility as a possibility so that it provides open and fair business environments and a variety of products and services to customers within the European Union. The main criticism of the EU approach is that it is slow and bureaucratic, causing it to lag behind the pace of ICT innovation. This explains the current dominance of private consortia.

There is a growing belief that there may be a complementary relationship between formal SSOs and private consortia (Bekkers & Seo, 2008; Rada & Ketchell, 2000). Formal SSOs can benefit from rich knowledge, technical expertise, and adoptive flexibility that consortia can provide, while private consortia can benefit from public oversight, transparency and legitimacy that formal SSOs can provide (Abbot & Snidal, 2000).

Efforts (e.g. ICT Standards Board [ICTSB] and CEN Workshop Agreements) have been made to combine these two approaches. The aim is to ensure a fair market for all businesses and consumers, while maintaining the swift approach to ICT standardization that private consortia use.

This situation leads to an interesting ICT standardization landscape, which all nations should recognize accordingly. For this reason, I first suggest that East Asian countries that are eager to play a significant role should consider this combinative approach. Asia has a unique opportunity to learn from the past mistakes of the E.U. and U.S.A. when developing this regulatory system. While it must ensure that it has a legitimized process, it should take steps to prevent this process from being too politicized and hence too slow. Therefore, Asian governments should actively cooperate with companies including foreign innovative firms to build a constructive standardization process.

Second, Asia should try to create a unified voice as the EU did in standardizing an ICT. Asia can coordinate and cooperate among its countries to create a harmonized proposal and push it forward as a global ICT standard. Considering that Asia has the largest ICT manufacturing capabilities, the largest ICT market, and capabilities to innovate ICT, Asian countries can standardize an ICT for their region if they want to standardize the ICT together. Despite the fact that Asia's innovative capabilities depend largely on South Korea, Japan, and lately China, it is likely that they can diffuse the standardized ICT to other Asian nations and regions as well.

For instance, the Japanese government and national firms pay attention to pursue a regional policy to develop and diffuse new technological ideas and standards in the East-Asia area (Yoshimatsu, 2007). Japan is now strongly motivated to establish and diffuse global ICT standards by actively searching cooperation with new strong partners in Asia. Since 2002, South Korean, Japanese, and Chinese ministers who were in charge of ICT industries had had annual meetings to discuss cooperation in ICT developments and standardizations until 2006. This was stopped due to their domestic political affairs, but they have reestablished this meeting in 2010 during the ASEAN+3 Telecommunications and IT Ministers meeting (TELMIN). ASEAN+3 refers to Association of Southeast Asian Nations plus 3 nations (Korea, Japan and China). The telecommunications and IT ministers of member countries of ASEAN, Korea, Japan, and China, regularly meet to reinforce their cooperation in the relevant fields. Korea, Japan, and China can expand their ICT standardization efforts to outside of their national boundaries by coinciding their meetings with the ASEAN+3 TELMIN meetings. It implies that the three nations are willing to find a common approach, even though these kinds of efforts have not been materialized yet.

One thing that Asia should NOT learn from the EU approach is to be so exclusive. When Asia tries to develop a harmonized proposal, it should be open to hear opinions and concerns from other non-Asian countries as it cooperates with private consortia. In this way, a pan-Asian proposal can be much stronger than others. However, the ques-

tions are whether there is a leadership in Asia to conduct this approach and furthermore whether the three Asian nations are ready to lead a global ICT standardization effort. Although Asia has enough market power and innovation capabilities as a whole, the ICT standardizations are not just about market size and technological issues, but require certain leadership to persuade others.

As the EU did in the GSM case at the beginning, these Asian countries have used ICT standards in developing their national industries and markets. It is proven that their leaderships have been successful in developing their domestic industries and markets through ICT standards. Now, the question is whether these leaderships can be transformed to a global level.

The leaderships of Korea, Japan, and China have not gone beyond their borders yet. This situation makes it difficult for them to lead unified ICT standards policies even among Asian nations. Considering that the economies of the three Asian countries are export-oriented, it is surprising to see that most patents (their technology innovation efforts) they have been granted in their own nations (see Figure 5).

For Asian countries, Figure 5 reveals that more than 60 percent of patents were granted in their nations. Especially, for Korea and China, the ratios went up to 75 percent and 94 percent in 2012, respectively, while the EU members had 21 percent of patents granted in their nations (EU by nation in Figure 5). However, considering the EU region as one domestic area (EU by EU in Figure 5), the percentage of patents granted in the EU region increased 39 percent. It implies that companies in many EU member nations are keen to apply patent applications in other EU member nations to freely trade their technologies within EU. Figure 5 indicates that the EU and U.S.A. are better at internationalizing their ICT innovations. Another interesting observation is that the U.S.A. and EU have slowly improved their capabilities in internationalizing ICT innovations, but Korea and China have not (see Figure 5), even though

Figure 5. Percentage of patents granted in its nation by country/region (WIPO, 2013)

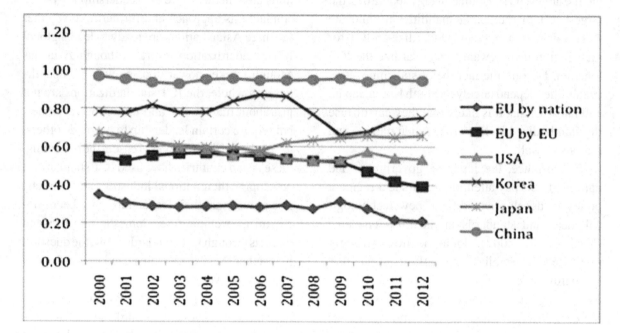

the ICT innovation capabilities of Korea, Japan and China have grown (see Figure 3 and Figure 4). Japan had improved and become competitive against EU and U.S.A. until 2006, but since then, Japan turned back to gain more patents in its nation.

Based on the above facts, Japan already has an ICT innovation capability to develop a potential global ICT standard, even though the percentage of patents granted in its nation grew lately, while Korea and China are still too domestic-centered in ICT innovations. What they need to do is to build capabilities to internationalize their technologies. Although the Japanese innovation capability is moving out of its national boundary, it has not played a strong leading role in standardizing an ICT yet, especially in the telecommunications arena.

5. CONCLUSION

Traditionally, the Asian countries relied on ICT standards from the EU and U.S.A. to produce and export products. However, this tradition has been changed.

Along with Japan, the newly emerging countries (e.g. Korea and China) in Asia represent large and growing forces in the ICT industry and market. We have seen that some of the Asian countries are rapidly becoming more prominent as ICT producers as well as consumers. However, we should remember that there are few countries that we can call an *ICT innovator*. Korea, Japan, and potentially China are three of the few true innovators in Asia. In addition, not all Asian countries have achieved the same economic and technological successes. However, Asia as a whole has tremendously developed.

Given these conditions, to what extent is Asia ready to lead global ICT standardizations?

Regarding the capacity and capability to produce a potential ICT standard, Asia is very much ready. Asia as one region is able to develop a variety of goods and services, ranging from high-tech products (e.g. Korea, Japan, and Taiwan) to cheap simple products (e.g. China, Vietnam, Indonesia, and others) and to specified software applications (e.g. India).

For the capacity to consume a potential ICT standard, the Asian market has the most potential, because its market for high-tech products and services is growing faster than any other region in the world.

Regarding the capability of developing an innovative ICT as a global standard, few Asian countries (e.g. South Korean, Japan, and potentially China) have achieved competitive resources and capabilities.

The lacking element for Asia to lead in global ICT standardizations is not in its technological capabilities, but in the leadership role itself. As mentioned, Asian nations can learn from the mistakes of the EU and U.S.A. in developing their global leaderships. If the EU wants to make its technologies global ICT standards beyond its boundary, it should include non-EU nations in the development of standards policies and strategies (Bekkers & Seo, 2008). The U.S.A. depends too much on market competition. These circumstances have made it difficult to harmonize a single global ICT standard, especially in the world telecommunications market. All Asian nations should realize that it is difficult for any one country in Asia to internationally standardize an ICT alone, particularly for *de jure* standards. For example, it seemed that Korea was successful in standardizing CDMA internationally, however it was based on a strong cooperation with Qualcomm (Seo, 2013). As explained, the successful commercialization of CDMA in South Korea and the cooperative efforts between Korea and Qualcomm made possible to internationally standardize the CDMA technology.

We need to clearly distinguish between a successful development of a national standard for a domestic market and a successful standardization of an ICT for an international market. For instance, Japan's PDC was a successful development of an indigenous standard for a domestic market, but not a successful standardization for an international market. China's Audio Video Coding Standard (AVS) is a successful development of an indigenous standard for the Chinese domestic market (Fomin, Su, & Gao, 2011), but there is no sign that it will be adopted outside of China yet. Another instance is the Chinese 3G standard, TD-SCDMA. Although China insists that it is an international standard issued by ITU, it has not been adopted in any other country except China. Additionally, China could not develop TD-SCDMA without help from foreign companies (Stewart, Shen, Wang, & Graham, 2011).

As shown, Asia as a whole has a great opportunity to lead global ICT standardizations, but none of its constituent nations has all of the ingredients. For example, Korea and Japan have ICT innovation capabilities, but do not have a consumption capacity as China and India have. Therefore, Asian countries must cooperate with each other to build a global leadership within Asia first. This must start with changing their perspective from a domestic centered view to a global centered view. If the Asian nations are able to find a way to cooperate with other governments and companies and form a harmonized and unified voice within Asia to present to the global community, this harmonized and unified voice will be able to steer international standards setting activities. For example, the EU has successfully presented and standardized its harmonized and unified standards, GSM, WCDMA, and Long Term Evolution (LTE) in the global market, even though CDMA 2000 and WiMax as competing technologies were commercialized earlier than WCDMA and LTE, respectively. Imagine that every country in Europe had tried to develop and internationally standardize its own indigenous technology. It would be very difficult for any one European country to standardize its technology in the global market. Due to the fact that GSM, WCDMA, and LTE are the European harmonized and unified standards, they became such strong international standards. Asian countries should learn a lesson studying this European model.

However, one thing we need to remember is that the global environment has been changed since the EU and U.S.A. led ICT standardizations decades ago. It was much easier for the EU and U.S.A. to standardize ICT when they were only regions that had innovation capabilities while the rest of world waited for them to come and diffuse their technologies. For the countries that had production capabilities, the most they hoped for was to have better license agreements with companies in the EU and U.S.A. at the time. Since the twenty first century started, a great amount of production capacities have moved to Asia. What is left for the EU and U.S.A are their strong innovation capabilities in term of ICT developments. However, we should not underestimate the political, economic and financial influence of the EU and U.S.A over other regions. This may mean that Asian countries will confront strong resistance from the EU and U.S.A. if they develop and standardize their own ICT without any technology from the EU and U.S.A., because the EU and U.S.A. may be totally excluded. The situation is different from when the EU and U.S.A used to standardize their ICTs, because Asian countries used to be included as production powerhouses even though they paid high royalties.

What this implies is that Asian countries should also try to find a way to include the EU and U.S.A. One way is cooperation with the EU and U.S.A. in innovating technologies and sharing patents. In this way, Asian countries can remove the burden of royalty fees and companies from the EU and U.S.A will have a fair chance to access the Asian market. Another way to include the EU and U.S.A. is making Asian innovative technologies open and compatible with those of the EU and U.S.A. Instead of fighting for royalties, it may be more advantageous for the Asian countries to compete in a market with open and compatible technologies, because of their capabilities in ICT productions. The openness and compatibility of a standard again provide companies from the EU and U.S.A. a fair chance to access to the Asian market. In addition, Asian countries should use their patents in accessing innovative technologies that the EU

and U.S.A. have through cross licensing. In this way, Asian nations are able to materialize their innovations and utilize the innovations from the EU and U.S.A.

These are a few suggestions that Asian countries can implement in moving toward global leadership in standardizing ICTs. The most fundamental idea to remember for Asian nations is to include the interests of many nations instead of excluding or antagonizing them. For example, they need to find a way to develop a harmonized and unified proposal within Asia that has shared interests with the EU and U.S.A. Now, it is time for Asian countries to move their attention from a nation-centered perspective to a world-oriented view as global leaders.

REFERENCES

Abbott, K. W., & Snidal, D. (2001). International 'standards' and international governance. *Journal of European Public Policy*, 8(3), 345–370. doi:10.1080/13501760110056013

Bekkers, R. and Seo, D. (2008). *Quick Scan for Best Practices in ICT Standardization: What ETSI could Learn from Other Standards Bodies*. Utrecht, The Netherlands: Dialogic Innovatie & interactie.

Bekkers, R., & Smits, J. (1998). *Mobile telecommunications: Standards, regulation, and applications*. Norwood, MA: The Artech House.

Blind, K., & Jungmittag, A. (2008). The impact of patents and standards on macroeconomic growth: A panel approach covering four countries and 12 sectors. *Journal of Productivity Analysis*, 29(1), 51–60. doi:10.1007/s11123-007-0060-8

David, P. A., & Steinmueller, W. E. (1994). Economics of Compatibility Standards and Competition in Telecommunication Networks. *Information Economics and Policy*, 6(3-4), 217–241. doi:10.1016/0167-6245(94)90003-5

De Vries, H. J. (2006). IT Standards Typology. In K. Jakobs (Ed.), *Information Technology Standards and Standardization Research* (pp. 1–26). Hershey, PA: Idea Group Publishing. doi:10.4018/978-1-59140-938-0.ch001

Ernst, D. (2013). Standards, Innovation, and Latecomer Economic Development – A Conceptual Framework. In *Proceedings of International Workshop on Asia and Global Standardization.* Seoul, Korea: Academic Press. doi:10.2139/ssrn.2388993

European Commission. (2004). The role of European standardisation in the framework of European policies and legislation. *Communication from the Commission to the European Parliament and the Council (COM), 674.*

Farrell, J., & Saloner, G. (1986). Installed Base and Compatibility: Innovation, Product Preannouncements, and Predation. *The American Economic Review, 76*(5), 940–955.

Fomin, V. V., Su, J., & Gao, P. (2011). Indigenous Standard Development in the Presence of Dominant International Standards: The case of the AVS standard in China. *Technology Analysis and Strategic Management, 23*(7), 745–758. doi: 10.1080/09537325.2011.592270

IPR-Helpdesk. (2010). *International patent filing declines due to financial crisis.* Available at http://www.iprhelpdesk.eu/news/news_6857.en.xml.html

ITU. (2010). *ITU ICT Statistics Database.* Available at http://www.itu.int/ITU-D/ICTEYE/Indicators/Indicators.aspx#

Jakobs, K. (2009). ICT Standardisation in China, the EU, and the US. In *Proceedings of the 2nd Kaleidoscope Conference. IEEE.*

Komiya, M. (1993, Spring). Personal Communications in Japan and its Implications for Asia. *Pan-European Mobile Communications, 52*-55.

Lathia, K. P. (1995). Standards Production in a Competitive Environment. In ETSI (Ed.), *European Telecommunications Standardization and the Information Society: The State of the Art 1995.* Sophia Antipolis: ETSI.

Lee, H., Chan, S., & Oh, S. (2009). China's ICT Standards Policy after the WTO Accession: Techno-national versus Techno-globalism. *Info, 11*(1), 9–18. doi:10.1108/14636690910932966

Lee, H., & Oh, S. (2008). The political economy of standards setting by newcomers: China's WAPI and South Korea's WIPI. *Telecommunications Policy, 32*(9-10), 662–671. doi:10.1016/j.telpol.2008.07.008

Mobile Broadband (2010). Asian-Pacific Region Mobile Broadband Lanscape. *Wireless Intelligence,* Q2.

Ping, W. (2013). *Global ICT Standards Wars in China, and China's Standard Strategy.* Paper presented at International Workshop on Asia and Global Standardization. Seoul, Korea.

Porter, M. E. (1990). *The Competitive Advantage of Nations.* New York: The Free Press.

Rada, R., & Ketchell, J. (2000). Standardizing the European Information Society. *Communications of the ACM, 43*(3), 21–25. doi:10.1145/330534.330552

Seo, D. (2013). *Evolution and Standardization of Mobile Communications Technology.* Hershey, PA: IGI Global. doi:10.4018/978-1-4666-4074-0

Seo, D., & Koek, J. W. (2012). Are Asian Countries Ready to Lead a Global ICT Standardization? *International Journal of IT Standards and Standardization Research*, *10*(2), 29–44. doi:10.4018/jitsr.2012070103

Seo, D. B. (2010, January). The Significance of Government's Role in Technology Standardization. *International Journal of IT Standards and Standardization Research*, *8*(1), 63–74. doi:10.4018/jitsr.2010120705

Steen, H. U. (2011). Limits to the Regulatory State in the Rule-making of Digital Convergence: A Case study of Mobile TV Standards Governance in the European Union and China. *Technology Analysis and Strategic Management*, *23*(7), 759–772. doi:10.1080/09537325.2011.592273

Stewart, J., Shen, X., Wang, C., & Graham, I. (2011). From 3G to 4G: Standards and the Development of Mobile Broadband in China. *Technology Analysis and Strategic Management*, *23*(7), 773–788. doi:10.1080/09537325.2011.592284

Suttmeier, R. & Yao, X. (2004). *China's Post-WTO Technology Policy: Standards, Software and the Changing Nature of Techno-Nationalism* (Special Report No. 7). The National Bureau of Asian Research.

UNESCO. (2010). *Beyond 20/20 WDS*. Available at http://stats.uis.unesco.org/unesco/TableViewer/tableView.aspx?ReportId=167

US Office of Technology Assessment (OTA). (1992). *Global Standards: Building Blocks for the Future*. Washington, DC: Government Printing Office.

Winn, J. K. (2005). US and EU Regulatory Competition in ICT Standardization Law & Policy. In *Proceedings of SIIT2005*. SIIT.

WIPO. (2010). *Statistics on patents*. Available at http://www.wipo.int/ipstats/en/statistics/patents/index.html

Yoshimatsu, H. (2007). Global competition and technology standards: Japan's quest for techno-regionalism. *Journal of East Asian Studies*, *7*(3), 439–468.

KEY TERMS AND DEFINITIONS

ICT Innovation: Introducing a new or different information and communications technology.

ICT Standardization: Bringing to or making of an established standard of an information and communications technology.

Intellectual Property: Property that comes from original creative thoughts as patents, copyright material, and trademarks.

Neo-Techno-Nationalism: Between Techno-nationalism and Techno-globalism, including policies such as adopting open competition with national interests.

Patent: Exclusive right granted by a government to an inventor to manufacture, use and sell an invention for a certain period.

Regulation: A rule, law or order prescribed by authority.

Techno-Globalism: Focusing on global interests based on market competition.

Techno-Nationalism: A technology policy that reflects national interests prior to others.

Section 5
About People

Chapter 14
The Role of the Individual in ICT Standardisation:
A Literature Review and Some New Findings

Kai Jakobs
RWTH Aachen University, Germany

ABSTRACT

This chapter discusses the influence individuals have in the ICT standards development process. The chapter draws upon ideas underlying the theory of the Social Shaping of Technology (SST). Looking through the SST lens, a number of non-technical factors that influence ICT standards development are identified. A literature review on the role of the individual in ICT standards setting and a case study of the IEEE 802.11 Working Group (WG) show that in a standards body's WG, the backgrounds, skills, attitudes, and behaviour of the individual WG members are crucially important factors. Yet, the case study also shows that in most cases employees tend to represent the ideas and goals of their respective employer. The chapter observes that the non-technical factors are ignored all too often in the literature. It argues that a better understanding of the impact and interplay of these factors, specifically including the skills and attitudes of the WG members, will have significant implications both theoretical and managerial.

1. INTRODUCTION AND MOTIVATION

E-business, mobile commerce, e-procurement, supply chain management – Information and Communication Technologies (ICT) have changed the way business is done, sometimes beyond recognition. One of their common characteristics is the electronic exchange of information between entities that may well be located anywhere on the globe. This, in turn, signifies the need for internationally accepted – and implemented – rules that govern this information exchange. Such rules are typically referred to as 'standards'.

Colloquially, the term 'standard' is used for specifications of very diverse origins. Windows is an industry/proprietary standard, http is a consortium standard and IEEE 802.11 (aka WiFi) is a formal standard. Yet, regardless of their respective origin, (successful) standards are crucial building blocks of all virtually all ICT systems. Think of

DOI: 10.4018/978-1-4666-6332-9.ch014

it – the success of the Internet, for instance, is to no small amount rooted in the simplicity and effectiveness of its core standards, TCP/IP[1].

In the 1980s standards and standardisation began to attract the attention of researchers. Initially, economists developed the greatest interest, although their focus was rather more on dominant designs that emerge through market forces than on consensus-based standards that emerge from standards bodies' committees or working groups. They used, for example, transaction cost theory to determine if and when a firm would switch from one standard to another or used the theory of network externalities to describe the uptake of a new product or service[2]. Subsequently, social scientists and some computer scientists joined the bandwagon. With the increasing importance of patents in ICT standardisation the importance of Intellectual Property Rights (IPR) increased as well and attracted researchers of the legal persuasion. These days, many other disciplines also contribute to standardisation research.

Nonetheless, one aspect of standardisation has received little attention so far – the role of the individual standards setter, i.e. those people who populate the working groups (WGs) and committees of the various Standards Setting Organisations (SSOs[3]). While many political decisions are made above WG level, these people are in charge of the actual standards development. Both technical and strategic decisions are made here, and the economic well-being of a firm that fails to have its Intellectual Property (IP) incorporated into an emerging standard may be severely damaged as a result.

In fact, and perhaps a bit surprisingly, I would consider these people to be one of the major influencing factors in standardisation. And since the development of an ICT standard may well take a couple of years, at least the core members of the individual WGs will over time form a tightly knit community. These communities have, for example, been described as "dense trans-national personal networks" (Henrich-Franke, 2008) or as a group for

whom "the value of the ... community ... exceeded corporate loyalty in many situations" (Isaak, 2006). Thus, we should look at the motivations, attitudes and views that influence these people's work if we want a better understanding of why a particular standard emerged the way it did. Once enough such knowledge has been accumulated it may help shape future standardisation activities in a way that maximises a new standard's value for society at large.

The remainder of the paper is organised as follows. Section 2 offers some more background and some further motivation for the subsequent study by discussing the importance of ICT standards. Section 3 introduces the theoretical background – the Social Shaping of Technology (SST) approach. Section 4 discusses the importance of the individual in standards setting based on a literature review. To test and perhaps complement these theoretical findings section 5 outlines some relevant findings from a case study. Finally, some concluding remarks are made in section 6.

2. A BIT ABOUT STANDARDS

2.1 Definition

The term 'standard' does not really lend itself to a useful definition. The Oxford Dictionaries[4], for example, define a standard as "something used as a measure, norm, or model in comparative evaluations". According to Merriam-Webster[5], a standard is "something established by authority, custom, or general consent as a model or example". ISO defines a standard as a, "document, established by consensus and approved by a recognized body, that provides, for common and repeated use, rules, guidelines or characteristics for activities or their results, aimed at the achievement of the optimum degree of order in a given context" (ISO, 2012).

All these definitions are too generic to be readily applied to a specific domain like ICT. However, when the term 'standard' appears throughout the remainder of this paper it will be meant in the sense of the ISO definition. Specifically, this will exclude proprietary standards (like e.g. MS Windows) that emerged through sheer market power as opposed to some form of (consensus-based) committee process.

2.2 Why ICT Standards are Important

"Standards are not only a technical question. They determine the technology that will implement the Information Society, and consequently the way in which industry, users, consumers and administrations will benefit from it." (EC, 1996). This quote conveys three important insights that are all too often ignored. The first one is that ICT systems simply would not work without underlying standards[6]. The second one is that today's ICT standards are tomorrow's technology, and that accordingly the shaping of such standards may to a considerable degree influence the network environment we will live with in the future. Insight number three directly follows from the others – standards have a considerable relevance for policy, economic importance and are crucial for companies that offer or deploy products or services in the ICT sector.

In fact, these days the economic importance of standards is no longer questioned. Swann (2010) provides a very thorough review of the relevant literature. The reported findings include, among many others, that e.g. "Standards contribute at least as much as patents to economic growth" (according to (DIN, 2000)). In addition, numerous case studies exist that highlight the economic benefits of standards for nation states and economies.

Moreover, standards frequently (albeit not necessarily) have a positive impact on innovation. For example, Blind (2009) argues that there are several ways in which standards can promote innovation. Specifically, he notes that in the ICT sector, "compatibility standards are the basis for innovation in network industries (e.g. GSM[7])".

For instance, GSM, as a platform standard, has been the basis for the numerous mobile services we are offered today.

Looking at the level of firms, standardisation is perhaps not always a matter of life or death, but success in standards setting may well have a significant impact on the economic well-being of a company. This impact may materialise through different channels. For example, a proprietary technology may be 'ennobled' by becoming a standard. This, in turn, may imply increased revenues due to, for instance, a faster diffusion of the technology. Likewise, a standard enables the emergence of complementing products or services.

Alternatively (or additionally), an organisation may capitalise on Intellectual Property (IP) that has been incorporated into a standard and for which licensing agreements may be made. Perhaps less obvious, but in many cases at least as important, a standard may help extend existing markets or even open up new ones (see e.g. (APEC Secretariat, 2010) or (den Uijl et al., 2013)). Along similar lines, a company may use standards setting to change the rules of the game and to get a competitive advantage. Lemstra & Hayes (2009) report a case where NCR successfully did that by initiating the development of a wireless local are network standard (to become known as WiFi or IEEE 802.11) rather than emulating the market leader's (IBM's) technology.

Standards are also of considerable interest to policy makers. In Europe, for example, harmonised standards contributed a great deal to the creation of a single market (see e.g. (CEU, 2011)). More recently, new regulations provide for a better integration of private consortium standards[8] into the European standardisation system and allow to make references to such standards in public procurement (see e.g. (EU, (2012)).

Hopefully, the above could show that (ICT) standards are not just boring technical documents that are a necessary evil at best and a pain in the neck at worst. Rather, they are of considerable relevance for policy makers and have a strong economic dimension. The latter is nicely highlighted in a paper by Hurd & Isaak (2009) aptly entitled 'IT Standardization: The Billion Dollar Strategy'.

3. THEORETICAL BACKGROUND: THE SOCIAL SHAPING OF TECHNOLOGY AND STANDARDS

3.1 The Social Shaping of Technology

Technological artefacts in general, and especially such powerful representatives as ICT systems, exert a potentially strong impact on their environment. Yet, this is not a one-way phenomenon; complex interaction between technology and its environment may be observed, where technology may assume both an active and a passive role. That is, technological artefacts and their environment are mutually interdependent. The environment within which technology is used and employed has, among others, social, cultural, societal, and organisational aspects, rules and norms. Technology cannot emerge completely independent from such external influences. However, the impact ICT may have on organisations, or indeed society as a whole, has thus far attracted considerably more attention than the powers that shape this technology in the first place. Especially the impact of ICT within organisational settings (e.g. on a company's performance, or its role as an enabler of business process re-engineering) has been subject to a vast number of studies and analyses. Terms such as 'management of change' (Wilson, 1992), 'management of technology' (Burgelman et al., 2008) or 'organisational change' (Tidd & Bessant, 2009) may frequently be found in the literature, typically denoting studies on how the introduction and subsequent use of ICT have changed a particular organisational environment – for better or worse.

Two mutually exclusive schools dominated research on technology and organisations until the early eighties. Proponents of the 'organisational choice' model consider technology as a vehicle to both reflect and foster the interests of particular groups; the process of change can be, and indeed is, shaped entirely by policy makers or organisation's managers. "Technology has no impact on people or performance in an organisation independent of the purposes of those who would use it, and the responses of those who have to work with it" (Huczynski & Buchanan, 1985). In contrast, 'technological determinism' in essence postulates that ICT determines the behaviour of organisations and that the consequences of manipulating a given technology will always be the same, independent of who manipulates it and within which context (Watad & Ospina, 1996). It follows that, according to this view, organisations have little choice but to adapt to the requirements of technology; particular paths of technological development are inevitable; like organisations, society at large also has no other choice but to adapt.

Research into the social shaping of technology (SST) largely emerged as a response to technological determinism. SST adopts a middle course between the two older approaches; it acknowledges that technology indeed has an impact on its environment, but states that at the same time it is framed through technical, but rather more through e.g. organisational, societal, cultural and economic factors (Williams & Edge, 1996). In particular, SST attempts to unveil the interactions between these technical and social factors. Abandoning the idea of inevitable technological developments implies that choices can be made regarding, for instance, acquisition, use and particularly design of technological artefacts. There may be a broad variety of reasons upon which these choices may be based. In an organisational context this may include purely technical reasons, as e.g. the need to integrate legacy systems, but decisions may also take into account company particulars, as for instance organisational or reporting structures. These choices, in turn, may lead to different impacts on the respective social or organisational environments. Thus, studying what shaped the particular technology offers a chance to proactively manipulate that very impact expected to result from this particular choice. At the same time this capability should also contribute to the prediction – and thus prevention – of undesirable side effects potentially resulting from a new technology. Technology tends to have other effects besides those actually intended, these effects need to be explored as well. On the other hand, the respective environment shapes technical artefacts and systems during design and also in use, i.e. at the site of the actual implementation.

3.2 The Social Shaping of Standards

"The shaping process begins with the earliest stages of research and development" (Williams & Edge, 1996). This observation points to a direct link between the shaping of technology and R&D activities.

Research is not normally conducted with the aim to transform its results into a standard. However, this does not preclude research findings from being fed into standardisation processes. Plus, research that indeed aims at standardisation does exist, in the form of pre- and co-normative research, respectively. Such research is carried out with the specific goal of integrating its findings into future standards. Yet, 'conventional' research as well may be relevant to standardisation, sometimes even without the researchers and their organisations being aware of it. The relation between research and standardisation can be described by the knowledge and information flows between the two realms, as shown in Figure 1 (Interest, 2007).

Especially information and communication technologies are in most cases based on international standards. Thus, while not necessarily representing the earliest stage of development, a standard clearly is an important early stage in the overall process that leads from R&D to products or services, and is thus also subject to a social shaping process.

Figure 1. The relation between research and standardisation (from Interest, 2007)

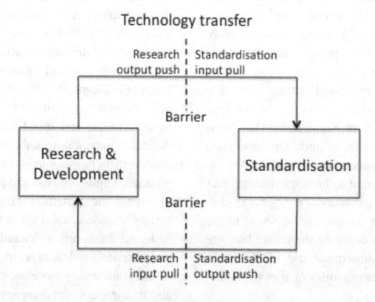

SST considers the interaction of different players in the process of appropriation of a technology to a specific environment. The fact that choices may be made regarding development and use of a technology (see sect. 3.1) implies a level of uncertainty about its precise nature at the end of this process and about its actual future use. "SST emphasises the negotiability of technologies – in the sense that artefacts typically emerge through a complex process of action and interaction between these heterogeneous players, rather than being determined by any one player" (Williams, 1997). According to Williams (1997), these players include technical specialists from supplier organisations, suppliers of complementary as well as competing products, consultants, policymakers, existing and potential users. They may have different understandings of a technology and, accordingly, attach different meanings to it (Pinch & Bijker, 1984). Against this background, the alignment of the interests and expectations of the players (not to forget the business interests of their employers) may be considered one of the major tasks of the negotiations.

Standards emerge through the co-operation and joint efforts of different individuals in technical committees and working groups. They aim to develop a technology whose eventual nature, use, utility and applications are not normally known from the outset. That is, their work is characterised by a level of uncertainty that is comparable to that of the corporate environment that is typically studied by SST. Moreover, the list of players identified by Williams (1997) bears a striking resemblance to the stakeholders typically represented in ICT standards setting. Specifically, it should be noted that the identified players are individuals (as opposed to organisations).

Most major SSOs have 'individual' membership. That is, WG members are supposed to act in a personal capacity (see e.g. (ISO, 2012)) and not, for example, as national or company representatives[9]. Their input to the process will be based on views, beliefs, and prejudices that have to a considerable degree been shaped by their previous experiences. Specifically, the corporate environment of the group members' respective employer (including its economic and strategic views and preferences) will have a major impact on the different visions of how a technology should function and be used, and on the ideas of how this can be achieved. That is, various factors that shape technology in use are also likely be channelled into the SSOs' working groups, thus shaping the future standards.

To summarise, according to Gerst et al. (2005), standardisation is shaped by social factors. More precisely,

- A range of choices is possible at every stage of the standardisation process;
- These choices depend on technical factors but also upon economic, social and organisational ones.

The discussion above suggests that the SST approach may indeed also be applied to standards setting.

A first attempt to put together in a pictorial form the individual non-technical factors that contribute to the shaping of a standard yields Figure 2.

Obviously, these factors come in addition to technical aspects like feasibility, provision of adequate interoperability, compatibility with a potentially installed base, etc.

4. THE INDIVIDUAL IN ICT STANDARDISATION

SST highlights the negotiability of technology and thus also of standards (see sect. 3.2 above). Therefore, this section will have a closer look at the role of the individual in ICT standards setting.

4.1 Overview

In almost all cases, a firm that actively participates in standards setting does so based on economic

Figure 2. Some factors that influence standards development (adapted from Jakobs, 2013)

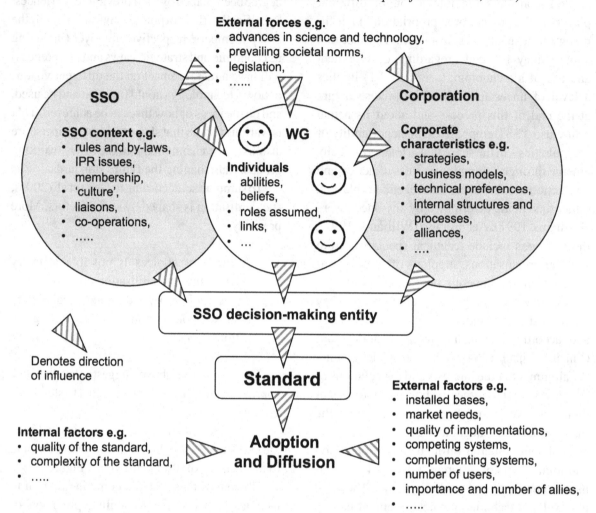

considerations. Whether these relate to the development of a new standard to open or extend a market, to have as much proprietary IP as possible incorporated into the standard or to prevent or delay the development of a new one does not really matter. In all these cases, a potentially significant amount of money may be at stake, perhaps even the survival of the firm. Accordingly, a firm should make sure that its interests are represented in the best possible way. This, in turn, implies that the capabilities and attitudes of its representatives need to be taken into account.

Kang et al. (2007) – rightly – observe that "Performance in standardization is naturally affected by that of individual standardization experts". That is, if a company (or a nation state) wants to participate effectively and efficiently in standards the education, training, and skills of its representatives in standards WGs play a role, but also their preferences, prejudices, and possibly hidden agendas. This becomes even more relevant if we assume that the Pareto Principle (the 80/20 law; see e.g. (Craft & Leake, 2002)) applies to the work done in standards WGs as well. In this case, the views of 20% of a WG's members may well influence the work of the whole group.

Despite all this and despite the economic importance of standards, the 'human' side of standards setting has attracted rather little attention. Yet, after all, the committees and working groups (WGs) of all SSOs and their respective decision-making bodies are comprised of individuals. That is, ultimately ICT standards are made by people, not by companies, nation states or standards bodies. And each of the individuals that make up an SSOs' WG will have possibly very diverse backgrounds, views, capabilities, preferences and prejudices that will, one way or other, have an impact on the final outcome of the WG's work – the standard.

In the following I will try and summarise what little is know about the value, roles and behaviour of individuals in the standards setting arena.

4.2 A Literature Recap

Papers that look at aspects to be associated with the individual standards setter are comparably few and far between. Broadly speaking, these papers adopt two different perspectives. One is the 'corporate view'; i.e. how firms seek to increase their influence in standards setting through the choice of personnel. The other one could be referred to as the 'personal view' that provides a look into the standards bodies' working groups and analyses e.g. the motivations and characteristics of the people who do the actual technical standardisation work. It should, however, be noted that these perspectives are not necessarily clearly distinguishable and may well overlap; this will also show in the discussion below.

Most (of the rather few) papers adopting a corporate perspective are based on social capital theory. According to Bourdieu & Wacquant (1992), social capital is "the sum of the resources, actual or virtual, that accrue to an individual or a group by virtue of possessing a durable network of more or less institutionalized relationships of mutual acquaintance and recognition". Social capital is related to, but clearly distinct from, human capital. Burt (1997) defines the difference between the two thus: "while human capital

refers to individual ability, social capital refers to opportunity". Still, social capital is inextricably associated with an individual. That is, from a corporate view the social capital of an employee in general and of a member of a standards working group (WG) in particular increases the value of this individual. On the other hand, social capital, once acquired, may well establish strong bonds between an individual and the 'source' of the social capital, in this case the standards WG. Isaak (2006) observes that standardisation of the Posix operating system benefitted from social capital accumulated by the WG members. He notes that social capital development was based on "repeated collaborative problem solving over an extended period of time building respect, trust and reinforcing common values". More specifically, he notes that in many cases loyalty to the WG was greater than loyalty to the employer – people changed the latter but were not prepared to give up their roles in the former, even if that implied self-funding of participation. Eventually, the importance of this phenomenon was also realised by organisations participating in the standardisation work; the US Department of Defense, for example, made sure that their representatives could work longer on the subject than the two year duty rotations would normally have allowed, in order be able to develop and deploy social capital (Isaak, 2006).

On a slightly different, more general note, Dokko & Rosenkopf (2010) argue that knowledge brought in by a new employee may help increase the employer's influence in standards setting. For one, this is due to an increased knowledge of another firms' positions, preferences and capabilities. On the other hand, the newly acquired social capital may come in handy in more political (as opposed to technical) activities, such as, for example, coalition forming. Typically, long-serving and well-connected individuals are much better positioned to conduct such political action (Dokko & Rosenkopf, 2010).

'Well-connected' is an important aspect here. Co-operation between individuals in WGs creates networks and a central position in such a network increases social capital and thus the 'usefulness' of an individual to his/her employer. Such a central position may, for example, be assumed by taking on a leading role in the standards setting process, e.g. that of a WG chairperson or of a document editor.

The importance of such networks in standards setting is also highlighted by Grundström & Wilkinson (2004). Specifically, such networks are crucial when it comes to informal discussions, deal-striking and compromise-finding before a vote or a crucial meeting. Moreover, they note that any newcomer will only have very limited influence on the process without such a network.

In addition, trust is of particular importance here and this can only be acquired over time. In general, 'trust' is an important aspect in relation to both, social capital and standards setting. A functioning personal network can hardly be established without it. Trust is particularly important in the informal negotiations and deal-striking in standardisation (Dokko & Rosenkopf, 2010). Zaheer et al. (1998) distinguish between interpersonal trust and inter-organisational trust and in standards setting the former is of particular importance ('just because my company trusts your company I do not necessarily trust you'). This is further corroborated by (Grundström & Wilkinson, 2004). They quote several high-level standards setters who in unison and emphatically stress the importance of trust.

Henrich-Franke observes that informal relations, also involving family members, have proved to be more important than the national needs and requirements of the WG members' respective home countries (this refers to a case in ITU where largely national positions are dealt with). Also, a common 'engineer habitus', rooted in a common background as radio amateurs, played a major role in the development of radio standards (Henrich-Franke, 2008).

Trust is also of importance in relation to boundary-spanners (Williams, 2002). These are individuals who facilitate communication between different groups or entities (Tushman, 1977), for example between a firm's marketing and engineering departments, between different firms or between different cultures. Given the international, multi-firm environment that characterises standards setting ideally each member of a standards WG were a boundary-spanner. At least, those who have assumed a leading role should be.

Spring et al. (1995) observe that the leadership (frequently, but not necessarily the chairperson) of a WG is crucially important. Along similar lines, Isaak (2006) notes that 'gurus' play an important leading role. According to Umapathy et al. (2007), hiring a guru as a representative in standards working groups may well be a way for an SME to punch above its weight in standardisation, thus potentially reversing the power distribution in the market.

The potentially strong impact one individual may have may also be exemplified through 'bulldogs'. According to Spring et al. (1995), a bulldog is "A person who dominates and disrupts a meeting against the majority opinion of that group". They estimate that 80% - 90% of all standards WGs have at least one such bulldog. Their influence is particularly prominent in standards bodies without clear decision-making procedures like voting. Most notably, this holds for the Internet Engineering Task Force (IETF), the Internet's standards setting body. Here, formal voting is replaced by 'rough consensus', a term very open for discussion. This is also reported in (Jakobs, 2003) – in the IETF process 'naysayers' and 'loudmouths' stand a good chance of delaying and possibly even obstructing the work; the process does not foresee any mechanisms to deal with such individuals.

In general, WG members can be classified based on their behaviour. Spring et al. (1995) distinguish between 'perfectionists' (attention to technical detail); 'doers' (ability to initiate proposals to get things moving); 'leaders' (ability to focus on objectives); 'diplomats' (ability to forge consensus); 'observers' (ability to listen attentively and monitor activities to ensure process is going in the right direction) and 'obstructionists' (ability to actively head-off bad ideas). Umapathy et al. (2007) have come up with a similar classification.

Apart from their actual behaviour in the standardisation process individuals may also assume very different roles in this process. While 'company representative' was the single most frequently assumed role by a mile, Jakobs et al. (2001) found that a majority of WG members saw themselves as either 'national representative', 'user advocate' or 'techie' (promoter of technically clean and advanced solutions). Similarly, Cargill (2011) notes that "a participant in a standardization effort wears many different hats simultaneously". According to him, these hats cover, among others, 'professional pride' (doing what's right), 'corporate or organisational goals' (doing what's right for your company) and 'personal friendships' (doing what's right to make you feel good and for social and professional strokes). Along similar lines, Nielsen (1996) observes that these 'hats' may also cover different standards bodies and different associated corporate strategies. Accordingly, an individual's behaviour in standard setting may also be context-dependent.

The above brief recap supports the 'prediction' of the SST approach that the individual standards setters are important elements in the process of ICT standardisation. From the 'corporate' perspective, they may become highly valuable assets through their accumulated social capital and/or their experience and capabilities. From the 'personal' perspective, links between members of a WG may become extremely strong; in some cases stronger than those to their employers (a fact that may be beneficially deployed by a wise employer).

However, this occasionally strong bond between WG members raises the issue of loyalty. More generally, it brings up the question 'Whom does the individual standards setter represent in his/her work in a WG?'. Strong bonds between members may suggest (part of) a WG setting its own agenda, independent of any employer's preferences. For example, a WG may decide to try and develop a standard that best addresses users' needs. Likewise, a personal agenda, driven by, for example, deep technical insights, personal preferences or simple prejudices may lead an individual or a small group to just represent themselves. In contrast, simple economics ('he who pays the piper calls the tune') may lead a standards setter to strictly represent his/her employer's position (perhaps even against own better judgement).

To know what drives WG members and what they stand for is clearly of considerable relevance for the outcome of a standardisation process. So, the next section will offer a look inside a particular standards working group.

5. THE CASE OF IEEE 802.11

The study outlined below will try and shed some light on two questions:

- Which factors are most important in ICT standardisation?
- To what extent do WG members represent the interests of their respective employers?

5.1 A Bit of Background

The IEEE WG 802.11 (Wireless LAN Working Group) is part of the IEEE 802 LAN/MAN Standards Committee. The WG has been in charge of the development of standards for wireless communication in unlicensed radio frequency bands. Today, these standards form the basis of the almost ubiquitous WiFi networks.

Today (December 2013) the working group has around 500 members, ca. 320 of whom have voting rights. They meet three times a year during the plenary sessions of the IEEE 802 group; 802.11 holds interim meetings an additional three times a year.

Like many other standards bodies (e.g. ISO and the IETF) IEEE 802.11 has 'individual' membership. That is, its members are supposed to act in an individual capacity, as opposed to acting e.g. as company or national representatives. The right to vote must be earned and subsequently maintained. Voting rights are conferred after attendance of three out of four consecutive plenary meetings and need to be maintained through continuing participation in both meetings and ballots. Moreover, members of all IEEE WGs are asked to disclose their affiliation in order to prevent the process from being dominated by any particular entity or interest category.

The individual voting right suggests that a direct association between employee's voting behaviour and employer's interest can not necessarily be taken for granted. Rather, other aspects like, for example, individual views, preferences, prejudices, and (hidden) agendas may influence voting behaviour.

A survey was conducted to find out if and to what degree this is actually the case. The survey was based on a questionnaire with 16 open-ended questions, subdivided into three sections. Section one asked for the interviewee's background, section two for his/her motivation and the role assumed during the process. Section three was they main part that asked for their observations regarding the activities and positions of fellow WG members in relation to the goals and views of their respective employers.

The questionnaire was sent to long-standing and experienced members of the 802.11 WG. They were identified with the help of Vic Hayes, the immediate past 802.11 chairman. The information presented in this section was compiled from twelve completed questionnaires.

5.2 Some Insights from the Survey

WGs are primarily populated by engineers. One would, therefore, assume the technical superiority of a proposal to be the decisive factor. However,

I honestly do not believe in anyone claiming technical superiority as that can be a very short term truth or as has been proven many times over, an untruth. <6>

Still, if not technical superiority than technical merits should be decisive. Yet, rather more non-technical aspects seem to be as important. Two typical responses:

Most influence came from 1/3 powerful organizations (companies), 1/3 strong technical proposals, 1/3 active and respected company representatives. <7>

The influence came through a combination of strong technical proposals, active representatives and powerful organizations. <2>

That at least some importance is assigned to strong technical proposals does not really come as a surprise. Neither does the fact that 'powerful organisations' play an important role. After all,

There are active/respected representatives from most large organizations because it costs so much to commit people to creating the standard, and active/respected representatives gravitate to organizations that support the standards effort. <3>

This suggests that at least in the ICT sector most large companies have a reasonably well developed idea of the importance of both standards and active participation in standardisation. Moreover, it is safe to say that 'powerful' and 'large' may be equated with 'deep pockets'. These companies can – and do – hire respected standards setters to competently present their proposals and to adequately defend and push them.

Persistence – which is closely related to 'deep pockets' – is another important factor.

Contributing something important to the process was only effective if you had the money to stick around and see it through to completion. <4>

While this is bad news for Small and Medium-sized Enterprises (SMEs) they too stand a chance to have their proposal standardised. All it takes are knowledgeable, enthusiastic and strong enough representatives.

… But there are also examples of small companies with very smart/respected representatives who took and got a lot of bandwidth. <1>

The responses so far suggest that the answer to the question "Which factors are important in ICT standardisation?" would be 'adequate funding', 'good proposal' and 'strong representative(s)'. The latter re-enforces the need to also answer the question "To what extent do WG members represent the interests of their respective employer?".

'Company representative' tops the list of the roles the respondents assumed[10]. However, there were other roles they assumed as well – some aimed at promoting a wireless standard (any standard, as opposed to a specific one e.g. supported by their respective employer), some wanted to support the user community. Also, these roles could change over time or several roles were assumed in parallel.

When asked if a company's representatives would typically act in unison, i.e. if they were they likely to represent their employer's interests, most responses were along the lines of

On the whole members or voters from or representing the same company acted in unison. <6>

Yet, deviating, more individualistic behaviour could occasionally be observed:

There were some groups of individuals that acted in unison and other groups of individuals from a different affiliation worked independently. <5>

However, it remains unclear whether this was due to strong individual positions, lack of relevant company directives, different departmental position with one large company or a simple misunderstanding

But there are examples of individuals who did [follow a personal agenda] (for whatever reason, sometimes they even self did not notice that they pleaded against their own company). <1>

Alternatively, company politics might have played a role:

Other times they would vote contrarily when it could be predicted, or sometimes just in case, the vote would confirm that alternate position anyway. That would ensure that the company had at least one vote on the prevailing side so that individual could later make a motion for reconsideration – again that's another political ploy. <4>

Yet, some had chosen to not necessarily represent their respective employer but – mostly – to work for the greater good:

Yes there were a number of individuals having their personal agendas, but this was not very frequent. They were usually very strong headed, but not very successful, but could consume a lot of meeting time. <2>

One respondent identified seven such individuals by name – not a very high number. But

These individuals I believe embody the essence of great standards creators for their efforts to create technical specifications which benefit everyone working in this technology space. <7>

The same respondent continued

Yes the ones who worked this way were generally very highly regarded and were generally successful (but not always). <7>

However, people had to be brave (or perhaps financially independent) to act this way. Several respondents mentioned loss of job as a consequence of deviating voting behaviour. One example

In general, when a company's rep did not represent the affiliations point of view, they tended not to appear at the next meeting. There are exceptions to this rule, but in general, if you work for a company, you are voting for their proposal. <8>

In cases where more than one person was needed to support a proposal or where interests of several people converged coalitions between individuals could occur independent of their respective employers' positions, albeit with an important qualification.

Groups of members would often form, particularly when there are issues where only a small number of members are passionate on a topic. This was typical when the issue was not critical to an employer's interests. <10>

And, at any rate, this seems to have been a rather infrequent occurrence as coalitions were mostly formed between companies, not between individuals.

No, coalitions I saw are primarily company-based. <9>

Moreover, clashes of egos could be observed. After all, 'being outspoken' and 'having a sense of purpose' are essential attributes for successful standards setters (Jakobs et al., 2001). Accordingly, one responded noted that

I have seen egos get in the way of many debates. <8>

Yet, such personal clashes might well go hand in hand with clashes of corporate interests,

… it was more of a combination of both ego and money. Many clashes were driven due to big investments in company technology directions where the direction of the standard was important to the financial health of the companies involved. <7>

5.3 Brief Summary and Discussion

At the end of the day, technical standards are developed by people, by those individuals who populate the Technical Committees and Working Groups of the various standards bodies. If they are good at what they are doing their respective employers and society in general stand to benefit.

While certainly not being an island, a standards WG is a more or less closed community whose members (most of them, anyway) work towards a common goal – a new standard. Views how exactly this standard should look like will differ in many cases, but the common goal remains.

To summarise the main factors that had influenced the technical decisions taken in the IEEE 802.11 context, one respondents' view was particularly helpful and enlightening, thanks to the quantification provided.

1. *Supporters/opponents present during discussion 30%.*
2. *Reputation of supports/opponents 30%.*

3. *Purely the technical merits of a proposal 20%.*
4. *Solution already implemented somewhere 10%.*
5. *Company/national/group interests 3%.*
6. *Individual interests 3%.*
7. *Anything else (users/implementers) 4%. <7>*

Another response paints a similar picture (note the qualification at the end).

The main factors influencing most technical decisions are:

1. *Relative technical strength of the proposal, i.e., ability to satisfy the requirements.*
2. *Relative cost of the solution (both manufacturability and impact on other parts of the system).*
3. *Encumbrance by intellectual property restrictions (this can be part of item 2, as well, considering licensing costs).*
4. *Reputation of individuals involved in the proposal.*
5. *Reputation of the companies involved in the proposal.*

By the time final technical decisions are made, all proposals are nearly equal with respect to items 1 and 2. <10>

That is, when it comes to voting the reputation of the supporters (and opponents) carries the greatest weight. This reinforces the assumption that companies should be very careful when selecting their representatives to standards bodies.

The importance of the qualifications and reputation of the individual representatives in ICT standards setting is out of the question. Yet, the comments given in sect. 5.2 suggest that in most cases these people tend to support their respective employer's interests (as opposed to their own agendas). There are exceptions to this rule, but they seem to be rather more infrequent. This holds all the more since apparently both individual ignorance and political considerations may also lead to a deviating voting behaviour. That is, the findings from this study (in line with those from an earlier one; see (Jakobs et al., 2001)) suggest that employers do not need to worry too much here.

6. SOME CONCLUDING REMARKS

Both the literature and the case study clearly demonstrate that standards setting is not just a technical activity. Rather, a fairly complex set of intertwined technical, legal, economic, social and psychological factors (and probably many others

Figure 3. Dependencies between people, technology, corporate environment and standards

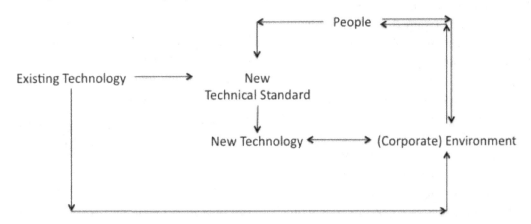

as well) together contribute to the shaping of a standard. These factors are either rather obvious (e.g. the legal boundary conditions), reasonably well understood (e.g. the technical specifics) or largely ignored and, accordingly, under-researched (e.g. the non-technical factors). Moreover, standards – through the technology they define – may have very considerable ramifications well beyond just the technical domain: The Internet as we know it, for example, would not exist without the underlying TCP/IP standards.

'Choice' is a central notion in the theory of the Social Shaping of Technology. Specifically, SST highlights the fact that choices are being made during the development of a standard and that these choices are the result of negotiations between members of an SSO's Working Group. Accordingly, these individuals' views, ideas, preferences etc. will exert a significant impact on the development of a standard (see sect. 3.2). This is further corroborated by the literature (see sect. 4) and also by the case study presented above (in sect. 5.2).

A person's values, beliefs, views and preferences are very much influenced by his or her respective environment. With respect to ICT standards, this holds particularly for the work environment. Studies into organisational culture also tell us as much: "Organisational culture refers to deeply held beliefs and values … the beliefs and values of culture … exist as cognitive schema which govern behaviour and actions to given environmental stimuli." (Ahmed, 1998). Combining this with the insights from SST yields Figure 3. The figure once more highlights the central role people play in the shaping process of standards and thus, ultimately, of technology (at least in the ICT sector).

The corporate environment comprises not just technical artefacts and systems which WG members use to perform their work or any new technologies they may currently develop. It also includes corporate strategies as well more intangible, but potentially deeply held corporate values or beliefs. The individual employees carry these characteristics, including any technical, strategic and economic goals or preferences, into a WG – they act as 'shape agents', typically on behalf of their employer, whether knowingly or unintentional.

This paper is, in a way, a successor to Nielsen (1996). Her paper "… has been written to provide some initial thoughts on human factors in standards development and to stimulate thinking on human behavior as a dimension of standards committee work". Sadly, it looks that so far she hasn't been overly successful. Let's hope this paper fares better.

REFERENCES

Ahmed, P. K. (1998). Culture and climate for innovation. *European Journal of Innovation Management, 1*(1), 30–43. doi:10.1108/14601069810199131

Biddle, B., White, A., & Woods, S. (2010). *How Many Standards in a Laptop? (And Other Empirical Questions). In Proceedings from K-2010: ITU-T Kaleidoscope Academic Conference – Beyond the Internet?* Geneva: ITU.

Blind, K. (2009): *Standardisation: A Catalyst for Innovation*. Retrieved from http://repub.eur.nl/pub/17558/EIA-2009-039-LIS.pdf

Bourdieu, P., & Wacquant, L. P. D. (1992). *An Invitation to Reflexive sociology*. Chicago: University of Chicago Press.

Burgelman, R.A., Christensen, C.M., & Wheelwright, S.C. (2008). *Strategic Management of Technology and Innovation* (5th ed.). New York: McGraw-Hill/Irwin.

Burt, R. S. (1997). The contingent value of social capital. *Administrative Science Quarterly, 42*(2), 339. doi:10.2307/2393923

Cargill, C. (2011): Why Standardization Efforts Fail. *Journal of Electronic Publishing, 14*(1). DOI:

CEU. (2011): *A strategic vision for European standards: Moving forward to enhance and accelerate the sustainable growth of the European economy by 2020* – COM(2011)311. Retrieved from http://eur-lex.europa.eu/LexUriServ/LexUriServ.do?uri=COM:2011:0311:FIN:EN:PDF

Choi, D. G., Kang, B. G., & Kim, T. H. (2010). *Standardization: Fundamentals, Impact, and Business Strategy*. Retrieved from http://publications.apec.org/publication-detail.php?pub_id=1032

Craft, R. C., & Leake, C. (2002). The Pareto principle in organizational decision making. *Management Decision, 40*(8), 729–733. doi:10.1108/00251740210437699

David, P. A., & Greenstein, S. (1990). The economics of compatibility standards: An introduction to recent research. *Economics of Innovation and New Technology, 1*(1-2), 3–41. doi:10.1080/10438599000000002

den Uijl, S., de Vries, H. J., & Bayramoglu, D. (2013). The Rise of MP3 as the Market Standard. *International Journal of IT Standards and Standardization Research, 12*(1), 1–26. doi:10.4018/jitsr.2013010101

DIN. (2000). *Economic Benefits of Standardization: Summary of Results*. Retrieved from http://www.din.de/sixcms_upload/media/2896/economic_benefits_standardization.pdf

Dokko, G., & Rosenkopf, L. (2010). Mobility of Technical Professionals and Firm Influence in Wireless Standards Committees. *Organization Science, 21*(3), 677–695. doi:10.1287/orsc.1090.0470

EC. (1996). *Communication from the Commission to the Council and the Parliament on 'Standardization and the Global Information Society: The European Approach, COM (96) 359*. Retrieved from http://eur-lex.europa.eu/LexUriServ/LexUriServ.do?uri=COM:1996:0359:FIN:EN:PDF

EU. (2013). *Regulation (EU) No 1025/2012 of the European Parliament and of the Council*. Retrieved from http://eur-lex.europa.eu/LexUriServ/LexUriServ.do?uri=OJ:L:2012:316:0012:0033:EN:PDF

Gerst, M., Bunduchi, R., & Williams, R. (2005). Social shaping & standardization: A case study from auto industry. In *Proceedings of HICSS-38: the 38th Annual Hawaii International Conference on System Sciences*. Piscataway, NJ: IEEE. DOI: doi:10.1109/HICSS.2005.547

Grundström, C., & Wilkinson, I. F. (2004). The role of personal networks in the development of industry standards: A case study of 3G mobile telephony. *Journal of Business and Industrial Marketing, 19*(4), 283–293. doi:10.1108/08858620410516763

Henrich-Franke, C. (2008). 'Cookies for ITU': The role of social networks in standardization processes. In Bargaining Norms – Arguing Standards (pp. 86-97). The Hague: STT.

Huczynski, A., & Buchanan, D. A. (1985). *Organizational Behaviour: An Introductory Text*. Englewood Cliffs, NJ: Prentice Hall.

Hurd, J., & Isaak, J. (2009). IT Standardization: The Billion Dollar Strategy. In Standardization Research in Information Technology: New Perspectives (pp. 20-26). Hershey, PA: IGI Global. DOI: doi:10.4018/978-1-59904-561-0.ch002

Interest. (2007). *A Guide to Standardisation for R&D Organisations and Researchers*. Retrieved from http://www-i4.informatik.rwth-aachen.de/Interest/Manual_R&D.pdf

Isaak, J. (2006). The Role of Individuals and Social Capital in POSIX Standardization. *International Journal of IT Standards and Standardization Research, 4*(1), 1–23. doi:10.4018/jitsr.2006010101

ISO. (2012). *ISO/IEC Directives, Part 1 – Procedures for the technical work*. Retrieved from http://isotc.iso.org/livelink/livelink?func=ll&objId=4230452&objAction=browse&sort=subtype

Jakobs, K. (2003): A Closer Look at the Internet's Standards Setting Process. In *Proceedings of the IADIS International Conference WWW/Internet*, (pp. 557–564). IADIS.

Jakobs, K. (2013). Strategic positioning in ICT Standardisation. In Boosting European Competitiveness. Aachen: Mainz Publishers.

Jakobs, K., Procter, R., & Williams, R. (2001). The Making of Standards – Looking Inside the Work Groups. *IEEE Communications Magazine*, *39*(4), 102–107. doi:10.1109/35.917511

Kang, S., Park, H. J., & Park, K. (2007). The Effect of Incentives on the Performance of International IT Standardization Experts. *ETRI Journal*, *29*(2), 219–230. doi:10.4218/etrij.07.0106.0188

Lemstra, W., & Hayes, V. (2009). The shaping of the IEEE 802.11 standard – The role of the innovating firm in the case of Wi-Fi. In Information and Communication technology standardization for e-business: Integrating supply and demand factors (pp. 98-126). Hershey, PA: IGI Global. doi:10.4018/978-1-60566-320-3.ch008

Nielsen, F. (1996). Human Behavior: Another Dimension of Standards Setting. *StandardView*, *4*(1), 36–41. doi:10.1145/230871.230878

Pinch, T., & Bijker, W. (1984). The Social Construction of Facts and Artefacts: Or How the Sociology of Science and the Sociology of Technology might Benefit Each Other. *Social Studies of Science*, *14*(3), 399–441. doi:10.1177/030631284014003004

Spring, M. B., et al. (1995). Improving the Standardization Process: Working with Bulldogs and Turtles. In Standards Policy for Information Infrastructure (pp. 220-252). Cambridge, MA: MIT Press.

Swann, G. M. P. (2010). The Economics of Standardization. Retrieved from https://www.gov.uk/government/organisations/department-for-business-innovation-skills

Tidd, J., & Bessant, J. (2009). *Managing Innovation: Integrating Technological, Market and Organizational Change*. Hoboken, NJ: John Wiley & Sons.

Tushman, M. (1977). Special boundary roles in the innovation process. *Administrative Science Quarterly*, *22*(4), 587–605. doi:10.2307/2392402

Umapathy, K., et al. (2007). Avatars of Participants in Anticipatory Standardization Processes. In The Standards Edge – Unifier or Divider? (pp. 295-302). Chelsea, MI: Bolin Group.

Watad, M., & Ospina, S. (1996). Information Technology and Organisational Change: The Role of Context in Moderating Change Enabled by Technology. In Diffusion and Adoption of Information Technology (pp. 202-220). London: Chapman & Hall.

Williams, P. (2002). The Competent Boundary Spanner. *Public Administration*, *80*(1), 103–124. doi:10.1111/1467-9299.00296

Williams, R. (1997). The Social Shaping of Information and Communications Technologies. In The Social Shaping of the Information Superhighways. Luxembourg: European Commission.

Williams, R., & Edge, D. (1996). The Social Shaping of Technology. *Research Policy*, *25*(6), 865–899. doi:10.1016/0048-7333(96)00885-2

Wilson, D.C. (1992). *A strategy of change: concepts and controversies in the management of change*. Cengage Learning EMEA.

Zaheer, A., McEvily, B., & Perrone, V. (1998). Does trust matter? Exploring the effects of interorganizational and interpersonal trust on performance. *Organization Science*, *9*(2), 141–159. doi:10.1287/orsc.9.2.141

KEY TERMS AND DEFINITIONS

ANSI: The American National Standards Institute, the US member of ISO.

IEEE 802.11: The standard that specifies the WiFi technology.

IETF: Internet Engineering Task Force; an entity that develops (most of) the standards for the Internet.

ISO: International Organisation for Standardisation; a global standards body whose members comprise the national standards bodies.

Social Capital: The sum of the resources, actual or virtual, that accrue to an individual or a group by virtue of possessing a durable network of more or less institutionalized relationships of mutual acquaintance and recognition.

Social Shaping of Technology (SST): SST is a model of the relation between technology and society. It claims that 'choices' can be made in the design of individual artefacts and systems and in the direction or trajectory of innovation programs.

Standard: A document, established by consensus and approved by a recognized body, that provides, for common and repeated use, rules, guidelines or characteristics for activities or their results, aimed at the achievement of the optimum degree of order in a given context.

Standardisation: The process that leads to the development of a standard.

Standards Setting Organisation: An entity that develops standards. This may either be a 'formal' body (e.g. ANSI and ISO) or a private standards consortium of forum (e.g. W3C, IETF).

W3C: World Wide Web Consortium; a private entity that develops standards for the WWW.

ENDNOTES

[1] Transmission Control Protocol/Internet Protocol.

[2] For a good overview see (David & Greenstein, 1990).

[3] This term denotes both formal bodies like International Organization for Standardization (ISO) and the International Telecommunication Union (ITU) as well as private standards consortia, e.g. the World Wide Web Consortium (W3C).

[4] http://oxforddictionaries.com.

[5] http://www.merriam-webster.com/.

[6] For example, Biddle et al. (2010) found that "251 technical interoperability standards [are] implemented in a modern laptop computer"; they reckon that the total number of standards relevant to such a device is much higher. And that's just one single machine.

[7] Global System for Mobile Communications, originally Groupe Spécial Mobile.

[8] I.e. those developed by private organisations like the W3C.

[9] Major exceptions include the ITU and the European Telecommunication Standards Institute (ETSI).

[10] Apparently, the same may be said for their peers. While no quantitative figures are available here, the responses suggest as much.

Chapter 15
How to Implement Standardization Education in a Country

Henk J. de Vries
Erasmus University, The Netherlands

ABSTRACT

This chapter explores how standardization education can be implemented at the national level. Previous studies form the main source for the chapter. This research shows that implementation of standardization in the national education system requires a national policy, a long-term investment in support, and cooperation between industry, standardization bodies, academia, other institutions involved in education, and government. The approach should combine bottom-up and top-down. The chapter is new in combining previous findings to an underpinned recommendation on how to implement standardization education.

INTRODUCTION

Interest in standardization education is growing. In Indonesia, for instance, the number of universities cooperating with the Indonesian national standards body BSN to address standardization has increased from none in 2007 to 23 in 2010 (Odjar Ratna Komala, 2011). South Korea is at the forefront of implementing standardization education in academic curricula and does more than Europe as a whole (Choi (Ed.) 2008, Czaya et al. 2010). Starting from scratch in 2003 (KSA, 2003) Korea has managed to get standardization education implemented at several levels, in particular universities and elementary schools,

amounting to thousands of students per year (Choi and De Vries, 2013). Standardization education is emerging in other Asian countries as well, both at the academic level and at lower levels including secondary and even elementary schools. Standardization education increases awareness of standards and standardization and prepares people for jobs in which they have standards-related tasks. In this paper, we investigate what could be done at the national level to stimulate standardization education.

The need for education about standardization has been addressed in several studies (Verman, 1973; Korukawa 2005; de Vries, 2005; de Vries and Egyedi, 2007; Krechmer, 2007; Cooklev,

DOI: 10.4018/978-1-4666-6332-9.ch015

2010). Implementing standardization education is not easy and despite its recent growth, it is an exception rather than a rule that the topic of standardization is included in education. A combination of barriers has to be overcome. A first barrier relates to the image of standardization. Students may perceive standardization to be 'dull' and if it is the main topic of an elective course, they may choose another, seemingly more appealing course. A second barrier is related to teachers: they may be reluctant to address standardization, because 1) they may be afraid that the topic fails to attract students (this is related to the first barrier), 2) they are not familiar with the topic, 3) they are not aware of its importance, and/or 4) the curriculum is already overloaded. The situation would be different if teachers were required to focus on standardization, but who should convince those who determine curricula and define the final attainment level for students? Standards bodies, of course, are aware of the importance of standards and standardization because it is their core business but should they take initiatives to promote standardization education? What about industry and governments? What role should they play and how aware are they of the importance of standardization as such and standardization education in particular? Lack of awareness on their side may be a third barrier (de Vries et al., 2009).

The 2006 standardization education workshop organized by the International Cooperation for Education about Standardization (ICES) concluded that if standards bodies or other stakeholders take the initiative to promote standardization education, success of implementation depends on (1) national policy, (2) the availability of resources at the national level, and (3) close cooperation between industry, standards bodies, academia, other organizations in the field of education, and government (de Vries and Egyedi, 2007). These elements will be addressed in the subsequent sections. The concluding section describes what steps could be taken to promote and implement standardization education.

NATIONAL POLICY

Developing and deploying a national standardization education strategy and policy is a prerequisite for a systematic national approach to standardization education (Choi et al., 2009; DeNardis and Levin, 2009). The creation of a national standardization education strategy in APEC member countries was stimulated by a decision taken at the 18th APEC Ministerial Meeting in Hanoi, Vietnam, in November 2006: 'The ministers of the Asia Pacific Economic Cooperation recognized the importance of standards education and encouraged their members to develop reference curricula and materials to address the significance of standards and conformance to trade facilitation in the region' (APEC, 2006). Following this decision, a project was set up and led by the Korean Standards Association (KSA) (Choi (Ed.), 2008). It includes the development of curricula and teaching materials, and the training of teachers. Most APEC member countries now have a national standardization education strategy. This strategy can be broad (addressing many areas of education) or limited and it can be detailed (specifying exactly what will be done when by whom) or global. It seems that the broader and more detailed the strategy, the more standardization education activities are in place in a country (Choi et al., 2009; Choi and de Vries, 2011). At the European level, the European Commission 'encourages the Member states to improve the position of standardisation in education programmes and academic curricula, in order to familiarise students with the strategic benefits and challenges of standardisation, drawing on the expertise of standardisation bodies' (Council of the European Union, 2008, Conclusion 27). Referring to this resolution, the CEN/CENELEC/ETSI Joint Working group on Education about Standardization (2011) has prepared a standardization education policy document which can serve as an example for national standardization education policies.

INVESTING IN ONGOING SUPPORT

However, a national strategy is not sufficient. Korean and Dutch examples show that a long-term investment in time (and thus money) is needed in the form of one or more dedicated people who actively approach and support schools in developing, implementing and maintaining education.

In the Korean case, the Korean Standards Association took the lead and managed to get education about standardization implemented in bachelor programs of engineering education all over the country. They established a Standards Education Development Committee composed of participating professors and lecturers. This committee networked with standards experts from various fields in the Republic of Korea and developed a curriculum and educational materials. The Korean government provided financial support (Choi and De Vries, 2013).

The Dutch case did not focus on standardization education but on a similar topic: intellectual property rights (IPR) in higher professional education. This subject has now been integrated in several compulsory courses in higher professional education and elective courses have been developed. It all began when the patent office approached an institution for higher professional education a few kilometres from their office. They established contacts with teachers, one of whom was offered for an internship at the patent office. He became the patent and IPR expert within his school and developed an elective course on patents together with patent office staff. The course is open to students from all technical disciplines. Other teachers were stimulated and started to introduce the topic into their courses. Starting with this one school, this approach was used at other schools of higher professional education in the country and 100% coverage has been achieved. The patent office stays in touch with the schools to increase awareness of the topic and its importance. It does so by arranging guest lectures, and providing teaching materials co-developed with teachers, exam questions, access to the patent database, and advice about how to include the topic in the final attainment level students should reach when leaving the school. The patent office is also in close contact with school boards, the national association of schools, and the national association of engineers. Moreover, there is a link to the education officer of the FME Association, the largest organization in the Netherlands representing employers and businesses in the technology sector. To enable these activities, the patent office has a dedicated officer for higher professional education available. From this level of education, the patent office has expanded its activities to a higher level (universities) and a lower level of technical education (intermediate technical schools) for which staff capacity is also available. As a governmental agency, the patent office is funded for these tasks by the national government (de Vries, 2003, pp. 14-15).

The Korean and Dutch examples and the literature show the following typical elements of a successful national approach:

- Leadership,
- Central coordination,
- Strategy,
- A steering group in which the most important stakeholders are represented (industry, standards bodies, government, organizations in the field of education),
- One or more dedicated staff members who are available for a period of years,
- An inventory of needs for education (de Vries & Egyedi, 2007),
- An action plan,
- Funding for salaries and other costs,
- Development of curricula and materials,
- A train-the-teachers programme,
- Promotional activities.

Activities can start with one or a few teachers from one or a few schools and from there expand to a growing number of schools. Additionally, an approach for teaching practitioners is needed (Choi & De Vries, 2011; Giossi, 2010).

BRIDGING FIVE WORLDS: INDUSTRY, STANDARDIZATION BODIES, ACADEMIA, OTHER INSTITUTIONS FOR EDUCATION, AND GOVERNMENT

A third requirement for successful implementation of standardization education is to bridge five worlds that are all involved in some way with standardization but are not always aware of each others' interests and capacities: industry, standards development organizations, academia, other institutions for education, and government. At the end of the day, industry and other stakeholders need employees' awareness of standards and standardization, and industry, government, standards development organization and other organizations need qualified people to do standards-related tasks. Academic and other education is needed to provide this qualification.

Standardization can be seen as a discipline for which education is needed (Verman, 1973; de Vries, 2002). But is it a discipline? 'Standards and standardization have yet to reach the status of an academic discipline in their own right, while on the other hand they cannot be classified under one of the accepted academic disciplines, such as engineering or social sciences' (Hesser, 1997, p. 3). De Vries (1999, Section 1.1.3) elaborates the idea of standardization as a discipline using the periods in the development of a scientific discipline developed by Kuhn (1962). The current trend to pay more attention to standardization education (Kurokawa, 2005; de Vries and Egyedi; 2007) should be seen as a normal step in the development of standardization into a more mature discipline (de Vries, 2002). A discipline needs professionals

with professional education, and professional and scientific journals publishing results of illustrative best practice cases and scientific research.

Industry

The need for standardization education in industry is latent rather than manifest. Take the example of industry participants in international standardization. Research has revealed more than a hundred factors that contribute to successful participation in international standardization committees (Brons, 2007). Most participants in international standardization are not aware of these factors. They spend several days or weeks a year in standardization activities and have the illusion they are doing a good job but are not aware that their efforts could be much more effective.

A professional community is needed to enhance professionalization of standards experts in industry. The national members of the International Federation of Standards Users IFAN, such as the Standards Engineering Society SES in the United States and Canada, form such communities where standards experts can share knowledge and experience. However, we can observe a paradoxical situation. Membership in both IFAN and most national standards users organizations, except in some Asian countries, has decreased recently although the importance of standards and standardization has increased (de Vries, 1999; Kurokawa, 2005; Swann, 2010). How can this paradox be explained? Traditionally, the members of these national organizations are managers of standardization departments in large companies or standards experts in medium-sized companies (Adolphi, 1997) and thus they are not only standards users (who use standards for their products, services, processes, etc.) but also standards developers (developers of company standards for use within their company or participants in standardization committees at the national or international level, in formal standards bodies or in industry consortia). However, many companies have eliminated standardization departments or reduced the number of staff. Reasons for this reduction include:

- Lack of awareness of the strategic importance of standardization.
- Standardization has an image problem. 'In Japan, there is a tendency for standardization personnel not to be assigned important roles in organizations, even in industries where standards are emphasized' (Kurokawa, 2005, p. 41). It is the author's experience that the same applies in other countries.
- Staff cost as a percentage of total cost has increased because the cost of machines and other equipment has decreased.
- Standardization requires a medium to long-term business perspective because standards, by definition, "freeze" a specification for a certain period of time until a new standard is developed, which may take several years. Cost precedes benefits. The growing emphasis on short-time financial returns makes it easy to justify cuts of standards-related activities.
- More standards-related tasks are being outsourced, e.g. updating the standards collection to a standardization body or a company.

These reasons, in particular the first one, provide a further underpinning of the need to address standards in technical but also in business education. However, the current under-evaluation of standards and standardization hinders the initiation of standardization education activities. What is needed is a clear and strong signal from industry that such education is needed. However, as long as industry and its associations lack awareness of the importance of standardization, this is not likely to happen. So to a certain extent there is a vicious circle. This could be broken by highlighting cases of companies that have managed to gain a competitive advantage by using standards or by being involved in standardization. For example, the German ISO member DIN presents an annual award for the best entries demonstrating the benefits of standardization.

If companies recruit fewer standards experts whereas standards and standardization are becoming more important, there should be a market for intermediary parties such as trade associations or consultancy firms to support companies in standards activities. Perhaps future standards experts will no longer be recruited by companies but by these intermediary parties instead. However, a mixed situation is more plausible, with big companies having their own experts and SMEs relying more on external advice (de Vries et al, 2009) and both companies and intermediaries represented in national associations of standards experts.

More about industry needs for standardization education can be found in Kurokawa (2005) and De Vries and Egyedi (2007). They conclude that general education should provide awareness about standards and standardization. This awareness should enable graduates, once they have a job in industry or in another sector, to recognize if they need further education. Additionally, regular education may prepare students, in particular in technical, business and economic and law studies, for their future jobs by teaching more than just awareness. And last but not least, thorough academic education is needed to prepare people who can improve the current standardization system and to further develop standardization as a discipline.

A few examples show that industry has taken initiative to stimulate standardization education. At the international level, the initiative to create the International Cooperation for Education about Standardization ICES was taken by industry (John Hill, Sun Microsystems, USA and Toshiaki Kurokawa, CSK Corporation, Japan). The International Federation of Standards Users IFAN has established a working group to stimulate standardization education. At the European level, Orgalime (European Engineering Industries Association) has emphasized the need for standardization education in policy papers (Orgalime, 2010a; Orgalime, 2010b).In the Netherlands, the FME Association, representing companies in the technology industry, has developed activities to support education including a working group of teachers in higher professional education. The Association has also stimulated the inclusion of standardization in curricula via this group (de Vries, 2003). SES, the standards users organization in Canada and the US, offers an introduction course about standardization (http://www.ses-standards.org).

Standardization Bodies

Standards and standardization are the core business of standardization bodies, so one would expect them to be centers of standardization expertise. In South Korea, it was the trade union of employees of KSA that saw the need to professionalize KSA staff and this is the reason that they initiated a workshop which formed the start of academic standardization education activities (KSA, 2003). DIN staff are required to successfully follow standardization courses (Behrens, 2010). However, such recognition of the importance of real standardization expertise for standardization bodies is not widespread.

Part of the professionalization of international standardization could thus be to better educate technical officers of standardization bodies. The system of international standardization could be upgraded by granting ISO and IEC secretariats only to technical officers with a recognized diploma in standardization. This is self-evident in other professional areas from accountants to bus drivers but so far not required for experts who provide standardization services. A first step

in this direction is the certification programme established by SES to recognize people who have demonstrated a high degree of professional competency in standardization (http://www.ses-standards.org).

Many standardization organizations provide standardization activities themselves, mostly for business people but sometimes also in regular education (Choi (Ed.), 2008). The academic week organized by the international standardization organizations ISO, IEC and ITU (http://www.iso.org/sites/WSCAW2010/index.html), the ISO award for Standardization in higher Education (ISO, 2011), the IEC lecture series (IEC, 2005; IEC, 2007) and the ITU Kaleidoscope conferences (http://www.itu.int/ITU-T/uni/kaleidoscope) are examples of how international standards bodies reach out to the academic community. National standards bodies have similar initiatives, for instance the Korean standards bodies, Korean Agency for Technology and Standards KATS and the Korean Standards Association KSA, established the Society for Standards and Standardization SSS, an academic association also open to practitioners. SSS took off in October 2010 with an international symposium on "Promotion of Research Activities on Standardization" (*ISO Focus+*, 2011).

Academia

A limited number of university professors pay attention to standardization in their education and research activities. In most cases, it is only one of the many topics they address. The number of standardization chairs is very limited. In terms of size of standardization staff, China Jiliang University in Hangzhou, winner of the first ISO Award on Higher Education in Standardization 2007, is the number one in the world (Song, 2007 and Yang, 2010). Until recently, the second largest standardization research group was at the Helmut Schmidt University in Hamburg (Hesser and Czaya, 1999).

Prof. Blind's Chair at the Technical University in Berlin can be seen as a successor though its scope is broader than just standardization. In Japan, the Tokyo University of Agriculture and Technology addresses standardization in its Management of Technology programme (Furukawa, 2007; Nonaka, 2010). Other universities with standardization programs include the Belarussian National Technical University (Serenkov, 2010), the French Ecole Internationale des Sciences du Traitement de l'Information (Beauvais-Schwartz and Bousquet, 2010) and the French University of Technology of Compiègne (Caliste and Farges, 2007).

The situation in the Netherlands is unique and might serve as a benchmark for other countries. The Dutch ISO member, NEN, created an endowed chair in standardization at the Rotterdam School of Management (RSM), Erasmus University in 1994. "Endowed" means that NEN pays the professor, currently Prof. Dr. Knut Blind, for his appointment on a one-day-a-week basis. NEN provides additional funding so that he can receive support. Besides providing standardization education at its own university, the chair does the following activities:

- Supports standardization research and education at other universities (by organizing, maintaining and supporting an informal network of academic researchers in standardization encompassing nine of the 12 Dutch universities).The Netherlands Standardization Institute NEN, the Dutch Council for Accreditation RvA, the Dutch standards users organization NKN and the Dutch Ministry of Economic Affairs also participate in this network, which allows for informal links with major stakeholders.
- Gives "status" to the topic of standardization by the simple fact the university has an endowed chair.

- Further develops standardization as a scientific discipline.
- Participates in policy debates, for instance, on how to improve national environmental policy by making use of standards. In some cases, the opinion of a professor is more convincing than that of the general director of a standards body.

Additionally, RSM students help NEN with feasibility studies for new standardization topics which has resulted in new activities for NEN. Five students educated at RSM have been recruited by NEN. RSM advice has contributed to better stakeholder involvement in NEN, the number of participants has increased by 30% which has also contributed to NEN's healthy financial results (NEN, 2010). Apparently, NEN gets a return on its investment in the chair.

Establishing an academic community is essential primarily for research but also for education. The European Academy for Standardisation EURAS (http://www.euras.org) is an established community of standardization researchers although membership is open to non-academics as well. EURAS' main activity is its annual conference. A EURAS working group is currently investigating user needs for standardization education. The organization is represented in the CEN/CENELEC/EURAS Working Group on Education about Standardization, and has prepared a White Paper on Standardization Education (Hesser and De Vries, 2011). The SIIT conferences (Standardization and Innovation in Information Technology) form another place for standardization researchers to meet. Four countries have an academic community at the national level: Korea, the Netherlands, Bulgaria and Greece. The Bulgarian Union of Standardization for European Integration of the Republic of Bulgaria was established in 1991 to support the transition of Bulgaria from a planned/

socialist economy to a market economy. Besides academic research and education, many seminars are organised for industry, in particular for SMEs (Ganeva et al., 2010). In Greece, Eneprot was established in 1997. This official organization focuses on academic research and education but supports SMEs. Eneprot took the initiative for a series of international conferences on "Standardization, Protypes and Quality: A means of Balkan Countries Collaboration" (Zachariadou et al., 2010).

Academic journals are another prerequisite for the development of a discipline. Standardization journals include the *EURAS Yearbook of Standardisation* (special issues of *Homo Oeconomicus*), the *International Journal of IT Standards and Standardization Research*, the *International Journal of Services and Standards*, and *Computer, Standards & Interfaces*. However, these journals have not yet achieved a scientific reputation in the set of management and economics journals needed to attract a sufficient number of excellent scientific contributions pushing the scientific progress in standardization research. Special issues on standardization of *Réseaux* (2000), *Knowledge, Technology, & Policy* (2001), *Telecommunications Policy* (2002), *MIS Quarterly* (2006), *Revue d'Économie Industrielle* (2006), *Organization* (2007), *Entreprises et Histoire* (2008), *Technology Analysis and Strategic Management* (2011), *Organization Studies* (2012) and *Technovation* (2015) have brought or are expected to bring standardization research to the attention of a broader academic audience. The more standardization is addressed in academic research, the more scientific researchers will be inclined to include it in their teaching activities.

OTHER EDUCATION INSTITUTIONS

Standardization education is not only relevant at the academic level. In the Netherlands, the first case of successfully implementing education about

IPRS was in higher professional education and this level was and is the first target group. From there, it was extended to senior secondary vocational education and universities. Also secondary schools are relevant and Thailand and Turkey are successful examples (Choi (Ed.), 2008). Compared with universities, other schools have less freedom to address their preferred subjects. Therefore, including standardization in the final attainment levels will stimulate adoption. However, this can only be achieved by involving individual teachers and schools but also associations and other organizations active in the organization of education at the national level.

GOVERNMENT

National governments play different roles related to standards and standardization (De Vries, 1999, Section 2.2.5). These include:

1. Supporting standardization as a part of their general role in stimulating business performance and international trade.
2. Creating a legal foundation for standardization – many countries have legislation setting criteria for the national standardization institute (Schepel, 2005).
3. Carrying out standardization activities themselves (in many countries, in particular in the former Soviet Union and in developing countries, the national standardization organisation is a governmental agency).
4. Supplementing, simplifying, or improving their legal system with standardization by making references to standards in laws.
5. Using standardization for specific public sector tasks (for instance, in the areas of public health, environmental protection, traffic infrastructure, army, and police. Then governmental interests are comparable to those of companies with a dominant market position or companies as main users).

6. Using standardization to improve their performance in areas that are not specifically governmental (for instance, procurement, IT systems, occupational health and safety of government workers).

In all these roles the government would benefit from better standardization education. Government officers in charge of roles 2, 3 and 4 need very specific standardization education. For role 1, standardization education is one of the policy instruments the government might use. Moreover, government has a seventh role: it is responsible for education. The government could include standardization knowledge in its criteria for accreditation of educational programs (Spivak and Kelly, 2003; Cooklev, 2010).

Many governments are insufficiently aware of these t roles and lack a policy that addresses them. An exception is the policy of the German government which focuses on the first role but also mentions all other roles except 3 (not applicable) and except the governmental responsibility for education (Die Bundesregierung, 2009).

THE PROCESS TOWARDS MORE STANDARDIZATION EDUCATION

We started this paper with three barriers for the implementation of standardization education. The first barrier might be the most difficult to overcome: how can we make the topic of standardization more appealing to students? Attractive teaching approaches and materials may partly solve this problem – and students may well pass on their enthusiasm to fellow students. De Vries and Egyedi (2007) have examined teaching materials and new materials and approaches including games are being developed. But this does not completely solve this problem. Elective courses focused on standardization only may lack appeal to students. Including it in other courses or as a compulsory part of the curriculum could be a solution.

The second barrier relates to teachers' willingness to include the topic in their courses. The Dutch and Korean examples suggest a combination of 'top-down' and 'bottom up'. The process is top-down in the sense that a decision is taken at central level, funding is available, and staff for coordination and support is available. The process is bottom-up in the sense that individual teachers and their management need to be convinced that standardization is an important subject and should form part of the curriculum. This is not easy because the curricula are already full and the topic has to compete with other more established ones. It would be particularly convincing if industry and government acknowledged the importance and the need for standardization and strongly urged (or recommended) it be included in educational programs. This can be achieved by setting up a standardization education steering group at the national level in which industry, government, standards body and academia plus other educational institutions are represented. This group can also facilitate another 'top-down' process: to get standardization included in the official final attainment level for graduating students. This may not apply for universities, but probably does for lower levels of education. This requires considerable lobbying which will be easier if some education is in place already. Where applicable, reference to APEC or EU policies or to national standardization strategies (APEC, 2006; Choi et al., 2009; Council of the European Union, 2008, Conclusion 27; European Commission, 2011) can be made. Participation in a national steering group increases awareness of the importance of standardization education for industry and government representatives – the third barrier. Their awareness and subsequent involvement is needed to gain momentum at the national level and this, in turn, may convince schools and their teachers to include standardization in the curriculum. Moreover, it may mobilize resources needed for the investment in standardization education.

Education is organized mainly at the national level so this is the natural level for starting initiatives. In some big countries, initiative taking could also occur at a regional level. Moreover, in a growing number of cases, national boundaries are no longer relevant – this applies to multinational companies and NGOs, and Internet communities. At the global level, ideas and approaches can be exchanged using the platform of the International Cooperation on Education about Standardization ICES (http://www.standards-education.org). International standardization have an additional role in developing teaching materials and in providing assistance or even education in countries where no standardization education is in place yet (Gerundino, 2010).

In South Korea, the initiative for standardization education was taken by an unexpected stakeholder: a trade union. This shows that any party can take the initiative – the standards body, industry, government, a university or any other stakeholder. The role of the initiator is to involve other stakeholders. The APEC inventory shows that national standards bodies play an important role in each country that has successfully implemented standardization education (Choi (Ed.), 2008). Next, resources are needed to employ dedicated people for some years, to develop educational materials and to organize train-the-trainer programs etc. These resources could come from industry, from standards bodies (with some delay, it will enhance their market position but cost precedes benefits), or from government (in the European case from the European Commission).

FUTURE RESEARCH

Meanwhile, initiatives for more standardization education are taken all over the world. Future research might make an inventory of initiatives and achievements and relate impact to measures taken. In-depth case studies might provide best practice examples. In particular, the Korean case deserves further investigation. Another opportunity is to benchmark the introduction of standardization education with other topics of education, such as the similar topic of IPR. Above we mentioned the example of IPR education in the Netherlands. Another country for such research is Japan where a steady increase in IPR education can be observed (Yamada, 2011). In such studies, authors might borrow from literature on 'educology' – the field of research that studies educational processes.

REFERENCES

Adolphi, H. (1997). *Strategische Konzepte zur Organisation der betrieblichen Standardisierung. DIN Normungskunde* (Vol. 38). Berlin: Beuth Verlag.

APEC. (2006). *The eighteenth APEC ministerial meeting joint statement*. Singapore: APEC.

Beauvais-Schwartz, N., & Bousquet, F. (2010). *France – Fostering competitive intelligence.* Retrieved May 26, 2010, from http://www.iso.org/iso/iso-focus-plus_index/iso-focusplus_online-bonus-articles/the-2009-iso-award/2009-award_france.htm

Behrens, H. (2010). *Education about Standardization – Competency of Standards Body Staff.* Paper presented at the first meeting of the CEN/CENELEC/ETSI Joint Working Group on Education about Standardization, 2010-03-09. Brussels, Belgium.

Brons, T. F. (2007). *Effective Participation in Formal Standardization: A Multinational Perspective.* Rotterdam: Rotterdam School of Management.

Caliste, J., & Farges, G. (2007). A French University: Encouraging hands-on experience. *ISO Focus, 4*(11), 13–14.

CEN/CENELEC/ETSI Joint Working group on Education about Standardization. (2011). *Policy on education about Standardization.* Brussels: CEN/CENELEC Management Centre. Retrieved February 15, 2014 from ftp://ftp.cencenelec.eu/CEN/Services/Education/Education/Policyon-EducationaboutStandardization.pdf

Choi, D. (Ed.). (2008). *APEC SCSC Education Guideline 1: Case Studies of How to Plan and Implement Standards Education Programs, Asia Pacific Economic Cooperation.* Singapore: APEC Secretariat.

Choi, D., & de Vries, H. J. (2013). Integrating standardization into engineering education: The case of forerunner Korea. *International Journal of Technology and Design Education, 23*(4), 1111–1126. doi:10.1007/s10798-012-9231-7

Choi, D., de Vries, H. J., & Kim, D. (2009). Standards Education Policy Development: Observations based on APEC Research. *International Journal of IT Standards and Standardization Research, 7*(2), 23–42. doi:10.4018/jitsr.2009070103

Choi, D. G., & Vries, H. J. (2011). Standardization as emerging content in technology education. *International Journal of Technology and Design Education, 21*(1), 111–135. doi:10.1007/s10798-009-9110-z

Cooklev, T. (2010). The Role of Standards in Engineering Education. *International Journal of IT Standards and Standardization Research, 8*(1), 1–10. doi:10.4018/jitsr.2010120701

Council of the European Union. (2008). *Council Conclusions on standardisation and innovation.* Paper presented at the 2891st Competitiveness Council meeting, 2008-09-25. Brussels: Council of the European Union.

Czaya, A., Egyedi, T., & Hesser, W. (2010). The current state of standardization education in Europe. In MijatovicI.ŽivkovićN. (Eds.), *Proceedings 7th International Conference "Standardization Protypes and Quality: A means of Balkan countries collaboration"*, (pp. 85-90). University of Belgrade, Faculty of Organizational Sciences.

de Vries, H. J. (1999). *Standardization – A Business Approach to the Role of National Standardization Organizations.* Boston: Kluwer Academic Publishers. doi:10.1007/978-1-4757-3042-5

de Vries, H. J. (2002). Standardization – Mapping a field of research. In S. Bollin (Ed.), *The Standards Edge* (pp. 99–121). Ann Arbor, MI: Bollin Communications.

de Vries, H. J. (2003). *Kenbaarheid Normalisatie en Normen – Deelproject 9b HBO-onderwijs – Tussenrapportage.* Delft: NEN.

de Vries, H. J., Blind, K., Mangelsdorf, A., Verheul, H., & van der Zwan, J. (2009). *SME Access to European Standardization - Enabling small and medium-sized enterprises to achieve greater benefit from standards and from involvement in standardization.* Brussels: CEN and CENELEC. Retrieved from http://www.cenelec.eu/NR/rdonlyres/88D06BD5-CA51-479D-A416-AB1F-3BE67E66/0/SMEAccessReport20090821.pdf

de Vries, H. J., & Egyedi, T. M. (2007). Education about Standardization. *International Journal of IT Standards and Standardization Research, 5*(2), 1–16. doi:10.4018/jitsr.2007070101

Denardis, L., & Levin, A. (2009). *Bridging the standardization gap – ITU-T Research Project: Measuring and Reducing the Standards Gap.* Geneva: International Telecommunication Union.

Die Bundesregierung. (2009). *Normungspolitisches Konzept der Bundesregierung.* Berlin: Die Bundesregierung.

European Commission. (2011). *A strategic vision for European standards: Moving forward to enhance and accelerate the sustainable growth of the European economy by 2020 - COM(2011) 311 final - Communication from the Commission tot he European Parliament, the Council and the European Economic and Social Committee.* Brussels: European Commission. Retrieved February 15, 2014 at http://eur-lex.europa.eu/LexUriServ/LexUriServ.do?uri=COM:2011:0311:FIN:EN:PDF

Focus, I. S. O. (2011). Society for standards and standardization launched. *ISO Focus, 2*(1), 36.

Furukawa, Y. (2007). A Japanese university: Educating standardization strategists in business. *ISO Focus, 4*(11), 15–16.

Ganeva, L., Sandalski, B., & Kotev, R. (2010). Contributions of the Bulgarian Union of Standardization for the European Integration of the Republic Bulgaria. In *Proceedings 7th International Conference "Standardization Protypes and Quality: A means of Balkan countries collaboration"*, (pp. 29-38). University of Belgrade, Faculty of Organizational Sciences.

Gerundino, D. (2010). Standards in economic development and trade. *ISO Focus, 1*(1), 35.

Giossi, S., & Papastamatis, A. (2010). *The effective teaching of standards in a lifelong learning world.* In *Proceedings 7th International Conference "Standardization Protypes and Quality: A means of Balkan countries collaboration"*, (pp. 118-125). University of Belgrade, Faculty of Organizational Sciences.

Hesser, W. (1997). *The need for interdisciplinary research on standardization.* Paper presented at the SCANCOR/SCORE Seminar on Standardization. Lund, Sweden.

Hesser, W., & Czaya, A. (1999). Standardization as a subject of study in higher education. *ISO Bulletin, 30*(6), 6–11.

Hesser, W., & de Vries, H. J. (2011). *White Paper Academic Standardisation education in Europe.* Hamburg, Germany: European Academy for Standardisation. Retrieved February 15, 2014 from http://www.euras.org/uploads/files/EURAS%20White%20paper%202011-08-13.pdf

IEC. (2005). *IEC Lecture Series – International Standardization in business, Industry, Society and Technology.* Geneva: International Electrotechnical Commission.

IEC. (2007). *IEC Lecture Series II – The Importance of Standards.* Geneva: International Electrotechnical Commission.

ISO. (2011). *The ISO 2011 Award for Higher Education in Standardization.* Geneva: International Organization for Standardization.

Ketchell, J. (2010) Education about standardization – Developing future generations of standardisers. Paper presented at WSC Academic Week. Geneva, Switzerland.

Krechmer, K. (2007). Teaching standards to engineers. *International Journal of IT Standards and Standardization Research*, 5(2), 1–12. doi:10.4018/jitsr.2007070102

KSA. (2003). *International workshop to develop a standardization education model*. Seoul: KSA.

Kuhn. (1962). *The Structure of Scientific Revolutions*. Chicago: University of Chicago Press.

Kurokawa, T. (2005). Developing Human Resources for International Standards. *Quarterly Review*, *17*. Retrieved from http://www.nistep.go.jp/achiev/ftx/eng/stfc/stt017e/qr17pdf/STTqr1703.pdf

NEN. (2010). *Annual Report 2009 – Crisis & Control*. Delft: NEN.

Nonaka, R. (2010). New approach on the pedagogy for standards education: A case of Applied Standards Education at TUAT. In *Proceedings of International Symposium on Standardization Education and Research 2010*, (pp. 156-167). Tokyo University of Agriculture and Technology.

Odjar Ratna Komala, D. (2011). *Mechanics of Developing a University Level Standards Education Program in Indonesia*. Paper presented at the 2011 PEC SCSC PAGE – ANSI CoE Workshop. Washington, DC.

Orgalime. (2010a). *Draft Orgalime comments on EP IMCO report on the Future of European Standardization*. Brussels: Orgalime.

Orgalime. (2010b). *Review of the European Standardization System*. Brussels: Orgalime.

Schepel, H. (2005). *The Constitution of Private Governance – Product Standards in the Regulation of Integrating Markets*. Portland, OR: Hart Publishing.

Serenkov, P. (2010). *Belarus – Training tomorrow's experts today*. Retrieved May 26, 2010, from http://www.iso.org/iso/iso-focus-plus_index/iso-focusplus_online-bonus-articles/the-2009-iso-award/2009-award_belarus.htm

Song, M. (2007). Guest View. *ISO Focus*, 4(11), 4–7.

Spivak, S. M., & Kelly, W. E. (2003). Introduce strategic standardization concepts during higher education studies … and reap the benefits! *ISO Bulletin*, 34(7), 22–24.

Swann, G. M. P. (2010). *The economics of standardization – An Update. report for the UK Department of Business, Innovation and Skills (BIS)*. Innovation Economics Limited.

Verman, L. C. (1973). *Standardization – A new discipline*. Hamden, CT: The Shoe String Press / Archon Books.

Yamada, H. (2011) *Development of Education on Standardization in Japan*. Paper presented at the 2011 PEC SCSC PAGE – ANSI CoE Workshop February 28, 2011. Washington, DC.

Yang, Y. (2010). China Institute of Metrology's Educational Model for Standardization. *China Standardization*, 37(1), 15-21.

Zachariadou, K., Zachariadis, A., & Latinopoulou, M. (2010). Contributions of the Bulgarian Union of Standardization for the European Integration of the Republic Bulgaria. In *Proceedings 7th International Conference "Standardization Protypes and Quality: A means of Balkan countries collaboration"*, (pp. 78-82). University of Belgrade, Faculty of Organizational Sciences.

KEY TERMS AND DEFINITIONS

Development: The act, process or result of developing (Webster Third New International Dictionary).

Education: The act or process of providing someone with knowledge, skills or competences (based on Webster Third New International Dictionary).

National: Of a nation.

Policy: A specific decision or set of decisions designed to carry out a definite course or method of action (based on Webster Third New International Dictionary).

Standardization: Activity of establishing and recording a limited set of solutions to actual or potential matching problems, prepared for the benefit of the party or parties involved, balancing their needs, and intended and expect to be used repeatedly or continuously, during a certain period, by a substantial number of the parties for whom they are meant (De Vries, 1997).

Strategy: The art of devising or employing plans towards a goal (based on Webster Third New International Dictionary).

Related References

To continue our tradition of advancing information science and technology research, we have compiled a list of recommended IGI Global readings. These references will provide additional information and guidance to further enrich your knowledge and assist you with your own research and future publications.

Adamich, T. (2012). Materials-to-standards alignment: How to "chunk" a whole cake and even use the "crumbs": State standards alignment models, learning objects, and formative assessment – methodologies and metadata for education. In L. Tomei (Ed.), *Advancing education with information communication technologies: Facilitating new trends* (pp. 165–178). Hershey, PA: Information Science Reference.

Abramowicz, W., Stolarski, P., & Tomaszewski, T. (2013). Legal ontologies in ICT and law. In *Digital rights management: Concepts, methodologies, tools, and applications* (pp. 34–49). Hershey, PA: Information Science Reference.

Adomi, E. E. (2011). Regulation of internet content. In E. Adomi (Ed.), *Frameworks for ICT policy: Government, social and legal issues* (pp. 233–246). Hershey, PA: Information Science Reference.

Akowuah, F., Yuan, X., Xu, J., & Wang, H. (2012). A survey of U.S. laws for health information security & privacy. [IJISP]. *International Journal of Information Security and Privacy, 6*(4), 40–54. doi:10.4018/jisp.2012100102

Aggestam, L. (2011). Guidelines for preparing organizations in developing countries for standards-based B2B. In *Global business: Concepts, methodologies, tools and applications* (pp. 206–228). Hershey, PA: Business Science Reference.

Akowuah, F., Yuan, X., Xu, J., & Wang, H. (2013). A survey of security standards applicable to health information systems. [IJISP]. *International Journal of Information Security and Privacy, 7*(4), 22–36. doi:10.4018/ijisp.2013100103

Alejandre, G. M. (2013). IT security governance legal issues. In D. Mellado, L. Enrique Sánchez, E. Fernández-Medina, & M. Piattini (Eds.), *IT security governance innovations: Theory and research* (pp. 47–73). Hershey, PA: Information Science Reference.

Alexandropoulou-Egyptiadou, E. (2013). The Hellenic framework for computer program copyright protection following the implementation of the relative european union directives. In *Digital rights management: Concepts, methodologies, tools, and applications* (pp. 738–745). Hershey, PA: Information Science Reference.

Al Hadid, I. (2012). Applying the certification's standards to the simulation study steps. In E. Abu-Taieh, A. El Sheikh, & M. Jafari (Eds.), *Technology engineering and management in aviation: Advancements and discoveries* (pp. 294–307). Hershey, PA: Information Science Reference.

Ali, S. (2012). Practical web application security audit following industry standards and compliance. In J. Zubairi, & A. Mahboob (Eds.), *Cyber security standards, practices and industrial applications: Systems and methodologies* (pp. 259–279). Hershey, PA: Information Science Reference.

Alirezaee, M., & Afsharian, M. (2013). Measuring the effect of the rules and regulations on global malmquist index. In J. Wang (Ed.), *Optimizing, innovating, and capitalizing on information systems for operations* (pp. 215–229). Hershey, PA: Business Science Reference.

Alirezaee, M., & Afsharian, M. (2011). Measuring the effect of the rules and regulations on global malmquist index. [IJORIS]. *International Journal of Operations Research and Information Systems*, 2(3), 64–78. doi:10.4018/joris.2011070105

Al Mohannadi, F., Arif, M., Aziz, Z., & Richardson, P. A. (2013). Adopting BIM standards for managing vision 2030 infrastructure development in Qatar. *International Journal of 3-D Information Modeling (IJ3DIM)*, 2(3), 64-73. doi:10.4018/ij3dim.2013070105

Al-Nu'aimi, A. A. (2011). Using watermarking techniques to prove rightful ownership of web images. [IJITWE]. *International Journal of Information Technology and Web Engineering*, 6(2), 29–39. doi:10.4018/jitwe.2011040103

Alves de Lima, A., Carvalho dos Reis, P., Branco, J. C., Danieli, R., Osawa, C. C., Winter, E., & Santos, D. A. (2013). Scenario-patent protection compared to climate change: The case of green patents. [IJSESD]. *International Journal of Social Ecology and Sustainable Development*, 4(3), 61–70. doi:10.4018/jsesd.2013070105

Amirante, A., Castaldi, T., Miniero, L., & Romano, S. P. (2013). Protocol interactions among user agents, application servers, and media servers: Standardization efforts and open issues. In D. Kanellopoulos (Ed.), *Intelligent multimedia technologies for networking applications: Techniques and tools* (pp. 48–63). Hershey, PA: Information Science Reference.

Anker, P. (2013). The impact of regulations on the business case for cognitive radio. In T. Lagkas, P. Sarigiannidis, M. Louta, & P. Chatzimisios (Eds.), *Evolution of cognitive networks and self-adaptive communication systems* (pp. 142–170). Hershey, PA: Information Science Reference.

Antunes, A. M., Mendes, F. M., Schumacher, S. D., Quoniam, L., & Lima de Magalhães, J. (2014). The contribution of information science through intellectual property to innovation in the Brazilian health sector. In G. Jamil, A. Malheiro, & F. Ribeiro (Eds.), *Rethinking the conceptual base for new practical applications in information value and quality* (pp. 83–115). Hershey, PA: Information Science Reference.

Atiskov, A. Y., Novikov, F. A., Fedorchenko, L. N., Vorobiev, V. I., & Moldovyan, N. A. (2013). Ontology-based analysis of cryptography standards and possibilities of their harmonization. In A. Elçi, J. Pieprzyk, A. Chefranov, M. Orgun, H. Wang, & R. Shankaran (Eds.), *Theory and practice of cryptography solutions for secure information systems* (pp. 1–33). Hershey, PA: Information Science Reference.

Ayanso, A., & Herath, T. (2014). Law and technology at crossroads in cyberspace: Where do we go from here? In *Cyber behavior: Concepts, methodologies, tools, and applications* (pp. 1990–2010). Hershey, PA: Information Science Reference.

Ayanso, A., & Herath, T. (2012). Law and technology at crossroads in cyberspace: Where do we go from here? In A. Dudley, J. Braman, & G. Vincenti (Eds.), *Investigating cyber law and cyber ethics: Issues, impacts and practices* (pp. 57–77). Hershey, PA: Information Science Reference.

Aydogan-Duda, N. (2012). Branding innovation: The case study of Turkey. In N. Ekekwe, & N. Islam (Eds.), *Disruptive technologies, innovation and global redesign: Emerging implications* (pp. 238–248). Hershey, PA: Information Science Reference.

Bagby, J. W. (2011). Environmental standardization for sustainability. In Z. Luo (Ed.), *Green finance and sustainability: Environmentally-aware business models and technologies* (pp. 31–55). Hershey, PA: Business Science Reference.

Bagby, J. W. (2013). Insights from U.S. experience to guide international reliance on standardization: Achieving supply chain sustainability. [IJAL]. *International Journal of Applied Logistics*, 4(3), 25–46. doi:10.4018/jal.2013070103

Baggio, B., & Beldarrain, Y. (2011). Intellectual property in an age of open source and anonymity. In *Anonymity and learning in digitally mediated communications: Authenticity and trust in cyber education* (pp. 39–57). Hershey, PA: Information Science Reference.

Balzli, C. E., & Fragnière, E. (2012). How ERP systems are centralizing and standardizing the accounting function in public organizations for better and worse. In S. Chhabra, & M. Kumar (Eds.), *Strategic enterprise resource planning models for e-government: Applications and methodologies* (pp. 55–72). Hershey, PA: Information Science Reference.

Banas, J. R. (2011). Standardized, flexible design of electronic learning environments to enhance learning efficiency and effectiveness. In A. Kitchenham (Ed.), *Models for interdisciplinary mobile learning: Delivering information to students* (pp. 66–86). Hershey, PA: Information Science Reference.

Bao, C., & Castresana, J. M. (2012). Interoperability approach in e-learning standardization processes. In *Virtual learning environments: Concepts, methodologies, tools and applications* (pp. 542–560). Hershey, PA: Information Science Reference.

Bao, C., & Castresana, J. M. (2011). Interoperability approach in e-learning standardization processes. In F. Lazarinis, S. Green, & E. Pearson (Eds.), *Handbook of research on e-learning standards and interoperability: Frameworks and issues* (pp. 399–418). Hershey, PA: Information Science Reference.

Barrett, B. (2011). Evaluating and implementing teaching standards: Providing quality online teaching strategies and techniques standards. In F. Lazarinis, S. Green, & E. Pearson (Eds.), *Developing and utilizing e-learning applications* (pp. 66–83). Hershey, PA: Information Science Reference.

Berleur, J. (2011). Ethical and social issues of the internet governance regulations. In D. Haftor, & A. Mirijamdotter (Eds.), *Information and communication technologies, society and human beings: Theory and framework (festschrift in honor of Gunilla Bradley)* (pp. 466–476). Hershey, PA: Information Science Reference.

Bhattathiripad, V. P. (2014). Software copyright infringement and litigation. In *Judiciary-friendly forensics of software copyright infringement* (pp. 35–55). Hershey, PA: Information Science Reference.

Bin, X., & Chuan, T. K. (2013). The effect of business characteristics on the methods of knowledge protections. In E. Carayannis (Ed.), *Creating a sustainable ecology using technology-driven solutions* (pp. 172–200). Hershey, PA: Information Science Reference.

Bin, X., & Chuan, T. K. (2013). The effect of business characteristics on the methods of knowledge protections. In *Digital rights management: Concepts, methodologies, tools, and applications* (pp. 1283–1311). Hershey, PA: Information Science Reference.

Bin, X., & Chuan, T. K. (2011). The effect of business characteristics on the methods of knowledge protections. [IJSESD]. *International Journal of Social Ecology and Sustainable Development*, 2(3), 34–60. doi:10.4018/jsesd.2011070103

Bogers, M., Bekkers, R., & Granstrand, O. (2013). Intellectual property and licensing strategies in open collaborative innovation. In *Digital rights management: Concepts, methodologies, tools, and applications* (pp. 1204–1224). Hershey, PA: Information Science Reference.

Bogers, M., Bekkers, R., & Granstrand, O. (2012). Intellectual property and licensing strategies in open collaborative innovation. In C. de Pablos Heredero, & D. López (Eds.), *Open innovation in firms and public administrations: Technologies for value creation* (pp. 37–58). Hershey, PA: Information Science Reference.

Bourcier, D. (2013). Law and governance: The genesis of the commons. In F. Doridot, P. Duquenoy, P. Goujon, A. Kurt, S. Lavelle, & N. Patrignani et al. (Eds.), *Ethical governance of emerging technologies development* (pp. 166–183). Hershey, PA: Information Science Reference.

Bousquet, F., Fomin, V. V., & Drillon, D. (2013). Anticipatory standards development and competitive intelligence. In R. Herschel (Ed.), *Principles and applications of business intelligence research* (pp. 17–30). Hershey, PA: Business Science Reference.

Bousquet, F., Fomin, V. V., & Drillon, D. (2011). Anticipatory standards development and competitive intelligence. [IJBIR]. *International Journal of Business Intelligence Research*, 2(1), 16–30. doi:10.4018/jbir.2011010102

Brabazon, A. (2013). Optimal patent design: An agent-based modeling approach. In B. Alexandrova-Kabadjova, S. Martinez-Jaramillo, A. Garcia-Almanza, & E. Tsang (Eds.), *Simulation in computational finance and economics: Tools and emerging applications* (pp. 280–302). Hershey, PA: Business Science Reference.

Bracci, F., Corradi, A., & Foschini, L. (2014). Cloud standards: Security and interoperability issues. In H. Mouftah, & B. Kantarci (Eds.), *Communication infrastructures for cloud computing* (pp. 465–495). Hershey, PA: Information Science Reference.

Briscoe, D. R. (2014). Globalization and international labor standards, codes of conduct, and ethics: An International HRM perspective. In *Cross-cultural interaction: Concepts, methodologies, tools and applications* (pp. 40–62). Hershey, PA: Information Science Reference.

Briscoe, D. R. (2012). Globalization and international labor standards, codes of conduct, and ethics: An International HRM perspective. In C. Wankel, & S. Malleck (Eds.), *Ethical models and applications of globalization: Cultural, sociopolitical and economic perspectives* (pp. 1–22). Hershey, PA: Business Science Reference.

Brooks, R. G., & Geradin, D. (2011). Interpreting and enforcing the voluntary FRAND commitment. [IJITSR]. *International Journal of IT Standards and Standardization Research*, 9(1), 1–23. doi:10.4018/jitsr.2011010101

Brown, C. A. (2013). Common core state standards: The promise for college and career ready students in the U.S. In V. Wang (Ed.), *Handbook of research on teaching and learning in K-20 education* (pp. 50–82). Hershey, PA: Information Science Reference.

Buyurgan, N., Rardin, R. L., Jayaraman, R., Varghese, V. M., & Burbano, A. (2013). A novel GS1 data standard adoption roadmap for healthcare providers. In J. Tan (Ed.), *Healthcare information technology innovation and sustainability: Frontiers and adoption* (pp. 41–57). Hershey, PA: Medical Information Science Reference.

Buyurgan, N., Rardin, R. L., Jayaraman, R., Varghese, V. M., & Burbano, A. (2011). A novel GS1 data standard adoption roadmap for healthcare providers. [IJHISI]. *International Journal of Healthcare Information Systems and Informatics*, *6*(4), 42–59. doi:10.4018/jhisi.2011100103

Campolo, C., Cozzetti, H. A., Molinaro, A., & Scopigno, R. M. (2012). PHY/MAC layer design in vehicular ad hoc networks: Challenges, standard approaches, and alternative solutions. In R. Aquino-Santos, A. Edwards, & V. Rangel-Licea (Eds.), *Wireless technologies in vehicular ad hoc networks: Present and future challenges* (pp. 70–100). Hershey, PA: Information Science Reference.

Cantatore, F. (2014). Copyright support structures. In *Authors, copyright, and publishing in the digital era* (pp. 81–93). Hershey, PA: Information Science Reference.

Cantatore, F. (2014). History and development of copyright. In *Authors, copyright, and publishing in the digital era* (pp. 10–32). Hershey, PA: Information Science Reference.

Cantatore, F. (2014). Research findings: Authors' perceptions and the copyright framework. In Authors, copyright, and publishing in the digital era (pp. 147-189). Hershey, PA: Information Science Reference. doi:10.4018/978-1-4666-5214-9.ch008

Cassini, J., Medlin, B. D., & Romaniello, A. (2011). Forty years of federal legislation in the area of data protection and information security. In H. Nemati (Ed.), *Pervasive information security and privacy developments: Trends and advancements* (pp. 14–23). Hershey, PA: Information Science Reference.

Charlesworth, A. (2012). Addressing legal issues in online research, publication and archiving: A UK perspective. In C. Silva (Ed.), *Online research methods in urban and planning studies: Design and outcomes* (pp. 368–393). Hershey, PA: Information Science Reference.

Chaudhary, C., & Kang, I. S. (2011). Pirates of the copyright and cyberspace: Issues involved. In R. Santanam, M. Sethumadhavan, & M. Virendra (Eds.), *Cyber security, cyber crime and cyber forensics: Applications and perspectives* (pp. 59–68). Hershey, PA: Information Science Reference.

Chen, L., Hu, W., Yang, M., & Zhang, L. (2011). Security and privacy issues in secure e-mail standards and services. In H. Nemati (Ed.), *Security and privacy assurance in advancing technologies: New developments* (pp. 174–185). Hershey, PA: Information Science Reference.

Ciaghi, A., & Villafiorita, A. (2012). Law modeling and BPR for public administration improvement. In K. Bwalya, & S. Zulu (Eds.), *Handbook of research on e-government in emerging economies: Adoption, E-participation, and legal frameworks* (pp. 391–410). Hershey, PA: Information Science Reference.

Ciptasari, R. W., & Sakurai, K. (2013). Multimedia copyright protection scheme based on the direct feature-based method. In K. Kondo (Ed.), *Multimedia information hiding technologies and methodologies for controlling data* (pp. 412–439). Hershey, PA: Information Science Reference.

Clark, L. A., Jones, D. L., & Clark, W. J. (2012). Technology innovation and the policy vacuum: A call for ethics, norms, and laws to fill the void. [IJT]. *International Journal of Technoethics, 3*(1), 1–13. doi:10.4018/jte.2012010101

Cooklev, T. (2013). The role of standards in engineering education. In K. Jakobs (Ed.), *Innovations in organizational IT specification and standards development* (pp. 129–137). Hershey, PA: Information Science Reference.

Cooper, A. R. (2013). Key challenges in the design of learning technology standards: Observations and proposals. In K. Jakobs (Ed.), *Innovations in organizational IT specification and standards development* (pp. 241–249). Hershey, PA: Information Science Reference.

Cordella, A. (2013). Emerging standardization. In A. Tatnall (Ed.), *Social and professional applications of actor-network theory for technology development* (pp. 221–237). Hershey, PA: Information Science Reference.

Cordella, A. (2011). Emerging standardization. [IJANTTI]. *International Journal of Actor-Network Theory and Technological Innovation, 3*(3), 49–64. doi:10.4018/jantti.2011070104

Curran, K., & Lautman, R. (2011). The problems of jurisdiction on the internet. [IJACI]. *International Journal of Ambient Computing and Intelligence, 3*(3), 36–42. doi:10.4018/jaci.2011070105

Dani, D. E., Salloum, S., Khishfe, R., & Bou-Jaoude, S. (2013). A tool for analyzing science standards and curricula for 21st century science education. In M. Khine, & I. Saleh (Eds.), *Approaches and strategies in next generation science learning* (pp. 265-289). Hershey, PA: Information Science Reference. doi:10.4018/978-1-4666-2809-0.ch014

Dedeke, A. (2012). Politics hinders open standards in the public sector: The Massachusetts open document format decision. In C. Reddick (Ed.), *Cases on public information management and e-government adoption* (pp. 1–23). Hershey, PA: Information Science Reference.

Delfmann, P., Herwig, S., Lis, L., & Becker, J. (2012). Supporting conceptual model analysis using semantic standardization and structural pattern matching. In S. Smolnik, F. Teuteberg, & O. Thomas (Eds.), *Semantic technologies for business and information systems engineering: Concepts and applications* (pp. 125–149). Hershey, PA: Business Science Reference.

De Silva, S. (2012). Legal issues with FOS-ERP: A UK law perspective. In R. Atem de Carvalho, & B. Johansson (Eds.), *Free and open source enterprise resource planning: Systems and strategies* (pp. 102–115). Hershey, PA: Business Science Reference.

den Uijl, S., de Vries, H. J., & Bayramoglu, D. (2013). The rise of MP3 as the market standard: How compressed audio files became the dominant music format. [IJITSR]. *International Journal of IT Standards and Standardization Research, 11*(1), 1–26. doi:10.4018/jitsr.2013010101

de Vries, H. J. (2013). Implementing standardization education at the national level. In K. Jakobs (Ed.), *Innovations in organizational IT specification and standards development* (pp. 116–128). Hershey, PA: Information Science Reference.

de Vries, H. J. (2011). Implementing standardization education at the national level. [IJITSR]. *International Journal of IT Standards and Standardization Research, 9*(2), 72–83. doi:10.4018/jitsr.2011070104

de Vuyst, B., & Fairchild, A. (2012). Legal and economic justification for software protection. [IJOSSP]. *International Journal of Open Source Software and Processes, 4*(3), 1–12. doi:10.4018/ijossp.2012070101

Dickerson, J., & Coleman, H. V. (2012). Technology, e-leadership and educational administration in schools: Integrating standards with context and guiding questions. In V. Wang (Ed.), *Encyclopedia of e-leadership, counseling and training* (pp. 408–422). Hershey, PA: Information Science Reference.

Dindaroglu, B. (2013). R&D productivity and firm size in semiconductors and pharmaceuticals: Evidence from citation yields. In I. Yetkiner, M. Pamukcu, & E. Erdil (Eds.), *Industrial dynamics, innovation policy, and economic growth through technological advancements* (pp. 92–113). Hershey, PA: Information Science Reference.

Ding, W. (2013). Development of intellectual property of communications enterprise and analysis of current situation of patents in emerging technology field. In T. Gao (Ed.), *Global applications of pervasive and ubiquitous computing* (pp. 89–96). Hershey, PA: Information Science Reference.

Ding, W. (2011). Development of intellectual property of communications enterprise and analysis of current situation of patents in emerging technology field. [IJAPUC]. *International Journal of Advanced Pervasive and Ubiquitous Computing, 3*(2), 21–28. doi:10.4018/japuc.2011040103

Dorloff, F., & Kajan, E. (2012). Balancing of heterogeneity and interoperability in e-business networks: The role of standards and protocols. [IJEBR]. *International Journal of E-Business Research, 8*(4), 15–33. doi:10.4018/jebr.2012100102

Dorloff, F., & Kajan, E. (2012). Efficient and interoperable e-business –Based on frameworks, standards and protocols: An introduction. In E. Kajan, F. Dorloff, & I. Bedini (Eds.), *Handbook of research on e-business standards and protocols: Documents, data and advanced web technologies* (pp. 1–20). Hershey, PA: Business Science Reference.

Driouchi, A., & Kadiri, M. (2013). Challenges to intellectual property rights from information and communication technologies, nanotechnologies and microelectronics. In *Digital rights management: Concepts, methodologies, tools, and applications* (pp. 1474–1492). Hershey, PA: Information Science Reference.

Dubey, M., & Hirwade, M. (2013). Copyright relevancy at stake in libraries of the digital era. In T. Ashraf, & P. Gulati (Eds.), *Design, development, and management of resources for digital library services* (pp. 379–384). Hershey, PA: Information Science Reference.

Egyedi, T. M. (2011). Between supply and demand: Coping with the impact of standards change. In *Global business: Concepts, methodologies, tools and applications* (pp. 105–120). Hershey, PA: Business Science Reference.

Egyedi, T. M., & Koppenhol, A. (2013). The standards war between ODF and OOXML: Does competition between overlapping ISO standards lead to innovation? In K. Jakobs (Ed.), *Innovations in organizational IT specification and standards development* (pp. 79–90). Hershey, PA: Information Science Reference.

Egyedi, T. M., & Muto, S. (2012). Standards for ICT: A green strategy in a grey sector. [IJITSR]. *International Journal of IT Standards and Standardization Research*, *10*(1), 34–47. doi:10.4018/jitsr.2012010103

El Kharbili, M., & Pulvermueller, E. (2013). Semantic policies for modeling regulatory process compliance. In *IT policy and ethics: Concepts, methodologies, tools, and applications* (pp. 218–243). Hershey, PA: Information Science Reference.

El Kharbili, M., & Pulvermueller, E. (2012). Semantic policies for modeling regulatory process compliance. In S. Smolnik, F. Teuteberg, & O. Thomas (Eds.), *Semantic technologies for business and information systems engineering: Concepts and applications* (pp. 311–336). Hershey, PA: Business Science Reference.

Ervin, K. (2014). Legal and ethical considerations in the implementation of electronic health records. In J. Krueger (Ed.), *Cases on electronic records and resource management implementation in diverse environments* (pp. 193–210). Hershey, PA: Information Science Reference.

Escayola, J., Trigo, J., Martínez, I., Martínez-Espronceda, M., Aragüés, A., Sancho, D., et al. (2013). Overview of the ISO/IEEE11073 family of standards and their applications to health monitoring. In User-driven healthcare: Concepts, methodologies, tools, and applications (pp. 357-381). Hershey, PA: Medical Information Science Reference. doi:10.4018/978-1-4666-2770-3.ch018

Escayola, J., Trigo, J., Martínez, I., Martínez-Espronceda, M., Aragüés, A., & Sancho, D. et al. (2012). Overview of the ISO/ieee11073 family of standards and their applications to health monitoring. In W. Chen, S. Oetomo, & L. Feijs (Eds.), *Neonatal monitoring technologies: Design for integrated solutions* (pp. 148–173). Hershey, PA: Medical Information Science Reference.

Espada, J. P., Martínez, O. S., García-Bustelo, B. C., Lovelle, J. M., & Ordóñez de Pablos, P. (2011). Standardization of virtual objects. In M. Lytras, P. Ordóñez de Pablos, & E. Damiani (Eds.), *Semantic web personalization and context awareness: Management of personal identities and social networking* (pp. 7–21). Hershey, PA: Information Science Reference.

Falkner, N. J. (2011). Security technologies and policies in organisations. In M. Quigley (Ed.), *ICT ethics and security in the 21st century: New developments and applications* (pp. 196–213). Hershey, PA: Information Science Reference.

Ferrer-Roca, O. (2011). Standards in telemedicine. In A. Moumtzoglou, & A. Kastania (Eds.), *E-health systems quality and reliability: Models and standards* (pp. 220–243). Hershey, PA: Medical Information Science Reference.

Ferullo, D. L., & Soules, A. (2012). Managing copyright in a digital world. [IJDLS]. *International Journal of Digital Library Systems*, *3*(4), 1–25. doi:10.4018/ijdls.2012100101

Fichtner, J. R., & Simpson, L. A. (2013). Legal issues facing companies with products in a digital format. In *Digital rights management: Concepts, methodologies, tools, and applications* (pp. 1334–1354). Hershey, PA: Information Science Reference.

Fichtner, J. R., & Simpson, L. A. (2011). Legal issues facing companies with products in a digital format. In T. Strader (Ed.), *Digital product management, technology and practice: Interdisciplinary perspectives* (pp. 32–52). Hershey, PA: Business Science Reference.

Folmer, E. (2012). BOMOS: Management and development model for open standards. In E. Kajan, F. Dorloff, & I. Bedini (Eds.), *Handbook of research on e-business standards and protocols: Documents, data and advanced web technologies* (pp. 102–128). Hershey, PA: Business Science Reference.

Fomin, V. V. (2012). Standards as hybrids: An essay on tensions and juxtapositions in contemporary standardization. [IJITSR]. *International Journal of IT Standards and Standardization Research*, *10*(2), 59–68. doi:10.4018/jitsr.2012070105

Fomin, V. V., & Matinmikko, M. (2014). The role of standards in the development of new informational infrastructure. In M. Khosrow-Pour (Ed.), *Systems and software development, modeling, and analysis: New perspectives and methodologies* (pp. 149–160). Hershey, PA: Information Science Reference.

Fomin, V. V., Medeisis, A., & Vitkute-Adžgauskiene, D. (2012). Pre-standardization of cognitive radio systems. [IJITSR]. *International Journal of IT Standards and Standardization Research*, *10*(1), 1–16. doi:10.4018/jitsr.2012010101

Francia, G. A., & Hutchinson, F. S. (2014). Regulatory and policy compliance with regard to identity theft prevention, detection, and response. In *Crisis management: Concepts, methodologies, tools and applications* (pp. 280–310). Hershey, PA: Information Science Reference.

Francia, G., & Hutchinson, F. S. (2012). Regulatory and policy compliance with regard to identity theft prevention, detection, and response. In T. Chou (Ed.), *Information assurance and security technologies for risk assessment and threat management: Advances* (pp. 292–322). Hershey, PA: Information Science Reference.

Fulkerson, D. M. (2012). Copyright. In D. Fulkerson (Ed.), *Remote access technologies for library collections: Tools for library users and managers* (pp. 33–48). Hershey, PA: Information Science Reference.

Gaur, R. (2013). Facilitating access to Indian cultural heritage: Copyright, permission rights and ownership issues vis-à-vis IGNCA collections. In *Digital rights management: Concepts, methodologies, tools, and applications* (pp. 817–833). Hershey, PA: Information Science Reference.

Galinski, C., & Beckmann, H. (2014). Concepts for enhancing content quality and eaccessibility: In general and in the field of eprocurement. In *Assistive technologies: Concepts, methodologies, tools, and applications* (pp. 180–197). Hershey, PA: Information Science Reference.

Geiger, C. (2013). Copyright and digital libraries: Securing access to information in the digital age. In *Digital rights management: Concepts, methodologies, tools, and applications* (pp. 99–114). Hershey, PA: Information Science Reference.

Geiger, C. (2011). Copyright and digital libraries: Securing access to information in the digital age. In I. Iglezakis, T. Synodinou, & S. Kapidakis (Eds.), *E-publishing and digital libraries: Legal and organizational issues* (pp. 257–272). Hershey, PA: Information Science Reference.

Gencer, M. (2012). The evolution of IETF standards and their production. [IJITSR]. *International Journal of IT Standards and Standardization Research*, *10*(1), 17–33. doi:10.4018/jitsr.2012010102

Gillam, L., & Vartapetiance, A. (2014). Gambling with laws and ethics in cyberspace. In R. Luppicini (Ed.), *Evolving issues surrounding technoethics and society in the digital age* (pp. 149–170). Hershey, PA: Information Science Reference.

Grandinetti, L., Pisacane, O., & Sheikhalishahi, M. (2014). Standardization. In *Pervasive cloud computing technologies: Future outlooks and interdisciplinary perspectives* (pp. 75–96). Hershey, PA: Information Science Reference.

Grant, S., & Young, R. (2013). Concepts and standardization in areas relating to competence. In K. Jakobs (Ed.), *Innovations in organizational IT specification and standards development* (pp. 264–280). Hershey, PA: Information Science Reference.

Grassetti, M., & Brookby, S. (2013). Using the iPad to develop preservice teachers' understanding of the common core state standards for mathematical practice. In D. Polly (Ed.), *Common core mathematics standards and implementing digital technologies* (pp. 370–386). Hershey, PA: Information Science Reference.

Gray, P. J. (2012). CDIO Standards and quality assurance: From application to accreditation. [IJQAETE]. *International Journal of Quality Assurance in Engineering and Technology Education*, *2*(2), 1–8. doi:10.4018/ijqaete.2012040101

Graz, J., & Hauert, C. (2013). The INTERNORM project: Bridging two worlds of expert- and lay-knowledge in standardization. In K. Jakobs (Ed.), *Innovations in organizational IT specification and standards development* (pp. 154–164). Hershey, PA: Information Science Reference.

Graz, J., & Hauert, C. (2011). The INTERNORM project: Bridging two worlds of expert- and lay-knowledge in standardization. [IJITSR]. *International Journal of IT Standards and Standardization Research*, *9*(1), 52–62. doi:10.4018/jitsr.2011010103

Grobler, M. (2013). The need for digital evidence standardisation. In C. Li (Ed.), *Emerging digital forensics applications for crime detection, prevention, and security* (pp. 234–245). Hershey, PA: Information Science Reference.

Grobler, M. (2012). The need for digital evidence standardisation. [IJDCF]. *International Journal of Digital Crime and Forensics*, *4*(2), 1–12. doi:10.4018/jdcf.2012040101

Guest, C. L., & Guest, J. M. (2011). Legal issues in the use of technology in higher education: Copyright and privacy in the academy. In D. Surry, R. Gray Jr, & J. Stefurak (Eds.), *Technology integration in higher education: Social and organizational aspects* (pp. 72–85). Hershey, PA: Information Science Reference.

Gupta, A., Gantz, D. A., Sreecharana, D., & Kreyling, J. (2012). The interplay of offshoring of professional services, law, intellectual property, and international organizations. [IJSITA]. *International Journal of Strategic Information Technology and Applications*, *3*(2), 47–71. doi:10.4018/jsita.2012040104

Hai-Jew, S. (2011). Staying legal and ethical in global e-learning course and training developments: An exploration. In V. Wang (Ed.), *Encyclopedia of information communication technologies and adult education integration* (pp. 958–970). Hershey, PA: Information Science Reference.

Halder, D., & Jaishankar, K. (2012). Cyber space regulations for protecting women in UK. In *Cyber crime and the victimization of women: Laws, rights and regulations* (pp. 95–104). Hershey, PA: Information Science Reference.

Han, M., & Cho, C. (2013). XML in library cataloging workflows: Working with diverse sources and metadata standards. In J. Tramullas, & P. Garrido (Eds.), *Library automation and OPAC 2.0: Information access and services in the 2.0 landscape* (pp. 59–72). Hershey, PA: Information Science Reference.

Hanseth, O., & Nielsen, P. (2013). Infrastructural innovation: Flexibility, generativity and the mobile internet. [IJITSR]. *International Journal of IT Standards and Standardization Research, 11*(1), 27–45. doi:10.4018/jitsr.2013010102

Hartong, M., & Wijesekera, D. (2012). U.S. regulatory requirements for positive train control systems. In F. Flammini (Ed.), *Railway safety, reliability, and security: Technologies and systems engineering* (pp. 1–21). Hershey, PA: Information Science Reference.

Hasan, H. (2011). Formal and emergent standards in KM. In D. Schwartz, & D. Te'eni (Eds.), *Encyclopedia of knowledge management* (2nd ed., pp. 331–342). Hershey, PA: Information Science Reference.

Hatzimihail, N. (2011). Copyright infringement of digital libraries and private international law: Jurisdiction issues. In I. Iglezakis, T. Synodinou, & S. Kapidakis (Eds.), *E-publishing and digital libraries: Legal and organizational issues* (pp. 447–460). Hershey, PA: Information Science Reference.

Hauert, C. (2013). Where are you? Consumers' associations in standardization: A case study on Switzerland. In K. Jakobs (Ed.), *Innovations in organizational IT specification and standards development* (pp. 139–153). Hershey, PA: Information Science Reference.

Hawks, V. D., & Ekstrom, J. J. (2011). Balancing policies, principles, and philosophy in information assurance. In M. Dark (Ed.), *Information assurance and security ethics in complex systems: Interdisciplinary perspectives* (pp. 32–54). Hershey, PA: Information Science Reference.

Henningsson, S. (2012). International e-customs standardization from the perspective of a global company. [IJITSR]. *International Journal of IT Standards and Standardization Research, 10*(2), 45–58. doi:10.4018/jitsr.2012070104

Hensberry, K. K., Paul, A. J., Moore, E. B., Podolefsky, N. S., & Perkins, K. K. (2013). PhET interactive simulations: New tools to achieve common core mathematics standards. In D. Polly (Ed.), *Common core mathematics standards and implementing digital technologies* (pp. 147–167). Hershey, PA: Information Science Reference.

Heravi, B. R., & Lycett, M. (2012). Semantically enriched e-business standards development: The case of ebXML business process specification schema. In E. Kajan, F. Dorloff, & I. Bedini (Eds.), *Handbook of research on e-business standards and protocols: Documents, data and advanced web technologies* (pp. 655–675). Hershey, PA: Business Science Reference.

Higuera, J., & Polo, J. (2012). Interoperability in wireless sensor networks based on IEEE 1451 standard. In N. Zaman, K. Ragab, & A. Abdullah (Eds.), *Wireless sensor networks and energy efficiency: Protocols, routing and management* (pp. 47–69). Hershey, PA: Information Science Reference.

Hill, D. S. (2013). An examination of standardized product identification and business benefit. In *Supply chain management: Concepts, methodologies, tools, and applications* (pp. 171–195). Hershey, PA: Business Science Reference.

Hill, D. S. (2012). An examination of standardized product identification and business benefit. In E. Kajan, F. Dorloff, & I. Bedini (Eds.), *Handbook of research on e-business standards and protocols: Documents, data and advanced web technologies* (pp. 387–411). Hershey, PA: Business Science Reference.

Holloway, K. (2012). Fair use, copyright, and academic integrity in an online academic environment. In V. Wang (Ed.), *Encyclopedia of e-leadership, counseling and training* (pp. 298–309). Hershey, PA: Information Science Reference.

Hoops, D. S. (2011). Legal issues in the virtual world and e-commerce. In B. Ciaramitaro (Ed.), *Virtual worlds and e-commerce: Technologies and applications for building customer relationships* (pp. 186–204). Hershey, PA: Business Science Reference.

Hoops, D. S. (2012). Lost in cyberspace: Navigating the legal issues of e-commerce. [JECO]. *Journal of Electronic Commerce in Organizations*, *10*(1), 33–51. doi:10.4018/jeco.2012010103

Hopkinson, A. (2012). Establishing the digital library: Don't ignore the library standards and don't forget the training needed. In A. Tella, & A. Issa (Eds.), *Library and information science in developing countries: Contemporary issues* (pp. 195–204). Hershey, PA: Information Science Reference.

Hua, G. B. (2013). The construction industry and standardization of information. In *Implementing IT business strategy in the construction industry* (pp. 47–66). Hershey, PA: Business Science Reference.

Huang, C., & Lin, H. (2011). Patent infringement risk analysis using rough set theory. In Q. Zhang, R. Segall, & M. Cao (Eds.), *Visual analytics and interactive technologies: Data, text and web mining applications* (pp. 123–150). Hershey, PA: Information Science Reference.

Huang, C., Tseng, T. B., & Lin, H. (2013). Patent infringement risk analysis using rough set theory. In *Digital rights management: Concepts, methodologies, tools, and applications* (pp. 1225–1251). Hershey, PA: Information Science Reference.

Iyamu, T. (2013). The impact of organisational politics on the implementation of IT strategy: South African case in context. In J. Abdelnour-Nocera (Ed.), *Knowledge and technological development effects on organizational and social structures* (pp. 167–193). Hershey, PA: Information Science Reference.

Jacinto, K., Neto, F. M., Leite, C. R., & Jacinto, K. (2014). Accessibility in u-learning: Standards, legislation, and future visions. In F. Neto (Ed.), *Technology platform innovations and forthcoming trends in ubiquitous learning* (pp. 215–236). Hershey, PA: Information Science Reference.

Jakobs, K., Wagner, T., & Reimers, K. (2011). Standardising the internet of things: What the experts think. [IJITSR]. *International Journal of IT Standards and Standardization Research*, *9*(1), 63–67. doi:10.4018/jitsr.2011010104

Juzoji, H. (2012). Legal bases for medical supervision via mobile telecommunications in Japan. [IJEHMC]. *International Journal of E-Health and Medical Communications*, *3*(1), 33–45. doi:10.4018/jehmc.2012010103

Kallinikou, D., Papadopoulos, M., Kaponi, A., & Strakantouna, V. (2013). Intellectual property issues for digital libraries at the intersection of law, technology, and the public interest. In *Digital rights management: Concepts, methodologies, tools, and applications* (pp. 1043–1090). Hershey, PA: Information Science Reference.

Kallinikou, D., Papadopoulos, M., Kaponi, A., & Strakantouna, V. (2011). Intellectual property issues for digital libraries at the intersection of law, technology, and the public interest. In I. Iglezakis, T. Synodinou, & S. Kapidakis (Eds.), *E-publishing and digital libraries: Legal and organizational issues* (pp. 294–341). Hershey, PA: Information Science Reference.

Kaupins, G. (2012). Laws associated with mobile computing in the cloud. [IJWNBT]. *International Journal of Wireless Networks and Broadband Technologies, 2*(3), 1–9. doi:10.4018/ijwnbt.2012070101

Kaur, P., & Singh, H. (2013). Component certification process and standards. In H. Singh, & K. Kaur (Eds.), *Designing, engineering, and analyzing reliable and efficient software* (pp. 22–39). Hershey, PA: Information Science Reference.

Kayem, A. V. (2013). Security in service oriented architectures: Standards and challenges. In *Digital rights management: Concepts, methodologies, tools, and applications* (pp. 50–73). Hershey, PA: Information Science Reference.

Kemp, M. L., Robb, S., & Deans, P. C. (2013). The legal implications of cloud computing. In A. Bento, & A. Aggarwal (Eds.), *Cloud computing service and deployment models: Layers and management* (pp. 257–272). Hershey, PA: Business Science Reference.

Khansa, L., & Liginlal, D. (2012). Regulatory influence and the imperative of innovation in identity and access management. [IRMJ]. *Information Resources Management Journal, 25*(3), 78–97. doi:10.4018/irmj.2012070104

Kim, E. (2012). Government policies to promote production and consumption of renewable electricity in the US. In M. Tortora (Ed.), *Sustainable systems and energy management at the regional level: Comparative approaches* (pp. 1–18). Hershey, PA: Information Science Reference.

Kinsell, C. (2014). Technology and disability laws, regulations, and rights. In B. DaCosta, & S. Seok (Eds.), *Assistive technology research, practice, and theory* (pp. 75–87). Hershey, PA: Medical Information Science Reference.

Kitsiou, S. (2010). Overview and analysis of electronic health record standards. In J. Rodrigues (Ed.), *Health information systems: Concepts, methodologies, tools, and applications* (pp. 374–392). Hershey, PA: Medical Information Science Reference.

Kloss, J. H., & Schickel, P. (2011). X3D: A secure ISO standard for virtual worlds. In A. Rea (Ed.), *Security in virtual worlds, 3D webs, and immersive environments: Models for development, interaction, and management* (pp. 208–220). Hershey, PA: Information Science Reference.

Kotsonis, E., & Eliakis, S. (2013). Information security standards for health information systems: The implementer's approach. In *User-driven healthcare: Concepts, methodologies, tools, and applications* (pp. 225–257). Hershey, PA: Medical Information Science Reference.

Kotsonis, E., & Eliakis, S. (2011). Information security standards for health information systems: The implementer's approach. In A. Chryssanthou, I. Apostolakis, & I. Varlamis (Eds.), *Certification and security in health-related web applications: Concepts and solutions* (pp. 113–145). Hershey, PA: Medical Information Science Reference.

Koumaras, H., & Kourtis, M. (2013). A survey on video coding principles and standards. In R. Farrugia, & C. Debono (Eds.), *Multimedia networking and coding* (pp. 1–27). Hershey, PA: Information Science Reference.

Krupinski, E. A., Antoniotti, N., & Burdick, A. (2011). Standards and guidelines development in the american telemedicine association. In A. Moumtzoglou, & A. Kastania (Eds.), *E-health systems quality and reliability: Models and standards* (pp. 244–252). Hershey, PA: Medical Information Science Reference.

Kuanpoth, J. (2013). Biotechnological patents and morality: A critical view from a developing country. In *Digital rights management: Concepts, methodologies, tools, and applications* (pp. 1417–1427). Hershey, PA: Information Science Reference.

Kuanpoth, J. (2011). Biotechnological patents and morality: A critical view from a developing country. In S. Hongladarom (Ed.), *Genomics and bioethics: Interdisciplinary perspectives, technologies and advancements* (pp. 141–151). Hershey, PA: Medical Information Science Reference.

Kulmala, R., & Kettunen, J. (2012). Intellectual property protection and process modeling in small knowledge intensive enterprises. In *Organizational learning and knowledge: Concepts, methodologies, tools and applications* (pp. 2963–2980). Hershey, PA: Business Science Reference.

Kulmala, R., & Kettunen, J. (2013). Intellectual property protection in small knowledge intensive enterprises. [IJCWT]. *International Journal of Cyber Warfare & Terrorism*, 3(1), 29–45. doi:10.4018/ijcwt.2013010103

Küster, M. W. (2012). Standards for achieving interoperability of egovernment in Europe. In E. Kajan, F. Dorloff, & I. Bedini (Eds.), *Handbook of research on e-business standards and protocols: Documents, data and advanced web technologies* (pp. 249–268). Hershey, PA: Business Science Reference.

Kyobe, M. (2011). Factors influencing SME compliance with government regulation on use of IT: The case of South Africa. In F. Tan (Ed.), *International enterprises and global information technologies: Advancing management practices* (pp. 85–116). Hershey, PA: Information Science Reference.

Lam, J. C., & Hills, P. (2013). Promoting technological environmental innovations: The role of environmental regulation. In Z. Luo (Ed.), *Technological solutions for modern logistics and supply chain management* (pp. 230–247). Hershey, PA: Business Science Reference.

Lam, J. C., & Hills, P. (2011). Promoting technological environmental innovations: What is the role of environmental regulation? In Z. Luo (Ed.), *Green finance and sustainability: Environmentally-aware business models and technologies* (pp. 56–73). Hershey, PA: Business Science Reference.

Laporte, C., & Vargas, E. P. (2014). The development of international standards to facilitate process improvements for very small entities. In *Software design and development: Concepts, methodologies, tools, and applications* (pp. 1335–1361). Hershey, PA: Information Science Reference.

Laporte, C., & Vargas, E. P. (2012). The development of international standards to facilitate process improvements for very small entities. In S. Fauzi, M. Nasir, N. Ramli, & S. Sahibuddin (Eds.), *Software process improvement and management: Approaches and tools for practical development* (pp. 34–61). Hershey, PA: Information Science Reference.

Lautman, R., & Curran, K. (2013). The problems of jurisdiction on the internet. In K. Curran (Ed.), *Pervasive and ubiquitous technology innovations for ambient intelligence environments* (pp. 164–170). Hershey, PA: Information Science Reference.

Layne-Farrar, A., & Padilla, A. J. (2013). Assessing the link between standards and patents. In K. Jakobs (Ed.), *Innovations in organizational IT specification and standards development* (pp. 19–51). Hershey, PA: Information Science Reference.

Layne-Farrar, A., & Padilla, A. J. (2011). Assessing the link between standards and patents. [IJITSR]. *International Journal of IT Standards and Standardization Research*, *9*(2), 19–49. doi:10.4018/jitsr.2011070102

Layne-Farrar, A. (2013). Innovative or indefensible? An empirical assessment of patenting within standard setting. In K. Jakobs (Ed.), *Innovations in organizational IT specification and standards development* (pp. 1–18). Hershey, PA: Information Science Reference.

Layne-Farrar, A. (2011). Innovative or indefensible? An empirical assessment of patenting within standard setting. [IJITSR]. *International Journal of IT Standards and Standardization Research*, *9*(2), 1–18. doi:10.4018/jitsr.2011070101

Lee, H., & Huh, J. C. (2012). Korea's strategies for ICT standards internationalisation: A comparison with China's. [IJITSR]. *International Journal of IT Standards and Standardization Research*, *10*(2), 1–13. doi:10.4018/jitsr.2012070101

Li, Y., & Wei, C. (2011). Digital image authentication: A review. [IJDLS]. *International Journal of Digital Library Systems*, *2*(2), 55–78. doi:10.4018/jdls.2011040104

Li, Y., Xiao, X., Feng, X., & Yan, H. (2012). Adaptation and localization: Metadata research and development for Chinese digital resources. [IJDLS]. *International Journal of Digital Library Systems*, *3*(1), 1–21. doi:10.4018/jdls.2012010101

Lim, W., & Kim, D. (2013). Do technologies support the implementation of the common core state standards in mathematics of high school probability and statistics? In D. Polly (Ed.), *Common core mathematics standards and implementing digital technologies* (pp. 168–183). Hershey, PA: Information Science Reference.

Linton, J., & Stegall, D. (2013). Common core standards for mathematical practice and TPACK: An integrated approach to instruction. In D. Polly (Ed.), *Common core mathematics standards and implementing digital technologies* (pp. 234–249). Hershey, PA: Information Science Reference.

Liotta, A., & Liotta, A. (2011). Privacy in pervasive systems: Legal framework and regulatory challenges. In A. Malatras (Ed.), *Pervasive computing and communications design and deployment: Technologies, trends and applications* (pp. 263–277). Hershey, PA: Information Science Reference.

Lissoni, F. (2013). Academic patenting in Europe: Recent research and new perspectives. In I. Yetkiner, M. Pamukcu, & E. Erdil (Eds.), *Industrial dynamics, innovation policy, and economic growth through technological advancements* (pp. 75–91). Hershey, PA: Information Science Reference.

Litaay, T., Prananingrum, D. H., & Krisanto, Y. A. (2013). Indonesian legal perspectives on biotechnology and intellectual property rights. In *Digital rights management: Concepts, methodologies, tools, and applications* (pp. 834–845). Hershey, PA: Information Science Reference.

Litaay, T., Prananingrum, D. H., & Krisanto, Y. A. (2011). Indonesian legal perspectives on biotechnology and intellectual property rights. In S. Hongladarom (Ed.), *Genomics and bioethics: Interdisciplinary perspectives, technologies and advancements* (pp. 171–183). Hershey, PA: Medical Information Science Reference.

Losavio, M., Pastukhov, P., & Polyakova, S. (2014). Regulatory aspects of cloud computing in business environments. In S. Srinivasan (Ed.), *Security, trust, and regulatory aspects of cloud computing in business environments* (pp. 156–169). Hershey, PA: Information Science Reference.

Lu, B., Tsou, B. K., Jiang, T., Zhu, J., & Kwong, O. Y. (2011). Mining parallel knowledge from comparable patents. In W. Wong, W. Liu, & M. Bennamoun (Eds.), *Ontology learning and knowledge discovery using the web: Challenges and recent advances* (pp. 247–271). Hershey, PA: Information Science Reference.

Lucas-Schloetter, A. (2011). Digital libraries and copyright issues: Digitization of contents and the economic rights of the authors. In I. Iglezakis, T. Synodinou, & S. Kapidakis (Eds.), *E-publishing and digital libraries: Legal and organizational issues* (pp. 159–179). Hershey, PA: Information Science Reference.

Lyytinen, K., Keil, T., & Fomin, V. (2010). A framework to build process theories of anticipatory information and communication technology (ICT) standardizing. In K. Jakobs (Ed.), *New applications in IT standards: Developments and progress* (pp. 147–186). Hershey, PA: Information Science Reference.

Macedo, M., & Isaías, P. (2013). Standards related to interoperability in EHR & HS. In M. Sicilia, & P. Balazote (Eds.), *Interoperability in healthcare information systems: Standards, management, and technology* (pp. 19–44). Hershey, PA: Medical Information Science Reference.

Madden, P. (2011). Greater accountability, less red tape: The Australian standard business reporting experience. [IJEBR]. *International Journal of E-Business Research*, *7*(2), 1–10. doi:10.4018/jebr.2011040101

Maravilhas, S. (2014). Quality improves the value of patent information to promote innovation. In G. Jamil, A. Malheiro, & F. Ribeiro (Eds.), *Rethinking the conceptual base for new practical applications in information value and quality* (pp. 61–82). Hershey, PA: Information Science Reference.

Marshall, S. (2011). E-learning standards: Beyond technical standards to guides for professional practice. In F. Lazarinis, S. Green, & E. Pearson (Eds.), *Handbook of research on e-learning standards and interoperability: Frameworks and issues* (pp. 170–192). Hershey, PA: Information Science Reference.

Martino, L., & Bertino, E. (2012). Security for web services: Standards and research issues. In L. Jie-Zhang (Ed.), *Innovations, standards and practices of web services: Emerging research topics* (pp. 336–362). Hershey, PA: Information Science Reference.

McCarthy, V., & Hulsart, R. (2012). Management education for integrity: Raising ethical standards in online management classes. In C. Wankel, & A. Stachowicz-Stanusch (Eds.), *Handbook of research on teaching ethics in business and management education* (pp. 413–425). Hershey, PA: Information Science Reference.

McGrath, T. (2012). The reality of using standards for electronic business document formats. In E. Kajan, F. Dorloff, & I. Bedini (Eds.), *Handbook of research on e-business standards and protocols: Documents, data and advanced web technologies* (pp. 21–32). Hershey, PA: Business Science Reference.

Medlin, B. D., & Chen, C. C. (2012). A global perspective of laws and regulations dealing with information security and privacy. In *Cyber crime: Concepts, methodologies, tools and applications* (pp. 1349–1363). Hershey, PA: Information Science Reference.

Mehrfard, H., & Hamou-Lhadj, A. (2013). The impact of regulatory compliance on agile software processes with a focus on the FDA guidelines for medical device software. In J. Krogstie (Ed.), *Frameworks for developing efficient information systems: Models, theory, and practice* (pp. 298–314). Hershey, PA: Engineering Science Reference.

Mehrfard, H., & Hamou-Lhadj, A. (2011). The impact of regulatory compliance on agile software processes with a focus on the FDA guidelines for medical device software. [IJISMD]. *International Journal of Information System Modeling and Design*, *2*(2), 67–81. doi:10.4018/jismd.2011040104

Mendoza, R. A., & Ravichandran, T. (2012). An empirical evaluation of the assimilation of industry-specific data standards using firm-level and community-level constructs. In M. Tavana (Ed.), *Enterprise information systems and advancing business solutions: Emerging models* (pp. 287–312). Hershey, PA: Business Science Reference.

Mendoza, R. A., & Ravichandran, T. (2013). An exploratory analysis of the relationship between organizational and institutional factors shaping the assimilation of vertical standards. In K. Jakobs (Ed.), *Innovations in organizational IT specification and standards development* (pp. 193–221). Hershey, PA: Information Science Reference.

Mendoza, R. A., & Ravichandran, T. (2011). An exploratory analysis of the relationship between organizational and institutional factors shaping the assimilation of vertical standards. [IJITSR]. *International Journal of IT Standards and Standardization Research*, *9*(1), 24–51. doi:10.4018/jitsr.2011010102

Mendoza, R. A., & Ravichandran, T. (2012). Drivers of organizational participation in XML-based industry standardization efforts. In M. Tavana (Ed.), *Enterprise information systems and advancing business solutions: Emerging models* (pp. 268–286). Hershey, PA: Business Science Reference.

Mense, E. G., Fulwiler, J. H., Richardson, M. D., & Lane, K. E. (2011). Standardization, hybridization, or individualization: Marketing IT to a diverse clientele. In U. Demiray, & S. Sever (Eds.), *Marketing online education programs: Frameworks for promotion and communication* (pp. 291–299). Hershey, PA: Information Science Reference.

Metaxa, E., Sarigiannidis, M., & Folinas, D. (2012). Legal issues of the French law on creation and internet (Hadopi 1 and 2). [IJT]. *International Journal of Technoethics*, *3*(3), 21–36. doi:10.4018/jte.2012070102

Meyer, N. (2012). Standardization as governance without government: A critical reassessment of the digital video broadcasting project's success story. [IJITSR]. *International Journal of IT Standards and Standardization Research*, *10*(2), 14–28. doi:10.4018/jitsr.2012070102

Miguel da Silva, F., Neto, F. M., Burlamaqui, A. M., Pinto, J. P., Fernandes, C. E., & Castro de Souza, R. (2014). T-SCORM: An extension of the SCORM standard to support the project of educational contents for t-learning. In F. Neto (Ed.), *Technology platform innovations and forthcoming trends in ubiquitous learning* (pp. 94–119). Hershey, PA: Information Science Reference.

Moon, A. (2014). Copyright and licensing essentials for librarians and copyright owners in the digital age. In N. Patra, B. Kumar, & A. Pani (Eds.), *Progressive trends in electronic resource management in libraries* (pp. 106–117). Hershey, PA: Information Science Reference.

Moralis, A., Pouli, V., Grammatikou, M., Kalogeras, D., & Maglaris, V. (2012). Security standards and issues for grid computing. In *Grid and cloud computing: Concepts, methodologies, tools and applications* (pp. 1656–1671). Hershey, PA: Information Science Reference.

Moreno, L., Iglesias, A., Calvo, R., Delgado, S., & Zaragoza, L. (2012). Disability standards and guidelines for learning management systems: Evaluating accessibility. In R. Babo, & A. Azevedo (Eds.), *Higher education institutions and learning management systems: Adoption and standardization* (pp. 199–218). Hershey, PA: Information Science Reference.

Moro, N. (2013). Digital rights management and corporate hegemony: Avenues for reform. In H. Rahman, & I. Ramos (Eds.), *Ethical data mining applications for socio-economic development* (pp. 281–299). Hershey, PA: Information Science Reference.

Mula, D., & Lobina, M. L. (2013). Legal protection of the web page. In *Digital rights management: Concepts, methodologies, tools, and applications* (pp. 1–18). Hershey, PA: Information Science Reference.

Mula, D., & Lobina, M. L. (2012). Legal protection of the web page. In H. Sasaki (Ed.), *Information technology for intellectual property protection: Interdisciplinary advancements* (pp. 213–236). Hershey, PA: Information Science Reference.

Mulcahy, D. (2013). Performativity in practice: An actor-network account of professional teaching standards. In A. Tatnall (Ed.), *Social and professional applications of actor-network theory for technology development* (pp. 1–16). Hershey, PA: Information Science Reference.

Mulcahy, D. (2011). Performativity in practice: An actor-network account of professional teaching standards. [IJANTTI]. *International Journal of Actor-Network Theory and Technological Innovation, 3*(2), 1–16. doi:10.4018/jantti.2011040101

Mustaffa, M. T. (2012). Multi-standard multi-band reconfigurable LNA. In A. Marzuki, A. Rahim, & M. Loulou (Eds.), *Advances in monolithic microwave integrated circuits for wireless systems: Modeling and design technologies* (pp. 1–23). Hershey, PA: Engineering Science Reference.

Nabi, S. I., Al-Ghmlas, G. S., & Alghathbar, K. (2014). Enterprise information security policies, standards, and procedures: A survey of available standards and guidelines. In *Crisis management: Concepts, methodologies, tools and applications* (pp. 750–773). Hershey, PA: Information Science Reference.

Nabi, S. I., Al-Ghmlas, G. S., & Alghathbar, K. (2012). Enterprise information security policies, standards, and procedures: A survey of available standards and guidelines. In M. Gupta, J. Walp, & R. Sharman (Eds.), *Strategic and practical approaches for information security governance: Technologies and applied solutions* (pp. 67–89). Hershey, PA: Information Science Reference.

Naixiao, Z., & Chunhua, H. (2013). Research on open innovation in China: Focus on intellectual property rights and their operation in Chinese enterprises. In *Digital rights management: Concepts, methodologies, tools, and applications* (pp. 714–720). Hershey, PA: Information Science Reference.

Naixiao, Z., & Chunhua, H. (2012). Research on open innovation in China: Focus on intellectual property rights and their operation in Chinese enterprises. [IJABIM]. *International Journal of Asian Business and Information Management, 3*(1), 65–71. doi:10.4018/jabim.2012010106

Ndjetcheu, L. (2013). Social responsibility and legal financial communication in African companies in the south of the Sahara: Glance from the OHADA accounting law viewpoint. [IJIDE]. *International Journal of Innovation in the Digital Economy, 4*(4), 1–17. doi:10.4018/ijide.2013100101

Ng, W. L. (2013). Improving long-term financial risk forecasts using high-frequency data and scaling laws. In B. Alexandrova-Kabadjova, S. Martinez-Jaramillo, A. Garcia-Almanza, & E. Tsang (Eds.), *Simulation in computational finance and economics: Tools and emerging applications* (pp. 255–278). Hershey, PA: Business Science Reference.

Noury, N., Bourquard, K., Bergognon, D., & Schroeder, J. (2013). Regulations initiatives in France for the interoperability of communicating medical devices. [IJEHMC]. *International Journal of E-Health and Medical Communications, 4*(2), 50–64. doi:10.4018/jehmc.2013040104

Null, E. (2013). Legal and political barriers to municipal networks in the United States. In A. Abdelaal (Ed.), *Social and economic effects of community wireless networks and infrastructures* (pp. 27–56). Hershey, PA: Information Science Reference.

O'Connor, R. V., & Laporte, C. Y. (2014). An innovative approach to the development of an international software process lifecycle standard for very small entities. [IJITSA]. *International Journal of Information Technologies and Systems Approach, 7*(1), 1–22. doi:10.4018/ijitsa.2014010101

Onat, I., & Miri, A. (2013). RFID standards. In A. Miri (Ed.), *Advanced security and privacy for RFID technologies* (pp. 14–22). Hershey, PA: Information Science Reference.

Orton, I., Alva, A., & Endicott-Popovsky, B. (2013). Legal process and requirements for cloud forensic investigations. In K. Ruan (Ed.), *Cybercrime and cloud forensics: Applications for investigation processes* (pp. 186–229). Hershey, PA: Information Science Reference.

Ortt, J. R., & Egyedi, T. M. (2014). The effect of pre-existing standards and regulations on the development and diffusion of radically new innovations. [IJITSR]. *International Journal of IT Standards and Standardization Research, 12*(1), 17–37. doi:10.4018/ijitsr.2014010102

Ozturk, Y., & Sharma, J. (2013). mVITAL: A standards compliant vital sign monitor. In IT policy and ethics: Concepts, methodologies, tools, and applications (pp. 515-538). Hershey, PA: Information Science Reference. doi:10.4018/978-1-4666-2919-6.ch024

Ozturk, Y., & Sharma, J. (2011). mVITAL: A standards compliant vital sign monitor. In C. Röcker, & M. Ziefle (Eds.), Smart healthcare applications and services: Developments and practices (pp. 174-196). Hershey, PA: Medical Information Science Reference. doi:10.4018/978-1-60960-180-5.ch008

Parsons, T. D. (2011). Affect-sensitive virtual standardized patient interface system. In D. Surry, R. Gray Jr, & J. Stefurak (Eds.), *Technology integration in higher education: Social and organizational aspects* (pp. 201–221). Hershey, PA: Information Science Reference.

Parveen, S., & Pater, C. (2012). Utilizing innovative video chat technology to meet national standards: A Case study on a STARTALK Hindi language program. [IJVPLE]. *International Journal of Virtual and Personal Learning Environments, 3*(3), 1–20. doi:10.4018/jvple.2012070101

Pawlowski, J. M., & Kozlov, D. (2013). Analysis and validation of learning technology models, standards and specifications: The reference model analysis grid (RMAG). In K. Jakobs (Ed.), *Innovations in organizational IT specification and standards development* (pp. 223–240). Hershey, PA: Information Science Reference.

Pina, P. (2013). Between Scylla and Charybdis: The balance between copyright, digital rights management and freedom of expression. In Digital rights management: Concepts, methodologies, tools, and applications (pp. 1355-1367). Hershey, PA: Information Science Reference. doi:10.4018/978-1-4666-2136-7.ch067

Pina, P. (2013). Computer games and intellectual property law: Derivative works, copyright and copyleft. In *Digital rights management: Concepts, methodologies, tools, and applications* (pp. 777–788). Hershey, PA: Information Science Reference.

Pina, P. (2013). The private copy issue: Piracy, copyright and consumers' rights. In *Digital rights management: Concepts, methodologies, tools, and applications* (pp. 1546–1558). Hershey, PA: Information Science Reference.

Pina, P. (2011). The private copy issue: Piracy, copyright and consumers' rights. In T. Strader (Ed.), *Digital product management, technology and practice: Interdisciplinary perspectives* (pp. 193–205). Hershey, PA: Business Science Reference.

Piotrowski, M. (2011). QTI: A failed e-learning standard? In F. Lazarinis, S. Green, & E. Pearson (Eds.), *Handbook of research on e-learning standards and interoperability: Frameworks and issues* (pp. 59–82). Hershey, PA: Information Science Reference.

Ponte, D., & Camussone, P. F. (2013). Neither heroes nor chaos: The victory of VHS against Betamax. [IJANTTI]. *International Journal of Actor-Network Theory and Technological Innovation*, 5(1), 40–54. doi:10.4018/jantti.2013010103

Pradhan, A. (2013). Pivotal role of the ISO 14001 standard in the carbon economy. In K. Ganesh, & S. Anbuudayasankar (Eds.), *International and interdisciplinary studies in green computing* (pp. 38–46). Hershey, PA: Information Science Reference.

Pradhan, A. (2011). Pivotal role of the ISO 14001 standard in the carbon economy. [IJGC]. *International Journal of Green Computing*, 2(1), 38–46. doi:10.4018/jgc.2011010104

Pradhan, A. (2011). Standards and legislation for the carbon economy. In B. Unhelkar (Ed.), *Handbook of research on green ICT: Technology, business and social perspectives* (pp. 592–606). Hershey, PA: Information Science Reference.

Prentzas, J., & Hatzilygeroudis, I. (2011). Techniques, technologies and patents related to intelligent educational systems. In G. Magoulas (Ed.), *E-infrastructures and technologies for lifelong learning: Next generation environments* (pp. 1–28). Hershey, PA: Information Science Reference.

Ramos, I., & Fernandes, J. (2013). Web-based intellectual property marketplace: A survey of current practices. In S. Chhabra (Ed.), *ICT influences on human development, interaction, and collaboration* (pp. 203–213). Hershey, PA: Information Science Reference.

Ramos, I., & Fernandes, J. (2011). Web-based intellectual property marketplace: A survey of current practices. [IJICTHD]. *International Journal of Information Communication Technologies and Human Development*, 3(3), 58–68. doi:10.4018/jicthd.2011070105

Rashmi, R. (2013). Biopharma drugs innovation in India and foreign investment and technology transfer in the changed patent regime. In *Digital rights management: Concepts, methodologies, tools, and applications* (pp. 846–859). Hershey, PA: Information Science Reference.

Rashmi, R. (2011). Biopharma drugs innovation in India and foreign investment and technology transfer in the changed patent regime. In P. Ordóñez de Pablos, W. Lee, & J. Zhao (Eds.), *Regional innovation systems and sustainable development: Emerging technologies* (pp. 210–225). Hershey, PA: Information Science Reference.

Rashmi, R. (2011). Optimal policy for biopharmaceutical drugs innovation and access in India. In P. Ordóñez de Pablos, W. Lee, & J. Zhao (Eds.), *Regional innovation systems and sustainable development: Emerging technologies* (pp. 74–114). Hershey, PA: Information Science Reference.

Reed, C. N. (2011). The open geospatial consortium and web services standards. In P. Zhao, & L. Di (Eds.), *Geospatial web services: Advances in information interoperability* (pp. 1–16). Hershey, PA: Information Science Reference.

Rejas-Muslera, R., Davara, E., Abran, A., & Buglione, L. (2013). Intellectual property systems in software. [IJCWT]. *International Journal of Cyber Warfare & Terrorism*, *3*(1), 1–14. doi:10.4018/ijcwt.2013010101

Rejas-Muslera, R. J., García-Tejedor, A. J., & Rodriguez, O. P. (2011). Open educational resources in e-learning: standards and environment. In F. Lazarinis, S. Green, & E. Pearson (Eds.), *Handbook of research on e-learning standards and interoperability: Frameworks and issues* (pp. 346–359). Hershey, PA: Information Science Reference.

Ries, N. M. (2011). Legal issues in health information and electronic health records. In *Clinical technologies: Concepts, methodologies, tools and applications* (pp. 1948–1961). Hershey, PA: Medical Information Science Reference.

Riillo, C. A. (2013). Profiles and motivations of standardization players. [IJITSR]. *International Journal of IT Standards and Standardization Research*, *11*(2), 17–33. doi:10.4018/jitsr.2013070102

Rodriguez, E., & Lolas, F. (2011). Social issues related to gene patenting in Latin America: A bioethical reflection. In S. Hongladarom (Ed.), *Genomics and bioethics: Interdisciplinary perspectives, technologies and advancements* (pp. 152–170). Hershey, PA: Medical Information Science Reference.

Rutherford, M. (2014). Implementing common core state standards using digital curriculum. In *K-12 education: Concepts, methodologies, tools, and applications* (pp. 383–389). Hershey, PA: Information Science Reference.

Rutherford, M. (2013). Implementing common core state standards using digital curriculum. In D. Polly (Ed.), *Common core mathematics standards and implementing digital technologies* (pp. 38–44). Hershey, PA: Information Science Reference.

Ryan, G., & Shinnick, E. (2011). Knowledge and intellectual property rights: An economics perspective. In D. Schwartz, & D. Te'eni (Eds.), *Encyclopedia of knowledge management* (2nd ed., pp. 489–496). Hershey, PA: Information Science Reference.

Ryoo, J., & Choi, Y. (2011). A taxonomy of green information and communication protocols and standards. In B. Unhelkar (Ed.), *Handbook of research on green ICT: Technology, business and social perspectives* (pp. 364–376). Hershey, PA: Information Science Reference.

Saeed, K., Ziegler, G., & Yaqoob, M. K. (2013). Management practices in exploration and production industry. In S. Saeed, M. Khan, & R. Ahmad (Eds.), *Business strategies and approaches for effective engineering management* (pp. 151–187). Hershey, PA: Business Science Reference.

Saiki, T. (2014). Intellectual property in mergers & acquisitions. In J. Wang (Ed.), *Encyclopedia of business analytics and optimization* (pp. 1275–1283). Hershey, PA: Business Science Reference.

Santos, O., & Boticario, J. (2011). A general framework for inclusive lifelong learning in higher education institutions with adaptive web-based services that support standards. In G. Magoulas (Ed.), *E-infrastructures and technologies for lifelong learning: Next generation environments* (pp. 29–58). Hershey, PA: Information Science Reference.

Santos, O., Boticario, J., Raffenne, E., Granado, J., Rodriguez-Ascaso, A., & Gutierrez y Restrepo, E. (2011). A standard-based framework to support personalisation, adaptation, and interoperability in inclusive learning scenarios. In F. Lazarinis, S. Green, & E. Pearson (Eds.), *Handbook of research on e-learning standards and interoperability: Frameworks and issues* (pp. 126–169). Hershey, PA: Information Science Reference.

Sarabdeen, J. (2012). Legal issues in e-healthcare systems. In M. Watfa (Ed.), *E-healthcare systems and wireless communications: Current and future challenges* (pp. 23–48). Hershey, PA: Medical Information Science Reference.

Sclater, N. (2012). Legal and contractual issues of cloud computing for educational institutions. In L. Chao (Ed.), *Cloud computing for teaching and learning: Strategies for design and implementation* (pp. 186–199). Hershey, PA: Information Science Reference.

Selwyn, L., & Eldridge, V. (2013). Governance and organizational structures. In *Public law librarianship: Objectives, challenges, and solutions* (pp. 41–71). Hershey, PA: Information Science Reference.

Seo, D. (2013). Analysis of various structures of standards setting organizations (SSOs) that impact tension among members. [IJITSR]. *International Journal of IT Standards and Standardization Research, 11*(2), 46–60. doi:10.4018/jitsr.2013070104

Seo, D. (2013). Background of standards strategy. In *Evolution and standardization of mobile communications technology* (pp. 1–17). Hershey, PA: Information Science Reference.

Seo, D. (2013). Developing a theoretical model. In *Evolution and standardization of mobile communications technology* (pp. 18–42). Hershey, PA: Information Science Reference.

Seo, D. (2013). The 1G (first generation) mobile communications technology standards. In *Evolution and standardization of mobile communications technology* (pp. 54–75). Hershey, PA: Information Science Reference.

Seo, D. (2013). The 2G (second generation) mobile communications technology standards. In *Evolution and standardization of mobile communications technology* (pp. 76–114). Hershey, PA: Information Science Reference.

Seo, D. (2013). The 3G (third generation) of mobile communications technology standards. In *Evolution and standardization of mobile communications technology* (pp. 115–161). Hershey, PA: Information Science Reference.

Seo, D. (2013). The significance of government's role in technology standardization: Two cases in the wireless communications industry. In K. Jakobs (Ed.), *Innovations in organizational IT specification and standards development* (pp. 183–192). Hershey, PA: Information Science Reference.

Seo, D. (2012). The significance of government's role in technology standardization: Two cases in the wireless communications industry. In C. Reddick (Ed.), *Cases on public information management and e-government adoption* (pp. 219–231). Hershey, PA: Information Science Reference.

Seo, D., & Koek, J. W. (2012). Are Asian countries ready to lead a global ICT standardization? [IJITSR]. *International Journal of IT Standards and Standardization Research, 10*(2), 29–44. doi:10.4018/jitsr.2012070103

Scheg, A. G. (2014). Common standards for online education found in accrediting organizations. In *Reforming teacher education for online pedagogy development* (pp. 50–76). Hershey, PA: Information Science Reference.

Sharp, R. J., Ewald, J. A., & Kenward, R. (2013). Central information flows and decision-making requirements. In J. Papathanasiou, B. Manos, S. Arampatzis, & R. Kenward (Eds.), *Transactional environmental support system design: Global solutions* (pp. 7–32). Hershey, PA: Information Science Reference.

Shen, X., Graham, I., Stewart, J., & Williams, R. (2013). Standards development as hybridization. [IJITSR]. *International Journal of IT Standards and Standardization Research, 11*(2), 34–45. doi:10.4018/jitsr.2013070103

Sherman, M. (2013). Using technology to engage students with the standards for mathematical practice: The case of DGS. In D. Polly (Ed.), *Common core mathematics standards and implementing digital technologies* (pp. 78–101). Hershey, PA: Information Science Reference.

Singh, J., & Kumar, V. (2013). Compliance and regulatory standards for cloud computing. In R. Khurana, & R. Aggarwal (Eds.), *Interdisciplinary perspectives on business convergence, computing, and legality* (pp. 54–64). Hershey, PA: Business Science Reference.

Singh, S., & Paliwal, M. (2014). Exploring a sense of intellectual property valuation for Indian SMEs. [IJABIM]. *International Journal of Asian Business and Information Management, 5*(1), 15–36. doi:10.4018/ijabim.2014010102

Singh, S., & Siddiqui, T. J. (2013). Robust image data hiding technique for copyright protection. [IJISP]. *International Journal of Information Security and Privacy, 7*(2), 44–56. doi:10.4018/jisp.2013040103

Spies, M., & Tabet, S. (2012). Emerging standards and protocols for governance, risk, and compliance management. In E. Kajan, F. Dorloff, & I. Bedini (Eds.), *Handbook of research on e-business standards and protocols: Documents, data and advanced web technologies* (pp. 768–790). Hershey, PA: Business Science Reference.

Spinello, R. A., & Tavani, H. T. (2008). Intellectual property rights: From theory to practical implementation. In H. Sasaki (Ed.), *Intellectual property protection for multimedia information technology* (pp. 25–69). Hershey, PA: Information Science Reference.

Spyrou, S., Bamidis, P., & Maglaveras, N. (2010). Health information standards: Towards integrated health information networks. In J. Rodrigues (Ed.), *Health information systems: Concepts, methodologies, tools, and applications* (pp. 2145–2159). Hershey, PA: Medical Information Science Reference.

Stanfill, D. (2012). Standards-based educational technology professional development. In V. Wang (Ed.), *Encyclopedia of e-leadership, counseling and training* (pp. 819–834). Hershey, PA: Information Science Reference.

Steen, H. U. (2013). The battle within: An analysis of internal fragmentation in networked technologies based on a comparison of the DVB-H and T-DMB mobile digital multimedia broadcasting standards. In K. Jakobs (Ed.), *Innovations in organizational IT specification and standards development* (pp. 91–114). Hershey, PA: Information Science Reference.

Steen, H. U. (2011). The battle within: An analysis of internal fragmentation in networked technologies based on a comparison of the DVB-H and T-DMB mobile digital multimedia broadcasting standards. [IJITSR]. *International Journal of IT Standards and Standardization Research, 9*(2), 50–71. doi:10.4018/jitsr.2011070103

Stoll, M., & Breu, R. (2012). Information security governance and standard based management systems. In M. Gupta, J. Walp, & R. Sharman (Eds.), *Strategic and practical approaches for information security governance: Technologies and applied solutions* (pp. 261–282). Hershey, PA: Information Science Reference.

Suzuki, O. (2013). Search efforts, selective appropriation, and the usefulness of new knowledge: Evidence from a comparison across U.S. and non-U.S. patent applicants. *International Journal of Knowledge Management (IJKM), 9*(1), 42-59. doi:10.4018/jkm.2013010103

Tajima, M. (2012). The role of technology standardization in RFID adoption: The pharmaceutical context. [IJITSR]. *International Journal of IT Standards and Standardization Research, 10*(1), 48–67. doi:10.4018/jitsr.2012010104

Talevi, A., Castro, E. A., & Bruno-Blanch, L. E. (2012). Virtual screening: An emergent, key methodology for drug development in an emergent continent: A bridge towards patentability. In E. Castro, & A. Haghi (Eds.), *Advanced methods and applications in chemoinformatics: Research progress and new applications* (pp. 229–245). Hershey, PA: Engineering Science Reference.

Tauber, A. (2012). Requirements and properties of qualified electronic delivery systems in egovernment: An Austrian experience. In S. Sharma (Ed.), *E-adoption and technologies for empowering developing countries: Global advances* (pp. 115–128). Hershey, PA: Information Science Reference.

Telesko, R., & Nikles, S. (2012). Semantic-enabled compliance management. In S. Smolnik, F. Teuteberg, & O. Thomas (Eds.), *Semantic technologies for business and information systems engineering: Concepts and applications* (pp. 292–310). Hershey, PA: Business Science Reference.

Tella, A., & Afolabi, A. K. (2013). Internet policy issues and digital libraries' management of intellectual property. In S. Thanuskodi (Ed.), *Challenges of academic library management in developing countries* (pp. 272–284). Hershey, PA: Information Science Reference.

Tiwari, S. C., Gupta, M., Khan, M. A., & Ansari, A. Q. (2013). Intellectual property rights in semi-conductor industries: An Indian perspective. In S. Saeed, M. Khan, & R. Ahmad (Eds.), *Business strategies and approaches for effective engineering management* (pp. 97–110). Hershey, PA: Business Science Reference.

Truyen, F., & Buekens, F. (2013). Professional ICT knowledge, epistemic standards, and social epistemology. In T. Takševa (Ed.), *Social software and the evolution of user expertise: Future trends in knowledge creation and dissemination* (pp. 274–294). Hershey, PA: Information Science Reference.

Tummons, J. (2013). Deconstructing professionalism: An actor-network critique of professional standards for teachers in the UK lifelong learning sector. In A. Tatnall (Ed.), *Social and professional applications of actor-network theory for technology development* (pp. 78–87). Hershey, PA: Information Science Reference.

Tummons, J. (2011). Deconstructing professionalism: An actor-network critique of professional standards for teachers in the UK lifelong learning sector. [IJANTTI]. *International Journal of Actor-Network Theory and Technological Innovation, 3*(4), 22–31. doi:10.4018/jantti.2011100103

Tuohey, W. G. (2014). Lessons from practices and standards in safety-critical and regulated sectors. In I. Ghani, W. Kadir, & M. Ahmad (Eds.), *Handbook of research on emerging advancements and technologies in software engineering* (pp. 369–391). Hershey, PA: Engineering Science Reference.

Tzoulia, E. (2013). Legal issues to be considered before setting in force consumer-centric marketing strategies within the European Union. In H. Kaufmann, & M. Panni (Eds.), *Customer-centric marketing strategies: Tools for building organizational performance* (pp. 36–56). Hershey, PA: Business Science Reference.

Unland, R. (2012). Interoperability support for e-business applications through standards, services, and multi-agent systems. In E. Kajan, F. Dorloff, & I. Bedini (Eds.), *Handbook of research on e-business standards and protocols: Documents, data and advanced web technologies* (pp. 129–153). Hershey, PA: Business Science Reference.

Uslar, M., Grüning, F., & Rohjans, S. (2013). A use case for ontology evolution and interoperability: The IEC utility standards reference framework 62357. In M. Khosrow-Pour (Ed.), *Cases on performance measurement and productivity improvement: Technology integration and maturity* (pp. 387–415). Hershey, PA: Business Science Reference.

van de Kaa, G. (2013). Responsible innovation and standardization: A new research approach? [IJITSR]. *International Journal of IT Standards and Standardization Research, 11*(2), 61–65. doi:10.4018/jitsr.2013070105

van de Kaa, G., Blind, K., & de Vries, H. J. (2013). The challenge of establishing a recognized interdisciplinary journal: A citation analysis of the international journal of IT standards and standardization research. [IJITSR]. *International Journal of IT Standards and Standardization Research, 11*(2), 1–16. doi:10.4018/jitsr.2013070101

Venkataraman, H., Ciubotaru, B., & Muntean, G. (2012). System design perspective: WiMAX standards and IEEE 802.16j based multihop WiMAX. In G. Cornetta, D. Santos, & J. Vazquez (Eds.), *Wireless radio-frequency standards and system design: Advanced techniques* (pp. 287–309). Hershey, PA: Engineering Science Reference.

Vishwakarma, P., & Mukherjee, B. (2014). Knowing protection of intellectual contents in digital era. In N. Patra, B. Kumar, & A. Pani (Eds.), *Progressive trends in electronic resource management in libraries* (pp. 147–165). Hershey, PA: Information Science Reference.

Wasilko, P. J. (2014). Beyond compliance: Understanding the legal aspects of information system administration. In I. Portela, & F. Almeida (Eds.), *Organizational, legal, and technological dimensions of information system administration* (pp. 57–75). Hershey, PA: Information Science Reference.

Wasilko, P. J. (2012). Law, architecture, gameplay, and marketing. In *Computer engineering: concepts, methodologies, tools and applications* (pp. 1660–1677). Hershey, PA: Engineering Science Reference.

Wasilko, P. J. (2011). Law, architecture, gameplay, and marketing. In M. Cruz-Cunha, V. Varvalho, & P. Tavares (Eds.), *Business, technological, and social dimensions of computer games: Multidisciplinary developments* (pp. 476–493). Hershey, PA: Information Science Reference.

White, G. L., Mediavilla, F. A., & Shah, J. R. (2013). Information privacy: Implementation and perception of laws and corporate policies by CEOs and managers. In H. Nemati (Ed.), *Privacy solutions and security frameworks in information protection* (pp. 52–69). Hershey, PA: Information Science Reference.

White, G. L., Mediavilla, F. A., & Shah, J. R. (2011). Information privacy: Implementation and perception of laws and corporate policies by CEOs and managers. [IJISP]. *International Journal of Information Security and Privacy*, 5(1), 50–66. doi:10.4018/jisp.2011010104

Whyte, K. P., List, M., Stone, J. V., Grooms, D., Gasteyer, S., & Thompson, P. B. et al. (2014). Uberveillance, standards, and anticipation: A case study on nanobiosensors in U.S. cattle. In M. Michael, & K. Michael (Eds.), *Uberveillance and the social implications of microchip implants: Emerging technologies* (pp. 260–279). Hershey, PA: Information Science Reference.

Wilkes, W., Reusch, P. J., & Moreno, L. E. (2012). Flexible classification standards for product data exchange. In E. Kajan, F. Dorloff, & I. Bedini (Eds.), *Handbook of research on e-business standards and protocols: Documents, data and advanced web technologies* (pp. 448–466). Hershey, PA: Business Science Reference.

Wittkower, D. E. (2011). Against strong copyright in e-business. In *Global business: Concepts, methodologies, tools and applications* (pp. 2157–2176). Hershey, PA: Business Science Reference.

Wright, D. (2012). Evolution of standards for smart grid communications. [IJITN]. *International Journal of Interdisciplinary Telecommunications and Networking*, 4(1), 47–55. doi:10.4018/jitn.2012010103

Wurster, S. (2013). Development of a specification for data interchange between information systems in public hazard prevention: Dimensions of success and related activities identified by case study research. [IJITSR]. *International Journal of IT Standards and Standardization Research*, 11(1), 46–66. doi:10.4018/jitsr.2013010103

Wyburn, M. (2013). Copyright and ethical issues in emerging models for the digital media reporting of sports news in Australia. In *Digital rights management: Concepts, methodologies, tools, and applications* (pp. 290–309). Hershey, PA: Information Science Reference.

Wyburn, M. (2011). Copyright and ethical issues in emerging models for the digital media reporting of sports news in Australia. In M. Quigley (Ed.), *ICT ethics and security in the 21st century: New developments and applications* (pp. 66–85). Hershey, PA: Information Science Reference.

Xiaohui, T., Yaohui, Z., & Yi, Z. (2013). The management system of enterprises' intellectual property rights: A case study from China. In *Digital rights management: Concepts, methodologies, tools, and applications* (pp. 1092–1106). Hershey, PA: Information Science Reference.

Xiaohui, T., Yaohui, Z., & Yi, Z. (2012). The management system of enterprises' intellectual property rights: A case study from China. [IJABIM]. *International Journal of Asian Business and Information Management*, 3(1), 50–64. doi:10.4018/jabim.2012010105

Xuan, X., & Xiaowei, Z. (2012). The dilemma and resolution: The patentability of traditional Chinese medicine. [IJABIM]. *International Journal of Asian Business and Information Management*, 3(3), 1–8. doi:10.4018/jabim.2012070101

Yang, C., & Lu, Z. (2011). A blind image watermarking scheme utilizing BTC bitplanes. [IJDCF]. *International Journal of Digital Crime and Forensics*, 3(4), 42–53. doi:10.4018/jdcf.2011100104

Yastrebenetsky, M., & Gromov, G. (2014). International standard bases and safety classification. In M. Yastrebenetsky, & V. Kharchenko (Eds.), *Nuclear power plant instrumentation and control systems for safety and security* (pp. 31–60). Hershey, PA: Engineering Science Reference.

Zouag, N., & Kadiri, M. (2014). Intellectual property rights, innovation, and knowledge economy in Arab countries. In A. Driouchi (Ed.), *Knowledge-based economic policy development in the Arab world* (pp. 245–272). Hershey, PA: Business Science Reference.

Compilation of References

DVB Project. (1994a, Sept. 27). *DVB Agrees conditional access Package. Press Release.* Retrieved May 25, 2010, from http://www.DVB.org/documents/press releases/pr005_DVB%20agrees%20conditional%20access%20package.940927. pdf

DVB Project. (2010). *History of the DVB Project.* Retrieved May 25, 2010, from http: //www.DVB.org/about_DVB/history/

DVB Project. (2013, May.). *DVB Fact Sheet.* Retrieved January 25, 2013, from http://www.dvb.org/resources/public/factsheets/DVB-Project_Factsheet.pdf

Aanestad, M., & Jensen, T. B. (2011). Building nation-wide information infrastructures in healthcare through modular implementation strategies. *The Journal of Strategic Information Systems, 20*(2), 161–176. doi:10.1016/j.jsis.2011.03.006

Abbate, J. (1994). The Internet Challenge: Conflict and Compromise in Computer Networking. In J. Summerton (Ed.), *Changing large technical systems* (pp. 193–210). Boulder, CO: Westview Press.

Abbate, J. (1999). *Inventing the Internet.* Cambridge, MA: MIT Press.

Abbott, K., & Snidal, D. (2001). International 'standards' and international governance. *Journal of European Public Policy, 8*(3), 345–370. doi:10.1080/13501760110056013

Abel, I. (2008). From technology imitation to market dominance: The case of iPod. *Journal of Global Competitiveness, 18*(3), 257–274. doi:10.1108/10595420810906028

ACEA. (2010, June 24). *Auto manufacturers agree on specifications to connect electrically chargeable vehicles to the electricity grid.* European Automobile Manufacturers' Association. Retrieved from http://www.acea.be/index.php/news/news_detail/auto_manufacturers_agree_on_specifications_to_connect_electrically_chargeab

Adolphi, H. (1997). *Strategische Konzepte zur Organisation der betrieblichen Standardisierung. DIN Normungskunde*(Vol. 38).Berlin: Beuth Verlag.

Afuah, A. (2013). Are network effects really all about size? The role of structure and conduct. *Strategic Management Journal, 34*(3), 257–273. doi:10.1002/smj.2013

Aggarwal, C. C., & Zhai, C. (2012). A survey of text clustering algorithms. In *Mining text data* (pp. 77–128). Springer. doi:10.1007/978-1-4614-3223-4_4

Ahmed, P. K. (1998). Culture and climate for innovation. *European Journal of Innovation Management, 1*(1), 30–43. doi:10.1108/14601069810199131

Ahrne, G., & Brunsson, N. (2011). Organization outside organizations: The significance of partial organization. *Organization, 18*(1), 83–104. doi:10.1177/1350508410376256

Akerlof, G. (1970). The Market for 'Lemons': Quality Uncertainty and the Market Mechanism. *The Quarterly Journal of Economics, 84*(3), 488–500. doi:10.2307/1879431

Alderman, J. (2001). *Sonic boom: Napster, MP3, and the new pioneers of music.* Cambridge, UK: Perseus Publishing.

Aldrich, H. (1999). Organizations evolving. *Sage (Atlanta, Ga.).*

Allen, R. H., & Sriram, R. D. (2000). The role of standards in innovation. *Technological Forecasting and Social Change, 64*(2-3), 171–181. doi:10.1016/S0040-1625(99)00104-3

Alter, S. (2003). Sorting Out Issues About the Core, Scope, and Identity of the IS Field. *Communications of the AIS, 12*(41).

Alvestrand, H. (2004, September). The role of the standards process in shaping the internet. *Proceedings of the IEEE, 92*(9), 1371–1374. doi:10.1109/JPROC.2004.832973

Anderson, P., & Tushman, M. L. (1990). Technological discontinuities and dominant designs: A cyclical model of technological change. *Administrative Science Quarterly, 35*(4), 604–633. doi:10.2307/2393511

ANEC. (2009). *ANEC Newsletter, No.102–December 2009.* Retrieved from http://www.anec.org/anec.asp?rd=453&ref=02-01.01-01&lang=en&ID=251

Anker, P. (2010) Cognitive radio, the market and the regulator.*Proc. IEEE Symposium on New Frontiers in Dynamic Spectrum Access Networks.* doi:10.1109/DYSPAN.2010.5457912

APEC. (2006). *The eighteenth APEC ministerial meeting joint statement.* Singapore: APEC.

Appelman, J. H., Osseyran, A., & Warnier, M. (Eds.). (2013). Standardization as ecodesign at sector level. In Green ICT & energy: From smart to wise strategies. London: CRC Press.

Apple Inc. (2004, August 10). *iTunes music store catalog tops one million songs.* Retrieved April 29, 2012, from http://www.apple.com/pr/library/2004/08/10iTunes-Music-Store-Catalog-Tops-One-Million-Songs.html

Apple Inc. (n.d.). *Form 10-Q (quarterly report).* Retrieved from http://investor.apple.com/sec.cfm?ndq_keyword=&DocType=Quarterly

Arthur, W.B. (1994). Positive feedbacks in the economy. *The McKinsey Quarterly, 1,* 81-95.

Arthur, W. B. (1989). Competing Technologies, Increasing Returns, and Lock-in by Historical Events. *The Economic Journal, 99*(394), 116–131. doi:10.2307/2234208

Arthur, W. B. (1996, July-August). Increasing Returns and the New World of Business. *Harvard Business Review,* 100–109. PMID:10158472

Augereau, A., Greenstein, S., & Rysman, M. (2006). Coordination versus differentiation in a standards war: 56K modems. *The Rand Journal of Economics, 37*(4), 887–909. doi:10.1111/j.1756-2171.2006.tb00062.x

Auriol, E., & Benaim, M. (2000). Standardization in decentralized economies. *The American Economic Review, 90*(3), 550–570. doi:10.1257/aer.90.3.550

Avital, M., & Te'eni, D. (2009). From Generative Fit to Generative Capacity: Exploring an Emerging Dimension of Information Systems Design and Task Performance. *Information Systems Journal, 19*(4), 345–367. doi:10.1111/j.1365-2575.2007.00291.x

Backhouse, J., Hsu, C., & Leiser, S. (2006). Circuits of power in creating de jure standards: Shaping an international information systems security standard. *Management Information Systems Quarterly, 30*(Special Issue), 413–438.

Baldwin, C. Y., & Woodard, C. J. (2009). The architecture of platforms: A unified view. In *Platforms, Markets and Innovation.* Cheltenham, UK: Edward Elgar Publishing Limited. doi:10.4337/9781849803311.00008

BAN/SVTC. (2002). *Exporting Harm: The High-Tech Trashing of Asia.* Seattle, WA: BAN/SVTC.

Bastian, M., Heymann, S., & Jacomy, M. (2009). Gephi: An open source software for exploring and manipulating networks. In Proceedings of International AAAI Conference on Weblogs and Social Media. AAAI.

Bauer, J. M., Ha, I. S., & Saugstrup, D. (2007). Mobile television: Challenges of advanced service design. *Communications of the Association for Information Systems, 20,* 621–631.

Bauman, Z. (2000). *Liquid modernity.* Cambridge: Polity Press.

Beauvais-Schwartz, N., & Bousquet, F. (2010). *France – Fostering competitive intelligence.* Retrieved May 26, 2010, from http://www.iso.org/iso/iso-focus-plus_index/iso-focusplus_online-bonus-articles/the-2009-iso-award/2009-award_france.htm

Behrens, H. (2010). *Education about Standardization – Competency of Standards Body Staff.* Paper presented at the first meeting of the CEN/CENELEC/ETSI Joint Working Group on Education about Standardization, 2010-03-09. Brussels, Belgium.

Bekkers, R. and Seo, D. (2008). *Quick Scan for Best Practices in ICT Standardization: What ETSI could Learn from Other Standards Bodies.* Utrecht, The Netherlands: Dialogic Innovatie & interactie.

Bekkers, R. (2001). *The development of European mobile telecommunications standards: An assessment of the success of GSM, TETRA, ERMES and UMTS.* Eindhoven: Eindhoven University of Technology.

Bekkers, R., & Seo, D. (2008). *Quick Scan for best practices in ICT standardisation: What ETSI could learn from other standards bodies. Commissioned by the Directorate of Energy and Telecommunications, Dutch Ministry of Economic Affairs.* Utrecht: Dialogic.

Bekkers, R., & Smits, J. (1998). *Mobile telecommunications: Standards, regulation, and applications.* Norwood, MA: The Artech House.

Beld, J.W. van den (1991). Technical standards not always commercially desirable. *Elektrotechniek- Elektronica, 2,* 22-24. (in Dutch)

Bender-Demoll, S., & Mcfarland, D. A. (2006). The art and science of dynamic network visualization. *Journal of Social Structure, 7*(2), 1–38.

Benkler, Y. (2006). *The Wealth of Networks. How Social Production Transforms Markets and Freedom.* New Haven, CT: Yale University Press.

Benyus, J. M. (2002). *Biomimicry: innovation inspired by nature.* New York: Perennial.

Besen, S. M., & Farrell, J. (1991). The role of the ITU in standardization. *Telecommunications Policy, 15*(4), 311–321. doi:10.1016/0308-5961(91)90053-E

Besen, S., & Levinson, R. (2009). Standards, intellectual property disclosure, and patent royalties after Rambus. *North Carolina Law Review, 10*(233). Retrieved from http://jolt.unc.edu/sites/default/files/Besen_Levinson_v10i2_233_282_0.pdf

Biddle, B., White, A., & Woods, S. (2010). *How Many Standards in a Laptop? (And Other Empirical Questions). In Proceedings from K-2010: ITU-T Kaleidoscope Academic Conference – Beyond the Internet?* Geneva: ITU.

Biggam, R. (2000). Public service broadcasting: The view from the commercial sector. *Intermedia, 28*(5), 21–23.

Bird, S., Klein, E., & Loper, E. (2009). *Natural language processing with python.* O'reilly.

Bjørn-Andersen, N., Razmerita, L., & Zinner-Henriksen, H. (2007). The streamlining of Cross-Border Taxation Using IT: The Danish eExport Solution. In G. O. J. Macolm (Ed.), *E-Taxation: State & Perspectives - E-Government in the field of Taxation: Scientific Basis, Implementation Strategies, Good Practice Examples* (pp. 195–206). Linz: Trauner Verlag.

Blei, D. M. (2012, April). Probabilistic topic models. *Communications of the ACM, 55*(4), 77–84. doi:10.1145/2133806.2133826

Blind, K. (2003). Patent Pools - A Solution to Patent Conflicts in Standardisation and an Instrument of Technology Transfer: The MP3 Case. In *Proceedings of the 3rd IEEE Conference on Standardisation and Innovation in Information Technology (SIIT 2003)*, (pp. 27-35) Delft: TUD-TBM. doi:10.1109/SIIT.2003.1251192

Blind, K. (2008a). Standardisation and Standards in Security Research and Emerging Security Markets. In *Proceedings of the Fraunhofer Symposium 'Future Security', 3rd Security Research Conference*, (pp. 63-72). Stuttgart: Fraunhofer IRB Verlag.

Blind, K. (2009). *Standardisation: A catalyst for innovation*. Retrieved from http://publishing. eur.nl/ir/repub/asset/17558/EIA-2009-039-LIS.pdf

Blind, K., & Gauch, S. (2007). Standardisation benefits researchers – Standards ought to be developed in parallel to the research processes. *Wissenschaftsmanagement*, Special 2/2007 (English Version), 16-17.

Blind, K., & Iversen, E. (2004). *The Interrelationship between IPR and Standardisation: Patterns and Policies*. Retrieved from http://eprints.utas.edu.au/1282/1/Blind_Iversen2004Euras.pdf

Blind, K. (2004). *The Economics of Standards: Theory, Evidence, Policy*. Cheltenham: Edward Elgar Publishing.

Blind, K. (2008b). Factors Influencing the Lifetime of Telecommunication and Information Technology Standards. In T. M. Egyedi, & K. Blind (Eds.), *The Dynamics of Standards* (pp. 155–180). Cheltenham: Edward Elgar Publishing. doi:10.4018/978-1-59904-949-6.ch024

Blind, K. (2011). An economic analysis of standards competition: The example of the ISO ODF and OOXML standards. *Telecommunications Policy*, *35*(4), 373–381. doi:10.1016/j.telpol.2011.02.007

Blind, K., Gauch, S., & Hawkins, R. (2010). How stakeholders view the impacts of international ict standards. *Telecommunications Policy*, *34*(3), 162–174. doi:10.1016/j.telpol.2009.11.016

Blind, K., & Jungmittag, A. (2008). The impact of patents and standards on macroeconomic growth: A panel approach covering four countries and 12 sectors. *Journal of Productivity Analysis*, *29*(1), 51–60. doi:10.1007/s11123-007-0060-8

Blondel, V. D., Guillaume, J.-L., Lambiotte, R., & Lefebvre, E. (2008, October). Fast unfolding of communities in large networks. *Journal of Statistical Mechanics*, *2008*(10), P10008. doi:10.1088/1742-5468/2008/10/P10008

Bloomberg. (2013). *Company Overview of Cwill Telecommunications, Inc.* Retrieved from http://investing.businessweek.com/research/stocks/private/snapshot.asp?privcapId=27274

Blundon, W. (1997). How Microsoft is broadening Java's scope. *Java World*. Retrieved from http://www.javaworld.com/article/2077608/learn-java/how-microsoft-is-broadening-java-s-scope.html

Boehlje, M., & Schiek, W. (1998). Critical success factors in a competitive dairy market. *Journal of Dairy Science*, *81*(6), 1753–1761. doi:10.3168/jds.S0022-0302(98)75744-3

Bonaccorsi, A., Giannangeli, S., & Rossi, C. (2006). Entry strategies under competing standards: Hybris business models in the open source software industry. *Management Science*, *52*(7), 1085–1098. doi:10.1287/mnsc.1060.0547

Borraz, O. (2007, January). Governing standards: The rise of standardization processes in France and in the EU. *Governance: An International Journal of Policy, Administration and Institutions*, *20*(1), 57–84. doi:10.1111/j.1468-0491.2007.00344.x

Borth, D., Ekl, R., Oberlies, B., & Overby, S. (2008). Considerations for successful cognitive radio systems in us tv white space. In *Proceedings of DySpan*. DySpan. doi:10.1109/DYSPAN.2008.61

Bourdieu, P., & Wacquant, L. P. D. (1992). *An Invitation to Reflexive sociology*. Chicago: University of Chicago Press.

Bowker, G. C., & Star, S. L. (1999). *Sorting things out: Classification and Its Consequences*. Cambridge, Massachusetts: The MIT Press.

Bradner, S. (1996, October). *The internet standards process – Revision 3* (No. 2026). RFC 2026 (Best Current Practice). IETF. (Updated by RFCs 3667, 3668, 3932, 3979, 3978, 5378, 5657, 5742)

Bradner, S. (1999, February 22). Open sources: Voices from the open source revolution (o'reilly open source). In *The Internet Engineering task Force*. O'Reilly.

Braithwaite, J. (2005). Neo-liberalism or regulated capitalism. *RegNet Occasional Paper, 5*.

Braithwaite, J. (2000). The New Regulatory State and the Transofrmation of Criminology. *The British Journal of Criminology*, *40*(2), 222–238. doi:10.1093/bjc/40.2.222

Brenner, M., Grech, M., Torabi, M., & Unmehopa, M. (2005). The open mobile alliance and trends in supporting the mobile services industry. *Bell Labs Technical Journal*, *10*(1), 59–75. doi:10.1002/bltj.20079

Brentani, U. (1991). Success Factors in Developing New Business Services. *European Journal of Marketing*, *25*(2), 33–59. doi:10.1108/03090569110138202

Brons, T. F. (2007). *Effective Participation in Formal Standardization: A Multinational Perspective*. Rotterdam: Rotterdam School of Management.

Brooks, R. G., & Geradin, D. (2010). *Interpreting and enforcing the voluntary FRAND commitment*. Available at http://papers.ssrn.com/sol3/papers.cfm?abstract_id=1645878

Brousseau, E. (1994). EDI and inter-firm relationships: Toward a standardization of coordination processes? *Information Economics and Policy*, *6*(3-4), 319–347. doi:10.1016/0167-6245(94)90007-8

Brown, A. W. (2005, Jan.). Interoperability, standards and sustainable receiver markets in the European Union. *EBU Technical Review*, 1–16.

Brown, A., & Picard, R. (2004). The long, hard road to digital television in europe. In *Proceedings of 6th World Media Economics Conference*, (pp. 12–15). Retrieved Apr. 14, 2010, from http://www.cem.ulaval.ca/pdf/brown_picard.pdf

Brown, M. (1995, Apr. 11). Who will rule the airwaves?; Those outside the BSkyB camp fear Murdoch is poised to 'do it again'. *The Independent* (London), p. 22.

Brunsson, N., & Jacobsson, B. (2000). *A world of standards*. Oxford, UK: Oxford University Press.

Brunsson, N., & Jacobsson, B. (2002). The Contemporary Expansion of Standardization. In N. Brunsson, & B. Jacobsson (Eds.), *Associates. A World of Standards*. New York: Oxford University Press. doi:10.1093/acprof:oso/9780199256952.003.0001

Brunsson, N., Rasche, A., & Seidl, D. (2012). The dynamics of standardization: Three perspectives on standards in organization studies. *Organization Studies*, *33*(5-6), 613–632. doi:10.1177/0170840612450120

Burgelman, R.A., Christensen, C.M., & Wheelwright, S.C. (2008). *Strategic Management of Technology and Innovation* (5th ed.). New York: McGraw-Hill/Irwin.

Burkart, P., & McCourt, T. (2006). *Digital music wars: Ownership and control over the celestial jukebox*. Lanham, MD: Rowman and Littlefield.

Burt, R. S. (1997). The contingent value of social capital. *Administrative Science Quarterly*, *42*(2), 339. doi:10.2307/2393923

Business Weekly. (2005). *Li Wanlin: 3G- the China's dream*. Retrieved from http://tech.sina.com.cn/t/2005-12-08/1632786691.shtml

Cai, J., & Tylecote, A. (2008). Corporate governance and technological dynamism of Chinese firms in mobile telecommunications: A quantitative study. *Research Policy*, *37*(10), 1790–1811. doi:10.1016/j.respol.2008.07.004

Caliste, J., & Farges, G. (2007). A French University: Encouraging hands-on experience. *ISO Focus*, *4*(11), 13–14.

Capek, P. G., Frank, S. P., Gerdt, S., & Shields, D. (2005). A history of ibm's open-source involvement and strategy. *IBM Systems Journal*, *44*(2), 249–257. doi:10.1147/sj.442.0249

Capgemini (2009). *Trends in mobility*. Utrecht: Cap Gemini/Transumo. (in Dutch)

Cargill, C. (2011): Why Standardization Efforts Fail. *Journal of Electronic Publishing, 14*(1). DOI:

Carley, K., Reminga, J., Storrick, J., & DeReno, M. (2009). *Ora users guide (Tech. Rep.)*. Carnegie Mellon University, School of Computer Science, Institute for Software Research.

Carroll, J. M., & Swatman, P. A. (2000). Structured-case: A methodological framework for building theory in information systems research. *European Journal of Information Systems*, *9*(4), 235–242. doi:10.1057/palgrave.ejis.3000374

Cave, M. (1997). Regulating digital television in a convergent world. *Telecommunications Policy*, *21*(7), 575–596. doi:10.1016/S0308-5961(97)00031-1

Cawley, R. A. (1997). European aspects of the regulation of pay television. *Telecommunications Policy*, *21*(7), 677–691. doi:10.1016/S0308-5961(97)00036-0

Cawson, A. (1995). High-Definition Television in Europe. *The Political Quarterly*, *66*(2), 157–173. doi:10.1111/j.1467-923X.1995.tb00460.x

CEN. (2005). *Standards are a concrete contribution for the relaunch of the Lisbon strategy for growth and employment in the European Union*. Retrieved from http://www.cen.eu/CENORM/news/pressreleases/interviewverheugen.asp

CEN. (2014a). *CEN Workshop Agreements (CWAs)*. Retrieved from http://www.cen.eu/pages/default.aspx

CEN. (2014b). *Technical Specifications (TS)*. Retrieved from http://www.cen.eu/pages/default.aspx

CEN/CENELEC/ETSI Joint Working group on Education about Standardization. (2011). *Policy on education about Standardization*. Brussels: CEN/CENELEC Management Centre. Retrieved February 15, 2014 from ftp://ftp.cencenelec.eu/CEN/Services/Education/Education/PolicyonEducationaboutStandardization.pdf

CEN-CENELEC STAIR. (2011). *The Operationalisation of the Integrated Approach: Submission of STAIR to the Consultation of the Green Paper "From Challenges to Opportunities: Towards a Common Strategic Framework for EU Research and Innovation funding"*. Retrieved from http://www.cencenelec.eu/research/pages/default.aspx

CEN-CENELEC. (2014). *CEN-CENELEC Research Helpdesk*. Retrieved from http://www.cen.eu/cen/Services/Innovation/Pages/default.aspx

CEPT. (2008). *CEPT Report 24: A Preliminary Assessment of the Feasibility of Fitting New/future Applica-Tions/services into Non-Harmonised Spectrum of the Digital Dividend (namely the so-Called 'White Spaces' between Allotments)*. Retrieved from http://www.erodocdb.dk/

CEU. (2011): *A strategic vision for European standards: Moving forward to enhance and accelerate the sustainable growth of the European economy by 2020*–COM(2011)311. Retrieved from http://eur-lex.europa.eu/LexUriServ/LexUriServ.do?uri=COM:2011:0311:FIN:EN:PDF

Chen, C., Watanabe, C., & Griffy-Brown, C. (2007). The co-evolution process of technological innovation—an empirical study of mobile phone vendors and telecommunication service operators in japan. *Technology in Society*, *29*(1), 1–22. doi:10.1016/j.techsoc.2006.10.008

China Spells out National Standard for Cell Phone Chargers. (2006, December 19). *People's Daily*. Retrieved from http://english.peopledaily.com.cn/200612/19/eng20061219_334047.html

China Youth Daily. (2009). *Guanghan Xu: the first one who helped China spawned into Chinese own 3G standard*. China Youth Daily.

Choi, D. G., Kang, B. G., & Kim, T. H. (2010). *Standardization: Fundamentals, Impact, and Business Strategy*. Retrieved from http://publications.apec.org/publication-detail.php?pub_id=1032

Choi, D. (Ed.). (2008). *APEC SCSC Education Guideline 1: Case Studies of How to Plan and Implement Standards Education Programs, Asia Pacific Economic Cooperation*. Singapore: APEC Secretariat.

Choi, D. G., Lee, H., & Sung, T. (2011). Research profiling for standardization and innovation. *Scientometrics*, *88*(1), 259–278. doi:10.1007/s11192-011-0344-7

Choi, D. G., & Vries, H. J. (2011). Standardization as emerging content in technology education. *International Journal of Technology and Design Education*, *21*(1), 111–135. doi:10.1007/s10798-009-9110-z

Choi, D., & de Vries, H. J. (2013). Integrating standardization into engineering education: The case of forerunner Korea. *International Journal of Technology and Design Education*, *23*(4), 1111–1126. doi:10.1007/s10798-012-9231-7

Choi, D., de Vries, H. J., & Kim, D. (2009). Standards Education Policy Development: Observations based on APEC Research. *International Journal of IT Standards and Standardization Research*, *7*(2), 23–42. doi:10.4018/jitsr.2009070103

Christensen, C. M. (1993). The rigid disk drive industry: A history of commercial and technological turbulence. *Business History Review*, *67*(4), 531–588. doi:10.2307/3116804

Christensen, C. M. (1997). *The Innovator's Dilemma: When New Technologies Cause Great Firms to Fail.* Boston, USA: Harvard Business School Press.

Clark, D. D., Sollins, K., Wroclawski, J., & Faber, T. (2003). Addressing Reality: An Architectural Response to Real-World Demands on the Evolving Internet. In *Proceedings of ACM SIGCOMM*. ACM. doi:10.1145/944760.944761

Clark, D. D., Wroclawski, J., Sollins, K. R., & Braden, R. (2002). Tussle in Cyberspace: Defining Tomorrow's Internet. In *Proceedings of SIGCOMM'02*. Pittsburgh, PA: ACM. doi:10.1145/633057.633059

Clarke, A. (1999). A practical use of key success factors to improve the effectiveness of project management. *International Journal of Project Management*, *17*(3), 139–145. doi:10.1016/S0263-7863(98)00031-3

Clark, K. B. (1985). The interaction of design hierarchies and market concepts in technological evolution. *Research Policy*, *14*(5), 235–251. doi:10.1016/0048-7333(85)90007-1

Clevers, S. H., & Verweij, R. (2007). *ICT in flow. Inventory of electricity use by the ICT sector & ICT-equipment.* The Hague: Ministry of Economic Affairs. (in Dutch)

Climate Group. (2008). *Smart 2020: Enabling the low carbon economy in the information age.* Retrieved from http://www.theclimategroup.org/publications/2008/6/19/smart2020-enabling-the-low-carbon-economy-in-the-information-age/

CNET. (2004, October 15). *MP3 losing steam?* Retrieved on April 29, 2012, from http://news.cnet.com/MP3-losing-steam/2100-1027_3-5409604.html

Collins, L. (2010). *'Whisky and soda' solution to software-defined radio architecture.* IET Collective Inspiration.

Cooklev, T. (2010). The Role of Standards in Engineering Education. *International Journal of IT Standards and Standardization Research*, *8*(1), 1–10. doi:10.4018/jitsr.2010120701

Cooper, R. G., & Kleinschmidt, E. J. (1987). Success Factors in Product Innovation. *Industrial Marketing Management*, *16*(3), 215–223. doi:10.1016/0019-8501(87)90029-0

Cooper, R. G., & Kleinschmidt, E. J. (1990). New Product Success Factors – A Comparison of Kills versus Successes and Failures. *R & D Management*, *20*(1), 47–63. doi:10.1111/j.1467-9310.1990.tb00672.x

Cooper, R. G., & Kleinschmidt, E. J. (1995). Benchmarking the Firm's Critical Success Factors in New Product Development. *Journal of Product Innovation Management*, *12*(5), 374–391. doi:10.1016/0737-6782(95)00059-3

COST. (2009). *Cost action ic0905 "Techno-economic regulatory framework for radio spectrum access for cognitive radio / software defined radio (terra)".* Retrieved from http://www.cost-terra.org

Council of the European Union. (2008). *Council Conclusions on standardisation and innovation.* Paper presented at the 2891st Competitiveness Council meeting, 2008-09-25. Brussels: Council of the European Union.

Craft, R. C., & Leake, C. (2002). The Pareto principle in organizational decision making. *Management Decision*, *40*(8), 729–733. doi:10.1108/00251740210437699

CREM. (2008). *An analysis of the flows of electronic waste in The Netherlands.* Amsterdam: Greenpeace. Retrieved from http://www.greenpeace.org/usa/en/

Cusumano, M. A., Mylonadis, Y., & Rosenbloom, R. S. (1992). Strategic maneuvering and mass-market dynamics: The triumph of VHS over Beta. *Business History Review*, *66*(1), 51–94. doi:10.2307/3117053

Czaya, A., Egyedi, T., & Hesser, W. (2010). The current state of standardization education in Europe. In Mijatovic I. Živković N. (Eds.), *Proceedings 7th International Conference "Standardization Protypes and Quality: A means of Balkan countries collaboration"*, (pp. 85-90). University of Belgrade, Faculty of Organizational Sciences.

Dai, X. (2008). Guiding the Digital Revolution: Is European Technology Policy Misguided? In J. Hayward (Ed.), *Leaderless Europe* (pp. 47–65). Oxford, UK: Oxford University Press. doi:10.1093/acprof:oso/9780199535026.003.0004

Damljanovic, Z., & Sippola, U. (2010). *Towards digital innovation theory: Cognitive radio report.* Academic Press.

Damsgaard, J., & Lyytinen, K. (2001). The role of intermediating institutions in the diffusion of electronic data interchange (EDI): How industry associations intervened in Denmark, Finland, and Hong Kong. *The Information Society, 17*(3), 195–210. doi:10.1080/019722240152493056

Damsgaard, J., & Trading, E. (1998). International trade at the speed of light: Building an electronic trading infrastructure in Denmark, Finland, and Hong Kong. In *Proceedings of the IFIP 8.2 and 8.6 Joint Working Conference on Information Systems: Current Issues and Future Changes.* IFIP.

Damsgaard, J., & Truex, D. (2000). Binary trading relations and the limits of EDI standards: The Procrustean bed of standards. *European Journal of Information Systems, 9*(3), 173–188. doi:10.1057/palgrave.ejis.3000368

Datang. (2010). *Datang history.* Retrieved from http://www.datanggroup.cn/templates/T_Contents/index.aspx?nodeid=16

David, P. A. (1985). Clio and the Economics of QWERTY. *American Economic Review, 75*(2), 332–336.

David, P. A. (2005). *The beginnings and prospective ending of "end-to-end": An evolutionary perspective on the internet's architecture.* SIEPR Discussion Paper No. 01-04. Retrieved from http://siepr.stanford.edu/publicationsprofile/567

David, P. A. (1985). Clio and the Economics of QWERTY. *The American Economic Review, 75*(2), 332–337.

David, P. A. (1990). Narrow windows, blind giants and angry orphans: the dynamics of systems rivalries and the dilemmas of technology policy. In F. Arcangeli (Ed.), *Innovation diffusion* (Vol. 3). New York: Oxford University Press.

David, P. A. (1995). Standardization policies for network technologies: The flux between freedom and order revisited. In R. W. Hawkins, R. Mansell, & J. Skea (Eds.), *Standards, innovation and competitiveness: The politics and economics of standards in natural and technical environments* (pp. 15–35). Aldershot, UK: Edward Elgar.

David, P. A., & Bunn, J. A. (1988). The economics of gateway technologies and network evolution: Lessons from the electricity supply history. *Information Economics and Policy, 3*(2), 165–202. doi:10.1016/0167-6245(88)90024-8

David, P. A., & Greenstein, S. (1990). The economics of compatibility standards: An introduction to recent research. *Economics of Innovation and New Technology, 1*(1-2), 3–41. doi:10.1080/10438599000000002

David, P. A., & Steinmueller, W. E. (1994). Economics of compatibility standards and competition in telecommunication networks. *Information Economics and Policy, 6*(3-4), 217–241. doi:10.1016/0167-6245(94)90003-5

de Bruin, R., & Smits, J. (1999). *Digital Video Broadcasting: Technology, Standards, and Regulations.* Boston, London: Artech House.

de Vries, H. J., Blind, K., Mangelsdorf, A., Verheul, H., & van der Zwan, J. (2009). *SME Access to European Standardization - Enabling small and medium-sized enterprises to achieve greater benefit from standards and from involvement in standardization.* Brussels: CEN and CENELEC. Retrieved from http://www.cenelec.eu/NR/rdonlyres/88D06BD5-CA51-479D-A416-AB1F-3BE67E66/0/SMEAccessReport20090821.pdf

De Vries, H. J., Verheul, H., & Willemse, H. (2003). *Stakeholder identification in IT standardization processes.* Paper presented at the Workshop on Standard Making: A Critical Research Frontier for Information Systems. Seattle, WA.

de Vries, H. J. (1999). *Standardization – A Business Approach to the Role of National Standardization Organizations.* Boston: Kluwer Academic Publishers. doi:10.1007/978-1-4757-3042-5

de Vries, H. J. (2002). Standardization – Mapping a field of research. In S. Bollin (Ed.), *The Standards Edge* (pp. 99–121). Ann Arbor, MI: Bollin Communications.

de Vries, H. J. (2003). *Kenbaarheid Normalisatie en Normen – Deelproject 9b HBO-onderwijs – Tussenrapportage.* Delft: NEN.

De Vries, H. J. (2006). IT Standards Typology. In K. Jakobs (Ed.), *Information Technology Standards and Standardization Research* (pp. 1–26). Hershey, PA: Idea Group Publishing. doi:10.4018/978-1-59140-938-0.ch001

de Vries, H. J., & Egyedi, T. M. (2007). Education about Standardization. *International Journal of IT Standards and Standardization Research, 5*(2), 1–16. doi:10.4018/jitsr.2007070101

de Vries, H., de Vries, H., & Oshri, I. (2008). *Standards-Battles in Open Source Software. The Case of Firefox.* London: Palgrave Macmillan. doi:10.1057/9780230595095

Delaere, S., & Ballon, P. (2008). Multi-level standardization and business models for cognitive radio: The case of the cognitive pilot channel. In *Proceedings of the 3rd IEEE Symposium on New Frontiers in Dynamic Spectrum Access Networks (DySPAN'08)*. Chicago, IL: IEEE.

Delaere, S., & Ballon, P. (2007). *Model implications of a cognitive pilot channel as enabler of flexible spectrum management. In Proceedings of 20th Bled eConference eMergence: Merging and Emerging Technologies*. Bled, Slovenia: Processes, and Institutions.

Den Uijl, S., & De Vries, H. J. (2008). Setting a technological standard: Which factors can organizations influence to achieve dominance?. In *Proceedings 13th EURAS Workshop on Standardisation. Aachener Beiträge zur Informatik, Band 40*. Aachen: Wissenschaftsverlag Mainz in Aachen.

den Uijl, S., de Vries, H. J., & Bayramoglu, D. (2013). The Rise of MP3 as the Market Standard. *International Journal of IT Standards and Standardization Research, 12*(1), 1–26. doi:10.4018/jitsr.2013010101

Denardis, L., & Levin, A. (2009). *Bridging the standardization gap – ITU-T Research Project: Measuring and Reducing the Standards Gap*. Geneva: International Telecommunication Union.

Denegri-Knott, J., & Tadajewski, M. (2010). The emergence of MP3 technology. *Journal of Historical Research in Marketing, 2*(4), 397–425. doi:10.1108/17557501011092466

Department for Culture, Media, and Sport. (2001). *Consultation on media ownership rules*. Retrieved Sept. 6, 2010, from www.culture.gov.uk/PDF/media_ownership_2001. pdf

Department of Justice. (2007). Response to Institute of Electrical and Electronics Engineers, Inc.'s Request for Business Review Letter. Washington, DC: DoJ.

DeWalt, K. M., & DeWalt, B. R. (2002). *Participant observation: a guide for fieldworkers*. Walnut Creek, CA: AltaMira Press.

Dickerson, K. (2004). Operator strategies for maximising the benefits of standardisation. Academic Press.

Die Bundesregierung. (2009). *Normungspolitisches Konzept der Bundesregierung*. Berlin: Die Bundesregierung.

DIN. (2000). *Economic Benefits of Standardization: Summary of Results*. Retrieved from http://www.din.de/sixcms_upload/media/2896/economic_benefits_standardization.pdf

DIN. (2012). *Research & Development Phase Standardisation*. Retrieved from http://www.ebn.din.de/cmd?level=tpl-home&languageid=en

Dokko, G., & Rosenkopf, L. (2010). Mobility of Technical Professionals and Firm Influence in Wireless Standards Committees. *Organization Science, 21*(3), 677–695. doi:10.1287/orsc.1090.0470

Dosi, G. (1982). Technological paradigms and technological trajectories. *Research Policy, 11*(3), 147–162. doi:10.1016/0048-7333(82)90016-6

Doyle, L. (2009). *Essentials of cognitive radio. Cambridge wireless essential series*. Cambridge, UK: Cambridge University Press. doi:10.1017/CBO9780511576577

DVB Project. (1993, Sept. 10). *Memorandum of understanding*. Retrieved May 25, 2010 http://www.immagic.com/eLibrary/ARCHIVES/GENERAL/DVB_CH/D001213M.pdf

DVB Project. (1994b). *DVB GA 2 (94) 9 rev. 1, Appendix 1: Code of Conduct -Access to Digital Decoders*. Author.

E2R II. (2007). *The e2r ii flexible spectrum management (fsm) - Technical, business & regulatory perspectives.* Author.

Eberlein, B., & Grande, E. (2005). Reconstituting Politcal Authority in Europe: Transnational Regulatory Networks and the Informalization of Governance in the European Union. In E. Grande, & L. Pauly (Eds.), *Complex sovereignty: reconstructing political authority in the twenty-first century* (pp. 146–167). Toronto, Canada: University of Toronto Press.

EC. (1996). *Communication from the Commission to the Council and the Parliament on 'Standardization and the Global Information Society: The European Approach, COM (96) 359.* Retrieved from http://eur-lex.europa.eu/LexUriServ/LexUriServ. do?uri=COM:1996:0359:FIN:EN:PDF

ECORYS. (2009). *Study on Competitiveness of the EU Security Industry.* Retrieved from http://ec.europa.eu/enterprise/policies/security/files/study_on_the_competitiveness_of_the_eu_security_industry_en.pdf

Egan, M. (2001). *Constructing a European market: standards, regulation, and governance.* Oxford, UK: OUP. doi:10.1093/0199244057.001.0001

Egyedi, T. M. (2002). Standards enhance system flexibility? Mapping compatibility strategies onto flexibility objectives. In *Proceedings from EASST 2002 Conference.* University of York.

Egyedi, T. M. (2006). Experts on causes of incompatibility between standard-compliant products. In Enterprise Interoperability, (pp. 553-563). Berlin: Springer.

Egyedi, T. M., & Dahanayake, A. (2003). Difficulties implementing standards. In *Proceedings of Standardization and Innovation in Information Technology.* Academic Press.

Egyedi, T., & Muto, S. (2010). Interoperability standards for ICT: A green strategy in a grey sector. In Yearbook ICT and Society 2010 (7th ed.). Gorredijk: Media Update. (in Dutch)

Egyedi, T. M. (2003). Consortium problem redefined: Negotiating democracy in the actor network on standardization. *International Journal of IT Standards and Standardization Research, 1*(2), 22–38. doi:10.4018/jitsr.2003070102

Egyedi, T. M. (2007). Standard-compliant, but incompatible?! *Computer Standards & Interfaces, 29*(6), 605–613. doi:10.1016/j.csi.2007.04.001

Egyedi, T. M., & Peet, D.-J. (2003). *Informatics & sustainable development.* Nijmegen: UCM/KU. (in Dutch)

Egyedi, T., & Spirco, J. (2011). Standards in transitions: Catalyzing infrastructure change. *Futures, 43*(9), 947–960. doi:10.1016/j.futures.2011.06.004

Egyedi, T., & Verwater-Lukszo, Z. (2005). Which standards' characteristics increase system flexibility? Comparing ICT and batch processing infrastructures. *Technology in Society, 27*(3), 347–362. doi:10.1016/j.techsoc.2005.04.007

Eisenhardt. (1989). Building Theories from Case study Research. *Academy of Management Review, 14*(4), 532-550.

Eisenhardt, K. M. (1989). Building Theories from Case Study Research. *Academy of Management Review, 14*(4), 532–550.

Eisenmann, T. (2008, Summer). Managing Proprietary and Shared Platforms. *California Management Review, 50*(4), 31–53. doi:10.2307/41166455

Eisenmann, T., Parker, G., & Van Alstyne, M. W. (2006, October). Strategies for two-sided markets. *Harvard Business Review, 84*(10), 92–101. PMID:16649701

Eltzroth, C. (2007, Dec. 31). *IPR Policy of the DVB Project: Commentary on Article 14 MoU DVB.* Retrieved July 9, 2010, from http://www.DVB.org/membership/ipr_policy/IPR_commentary0712.pdf

Ely, S. (1995, Winter). MPEG video coding. A simple introduction. *EBU Technical Review,* 12–23. Retrieved July 6, 2010, from http://www.ebu.ch/en/technical/trev/trev_frameset-index.html

Ernst, D. (2013). Standards, Innovation, and Latecomer Economic Development – A Conceptual Framework. In *Proceedings ofInternational Workshop on Asia and Global Standardization*. Seoul, Korea: Academic Press. doi:10.2139/ssrn.2388993

Ernst, D. (2007). Beyond the 'Global Factory' model: Innovative capabilities for upgrading China's IT industry. *International Journal of Technology and Globalisation*, *3*(4), 437–459. doi:10.1504/IJTG.2007.015459

Ernst, H. (2002). Success factors of new product development: A review of the empirical literature. *International Journal of Management Reviews*, *4*(1), 1–40. doi:10.1111/1468-2370.00075

ESRIF. (2009). *ESRIF Final Report*. Retrieved from http://ec.europa.eu/enterprise/policies/security/ files/ esrif_final_report_en.pdf

Ethier, S. (2008). *The Worldwide PMP/MP3 Player Market: Shipment Growth to Slow Considerably*. In-Stat report.

ETSI (2014). *Final Draft Standard EN 301 598: White Space Devices (WSD); Wireless Access Systems operating in the 470 MHz to 790 MHz TV Broadcats band; Harmonised EN covering the essential requirements of Article 3.2 of the R&TTE Directive. ETSI, February 2014*. Author.

ETSI. (2012). *Making better standards: Practical ways to success*. Retrieved from http://portal.etsi.org/mbs

EU. (2013). *Regulation (EU) No 1025/2012 of the European Parliament and of the Council*. Retrieved from http://eur-lex.europa.eu/LexUriServ/LexUriServ.do?uri=OJ:L:2012:316:0012:0033:EN:PDF

European Commission. (1993, Nov. 17). *Digital Video Broadcasting: A Framework for Community Policy*. COM(93) 557 final. Retrieved Aug. 26, 2010, from aei. pitt.edu/3116/

European Commission. (2004). *Critical Infrastructure Protection in the fight against terrorism (COM/2004/0702)*. Retrieved from http://eur-lex.europa.eu/LexUriServ/LexUriServ.do?uri=COM:2004:0702:FIN:EN:PDF

European Commission. (2004a). *The role of European standardisation in the framework of European policies and legislation*. Communication from the Commission to the European Parliament and the Council. Retrieved from http://ec.europa.eu/enterprise/standards_policy/role_of_standardisation/doc/context_en.pdf

European Commission. (2004b). *Commission staff working document: The challenges for European standardisation*. Retrieved from http://ec.europa.eu/enterprise/standards_policy/role_of_standardisation/doc/staff_working_document_en.pdf

European Commission. (2008). Communication from the Commission to the Council, the European Parliament and the European Economic and Social Committee. *Towards an increased contribution from standardisation to innovation in Europe*. COM(2008) 133 final. Retrieved from http://ec.europa.eu/enterprise/standards_policy/standardisation_innovation/doc/com_2008_133_en.pdf

European Commission. (2008). *Towards an increased contribution from standardisation to innovation in Europe*. Retrieved from http://eur-lex.europa.eu/LexUriServ/LexUriServ.do? uri=COM:2008:0133:FIN:en:PDF

European Commission. (2009, June 29). *Harmonisation of a charging capability of common charger for mobile phones – Frequently Asked Questions* [Press Release]. Retrieved from http://europa.eu/rapid/pressReleasesAction.do?reference=MEMO/09/301

European Commission. (2009a). *Future networks. The way ahead!* Brussels: Information Society and Media Directorate General.

European Commission. (2009b). *Radio spectrum policy group report on "Cognitive technologies". Final draft*. Brussels: Information Society and Media Directorate-General.

European Commission. (2010, June 29). *Towards a European common charger for electric vehicles* [Press Release]. Retrieved from http://europa.eu/rapid/pressReleasesAction.do?reference=IP/10/857&format=HTML&aged=0&language=EN&guiLanguage=en

European Commission. (2011). *A strategic vision for European standards: Moving forward to enhance and accelerate the sustainable growth of the European economy by 2020 - COM(2011) 311 final - Communication from the Commission tot he European Parliament, the Council and the European Economic and Social Committee.* Brussels: European Commission. Retrieved February 15, 2014 at http://eur-lex.europa.eu/LexUriServ/LexUriServ.do?uri=COM:2011:0311:FIN:EN:PDF

European Commission. (2011a). *Programming Mandate Addressed to CEN, CENELEC and ETSI to Establish Security Standards.* Retrieved from ftp://ftp.cencenelec.eu/CENELEC/EuropeanMandates/M_487.pdf

European Commission. (2011b). *Communication from the Commission to the European Parliament, the Council and the European Economic and Social Committee: A strategic vision for European standards: Moving forward to enhance and accelerate the sustainable growth of the European economy by 2020, COM(2011) 311 final.* Retrieved from http://eur-lex.europa.eu/LexUriServ/LexUriServ.do?uri=COM:2011:0311:FIN:EN:PDF

European Council. (1985). *Council Resolution on a new approach to technical harmonisation and standards.* Retrieved Sept. 1, 2013, from http://eur-lex.europa.eu/legal-content/EN/TXT/PDF/?uri=CELEX:31985Y0604(01)&from=EN

European Council. (2010). *The Stockholm Programme - An Open and Secure Europe Serving and Protecting Citizens.* Retrieved from http://eur-lex.europa.eu/LexUriServ/LexUriServ.do?uri=OJ:C:2010

European Parliament (EP). (2001, Dec. 10). *Debate on electronic communications networks and services.* Retrieved Sept. 1, 2010, from http://www.europarl.europa.eu/sides/getDoc.do?type=CRE&reference=20011210&secondRef=ITEM-005&format=XML&language=EN

EXPRESS [Expert Panel for the Review of the European Standardisation System]. (2010). *Standardization for a competitive and innovative Europe: a vision for 2020. Report delivered to the European Commission in February 2010.* Retrieved from http://ec.europa.eu/enterprise/policies/european-standards/files/express/exp_384_express_report_final_distrib_en.pdf

Fan, P. (2006). Catching up through developing innovation capability: Evidence from China's telecom-equipment industry. *Technovation*, *26*(3), 359–368. doi:10.1016/j.technovation.2004.10.004

Farrell, J., & Saloner, G. (1985). Standardization, compatibility, and innovation. *The Rand Journal of Economics*, *16*(1), 70–83. doi:10.2307/2555589

Farrell, J., & Saloner, G. (1986). Installed Base and Compatibility: Innovation, Product Preannouncements, and Predation. *The American Economic Review*, *76*(5), 940–955.

Farrell, J., & Saloner, G. (1987). Competition, Compatibility and Standards: The Economics of Horses, Penguins, and Lemmings. In H. L. Gabel (Ed.), *Product Standardisation as a Competitive Strategy* (pp. 1–21). Amsterdam: Elsevier Science.

Federal Communications Commission. (2010a). *Second memorandum opinion and order 10-074 in the matter of unlicensed operations in the tv broadcast bands* (Technical paper). Federal Communications Commission (FCC).

Federal Communications Commission. (2010b). *Spectrum analysis: Options for broadcast spectrum (Technical paper): Federal Communications Commission.* FCC.

Flick, U. (2002). An introduction to qualitative research (2nd ed.). London: SAGE Publications.

Fligstein, N. (1996). Markets as politics: A political-cultural approach to market institutions. *American Sociological Review*, *61*(4), 656–673. doi:10.2307/2096398

Focus, I. S. O. (2011). Society for standards and standardization launched. *ISO Focus*, *2*(1), 36.

Folmer, E., Bekkum, M., & Verhoosel, J. (2009). Strategies for using international domain standards within a national context: The case of the Dutch temporary staffing industry. In *Proceedings of Innovations for Digital Inclusions, 2009. K-IDI 2009. ITU-T Kaleidoscope.* IEEE.

Fomin, V. V. (2001). *Innovation, standardization, and sustainable development of cellular mobile communications on three continents.* Paper presented at the The 6th EURAS Workshop on Standards, Compatibility and Infrastructure Development. Delft, The Netherlands.

Fomin, V. V., & Medeisis, A. (2012). In search of sustainable business models for cognitive radio evolution. *Technological and Economic Development of Economy*.

Fomin, V. V. (2012). Standards as Hybrids. *International Journal of IT Standards and Standardization Research*, *10*(2), 59–68. doi:10.4018/jitsr.2012070105

Fomin, V. V., & Lyytinen, K. (2000). How to distribute a cake before cutting it into pieces: Alice in wonderland or radio engineers' gang in the nordic countries? In K. Jakobs (Ed.), *Information technology standards and standardization: A global perspective* (pp. 222–239). Hershey, PA: Idea Group Publishing. doi:10.4018/978-1-878289-70-4.ch014

Fomin, V. V., Pedersen, M. K., & de Vries, H. J. (2008). Open standards and government policy: Results of a delphi survey. *Communications of the Association for Information Systems*, *22*(April), 459–484.

Fomin, V. V., Su, J., & Gao, P. (2011). Indigenous Standard Development in the Presence of Dominant International Standards: The case of the AVS standard in China. *Technology Analysis and Strategic Management*, *23*(7), 745–758. doi:10.1080/09537325.2011.592270

Fomin, V. V., Sukarevičienė, G., & Lee, H. (2014). State-of-the-Art in Policy and Regulation of Radio Spectrum. In *Cognitive Radio Policy and Regulation Techno-Economic Studies to Facilitate Development of Cognitive Radio*. Springer.

Foray, D. (1994). Users, Standards and the Economics of Coalitions and Committees. *Information Economics and Policy*, *6*(3-4), 269–293. doi:10.1016/0167-6245(94)90005-1

Forge, S., Blackman, C., Bohlin, E., & Cave, M. (2009). A green knowledge society: An ICT policy agenda to 2015 for Europe's future knowledge society. A Report for the Ministry of Enterprise, Energy and Communications, Government Offices of Sweden. Chiltern Close, UK: SCF_Associates.

Foster, R. (1986). *Innovation; The Attacker's Advantage*. New York: Summit Books.

FP7. (2011). *Fp7 project ""End-to-end efficiency (e3)"*. Retrieved from https://ict-e3.eu

Frainhofer, I. I. S. (2012, March 22). *Die MP3 Geschichte*. Retrieved March 22, 2012, from http://www.iis.fraunhofer.de/en/bf/amm/diemp3geschichte/zeitleiste/

Friedman, B., Kahn, P. H., & Borning, A. (1996). Value Sensitive design and information systems. In P. Zhang, & D. Galletta (Eds.), *Human-computer Interactions and Management Information Systems: Foundations* (Vol. 6, pp. 348–372). Armonk, NY: M.E. Sharp.

Furukawa, Y. (2007). A Japanese university: Educating standardization strategists in business. *ISO Focus*, *4*(11), 15–16.

Gallagher, S. R. (2012). The battle of the blue laser DVDs: The significance of corporate strategy in standards battles. *Technovation*, *32*(2), 90–98. doi:10.1016/j.technovation.2011.10.004

Gallagher, S., & Park, S. H. (2002). Innovation and Competition in Standard-Based Industries: A Historical Analysis of the U.S. Home Video Game Market. *IEEE Transactions on Engineering Management*, *49*(1), 67–82. doi:10.1109/17.985749

Galperin, H. (2002). Can the US transition to digital TV be fixed? Some lessons from two European Union cases. *Telecommunications Policy*, *26*(1-2), 3–15. doi:10.1016/S0308-5961(01)00050-7

Gal, U., Lyytinen, K., & Yoo, Y. (2008). The Dynamics of IT Boundary Objects, Information Infrastructures, and Organisational Identities: The Introduction of 3D Modelling Technologies into the Architecture, Engineering, and Construction Industry. *European Journal of Information Systems*, *17*(3), 290–304. doi:10.1057/ejis.2008.13

Gamber, T., Friedrich-Nishio, M., & Grupp, H. (2008, January 21). Science and technology in standardization: A statistical analysis of merging knowledge structures. *Scientometrics*, *74*(1), 89–108. doi:10.1007/s11192-008-0105-4

Ganeva, L., Sandalski, B., & Kotev, R. (2010). Contributions of the Bulgarian Union of Standardization for the European Integration of the Republic Bulgaria. In *Proceedings 7th International Conference "Standardization Protypes and Quality: A means of Balkan countries collaboration"*, (pp. 29-38). University of Belgrade, Faculty of Organizational Sciences.

Gao, P. (2007). Counter-networks in standardization: A perspective of developing countries. *Information Systems Journal, 17*(4), 391–420. doi:10.1111/j.1365-2575.2007.00262.x

Gao, P., & Lyytinen, K. (2000). Transformation of China's telecommunications sector: A macro perspective. *Telecommunications Policy, 24*(8-9), 719–730. doi:10.1016/S0308-5961(00)00059-8

Gao, X. D., & Liu, J. X. (2012). Catching up through the development of technology standard: The case of TD-SCDMA in China. *Telecommunications Policy, 36*(7), 531–545. doi:10.1016/j.telpol.2012.01.006

Garcia, D. L. (1992). Standard setting in the united states: Public and private sector roles. *Journal of the American Sociaety for Information Science, 43*(8), 531–537. doi:10.1002/(SICI)1097-4571(199209)43:8<531::AID-ASI3>3.0.CO;2-Q

Garud, R., Jain, S., & Kumaraswamy, A. (2002). Institutional entrepreneurship in the sponsorship of common technological standards: The case of Sun Microsystems and JAVA. *Academy of Management Journal, 45*(1), 196–214. doi:10.2307/3069292

Garud, R., & Kumaraswamy, A. (1993). A., Changing Competitive Dynamics in Network Industries: An Exploration of Sun Microsystems' Open Systems Strategy. *Strategic Management Journal, 14*(5), 351–369. doi:10.1002/smj.4250140504

Gawer, A. (2009). *Platforms, Markets and Innovation*. Cheltenham, UK: Edvard Elgar. doi:10.4337/9781849803311

Geek.com. (2000, November 1). *Warner Music likes Windows Media*. Retreived on April 29, 2012, from http://www.geek.com/articles/news/warner-music-likes-windows-media-2000111

Gençer, M., Oba, B., Özel, B., & Tunaloğlu, V. S. (2006). Open source systems, ifip working group 2.13 foundation on open source software 2006. In E. Damiani, B. Fitzgerald, W. Scacchi, & M. Scotto (Eds.), Organization of Internet Standards. Springer.

Gencer, M. (2012). The evolution of ietf standards and their production. *International Journal of IT Standards and Standardization Research, 10*(1), 17–33. doi:10.4018/jitsr.2012010102

Gerst, M., Bunduchi, R., & Williams, R. (2005). Social shaping & standardization: A case study from auto industry. In *Proceedings of HICSS-38: the 38th Annual Hawaii International Conference on System Sciences*. Piscataway, NJ: IEEE. DOI: doi:10.1109/HICSS.2005.547

Gerundino, D. (2010). Standards in economic development and trade. *ISO Focus, 1*(1), 35.

Ghezzi, C., Jazayeri, M., & Mandrioli, D. (2002). *Fundamentals of software engineering*. Upper Saddle River, NJ, USA: Prentice Hall PTR.

Giddens, A. (1984). *The Constitution of Society*. Berkeley, CA: University of California Press.

Giossi, S., & Papastamatis, A. (2010). *The effective teaching of standards in a lifelong learning world*. In *Proceedings 7th International Conference "Standardization Protypes and Quality: A means of Balkan countries collaboration"*, (pp. 118-125). University of Belgrade, Faculty of Organizational Sciences.

Grimme, K. (2001). *Digital television standardization and strategies*. Boston: Artech House Publishers.

Grimsley, M., & Meehan, A. (2007). e-Government information systems: Evaluation-led design for public value and client trust. *European Journal of Information Systems, 16*(2), 134–148. doi:10.1057/palgrave.ejis.3000674

Grindle, P. (2002). *Standards, Strategy, and Policy. Cases and Stories*. Oxford, UK: Oxford University Press.

Group, N. P. D. (2012, March 6). *Maintaining customers has been the key to a reinvigorated music market, according to NPDs annual music study*. Retreived on April 29, 2012, from www.npd.com/wps/portal/npd/us/news/pressreleases/pr_120306

Group, N. P. D. (2006). *Annual digital music study survey of U.S. consumers 2006*. Author.

Group, N. P. D. (2007). *Annual digital music study survey of U.S. consumers 2007.* Author.

Group, N. P. D. (2009). *Annual digital music study survey of U.S. consumers, 2009.* Author.

Grundström, C., & Wilkinson, I. F. (2004). The role of personal networks in the development of industry standards: A case study of 3G mobile telephony. *Journal of Business and Industrial Marketing, 19*(4), 283–293. doi:10.1108/08858620410516763

GSMA. (2009, February 17). *GSM World agreement on Mobile phone Standard Charger* [Press Release]. Retrieved from http://www.gsmworld.com/newsroom/press-releases/2009/2548.htm

Gustafsson, M. R., Karlsson, T., & Bubenko, J. J. (1982). A declarative approach to conceptual information modelling. In T. W. Olle, H. G. Sol, & A. A. Verrijn-Stuart (Eds.), *Information Systems Design Methodologies: A Comparative Review* (pp. 93–142). Amsterdam: North-Holland.

Hall, R., & Biersteker, T. (Eds.). (2002). *The emergence of private authority in global governance.* Cambridge, UK: Cambridge Univiversity Press. doi:10.1017/CBO9780511491238

Handelsblatt. (2000, September 6). *Interview: Die Musikindustrie schläft weiter.* Retrieved on March 22, 2012, from http://www.handelsblatt.com/archiv/interview-mit-den-mp3-erfindern-interview-die-musikindustrie-schlaeft-weiter/2003290.html

Hanseth, O., & Monteiro, E. (1997). *Understanding Information Infrastructures.* Unpublished Manuscript. Retrieved from http://heim.ifi.uio.no/~oleha/Publications/bok.pdf

Hanseth, O., Nielsen, P., & Alhponse, J. (2012). *Fluid Standards: The Case of Mobile Content Serices.* Unpublished manuscript. Retrieved from http://heim.ifi.uio.no/~oleha/Publications/FluidStandardsNielsenHanseth.pdf

Hanseth, O. (2000). The economics of standards.. In C. U. Ciborra (Ed.), *From control to drift: The dynamics of corporate information infrastructures* (pp. 56–70). Oxford, UK: Oxford University Press.

Hanseth, O. (2014). *Developing Pan-European e-Government Solutions: From Interoperability to Installed Base Cultivation The Circulation of Agency in E-Justice* (pp. 33–52). Netherlands: Springer.

Hanseth, O., & Braa, K. (2001). Hunting for the treasure at the end of the rainbow. Standardizing corporate IT infrastructure. *Computer Supported Cooperative Work, 10*(3-4), 261–292. doi:10.1023/A:1012637309336

Hanseth, O., Jacucci, E., Grisot, M., & Aanestad, M. (2006). Reflexive Standardization: Side Effects and Complexity in Standard Making. *Management Information Systems Quarterly, 30*, 563–581.

Hanseth, O., Monteiro, E., & Hatling, M. (1996). Developing information infrastructure: The tension between standardisation and flexibility. *Science, Technology & Human Values, 21*(4), 407–426. doi:10.1177/016224399602100402

Hart, J. A. (2004). *Technology, Television, and Competition - The Politics of digital TV.* Cambridge, UK: Cambridge University Press. doi:10.1017/CBO9780511490941

Harwit, E. (2008). *China's telecommunications revolution.* Oxford: Oxford University Press. doi:10.1093/acprof:oso/9780199233748.001.0001

Hatto, P. (2013). *Standards and Standardisation. A practical guide for researchers.* Retrieved from http://ec.europa.eu/research/industrial_technologies/pdf/practical-standardisation-guide-for-researchers_en.pdf

Haug, T. (2002). A commentary on standardization practices: Lessons from the nmt and gsm mobile telephone standards histories. *Telecommunications Policy, 26*(3-4), 101–107. doi:10.1016/S0308-5961(02)00003-4

Hause, K. (2000). *The future of the music industry: MP3, DVD audio and more.* IDC report.

Haykin, S. (2005). Cognitive radio: Brain-empowered wireless communications. *IEEE Journ. on Sel. Areas in Communicatons, 23*(2), 201–220. doi:10.1109/JSAC.2004.839380

Hazlett, T. (2010). Putting economics above ideology. *Barron's Editorial Commentary*. Retrieved from http://online.barrons.com/

Henfridsson, O., & Bygstad, B. (2013). The generative mechanisms of digital infrastructure evolution. *Management Information Systems Quarterly, 37*(3).

Henningsson, S., & Bjørn-Andersen, N. (2009). *When standards is not enough to secure interoperability and competitiveness for European exporters*. Paper presented at the 17th European Conference on Information Systems. Verona, Italy.

Henningsson, S., Bjorn-Andersen, N., Schmidt, A., Fluegge, B., & Zinner Henriksen, H. (2011). Food Living Lab – Complexity of Export Trade. In Y.-H. Tan, N. Bjørn-Andersen, S. Klein, & B. Rukanova (Eds.), *Accelerating Global Supply Chains with IT-Innovation* (pp. 3–29). Berlin: Springer. doi:10.1007/978-3-642-15669-4_5

Henningsson, S., Budel, R., Gal, U., & Bjorn-Andersen, N. (2010). ITAIDE Information Infrastructure (I3) Framework. In Y.-H. Tan, N. Bjørn-Andersen, S. Klein, & B. Rukanova (Eds.), *Accelerating Global Supply Chains with IT-Innovation*. Berlin: Springer.

Henningsson, S., & Zinner Henriksen, H. (2011). *Inscription of Behaviour and Flexible Interpretation in Information Infrastructures: The case of European e-Customs. Journal of Strategic Information Systems.*

Henrich-Franke, C. (2008). 'Cookies for ITU': The role of social networks in standardization processes. In Bargaining Norms – Arguing Standards (pp. 86-97). The Hague: STT.

Hesser, W. (1997). *The need for interdisciplinary research on standardization*. Paper presented at the SCANCOR/SCORE Seminar on Standardization. Lund, Sweden.

Hesser, W., & de Vries, H. J. (2011). *White Paper Academic Standardisation education in Europe*. Hamburg, Germany: European Academy for Standardisation. Retrieved February 15, 2014 from http://www.euras.org/uploads/files/EURAS%20White%20paper%202011-08-13.pdf

Hesser, W., & Czaya, A. (1999). Standardization as a subject of study in higher education. *ISO Bulletin, 30*(6), 6–11.

Hesser, W., Feilzer, A. J., & de Vries, H. J. (2007). *Standardisation in Companies and Markets*. Hamburg: Helmut Schmidt University.

Hilty, L. M. (2008). *Information Technology and Sustainability. Essays on the Relationship between ICT and Sustainable Development*. Books on Demand GmbH, Norderstedt.

Hofmann, T. (1999). Probabilistic latent semantic indexing. In *Proceedings of the 22nd annual international acm sigir conference on research and development in information retrieval* (pp. 50–57).

Homer, S. (1994, May 16). Science: The day of digital TV is dawning; Steve Homer charts the progress of technology that is going to give us clearer television pictures. *The Independent* (London), 21.

Hong, Y., Bar, F., & An, Z. (2012). Chinese telecommunications on the threshold of convergence: Contexts, possibilities, and limitations of forging a domestic demand-based growth model. *Telecommunications Policy, 36*(10-11), 914–928. doi:10.1016/j.telpol.2012.07.013

Hotelling, H. (1929). Stability in competition. *The Economic Journal, 39*(153), 41–57. doi:10.2307/2224214

Hoyer, P. O. (2004). Non-negative matrix factorization with sparseness constraints. *Journal of Machine Learning Research, 5*, 1457–1469.

Hsueh, R. (2011). *China's regulatory state: a new strategy for globalization*. Ithaca: Cornell University Press.

Huczynski, A., & Buchanan, D. A. (1985). *Organizational Behaviour: An Introductory Text*. Englewood Cliffs, NJ: Prentice Hall.

Hughes, T. P. (1993). The evolution of large technological systems. In W. E. Bijker, T. P. Hughes, & T. J. Pinch (Eds.), *The social construction of technological systems: New directions in the sociology and history of technology* (pp. 51–82). Cambridge, MA: MIT Press.

Hurd, J., & Isaak, J. (2009). IT Standardization: The Billion Dollar Strategy. In Standardization Research in Information Technology: New Perspectives (pp. 20-26). Hershey, PA: IGI Global. DOI: doi:10.4018/978-1-59904-561-0.ch002

ICT~Milieu (2009). *ICT environmental monitor*. Woerden: ICT~Office/ICT~Milieu. (in Dutch)

IEC. (2005). *IEC Lecture Series – International Standardization in business, Industry, Society and Technology*. Geneva: International Electrotechnical Commission.

IEC. (2007). *IEC Lecture Series II – The Importance of Standards*. Geneva: International Electrotechnical Commission.

IEEE. (2013). *IEEE Standards Association Operations Manual*. New York: Authors.

IEEE. (2014a). *IEEE Constitution and Bylaws*. New York: Authors.

IEEE. (2014b). *IEEE Policies*. New York: Authors.

Iivari, J. (2003). Towards Information Systems as a Science of Meta-Artifacts. *Communication of the AIS, 12*, 568–581.

INTEREST. (2006). *INTEREST: Integrating Research and Standardisation: A Guide to Standardisation for R&D Organisations and Researchers*. Retrieved from http://www-i4.informatik.rwth-aachen.de/Interest/Manual_R%26D.pdf

Interest. (2007). *A Guide to Standardisation for R&D Organisations and Researchers*. Retrieved from http://www-i4.informatik.rwth-aachen.de/Interest/Manual_R&D.pdf

International Federation of the Phonographic Industry (IFPI). (2001, April). *2000 recording industry world sales*. IFPI.

International Federation of the Phonographic Industry (IFPI). (2011, March). *The recording industry in numbers: The recorded music market in 2010*. IFPI.

Iosifidis, P. (2007). Digital TV, digital switchover and public service broadcasting in Europe. *Javnost-The Public, 14*(1), 5.

Iosifidis, P., Steemers, J., & Wheeler, M. (2005). *European television industries*. London: British Film Institute.

IPR-Helpdesk. (2010). *International patent filing declines due to financial crisis*. Available at http://www.iprhelpdesk.eu/news/news_6857.en.xml.html

Isaak, J. (2006). The Role of Individuals and Social Capital in POSIX Standardization. *International Journal of IT Standards and Standardization Research, 4*(1), 1–23. doi:10.4018/jitsr.2006010101

ISO. (2005). *FAQ*. Retrieved from http://www.iso.org/iso/en/faqs/faq-standards. html

ISO. (2011). *The ISO 2011 Award for Higher Education in Standardization*. Geneva: International Organization for Standardization.

ISO. (2012). *ISO/IEC Directives, Part 1 – Procedures for the technical work*. Retrieved from http://isotc.iso.org/livelink/livelink?func=ll&objId=4230452&objAction=browse&sort=subtype

ISO. (2014). *ISO deliverables*. Retrieved from http://www.iso.org/iso/home/standards_development/deliverables-all.htm?type=pas

ITU. (2008). *ITU and Climate Change*. Geneve: ITU.

ITU. (2009a). ITU-T Focus Group on CT and Climate Change. In *Deliverable 1: Definitions*. Geneva: ITU. Retrieved from http://www.itu.int/dms_pub/itut/oth/33/07/T33070000030001MSWE.doc

ITU. (2009b). *ITU-T Focus Group on CT and Climate Change. Deliverable 2: Gap Analysis*. Geneva: ITU.

ITU. (2009c, October 22). *Universal phone charger standard approved — One-size-fits-all solution will dramatically cut waste and GHG emissions* [Press Release]. Retrieved from http://www.itu.int/newsroom/press_releases/2009/49.html

ITU. (2010). *ITU ICT Statistics Database*. Available at http://www.itu.int/ITU-D/ICTEYE/Indicators/Indicators.aspx#

Iversen, E. (2004). Case Study: TETRA. In *Study on the Interaction between Standardisation and Intellectual Property Rights* (pp. 167–174). Retrieved from http://ftp.jrc.es/EURdoc/eur21074en.pdf

Iversen, E., Bekkers, R., & Blind, K. (2006). Emerging coordination mechanisms for multi-party IPR holders: Linking research with standardisation. *Industrial and Corporate Change, 21*(4), 901–931.

Jakobs, K. (2013). Strategic positioning in ICT Standardisation. In Boosting European Competitiveness. Aachen: Mainz Publishers.

Jakobs, K. (2000). *User Participation in Standardization Processes - Impact, Problems and Benefits*. Berlin: Vieweg Publishers.

Jakobs, K. (2003): A Closer Look at the Internet's Standards Setting Process.In*Proceedings of the IADIS International Conference WWW/Internet*, (pp. 557–564). IADIS.

Jakobs, K. (2008). *The IEEE 802.11 WLAN Installation at RWTH Aachen University: A Case of Voluntary Vendor Lock-In The dynamics of standards*. London: Edward Elgar.

Jakobs, K. (2009). ICT Standardisation in China, the EU, and the US. In *Proceedings of the 2nd Kaleidoscope Conference. IEEE*.

Jakobs, K. (2011). How People and Stakeholders Shape Standards - The Case of IEEE 802.11. In J. Filipe, & J. Cordeiro (Eds.), *Web Information Systems and Technologies 2010, LNBIP*. Springer. doi:10.1007/978-3-642-22810-0_1

Jakobs, K., Lemstra, W., Hayes, V., Tuch, B., & Links, C. (2010). Creating a Wireless LAN Standard: IEEE 802.11. In J. Groenewegen, & V. Hayes (Eds.), *The Innovation Journey of WiFi*. Cambridge University Press. doi:10.1017/CBO9780511666995.006

Jakobs, K., Procter, R., & Williams, R. (2001). The Making of Standards – Looking Inside the Work Groups. *IEEE Communications Magazine, 39*(4), 102–107. doi:10.1109/35.917511

Janecek, V., & Hynek, J. (2010). Incentive System as a Factor of Firms' Efficiency Improvement. *E & M Ekonomia Management, 13*(1), 76-90.

Jobs, S. (2007). *Thoughts on Music*. Apple Inc. Press Release. Retrieved from http://www.apple.com/fr/hotnews/thoughtsonmusic/

Jones, K. S. (1972). A statistical interpretation of term specificity and its application in retrieval. *The Journal of Documentation, 28*(1), 11–21. doi:10.1108/eb026526

Jones, P., & Hudson, J. (1996). Standardization and the cost of assessing quality. *European Journal of Political Economy, 12*(2), 355–361. doi:10.1016/0176-2680(95)00021-6

Josephson, I. (2005, April 4). Presentation for NARM. *NPD Music Year*.

Kang, S., Park, H. J., & Park, K. (2007). The Effect of Incentives on the Performance of International IT Standardization Experts. *ETRI Journal, 29*(2), 219–230. doi:10.4218/etrij.07.0106.0188

Katz, M. L., & Shapiro, C. (1985). Network externalities, competition, and compatibility. *The American Economic Review, 75*(3), 424–440.

Katz, M., & Shapiro, C. (1994). Systems Competition and Network Effects. *The Journal of Economic Perspectives, 8*(2), 93–115. doi:10.1257/jep.8.2.93

Kennedy, S. (2006). The Political Economy of Standards Coalitions: Explaining China's Involvement in High-Tech Standards Wars. *Asia Policy,* (2), 41-62.

Kennedy, S., Suttmeier, R. P., & Su, J. (2008). *Standards, Stakeholders, and Innovation: China's Evolving Role in the Global Knowledge Economy*. Academic Press.

Ketchell, J. (2010) Education about standardization – Developing future generations of standardisers. Paper presented at WSC Academic Week. Geneva, Switzerland.

Khazam, J., & Mowery, D. (1994). The commercialization of RISC: Strategies for the creation of dominant designs. *Research Policy, 23*(1), 89–102. doi:10.1016/0048-7333(94)90028-0

Kindleberger, C. P. (1983). Standards as public, collective and private goods. *Kyklos, 36*(3), 377–396. doi:10.1111/j.1467-6435.1983.tb02705.x

King, J. L., Gurbaxani, V., Kraemer, K. L., McFarlan, F. W., Raman, K. S., & Yap, C. S. (1994). Institutional factors in information technology innovation. *Information Systems Research*, 5(2), 139–169. doi:10.1287/isre.5.2.139

Kipnis, A. B. (2012). Constructing Commonality: Standardization and Modernization in Chinese Nation-Building. *The Journal of Asian Studies*, 71(3), 731–755. doi:10.1017/S0021911812000666

Kisielnicki, J., & Sroka, S. (2005). Efficiency and Effectiveness of Management in Project Oriented Organizations: The Role of Information Technology in the Organizations. In *Proceedings of the 2005 Information Resources Management Association International Conference: Managing Modern Organizations Through Information Technology*, (pp. 83-87). Hershey, PA: IGI Global.

Klein, S., Reimers, K., Johnston, R. B., Barrett, M., Modol, J. R., Tan, Y.-H., & Henningsson, S. (2012). Inter-organizational information systems: from strategic systems to information infrastructures. In *Proceedings of the 25th Bled eConference*, (pp. 302-319). Academic Press.

Klein, H. K., & Myers, M. D. (1999). A set of principles for conducting and evaluating interpretive field studies in information systems. *Management Information Systems Quarterly*, 23(1), 67–94. doi:10.2307/249410

Klievink, B., & Lucassen, I. (2013). Facilitating Adoption of International Information Infrastructures: A Living Labs Approach. In M. A. Wimmer, M. Janssen, & H. J. Scholl (Eds.), *Electronic Government* (pp. 250–261). Berlin: Springer. doi:10.1007/978-3-642-40358-3_21

Kloch, C., Bilstrup, B., Vesterholt, C. K., & Pedersen, T. P. (2009). *Roadmap for software defined radio - a technology, market and regulation perspective*. Danish Technological Institute.

Knill, C., & Lehmkuhl, D. (2002). Private actors and the state: Internationalization and changing patterns of governance. *Governance: An International Journal of Policy, Administration and Institutions*, 15(1), 41–63. doi:10.1111/1468-0491.00179

Kobayashi, B., & Wright, J. (2009). Substantive preemption, and limits on antitrust: An application to patent holdup. *Journal of Competition Law & Economics*, 5(469).

Kogut, B. (2000). The network as knowledge: Generative rules and the emergence of structure. *Strategic Management Journal*, 21(3), 405–425. doi:10.1002/(SICI)1097-0266(200003)21:3<405::AID-SMJ103>3.0.CO;2-5

Kolltveit, B. J., Hennestad, B., & Grønhaug, K. (2007). IS projects and implementation. *Baltic Journal of Management*, 2(3), 235–250. doi:10.1108/17465260710817465

Komiya, M. (1993, Spring). Personal Communications in Japan and its Implications for Asia. *Pan-European Mobile Communications*, 52-55.

Koomey, J., Kawamoto, K., Nordman, B., Piette, M. A., & Brown, R. E. (1999). *Initial comments on "The Internet begins with coal"*. Memorandum (LBNL-44698). Berkeley: Berkeley Lab. Retrieved from http://www.zdnet.com/news/networking/2007/09/20/micro-usb-to-be-phone-charger-standard-39289524/

Kraidy, M. (2005). Hybridity, or the cultural logic of globalization. Philadelphia, PA: Temple University Press.

Kraidy, M. M. (2002). Hybridity in cultural globalization. *Communication Theory*, 12(3), 316–339. doi:10.1111/j.1468-2885.2002.tb00272.x

Krechmer, K. (2006). Open Standards Requirements. *The International Journal of IT Standards and Standardization Research, 4* (1).

Krechmer, K. (2007). Teaching standards to engineers. *International Journal of IT Standards and Standardization Research*, 5(2), 1–12. doi:10.4018/jitsr.2007070102

KSA. (2003). *International workshop to develop a standardization education model*. Seoul: KSA.

Kshetri, N., Palvia, P., & Dai, H. (2011). Chinese institutions and standardization: The case of government support to domestic third generation cellular standard. *Telecommunications Policy*, 35(5), 399–412. doi:10.1016/j.telpol.2011.03.005

Kuhn. (1962). *The Structure of Scientific Revolutions*. Chicago: University of Chicago Press.

Kurokawa, T. (2005). Developing Human Resources for International Standards. *Quarterly Review, 17*. Retrieved from http://www.nistep.go.jp/achiev/ftx/eng/stfc/stt017e/qr17pdf/STTqr1703.pdf

Kwak, J., Lee, H., & Chung, D. B. (2012). The evolution of alliance structure in China's mobile telecommunication industry and implications for international standardization. *Telecommunications Policy*, 36(10-11), 966–976. doi:10.1016/j.telpol.2012.07.017

Kwak, J., Lee, H., & Fomin, V. V. (2011). The governmental coordination of conflicting interests in standardisation: Case studies of indigenous ict standards in china and south korea. *Technology Analysis and Strategic Management*, 23(7), 789–806. doi:10.1080/09537325.2011.592285

Lane, D. A. (2011). Complexity and innovation dynamics. In C. Antonelli (Ed.), *Handbook on the Economic Complexity of Technological Change*. Cheltenham, UK: Edward Elgar Publishing. doi:10.4337/9780857930378.00008

Langlois, R. N., & Robertson, P. L. (1992). Networks and innovation in a modular system: Lessons from the microcomputer and stereo component industries. *Research Policy*, 21(4), 297–313. doi:10.1016/0048-7333(92)90030-8

Lathia, K. P. (1995). Standards Production in a Competitive Environment. In ETSI (Ed.), European Telecommunications Standardization and the Information Society: The State of the Art 1995. Sophia Antipolis: ETSI.

Laven, P. (2002). Workshop OBS/IViR/EMR 2002: Co-regulation of the Media in Europe. In Proceedings of Co-regulation of the Media in Europe: Co-regulation of the Media in Europe. Florence: European University Institute.

Layne-Farrar, A., Llobet, G., & Padilla, J. (2014). Payments and participation: The incentives to join cooperative standard setting efforts. *Working Paper*. Retrieved from http://papers.ssrn.com/sol3/papers.cfm?abstract_id=1904959

Lee, H. J., & Oh, S. J. (2008). The political economy of standards setting by newcomers: China's WAPI and South Korea's WIPI. *Telecommunications Policy*, 32(9-10), 662–671. doi:10.1016/j.telpol.2008.07.008

Lee, H., Chan, S., & Oh, S. (2009). China's ICT Standards Policy after the WTO Accession: Techno-national versus Techno-globalism. *Info*, 11(1), 9–18. doi:10.1108/14636690910932966

Lee, H., & Oh, S. (2006). A standards war waged by a developing country: Understanding international standard setting from the actor-network perspective. *The Journal of Strategic Information Systems*, 15(3), 177–195. doi:10.1016/j.jsis.2005.10.002

Lemley, M. A., & Lessig, L. (2000). The End of End-to-End: Preserving the Architecture of the Internet in the Broadband Era. *UCLA Law Review*, 48(925). doi:10.2139/ssrn.247737

Lemstra, W., & Hayes, V. (2009). The shaping of the IEEE 802.11 standard – The role of the innovating firm in the case of Wi-Fi. In Information and Communication technology standardization for e-business: Integrating supply and demand factors (pp. 98-126). Hershey, PA: IGI Global. doi:10.4018/978-1-60566-320-3.ch008

Lemstra, W., Groenewegen, J., & Hayes, V. (2010). *The Innovation Journey of WiFi*. Cambridge University Press. doi:10.1017/CBO9780511666995

Lessig, L. (2001). *The future of ideas: the fate of the commons in a connected world*. New York: Random House.

Levinthal, D. A. (1998). The slow pace of rapid technological change: Gradualism and punctuation in technological change. *Industrial and Corporate Change*, 7(2), 217–247. doi:10.1093/icc/7.2.217

Levy, D. A. L. (1997). The regulation of digital conditional access systems. A case study in European policy making. *Telecommunications Policy*, 21(7), 661–676. doi:10.1016/S0308-5961(97)00035-9

Levy, D. A. L. (1999). *Europe's Digital Revolution: Broadcasting regulation, the EU and the nation State*. London: Routledge. doi:10.4324/9780203278284

Li, J. (2007, September 10). Behind the Curtain of 3G Standard. *Commercial Weekly*.

Liebowitz, S. J., & Margolis, S. E. (1994). Network Externality: An Uncommon Tragedy. *The Journal of Economic Perspectives*, 8(2), 133–150. doi:10.1257/jep.8.2.133

Li, G. (2008). Moving towards unsustainability: A study of the Chinese telecommunications regulation. *International Journal of Private Law*, 1(1/2), 47–68. doi:10.1504/IJPL.2008.019432

Liikanen, E. (2001, Mar. 27). *EBU Conference, Public service broadcasting in eEurope*. Brussels: RAPID 01/143.

Lipsey, R. G., & Steiner, P. O. (1979). *Economics: An Introductory Analysis*. New York: Addison Wesley.

Liu, X. (2010). China's catch-up and innovation model in IT industry. *International Journal of Technology Management, 51*(2/3/4), 194 - 216.

Liu, C., & Arnett, K. P. (2000). Exploring the factors associated with Web site success in the context of electronic commerce. *Information & Management*, 38(1), 23–33. doi:10.1016/S0378-7206(00)00049-5

Loewer, U. M. (2006). *Interorganisational standards*. Heidelberg: Physica.

Low, B., & Johnston, W. J. (2010). Organizational network legitimacy and its impact on knowledge networks: The case of China's TD-SCDMA mobility technology. *Journal of Business and Industrial Marketing*, 25(6), 468–477. doi:10.1108/08858621011066053

Luna, L. (2007, January). Reality game. *Mobile Radio Technology*.

Lyle, D. (2008). The Digital Revolution -What Does it Mean for Advertising? In G. Terzis (Ed.), *European Media Governance: The Brussels Dimension* (pp. 121–128). Bristol: Intellect Ltd.

Lyytinen, K. J., Keil, T., & Fomin, V. V. (2008). A framework to build process theories of anticipatory information and communication technology (ict) standardizing.[JITSR]. *International Journal of IT Standards and Standardization Research*, 6(1), 1–38. doi:10.4018/jitsr.2008010101

Lyytinen, K., & King, J. L. (2002). Around the cradle of the wireless revolution: The emergece and evolution of cellular telephony. *Telecommunications Policy*, 26(3-4), 97–100. doi:10.1016/S0308-5961(02)00002-2

Lyytinen, K., & King, J. L. (2006). Standards making: A critical research frontier for information systems research. *Management Information Systems Quarterly*, 30(5), 205–411.

Markus, M. L., & Bjørn-Andersen, N. (1987). Power Over Users: Its Exercise By System Professionals. *Communications of the ACM*, 30(6), 498–504. doi:10.1145/214762.214764

Mayntz, R. (2004). Governance im modernen Staat. In A. Benz (Ed.), *Governance – Regieren in Komplexen Regelsystemen: Eine Einführung* (pp. 65–76). Wiesbaden: Verlag für Sozialwissenschaften. doi:10.1007/978-3-531-90171-8_4

McDonough, W., & Braungart, M. (2002). *Cradle to Cradle: Remaking the Way We Make Things*. New York: North Point Press.

McHale, J. (2010). *Software-defined radio technology is enhancing communications in military and commercial applications worldwide*. Military & Aerospace Electronics.

Medeišis, A. (2014). European Regulatory Developments Related to CR. In Cognitive Radio Policy and Regulation Techno-Economic Studies to Facilitate Development of Cognitive Radio. Academic Press.

Miller, A. R., & Tucker, C. (2009). Privacy Protection and Technology Diffusion: The Case of Electronic Medical Records. *Management Science*, 55(7), 1077–1093. doi:10.1287/mnsc.1090.1014

Mills, M. P. (1999). *The Internet begins with coal: A preliminary exploration of the impact of the Internet on electricity consumption*. Arlington, VA: The Greening Earth Society.

Mitola, J. I. (2009). Cognitive radio architecture evolution. *Proceedings of the IEEE*, 97(4), 626–641. doi:10.1109/JPROC.2009.2013012

Mitola, J., & Maguire, G. (1999). Cognitive radio: Making software radios more personal. *IEEE Personal Communications, 6*(4), 13–18. doi:10.1109/98.788210

Mobile Broadband (2010). Asian-Pacific Region Mobile Broadband Lanscape. *Wireless Intelligence*, Q2.

Mock, D. (2005). *The Qualcomm Equation: How a Fledgling Telecom Company Forged a New Path to Big Profits and Market*. New York: AMACOM.

Moore, G. E. (1965). Cramming more components onto integrated circuits. *Electronics, 38* (8).

Motorola Inc. (2007). *Minimizing the cost of umts/hsxpa networks*. Motorola, Inc.

Mueck, M., Piipponen, A., Kalliojarvi, K., Dimitrakopoulos, G., Tsagkaris, K., & Demestichas, P. et al. (2010). Etsi reconfigurable radio systems – status and future directions on software defined radio and cognitive radio standards. *IEEE Communications Magazine, 48*(9), 78–86. doi:10.1109/MCOM.2010.5560591

Musmann, H. G. (2006, August). Genesis of the MP3 audio coding standard. *IEEE Transactions on Consumer Electronics, 52*(3), 1043–1049. doi:10.1109/TCE.2006.1706505

Nakatsuji, K. (2001). Essence of Trade Negotiation: A Study on China's Entry for WTO. *Ritsumeikan Annual Review of International Studies, 14*(1), 15–34.

Narayanan, V., & Chen, T. (2012). Research on technology standards: Accomplishment and challenges. *Research Policy, 41*(8), 1375–1406. doi:10.1016/j.respol.2012.02.006

Nekovee, M. (2009). A survey of cognitive radio access to tv white spaces. *International Journal of Digital Multimedia Broadcasting*.

NEN. (2010). *Annual Report 2009 – Crisis & Control*. Delft: NEN.

Nickerson, J. V., & Muehlen, M. Z. (2006). Standard making, legitimacy, organizational ecology, institutionalism, internet standards, web services choreography. *MIS Quarterly, 30*(SI), 467–488.

Nickerson, J. V., & Zur Muhlen, M. (2006). The Ecology of Standards Process: Insights from Internet Standard Making. *Management Information Systems Quarterly, 30*(Special issue), 467–488.

Nielsen, F. (1996). Human Behavior: Another Dimension of Standards Setting. *StandardView, 4*(1), 36–41. doi:10.1145/230871.230878

Nihon Keizai Shimbun. (2000, August 9). *Minidisc player/recorder shipments rise*. Retreived on April 29, 2012, from http://www.telecompaper.com/news/minidisc-playerrecorder-shipments-rise

Nolan, D. (1997). Bottlenecks in pay television: Impact on market development in Europe. *Telecommunications Policy, 21*(7), 597–610. doi:10.1016/S0308-5961(97)00037-2

Nonaka, R. (2010). New approach on the pedagogy for standards education: A case of Applied Standards Education at TUAT. In *Proceedings of International Symposium on Standardization Education and Research 2010*, (pp. 156-167). Tokyo University of Agriculture and Technology.

Nooteboom, B. (2008). In S. Cropper, M. Ebers, C. Huxham, & P. S. Ring (Eds.), *The oxford handbook of inter-organizational relations* (pp. 607–634). Oxford University Press.

North, D. C. (1990). *Institutions, institutional change and economic performance. Political economy of institutions and decisions*. Cambridge: Cambridge University Press. doi:10.1017/CBO9780511808678

O'Meara, M. (2000). Harnessing Information Technologies for the Environment. In *State of the World 2000* (pp. 121–141). Washington, US: The Worldwatch Institute.

Odjar Ratna Komala, D. (2011). *Mechanics of Developing a University Level Standards Education Program in Indonesia*. Paper presented at the 2011 PEC SCSC PAGE – ANSI CoE Workshop. Washington, DC.

OECD. (2009a). *OECD communications outlook 2009*. Paris: OECD.

OECD. (2009b). *Towards Green ICT Strategies: Assessing Policies and Programmes on ICT and the Environment*. Paris: OECD. Retrieved from www.oecd.org/dataoecd/47/12/42825130.pdf

Ofcom. (2008). Ofcom awards spectrum licence to qualcomm uk spectrum ltd (news release). *Office of Communications* Retrieved May 23rd 2008, from http://www.ofcom.org.uk/media/news/2008/05/nr_20080516b

Ohanjanyan, O. & Haven, A. (2000). *From Microchip to Megamarket*. Internal document. (in Dutch)

Oliphant, T. E. (2007). Python for scientific computing. *Computing in Science & Engineering*, 9(3), 10–20. doi:10.1109/MCSE.2007.58

OMA. (2014). *Open Mobile Alliance: Policies and Terms of Use*. Retrieved from http://openmobilealliance.org/about-oma/policies-and-terms-of-use

Orgalime. (2010a). *Draft Orgalime comments on EP IMCO report on the Future of European Standardization*. Brussels: Orgalime.

Orgalime. (2010b). *Review of the European Standardization System*. Brussels: Orgalime.

Orlikowski, W. J., & Baroudi, J. J. (1991). Studying information technology in organizations: research approaches and assumptions. *Information Systems Research*, 2(1), 1–28. doi:10.1287/isre.2.1.1

Ostry, S., & Nelson, R. R. (1995). *Techno-nationalism and techno-globalism: conflict and cooperation*. Washington, D.C.: Brookings Institution.

Overeem, P. (2009). *Reset: Corporate social responsibility in the global electronics supply chain*. Amsterdam: GoodElectronics & MVO Platform.

Owen, R., Macnaghten, P., & Stilgoe, J. (2012). Responsible research and innovation: From science in society to science for society, with society. *Science & Public Policy*, 39(6), 751–760. doi:10.1093/scipol/scs093

Paetsch, M. (1993). *The evolution of mobile communications in the u.S. And europe: Regulation, technology, and markets*. London: Artech House.

Paxton, M. (2000). *Portable Digital Music Players Ride the MP3 Wave*. Cahners In-Stat Group Report.

Pearson, M. (2005). China's WTO Implementation in Comparative Perspective. In R. Keith (Ed.), *China as a Rising World Power and its Response to Globalization*. London: Routledge.

Pedregosa, F., Varoquaux, G., Gramfort, A., Michel, V., Thirion, B., & Grisel, O. et al. (2011). Scikit-learn: Machine learning in Python. *Journal of Machine Learning Research*, 12, 2825–2830.

Peters, B., & Pierre, J. (1998). Governance without government? Rethinking public administration. *Journal of Public Administration: Research and Theory*, 8(2), 223–243. doi:10.1093/oxfordjournals.jpart.a024379

Peterson, J., & Sharp, M. (1998). Technology Policy in the European Union. In N. Nugent, W. E. Paterson, & V. Wright (Eds.), *The European Union Series*. London: Macmillan Press.

Pew Research Center. (2012, March 22). *Internet use over time*. Retrieved on March 22, 2012, from http://www.pewinternet.org/data-trend/internet-use/internet-use-over-time/

Pfetsch, F. (2008). Bargaining and Arguing as Communicative Modes of Strategic, Social, Economic, Political Interaction. In J. Schueler, & A. Hommels (Eds.), *Bargaining Norms. Arguing Standards* (pp. 52–65). The Hague: STT Netherlands Study Centre for Technology Trends.

Pieterse, J. N. (1994). Globalization as hybridization. *International Sociology*, 9(2), 161–184. doi:10.1177/026858094009002003

Pinch, T., & Bijker, W. (1984). The Social Construction of Facts and Artefacts: Or How the Sociology of Science and the Sociology of Technology might Benefit Each Other. *Social Studies of Science*, 14(3), 399–441. doi:10.1177/030631284014003004

Ping, W. (2013). *Global ICT Standards Wars in China, and China's Standard Strategy*. Paper presented at International Workshop on Asia and Global Standardization. Seoul, Korea.

Porter, M. E. (1990). *The Competitive Advantage of Nations*. New York: The Free Press.

Porter, T. (2005). The Private Production of Public Goods: Private and Public Norms in Global Governance. In E. Grande, & L. Pauly (Eds.), *Complex sovereignty: reconstituting political authority in the twenty-first century* (pp. 217–237). Toronto, Canada: University of Toronto Press.

R Development Core Team. (2009). R: A language and environment for statistical computing. Vienna, Austria: Author.

Rada, R., & Ketchell, J. (2000). Standardizing the European Information Society. *Communications of the ACM*, *43*(3), 21–25. doi:10.1145/330534.330552

Reddy, N. M. (1990). Product of self-regulation: A paradox of technology policy. *Technological Forecasting and Social Change*, *38*(1), 49–63. doi:10.1016/0040-1625(90)90017-P

Rediske, M. (1996, May 11). Die Telekom als Kontrolleur. *TAZ*, 7.

Reimers, U. (1997, February). DVB-T: the COFDM-based system for terrestrial television. *Electronics & Communication Engineering Journal*, 28.

Reimers, K., & Li, M. (2007). Effectiveness of the international 3G standardisation process and implications for China's 3G policy. *International Journal of Public Policy*, *2*(1/2), 124–139. doi:10.1504/IJPP.2007.012279

Reimers, U. (2006, January). DVB: The Family of International Standards for Digital Video Broadcasting. *Proceedings of the IEEE*, *94*(1), 173–182. doi:10.1109/JPROC.2005.861004

Riefler, B. (2008). *The Composition of Working Groups in Industry-Specific Standardisation Organizations*. Retrieved from http://www.ivr.uni-stuttgart.de/mikro/RePEc/stt/ download_dpaper/composition_of_ working_groups.pdf

Rosenbloom, R. S., & Cusumano, M. A. (1987). Technological Pioneering and Competitive Advantage: The Birth of the VCR Industry. *California Management Review*, *29*(4), 51–76. doi:10.2307/41162131

Rukanova, B., Bjorn-Andersen, N., van Ipenburg, F., Klein, S., Smit, G., & Tan, Y. H. (2010). Introduction. In Y.-H. Tan, N. Bjørn-Andersen, S. Klein, & B. Rukanova (Eds.), *Accelerating Global Supply Chains with IT-Innovation* (pp. 3–29). Berlin: Springer.

Rysman, M. (2009). The economics of two-sided markets. *The Journal of Economic Perspectives*, *23*(3), 125–143. doi:10.1257/jep.23.3.125

Saltzer, J. H., Reed, D. P., & Clark, D. D. (1984). End-to-End Arguments in Systems Design. *ACM Transactions on Computer Systems*, *2*(4), 277–288. doi:10.1145/357401.357402

Scapolo, F., Churchill, P., & Viaud, V. (2013). *A possible future for the standardization system through the lens of additive manufacturing*. Paper presented at the Kick-Off meeting of the STAIR AM platform. Brussels, Belgium.

Scharpf, F. W. (1988). The Joint-Decision Trap. Lessons From German Federalism an European Integration. *Public Administration*, *66*(3), 239–278. doi:10.1111/j.1467-9299.1988.tb00694.x

Schepel, H. (2005). *The Constitution of Private Governance – Product Standards in the Regulation of Integrating Markets*. Portland, OR: Hart Publishing.

Schilling, M. A. (1998). Technological lockout: An integrative model of the economic and strategic factors driving technology success and failure. *Academy of Management Review*, *23*(2), 267–284.

Schilling, M. A. (2002). Technology success and failure in winner-take-all markets: The impact of learning orientation, timing, and network externalities. *Academy of Management Journal*, *45*(2), 387–398. doi:10.2307/3069353

Schilling, M. A. (2003). Technological Leapfrogging: Lessons from the U.S. Video Game Console Industry. *California Management Review, 45*(3), 6–32. doi:10.2307/41166174

Schilling, M. A. (2005). *Strategic Management of Technological Innovation*. New York: McGraw-Hill.

Schot, J., & Geels, F. (2007). Niches in evolutionary theories of technical change. *Journal of Evolutionary Economics, 17*(5), 605–622. doi:10.1007/s00191-007-0057-5

Schot, J., Hoogma, R., & Elzen, B. (1994). Strategies for shifting technological systems. *Futures, 26*(10), 1060–1076. doi:10.1016/0016-3287(94)90073-6

Scott, J. (2000). Social network analysis. *Sage (Atlanta, Ga.)*.

Scott-Joynt, J. (1998). *ETSI Pulls Off 3G Deal And Wins Asian Support*. Retrieved from http://www.totaltele.com/view.aspx?ID=425641

Seo, D. (2013). *Evolution and Standardization of Mobile Communications Technology*. Hershey, PA: IGI Global. doi:10.4018/978-1-4666-4074-0

Seo, D. B. (2010, January). The Significance of Government's Role in Technology Standardization. *International Journal of IT Standards and Standardization Research, 8*(1), 63–74. doi:10.4018/jitsr.2010120705

Seo, D., & Koek, J. W. (2012). Are Asian Countries Ready to Lead a Global ICT Standardization? *International Journal of IT Standards and Standardization Research, 10*(2), 29–44. doi:10.4018/jitsr.2012070103

Serenkov, P. (2010). *Belarus – Training tomorrow's experts today*. Retrieved May 26, 2010, from http://www.iso.org/iso/iso-focus-plus_index/iso-focusplus_online-bonus-articles/the-2009-iso-award/2009-award_belarus.htm

Seung, D., & Lee, L. (2001). Algorithms for non-negative matrix factorization. *Advances in Neural Information Processing Systems, 13*, 556–562.

Shankar, V., & Bayus, B. L. (2003). Network effects and competition: An empirical analysis of the home video game industry. *Strategic Management Journal, 24*(4), 375–384. doi:10.1002/smj.296

Shapiro, C., & Varian, H. R. (1999a). Art of Standard Wars. *California Management Review, 41*(2), 8–32. doi:10.2307/41165984

Shapiro, C., & Varian, H. R. (1999b). *Information Rules: A Strategic Guide to the Network Economy*. Cambridge: Harvard Business Review Press.

Shen, X. (1999). *The Chinese Road to High Technology., 256*. doi:10.1057/9781403905505

Sherif, M. H. (2001). *Contribution Towards A Theory Of Standardisation In Telecommunications*. Retrieved from www-i4.informatik.rwth-aachen.de/~jakobs/siit99/proceedings/Sherif.doc

Sherif, M. H. (2007). *Standardization of business-to-business electronic exchanges*. Paper presented at the Standardization and Innovation in Information Technology. New York, NY. doi:10.1109/SIIT.2007.4629329

Sherif, M. H., Jakobs, K., & Egyedi, T. M. (2007). Standards of quality and quality of standards for Telecommunications and Information Technologies. In M. Hoerlesberger, Elnawawi, & M., Khalil, T. (Eds.), Challenges in the Management of New Technologies (pp. 427-447). Singapore: World Scientific.

Simcoe, T. S. (2006). Open innovation: Reaching a new paradigm. In H. Chesbrough, W. Vanhverbeke, & J. West (Eds.), Open standards and intellectual property rights. Oxford University Press.

Simon, H. A. (1962). The architecture of complexity. *Proceedings of the American Philosophical Society, 106*(6), 467–482.

Sinay, J. (2011). Security Research and Safety Aspects in Slovakia. In K. Thoma (Ed.), *European Perspectives on Security Research* (pp. 81–89). Berlin: Springer. doi:10.1007/978-3-642-18219-8_7

Singhal, P. (2006). *Integrated Product Policy Pilot on Mobile Phones, Stage III Final Report: Evaluation of Options to Improve the Life-Cycle Environmental Performance of Mobile Phones*. Espoo, Finland: Nokia Corporation.

Smit, F. C., & Pistorius, C. W. I. (1998). Implications of the Dominant Design in Electronic Initiation Systems in the South African Mining Industry. *Technological Forecasting and Social Change, 59*(3), 255–274. doi:10.1016/S0040-1625(98)00006-7

Smith, E., & Wingfield, N. (2003, September 9). The high cost of sharing. *The Wall Street Journal,* pp. B1, B8.

Söderström, E. (2004). *B2B Standards implementations: issues and solutions.* (Ph D Doctoral Dissertation). Stockholm.

SOMO (2008), *Mobile Connections: Supply Chain Responsibility of Five Mobile Phone Companies.* Amsterdam: SOMO.

Song, M. (2007). Guest View. *ISO Focus, 4*(11), 4–7.

Spanias, A., Painter, T., & Venkatraman, A. (2007). *Audio signal processing and coding.* Hoboken, NJ: John Wiley & Sons, Inc. doi:10.1002/0470041978

Spilker, H. S., & Höier, S. (2013). Technologies of Piracy? Exploring the Interplay Between Commercialism and Idealism in the Development of MP3 and DivX. *International Journal of Communication, 7,* 2067–2086.

Spivak, S. M., & Kelly, W. E. (2003). Introduce strategic standardization concepts during higher education studies … and reap the benefits! *ISO Bulletin, 34*(7), 22–24.

Spring, M. B., et al. (1995). Improving the Standardization Process: Working with Bulldogs and Turtles. In Standards Policy for Information Infrastructure (pp. 220-252). Cambridge, MA: MIT Press.

Stango, V. (2004). The Economics of Standards Wars. *Review of Network Economics, 3*(1), 1. doi:10.2202/1446-9022.1040

Star, S. L. (1999). The Ethnography of Infrastructure. *The American Behavioral Scientist, 43*(3), 377–391. doi:10.1177/00027649921955326

Steen, H. U. (2011). Indicators of development or dependency in disguise? Assessing domestic inventive capacity in South Korean and Chinese infrastructural ICT standards. *Telecommunications Policy, 35*(7), 663–680. doi:10.1016/j.telpol.2011.06.004

Steen, H. U. (2011). Limits to the Regulatory State in the Rule-making of Digital Convergence: A Case study of Mobile TV Standards Governance in the European Union and China. *Technology Analysis and Strategic Management, 23*(7), 759–772. doi:10.1080/09537325.2011.592273

Sterne, J. (2012). *The meaning of a format.* Durham, NC: Duke University Press. doi:10.1215/9780822395522

Stewart, J., Dorfer, W., Pitt, L., Eskedal, T., Gaarder, K., & Winskel, M. et al. (2003). *Cost and benefit of use scenarios. The selection environment for mimo-enabled multi-standard wireless devices including cost benefit analysis of various convergence technologies.* Edinburgh, UK: University of Edinburgh.

Stewart, J., Shen, X., Wang, C., & Graham, I. (2011). From 3g to 4g: Standards and the development of mobile broadband in china. *Technology Analysis and Strategic Management, 23*(7), 773–788. doi:10.1080/09537325.2011.592284

Stilgoe, J., Owen, R., & Macnaghten, P. (2013). Developing a framework for responsible innovation. *Research Policy, 42*(9), 1568–1580. doi:10.1016/j.respol.2013.05.008

Suarez, F. F. (2004). Battles for technological dominance: An integrative framework. *Research Policy, 33*(2), 271–286. doi:10.1016/j.respol.2003.07.001

Sukarevičienė, G. (2014). Business Scenarios and Models for Use of Geo-Location Database in TV White Spaces. In Cognitive Radio Policy and Regulation Techno-Economic Studies to Facilitate Development of Cognitive Radio. Academic Press.

Suttmeier, R. & Yao, X. (2004). *China's Post-WTO Technology Policy: Standards, Software and the Changing Nature of Techno-Nationalism* (Special Report No. 7). The National Bureau of Asian Research.

Suttmeier, R. P., & Xiangkui, Y. (2004). China's Post-WTO Technology Policy: Standards, Software, and the Changing Nature of Techno-Nationalism. *NBR Special Report, 7.*

Swann, G. M. P. (2000). *The Economics of Standardization.* London: Department of Trade and Industry, Standards and Technical Regulations Directorate. Retrieved from https://www.gov.uk/government/uploads/system/uploads/attachment_data/file/16506/The_Economics_of_Standardization_-_in_English.pdf

Swann, P. (2000). *The Economics of standardization: Final Report for Standards and Technical Regulations Directorate Department of Trade and Industry.* Retrieved from http://www.dti.gov.uk/files/file11312.pdf

Swann, G. M. P. (2010). *The economics of standardization – An Update. report for the UK Department of Business, Innovation and Skills (BIS).* Innovation Economics Limited.

Tardy, I., & Grøndalen, O. (2010). Which regulation for cognitive radio? An operator's perspective. *Telektronikk, 1,* 105–120.

Tassey, G. (2000). Standardization in technology-based markets. *Research Policy, 29*(4-5), 587–602. doi:10.1016/S0048-7333(99)00091-8

Tee, R., & Gawer, A. (2009). Industry Architecture as a Determinant of Successful Platform Strategies: A Case Study of the I-Mode Mobile Internet Service. *European Management Review, 6*(4), 217–232. doi:10.1057/emr.2009.22

Three-G.net. (2011). *3G Standards.* Retrieved from http://three-g.net/3g_standards.html

Tidd, J., & Bessant, J. (2009). *Managing Innovation: Integrating Technological, Market and Organizational Change.* Hoboken, NJ: John Wiley & Sons.

Tilson, D., Sørensen, C., & Lyytinen, K. (2012). Change and Control Paradoxes in Mobile Infrastructure Innovation: The Android and iOS Mobile Operating Systems Cases. In *Proceedings of the 45th Hawaii International Conference on System Science (HICSS 45).* IEEE. doi:10.1109/HICSS.2012.149

Tiwana, A., Konsynski, B., & Bush, A. A. (2010). Platform Evolution: Coevolution of Platform Architecture, Governance, and Environmental Dynamics. *Information Systems Research, 21*(4), 675–687. doi:10.1287/isre.1100.0323

Todd, C. C., Davidson, G. A., Davis, M. F., Fielder, L. D., Link, B. D., & Vernon, S. (1994). *AC-3: Flexible Perceptual Coding for Audio Transmission and Storage.* Paper presented at the 96th Convention of the Audio Engineering Society. New York, NY.

Trimintzios, P., Hall, C., Clayton, R., Anderson, R., & Ouzounis, E. (2011). *Resilience of the Internet Interconnection Ecosystem.* European Network and Information Security Agency. Retrieved from https://www.enisa.europa.eu/activities/Resilience-and-CIIP/critical-infrastructure-and-services/inter-x/interx/report

Tripsas, M. (1997). Unraveling the Process of Creative Destruction: Complementary Assets and Incumbent Survival in the Typesetter Industry. *Strategic Management Journal, 18*(S1), 119–142. doi:10.1002/(SICI)1097-0266(199707)18:1+<119::AID-SMJ921>3.3.CO;2-S

Tushman, M. (1977). Special boundary roles in the innovation process. *Administrative Science Quarterly, 22*(4), 587–605. doi:10.2307/2392402

Tushman, M., & Anderson, P. (1986). Technological discontinuities and organizational environments. *Administrative Science Quarterly, 31*(3), 439–465. doi:10.2307/2392832

Ulankiewicz, S., Henningsson, S., Bjorn-Andersen, N., & Fluegge, B. (2010). Interoperability Tools. In Y.-H. Tan, N. Bjørn-Andersen, S. Klein, & B. Rukanova (Eds.), *Accelerating Global Supply Chains with IT-Innovation.* Berlin: Springer.

Umapathy, K., et al. (2007). Avatars of Participants in Anticipatory Standardization Processes. In The Standards Edge – Unifier or Divider? (pp. 295-302). Chelsea, MI: Bolin Group.

UNEP. (2009a). *Guideline on the Awareness Raising-design considerations: Mobile Phone Partnership Initiative – Project 4.1*. Basel: United Nations Environment Programme. Retrieved from http://www.basel.int/industry/mppi/MPPI%20Guidance%20Document.pdf

UNEP. (2009b) *Recycling – From E-Waste to Resources*. Nairobi: United Nations Environment Programme. Retrieved from www.unep.org/pdf/Recycling_From_e-waste_to_resources.pdf

UNEP. (2010). *UNEP yearbook 2010: New science and developments in our changing environment.* Nairobi: United Nations Environment Programme. Retrieved from http://www.unep.org/yearbook/2010

UNESCO. (2010). *Beyond 20/20 WDS*. Available at http://stats.uis.unesco.org/unesco/TableViewer/tableView.aspx?ReportId=167

Updegrove, A. (2003). Darwin, Standards and Survival. In The standards edge: Dynamic tension. Ann Arbor, MI: Bolin Communications.

Ure, J. (2007). *China Standards and IPRs*. Hong Kong: Working Paper for the EU-China Trade Project.

US Office of Technology Assessment (OTA). (1992). *Global Standards: Building Blocks for the Future*. Washington, DC: Government Printing Office.

Utterback, J. M., & Abernathy, W. J. (1975). A dynamic model of process and product innovation. *Omega, 3*(6), 639–656. doi:10.1016/0305-0483(75)90068-7

van de Kaa, G. (2009). *Standards Battles for Complex Systems. Empirical Research on the Home Network.* Rotterdam: Erasmus Research Institute of Management.

van de Kaa, G. (2013). Responsible innovation and standardization: A new research approach? *International Journal of IT Standards and Standardization Research, 11*(2), 61–65. doi:10.4018/jitsr.2013070105

van de Kaa, G., Greeven, M., & van Puijenbroek, G. (2013). Standards battles in China: Opening up the black-box of the Chinese government. *Technology Analysis and Strategic Management, 25*(5), 567–581. doi:10.1080/09537325.2013.785511

van de Kaa, G., Rezaei, J., Kamp, L., & De Winter, A. (2014). Photovoltaic Technology Selection: A Fuzzy MCDM Approach. *Renewable & Sustainable Energy Reviews, 32*, 662–670. doi:10.1016/j.rser.2014.01.044

van de Kaa, G., Van den Ende, J., De Vries, H. J., & Van Heck, E. (2011). Factors for winning interface format battles: A review and synthesis of the literature. *Technological Forecasting and Social Change, 78*(8), 1397–1411. doi:10.1016/j.techfore.2011.03.011

van de Kaa, G., Van Heck, H. W. G. M., De Vries, H. J., Van den Ende, J. C. M., & Rezaei, J. (2014). Supporting Decision-Making in Technology Standards Battles Based on a Fuzzy Analytic Hierarchy Process. *IEEE Transactions on Engineering Management, 61*(2), 336–348. doi:10.1109/TEM.2013.2292579

Van de Ven, A. H. (2005). Running in packs to develop knowledge-intensive technologies. *Management Information Systems Quarterly, 29*(2), 368–378.

Van de Ven, A. H., Polley, D., Garud, R., & Venkataraman, S. (1999). *The innovation journey*. New York: Oxford University Press.

van den Ende, J., van de Kaa, G., den Uijl, S., & de Vries, H. J. (2012). The paradox of standard flexibility: The effects of co-evolution between standard and interorganizational network. *Organization Studies, 33*(5-6), 705–736. doi:10.1177/0170840612443625

van Huijstee, M., & de Haan, E. (2009). *E-Waste*. Amsterdam: SOMO. Retrieved from http://somo.nl/publications-nl/Publication_3289-nl/at_download/fullfile

van Huijstee, M., de Haan, E., Poyhonen, P., Heydenreich, C., & Riddselius, C. (2009). *Fair Phones: It's Your Call: How European mobile network operators can improve responsibility for their supply chain*. Amsterdam: SOMO.

van Lieshout, M., & Huygen, A. (2010). ICT and the environment – Could it be a byte more? In Yearbook ICT and Society 2010 (7th ed.). Gorredijk: Media Update. (in Dutch)

van Osch, W., & Avital, M. (2010). Generative Collectives. In *Proceedings of ICIS 2010*. ICIS.

van Schewick, B. (2010). *Internet Architecture and Innovation*. Cambridge, MA: The MIT Press.

Verman, L. C. (1973). *Standardization – A new discipline*. Hamden, CT: The Shoe String Press / Archon Books.

Verse, A. (2008). Conditional access für das Digitale Fernsehen. In U. Reimers (Ed.), DVB-Digital Fernsehtechnik: Datenkompression und Übertragung (3rd ed., pp. 221–228). New York: Springer-Verlag.

Vialle, P., Song, J. J., & Zhang, J. (2012). Competing with dominant global standards in a catching-up context. The case of mobile standards in China. *Telecommunications Policy*, 36(10-11), 832–846. doi:10.1016/j.telpol.2012.09.003

Vogt, W. P. (1999). *Dictionary of Statistics and Methodology*. Thousand Oaks, CA: SAGE Publications.

Von Schomberg, R. (2011). Prospects for technology assessment in a framework of responsible research and innovation. In Technikfolgen abschatzen lehren: Bildungspotenziale transdisziplinarer Methoden (pp. 39–61). Springer

Wade, J. (1995). Dynamics of Organizational Communities and Technological Bandwagons: An Empirical Investigation of Community Evolution in the Microprocessor Market. *Strategic Management Journal*, 16(S1), 111–133. doi:10.1002/smj.4250160920

Walsham, G. (1993). *Interpreting information systems in organizations*. Chichester, UK: Wiley.

Walsham, G. (1995). Interpretive Case Studies in IS Research: Nature and Method. *European Journal of Information Systems*, 4(2), 74–81. doi:10.1057/ejis.1995.9

Wasserman, S., & Faust, K. (1994). *Social network analysis*. Cambridge. doi:10.1017/CBO9780511815478

Watad, M., & Ospina, S. (1996). Information Technology and Organisational Change: The Role of Context in Moderating Change Enabled by Technology. In Diffusion and Adoption of Information Technology (pp. 202-220). London: Chapman & Hall.

Watson, A. B. (2005, January). Interoperability standards and sustainable receiver markets in the European Union. *EBU Technical Review*, 1-16. Retrieved May 3, 2014, from https://tech.ebu.ch/docs/techreview/trev_301-eu.pdf

Watts, D. J. (1999). Networks, dynamics, and the Small-World phenomenon. *American Journal of Sociology*, 105(2), 493–527. doi:10.1086/210318

Watts, D. J., & Strogatz, S. H. (1998, June04). Collective dynamics of 'small-world' networks. *Nature*, 393(6684), 440–442. doi:10.1038/30918 PMID:9623998

West, J. (2003). *Proceedings of the workshop on standard making: A critical research frontier for information systems*. Academic Press.

Wilde, J., & de Haan, E. (2006). *The High Cost of Calling: Critical Issues in the Mobile Phone Industry*. Amsterdam: SOMO.

Willard, G. E., & Cooper, A. C. (1985). Survivors of Industry Shake-Outs: The Case of the U.S. Color Television Set Industry. *Strategic Management Journal*, 6(4), 299–318. doi:10.1002/smj.4250060402

Williams, R. (1997). The Social Shaping of Information and Communications Technologies. In The Social Shaping of the Information Superhighways. Luxembourg: European Commission.

Williams, E., Kahhat, R., Allenby, B., Kavazanjian, E., Kim, J., & Xu, M. (2008). Environmental, Social, and Economic Implications of Global Reuse and Recycling of Personal Computers. *Environmental Science & Technology*, 42(17), 6446–6454. doi:10.1021/es702255z PMID:18800513

Williamson, O. (1979). Transactions-Cost Economics: The Governance of Contractual Relations. *The Journal of Law & Economics*, 22(2), 233–262. doi:10.1086/466942

Williams, P. (2002). The Competent Boundary Spanner. *Public Administration, 80*(1), 103–124. doi:10.1111/1467-9299.00296

Williams, R., & Edge, D. (1996). The Social Shaping of Technology. *Research Policy, 25*(6), 865–899. doi:10.1016/0048-7333(96)00885-2

Wilson, D.C. (1992). *A strategy of change: concepts and controversies in the management of change.* Cengage Learning EMEA.

Winn, J. K. (2005). US and EU Regulatory Competition in ICT Standardization Law & Policy. In *Proceedings of SIIT2005.* SIIT.

WIPO. (2010). *Statistics on patents.* Available at http://www.wipo.int/ipstats/en/statistics/patents/index.html

Wood, D. (1995, Winter). Satellites, science and success: The DVB story. *EBU Technical Review,* 4–11. Retrieved May 25, 2010, from http://www.ebu.ch/en/technical/trev/trev_266-wood.pdf

World at War. (1990, August 4). *The Economist, UK Edition,* 65.

Wu, I. S. (2009). *From iron fist to invisible hand: the uneven path of telecommunications reform in China.* London: Eurospan.

Wüstenhagen, R., Wolsink, M., & Bürer, M. J. (2007). Social acceptance of renewable energy innovation: An introduction to the concept. *Energy Policy, 35*(5), 2683–2691. doi:10.1016/j.enpol.2006.12.001

Wu, T. (2010). *The Master Switch: The Rise and Fall of Information Empires.* New York: Knopf Publishing Group.

Xu, X. Y. (2005). *TD-SCDMA Testing.* Retrieved from http://www.tdscdma-forum.org/en/pdf-word/200561413101910889.doc

Yamada, H. (2011) *Development of Education on Standardization in Japan.* Paper presented at the 2011 PEC SCSC PAGE – ANSI CoE Workshop February 28, 2011. Washington, DC.

Yamada, A. (2000). *Neo-Techno-Nationalism: How and Why It Grows.* Columbia International Affairs Online.

Yan, H. (2007). *The 3G Standard Setting Strategy and Indigenous Innovation Policy in China: Is T-SCDMA a Flagship?* (DRUID Working Paper No. 07-01). Academic Press.

Yang, Y. (2010). China Institute of Metrology's Educational Model for Standardization. China Standardization, 37(1), 15-21.

Yin, R. K. (1994). *Case study research: designs and methods.* Thousand Oaks, CA: Sage Publications Inc..

Yin, R. K. (2008). *Case study research, design and methods* (3rd ed.). Newbury Park: Sage Publications.

Yin, R. K. (2011). *Qualitative Research. From Start to Finish.* New York: Guilford Pubn.

Yoo, Y., Lyytinen, K., & Yang, H. (2005). The role of standards in innovation and diffusion of broadband mobile services: The case of south korea. *The Journal of Strategic Information Systems, 14*(3), 323–353. doi:10.1016/j.jsis.2005.07.007

Yoshimatsu, H. (2007). Global competition and technology standards: Japan's quest for techno-regionalism. *Journal of East Asian Studies, 7*(3), 439–468.

Ypsilanti, D., & Sarrocco, C. (2009). *OECD Communications Outlook 2009.* Retrieved May 3, 2014, from http://www.oecd.org/sti/broadband/oecdcommunicationsoutlook2009.htm

Zachary, G. P. (2000). *The global me: new cosmopolitans and the competitive edge: picking globalism's winners and losers.* London: Nicholas Brealey Pub.

Zaheer, A., McEvily, B., & Perrone, V. (1998). Does trust matter? Exploring the effects of interorganizational and interpersonal trust on performance. *Organization Science, 9*(2), 141–159. doi:10.1287/orsc.9.2.141

Zhan, A. L., & Tan, Z. X. (2010). Standardisation and innovation in China: TD-SCDMA standard as a case. *International Journal of Technology Management, 51*(2-4), 453–468.

Zittrain, J. (2006). The Generative Internet. *Harvard Law Review, 119,* 1974–2040.

About the Contributors

Kai Jakobs joined RWTH Aachen University's Computer Science Department as a member of the technical staff in 1985. Since 1987, he has been Head of the Technical Staff at the Chair of Informatik 4. He holds a PhD in Computer Science from the University of Edinburgh and is a Certified Standards Professional. Kai's research interests and activities focus on various aspects of ICT standards and the underlying standardisation process. Over time, he (co)-authored/edited a text book on data communication networks and more recently, 24 books on standards and standardisation processes, with a focus on the ICT sector. More than 200 of his papers have been published in conference proceedings, books, and journals. He has been on the programme committee and editorial board of numerous international conferences and journals, respectively, and has served as an external expert on evaluation panels of various European R&D programmes, on both technical and socio-economic issues. He is also Vice President of the European Academy for Standardisation (EURAS), as well as founder and editor-in-chief of the *International Journal on IT Standards & Standardization Research*, and of the *Advances in Information Technology Standards and Standardization Research* and the *EURAS Contributions to Standardisation Research* book series.

* * *

Deniz Kaan Bayramoglu is Patent- and Innovation Manager at Darmstadt University of Technology, in the department of Technology Transfer. His focus lies on the commercialization of technologies and intellectual property rights via license agreements, sale of rights, and through the foundation of spin-off companies.

Henk J. de Vries is Associate Professor of Standardisation at the Rotterdam School of Management, Erasmus University. His research and teaching focus is on the standardisation from a business point of view. Henk is President of the European Academy for Standardisation EURAS, Special Advisor to the International Federation of Standards Users IFAN, and Immediate Past President of the International Co-operation for Education about Standardization ICES. He is (co-)author of more than 300 publications in the field of standardisation. See http://www.rsm.nl/hdevries.

Simon den Uijl is a Standardization Manager at Royal Philips Electronics, department of Intellectual Property and Standards. In addition, Simon is a PhD candidate at Rotterdam School of Management, Erasmus University, Department of Technology and Operations Management. Simon has published in the *California Management Review*, *Organization Studies*, and *Business History*.

Tineke M. Egyedi works as a senior researcher at DIRoS. Her current interests include how standards affect innovation, and participatory issues in standardization. She has collaborated in projects for the EU, the Next Generation Infrastructures Foundation, the Dutch Science Foundation, Dutch ministries, international IT companies and standards bodies. She publishes in journals ranging from *IEEE Communications Magazine* to the *International Journal of Hydrogen Energy*. Her latest book is on Inverse Infrastructures: Disrupting Networks from Below (2012). She initiated the game Setting Standards, which is used for US policy makers. She is board member of the European Academy for Standardization (president from 2005-2011), treasurer of the IEEE SIIT conference series, and member of the Standards Education group of the UNECE Working Party on Regulatory Cooperation and Standardization Policies.

Vladislav Vladimirovich Fomin is a professor at the department of Applied Informatics at Vytautas Magnus University in Kaunas, Lithuania, and holds visiting positions at the University of Latvia and Turība University in Riga, Latvia. After earning his PhD degree in 2001, Vladislav V. Fomin held academic positions at the University of Michigan in Ann Arbor (2001-3), Copenhagen Business School (2004-6), Delft University of Technology (2006), Montpellier Business School (2007), and Rotterdam School of Management, and Erasmus University (2008). Dr. Fomin has extensive experience in international research and professional projects. Vladislav is serving on the editorial board of the International Journal of IT Standards & Standardization Research (JITSR) and Baltic Journal of Modern Computing (BJMC), is serving as a reviewer for many recognized journals and is regularly invited to serve as a scientific committee member to recognized international conferences. Fomin is a member of European Academy of Standardization (EURAS) and The Association for Information Systems (AIS). Vladislav has over 70 scientific publications in journals, conferences, and as book chapters, including *Journal of Strategic Information Systems, Communications of the Association for Information Systems, International Journal of IT Standards & Standardization Research, Telecommunications Policy,* and *Knowledge, Technology & Policy*. Conference publications and presentations include The International Conference on Information Systems, European Conference on Information systems, Hawaii International Conference on System Sciences, Academy of Management, and others.

Mehmet Gençer is Associate Professor of Organization Studies at Istanbul Bilgi University, Faculty of Engineering. His research areas include empirical studies on collaboration in virtual communities, innovation dynamics, and computational socio-economic system models. He has published several journal articles and book chapters nationally and internationally, in the areas of strategic management, innovation ecosystems, and software innovation. His articles appeared in *Technology Analysis & Strategic Management Journal, International Journal of IT Standards and Standardization Research,* and *IEEE Computers and Communications* among others.

Ian Graham is a Senior Lecturer in Innovation at the University of Edinburgh Business School. Dr. Graham participated in the China EU Information Technology Standards Research Partnership, an EU funded consortium of academic researchers in China, UK, Norway, Germany and Lithuania that studied the emerging processes of standards collaboration between China and the European Union.

Ole Hanseth is Professor in the Department of Informatics, University of Oslo. His research focuses mainly on the interplay between social and technical issues in the development and use of large-scale networking applications. He is also a visiting professor at the Department of Information Systems, London School of Economics.

Stefan Henningsson is an Associate Professor at Copenhagen Business School, Department of IT Management. His current research addresses managerial aspects of IT in contexts that include corporate mergers and acquisitions, digital payments, and international trade processes. Previous publications include more than 70 peer-refereed papers published in journals such as *Information Systems Journal, European Journal of Information Systems, Journal of Strategic Information Systems*, and *Management Information Systems Quarterly Executive*.

Anne Layne-Farrar is a vice president in the Antitrust and Competition Economics Practice of CRA. She specializes in antitrust and intellectual property matters, especially where the two issues are combined. She advises clients on competition, intellectual property, regulation, and policy issues across a broad range of industries with a particular focus on high-tech and has worked with some of the largest information technology, communications, and pharmaceuticals companies in the world. Dr. Layne-Farrar's expert work for industry leading clients has included analyzing reasonable licensing, including F/RAND, analyzing patent portfolios for licensing negotiations, assessing economic incentives and firm behavior within standard setting organizations, reviewing the competitive implications of licensing, calculating damages, conducting empirical cost-benefit research, including for payment instruments in the US, for legislative proposals covering credit and debit cards, labor unions, television ratings, software security, and e-commerce. She has given oral and written expert testimony in a variety of courts and has presented in industry conferences around the world. Additionally, she has coauthored a book, published articles in *Antitrust, Global Competition Review*, and *Regulation Magazine* and has numerous publications in academic journals, including *Antitrust Law Journal, International Journal of Industrial Organization*, and *Journal of Competition Law and Economics*.

Arturas Medeisis graduated with a BSEE from Vilnius Gediminas Technical University, later obtaining an MS in Telecommunications Engineering and a PhD with a thesis in radio spectrum management from Kaunas University of Technology, Lithuania. Since graduation in 1995, he had been working in the field of radio spectrum management, first with the VRDT – the national regulatory authority of Lithuania, then moving on to the European Radiocommunications Office in Copenhagen, Denmark. Throughout his work in VRDT and ERO he had been engaged in many CEPT, ITU and ETSI activities, including chairing of international project teams on spectrum management and spectrum engineering related aspects. Since 2007, Arturas holds a position of Associate Professor. Since 2012, he is the Head of the Telecommunications Engineering Department at the Vilnius Gediminas Technical University in Lithuania.

Niclas Meyer initially studied European politics at the University of Maastricht. In 2007, he obtained a masters degree in political economy from the London School of Economics and Political Science, where he also obtained a PhD in 2012. His dissertation dealt with governmental interventions in self-regulatory processes at the example of technical standardization. In 2012, he joined the Fraunhofer Institute for Systems and Innovations Research ISI in Karlsruhe as a researcher and project manager.

Sachiko Muto is an external PhD candidate at TU Delft and currently a Visiting Scholar at the UC Berkeley Center for Science, Technology, Medicine & Society (CSTMS). With degrees in Political Science from the University of Toronto and the London School of Economics, her research is focused on public policy and standardization - particularly in areas where standards are needed to achieve societal objectives, such as the realisation of Smart Grids. She also takes a wider interest in the social and political implications of technological change. Sachiko serves as the Director of OpenForum Europe, an organisation that promotes the use of Open Standards.

Petter Nielsen is a Researcher at Telenor Research and Future Studies and an Associated Professor in the Department of Informatics, University of Oslo. His research circles around the construction, evolution, and adoption of large scale and heterogeneous information infrastructures in the telecom domain.

DongBack Seo earned her Doctor of Philosophy and Masters of Science in Management Information Systems from the University of Illinois at Chicago and her Bachelors of Engineering from Hansung University. Prior to entering the PhD program, she worked as a software engineer in a wireless communications firm and as a small business owner. Her publications include three books, recently published Evolution and Standardization of Mobile Communications Technology, as well as a class manual and several chapters. Her papers have been published in many journals (e.g., *Communications of the ACM, European Journal of Information Systems, Telecommunications Policy*, etc.) and conference proceedings (e.g., International Conference on Information Systems, European Conference on Information Systems, etc.). Her research interests include the areas of adoption of IT/IS-enabled services from the perspectives of individuals and organizations, organizational standards strategy, business convergence, mobile commerce, and analysis of competitive dynamics in rapidly changing industries.

Xiabao Shen is a Senior Lecturer in International Business at the University of Edinburgh Business School. Dr. Shen participated in the China EU Information Technology Standards Research Partnership, an EU funded consortium of academic researchers in China, UK, Norway, Germany and Lithuania that studied the emerging processes of standards collaboration between China and the European Union.

Geerten van de Kaa received his MSc degree from the Faculty of Economics, Erasmus University, Rotterdam, The Netherlands, and his PhD degree from Rotterdam School of Management, Erasmus University. He is currently an Assistant Professor of strategy and innovation at Delft University of Technology, Delft, The Netherlands. He has been a Visiting Scholar at Berlin University of Technology, Berlin, Germany. His research interests include platform wars for complex systems, smart and network governance, and responsible innovation. He has published in high ranking international journals including *Organization Studies, IEEE Transactions on Engineering Management, Renewable and Sustainable Energy Reviews, Technological Forecasting and Social Change, Technology Analysis & Strategic Management,* and *Computer Standards & Interfaces.*

Robin Williams is Director of the Institute for the Study of Science, Technology, and Innovation (ISSTI) at the University of Edinburgh. Professor Williams participated in the China EU Information Technology Standards Research Partnership, an EU funded consortium of academic researchers in China, UK, Norway, Germany, and Lithuania that studied the emerging processes of standards collaboration between China and the European Union.

Simone Wurster studied at the Brandenburg University of Applied Sciences and at the University of Potsdam and received a degree in business administration. After her graduation, she worked at a German consulting company as project manager and consultant. Since 2003, she has been working as a researcher, lecturer, and project coordinator and wrote her PhD thesis about 'Born Global Standard Establishers' at the University of Potsdam. Her research focus is on standards and standardization strategies, security technologies, early warning systems, and Entrepreneurship. Since March 2010, she has been working as a researcher at the chair of Innovation Economics at the Faculty of Economics and Management at the Berlin University of Technology. Dr. Wurster has been involved in diverse research and consulting projects in the standardization field including the projects InfraNorm, E-STAN (Entrepreneurship and Standardization), NormPlas, TransFuE, TransCase, and CRISP - Evaluation and certification schemes for security products. She is also a member of the German mirror committee of the CEN/CENELEC Project Committee "Services for fire safety and security systems."

Index